HOME MOVIES

A History of the American Industry, 1897-1979

Alan D. Kattelle

ISBN: 0-9654497-8-5

Library of Congress Control Number 00-136151

Copyright © 2000 by Alan D. Kattelle
All rights reserved.

First Edition
Printed in the United States of America

Publisher: Transition Publishing
Nashua, New Hampshire

Alan D. Kattelle
50 Old County Road
Hudson, MA 01749

Stereo view of author Alan D. Kattelle, taken by Nicholas M. Graver, 20 October 1990.

To Natalie

For patience, support, understanding,
and love.

Charles H. Percy
Chairman

In these days of ubiquitous camcorder and rented videos, it is easy to forget how important home movies once were as home entertainment just a generation ago. In fact to anyone under thirty, the home movie projector probably seems as quaint as the stereopticon does to those of us "of a certain age". It is an inescapable fact that most of the pioneers of amateur cinematography are no longer with us, just as amateur movies themselves are declining. Alan Kattelle, a retired engineer, some twenty years ago became fascinated with the technology of amateur motion pictures, and began collecting the cameras and projectors that were rapidly being displaced by the camcorder and VCR. His interest in the history of the technology behind these machines led him to seek out, interview and record the stories of many the leading executives, scientists and engineers who worked in this field, myself included. The result of his efforts is this absorbing and valuable account of this once-vigorous American industry.

Charles H. Percy
9/23/98

Charles Percy & Associates, Inc.
International Investment and Trade Consultants

Charles H. Percy was President and Chief Executive Officer of Bell & Howell Company—a world leader in the development and manufacturing of motion picture cameras and projectors—for 26 years. He then served in the United States Senate for 18 years. From 1980 to 1985 he was Chairman of the Foreign Relations Committee.

ACKNOWLEDGMENTS

As I look back on the 15 years or so that this book has been in gestation, I am struck by the number of people who have given of their time and knowledge to help me in my endeavors. As trite as it may sound, it is absolutely true that this book could not have been written without their contributions.

Foremost among my benefactors has been my good friend and yes, severest critic, "Nick" Graver. His vast knowledge of photographic history and processes, his discerning eye for the non sequitur, the redundancy, and other ills the writer is heir to has rescued me from many of those pitfalls. Those that the reader may discover undoubtedly are there because Nick did not see that section!

The many present or retired Eastman Kodak employees who have helped me include the following: Linda Bouchard and Luanne Cenci of the Legal Department, Raymond Curtin, Archives Manager, Heidi Dilmore in Imaging Services, Lois Gouch and Andrea Imburgia of the Business Information Center

It has been my good fortune to meet or correspond with many of the Kodak engineers or scientists whose work impinged on amateur cinematography. Without exception they have been generous with help on technical matters. These include: William Allen, Joe Bailey, Blanchard Brock, M. E. Brown, Jasper Chandler*, Pete Chiesa*, Paul Doering, Donald Easterly, Evan Edwards, William Fujimura*, David Gibson, Don Gorman*, Vern Jungjohann, Myron Kerney, Rudolf Kingslake, Roger Loveland*, Leslie Quigley, Martin Scott, Willis Stockdale, Harris Tuttle*, and Rollie Zavada.

At the George Eastman House I have received invaluable help from Kathy Connor, Todd Gustafson, Becky Simmons, and Ed Stratmann. Other individuals in the Rochester community on whom I have called are: Betsy Brayer, historian and author of the definitive biography of George Eastman, Warren Doremus, Jim Dierks of Movies on a Shoestring (a film festival), Bob Herden, Bausch & Lomb retiree, Tom Hope of *Hope Reports*, Karl Kabelac of the University of Rochester Library, good friend Frank Mehlenbacher, and Carol Sandler of the Strong Museum.

At Bell & Howell were Denise Antablian, George Krtous, Tom Rappel, Lois and Jack Fay Robinson, Carl Schreyer, Malcolm Townsley, Bill White, and of course Senator Charles Percy, all of whom were gracious and helpful. One of my biggest fans at Bell & Howell, Jack Bray, was always encouraging, but sadly did not live to see this book finished. Kirk Kekatos of the Chicago Photographic Collectors Society was also very helpful on Bell & Howell history.

The account of the Revere Camera Company could not have been written without the help of Fred Pellar*. Similarly, Emil Bolsey has generously provided fine insights to his father's career. Well-known historians George Gilbert, Richard Koszarski, Eaton Lothrop, Ray Phillips, Cynthia Repinski, and Don Sutherland have generously shared their expertise. Tony Galluzzo of *Modern Photography,* and Elinor Stecker-Orel and Leendert Drukker of *Popular Photography,* have patiently reviewed sections. Paul Beck of Emerson College has tried valiantly to educate me on video history, as has Jim Beach of the L.A. Cinema Club, while Henry Weisenburger has done his best to make me a passable document photographer.

Closer to home, Miss Phyllis Brooks, reference librarian at the Hudson Public Library, has cheerfully and skillfully guided me through frequents searches for elusive data in the stacks and the Library Internet.

Finally, I want to thank my good friend, publisher Bud Swanson, and Nita Van Zandt, editor, for their patience, skills, and untiring efforts in helping transform the reams of manuscript and hundreds of illustrations into a finished book.

To all I have named, and to those whom I may have overlooked, my heartfelt thanks.

Alan D. Kattelle

* Deceased

APOLOGIA PRO LIBRO MEO

In all ages wherein Learning hath Flourished, complaint hath been made of the Itch of Writing, and the multitude of worthless Books, wherein importunate Scriblers have pestered the World. I am sensible that this Tractate may likely incur the Censure of a superflous Piece. First therefore, in Excuse of it, I plead, That there are in it some Considerations new and untoucht by others: wherein if I be mistaken, I alledge Secondly, that manner of Delivery and Expression may be more suitable to some Mens Apprehension, and facile to their Understandings. If that will not hold, I pretend Thirdly, That all the Particulars contained in this Book, cannot be found in any one Piece known to me, but ly scattered and dispersed in many, and so this may serve to relieve those Fastidious Readers, that are not willing to take the Pains to search them out: and possibly, there may be some whose Ability (whatever their Industry might be) will not serve them to purchase, nor their opportunity to borrow, those Books, who yet may spare Money enough to buy so inconsiderable a Trifle.

So begins John Ray's Preface to his *The Wisdom of God manifested in the Works of Creation* (1691) and quoted by William T. Stearn as part of his preface to the third edition of his classic *Botanical Latin.**

While I hasten to deny any suggestion that I thus appropriate to this book any of the virtues of either John Ray's or William Stearn's books, I would like to think that the venerable linguist's first and third delightfully worded pleadings for his work can be applied to my book. While I do not yet know what the cost of this book will be as I write this, I suspect that John Ray would hardly find it an "inconsiderable Trifle," and for that *I* apologize.

Alan D. Kattelle

* From *Botanical Latin*, published by David & Charles at £20.00

On January 8, 1923, Dr. C.E.K. Mees of the Eastman Kodak Company delivered a lecture to the Rochester Chapter of the American Chemical Society, entitled "Motion Picture Photography for the Amateur." With this modest introduction, the public first learned of a brand new product that, over the next 50 years, would create thousands of jobs, produce hundreds of millions of sales dollars, and delight generations of amateur cinematographers.

There were amateurs taking movies before 1923, of course, but only a relative handful, for the hobby was very expensive and the equipment cumbersome. Eastman Kodak's perfection of a system of film and equipment utilizing a narrow gauge of safety film made home movies immediately available to the merely well-to-do and, ultimately, within the reach of anyone who could afford to take snapshots. At the same time, this development spurred the growth of dozens of other companies in the field.

As well as creating new businesses, the new technology created a new genre of social document: the home movie. Millions of people found a new way to record family history; to relive that once-in-a-lifetime vacation; and many thousands became vicarious DeMilles and Hitchcocks. A number of excellent books have described the technology of professional motion pictures; two or three books have pictured amateur motion picture equipment; and a handful of learned treatises have discussed the home movie as a social document. No one volume, to my knowledge, has attempted to cover all facets of amateur motion pictures—how they were made, who made them, and what they were all about.

My objectives with this book have been four-fold:

1. to record the most significant elements of amateur motion picture technology;

2. to describe the major corporations that prospered or failed in it, and the individual inventors, scientists, engineers, executives, and entrepreneurs that contributed to this technology;

3. to give a brief history of the literature and the organizations that served the amateur movie maker;

4. to record the stories of some of the more accomplished amateurs and their films.

I have limited myself to the American amateur motion picture industry, simply because I felt that an adequate treatment of the European and Japanese industries could only be done properly by a resident of those countries. However, foreign suppliers and technologies are discussed where significant to the United States market.

I have begun the book with chapters on the origins of the motion picture, including that of photography itself. This has of course been done well by many other authors, and in considerably more detail. I have included them nonetheless, because I find the lives of the pioneers to be so interesting that it pleased me to research them and write about their achievements, which I hope you will find of interest also. They were also included for the reader who might find it convenient to review that history without having to resort to another book.

So, it is on the plate; you may leave it if you like and go on to the main course—and *bon appétit!*

Alan D. Kattelle

TABLE OF CONTENTS

LIST OF ILLUSTRATIONS

"It all started with an ordinary Ciné Kodak."

1   The Ancestry of the Motion Picture

Fig. 1. Athanasius Kircher.

The Beginnings

cin-e-ma-tog-ra-phy (sin a ma tog ra fe) n. The technique of making motion pictures. (Greek kinema, motion + graph, an apparatus that writes or records.)

Taken with the etymology, that is a remarkably concise definition of cinematography. But what are "motion pictures," physically? A reasonably simple answer might be:

A motion picture is a continuous series of still pictures, projected from a strip of transparent photographic film on to a viewing surface, in which the images succeed each other at the rate of 16 (or more) images per second.

The art of making motion pictures is thus seen to rest on three supports, two of which are reasonably self-evident the art of projection and the art of photography. The third support, which is hinted at in the phrase "at the rate of 16 images per second," is: the art which exploits several physiological phenomena popularly known as "persistence of vision," that quirk of the human eye-brain system that is familiar to every schoolchild who has drawn a succession of stick figures on the page corners of a book.[1]

Projection

The art of projection is by far the older of the two arts; man has been projecting images of a sort from prehistoric days. It seems entirely possible that our cave-dwelling ancestors might have discovered ways of making frightening shadows appear on cave walls, and the ancients have written of sorcerers casting shadows on columns of smoke that arose from their ceremonial fires. A German Jesuit priest named Fr. Athanasius Kircher (1601-1680) (Fig. 1) published the first record of a special apparatus to accomplish projection in 1646.[2] Fr. Kircher described a system of image projection known as "mirror writing," in which a design or message painted on a mirror was projected through a bi-convex lens, using the sun as a light source (Fig. 2).

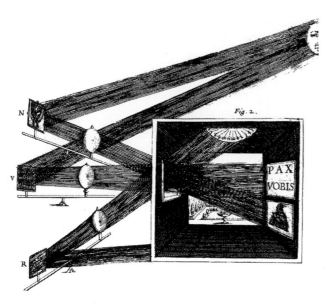

Fig. 2. Kircher's mirror projection.

Fig. 3. Zahn's lantern.

In the second edition of his book, published in 1671, Kircher gave some quite incorrect illustrations of magic lanterns, but also reported that the Danish astronomer, Thomas Walgenstein, had constructed a working magic lantern and had demonstrated it in several major European cities. Walgenstein's lantern, while crude, contained all the essential elements: light source, reflector, lens tube, and means for holding slides or transparent drawings in the light path. More sophisticated lanterns and elaborate slides were illustrated in a treatise by Johannes Zahn (Fig. 3) published in 1686. Zahn also proposed projecting the images of small living animals held in a water-cell, a technique employed two centuries later by Professor Morton of Philadelphia. The magic lantern held a great fascination for the philosophers and scientists of the period: many advances in lantern design were made by such men. Both William Molyneux, the Irish astronomer, and Christiaan Huygens (1629-1695), the Dutch discoverer of the Orion Nebula, made improvements in the optics of the lantern in the closing years of the seventeenth century.[3]

The magic lantern was also taken up by itinerant showmen, who carried crude lanterns on their backs, through the cities and villages of Europe, giving shows wherever a crowd of the curious might assemble (Fig. 4).

The lantern was little noted by the general populace however until late in the eighteenth century when a French impresario, Etienne Gaspard Robert

(1763-1837), who called himself Robertson, invented a new type of lantern, mounted on wheels (Fig. 5). The lantern thus mounted could be moved closer or further from the screen, thus changing the size of the image. Robertson took what had been a generally static display of dimly lit images projected against any convenient wall and transformed it into a full-fledged spectacle, with frightening images that

Fig. 4. A traveling showman, Europe, eighteenth century.

Fig. 5. Robertson's Fantascope lantern, equipped with two lenses.

mysteriously grew and shrank, accompanied by terrifying sound effects. He called his shows "Phantasmagoria."[4] (See Fig. 6.)

Robertson's showmanship and techniques drew great crowds; his commercial success caught the attention of other showmen in England and France, and his lantern was widely copied. But what was needed was greater illumination than could be coaxed from the whale oil lamps generally in use at that time. From the inception of the lantern in the seventeenth century through most of the eighteenth century, illumination for the magic lantern paralleled that for domestic lighting: simple wick lamps fueled by animal or vegetable oils. The lamps gave minimum light and produced quantities of unpleasant smoke, as is clearly shown in the woodcut of one of Zahn's lanterns.[5]

A quantum leap came in 1820, with the invention of the limelight. This device, patented by an English surgeon-scientist named Dr. Goldsworthy Gurney, consisted of a small cylinder of calcined lime held in the flame of an oxy-hydrogen burner (Fig. 7). Under this intense flame, the lime becomes incandescent, giving off a brilliant white light. This advance did not come without a price—oxygen and

Fig. 6. Robertson's Phantasmagoria. A performance at the former Capucine Convent in Paris, late eighteenth century.

hydrogen do not make good neighbors unless handled with the utmost care, as many a projectionist learned to his dismay, providing he survived the lesson.

Fortunately, an equally powerful but considerably safer light source was soon discovered: the electric arc. In 1850, the renowned French optician and instrument maker, Jules DuBoscq (1817-1886), patented a self-regulating arc lamp (Fig. 8). This invention greatly reduced the hazards attendant on a magic lantern presentation, while giving a truly brilliant light that permitted exhibitions to large audiences. Since the limelight did not require a source of electric power, it continued to be used, particularly by traveling exhibitors, well into the closing years of the nineteenth century.

Just which lanternist first hit upon the idea of using two lanterns for "dissolving views" is somewhat in dispute; it may have been Robertson, but in England, a showman named Henry Langdon Childe is given that credit, the date being about 1811. With the two "combs" (shutters) manipulated in front of the lenses, the lanternist could make a smooth transition from the slide being shown in the top lantern to the one in the bottom. A lantern of this design was called a "biunial" (Fig. 9). Somewhat later, three lanterns were stacked on top of one another, and the machine was designated a "triunial" (Fig. 10). Such machines required more than one operator, but with them, and elaborate mechanical slides, truly absorbing programs could be presented, showing such effects as a landscape progressing through all the seasons of the year, winter ice giving way to sparkling waters, snowy fields replaced with drifts of daffodils, midnight shadows yielding to sunrise, high noon, and glowing sunset.[6]

The lanterns described thus far were generally built by opticians and were sold to professional showmen, or as noted, to scientists or scientific investigators. The first commercially manufactured lanterns designed for non-theatrical use were produced in France in 1843 by one August LaPierre, a tinsmith who reportedly wanted a lantern to entertain his own children. Lapierre's lanterns were simple and inexpensive and became a very popular form of family entertainment. Numerous competitors sprang up in France and Germany, producing lanterns in a great variety of designs. Materials were "tin," (enameled sheet iron), painted iron, brass, and even ceramics.

One American who made a substantial improvement in lantern design was Lorenzo James Marcy (1819-1896), a Rhode Island school teacher who became interested in visual aids to classroom lectures, but found the lanterns available in the 1850s to be unsatisfactory in several respects. Between April

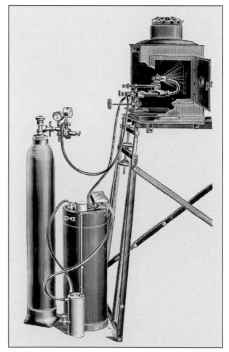

Fig. 7. Lantern equipped with oxy-acetylene tanks and limelight, ca. 1915.

Fig. 8. Self-regulating arc lamp.

Fig. 9. Biunial lantern, with lime-light.

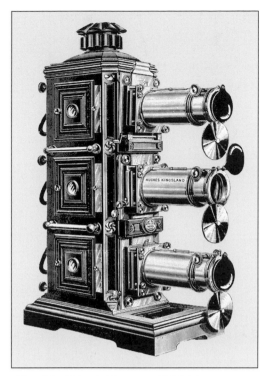

Fig. 10. Triunial lantern (British).

1868 and July 1869, Marcy received three patents for improved lantern and burner design. In its final form, the Marcy Sciopticon utilized two broad flat wicks parallel to the axis of the lantern, with a perforated vent plate between the wicks, a lantern body constructed of two concentric cylinders, with an air space between, with the reflector at one end and the lens at the other (Fig. 11). This made for a very rigid and compact lantern, at the same time one in which the outer body was kept reasonably cool, a great boon to the operator. The new burner gave

the most brilliant flame achieved at that time by an oil lamp. For the first time, a lantern was available with sufficient "throwing power" to effectively display detailed slides to a classroom, yet fueled with cheap, reliable, non-explosive kerosene.[7]

As the nineteenth century drew to a close, there were four classes of magic lanterns in use: high quality, special purpose lanterns used primarily by scientists; powerful biunial and triunial lanterns known as stereopticons, used by showmen and lecturers; lanterns such as Marcy's Sciopticon used principally by the clergy and educators; and small inexpensive lanterns for home use. There was a degree of overlapping between classes, and within each class there was a considerable range of quality, with many of the home-use lanterns being very cheaply made toys. Taken as a whole, however, the art of projection had reached a high level of performance.

Lantern slides were at first hand-painted and fairly crude, commonly depicting grotesqueries such as half-animal, half-human figures with distorted features, monsters, and the like. Hand-painting gave way to stenciled outlines filled in by hand. Photographically produced slides were introduced by the Langenheim brothers of Philadelphia about 1850, and decalcomania designs appeared in 1902 (Fig. 12).

One effect that every lanternist wanted to include in his repertoire, from the professional showmen like Robertson, Childe, and Norton to the devoted amateur amusing his family, was the projection of life-like motion.

Fig. 11. Marcy's Sciopticon, ca. 1868.

Fig. 12. Storytelling lantern slides.

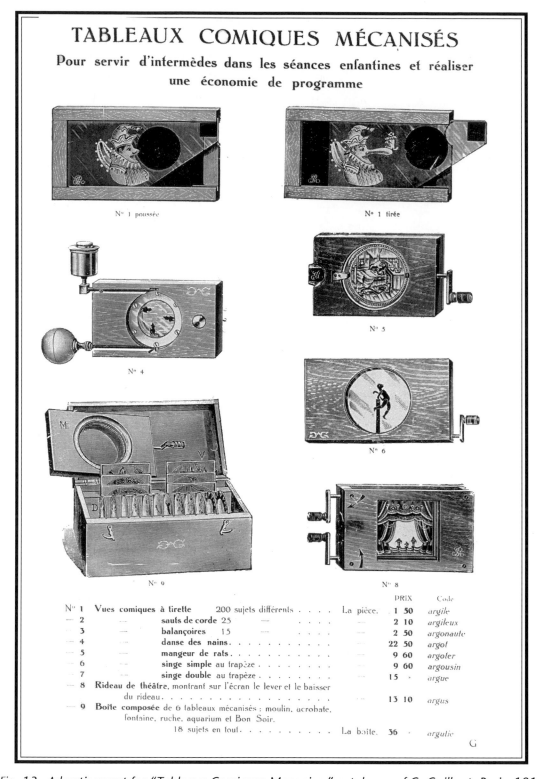

Fig. 13. Advertisement for "Tableaux Comiques Mecanise," catalogue of G. Guilbert, Paris, 1914.

Mechanical slides, in which some motion is given to the image, were noted as early as Zahn's time. Very elaborate ones were produced in later years, such as those that could depict the motions of the planets, phases of the moon, action of the tides, and so on. Several of these mechanisms are illustrated in the French advertisement shown in Fig. 13. One very popular mechanical slide was "The Man Swallowing Rats," in which a sleeping gentleman is made to do just that, by a clever combination of a slipping slide and a rotating element (No. 5 in Fig. 13).

Here is a translation of the French text that

appears below the illustrations in Figure 13:

No.		Price per piece
1 Comic moveable slides	200 different subjects . 1.50 fr.	
2 without cords	25 .... 2.10 fr.	
3 seesaws	15 .... 2.50 fr.	
4 dance of the dwarves	.... 22.50 fr.	
5 the rat eater	.... 9.60 fr.	
6 single monkey on trapeze	.... 9.60 fr.	
7 double monkey on trapeze	.... 15.0 fr.	
8 Theatre curtain, showing on the screen the raising and lowering of the curtain	.... 13.10 fr.	
9 Box containing 6 mechanical slides: mill acrobat, fountain, beehive, aquarium, and Good Evening. the box	.... 36 fr.	

(Numbers 2 and 3 are not illustrated in the ad.)

As entertaining as these effects were, not even the most ardent supporter could pretend that they truly "imitated life." It remained for a Belgian physicist to harness the phenomenon that would bring the "magic shadows" to life.

The Second Support—Persistence of Vision

Today's neuroscientists assert that there is no such thing as persistence of vision, that the eye does not retain an image, but that the motion picture depends on the combined effects of two physiological phenomena known as "critical fusion frequency" [8] and "(detection of) apparent movement." These phenomena are the mechanisms by which the retina receives light signals, transmits these signals to the brain, which then processes them into what we see as "moving images." That being said, for convenience's sake in this text the process shall be referred to as persistence of vision.

While the phenomenon of persistence of vision was probably known to the ancients, the first scientist to note this trait of the human visual system appears to have been Sir Isaac Newton (1642-1727), sometime about 1655, while he was investigating the properties of light. He does not appear to have been greatly intrigued by the phenomenon, being much more enthused about his discovery that white light was actually the combination of all the colors. He did, however, construct a device that demonstrated both persistence of vision and the constitution of white light, the Newton Disk. This is a flat disk on which are drawn six pie-shaped segments of the primary colors; when spun rapidly, the disk appears white. Some 100 years later, a French philosopher, the Chevalier D'Arcy, experimented with a large wheel to the rim of which was attached a burning coal. D'Arcy noted that the ring of light produced appeared continuous and determined that the duration of persistence was about one-tenth of a second. Both Newton and D'Arcy were exploring the "critical fusion frequency" referred to above.

Sometime in 1824, a London paper published a letter from a gentleman who requested an explanation of a curiosity he had observed from his window, when a carriage passed by on the other side of a picket fence. When the wheels of the carriage were seen through the fence, the spokes of the wheels seemed to become visible, but distorted, and sometimes even appeared to stand still (Fig. 14).

Fig.14. What Roget explained, moving carriage wheels seen through a picket fence.

Fig. 15. Joseph Plateau.

Fig. 16. Plateau's Phenakistoscope, 1832.

A London physician, Dr. Peter Mark Roget, (later to write his Thesaurus) responded to the query with an explanation in which he correctly ascribed the effect to persistence of vision. Roget's reply attracted the attention of many scientists of the day, including the eminent Michael Faraday (1791-1867), then director of Sir Humphry Davy's laboratory and soon to be appointed professor of chemistry at the Royal Institution. Faraday constructed a device to reproduce the phenomenon, called Faraday's Wheel, which he demonstrated to the Royal Society in 1831. It is a measure of Faraday's brilliance that while he found the time to explore this physiological quirk of the human eye, he was at the same time discovering benzene, assisting Davy in cryogenic research, and making important discoveries in electrolysis. [9, 10]

Among the scientists who read Roget's paper was a truly remarkable Belgian physicist and physiologist, Joseph Antoine Ferdinand Plateau (1801-1883) (Fig. 15). While still in his teens he decided on optics as his field of study, particularly the function of the eye, and pursued that career with incredible devotion throughout his long life. At the age of twenty-eight, while studying the effect of sunlight on the eye, he exposed his own eyes to the full blaze of the sun for some period of time, as a result of which he immediately lost most of his sight and ultimately became totally blind. He continued to work in his chosen field, assisted by his wife, who carried out the experiments under his direction.

Plateau actually anticipated some of Faraday's work, and in turn, building on Faraday's Wheel, went on to produce in 1832 the first device utilizing the phenomenon of persistence of vision to create the illusion of a moving image. Plateau named his invention the Phenakistoscope. It consisted of a flat disk on which are drawn a series of images of some repetitive action, each drawing showing the action slightly advanced from the last. Around the perimeter of the disk are cut a series of slots, one slot for each drawing. The disk is then mounted on a spindle on a handle. If the disk is then held up to a mirror, so that the illustrated side of the disk is visible through one of the slots, and then spun with the other hand, the drawings seen in the mirror come alive with smooth continuous motion (Fig. 16).

The explanation is as follows: consider that you are looking at one drawing through one of the slots. You eye receives that image, then the image is obscured by the area between the slots, until the next slot comes in place before your eye. Now your eye sees the next image, which is slightly advanced from the previous one. If the interval between the receiving of those two images was less than the critical tenth of a second, your visual system retained the first image long enough for it to be blended with the image that supplanted it. If you look with both eyes through the entire rim of the disk, the result will be that you will see the entire disk in motion. [11]

By a curious happenstance, at the very time that Plateau was displaying his Phenakistoscope, an Austrian inventor named Simon Stampfer quite independently developed an identical device, which he named the Stroboscope, a name which became generic for any device which stopped motion by means of intermittent illumination.

The phenakistoscope had two drawbacks—only one person could view the action at a time, and the

Fig. 17. Horner's Daedaleum (Zoetrope), 1834.

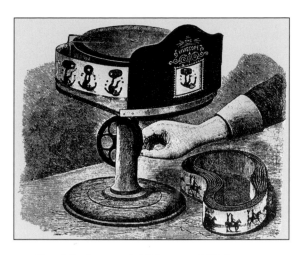

Fig. 18. Farnum's Viviscope, 1895.

drawings were difficult to construct properly. In 1834, an Englishman named William George Horner invented a device he named the Daedaleum, which solved both of those problems (Fig. 17).

The slotted disk was replaced by a slotted cylinder, and the drawings, now on a band, could be easily reproduced. As many people as could cluster around the cylinder could view the action simultaneously. The device did not achieve great popularity, however, until some thirty-odd years later, when an American, William E. Lincoln, of Providence, Rhode Island, was issued Pat. No. 64,117 on April 23, 1867, for basically the identical device, which he named the Zoetrope, or Wheel of Life. Lincoln assigned his patent to the Milton Bradley Company, under which imprint they became somewhat of a craze and were turned out by the thousands. Generally made of cardboard or light metal, and usually given to children, relatively few of them have survived.

A curious optical toy was devised by W.C. Farnum of Arlington, Vermont. Farnum called his device the "Viviscope" and was issued U. S. Patent No. 547,775, on October 15, 1895. A loose band of images was placed around a cylinder and kept in contact except where a smaller roller, rotating between the fixed cylinder and the band, kept the band away from the cylinder. As the small roller passed around the cylinder, it advanced the band by one image for each revolution. Farnum also patented the machine in Britain, as a Zoetrope. The device is particularly interesting because it was marketed in the United States by E. B. Koopman's Magic Introduction Company of New York (Fig. 18).

Koopman was at this time about to join forces with W.K.L. Dickson, Herman Casler, and Harry Marvin to form the American Mutoscope Company. This company went on to produce the Mutoscope, the arcade machine that supplanted Edison's Kinetoscope, and the Biograph, which drove out Edison's Vitascope theater projector. It seems possible that Farnum's Viviscope, with its intermittent motion, might have influenced Casler and Dickson in their work on the Mutoscope and the Biograph. In that same October of 1895, Farnum received British Patent No. 18,317 for a device which seems to have been a form of mutoscope.[12] There is no record of it having been patented in America, nor whether it was ever manufactured. The Viviscope deserves a place in the history of the motion picture as it appears to be the first of the zoetrope family of devices that incorporated intermittent motion of the image.

In 1886, a London optician, L.S. Beale, constructed a device which appears to have been the first to incorporate the "image at rest" principle with a magic lantern slide to achieve true stroboscopic projection. He called the instrument the Choreutoscope (Fig 19).

A long slide with six images of an action sequence was moved intermittently through the light path by a linear Maltese Cross operated by a crank. The same crank operated a shutter that was arranged to cut off the light while the slide advanced to the next image. In place of the painted glass slide, a metal slide with the images cut out in the form of a stencil was also used. The dancing skeleton was a popular design.[13]

A somewhat similar device was constructed by an American, O.B. Brown, of Malden, Massachusetts,

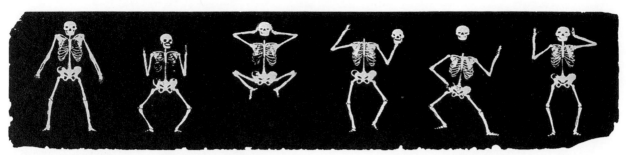

Fig. 19. Beale's Choreutoscope, ca. 1866.

who received U.S. Patent 93,594 on August 10, 1869, for his Optical Instrument (Fig. 20). The image sequences in Brown's machine were painted on the polygonal glass plate P, which was moved intermittently by a Maltese cross action, while a two-bladed shutter positioned in front of the lens and driven by the same operating crank provided the necessary periodic obscuration.

While Brown's invention appears to have been capable of meeting the patent claims, there is no record of its demonstration, nor any evidence that it was ever produced. The credit for actual projection of a phenakistoscope device belongs to an Austrian officer named Franz von Uchatius (1811-1881). While still a very junior officer, Uchatius invented an artillery shell fuse in 1843. His talents came to the attention of a field marshal, who suggested that

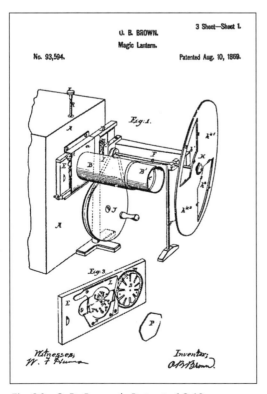

Fig 20. O.B. Brown's Patent, 1869.

he develop a projection device as an aid to military instruction. Uchatius's first attempt used a variation of one of Plateau's slotted disk machines, illuminated by an oil lamp, but the results were not satisfactory.

In 1853, he demonstrated a machine using a limelight. A series of images painted on glass were mounted in a circle on the perimeter of a stationary wooden holder. A second stationary holder in front of the first carried a series of objectives, one for each image, and all focused on a common area on the projection surface. Behind the image holder was a limelight and condenser, mounted so that by turning a crank the light passed behind each of the images in turn. This was the only moving part in the projector. Each image was *momentarily* projected, but with the full power of the light, with no loss through slots or a shutter. The results were so successful that Uchatius' original machine was purchased by a well-known showman, Ludwig Dobler, who gave performances with it all over Europe, thereby making himself wealthy, while fortune escaped General Uchatius, despite the importance of his invention in the history of cinematography.[14]

An experimenter who was also trying to improve on the phenakistoscope made the next significant event in the evolution of projection of motion.

Charles Emile Reynaud (1844-1918) (Fig. 21), a French artist and inventor who had served apprenticeships in a photographic studio and a precision machine shop, read an article on optical toys in the philosophical journal *La Nature*, which prompted him to build a simple model of a phenakistoscope. Dissatisfied with viewing the images in a mirror, Reynaud constructed a new device that was actually an improvement on the Zoetrope.

The slots in the cylinder were replaced by a centrally mounted, multi-faceted mirror—one facet for each image on the drawing strip. Each mirror-reflected image moved smoothly past the eye, with

Fig 21. Charles Emile Reynaud.

no intervening slots to cause distortion or diminution of light. The result was a bright image that gave an excellent simulation of motion. The device that Reynaud christened the Praxinoscope was patented in 1876 (Fig. 22).

One year later, Reynaud patented a delightful refinement of the Praxinoscope, the Praxinoscope Theater (Fig. 23).

The viewer sees the action as apparently taking place on a stage, with the animated figure seeming to appear in relief and performing against the appropriate scenery (e.g., an acrobat in a circus ring, a swimmer in a pool, and so on). The device was sold with ten picture bands and ten sets of scenery and backdrops. In 1880, Reynaud carried his design one step further. By combining his Praxinoscope Theater with a magic lantern, he produced the Projecting Praxinoscope (Fig. 24).

Reynaud's toys became a lively commercial success, and Reynaud found himself a manufacturer, with two or three employees assembling mirrors and lanterns. In 1881, he conceived the idea of using a long band of images, which would permit an exhibition of several minutes duration. The images were painted on thin glass plates, later supplanted by celluloid, and mounted in bands of strong canvas or linen, containing as many as 700 frames. The band was carried from a supply reel around the central mirror prism by a toothed feed wheel, the teeth engaging eyelets in the picture band. A beam from an arc lamp passed through the pictures to the mirror prism where it was reflected by two more mirrors to

Fig. 22. Reynaud's Praxinoscope.

Fig. 23. Reynaud's Praxinoscope Theatre.

Fig. 24. The Projecting Praxinoscope.

Fig. 25. Reynaud's Theatre Optique. The inventor is shown operating the machine.

the back of a translucent screen that faced the audience. A second lantern threw a background scene on the screen, against which the band images moved. Through the combination of Reynaud's artistic ability in making the paintings, and his skill at constructing and operating his apparatus, his Theatre Optique, which he patented in December 1888, presented a truly magical spectacle (Fig. 25).

Reynaud had hoped to sell his Theatre Optique to itinerant showmen or impresarios, but after three years of unsuccessful efforts, he signed an exclusive contract with the Musée Grévin, a popular exhibition hall in Paris, to produce five performances daily and twelve on Sundays and holidays. Reynaud was responsible for all expenses of the apparatus, scenery, personnel, and maintenance of the equipment, as well as all expenses for providing new exhibits; the Musée furnished electricity and the musical accompaniment. In exchange, Reynaud received 500 francs per month, plus ten percent of the gross.

His performances were called *Les Pantomimes Lumineuses*, and a typical presentation was Pauvre Pierrot, a band of 500 frames, 22 meters long, being ten or twelve minutes on the screen.[15] It opens with Harlequin jumping over a garden wall, serenading Columbine, then hiding on the return of Pierrot,

who offers Columbine a bouquet and gets beaten by Harlequin. As an example of the lengths to which Reynaud went to refine his performances, the above playlet was not only accompanied by the Musée Grévin orchestra, but by appropriate sound effects which were made operative by electrical switches tripped at the proper times by contacts on the film band. Many of Reynaud's techniques would be familiar to the Disney animators: the separation of background from characters, the use of transparencies over a static background, reversing the band for reversing the motion, etc.

While his performances were extremely popular and well attended, Reynaud soon found himself in trouble. The Théatre Optique mechanism was delicate, and Reynaud could not trust anyone to operate it other than himself. As a result, he had the formidable task of staging all forty-four of those weekly shows, plus maintaining the bands, plus creating new ones. On top of all this, the celluloid frames were not standing up well under the heavy use and the high temperature of the arc lamps. The constant demand for new episodes from the Musée management finally forced Reynaud to abandon his hand-painting of the frames and employ a camera that he built himself, patterned after Étienne Jules Marey's chronophotographe. Even then, he used the photographs so obtained simply as models, from which he continued to paint individual frames.

But far more threatening than these problems was a new diversion that was catching the public fancy, and increasingly, the attention of the management of the Musée Grévin. In July 1898, Reynaud shared billing with a program of *Animated Projections of the Cinematographe*. And on March 1, 1900, Reynaud's Théatre Optique was replaced by a troupe of English marionettes. Reynaud fought back, nonetheless, even building a camera for stereoscopic photography of motion, which attracted little attention. Sales of the praxinoscope toys shrank to near zero, and Reynaud sank into depression. Finally, in 1911, he smashed the three remaining Théatre Optiques in his possession and threw all his bands into the Seine. Illness followed depression and disillusionment, and this brilliant pioneer died on the ninth of January, 1918, in a hospital for incurables, attended only by his wife.[16]

The Third Support—Photography

As artistic and entertaining as Reynaud's presentations were, they were not motion pictures, on two counts: while they were (occasionally) projected intermittently, the period of rest and replacement was far longer than that required for persistence of vision to be effective; and they were *drawings* of life, not photographs.

Photography had its beginnings in the eighteenth and early nineteenth centuries when scientists such as Schulze in 1727, Wedgwood in 1802, and Davy in 1814, discovered the dramatic change in the color of silver salts under the action of light. It was not until the camera obscura came into general use, however, that the search began in earnest for ways in which to capture an image by the action of light.

The camera obscura, Latin for "dark room," was first described by Leonardo da Vinci (1452-1519). However, his account written in cipher was not discovered until many years after his death. The first person to make the device widely known was Giovanni Baptista della Porta, in his book *Magica Naturalis*, published in 1558.[17] As described by della Porta, the camera obscura was a windowless room, through one wall of which a small hole admitted light. The hole acted as a lens, so that a fully detailed

Fig. 26. A camera obscura in use.

but inverted image of the exterior scene was projected on the opposite interior wall (Fig. 26).

It was soon discovered that the substitution of a lens for the hole gave a much sharper image; it was also soon realized that the device could be reduced to a portable version, whereupon it became popular with artists who had trouble with perspective and proportion. The instrument shown incorporates an objective lens, an angled mirror, and a pane of glass on which a piece of paper may be placed for tracing the image. A few of the large camera obscurae are to be found in Europe, and the George Eastman House in Rochester, New York, has recently installed one at the entrance to the Mees Gallery.

Probably every artist who used a camera obscura wished for some way to fix the image that appeared on the tracing paper, and many of them made serious efforts toward this objective. The story of how an image was finally captured is the story of two men of France whose lives and fortunes became entwined in a curious contractual relationship which resulted in world-wide recognition for one and near-obscurity for the other.

Joseph Nicéphore Niepce (1765-1833) was born to a wealthy family at Chalon-sur-Saône, an ancient town in eastern France where the Canal du Centre meets the Saône (Fig. 27).[18] Well-educated, Joseph and his older brother Claude, after relatively brief services in Napoleon's forces, embarked on careers of invention. Their first notable achievement was an internal combustion engine fueled by the explosive combustion of lycopodium powder.[19] As impractical as that may sound, their curious invention was

Fig. 27. Joseph Nicéphore Niepce.

Fig. 28. View From the Window at Gras, by Niepce, the world's first photograph, 1824.

a forerunner of the internal combustion engine and was so noted by the eminent French physicist, Nicolas Carnot. Beginning about 1816, Joseph's interests shifted to the newly invented process of lithography.

Lithography, literally "writing on stone," is the process of transferring an original drawing to the surface of a stone, so that the stone becomes a printing block from which multiple copies of the original can be printed. Invented in 1797 by the Bavarian Alois Senefelder, it revolutionized the printing of drawings and artwork of all kinds, virtually supplanting the more laborious techniques of wood and steel engravings.

Niepce set out to transfer drawings to the lithographic stone by the action of light. The photosensitive material he used was an asphaltic substance known as bitumen of Judea, which has the property of hardening on exposure to light. Finding the local stone unsatisfactory, Niepce switched to pewter plates, and with this combination he ultimately succeeded in producing lithographic plates, in a process which he named heliography.

At some point, Niepce began experiments with a camera obscura, attempting to capture the image on the camera's screen with his bitumen-coated plate, and while the relative insensitivity of the bitumen made inordinately long exposures necessary, he did succeed in producing a permanent photographic image and was the first person to do so. Of the handful of actual "photographs" attributed to Niepce which have survived, the best known is the "View from the Window at Gras," a rather faint im-

age of three or four roofed buildings, on a pewter plate (Fig. 28). This image is in the Gernsheim Collection at the University of Texas in Austin and is thought to have been taken in 1826.

Niepce bought his camera and lenses from the noted optical firm of Chevalier, which was also supplying lenses to a prominent French painter named Daguerre. The two experimenters were introduced through this connection and thus began an association that was to have momentous results.[20]

Louis Jacques Mandé Daguerre (1787-1851) was born in a suburb of Paris on November 18, 1787 (Fig. 29). His father was a minor government official. Daguerre showed artistic talent at an early age and, after an apprenticeship to a noted scene painter,

Fig. 29. Louis Jacques Mandé Daguerre.

14

Fig. 30. Diorama Building, Rue Sanson, Paris, designed by Daguerre for showing his dioramas, 1822.

went on to a successful career as a painter and set designer for Paris opera houses and theaters. It may be presumed that he worked on some of the several panoramas that had been established in Paris after their introduction in 1804 by Robert Barker.

The panorama was a huge painting as much as 20 feet tall by several hundred feet long, mounted inside a rotunda. The spectators were seated in a central area, separated from the painting by a sort of dry moat. The canvas was mounted on rollers so that it could be scrolled past the audience. The painting on the canvas depicted some topical event, such as "Mr. Albert Smith's Ascent of Mont Blanc," or some classic scene from Egypt or the Holy Lands. The lighting of the canvas could be varied by manipulation of skylights and/or reflectors.

In 1822, Daguerre, in association with a M. Bouton, launched a greatly augmented version of the panorama that he called the Diorama (Fig. 30). The huge painting was now stationary, with the audience on a rotating platform which carried them slowly past the varied scenes spread out before them. The paintings were executed on a translucent material and could be lit from front or back, enabling the operator to make dramatic changes in atmosphere and mood—from broad daylight to darkest night, scenes of conflagrations, volcanic eruptions, and so on.

Typical pieces were: "The Valley of Goldau before and after the Catastrophe" and "The Earthquake

at Lima." The foreground of the scene might contain actual objects, skillfully placed against the backdrop to give a strong three-dimensional effect. On at least one instance, Daguerre is known to have embellished a Swiss scene with the sound of alpenhorns and tinkling cowbells. There is even an account of refreshments being served, quite in the manner of our present day "dinner theatres." [21]

Painting these huge scenes from life was greatly facilitated by the use of the camera obscura, a technique that Daguerre employed extensively. Daguerre was also fascinated with the idea of capturing an image with the camera obscura, and his experiments apparently paralleled those of Niepce. Both had experimented with plates coated with salts of silver, without any substantial results. It took the two men several years after their introduction to decide to collaborate, but on December 14, 1829, they signed a ten-year contract of partnership. The first paragraph of the contract read:

Between Niepce and Daguerre, formed to co-operate for the further improvement of the invention of Niepce which was perfected by Daguerre.

As part of the partnership agreement, Niepce wrote out a full description of his heliographe process, which is the "invention" referred to above; the "perfection by Daguerre" referred to improvements in the camera obscura. Following the signing, both men worked tirelessly to find a more responsive material. It fell to Daguerre to make the all-important discovery, namely, the sensitizing of the silver-coated plate with iodine vapor. Daguerre, who was apparently unaware of Sir Humphry Davy's discovery of the light-sensitivity of silver iodide in 1814, immediately wrote to Niepce suggesting the use of iodized silver plates. Niepce acted on the suggestion, but after some months, reported that he had no more success with that material this time than he had had some years previously.

Sadly, Joseph Nicèphore Niepce did not live to see the eventual triumph of their efforts, dying on July 5, 1833. His son Isidore, as heir, took his place in the partnership. Daguerre carried on his experiments and in 1835 made another crucial discovery—the development of the latent image in silver iodide by exposing it to mercury vapor. The realization that a latent image was produced long before any visible change occurred meant that exposure times were at once reduced from hours to minutes, and the mercury-developed image was permanent, albeit fragile.

On May 9, 1835, Daguerre had an "addition" to the original contract drawn. This addition, with a slight bow to the contribution of the late partner, took note of Daguerre's "new process" and changed the name of the firm to "Daguerre and Isidore Niépce." Two years later, on June 13, 1837, a final contract was signed between Isidore and Daguerre which called for the new process to be made public and gave Daguerre the right to call the new process by the name "Daguerre" alone. After two years of

unsuccessfully attempting to sell subscriptions to their company to the public, the partners gave their process to the French government, who rewarded Daguerre and Niepce with pensions, and gave the process to the world.[22] The daguerreian process took the world by storm (Fig. 31). The images became known as daguerreotypes (Fig. 32). Within months of the announcement, daguerreian studios sprang up throughout Europe and in the United States.

Beautiful as it was, the daguerreotype had a major shortcoming—it was a one-of-a-kind. Copies were made only by re-photographing the original or making multiple exposures the first time. The process had no relevance to cinematography, or even to modern photography except as it stimulated interest in the photographic process.[23]

An English archaeologist and scientist, William Henry Fox Talbot (1800-1877), announced almost simultaneously with Daguerre, a negative/positive process that is the foundation of modern photography. Talbot's photographs were made on paper that had been impregnated with silver chloride, exposed in the camera obscura, and then developed to a negative image, from which as many positives as desired could be printed. "Calotypes," as he called them, did not have the sharpness of the daguerreotype, due to the grain of the paper, but they were beautiful images nonetheless. Talbot used twenty-four of these prints in 1844 to produce *The Pencil of Nature*, the first book ever illustrated with photographs.[24]

Frederick Scott Archer (1813-1857) made the

Fig. 31. Daguerreotype outfit, French, 1847.

Fig. 32. Paris street scene, photographed by Daguerre, ca 1838. Note the gentleman getting a shoeshine. (Courtesy Bayerisches National Museum, Munich.)

next major advance in photographic technology public in 1851. Archer made his negatives on glass plates which had been coated with collodion, a form of nitrocellulose, in which potassium iodide had been dissolved. The plate was then sensitized by immersion in a silver nitrate solution and, while still wet, placed in the camera for exposure.

This emulsion turned out to be amazingly fast, an exposure of as little as four to six seconds being sufficient for well-lit subjects. After exposure the plate was immersed in a developer, and the negative could then be stripped from the glass support. Archer's "wet-plate" process, so called because of the necessity of keeping the plate moist from sensitizing through development, made for some cumbersome equipment, particularly for fieldwork. The operator was required to carry a portable darkroom, as shown in a well-known cartoon showing a youthful George Eastman supposedly setting out on a photographic expedition (Fig 33).

Recalling the earliest days of photography, this cartoon pictures George Eastman loaded down with a camera, tripod, chemicals and even a tent to use as a darkroom.

Fig. 33. Cartoon of Eastman from a Rochester paper in the 1920s.

Fig. 34. George Eastman in his early thirties.

Fig. 35. Col. Henry A. Strong.

Cumbersome or not, the wet collodion process dominated photography for the next 25 years, until it was supplanted by the development of the dry plate, accomplished again by a number of English workers, including Richard Maddox (1816-1902), Charles Bennet (1840-1927), and F. C. L. Wratten (1840-1926). Along with the boon of freeing the photographer from the wet plate came greatly increased speed. Wratten's "Drop Shutter Plates," announced in 1882, could be exposed at speeds of one one-thousandth of a second.[25]

At last the photography of motion was possible; such emulsion speed could stop a bird in flight or a speeding locomotive. The chief problem was now one of mechanics: how to move the photographic medium through the camera fast enough to meet the physiological necessity of presenting successive images to the eye at intervals short enough to satisfy the so-called "persistence of vision" interval. Glass was a terrible support, heavy and breakable; paper was possible, but not very strong. The answer finally came from the other side of the Atlantic when George Eastman announced his flexible transparent film in 1889.

George Eastman (1854-1932) (Fig. 34) was a promising young clerk in his early twenties at a Rochester, New York, savings bank when an acquaintance suggested that he take a camera with him on his proposed vacation trip to Santo Domingo. The trip did not materialize, but Eastman did buy a wet-plate outfit, and with characteristic thoroughness, engaged the services of a local photographer, one George Monroe, to teach him the intricacies of this new art. In Eastman's own words:

My layout, which included only the essentials, had in it a camera the size of a soap box, a tripod which was strong enough to support a bungalow, a big plate holder, a dark-tent, a nitrate bath, and a container for water. The glass plates were not, as now, in the holder ready for use; they were what is known as "wet plates," that is glass which had to be coated with collodion and then sensitized with nitrate of silver in the field just before exposure.

Eastman was reading every photographic magazine that he could lay his hands on, and when he read an article in the British Journal of Photography on making dry plates, he began making his own emulsions in the kitchen of the home he shared with his widowed mother. His experiments were so encouraging, and his enthusiasm so great, that by 1878 he was ready to quit his job at the bank and start his own business of making dry plates. Eighteen months after taking up photography he had settled on a formula for an emulsion and designed and built a machine for coating plates mechanically. With supreme confidence in his accomplishments, he withdrew four hundred dollars from his savings and sailed to London, then the capital of the photographic world, and obtained his first patent for the coating machine on July 22, 1879.[26]

By the close of 1880, Eastman was in business; he had leased the top floor of a building in downtown Rochester, he had labels, developing instructions and boxes for his plates, and he had a substantial order from E. & H.T. Anthony, one of the leading distributors of photographic materials. And he had acquired a partner with a purse, Colonel Henry A. Strong, who is discussed later (Fig. 35).

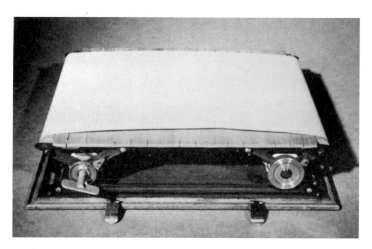

Fig. 36. Eastman-Walker Roll Holder.

Fig. 37. Frank A. Brownell, ca 1900.

The dry plate business went well, but Eastman continued his search for a replacement for glass as the support for the sensitive material. Roll film systems had begun to evolve in the 1850s, and a notable one was invented in 1875 by the Russian-born Leon Warnerke (1837-1900). Warnerke devised a complex paper-based collodion and rubber film and a camera with a pair of rollers to carry the film. The system was workable, but not a commercial success.

In 1883, Eastman hired William H. Walker (1846-1917), a local manufacturer of dry plate cameras, to help design a roll film system. Walker and Eastman decided to focus on three basic system components: a film, a film holder mechanism, and the film making machinery.[27]

From this resolve, there emerged in 1884 a product designed by Eastman that consisted of a gelatin emulsion carried on a paper support, which after exposure and development was treated with oil or wax to reduce the opacity of the paper. This was never very satisfactory and was soon replaced by a product called "American Stripping Film." This consisted of a non-soluble emulsion layer on a soluble gelatin layer on a paper backing. After exposure and development, the film was subjected to a complex multi-step process that nevertheless resulted in a flexible and reasonably durable negative.

In the meantime, Walker had completed a roll-holder design, similar to the Warnerke roll holder [28] but with a number of improvements, including the important one of making the roll holder separate from the camera. In that same year, the two designed and patented a plate holder for sheet film and a continuous paper coating and drying machine.

The Eastman-Walker roll holder (U. S. Patent No. 317,049) (Fig. 36) came on the market in the spring of 1885 and was well received by the industry, even gaining admiration from Warnerke himself. The stripping film, marketed as "American Film," did not fare as well, due to its complex method of processing, and Eastman felt compelled to continue to offer the paper negative film to encourage the use of the film holders. The roll holders were largely manufactured by a Rochester camera manufacturer, the Brownell Manufacturing Company.

Frank A. Brownell (1859-1939), was born in Vienna, Canada, and moved to Rochester in 1875 (Fig. 37). He apprenticed to a cabinet-maker and became a skilled metal and woodworking craftsman. In 1883 he began as a camera manufacturer, producing high quality cameras for both amateur and professional use, including a dry-plate stereo camera. The Brownell workmanship was so good that Eastman soon turned over the manufacture and much of the design of all cameras and related equipment to Brownell. Among the cameras that Brownell designed and patented: the first Folding Kodak of 1889, the 1895 Pocket Kodak that was Kodak's first daylight-loading camera, the Cartridge Kodaks, and the Folding Pocket Kodaks.

In 1892, following a fire at Brownell's plant, Eastman decided the time was right for a new and better camera manufacturing facility, and construction was begun on a new factory adjacent to the existing Kodak buildings. The completed building and necessary machinery cost about $60,000 and was leased to Brownell at six percent of that cost per annum.

Despite being Eastman's sole source for quality camera work and Brownell's own designing skill, Brownell apparently enjoyed a poor bargaining position. His contract with Eastman required him to work on a cost plus a percentage basis, and Eastman set his profit percentage at 10 percent. On the Pocket Kodak, for example, Brownell's cost was 80 cents, Eastman paid him 87 cents, and the camera retailed for $5.00. It is difficult to imagine George Eastman allowing the dealer as much as a 50 percent markup, but assuming for the sake of argument that he did, then he pocketed $2.50 for a camera for which he paid 87 cents.

But even that 10 percent going to Brownell bothered Eastman, so effective July 1, 1898, Brownell was advised that his profit would be reduced to 5 percent. The result of this move, perhaps as Eastman intended, was to cause Brownell to sell the Brownell Manufacturing Company to the Eastman Kodak Company, in October of 1902. Brownell was retained by Eastman as a camera design consultant for several years, resigning in 1906 to found a gasoline engine manufacturing company, the F. A. Brownell Motor Company. One of the company's engines was installed in the first gasoline-powered motor yacht accepted by the U. S. Navy, a motor yacht designed for the private use of a ranking rear admiral. Brownell's ventures suffered some reverses during the great depression of 1929 to 1933, and the inventor died in rather straitened circumstances in 1939.[29]

Despite the good reception of the Eastman dry plates, the roll holder, and a burgeoning business in both photographic printing papers and negative paper, Eastman still did not have a product of great mass appeal, and he continued to explore avenues to this goal. One such avenue appeared to be that of a small, easy-to-use camera, and in 1888, possibly the single most important photographic product that has ever been produced, "The Kodak," was announced at a photographer's convention in Minneapolis. George Eastman attended the conference himself to exhibit the revolutionary new product (Fig. 38).

The camera measured 3-1/4" by 3-1/2" by 6-3/4" long and came loaded with sufficient "stripping film" for 100 exposures. It cost $25. The user was instructed: "You press the button, we do the rest." On completing the 100 exposures, the user simply

Fig. 38. The Kodak Camera of 1888.

mailed the entire camera back to Rochester, where the film was developed and printed, the camera reloaded with film and returned to the owner with the finished prints, all for just $10. Instructions were included for home processing, but most customers preferred to let Eastman do the work.

The panel of judges at the convention awarded the Kodak camera the medal for "the photographic invention of the year." The public's reaction was equally enthusiastic and within two years the Eastman Company, as it was then named, was unable to process films as fast as they poured in to Rochester. Construction was begun on new facilities that would eventually become the fabled Kodak Park.[30]

More than a new product had been launched: there was added to the world's vocabulary a new word, recognized in a hundred languages; an advertising slogan that became as familiar to most Americans as the words of their national anthem; a new industry, photo-finishing. There was also created a new hobby, pastime, diversion that changed the way we look at ourselves. It is impossible to estimate how many careers were begun because of that little black box that gave everyone the power to capture an image of whatever in the wide world caught their attention, spurred their imagination, made them think.[31]

What does all this have to do with amateur motion pictures? The answer is: a great deal. To begin with, the incredible success of the Kodak camera made the search for a better film support of utmost importance to Eastman. His solution to that problem, transparent flexible film, provided the material that made movies possible. And the financial success of the Kodak system made the Kodak

Research Laboratories possible and from these laboratories came the first successful amateur motion picture system.

The search for a flexible film base began to focus on celluloid, a form of nitrocellulose which was being produced commercially as a substitute for glass in the manufacture of dry plates by the brothers John and Isaiah Hyatt, who formed the Celluloid Corporation in Newark, New Jersey, in 1874. The product was quite transparent, but relatively inflexible, and thus was not usable for roll film. There were three people who were responsible for creating a transparent, flexible film of nitrocellulose: George Eastman, Henry M. Reichenbach, and the Rev. Hannibal Goodwin (Fig. 39). There is only space to give the barest outline of the complex chain of events in which these three men were to become involved over the next 25 years.

Henry M. Reichenbach was an assistant in the Chemistry Department of the University of Rochester when he was hired in August of 1886 by George Eastman to work on improved emulsions. The Reverend Hannibal W. Goodwin (1822-1900), an Episcopal minister in Newark, New Jersey, was an ardent amateur photographer who began experimenting with nitrocellulose circa 1886.

On May 2, 1887, Goodwin filed a patent application for a synthetic substitute for glass plates and for paper film for roll film cameras. His claims were very broad, covering practically any film that was formed by flowing and evaporation of solvents. Partly because of his broad claims, but also undoubtedly because of inexperience and poor legal counsel, his application was rejected and re-filed five times in the year following its submission. There followed many more submissions and rejections, but Goodwin was finally issued a patent on September 13, 1898.

In the fall of 1888, with the Kodak securely launched, Eastman assigned Reichenbach to the task of developing a flowed-on film. Reichenbach's progress was no less than astounding; by January of 1889 Eastman was so satisfied with Reichenbach's discoveries that he had begun getting estimates on raw materials and machinery with which to equip a plant. He also alerted his lawyers to gather all existing patents on celluloid and prepare for drawing up patent applications. In February, he submitted to the

Fig. 39. The Reverend Hannibal Goodwin.

board of directors samples of the new film and an ambitious plan for manufacture, all of which was enthusiastically approved. In April, patent applications were filed, in Reichenbach's name for the chemistry of the new film and in Eastman's name for the mechanical aspects of the film.

Early in 1892, the Patent Office notified the Eastman Company that an interference had been declared between the Goodwin application and the Reichenbach patent; thus began a legal struggle that would last for almost 25 years, one that blocked Goodwin from any benefit from his labors and impoverished him in the process, that kept scores of lawyers employed, and that had almost no effect whatsoever on the Eastman Company.

In 1914, the Circuit Court of Appeals heard the last appeal in the case of Goodwin vs. Eastman Kodak Company and, reversing a lower court, found that the Goodwin patent of 1898 was valid and that Eastman Kodak had been infringing for many years. By this time, Rev. Goodwin had been dead for 14 years, his Goodwin Camera and Film Co. had been sold along with his patent rights to the Ansco Corporation. Eastman negotiated a settlement with Ansco that called for a five million dollar payment, a small portion of which trickled down to Goodwin's heirs through their ownership of some Ansco stock.[32]

Back to 1889: when Eastman Dry Plate and Film Company marketed those first lots of transparent, flexible celluloid film, produced under the Reichenbach and Eastman patents, the last obstacle to capturing motion on film was surmounted. The path was clear for a new set of inventors.

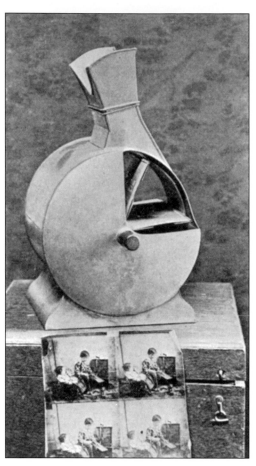

Fig. 40. Coleman Sellers' Kinematoscope.

First Steps

As long as an exposure had to be measured in minutes, or even seconds, photographers realized that capturing a moving target on film was impossible, but the appearance of motion could be obtained by taking sequential photographs of a posed subject. Among the first experimenters to try this approach was an American, Coleman Sellers (1827-1907) of Philadelphia.

Dr. Sellers, grandson of the famed painter Charles Wilson Peale, was a man of remarkably varied interests and accomplishments. Born in Philadelphia in 1827, Sellers was interested from childhood in "natural philosophy," as it was then called. Employed in his uncle's wire mill which was turning out wire for the new telegraph lines that were pushing westward, he was deeply stirred to read of Faraday's experiments with electricity and, in a makeshift laboratory, succeeded in duplicating the scientist's results. Sellers' industrial career included managing a rolling mill, designing power transmission systems, designing locomotives for the Panama Canal, and consulting to the International Niagara Commission.

After retirement from industry, Sellers served for many years as vice-president and, finally, president of the Franklin Institute.[1] Somewhere along the line he found time to invent and patent the "Kinematoscope" in 1861 (Fig. 40).

This was an instrument for viewing a series of stereoscopic pairs of posed photographs of successive phases of some action. Six stereo pairs were mounted by their inner edge on a central mandrel, with their outer edge fixed in a cylindrical cage. Two viewing slots for each pair were cut in the cage so that the images appeared moving towards the viewer as the respective slots aligned with the stereo viewing lenses. The motion of the axle was continuous, and Sellers explains this in his patent,[2] stating:

It is absolutely necessary that the pictures should be entirely at rest during the moment of vision, or that motion should be in a direction of the line of vision, that is, advancing toward the eye, or receding from it.

His patented apparatus took the second alternative: motion in a direction of the line of vision.[3]

Sellers' subjects for this reconstructed motion were his two sons, Coleman Jr., aged about 5, and Horace, about 2. Coleman Jr. is hammering a nail, while Horace looks on from a rocker. What could be a more prototypical home movie? [4]

Probably the first public demonstration of projected sequence motion using photographic images was that given by Henry Renno Heyl, a machinery designer from Columbus, Ohio, and friend and associate of Coleman Sellers on the Board of Trustees of the Franklin Institute. Heyl exhibited his Phasmatrope in February of 1870 to the Academy of Music in Philadelphia. Heyl's instrument was basically a projecting phenakistoscope with nine pairs of transparencies arranged around the perimeter of a large disk, which was revolved intermittently by a ratchet and pawl worked by hand by a reciprocating bar. The same mechanism operated a shutter that provided obscuration during image advance. The transparencies, approximately 3/4" x 1", were photographed from posed subjects, the slowness of film available at that time necessitating the posing of the subjects, which were dancers and acrobats. [5, 6]

In 1872, an English-born photographer, Eadweard James Muybridge,[7] (1830-1904) (Fig. 41) who had been making an extensive photographic

Fig. 41. Eadweard Muybridge.

survey of the American far west, was invited by Leland Stanford, former governor of California, to attempt the settlement of a long-standing debate among horsemen: does a trotting horse at any time have all four hooves off the ground? After a few failures, in 1873 Muybridge, using a wet-plate camera, succeeded in taking a sequence of photographs as the horse passed in front of his camera, several of which clearly showed that at one point in the horse's stride, all four feet were off the ground (Fig. 42).

Fig. 42. One of a series of photographs by Muybridge of Governor Stanford's horse Occident (1878).

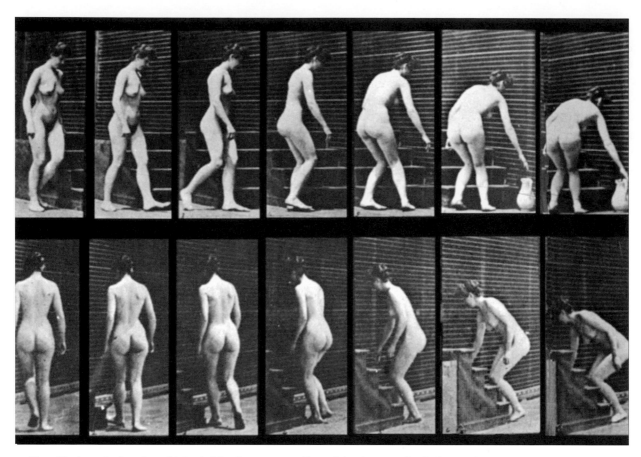

Fig. 43. A typical series of Muybridge's many studies of the human body in motion.

Muybridge published several books on animal and human locomotion; Fig. 43 is from *The Human Figure in Motion*, published in 1901.

Muybridge's photographic career was interrupted in 1874, when he learned that his young bride had been dallying with a dashing young mining engineer, Major Henry Larkyns. Muybridge hunted down the unfortunate Larkyns, shot him dead, then peacefully gave himself up. He stood trial but was eventually released, the jury, not surprisingly for those days, finding for a verdict of justifiable homicide. Muybridge nevertheless found it expedient to leave shortly thereafter for an extended tour of Central America.

He returned to Sacramento in 1877 with an improved camera boasting a shutter capable of one one-thousandth of a second speed and, with continued financing from Stanford, embarked on an elaborate scheme to take sequence photographs of moving horses. A long shed to house 12 wet-plate cameras, later increased to 24, was built alongside a special whitened track, on the other side of which was erected a white wall to serve as background (Fig. 44).

The camera shutters were tripped by wires or strings stretched across the track, depending on whether the subject was a horse or a horse and vehicle.

The results astonished sportsmen, artists, and scientists alike. Far from the conventional artist's rendition of the horse with forelegs extended forward and hind legs stretched out behind, the horse was seen to gather all four legs under his belly and, even more astounding, to put his hooves down one at a time!

Scientific American for October 19, 1878, published a set of drawings made from Muybridge's photographs, with the suggestion to the reader to paste the drawings on a cardboard strip and place the strip in a zoetrope to see the full effect of a galloping horse. Muybridge went this scheme one better. Recreating his photographic images with paintings on the rim of a phenakistoscope disc, he constructed a projector somewhat similar to Uchatius's projector of 1853. Muybridge called his machine the "Zoopraxiscope," (Fig. 45) and in 1879 took the machine to Europe on a triumphal lecture tour.[8]

Fig. 44. Muybridge's track set up for photographing horses in various gaits.

Etienne Jules Marey (1830-1904) (Fig. 46), whose life span exactly coincided with Muybridge's, was a brilliant French physiologist with a da Vinci-like gift for mechanical devices. While he never practiced

Fig. 45. Muybridge's Zoopraxiscope.

medicine as such, he was the originator of many of the physiological measuring and recording instruments upon which modern medicine depends, such as those that measure pulse, respiration, blood pressure, and heart function. His first such machine, developed in 1859 while he was still a medical student, was a sphygmograph, or pulse recorder. Physicians immediately recognized the value of this instrument, and the royalties from its sale enabled Marey to build his first laboratory.

Marey's contributions to the motion picture grew out of his consuming interest in and study of animal locomotion, for which he devised some marvelously complex machines, including several that were designed for the study of the flight of birds. Extremely light motion sensors were fitted to the birds, the signals from which were transmitted by air pressure through light rubber tubes to recording instruments on the ground. With these machines, Marey succeeded in obtaining a graphic record of the intricacies of the various motions of a bird's wing in flight. But he had hoped for more, and he was among the first scientists to recognize the potential value of the lowly zoetrope as a means of reproducing the actual motions of animals as they appear to the human eye.

Fig. 46. Etienne-Jules Marey.

Muybridge's photographs had also appeared in the December 1878 issue of *La Nature*, a popular science journal that followed the latest news in the burgeoning field of photography. Marey saw the photographs and immediately wrote to the editor expressing his admiration for Muybridge's work and asking to be put in touch with him. Muybridge not only replied but sent a set of his photographs.

When Muybridge took his Zoopraxiscope to Europe in 1881, Marey graciously invited Muybridge to demonstrate his machine at Marey's home to a gathering of many of the leading scientists of the day.

Word of this fascinating device and its revolutionary images spread through Paris, and a few months later a second party for Muybridge was arranged by one of Marey's artist friends. Interestingly, the artists and photographers were entranced and showered Muybridge with praise; the scientists, including Marey, were less enthusiastic, recognizing Muybridge's lack of scientific training and the scientific shortcomings of his methodology. Marey's chief complaint with Muybridge's system of an array of cameras actuated by the horse's hooves was that the time interval between the exposures was not uniform, nor was it recorded.

Several years previously, in 1876, the French astronomer Pierre Janssen (1824-1907), director of the Astrophysical Observatory in Paris, gave a lecture to the Academie des Sciences on the "photographic revolver" which he had designed and carried to Japan two years previously to record the transit of Venus across the face of the sun. Janssen's objective was not to record motion. He simply wished to capture the moment (of most interest to astronomers) when the planet's path first intercepts the observer's line of sight with the sun's disk. The most certain way to do that was to take a rapid sequence of pictures just as the planet approached the sun's rim. Janssen was an intrepid traveler, going all over the globe to observe astronomical phenomena. His most daring exploit occurred during the Franco-Prussian War on December 2, 1870. He escaped from besieged Paris in a balloon to catch an eclipse of the sun in Algeria.[9]

Marey in 1882 adapted Janssen's design to produce a photographic gun with which he photographed birds in flight, at the remarkable speed of twelve exposures per second. Unfortunately, his photosensitive material being a heavy glass plate, one second's worth of exposures was all he could make before re-loading the gun (Fig. 47). He subsequently made a greatly enlarged version, with a single fixed plate and rotating disk shutter four and one half feet in diameter, with which he recorded multiple images on the single plate, some of which resemble Dr. Harold Edgerton's multi-image photographs made with his stroboscope.[10]

Marey continued to struggle with the inherent limitations of the plate camera, even constructing one that moved the image across a fixed plate by means of an oscillating mirror. Of course he was still limited to the number of images that could be fitted on one plate, but the cure for this problem was soon to arrive.

Another student of animal locomotion was the Polish-born German professional photographer, Ottomar Anschutz (1846-1907). His method of photography was inspired by Muybridge—a series of still cameras—but his technique for viewing the results was entirely original and a great improvement on Muybridge's Zoopraxiscope.

Anschutz mounted his photos, which were in the form of glass transparencies, around the perimeter of a large vertical wheel, rotating behind a wall with an opening at the top for viewing. As each glass came by, it was illuminated from behind by the flash from a Geissler tube, the predecessor of our modern electronic flash gun. While the wheel revolved continuously, the flash of the Geissler tube was of such

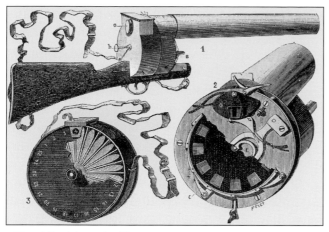

Fig. 47. Marey's rifle camera.

short duration, on the order of one thousandth of a second, that the signal to the retina was as of a stationary view, and as the images replaced each other at approximately 1/30th of a second, the effect was of smooth continuous motion. The Electro-Tachyscope (Fig. 48) was so successful that Anschutz had a number of coin-operated versions built which were exhibited throughout Europe and America, including one unit at the Chicago World's Columbian Exposition of 1893.[11]

The Arrival of Film

When Eastman's roll film became available in 1888, Marey constructed a camera to use the new flexible film, which he described to the Academie des Sciences in October of 1888. A strip of sensitive film 3-1/2 inches wide was moved continuously from a supply reel to a take-up reel, but clamped momentarily in the film gate as the exposure was made. As the film was not perforated, film advance was not uniform, and projection was not entirely satisfactory.[12]

The results were good enough however to lead Marey to demonstrate his film camera and films at the Universal Exposition in Paris of 1889. The individual images were mounted on strips and shown in a zoetrope. Incredibly, both Edison and Emile Reynaud were also exhibitors at the Exposition. What a constellation of geniuses! Edison's presence in Paris at this time was to have important consequences, as we shall see.

By November 1890 Marey had redesigned the entire camera, replacing the single disk shutter with two counter-rotating shutters and replacing the electrically driven clamping mechanism with a gear and cam mechanism (Fig. 49).

On June 29, 1893, Marey received Patent No. 231,209 for yet another design that Hopwood describes as follows:

The arrangement of its several mechanical details rendered the spacing of the individual photographs somewhat irregular, and the views were therefore of comparatively little use for subsequent projection. At a considerably later

Fig. 48. Anschutz's Electrical Tachyscope.

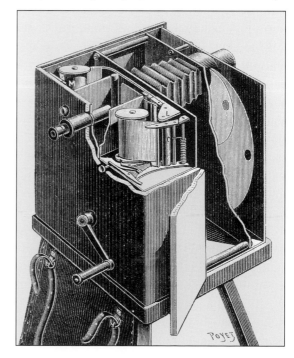

Fig. 49. Marey's film camera of 1890.

date M. Marey overcame these difficulties, and his final apparatus will be described in the next chapter. [13]

The "final apparatus," as illustrated in Hopwood, which he calls "Marey's Latest Chronophotograph," does not appear to be radically different; there is still a spring detent and a cam-operated clamp, but Hopwood declares, "These modifications have rendered the machine perfectly effective in the matter of equal spacing." [14] Hopwood's book was published in 1899.

Except for the use of unperforated film, Marey's last camera embodied all the elements of the modern ciné camera; flexible film moved intermittently through the gate, exposed behind a rotary shutter. This has been sufficient for many of Marey's partisans to consider him the true father of cinematography. It is ironic that Marey had actually no interest in producing moving images for any other purpose than the study of animal locomotion, yet he is perhaps the pre-eminent figure in the roster of individuals whose work led to the motion picture technology as we know it today. Quite aside from his chronophotography, he was a giant in scientific circles of the day; in 1901 he was named president of the Scientia Conference, an international body formed in 1886 to pay respects to the most illustrious representatives of science. Previous holders of the title included Pasteur, Lister, and Lord Kelvin.[15]

While the introduction of flexible film greatly facilitated the design of cameras for taking a rapid sequence of pictures, the successful moving of the film intermittently yet uniformly through the camera remained a challenging problem for many years after film was available. Hopwood describes no less than fourteen distinct ways that this was accomplished with more or less success by the date of his book, 1899.

Ironically, the man who devised a film advance mechanism that proved to have a longer life than Marey's system was none other than his long-time assistant, Georges Demeny. Demeny's invention was the "beater movement," which enjoyed some popularity in both cameras and projectors for the first two decades of commercial motion picture machines.

Georges Demeny (1850-1917) was a young physical fitness enthusiast when he applied to and was hired by Marey in 1881. Demeny was interested in the practical application of Marey's physiological studies, and was soon installed as Marey's "préparateur," or assistant, a relationship that thrived for thirteen years. Demeny proved to be a good mechanic and photographer and was soon left in charge of the Station Physiologique during Marey's annual winter sojourns in Naples.

The dissolution of the relationship came about at least in part when Demeny developed and patented his Phonoscope (Fig. 50), a curious sort of

Fig. 50. Georges Demeny with his Phonoscope.

Fig. 51.   The Phonoscope in operation.

phenakistoscope that was to be used to teach deaf children the elements of speech. Using one of Marey's cameras, Demeny took close-up photographs of a model (sometimes himself) enunciating some common phrase such as "Je vous aime." The individual photos were made translucent and placed around the edge of a glass disc, behind which was a shutter. The disc and shutter were turned by a crank; the images could be viewed in the machine or, with the addition of a lamp, projected (Fig. 51).

The Phonoscope was demonstrated at the first International Photography Exposition at Paris in May 1892 and was hailed as the next companion to the then immensely popular phonograph. However it was never successfully marketed, and Demeny lost a considerable sum in the process.

Chafing at his secondary role at Marey's Station and determined to make a name for himself, Demeny saw an opportunity in an improvement on Marey's camera. Replacing Marey's spring and clamp film advance action, Demeny positioned a rotating arm to periodically "beat" on the film, pulling one frame length through the gate each time the "beater" came around. The great advantage of this mechanism was its extreme simplicity and hence economy of manufacture. Demeny received a patent for the movement in 1893.

Demeny tried to interest the Lumières, but they had already settled on their much more elaborate

intermittent mechanism, which they patented in 1895. Demeny's camera came to the attention of Leon Gaumont, head of Le Comptoir General de Photographie, who asked Demeny to redesign his camera to take film 60mm wide with perforations on both edges. The result was the Demeny-Gaumont Chronographe, patented in 1896 (Fig. 52). The camera could also serve as a projector. The apparatus apparently functioned well and the large frames with

Fig. 52.   The Demeny-Gaumont Chronographe. The inset shows the beater movement at D.

Fig. 53. *Louis Aime Augustin LePrince, ca. 1880.*

Fig. 54. *Le Prince's multi-lens camera.*

four times the area of the Edison style film gave an excellent projected image. An exhibition in England elicited this comment from the British Journal of Photography: "[the performance was] . . . the best, photographically and mechanically, that we have seen."[16]

Despite such high praise for his equipment, fortune still eluded Demeny. Perhaps the higher cost of 60mm film kept the Chronographe from commercial success. Braun reports that Demeny ceded all his rights in the camera to Gaumont, retired from invention, and died in penury on December 26, 1917.

At the very time that Marey was describing his camera to the Academie in 1888, another dedicated experimenter was actually taking motion pictures with a film camera. This historic event was taking place in Leeds, England, and the cameraman was the ill-fated Louis Aimé Augustin Le Prince.[17]

Louis Le Prince (1841-1890) (Fig. 53) was born in Metz, to the family of a French artillery officer, who was reported to be a friend of Daguerre. Le Prince received a good education, studying in Paris and doing post-graduate work in chemistry at the University of Leipzig. In his mid-twenties he moved to England where he married the daughter of a well-to-do industrialist. After some years in his father-in-law's firm, he moved his family to the United States. In New York City, he became manager of a group of

artists who were producing large panoramas, one of which depicted the battle between the Merrimac and the Monitor.

Although hard evidence of Le Prince's earliest experiments is almost non-existent, it appears that around 1883 Le Prince began his attempts to build a motion picture machine. His first and only American patent, applied for on November 2, 1886, was for a multi-lens camera using flexible film such as Eastman's paper negative film and a similar multi-lens projector. Each machine had a rectangular array of sixteen lenses and shutters, arranged in two parallel bands of eight, to operate on two parallel bands of film (Fig. 54).[18]

As a camera, one band was clamped in place and eight sequential exposures made, during which time the other band was advanced an appropriate amount, and then the process repeated for the second band. Since the film was not perforated, the length of film per frame would vary as the diameter of the take-up spool increased—the same problem that Marey had. But as the negative frames had to be cut apart to make the positives, that deficiency could be overcome. The projector lenses were similar except they had to be arranged for convergent focus on the viewing surface. There was no flexible positive film available to Le Prince at that time, but in the words of the patent, this was his solution:

The sensitive film for the transparencies or positives must be on a transparent flexible material—such as gelatine, mica, horn, etc.,—for the larger deliverer with drums.

The positives were to be carried in perforated metal bands for projection. The reason for the reference to a "larger deliverer" is that Le Prince had originally proposed an alternate "small deliverer," or projector, which was to use glass plates and sounded very much like O.B. Brown's machine of 1869. This alternate was probably rejected by the patent examiner and the drawings removed, but the wording left in.

There is some disagreement among historians as to Le Prince's reasons for the two-strip, multiple lens design. The most plausible explanation would seem to be that it was a means of reducing the speed at which the film had to be moved through the camera. Le Prince lays considerable emphasis in his patent as to how the design permits nine hundred and sixty pictures per minute with only one revolution per second of the film drum.

Christopher Rawlence believes that Le Prince's intent was to produce stereoscopic motion pictures; however, there is no mention of any such intent in either his American patent nor his English patent for the same machine. In his initial application, Le Prince had stated that one or two lenses could be utilized, but the patent examiner rejected these options on the erroneous grounds of "anticipation" by other inventors such as Muybridge, DuMont, and even Simon Wing. These rejections were unfortunately accepted by Le Prince's attorneys while Le Prince was in England, unaware of this alteration.

Le Prince returned to England in May of 1888, and began work on a single lens camera. This camera used a single lens, a single band of film fed again by the take-up reel, and a rotary shutter (Fig. 55). With this camera, Le Prince filmed a touching "home movie." He set up the camera in the garden of his in-laws on a sunny October afternoon and persuaded the elderly couple and his son Adolphe to do a little dance. As Fate would have it, his mother-in-law died a few days after the filming, and since that date is inscribed on her tombstone there is an incontrovertible "no later than" date for LePrince's achievement—October 24, 1888. This film and a few more frames of other films survive and have been success-

fully projected, demonstrating that Le Prince had achieved a workable camera by that date.

The multiple-strip projector as described in the patent apparently did not function well, and in its place LePrince devised a single-lens projector, which he described in a May 1889 letter to his wife. The positive images, in effect glass slides, were carried in an endless "belt chain" to the top of a tube, where they dropped by gravity to a position behind a lens, held there momentarily for projection, then dropped to the bottom to be picked up again by the chain. As might be imagined, Le Prince had a great deal of trouble reaching a satisfactory "frame rate" with this arrangement, and the fall of 1889 found him working with a 3-lens and 3-belt projector. By this time, Eastman's celluloid film was available for positives, which made projection somewhat easier, but despite months of tinkering the mechanism could not be made to perform satisfactorily.

While he struggled with his projection apparatus, Le Prince was beset with other problems—family

Fig. 55. Le Prince single-lens camera.

illnesses, lack of steady income, demands of creditors, and the nagging fear that someone might overtake him putting a workable projector on the market. The latter concern was well founded. As we have seen, it was a time of great ferment in the art of "chrono-photography," with the achievements of Muybridge, Anschutz, and Marey well known and Edison having filed his first motion picture caveat in October 1888.

In September of 1890, Le Prince set off with two old friends for a vacation in France. Leaving his friends in Paris with an understanding to meet them in a few days, Le Prince left for a brief visit with his brother in Dijon, possibly to discuss the settlement of their mother's estate. On September 16, he boarded the train for Paris, and was never heard from again. No trace of him or any luggage was ever found, despite the efforts of both French and English police.

At the time of his disappearance, his family believed that he was close to success in his efforts to produce a workable motion picture system. They were extremely frustrated with the failure of the authorities to turn up any leads on his whereabouts and with the legal bar to their prosecution of his patent rights until seven years after his disappearance. At the same time they became ever more convinced that Thomas Edison's forces were somehow involved in his disappearance. His eldest son, Adolphe, was to spend a great deal of time and effort over the next ten years in futile attempts to prove his father's precedence over Edison in the invention of the motion picture.

Almost all of Le Prince's equipment was lost when a well-meaning friend "cleaned out" his workshop in Leeds some time after Le Prince's disappearance. Fortunately, a single-lens camera and parts of a multiple-lens camera survived, along with a few frames of the films taken with the single-lens camera, and are now in the Science Museum in London.

The Kinetoscope and Its Offspring

Thomas Alva Edison (1847-1931) (Fig. 56) was already a world-famous inventor and wealthy industrialist when the photography of motion came to his attention. Exactly when this occurred is in some doubt. Edison himself claimed the year 1887 but it is now believed to have been at least one year later. Gordon Hendricks' exhaustive study goes a long way toward dispelling the commonly held notion that

Edison single-handedly invented the motion picture, largely by showing that the bulk of the work on motion pictures was done by one of his assistants.[19]

Unlike other workers in the field, Edison had at his command a thriving experimental laboratory and a staff who were accustomed to turning the great man's ideas and sketches into solid working prototypes. One member of his staff was a young Britisher with an interest in photography, William Kennedy Laurie Dickson, and it was to this young man that Edison assigned his oft quoted idea—"to do for the eye what the phonograph does for the ear."

William Kennedy-Laurie Dickson (1860-1935) (Fig. 57) was born in France to a Scotswoman born in the United States and an Englishman. At age 19, Dickson, engrossed by the exploits of the "Wizard of Menlo Park," wrote from London to the famous inventor asking for a job in Edison's laboratories. The reply was brief: Edison was not taking on any new employees. Undaunted, Dickson persuaded his mother and two sisters to pull up stakes and immigrate to Virginia, Mrs. Dickson's birthplace.

Fig. 56. *Thomas Alva Edison, posing with "Edison effect" bulb.*

Two years later, Dickson presented himself at Edison's office in New York and was granted an interview, where he offered his credentials. Edison ignored the portfolio but, perhaps admiring Dickson's persistence, took him on and assigned him to the testing department of the Edison Electric Works. Dickson was bright and industrious; he did well at every assignment and by 1885 was in charge of Edison's ore milling experiments.

An event occurred in 1888 that may well have been the impetus for Edison's pregnant thought expressed above. On the 25th of February of that year, Muybridge visited Edison at the new laboratories in West Orange, and the two men discussed the possibility of combining the capabilities of Edison's phonograph with Muybridge's Zoopraxiscope. Edison even suggested that he record two well-known performers of the day, Edwin Booth and Lillian Russell, while Muybridge photographed them.[20]

While the idea never came to fruition, Edison filed his first caveat for a camera on October 8 of that year.[21, 22] The machine described in the caveat was largely the work of Dickson and was an adaptation of Edison's original phonograph mechanism: a horizontal cylinder turned with intermittent motion by a crank, bearing a photo-sensitive material, to receive a spiral of images on its surface. The machine had two serious drawbacks—the difficulty of getting a photosensitive material to conform to the cylin-

drical shape and the almost microscopic size of the images (Fig. 58).

While Dickson was struggling with these problems, Edison left for a tour of Europe in August of 1889. The tour was a triumphal one: he was named a Commander of the Legion of Honor of France, a Grand Officer of the Crown of Italy, and lunched with Gustave Eiffel at the top of the eponymous tower. But perhaps his greatest pleasure came from a visit with Dr. Marey, where Marey showed Edison his newly improved film camera. "I knew instantly that Marey had the right idea," he told Albert Smith, the film historian, and while returning across the Atlantic he sketched the machine he wanted.[23]

The accounts of what happened on Edison's return from Europe are typical of the inconsistencies and contradictions that permeate the history of this period as recorded by its participants. Dickson, in a memoir written for the *Journal of the Society of Motion Picture Engineers* in 1933, stated that he greeted Mr. Edison with a talking picture on the "Kinetophone," adding, "There was no hitch, and a pretty steady picture."[24] Eugene Lauste, another of Edison's assistants, who later became an important figure in the development of sound films, recalled that day and characterized Dickson's attempt at projection as a failure, with Edison leaving the room with dissatisfaction.[25] Edison himself, when queried about the demonstration several years later, denied under oath that there had been any projection.[26]

Fig. 57. William Kennedy Laurie Dickson.

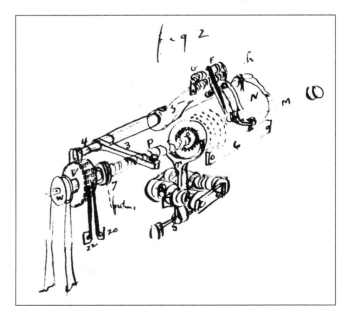

Fig. 58. Edison's sketch of his cylinder camera.

In any event, Edison's meeting with Marey brought a halt to efforts with the cylinder mechanism, and in November of 1889 Edison drafted a caveat describing the use of a long band of edge-perforated film carried from a supply reel to a take-up reel by toothed sprocket wheels, and intermittent motion.[27] The patent records show that on August 24, 1891, Edison filed applications for a camera called a Kinetographic Camera, an "Apparatus for Exhibiting Photographs of Moving Objects." The latter application resulted in Patent No. 493,426 issued March 14, 1893, and from the patent drawings is clearly the Kinetoscope. The camera patent, No. 589,168, was granted four and a half years later on August 31, 1897 (Fig 59). The patent drawing shows a horizontal disc escapement that Hendricks says was used in Black Maria production.[28]

Even before these applications were filed, the machines had been constructed and a successful demonstration made of the Kinetoscope for a delegation of the National Federation of Women's Clubs who visited West Orange on the 20th of May 1891. What the ladies saw was nevertheless a prototype, and experiments and improvements continued. By June of 1892, Dickson had completed a new Kinetograph camera, and construction of a special studio building, nicknamed "The Black Maria," had begun for making films with the new camera. The camera used Eastman Kodak film 1-3/8" wide, with four perforations on each side of the frame. The most generally accepted explanation for the use of this width is that it was the most convenient for Eastman to supply, being exactly one half of the width of the film being made for the original Kodak.

Externally, the Kinetoscope was an oak cabinet standing about four feet high with a "peep-hole" eyepiece on top and, as an option, a slot for coin operation (Fig. 60). Inside was a bank of spools holding an endless loop of film forty-two feet long, enough for about twenty seconds of viewing. The film, driven by an electric motor, ran continuously over a small light bulb. A rheostat in the motor circuit permitted the motor speed to be varied to adjust for the speed at which the film had been exposed, which might have been anywhere from eighteen to forty frames per second. A large shutter wheel with a very small slot was interposed between the film and the viewing lens. The high rate of frames

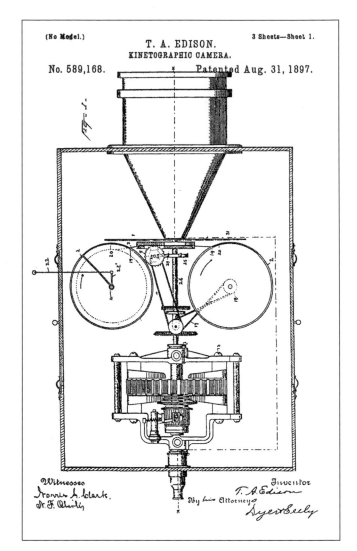

Fig. 59. Patent drawing for Edison's "Kinetographic Camera."

per second, plus the narrow aperture, obviated the need for intermittent motion, but did not yield a very bright image.

In 1894 Edison engaged the firm of Raff & Gammon as sales agents for the Kinetoscope. On April 14, 1894, the first Kinetoscope parlor was opened at the Holland Brothers Theatre at 1155 Broadway, New York City. The "parlor" system was a natural for Edison, since that merchandising system had been so successful for the phonograph. In a curious lapse of judgment, Edison declined to patent the Kinetoscope in Europe, reputedly saying that it was not worth the $100 fee. This decision turned out to be quite costly for him and to have far reaching consequences for the industry.

The Kinetoscope parlor was an immediate and astonishing success, and word of the success spread

Fig. 60. The Kinetoscope, side removed to show film-carrying spools.

rapidly (Fig. 61). By the end of 1894 no less than 54 Kinetoscope parlors had been opened, not only in major cities but also in towns like Sherman, Texas and Rutland, Vermont. Parlors were also opened in London, Paris, and Sydney, Australia. The Black Maria studio was kept busy churning out films, chiefly of popular vaudeville acts that were enticed to come to West Orange, such as Sandow, the Strong Man, Boxing Cats, and the dancer Carmencita.[29]

A New Entertainment

In July of 1894, a landmark film was produced when three would-be impresarios had the idea of staging a boxing match before the magic camera. Major Woodville Latham and his sons Otway and Grey Latham, scions of an aristocratic Virginia family had come north to recoup the family fortunes. Having witnessed the steady traffic at the Kinetoscope parlors, the Lathams decided to open their own Kinetoscope parlor but with a more exciting program than mere vaudeville acts.

Edison was approached and was amenable, but the limited film capacity of the Kinetograph was a problem—one film load would not be enough for

Fig. 61. Interior of Thomas Tally's phonograph and picture parlor, Los Angeles, 1897-98. Kinetoscopes on left, mutoscopes in center, phonographs right.

even one round. Working with the Lathams was a young electrical engineer named Enoch J. Rector, who enlarged the Kinetograph to take 150 feet of film, enough for a one-minute round. Michael Leonard, a prominent lightweight boxer of the day, and one unknown, Jack Cushing, were persuaded to go before the enlarged Kinetograph in a specially built 12-foot ring, designed to keep the fighters in the range of the camera. Six one-minute rounds were fought, with seven minutes between rounds, this long interval apparently needed to reload and adjust the camera.

The Lathams, now organized as the Kinetoscope Exhibition Company, opened a parlor at 83 Nassau Street with six Kinetoscopes, each showing one round of the Cushing-Leonard fight. The program was successful, but a new attraction was soon needed. Another bout was organized, this one between "Gentleman Jim" Corbett and Peter Courtney, heavyweights this time and much more in the public eye, Corbett having taken the title from the famed John L. Sullivan just two years earlier (Fig. 62).

Despite the fact that prize fighting was totally illegal in New Jersey, the fight took place without interference from the police on September 7, 1894, again in a small ring in the Black Maria. According to Ramsaye, the fight was "fixed." The Latham people had arranged with the fighters that the bout would go exactly six rounds and end with a knockout by Corbett in the sixth round.[30] The success of these two films in the peep show Kinetoscopes spurred the Lathams to pursue the idea of projecting the "living pictures" on to a screen. They may have even broached the idea to Edison himself, without success, since he was known to have felt that such a development would be the death knell of Kinetoscope sales, then still strong. Dickson had apparently long nurtured the thought of projection, and soon was discussing the possibility with the Lathams without letting on to Edison that he was doing so.

About this time, Edison had hired a new general manager, William E. Gilmore, who took an almost instant dislike to Dickson. When Gilmore discovered that Dickson had been secretly working with the Lathams, presumably not in the interests of the Edison Company, he confronted Dickson with his suspicions in Edison's presence. Dickson denied any wrongdoing and suggested that either he or Gilmore should leave the company. When Edison's demurrers were too equivocal, Dickson resigned on the spot. The date was April 2, 1895.

Curiously, despite this rather callous treatment by the man who had been his idol, and for whom he had performed great service, Dickson did not seem to harbor ill feelings toward Edison. A paper he prepared for the Society of Motion Picture Engineers in 1933, ended with this gracious statement:

In conclusion, it is with considerable pleasure that I look back on these days and nights at Edison's laboratories; of strenuous work, defeat, and triumph. My friendship and close association with Edison will always remain as a happy memory shadowed by his loss. I still watch with keen interest the development of this great industry—Edison's dream materialized. [31]

To what extent Dickson had helped the Lathams in pursuit of projection is not clearly recorded, but within weeks of his departure from Edison the Lathams demonstrated a projector they called the "Panoptikon," later renamed the "Eidoloscope." It took film twice as wide as the Kinetoscope film but retained the latter's continuous motion. It was demonstrated to the press on April 21, 1895.

The press reaction was favorable enough to encourage the Lathams to produce another boxing match, which went on public exhibition on May 20, 1895, at a store front theater at 153 Broadway in New York City. The record does not show whose camera was used, but it was possibly the enlarged Kinetograph used to film the Leonard/Cushing fight.[32] An improved projector, the Eidoloscope, incorporating intermittent motion, was announced, but it came under attack from Edison for patent infringement and was soon abandoned. This marked the end of the Latham enterprises.

Enoch J. Rector (1863-1957) was a classmate of the Latham sons at the University of West Virginia and a graduate engineer. He worked with the Lathams in their first efforts to achieve projection, but left them before their "Eidoloscope" was launched. Leaving with him was one Samuel J. Tilden, Jr., whose chief asset seems to have been the fact that he was the nephew and namesake of a former governor of New York State and a one-time Democratic candidate for president of the United States.

Fig. 62. The Corbett-Courtney Bout, as staged at Edison's Black Maria, September 7, 1874.

Rector and Tilden had acquired and retained an exclusive fight picture contract with Corbett on the strength of which they set about organizing a bout between Corbett and Bob Fitzsimmons, to be held in Dallas. Rector had remained on good terms with Edison and was able to order four cameras from him. The Dallas bout was canceled, but eventually re-scheduled for March 17, 1897, in Carson City, Nevada (Fig. 63).

Curiously, Rector did not use the Edison cameras but built three of his own design, christened the Veriscope. The camera took an image 2-3/16 inches wide and could be converted to a projector. When the fight was over, Rector had exposed over 11,000 feet of film, which if exhibited in its entirety would certainly have qualified as the world's first feature-length film.

The first screening of the Corbett-Fitzsimmons fight via the Veriscope projector was at the Academy of Music on 14th Street in Manhattan, followed by a long engagement at the Park Theater in Brooklyn. Despite these apparent successes, Rector and the Veriscope soon dropped from sight. Undoubtedly the relatively high per foot cost of the Veriscope film, plus the arrival of other systems using the Edison format, would have contributed to the demise of the Veriscope system.

If the growth of the motion picture industry is thought of as a tree whose roots are the Phenakistoscope, the Praxinoscope, and the Zoetrope, and whose trunk is the Kinetoscope, then Dickson's brief

Fig. 63. Corbett-Fitzimmons Fight, Carson City, Nevada, March 17, 1897.

excursion with the Lathams produced two branches which were not destined to bear much fruit—the Latham Eidoloscope and the Rector Veriscope.

The Mutoscope and the Biograph

An earlier Dickson sortie, begun before the Lathams appeared, was of great significance in the course of motion picture history. It began with a little toy known to children for years—the flip book—and was to end with a motion picture system that provided a vehicle for the industry's first master cinematographer and produced one of the greatest film directors of all times.

There were, besides Dickson, three men involved in this development. The chronology and relative degree of their participation has been treated at length by Hendricks in his *Beginnings of the Biograph* and, in a sometimes more romanticized fashion, by Ramsaye in *A Million and One Nights* (Fig. 64).

Harry N. Marvin (1862-?) was an electrical engineer who had once worked at the same Edison plant in New York with Dickson. He went on to invent an electric rock drill, patented in 1889, in which Edison was interested and had at one time planned to market under his own name.[33]

To produce the drill, Marvin induced another former Edison employee to join him in founding the Marvin Electric Rock Drill Works in Canastota, New York.

Herman Casler (1867-1939) was a brilliant engineer/mechanic who invented among other things, the "Photoret," a remarkable miniature camera in the shape of a pocket watch, and another "spy" camera called the "Presto," both highly valued today by collectors. Casler's Photoret was marketed by a New York City entrepreneur named Koopman.

Elias B. Koopman (?-1929), the least well known of the group, played a major role through his personal involvement in the company that was eventually formed and through his contacts with New York businessmen. Koopman was the proprietor of the charmingly named "Magic Introduction Company," a dealership in various toys and novelties, including Farnum's Viviscope.[34]

While still in Edison's employ, Dickson approached his friend Marvin with an idea for a simple, inexpensive device that would permit viewing of some short dramatic event, such as the last few seconds of a knockout punch in a boxing match. Marvin later recounted that Dickson had made up an experimental batch of cards on which were drawn a series of crosses in varying positions. When the cards were thumbed the cross seemed to whirl and dance.

Fig. 64. The founders of the K.M.D.C. Syndicate, later Biograph. L to R: H.N. Marvin, William K-L Dickson, Herman Casler, E.B. Koopman. Posed on Casler's lawn, Canastota, New York, September 22, 1895.

This idea was not new, of course. An Englishman named Linnet had patented in 1868 a flip-card device he called the Kineograph and that was anticipated by Coleman Sellers' 1861 Kinematoscope. Marvin discussed the idea with his friend Casler, who consulted Koopman, who was marketing Casler's Photoret. All agreed that the idea had merit, and work was begun at the Marvin Rock Drill works in Canastota. Hendricks says that a Mutoscope was completed by November 1894, but gives no source for this assertion.

As realized by Casler, the Mutoscope consisted of a spool of sequential photographs mounted on cards arranged radially on a core (Fig. 65). The cards were approximately 2-1/2" wide by 3-1/2" long, with the image placed on the outer two inches of each card. The cards were interleaved with blank cards slightly shorter than the image cards. In operation, the viewer deposited a nickel, which released the hand crank permitting one full revolution of the reel. Approximately 1,000 cards were in each reel, yielding about a one-minute show.[35]

Casler filed for a patent on the Mutoscope on November 21, 1894, but if a machine had been built by that time, it is a mystery whence came the photographs, as the quadrumvirate did not have a camera as of that date.

The Mutoscope was not offered to the public until 1897. It required the development of a camera and, by the time the camera was ready, Dickson and his group had their eyes on projection. Work on the camera commenced in January of 1895 and progressed rapidly, with a prototype being ready in June. Dickson had left Edison in April and it may be assumed that he was the major contributor to the design of the camera. The Mutograph, as the camera was now called, was a massive affair. The mahogany case measured about 30" high by nearly 60" long, on top of which was mounted a 2-1/2 horsepower motor which itself weighed 200 pounds. The well-known illustration from Scientific American shows that set up on location, the outfit standing about seven feet high.[36] (See Figs. 66 and 67.)

The first film made with the Mutograph was a bit of "clowning." On a June day in Canastota Marvin and Casler squared off in front of a sheet outside one of their shops while Dickson ran off a

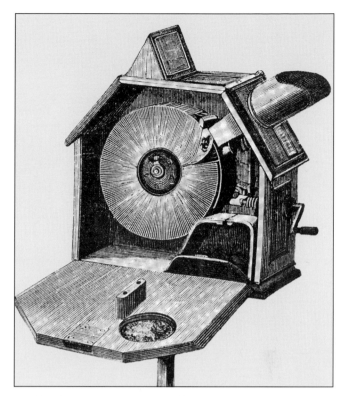

Fig. 65.   1897 version of the Mutoscope.

few feet of film. A few weeks later two professionals were hired to go a few rounds in front of the camera. This film was shown to the four principals and a few guests at the shop of one James Mahan in Canastota in November 1895.

The showing so pleased the principals that the American Mutoscope Company was organized on December 27, 1895, with a capital stock of $2,000,000. Headquarters was established at 837-841 Broadway in New York City, and a "state-of-the-art" studio constructed on the roof of that building, doubtless designed by Dickson (Fig. 68). About this time the company name was changed to the American Mutoscope and Biograph Company, evidently in recognition of the two distinct lines of the company's business, "Biograph" being the projected film division.

The new camera was kept very busy in 1896, not only at the stage but on numerous "location" shots for such films as *Shooting the Shutes, Atlantic City, Pennsylvania R.R. at New Brunswick*, and a series of eleven films of Niagara Falls. Considering the weight and bulk of the camera and the batteries that were required in the field, one must admire the determination of the camera crew.

Fig. 66. Filming with the Mutograph: Pennsylvania Railroad Limited Express.

Fig. 67. The Mutograph, open.

Fig. 68.   The Biograph rooftop studio, New York City.

The first person other than Dickson to operate the camera was a young man named W.G. Bitzer (1872-1944) (Fig. 69). Billy, as he was universally known, was born in Roxbury, Massachusetts, into a family of silversmiths. Bitzer worked at Gorham's and other places, but at the age of 22, tiring of the family craft, enrolled in evening courses in "electri-

Fig. 69.   William G. "Billy" Bitzer.

cal engineering" at Cooper Union in New York. He shortly thereafter was hired by Koopman to work in the Magic Introduction Company. He became a cameraman under Dickson's tutelage in 1896.

The first Biograph projector was apparently made by conversion of a Mutograph camera. To keep the arc flame as far from the massive rolls of nitrate film as possible, the lamphouse was placed entirely outside the camera body, at right angles to the film, with the light beam directed through the film by a suitably placed mirror. It too was a very large and unwieldy piece of equipment.[37]

In 1907 or thereabouts, a young actor/writer, then using the name Larry Griffith, came looking for work with The American Mutoscope and Biograph Company (Fig. 70). After appearing in a few of the company's one-reelers, he applied for a directing job and was put to work on "off-color" pictures intended for the arcade Mutoscopes, where Billy Bitzer was also working. After one of Biograph's directors left, Griffith was given his first chance at a good script about a girl named Dolly who is kidnapped by gypsies, sealed in a barrel, then rescued from a river. Billy Bitzer had taken a liking to Griffith and gave him some pointers on organizing the shooting, although another cameraman was assigned to Griffith.[38] The result was The Adventures of Dollie, released July 14, 1908. This charming little

Fig. 70. David Wark Griffith.

melodrama proved so popular with the public that distributors demanded more films like it and the careers of David Wark Griffith (1875-1948) and Billy Bitzer were securely launched (Fig. 71).

Griffith and Bitzer would remain another five years with Biograph, during which time the team of director and cameraman made stars of such as Mary Pickford, Dorothy and Lillian Gish, Blanche Sweet, Mabel Normand, Donald Crisp, Wallace Reid, and Harry Carey. Both men are generally acknowledged to rank among the very top practitioners of their respective professions; they were originators of many effects and techniques that were revolutionary at the time, but today are taken for granted.

Biograph itself faded from the scene shortly after Griffith and Bitzer left. Griffith had a burning desire to make feature-length films, while Biograph's management and most of the other studios were more interested in turning out one- and two-reeler for the nickelodeons. In their view, films were commodities to be sold by length with little regard for content. When Griffith joined Mutual in 1914, Bitzer and most of the company of actors went with him.[39]

Ironically, the Mutoscope far outlived its Biograph offspring and most other primitive viewing machines. As Gerald Mast observed, the large cards offered the viewer much clearer pictures than the Kinetoscope, and the fact that the viewer controlled the speed of the machine by the hand crank added greatly to the sensory pleasure. Mutoscopes remained a popular feature of arcades and amusement parks well into the middle of the twentieth century.

Armat/Jenkins and the Vitascope

Thomas Armat (1866-19?) (Fig. 72) was a partner in a Washington D.C. real estate office when he first became involved in motion pictures. Unfortunately, almost nothing is known of his life prior to that time. In 1934, he prepared a biographical reminiscence at the request of the Historical and Museum Committee of the Society of Motion Picture Engineers, received by them on January 1, 1935, from which most of the following account is taken.[40]

From this well-written paper we learn that two of Armat's fondest childhood possessions were a toy Zoetrope and a small magic lantern. From the latter he learned the delight of enlarged projection of small objects. With this background, one can understand his interest at the Anschutz Tachyscope that he viewed at the World's Columbian Exposition in Chicago in 1893.

One year later, at the insistence of a friend, Armat attended the first exhibition of the Edison Kinetoscope in Washington, D.C., on October 8, 1894, at the Columbia Phonograph Musical Palace.

Fig. 71   Bitzer at the Pathé with David Wark Griffith, on location for "Way Down East," 1920.

Fig. 72. Thomas Armat.

Fig. 73. C. Francis Jenkins.

The friend was a man who knew both Raff and Gammon, Edison's agents for the Kinetoscope, and thought that this was a business Armat might look into.

Armat's reaction to the demonstration was guarded; he told his friend that he thought it unlikely that the Kinetoscope would be a commercial success, unless some way could be found to project the images. Despite his rather prosaic occupation, Armat was a many-faceted man. He held several patents in rather disparate fields, among them an automatic railroad car coupler and a conduit electric railway system. The latter received high praise from an authority in the field.[41]

The Kinetoscope had touched Armat's imagination, and he began to consider the problems of projection. To begin with, it seemed likely that the first requirement be a stronger light source, such as an arc lamp. To learn about this technology, Armat enrolled in the Bliss School of Electricity in Washington. He was shortly introduced to Charles Jenkins, another student at the school known to be interested in motion pictures.

C. (Charles) Francis Jenkins (1867-1934) (Fig. 73) was just about Armat's age and was also of an in- ventive mind. His occupation at the time was just as prosaic as Armat's—he was a stenographer/clerk at the United States Treasury Department.

The two became friends, and Jenkins showed Armat some designs he had already developed for motion picture machines, including two varieties of cameras, and a projector he called the "Phantoscope," on which he had just filed his patent application.[42] Armat considered the machine "simply an adaptation of the Kinetoscope" and argued that if it retained the Kinetoscope's continuously moving film, it would not be successful.

After working together for a while, they drew up a formal partnership agreement, signed on March 25, 1895, that provided for: a) Jenkins to drop his an application for a beater type intermittent projector, b) Armat to build a projector based on a modification of Jenkins' Phantoscope and advance the funds necessary thereto, and c) Armat to have the use of several of Jenkins' rotating lens cameras.

They shortly completed a projector as called for in (b) above, which Armat labeled a complete failure.[43] He then took over the project and built what he described as the first projector using intermittent motion of the film, using a "mutilated gear," his name for a variation of the Geneva movement. The machine was designated the "Jenkins & Armat Phantoscope." [44]

Again a failure; this time because the "mutilated gear" mechanism could not stand up to the Edison film rate of 40 frames per second. However, it did demonstrate that the intermittent motion of the film was essential for successful projection. Armat decided to revert to the beater movement.

One machine was built, proved satisfactory, and two more machines were ordered, to be shipped on completion to the Cotton States Exposition in Atlanta, Georgia, where Armat and Jenkins hoped to attract enough customers to pay for the trip. The machines worked well, but the anticipated crowds did not materialize and the partners lost a considerable sum of money, chiefly Armat's, one supposes.

Jenkins borrowed one of the machines to take to Richmond, Indiana, where his brother-in-law was getting married. Armat returned to Washington to work on further improvements on the projectors. On his next visit to Jenkins, he discovered that his partner was about to file for a patent on the Atlanta projector as his sole invention.

For this move, and possibly other reasons, the two men severed their relationship, not without rancor. Armat obtained a writ of replevin to recover the "borrowed" projector. Jenkins proceeded with his patent application; however, it was ultimately declared in interference with the Armat/Jenkins patent, and the latter was upheld.

There followed an unhappy period of claims and counter-claims. Jenkins read a paper before the Franklin Institute, presenting himself as the sole inventor of the first successful motion picture projector, on the strength of which the Institute awarded him a gold medal. Armat understandably protested and offered the Patent Office ruling on the Armat/Jenkins projector as evidence of his claim. Nothing came of Armat's protest; Jenkins kept his gold medal and has received most of the recognition by historians.

After further modifications to the Atlanta projector, on February 19, 1896, Armat filed for a patent on a machine he called the Vitascope (Fig. 74). This touched off a long Patent Office "Interference Procedure." [45] The claimants of interference were, besides Armat: Herman Casler, of Biograph, Edwin H. Amet[46], and Woodville Latham. The hearing dragged on for five years, produced volumes of testimony, and eventually, a finding in Armat's favor.[47]

Meanwhile, Raff & Gammon was becoming increasingly unhappy with the Kinetoscopes. The public was tiring of one minute vaudeville turns, dimly seen through a peep hole, and Edison was slow in providing new films. The Lathams had given a glimpse of what might be expected of projection, if someone could contrive a satisfactory machine. Edison continued to ignore the pressure or make empty claims to having a better machine in the offing.

Finally, Armat succeeded in demonstrating his Vitascope to Gammon, by dint of paying his fare to

Fig. 74. Armat's Vitascope.

Washington, and bowled the entrepreneur over with what he saw. Negotiations were begun under which the Edison Company would manufacture the projectors for a certain fee, the machines to be leased only, never sold. Then Mr. Edison began to think about the situation, and Armat received a most curious letter.

It seems that Raff & Gammon and Mr. Edison were concerned that the machine, as excellent as it appeared to be, would hardly command the public's attention as an "Armat" Vitascope. How much more quickly it would seize the public if announced under the magic of Mr. Edison's name! Of course Mr. Edison had no intention of passing the invention off as his own and as soon as the machine was well established in the marketplace, a suitable place would be found to identify the machine as "Armat Design," or something of that kind. Then of course when everyone was making lots of money, Mr. Edison would definitely make it his business to attach Mr. Armat's name to the machine as inventor, and Raff & Gammon was confident that Mr. Armat would eventually receive the credit which was due him for his invention.[48]

How much stock Armat put in these slippery phrases is not known, but he evidently considered the alternatives and, deciding that he had few options, went along with the proposed contract. Construction of the Edison Vitascope began, with Armat's brother J. Hunter Armat installed as supervisor of production. On April 3, 1896, a demonstration for the press was held at West Orange.

If it really was Edison's intent to credit Armat, the newspapers that reported the demonstration the next day did not get the message. The New York Herald, presumably quoting Edison, reported:

The vitascope, which has been in process of perfection at the Llewellyn laboratory for the last seven or eight months under Mr. Edison's direction, is the ideal which he had in mind, he says, when he began work on the kinetoscope machine, with which he has never been satisfied.

The first commercial showing was scheduled for the week beginning April 20 at Koster and Bial's Music Hall. However, some difficulties arose in installing the two projectors in the balcony of the theater and the actual opening took place on April 23, 1896. The films shown included: *Umbrella Dance, Burlesque*

Boxing, Kaiser Whilhelm Reviewing His Troops, and *Sea Waves.* The first two were Edison productions, while the last two obviously could not have been. Sea Waves was actually Robert Paul's Rough Seas at Dover, which Raff & Gammon had acquired in their desperate search for new titles.[49] (Fig. 75)

The audience reaction to the Vitascope was all that any showman could have wished. When the "rough seas" came rolling up at the audience, the first few rows hastily vacated their seats, fully expecting to be drenched. When the house lights came on the audience broke into cheers, with cries of "Edison! Edison! Speech! Speech!" but Edison sat

Fig. 75. Koster and Bial's Program for the week of April 20, 1896.

mute in his box. What Armat's reaction was as he supervised the debut of his creation is unrecorded.

Despite this auspicious beginning, the relationship between Armat and Raff & Gammon began to deteriorate. The latter company was finding that the carefully delineated territories for which it had given exclusive contracts to its Vitascope clients were being invaded by purveyors of pirated projectors of various designs. To make matters worse, Edison was reported to be planning the introduction of an improved machine to be called "Edison's Projecting Kinetoscope," which would be sold, not leased.

Edison had actually approached Armat about permitting sale of his machines, which Armat flatly refused, feeling that the small but steady royalty revenue from exhibitors would in the aggregate be much greater than the profit from a relatively small number of projectors sold outright.[50]

In November of 1896, Edison announced the Projecting Kinetoscope, described as "an improvement over the Vitascope" (See Figs. 76 and 77.) This naturally diminished the value of Raff & Gammon's franchise for the Vitascope. The latter machine was dealt another blow with the appearance of the American Biograph at Hammerstein's Olympia Music Hall in October and, even more seriously, by the arrival in New York of a French machine whose

pictures were said to have been superior to those of the Vitascope.

The Edison Company continued to produce motion pictures at the West Orange complex until a an explosion and subsequent fire destroyed the film department and other buildings on the night of December 9, 1914.

The Kinetoscope Goes Abroad

News of the Kinetoscope had arrived in England in early 1894 via several publications, including a long descriptive piece in *Century Magazine*, written by Dickson and his sister, Antonia. The machine was first exhibited by Maguire and Baucus, European agents for Edison, who had the machines shipped to their "parlour" at 70 Oxford Street, London. The debut received mixed notices from the press, but an enthusiastic welcome from the general public. Other parlors were opened in Paris and Sydney, Australia.

Several more parlors were opened in England and the demand for more machines quickly outstripped Edison's agents' ability to supply them. Not surprisingly, someone with more business acumen than scruples stepped in to take advantage of the situation. George Georgiades and George Trajedes, two Greek businessmen who were the English agents of Holland Brothers, having brought some Kinetoscopes, films, and spare parts to England,

Fig. 76. Edison Projecting Kinetoscope, spoolbank model.

Fig. 77. Edison Projecting Kinetoscope.

Fig. 78.   Robert W. Paul.

Fig. 79.   Birt Acres.

decided that a local source of machines would increase their profit margins. Looking about for someone to duplicate the Kinetoscopes, they were led to Robert W. Paul (1868-1943), an electrical engineer and scientific instrument maker in London (Fig. 78). Paul at first refused, assuming that Edison would certainly have patented his machine in England, and warned the two entrepreneurs what might ensue if they proceeded with their plan.

After they left, Paul decided to investigate Edison's patent and, of course, discovered to his great surprise that there was no such patent. He then summoned Georgiades and Trajedes and advised them that he would be happy to make them as many machines as they wanted plus a few for himself. The offer was accepted, and by Paul's later recollection he produced six machines in 1894 and about 60 in 1895.

Paul became an exhibitor and soon was confronted with the problem of obtaining replacement films for those that wore out and demands from coustomers for new subjects. Unlike the Kinetoscope, Edison had copyrighted the films and they were only sold to registered owners of Kodascopes, bought from a Kodascope dealer.[51]

From this point on, the record is very confusing. In another case reminiscent of the Armat/Jenkins controversy, two investigators meet and pool their resources and ideas, come to disagree, part company, then forever after issue conflicting statements as to who contributed what.

According to Paul, he began to design a camera in 1894 which he completed by February 1895.[52] He then looked about for someone to operate the camera and was introduced to a professional photographer named Birt Acres (1854-1918) (Fig. 79). It is also possible that Paul was looking for someone with photographic experience to apply that knowledge to the camera design.

Acres had designed a device for making prints from glass negatives in rapid succession and showed sketches of his ideas to Paul. Acres seems to have felt that his design was applicable to a motion picture camera. However, Paul pointed out that the mechanism would be far too clumsy for cinematography. The device did start him thinking along lines that ultimately resulted in a working camera.

Acres felt that the successful design was as much his as Paul's and filed a patent application for a Kinetic Camera, which was issued on May 27, 1985. The patent claimed the intermittent movement and other features of the camera that Paul had designed independently of Acres but, curiously, had never patented.

Paul recalled that Acres did provide a lens for their first camera but, other than that, had no part in its design. Despite this contretemps, the two then entered into an agreement under which Acres would use the Paul-Acres camera to supply films exclusively for Paul. The camera was apparently completed by March 29, 1895, because on that date Paul wrote to

Thomas Edison, enclosing samples of his film and proposing an exchange of films. Edison declined the offer.

On March 30, Acres filmed the *The Boat Race*, their first salable film. On May 29, Acres filmed the 1895 Derby and was himself photographed as he operated the Paul-Acres camera. On July 12, Acres announced that he could no longer make films without being financed, which may be assumed to mean "paid in advance." This was unacceptable to Paul, whereupon the agreement was canceled. Acres paid for the camera and set out on his own as a producer and exhibitor of films. Paul also went on to a successful, if relatively brief, career designing new cameras, printers, perforators, and projectors.[53] The projectors were known as Theatrographs and were widely used throughout England.

Acres' account of his association with Paul, written after their parting, differs radically from the above. First, he denied that there was ever any part-

nership between them. In another letter he stated that at the time of their first meeting Paul "admitted to me that he had no idea how to make such an apparatus (a camera)." Acres also maintained that he had constructed and used a "machine" as early as 1893, but did not get around to applying for a patent until 1895. That Acres could have had a working camera and projector one year before the Kinetoscope arrived, without anyone hearing of it, seems extremely unlikely since he was quite diligent at self-promotion.

In evaluating these conflicting stories, the reader should consider that Paul was, at the time of meeting Acres, a well-established manufacturer of scientific instruments, while Acres was an accomplished photographer with no mechanical achievements of particular merit. Regardless of their final disenchantment, the two must be recognized as the two most significant figures in the establishment of the cinema in England.

Fig. 80. Louis and Auguste Lumière, taken at Lyon-Montplaisir.

Fig. 81. The Lumière Cinematographe in use.

Across the Channel, the Lumières

August and Louis Lumière (Fig. 80) were the owners of one of France's leading photographic supply houses, founded in 1882 in Lyons by their father Antoine. Sometime in 1894, a local exhibitor of the Kinetoscopes showed the brothers a piece of Kinetoscope film. Because of the high prices being charged by the Edison dealer, the exhibitor asked the Lumières if they could supply films. Auguste began designing a camera. As the story goes he was having difficulty with the intermittent movement when his brother Louis remembered how his wife's sewing machine worked and suggested that Auguste try a similar mechanism. The concept worked and a French patent was issued on February 13, 1895.[54]

The Lumière machine (Fig. 81), called the Cinematographe, could also function as a projector by removing the back of the camera, mounting a magic lantern or other light source behind the camera, and substituting a projection lens for the taking lens. The camera was hand-cranked like the Paul-Acres camera, but even more compact and lighter, making it ideal for outdoor, or what we would call "location" shooting. Compare this with the Kineto-graph, or Bioscope, each of which weighed close to 200 pounds and required hundreds of pounds of batteries for their electric drives when they were in the field.

This portability encouraged the Lumières to take impromptu movies of scenes that heretofore had not been attempted, such as workers streaming out of the Lumière factory, Madame Lumière feeding the baby, and so on. The first public exhibition of the Cinematographe was in Paris on March 22, 1895, to the members of a learned society, and the film shown was "La sortie des Usines Lumières." [55] (See Fig. 82.) The effect on the audience was electric, and the Lumières were obliged to repeat the one-minute showing several times for the thunderstruck audience.

Encouraged by this reception, the Lumières quickly shot more films, and put together a 30-minute show of 12 films which they launched commercially at the Grand Café, 14 Boulevard des Capucines, on December 28, 1895.

Fig. 82. La Sortie des Usines Lumières.

For this showing, Lumière had invited Carpentier, the builder of his Cinematographe, reporters on science, and Georges Méliès (1861-1938), the celebrated conjurer and proprietor of the Theatre Robert-Houdin, a house devoted to sleight-of-hand and mechanical magic shows. Some 20 years later, Méliès gave this account of his reaction:

The spectacle left us with mouth agape, struck with wonder and almost speechless. At the end of the presentation, I made an offer to M. Lumière to buy one of his machines for my theatre. He refused. I had offered as much as 10,000 francs, a sum that seemed enormous to me. M. Thomas, director of the Musée Grevin, offered 20,000 francs with the same result. Finally M. Lallemand, director of the Folies-Bergère, went up to 50,000 francs. M. Lumière remained unmoved, and advised us with good humor: 'This machine is a secret, and I do not wish to sell it. I intend to exploit it myself.' [56, 57]

And exploit it he did, contracting with Carpentier to build 200 Cinematographes, which Lumière agents took all over Europe and America. The first American showing was at Keith's Union Square Theatre in New York City on June 29, 1896.[58]

The fruits of the Kinetoscope tree had taken root in England and the Continent, and hardy hybrids were springing up all over the world. The motion picture machine, whether it was called Kinetoscope, Panoptikon, Biograph, Vitascope, Veriscope, Theatrograph, or Cinematographe, was irretrievably launched on the world and the world would never be quite the same.

Of the men who labored in this orchard, debate has boiled or simmered for years as to who deserves the laurels. Each country has its own hero or heroes; probably a half-dozen countries have a plaque somewhere marking "the birthplace of the motion picture." But as we have seen, it is impossible to single out one individual and say, "without this man's work the motion picture would not exist." It seems evident to this writer at least that the absence of any one individual would have delayed the eventual outcome by six months perhaps, a year or two at the most.

So let us remember them all, with their foibles, their occasional human weaknesses, their indomitable will, and their flashes of genius. They built an amazing structure—their hands provided the tools for a new art form which has endured for a century (Fig. 83). Who knows what the next century will bring? Perhaps an entirely new form and a new pantheon of heroes.

Fig. 83. Auguste and Mme Lumière and their infant daughter at breakfast. The first home movie?

3   Amateur Equipment Prior to 1923

Fig. 84. Birt Acres' Birtac, 17.5 mm, 1898.

Cheaper and Safer

Almost as soon as motion pictures became commercially successful in the closing years of the nineteenth century, entrepreneurs began looking for ways to bring this new amusement into the home. To do so successfully required reducing the bulk and cost of professional equipment and, insofar as possible, reducing the hazards associated with nitrate film. The introduction took at least two distinct courses. At one level were some quite sophisticated and fairly expensive machines generally designed for smaller than standard gauge film, this being the simplest way to reduce operating cost. At the other extreme, and appearing simultaneously, was a class of machines which continued to use full size standard film but were primarily toys, limited to showing very short lengths of film and generally selling at a much lower price. Further, there arose a category of machines using other than conventional film, of such diverse mechanisms that they can only be classified as "special."

While acetate-based "safety" film was available from both Eastman Kodak and Pathé as early as 1911, the ready availability of commercially produced 35mm films plus the generally lax standards of safety at the time resulted in many machines being offered for home use which were designed for the dangerously flammable nitrate film.

Origins in Europe

With a few exceptions, the first efforts to accommodate movie machinery to home use took place in Europe, particularly in England. By the 1890s the magic lantern was a popular fixture in mid- to upper-class homes, thus it was natural that many of the first projection devices to permit showing movies at home were designed to utilize the magic lantern as a light source. The first four machines designed specifically for the amateur were all British: the 1898 Birtac, the 1897 Motorgraph, the 1899 Biokam, and the 1900 La Petite.

Fig. 85. *The Motorgraph, by W. Watson & Sons, 35mm film, 1897.*

The Birtac (Fig. 84) was designed by Birt Acres, the London photographer who was for a time associated with Robert W. Paul, generally regarded as the father of the British film. Acres designed this camera to take 35mm film split lengthwise to 17.5mm, with two round perforations per frame on each edge. The camera was compact and well made. It came with a fitted leather case, permitting it to be used, as Coe puts it, "unobtrusively, in the manner of the detective still cameras of the time." The Birtac outfit, with case and lamp house, sold for ten guineas.[1, 2]

The Motorgraph, by W. Watson & Sons, was a sturdy mechanism designed to mount in front of a stereopticon, or magic lantern (Fig. 85). It took standard 35mm film and could be used as a camera. It sold for twelve guineas. A guinea (21 shillings) equaled five dollars (U.S.) at that time; applying U.S. Dept. of Labor Statistics Consumer Price Index, 12 guineas of 1897 are seen to be nearly $900 in year 2000 dollars.[3]

The Biokam was similar to the Birtac and also used 17.5mm film, with, however, slot perforations in the center of the film between frames (Fig. 86). This placement of the perforations, rather than at the edge of the film, was done to get the most image area possible out of the width of the film. The Biokam had single frame capability, and thus was advertised as useful as a combined "Cinematograph & Snapshot Camera, Printer, Projector, Reverser and Enlarger." The basic camera sold for six guineas and the complete outfit for 11 guineas. Each of the three foregoing cameras could be adapted to projection by the addition of a light source.

The La Petite, made in London by Hughes, took 17.5mm film with one square perforation per frame.[4] Across the Channel, two cameras for smaller-than-

Fig. 86. *The Biokam, 17.5 mm film, 1899.*

standard film were introduced in France, in 1900. The Mirographe, manufactured by the Paris firm of Reulos & Goudeau, used film 20mm wide which, in place of perforations, was notched on one edge (Fig. 87). To advance the film, the notches were engaged by the rim of a spiral wheel, which the French descriptively called a "snail." The Mirographe was patented in 1898 and was the first French apparatus to use sub-standard film.[5]

Another Paris firm, L. Gaumont & Cie., produced the "Chrono de Poche," a combination camera and projector using 15mm center-perforated film (Fig. 88). Film advance was by the Demeny beater movement. The camera could be hand-cranked or driven by a detachable spring motor, the first instance of such a drive applied to an amateur camera.[6]

One of the earliest amateur motion picture cameras produced in Germany was the Kino, introduced

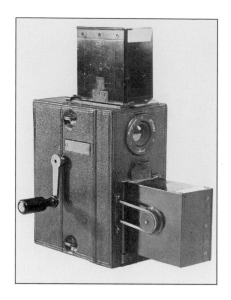

Fig. 87. *The Mirographe, Reulos & Goudeau, 20mm film.*

Fig. 88. *Chrono de Poche, Gaumont & Cie, 15mm film.*

Fig. 89. *Ernemann's Kino, 17.5mm film, 1903.*

in 1903 by the prominent Dresden firm, H. Ernemann A. G. (Fig. 89). The camera took 17.5mm film with one center perforation per frame, and as with others of its time, could be converted to projection.[7]

As ingenious and effective as these machines were, however, very few of them seem to have reached the United States. Merritt Crawford, one of cinematography's earliest historians, writing in 1930, remarked that he had been unable to find evidence of any effort to market these machines in the United States.[8]

Developments in the United States

The first U.S.-made home movie machine of record was hardly more than a toy, but certainly an engaging one. The Parlor Kinetoscope, manufactured by the American Parlor Kinetoscope Company of Washington, D.C., was patented August 24, 1897 (Fig. 90). Inside a wooden box approximately 11" wide, 12" high and 3" deep, an endless loop of paper images was carried past a peephole in the top of the box. The images, 1-3/4" wide by 1-3/8" high, were illuminated by light coming through a hole in one side of the box. As its name implies, the device appears to have been inspired by the Edison Kinetoscope. The Parlor Kinetoscope sold for six dollars and "picture belts" were available in lengths from 15 feet to 60 feet, costing from three to six dollars per dozen. Among the titles listed in the Parlor Kinetoscope catalog were *Dance of the Rustic, The Elephants,* and *General View of the Beach at Atlantic*

City. The source of these films is unknown.[9]

The next movie machine to appear in this country used 11mm film and was also a toy. The Vitak of 1902 (Fig. 91), designed and patented by Enoch J. Rector, the designer of the 1897 professional Veriscope camera, as noted in Chapter 2. It is believed to be the first U.S.-made projector using non-standard film designed specifically for amateur use. Films supplied with the projector were short lengths of reduction prints from commercially produced short subjects. The projector was hand-cranked and

Fig. 90. *The Parlor Kinetoscope, paper film.*

Fig. 91. The 1902 Vitak, 11mm film, patented by E. J. Rector.

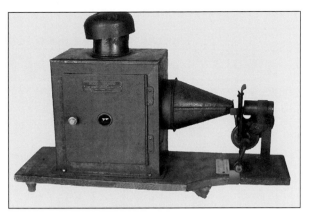

Fig. 92. E. J. Rector's Ikonograph Model 4, 17.5mm film, ca. 1905.

provided with a small carbide lamp for illumination. It was very cheaply constructed of scrap wood and sheet steel. It wholesaled for two dollars, but was also distributed as a premium to promote the sale of other products.

Another machine for 11mm film was the curiously-shaped Duplex, designed by one G. J. Badgley, and marketed from circa 1915 to 1927 by the Duplex Corporation. The film was slit from 35mm nitrate stock, and thus measured somewhat over 11mm and had one perforation per frame on the frame line. A camera, printer, splicer and developing machine were reportedly also marketed.[10]

Following the Vitak, Rector designed the Ikonograph (Fig. 92), a much more substantial projector. According to Brummit, Rector demonstrated both the new projector and a camera called an Ikonoscope to George Eastman early in 1902. Brummit reports that Eastman was impressed and expressed a particular wish to have some footage of his mother. However, since the film that Rector had was too slow for indoor filming and Rochester was too cold for outdoor filming, Eastman asked Rector to come back in the spring and film Eastman's mother walking in the garden.[11]

It is not recorded whether Rector ever returned to Rochester, nor is there any further evidence of a camera having been constructed; however the Ikonograph projector did reach the market. The Ikonograph Commercial Company was organized about 1904 by Eberhard Schneider of New York.[12] The projector took 17.5mm film with a single slot perforation per frame, centered at the frame line, and advance was by a claw movement. There was no shutter, but the top-of-the-line model did have a

fire-shutter. Illumination was by acetylene burner or incandescent lamp. Films were presumably obtained as reduction prints of commercial films. The projector was offered in three models, priced at $10, $15, and $25.[13]

A camera was advertised in the company catalog, but no price was listed, and it appears that none was ever produced.

The Premier projector, listed in a Sears Roebuck catalog of the 1905-1910 period, strongly resembled the Ikonograph Model D and also took 17.5mm film, however the film had two slot perforations per frame (Fig. 93). This projector was equipped with an acetylene lamp and sold for $8.95, or $9.95 with a 50-candlepower electric light. Films were offered in 10, 20 or 30-foot lengths and were priced at nine cents per foot. A lengthy list of titles available were in categories of "Comic," "Scenic and Travel," and "Miscellaneous." Judging by the catalog description, many of the so-called "comic" subjects were racially derogatory.

1910 brought the introduction of several machines designed for standard film, among them the Picturescope invented by Charles E. Dressler. As described by Crawford, it incorporated the novel idea of exposing just one half the width of the film on its first run through the camera; the reel was then reversed in the camera and the other half exposed, precisely the system to be used 22 years later when Eastman Kodak introduced 8mm film.

Singer describes the Homograph projector, dating from 1912, manufactured by the James Coughlin Company of Union Square, New York, from a promotional pamphlet found in the Edison Archives.[14] This machine was designed to project short lengths

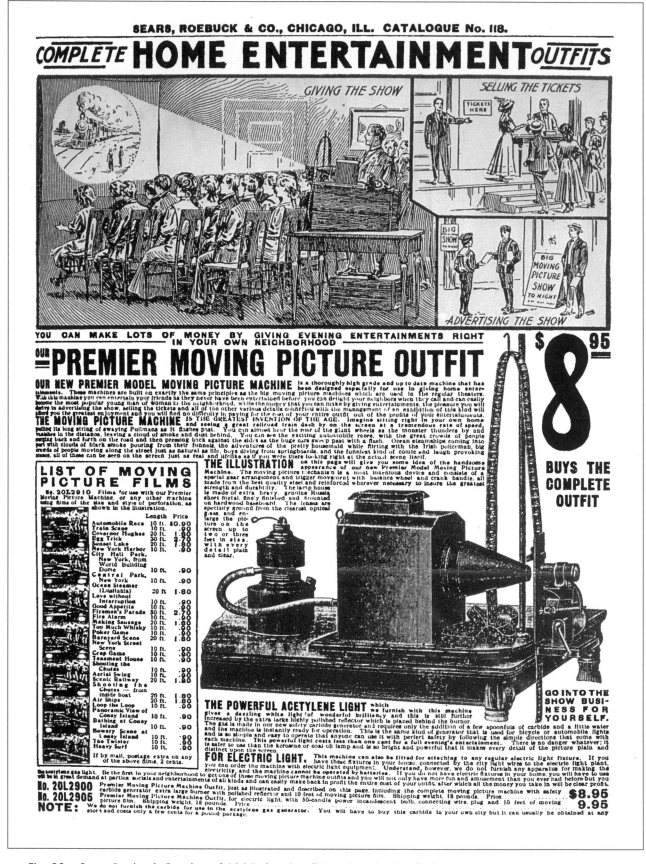

Fig. 93.   Sears Roebuck Catalog of 1905 showing "New Premier Outfit."

Fig. 94.   Phantoscope 35mm camera, ca. 1912.

of standard size film. Neither supply nor take-up reels were provided but the projector offered one unusual feature: illumination by battery powered lamp. An identical machine is described in a pamphlet found in the George Eastman House archives, except that the name was "Kodagraph," and the manufacturer was the H. L. Brittain Company. One might guess that Eastman Kodak lawyers had something to do with the name change.

The name "Phantoscope" must be introduced at this point, with this caveat: the same name appears to have been given by C. F. Jenkins to several different machines. As noted in Chapter 2, that was the name of two professional 35mm projectors, one patented by Jenkins and one by Jenkins and Armat. The name was also applied to an amateur camera and a portable projector. The camera is known to this author only through the existence of one example in private hands, which is of mahogany frame, 6" x 8" x 13-1/2", with a label marked "Phantoscope Manufacturing Company, Washington, D.C." (See Fig. 94.)

The undated pamphlet describing the portable projector lists the following attributes:

1. Takes standard motion picture film used the world over.
2. Takes electric current from ordinary incandescent lamp socket.
3. Can be stopped at any time, film will not be ignited, besides, the new picture film of today is non-inflammable stock.
4. Works equally well in rural districts without electric current.

While there is no date on the pamphlet, statements 1 and 3 are very curious since "standard motion picture film used the world over" almost always referred to nitrate-based flammable film. Although 35mm safety film was available from Eastman Kodak, it was not widely used. No explanation is offered as to how the projector could function in districts without electric current.

The Movee, a combined motion picture camera and projector, was the design of a man named F. E. Oiler, who had been an exhibitor and photo-supply salesman for Cramer Dry Plate Company. It appeared circa 1917 and sold for $35. It was designed for standard film and does not appear to have had any unusual attributes, nor to have been commercially successful.

The Actograph, introduced circa 1917 by the Wilart Instrument Company of New Rochelle, New York, was a 17.5mm camera described by McKay[15] as: "one of the most perfect small cameras ever built . . . it made use of professional outside magazines, reverse film travel, and other professional features." The same design was later enlarged to a 35mm version with 200-foot capacity, known as the "Wilart News Camera." Still later, a simplified version was marketed by the New York Institute of Photography and was known as the "Institute Standard."[16] (See Fig. 95.)

The Alamo, manufactured by Simplex Photo Products Company of Morris Park, New York, was another small camera using standard film, but appears to have been a much better design. It had an aluminum body, leather covered, and was available with an Aplanat f/6 lens at $35, or a Zeiss Tessar f/3.5 focusing lens at $58. A carrying case with 4 extra magazines cost $7.50, and a tripod with rotating cradle top cost $15.[17] This camera may also have been known as the "Simplex."

As an example of the puffery and obfuscation typical of the advertising of the period, the brochure of the 1918 Klix Manufacturing Company of Chicago is hard to surpass. After pointing out to the reader how the enormous expense and bulk of professional equipment has heretofore prevented the average person from making his own movies, the brochure continues:

But now, at last, the problem has been solved for all by the invention of the Klix which brings motion pictures into the home at low cost and in safe, convenient form . . . .

Fig. 95. Wilart News Camera, 35mm (left) and the Actograph, 17.5mm (right).

Fig. 96. The Sept, Andre Debrie, Paris 1920.

Motion picture films of standard width are used in handy lengths of 20 feet and are furnished in lightproof magazines for easy loading. The action you can secure on 20 feet of film with the Klix is equal to that necessitating 40 to 50 feet of film of professional movie cameras.

A few lines further on it states that on 20 feet of film with the Klix, one secures "more than three hundred pictures." Yet 20 feet, or 240 inches, divided by 300 images yields a frame height of 0.8 inches, just about standard. The brochure also claims that the risk of fire has been completely eliminated and that the film may be stopped to project one image for "hours at a time" without the film becoming heated. This is hard to accept until one reads that the projection lamp is a 6-8 volt, 2-1/2 amp Mazda. And of course the projector is illustrated as throwing a dazzling image on a screen at least ten feet away! The Klix was the invention of Varian M. Harris of Chicago.[18]

A small 35mm camera of decidedly high quality was the Sept, manufactured by Etablissements André

Debrie of Paris, introduced in France in 1920, and a few years later in the United States (Fig. 96). The camera was spring-motor driven and extremely compact, measuring less than 6" tall, 4" wide, and less than 3" deep, with motor attached. The capacity, which supposedly gave it its name, was seven meters of film, carried in plated brass cassettes.

The camera was extremely versatile, described as being capable of operation as a movie or still camera, contact printer, enlarger or projector. McKay reports that a falcon fight sequence in Douglas Fairbanks' *Robin Hood* (1922) was filmed with a Sept.[19] It was widely marketed in this country, despite being quite expensive at introduction. According to Schneider this price was over $200, nearly $2,000 in year 2000 dollars, but because of strong demand, and thus volume production, the price was soon reduced to a mere $100 in 1928.[20] A 1926 Willoughby's ad in the author's collection offers: "Only a limited quantity left—regularly $100 now $37.50."

A New Tack—Away From Ribbon Film

Up to this point we have described only machines using flexible film in ribbon form, either standard 35mm width or narrower. There also came into being an entirely different class of moving picture machines. As inventors sought ways to avoid the danger of flammable film, or reduce the cost of taking numerous pictures, some amazingly diverse designs evolved, some manifestly impractical, some showing considerable promise.

To the working photographer of the 1890s, one obvious alternative to film was the glass plate, and one of the first inventors to use this approach for motion pictures was an American, Nicolay Nelson of Waukegan, Illinois. Nelson was associated with Edwin Hill Amet in the development of the Magniscope about 1895.[21] On November 23, 1897, Nelson received U.S. Patent No. 594,094 for a "Kinetographic Camera—apparatus for Taking, Enlarging, and Projecting successive pictures of moving objects." The patent described a plate holder or film given rotary and lateral motion, in front of a fixed lens, with an intermittent advance.

Substitution of a glass plate for flexible film was taken up by numerous other inventors, including L. U. Kamm of London with his 1900 Kammatograph,[22] Alexander Victor in 1910, and Sig. Gianni Bettini in Italy about 1912 (Fig. 97).

Alexander F. Victor's Animato-Graph was reported in the June 17, 1910, issue of the Davenport (Iowa) *Daily Times* as a machine that "promises to revolutionize the motion picture business. . . . It gives promise of making the motion picture machine as common and as popular in the home as the gramophone."[23] The Animato-Graph utilized a metal disc on which a number of individual frames of standard motion picture film were mounted in a spiral. The disc was advanced at a slow rate, less than 16 frames per second, with a flicker blade interrupting each image several times. The projected image was rather dim, and the individual frames tended to buckle and go out of focus. Victor abandoned the idea before any machines were manufactured, but the disc and its advance mechanism were incorporated in another device called the Stereotrope, which could be used for the projection of a series of still pictures or a 30-frame animated cartoon. The Stereotrope was first marketed in December 1910.[24, 25]

Charles Urban proposed a variation of the disc design in 1913. Urban was an American-born entrepreneur who moved to England circa 1898 and founded a very successful equipment and film supply company, Warwick Trading Company. Urban provided the financial support and encouragement for the development of Kinemacolor.[26]

Urban and one Henry W. Joy devised a projector using a spiral of images on a disc of nitrate film (later changed to safety film). The images were printed from a master glass negative, which had been formed by reduction printing from standard commercial

Fig. 97. Sr. Bettini's Apparatus of 1912.

films. The Spirograph trademark was registered in England in 1909; however, Urban seems to have done little more than that until he returned to the United States and established Urban Motion Picture Industries, Inc., in Irvington, New York.[27] From this address, the Spirograph was announced in 1923, a most inauspicious time, as will appear (Fig. 98).

The Spirograph projector took a disc of Eastman Safety film 10-1/2" in diameter on which 1,200 images, each 7/32" by 5/32", were arranged in a spiral. The discs, called "records" by Urban, were advertised as being the equivalent of 75 feet of conventional film and sold for one dollar. Projection was by either a 6- or 24-volt lamp, depending on the size of picture desired. By removing the lamp and changing the projection lens to a microscope, the images could be viewed by reflected daylight. No camera was provided, the company pointing out that direct photographs of such small size would be impractical for projection.

A library of Spirograph records was promised, which would encompass films of Popular Science,

Fig. 98. Charles Urban's Spirograph of 1923.

Prominent People, Animal Kingdom, Travel, all to be drawn from the Urban Negative Library of two million feet of popular classics. The machines are quite rare, suggesting that not many were produced. The venture was of course doomed by the arrival of Eastman Kodak's 16mm system within months of the Spirograph debut.

C.F. Jenkins proposed another disc machine, the Discrola, no less, in one of the most wildly improbable machines of the era. In a paper read to the Society of Motion Picture Engineers in May 1923, Jenkins proposed printing commercially produced movies on paper discs, the opaque images to be projected by reflected light through a system of mirrors to a small screen. Each disc held just 20 images printed at the periphery and a plurality of discs would be stacked into a sort of circular book form. The discs were to have one radial slit, so that the leaves could be interlaced. The stack of discs was then placed on a turntable in a machine looking much like a 1920s Victrola, which might explain Jenkins' name for the machine. As the turntable rotated, an arm would lift the outer edge of each disc, bringing the row of images into position behind the projection lens.

In the customary discussion period following the reading of the paper, at which Jenkins was not present, Mr. F. H. Richardson, a well-known authority on projection, remarked with considerable restraint: "With all due respect to Mr. Jenkins, I doubt if a projector of this type will be found satisfactory." [28]

Still another camera/projector system for opaque images was called the "Daypho," and was probably introduced between 1910 and 1915. The Daypho was the creation of F.W. Hochstetter, whose company was the Dayton Photo Products Company. The descriptive brochure explained that there were three obstacles to more general use of motion pictures in schools, churches, business places, hospitals and homes: the cost and highly flammable nature of film and the cost and complexity of both camera and projector.

The Daypho supposedly surmounted these obstacles by combining camera and projector in one "simple" machine, by the use of paper prints furnished by the company that simultaneously solved the cost and hazard problems of ordinary film. The machine was in essence an animated postcard projector. Anyone who has used an opaque projector will recognize at once the difficulty of getting a bright image; couple this with the impossibility of moving such images at anything approaching 16 frames per second, and one will realize that Mr. Hochstetter's machine could hardly have been any more practical than the Jenkins machine.

The Advent of Safety Film

One pleasant spring evening in Paris, on May 14, 1897, some 200 or more grandes dames et messieurs of the city's aristocracy gathered for the annual *Bazar de la Charité*, an elegant affair held at a theater on the Champs Elyseé. One of the entertainments was to be a showing of the new craze that was sweeping the city: "living pictures." The show went on, the screen filled with those astounding images; a train rushed towards the audience, causing squeals of mixed delight and fright for those in the front row.

Suddenly the squeals turned to shrieks of genuine terror—the projection platform had exploded in flames, which quickly spread to the flimsy decor throughout the hall. Dense smoke and flames engulfed the terrified audience as men, women and children struggled to reach the single exit.[29]

When the carnage was over, more than 140 members of France's most prominent families had perished, and the reputation of the cinema had been dealt a severe blow. The immediate result of the tragedy was the enactment of laws and regulations governing the operation and outfitting of theaters that exhibited films, not only in France but in other countries as well. This fire and others also spurred the search for non-flammable film in all countries with a nascent film industry.[30]

Eastman Kodak began research on non-flammable motion picture film support as early as 1906 and made sufficient progress to announce in 1909 that it was prepared to give up cellulose nitrate-based film production all together and switch to a cellulose diacetate film support. This did not please the film distributors and exhibitors, however, who complained that the acetate-based film was not as strong as nitrate-based and did not have good dimensional stability. Acetate-based film was abandoned except for small quantities supplied for some special uses.

Work on cellulose acetate was resumed in earnest in 1925 at the Kodak Research Laboratories, and by 1929, X-ray film was made exclusively on acetate base. Achieving the necessary properties for commercial motion picture film took somewhat longer, but by 1951 the industry had changed over almost totally to acetate-based film, and as Dr. Mees wrote in 1961: "the hope of many years was realized in 1951, when the plant for the manufacture of cellulose nitrate was dismantled."[31]

In Europe, the Lumières had made non-flammable film in 1908, and in 1912 a market for such film appeared. That year Pathé Frères announced the first complete system of safety film, camera, and projector for the amateur. The projector was the famed Pathé Kok, named for the Pathé Company logo, a crowing rooster. The film was cellulose acetate, 28mm wide, with three perforations per frame on one side, and one on the other. This configuration was designed to provide the most accurate registration (Fig. 99).

As domestic electric lighting was not widespread in France at that time, a small generator that was driven by the same hand-cranked mechanism that advanced the film powered the projection lamp. To permit showing of "stills," a small battery was available at extra charge. The projector including screen, carrying case and cleaning unit sold for approximately $75.[32] Films for the projector were abbreviated versions of Pathé's commercial films, reduction printed to the smaller gauge.

While it was Pathé's expectation that most customers would only be interested in the projector for showing such films, a camera was also produced. The camera, also hand-cranked, was of leather-covered wood, measuring 6-1/4" wide x 12" deep x 10" high, with two co-axial 400-foot metal magazines. The lens was an Anastigmat f/4.5, 45mm. The camera does not appear to have reached this country in

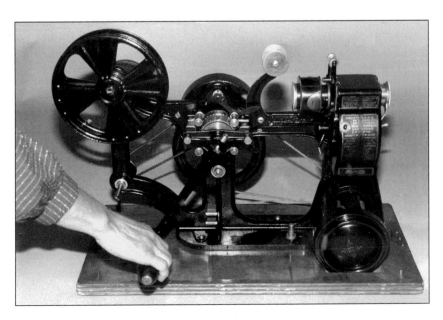

Fig. 99. The Pathé Kok Projector of 1912, 28mm safety film.

Fig. 100. Pathé Freres 28 mm camera.

Fig. 101. The New Premier Motion Picture Projector.

any quantity; however, the Pathéscope Company of America, Inc marketed a motor-driven version of the projector in the United States in 1913.[33] (See Fig.100.)

In the United States, Willard B. Cook, who registered the Pathéscope trademark under his own name in May 1913, assumed distribution rights.[34] Cook began by importing the Pathéscope from France, but soon introduced a greatly improved projector of his own design, called the New Premier Pathéscope. This projector was very sturdily built, motor-driven, or could be had as hand-cranked, with the projection bulb battery-powered.

After the Society of Motion Picture Engineers adopted the Safety Standard in 1918, Cook, brought out a Pathéscope designed for the new standard film, with three perforations per frame on each side. This machine probably appeared about the same time as Victor's Safety Cinema and was called the "Flickerless Safety Standard Motion Picture Projector." (See Fig. 101.)

While the Pathéscopes were designed to serve the educational, fraternal, and religious markets, enabling those users to show the growing libraries of films on safety stock, Cook, as did Victor, hoped to expand the horizons for those applications and the home user. To this end, Cook introduced a 28mm camera called the New Premier Daylight Loading Safety Standard Motion Picture Camera. An instruction book of that title describes a fairly simple camera taking daylight loading spools of 100-foot length, nitrate negative. Two models were described: the

"DeLuxe" model being equipped with an f/3.1 lens in focusing mount, the camera covered in genuine Morocco; the "Favorite" model was covered in imitation leather, and came with a fixed-focus f/7.7 lens. (See Fig. 102.)

The existence of the Safety Standard Pathéscope mentioned above is predicated on the following sentence from the instruction book just described:

With the New Premier Daylight Loading Safety Standard Camera and the Pathéscope Flickerless Safety Standard Motion Picture Projector, you can now enjoy taking pictures that may be projected at home with perfect safety, and that add to the lure of taking, the thrill of living action.

Somewhat later, the New Premier Pathéscope appeared under a new name: "The Peerless Standard Projector," manufactured by the Peerless Projector Company, a subsidiary of the Pathéscope Company of America.

Almost simultaneously with Pathé's announcement of their 28mm safety film system in 1912, Thomas Edison announced the Edison Home Kinetoscope. This novel projector used Eastman Kodak acetate-based film in a new format and was the invention of A. F. Gall, an Edison employee, who filed for a patent on a "Kinetoscope" on October 12, 1911, and was issued U.S. Patent No. 1,204,424 on November 14, 1916, assigned to Thomas Edison (Fig. 103).

The film was 22mm wide and carried three rows of images, with two perforations per frame on either

Fig. 102. New Premier Motion Picture Camera.

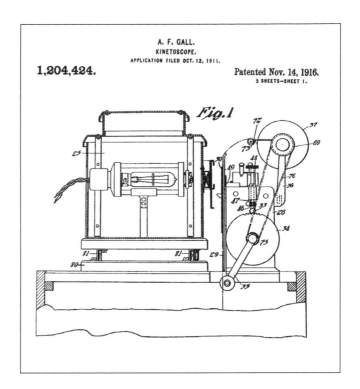

Fig. 103. Gall's patent for the Edison Home Kinetoscope.

side of the central row. The image size was 5.08mm x 3.76mm, just slightly smaller than today's Super 8. The three rows were arranged head-to-tail, so that by shifting the film at the ends of each row, and reversing direction, a continuous length of images three times the length of the film segment would be obtained. The perforation pitch happens to be identical to that of Super 8, thus a 50-foot reel of Home Kinetoscope film was equivalent to 150 feet of today's Super 8, which means that a 50-foot reel of Kinetoscope film had a running time of ten minutes. The projector consisted of a cast-iron gear case mounted on an oak base carrying the lamp housing. The gear case contained the film advance mechanism and supported the reel arms, lenses, film gate and the film transport shifting mechanism. Illumination could be by "baby arc," acetylene burner, or originally, a Nernst lamp; the latter subsequently was replaced with a conventional incandescent lamp.[35] (See Fig. 104.)

In use, the projector was placed on top of the carrying case as a base, the illumination turned on, and the first row of film cranked through the gate. When the end of that row was reached, the film transport was shifted over to the next row and the film cranked back in the other direction, then the process repeated for the third row. At first the projector was provided with just a supply reel, the film passing through a cutout in the base permitting the film to coil up in the bottom of the case. This frequently caused problems, and later models were equipped with a take-up reel.

Films for the Home Kinetoscope were initially all reduction prints of the 35mm commercial films being produced at the Edison Studios between 1910 and 1914, but later the list included many films made by other studios or filmmakers. Films were supplied in eight classes (lengths), "A" through "H." Film prices ranged from $2.50 for the shortest, about 13 feet, to $20.00 for the Class H film which was about 80 feet long. The films were mounted on wooden cores, and were sold in airtight metal cans, which could be mailed back to the dealer in an exchange program. A library of over 250 titles in categories of Comedy, Drama, Trick, Educational, Religious, and Juvenile was maintained.

The projector came equipped with an auxiliary stereopticon lens mounted parallel to the motion picture lens. The front of the lamp house carried a slide channel and a suitable mask with a round opening for movies and a smaller rectangular opening for slide projection. To operate as a stereopticon, the lamp house could be moved laterally to align the light beam with the stereopticon lens. Special Edison

Fig. 104. Edison posing by Home Kinetoscope.

Lantern Slides were available, glass slides carrying two rows of five images, each image approximately 1/2" by 5/8". The slides, of which few have survived, were made from views copyrighted by Underwood & Underwood and licensed to Edison. They cost 50 cents each and came with a brief explanatory "lecture" for each slide. Typical titles were: *Panama Canal,* showing President Taft and Colonel Goethals inspecting the partially completed Gatun Locks, and *American Indians,* showing Hopi Indians performing the Katchina dance to the rain gods.[36]

The price of the projector varied according to the choice of illuminant, the voltage and current specified, and the lens system chosen. Including carrying case and transformer or rheostat, the price ranged from a low of $72.00 to a high of $97.50.

By all evidence, the Home Kinetoscope fared very poorly in the marketplace. Ben Singer has written an excellent monograph on the Kinetoscope after an exhaustive study of the archives at the Edison National Historic Site in West Orange, New Jersey.[37]

The records show that the Home Kinetoscope was a failure from every aspect.

To begin with, despite an offer from George Eastman to distribute the Kinetoscope through Eastman Kodak dealers, Edison elected to distribute through his existing network of phonograph jobbers and dealers. This turned out to be a bad decision, since the jobbers had not been given any training to acquaint them with this new and different product. They in turn could offer no help to the retailer, with the result that customer complaints, whether justified or not, were seldom resolved.

The price of the Kinetoscope and films was also a deterrent to widespread appeal. At a price of almost $100 the projector was more expensive than a medium-priced phonograph, which cost about $50. At a time when a factory worker might be earning as little as $2 per day[38] the Home Kinetoscope was another amusement primarily for the well-to-do.

Overshadowing all of the foregoing problems, however, was the functioning of the machine.

Almost as soon as Kinetoscopes reached the first customers, complaints rolled in. The most common complaint was that of tangled film due to the lack of a take-up reel as mentioned above. On reverse cranking, the film tended to kink and catch in the base, causing projection to stop, and/or torn film. The fire shutter, supposed to move out of the way when the projector was cranked at the proper speed, did not always completely clear the aperture, thus obscuring part of the scene. Indexing of the side-shift was not always exact, producing an annoying double image on the screen. The machines at first had no provision for adjusting the "framing," resulting in the annoying appearance of a portion of the next frame appearing at the top or bottom of the picture. A customer-installable framing device was later supplied. The baby arc was described by one of Edison's own engineers as a "joke." [39] Dealers and jobbers began returning unsold machines. Singer estimates that of the 2,476 machines shipped to U.S. jobbers as of March 1915, only 500 or so were actually sold, and practically all of the 1,185 machines shipped to Europe were returned.

If Edison had any plans for solving any of the Home Kinetoscope problems, the need for such plans went up in smoke on December 9, 1914, when a disastrous fire at the West Orange complex destroyed ten buildings, or approximately three-quarters of the complete works. [40] Ironically, the fire began in the film-finishing house, and it marked the beginning of the end of Edison's efforts in the film industry, both amateur and professional.

While nitrate-based film was dangerous to use in home projectors because of the proximity of either an arc or a gas flame, there was no such risk for its use in a camera. Thus the amateur could safely utilize nitrate stock in his camera, then have it printed on safety stock for projection.

An example of such an arrangement was the Movette, manufactured in Rochester and patented in 1917. [41] The Movette camera was of unusual design, as the film path was at right angles to the long axis of the camera, much like the Zeiss Movikon 8mm camera of 1952. The film was Eastman nitrate negative, 17.5mm with two round perforations per frame on each side, put up by Movette in 50-foot paper-covered steel "packages" (Movette's terminology). In use, a short loop of film was pulled from the "package," enough to thread over the single sprocket and through the gate.

When the film was totally exposed, the user was instructed to return the package to the dealer, along with a special projection magazine. The dealer would process and print the film to a safety positive. The negative was returned in the original container, while the positive was returned in the projection magazine, which would hold 200 feet of film. Each time the customer brought in a 50-foot exposed film package, the dealer would splice the new film onto that already in the projection magazine until the 200-foot capacity was reached. The camera sold for $40 and the projector for $60. As ingenious as the Movette system appeared, the camera did not function well and the company did not survive for more than a few years. [42] (Fig. 105)

Very little is known of the Sinemat, introduced circa 1915 by the Sinemat Motion Picture and Radio Machine Company of 324 Avenue A, New York City. [43] A brochure in the George Eastman House archives describes it as using a daylight-loading cartridge and that camera, projector attachment, and tripod were available at $30, $20, and $6, respectively.

On April 11, 1914, Herman C. Schlicker, an obscure German national living in New York City filed a patent application for a "Kinetograph," the principal object of which was "to produce an improved . . . (motion picture machine) . . . that is especially adapted for use by amateurs." Thus began a sequence of events, which would engage the time and money of a leading motion picture executive and create one of the most unusual and short-lived motion picture machines to appear before the fateful year of 1923.

Schlicker's objective, as with many of his predecessors, was to get as many images on a given area of film surface as possible. His method was to arrange 1,664 images in a slow helix on an endless belt of Eastman Safety Film, 5" wide and 17-1/2" long. Schlicker received U. S. Patent 1,256,931 on February 19, 1918, for his "Kinetograph." On August 12, 1924, he received U.S. Patent No. 1,504,722 for a projector.

The patents somehow caught the eye of John R. Freuler, co-founder and then president of the Mutual Film Company in Milwaukee, Wisconsin. Freuler's greatest public recognition came in 1916 when he signed Charles Spencer Chaplin to a

Fig. 105. Movette ad of 1917.

contract that rocked the movie world. The contract gave Chaplin, then just 26 years old, the unheard of sum of $10,000 per week, plus a $150,000 bonus to appear in twelve films over the next year.

Freuler decided Schlicker's scheme had potential, so he bought the patent, moved Schlicker to Milwaukee, and set up a plant to manufacture the camera (Fig. 106) and projector (Fig. 107). The company and the product were called "Vitalux," and by 1922, cameras, projectors, and films were being produced. A dealer network had been established, and a company brochure proclaimed: "Vitalux Makes Yesterday Today." [44] (See Fig. 108.)

The Vitalux camera in a die-cast aluminum body, was hand-cranked, magazine loaded. It measured 8-1/2" x 11" x 4-1/4" and weighed nearly 11 pounds. A metal magazine carried the film band, which remained entirely within the magazine, exposure being made through a vertical slot, opened only when the magazine was fully inserted in the camera. Turning the crank set in motion four sets of gears, two scotch-yoke mechanisms for the double-claw film advance, a lead screw for the vertical traverse of the lens, and the drive of the rotary disc shutter. The intermittent motion of the film, plus the continuous motion of the lens produced the spiral pattern of images on the film belt. While the lens motion was continuous, it was so gradual (0.065mm per frame) that no appreciable blurring occurred.

The Vitalux projector was a chunky, slope-backed

Fig. 106. The Vitalux Camera.

Fig. 107. The Vitalux Projector.

box of cast iron, weighing 25 pounds including the motor drive. A 5-inch diameter vertical cylinder served as the spool for the film. The front of the projector enclosed the mass of cams, gears, shafts, clutches, rocker arms and springs required to give the film and projection lens the same motions that went on in the camera, plus the need to have the lamp and its socket, reflector and heat shield travel vertically with the projection lens. In addition, the designer thoughtfully added a gear change feature, so that when the lens reached the top of its slow climb up the width of the film, it could be returned to the starting position at twice the showing speed! It is interesting to speculate on the hours of casting, machining and assembly that must have gone in to this remarkable piece of machinery.

Fig. 108. John R. Freuler photographing his grandaughter with the Vitalux camera.

The camera, complete with one magazine and a Goerz f/3.5 lens carried a list price of $125. The projector with motor drive, ten-foot cord and 250-watt lamp was priced at $175. A single film magazine cost $7.50. Film was cheap: either positive of negative was 75 cents, negative developing 10 cents each, positive developing 15 cents each. The initial investment came to $350, not far from the introductory price of the Ciné-Kodak outfit, whose debut was just around the corner.

What became of the Vitalux is somewhat of a mystery. It seems unlikely that many were made, as only two are known to exist,[45] yet the apparatus attracted sufficient attention to be described by Herbert C. McKay in his seminal 1924 book, *Motion Picture Photography for the Amateur*. McKay offered a cost analysis showing the costs per minute of screen time for 35mm professional film, Kodak 16mm reversal safety film, and the Vitalux "belt" as $6.25, $1.50, and 88 cents, respectively. So Schlicker achieved one of his objectives, low film cost.

Commercially produced films were available for $1.25, with such titles as *Sweet Revenge, The U. S. Naval Academy, Hawaiian Blues, Douglas Fairbanks at the Rodeo*, etc.

The two most serious drawbacks of the Vitalux system were the impossibility of editing the film and the two-minute length of run of the Vitalux belt, which obviously could not be spliced. The Kodak, Bell & Howell, and Victor cameras that came on the market in 1923 and 1924 had only 100' capacity, but their films could readily be spliced to give an hour or more of projection. Despite the apparent care with which the Vitalux projector was constructed, the presence of many "blisters" on films in the author's collection suggest that the projector's performance was less than perfect.

The Vitalux Company struggled on for four years, changing its name to The Automatic Movie Display Corporation and even teaming up for a time with Willoughby's, the large New York City camera retailer, in a 16mm commercial film rental plan, but this too failed, and in August 1927 the corporation was dissolved.

The revolutionary product, 16mm direct-reversal safety film, introduced by Eastman Kodak in 1923, with one exception, swept away every other amateur format and scheme that had been essayed

since 1894. Its economy of film, absolute safety, universal availability of film, and film processing were more than any competitive system could match.

Nine Point Five

The "one exception" was of course Pathé's 9.5mm system. The Pathé KOK 28mm system had not proved a commercial success, principally because of cost. Acetate film was more expensive than nitrate to begin with, and the reduction of width from 35mm to 28mm still did not give sufficient cost advantage to attract many customers.

In 1922 the company introduced an entirely new gauge of safety film, now reduced to just 9.5mm wide with a single slot perforation centered on the film width at the frame line. The projector, called the Pathé Baby (Fig. 109), was launched in time for the Christmas market, and as with the earlier 28mm Pathé Kok, was designed to permit home showing of selected portions of commercial films, reduction printed to the new gauge. Films were sold in small steel-enclosed canisters holding 8.5 meters (28 feet) of film.

In operation, the film canister was placed in a receptacle in the top of the projector, a length of film extracted and placed in the film channel. Turning the operating crank fed the film into a glass-enclosed chamber at the bottom of the projector. Rewinding was manual, but did not require re-threading the film.

An ingenious method of economizing on film was accomplished by placing one or more notches in the edge of the film where a title appeared. The notch triggered a mechanism that stopped the film advance for three or four seconds, then the film moved on normally. By judicious selection of the number of title frames and notches, depending on title length, a title might occupy as few as four or five frames, as against 50 or more that would be required by the conventional method.

By 1923, more than 100 titles were available, and more were being added at the rate of 50 per month. A rental service was later established.[46] The projector sold for 275 francs at introduction, and films cost five to six francs each. An improved model projector capable of showing 20-meter (66 feet) films was introduced in 1924 at a price of 385 francs.[47]

The Pathé Baby projector was immediately

Fig. 109. The Pathé Baby projector, with motor drive.

Fig. 110. The Pathé Baby camera.

successful, and thus encouraged, Pathé began work on a camera. The result was the Pathé Baby camera, announced on April 1, 1923 (Fig. 110). The camera was hand-cranked, but a clamp-on spring motor was available in 1926. Both camera and projector were actively marketed in the United States, but were named "Pathex" when sold in this country.

Pathé was determined that the user should be entirely self-sufficient, including the ability to process his own film at home. To this end, its engineers, led by Louis J. J. Didée, investigated the various methods of "reversal development" known at the time, one of which would be used by Eastman Kodak in their 16mm system. Kodak's system, however, required a four-step process that included a carefully controlled second exposure. The Pathé

engineers realized this would be completely beyond the capability of any amateur working at home, so a process was devised which while fairly elaborate, was deemed to be within the average amateur's abilities. Pathé recognized that many users would probably prefer to have the processing done professionally, so established a professional processing laboratory. Most users did find it difficult to achieve consistently good results, and home processing was gradually phased out.[48]

The Pathé 9.5mm system quickly became extremely popular in Europe, and has remained so in some quarters to this day. The image size was nearly as large as 16mm, yet the cost was about half the cost of 16mm. As recently as 1990, The French firm of Beaulieu offered "La Camera Ciné 9.5 Quartz," a machine incorporating all the amenities of a professional Super 8 or 16mm camera. An International Festival of 9.5 is still held annually in Albi, France. While the gauge never achieved similar popularity in this country, the company's products have played a significant role in amateur motion pictures.

4 George Eastman and His Company

Fig. 111. George Eastman.

Recapitulation: 1881 to 1889

The Eastman Kodak Company of today began as a partnership formed in 1881 between George Eastman (Fig. 111) and Colonel Henry A. Strong, a partner in a highly successful Rochester buggy whip manufacturing business. Strong, seventeen years Eastman's senior, became the younger man's co-executive and confidant for almost forty years. He had no knowledge of photography whatsoever, but as well as providing some needed start-up capital, he brought encouragement and wise counsel to the enterprise.

As recounted in Chapter 1, the company's first product was a line of photographic dry plates, followed in 1884 by two revolutionary new products, Eastman negative paper and the Eastman-Walker roll holder. The success of these products and the need for additional capital to finance their production and marketing led Strong and Eastman to dissolve their partnership and incorporate the company as the Eastman Dry Plate and Film Company, effective October 1,1884. The officers of the new company were: Henry Strong, president; John H. Kent, vice-president; George Eastman, treasurer, and William H. Walker, secretary.[1]

With the perfection of the Eastman-Walker roll holder, Eastman's invention of the Kodak camera, and Reichenbach's achievement of flexible celluloid film, the corporation possessed the "wheels" which would carry it forward for many years. The Kodak Camera (original 1888 model) and the roll holder paved the way for dozens of subsequent Kodak cameras, the flexible celluloid film provided the fodder for these and the myriad competitive cameras and, of course, was the essential raw material for the budding motion picture industry.

Fig. 112. William G. Stuber.

Becoming an International Force: 1890 to 1918

With the phenomenal success of the Kodak camera and celluloid film, the company's physical plant quickly became inadequate. Eastman's vision was bold; property must be acquired with ample clean water, clean air, and room to grow. One of the corporate directors was instructed to quietly start buying up farmland at a location almost three miles north of the headquarters and factory buildings in the city, a site then in the village of Greece, to the west of the Genesee River. On October 1, 1890, ground was broken at what would later be called Kodak Park, for three new buildings: a power plant, a film factory, and a "laboratory."

To oversee the work at Kodak Park, Eastman made his first hire of a Massachusetts Institute of Technology graduate, a young mechanical engineer named Darragh deLancey. In addition to his other duties, deLancey was charged with seeing that the identical film making machinery being installed in Kodak Park was shipped to Harrow. DeLancey performed brilliantly, but sadly his career was cut short by illness in 1899. Years later, Eastman was quoted as saying: "deLancey switched Kodak Park from the empirical to the scientific path."[2]

As well as film support, emulsion production was also moved to Kodak Park. Eastman chose Henry Reichenbach to be chief emulsion maker and eventually placed him in charge of the entire Kodak Park operation. This was one of the rare occasions when Eastman's trust was misplaced; on December 31, 1891, Eastman discovered that Reichenbach and two other key employees were planning to start their own company, using the expertise they had acquired at Kodak. Eastman fired them the next day and began legal action to prevent them from using any Eastman Kodak trade secrets in any venture of their own.

Emulsion problems arose soon after Reichenbach's departure and persisted for some time. Late in 1893 Eastman began making overtures to a well-known Louisville, Kentucky, photographer, William G. Stuber (Fig. 112) for a position at Eastman Kodak. Stuber at this time had gained wide recognition for his ability to produce his own sensitized plates of exceptional quality, as well as his skill as a photographer.

Largely self-taught, without a college education, Stuber while still a young man had begun experimenting with dry plate emulsion formulas, much as Eastman had. Dissatisfied with his progress, Stuber journeyed to Zurich, Switzerland, in 1890 to study emulsion making under one Dr. John H. Smith, a manufacturer of dry plates and paper in Europe. Stuber not only learned from him, but also returned to the States with the U.S. rights to a coating machine that Smith had developed.[3] After some reluctance, Stuber was won over and moved to Rochester in 1894 and in a short time was placed in charge of both plate and film emulsions.[4]

Up to this point, Eastman's method of making celluloid film base was one that he and Reichenbach had developed in 1889, which consisted of spreading the nitrocellulose solution, called "dope," out on long plate glass tables, 3-1/2 feet wide by 80 feet long. The dope was allowed to dry overnight, then the sensitive emulsion was spread over the base and dried under a wooden hood carrying a current of warm air. When dry, the completed film was stripped from the tables, wound and slit to the desired widths.

This rather cumbersome batch method had been supplanted some years before by a continuous process at the Celluloid Company and the American Camera Company. When Eastman acquired the latter firm in 1898, along with the rights to the process, he directed deLancey to convert Kodak Park to the new process.[5] DeLancey by this time had hired an assistant, Frank W. Lovejoy (Fig. 113), a mechanical engineering graduate of "Tech," class of 1894. When deLancey's health forced him to resign, Lovejoy took over his responsibilities.

71

Fig. 113. Frank W. Lovejoy.

In the continuous casting process a thin layer of dope is deposited on the highly polished surface of a large heated drum, as much as 12 feet in diameter, which revolves continuously beneath the dispensing hopper. By proper adjustment of solvents, drum temperature, and speed, the solvents evaporate and the film is dry just before the drum has completed one revolution, allowing the dried film to be continuously stripped from the drum and led off to the coating station, where a similar operation is performed (Fig. 114).

While Lovejoy was designing the new production layout, Eastman suggested to Lovejoy that he hire someone to supervise the fabrication of the machines and that the person be placed in charge of the casting department once it was in operation. Lovejoy found his man in the person of Perley Smith Wilcox, an 1897 mechanical engineering graduate of Cornell University, who had been working at Swift & Co.

These hirings illuminate a significant factor in Eastman Kodak's phenomenal growth and progress over the years. Of the next five chief executives who succeeded Eastman, all but one were engineers who had come up through manufacturing responsibilities and would successively guide the company at the highest level for the next 35 years.[6] Stuber succeeded Eastman as president in 1925, Lovejoy succeeded Stuber in 1934, Hargrave succeeded Lovejoy in 1941, Wilcox was elected chairman in 1944, and Chapman was president from 1952 to 1960.

None of these men came up through sales or marketing or finance. Stuber was once quoted as saying: "I couldn't sell gold dollars for ninety cents apiece!"[7] Eastman Kodak Company was the quintessential technology-driven company, but aggressive marketing, and knowledge of its customer base also

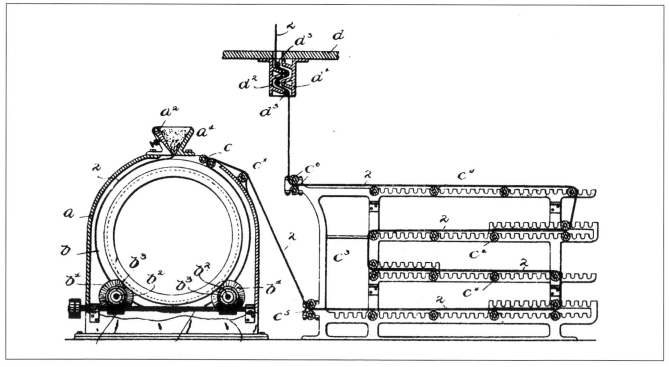

Fig. 114. Blair-Waterman Continuous Casting Machine. Feed hopper at top of casting drum; film is drawn off to drying racks to right.

contributed to its success. George Eastman, of course, was unusual, combining as he did a thorough understanding of the technology, a shrewd business sense, and a superb sense of marketing. And he had instilled many of these qualities in the men such as Stuber and Lovejoy who served under him.

Growth of the Film Market, and the Motion Picture Patents Company

With the ever-expanding lines of still cameras being sold by Eastman Kodak and others came demands for more film, while at the same time the nascent motion picture industry was becoming a very important consumer

In the years from 1897 to 1902, Kodak's domestic sales of raw motion picture film averaged just over $100,000 a year, less than ten percent of the company's total sales, while cartridge film sales grew from $500,000 to nearly $1 million. By 1906, motion picture film sales had reached $285,000 per year, and $2 million plus by 1909, a ten-fold increase, while cartridge film sales increased just 35 percent in the same period, from $1,578,000 to $2,098,000, each being approximately 22 percent of total company sales. [8, 9]

While Eastman Kodak was enjoying the fruits of the expanding motion picture industry, other members of the industry were not as happy. In particular, the man who had been first out of the gate. Thomas Edison was losing customers for his movies to upstart producers who were quite willing to cut prices.

At this time, all producers made essentially the same product: 1,000-foot reels of some simple drama or comedy turned out like sausage. These films were at first sold directly to the exhibitor, at prices ranging from five cents to 25 cents per foot, depending on how much it had cost to produce, how popular the producer thought it would be, whether hand-colored or not, etc. As the exhibitor owned the film, he could show it as many times as he wished. Since his clientele would tire of it long before it wore out, the inefficiency of this arrangement was apparent.

In 1902, two photographer brothers, Harry and Herbert Miles hit on the idea of serving as the middleman between the movie producer and the movie exhibitor. Instead of the exhibitor having to buy a film for $100 to show for one week and then have no further use for it, the Miles brothers would buy the film, rent it to the exhibitor for $50 for one week, get it back and rent it to the next exhibitor. They set up shop at 116 Turk Street in San Francisco, and thus was the first "film exchange" born.[10]

Ramsaye called this the most important development in the movie industry since the development of the projector, a bit of an exaggeration perhaps, but it did create the third element in the three-tier structure of the motion picture industry that is basically still in effect—the producer of the motion picture, the distributor (or exchange), and the exhibitor.

In this structure, Edison perceived a way to control the production and distribution of films, stabilize prices, and guarantee himself a return on the use of his patented cameras and projectors. The mechanism would be to create an entity which would hold all the valid patents in the field, and which would then license their use, for a fee, to all the members who would sign on to the new organization.

A 1907 court decision in favor of Edison in a suit brought against William N. Selig, ruling that the latter's Selig Polyscope projector infringed on an Edison patent, encouraged Edison to go ahead with his plan. Discussions were held with other movie producers and, by 1908, Edison, Essanay, Kalem, Biograph, Lubin, Selig, Vitagraph, Méliès and Pathé had signed a document creating the Motion Picture Patents Company.[11] (See Fig. 115.)

George Eastman had been kept informed of these machinations by Edison; in fact he had encouraged the latter, going so far as to act as Edison's emissary to Pathé about the scheme. Eastman's interest and even willingness to participate is somewhat difficult to understand since he of all the players in this struggle had the least to fear from competitors. While there were European manufacturers of raw film, the quality of their product was far below that of Kodak's. Eastman nonetheless was concerned that these producers could eventually cut into his export sales significantly.

For a relatively brief time, Eastman had what appeared to be an ace in the hole—the Kodak Park progress in producing a non-flammable film support. A series of disastrous fires in the United States and Europe had aroused many municipalities to mandate drastic safety measures surrounding the exhibition of nitrate film. The rumors that the

Fig. 115. The principal members of the Motion Picture Patents Company, posed on the steps of Edison's laboratory, December 19, 1908.

powerful Rochester company was on the verge of launching a product that would make nitrate film obsolete made the European film producers extremely nervous, including Pathé and Lumière. However, the political strength of the exhibitors in this country in fighting any move to outlaw nitrate, coupled with the ultimate failure of Eastman Kodak to produce a non-flammable film that would meet the producers' and exhibitors' requirements as to strength and durability, led Eastman to withdraw acetate-base film for professional use early in 1911.[12] The company did continue to make acetate-base film available for small non-professional use such as for the Edison Home Kinetoscope in 1912, the Movette in 1917 and, in 1918, for Safety Standard 28mm film.

Eastman did assume a critical role in the Motion Picture Patents Company. As the de facto sole supplier of raw film, Eastman was designated the "toll collector" for the Patents Company. The contract that the nine producers and Eastman had signed stipulated that Eastman Kodak would be the sole source of film, and would sell film only to the members of the Patents Company. All purchasers of raw film would pay Eastman Kodak a fee of a half cent per foot of film over and above the base cost of the film, said fees to be turned over to the Patents Company at the close of each year. These sums would be then paid to the machinery patent holders, in

proportion to the agreed-upon value of their patents, chiefly Edison and Biograph. In addition, the licensed producers could sell their finished films only to distributors and exhibitors licensed by the Patents Company, passing on the half-cent fee plus any other markup they desired. And lastly, each exhibitor would be assessed a two dollar weekly fee for each projector operated.

These new "rules of the game" were announced in 1909 to a gathering of exchange operators and exhibitors as a *fait accompli,* with no prior notice whatsoever. As may be imagined, there were immediate anguished howls from the exhibitors particularly, for whom the new arrangement meant higher rental fees in addition to the two dollar weekly license fee for using their own projectors, with no compensating benefits.

One of the most vociferous objectors was Carl Laemmle (1867-1939) the diminutive and dynamic future head of Universal Studios, then just getting started at building his exchange business. Laemmle not only refused to join the Patents Company, but announced that he would start his own production company, which he did, naming it the Independent Motion Picture Company of America, or "IMP" as it soon became known.

Laemmle then mounted an enormous publicity campaign excoriating and ridiculing the Patents

Fig. 116. Cartoons pro and con of the Motion Picture Patents Co.

Company and its offspring, the General Film Company. Encouraged by Laemmle's action, and the availability of imported Lumière film, other independents began producing movies (Fig. 116).[13] The Patents Company fought back, by fair means and foul. A patent infringement suit was filed against IMP, and gangs of toughs were sent to break up independents' sets and productions.[14]

Eastman was not happy to lose business to Lumière and other imported films and in 1911 amended his contract with the Patents Company so that he could sell film to the independents. The next crack in the dike came in 1912 when a Federal Court dismissed the Patents Company's suit against Laemmle's IMP. An anti-trust petition filed against the Patents Company by the U. S. Attorney General's office followed. Finally, when the Supreme Court ruled in 1917 that the very heart of the Patents

Company's corporate body, the "tying in" of forced purchase of one product (raw film) as a condition of using a patented product (projectors) was illegal, then the Patents Company was truly dead.

It had been brought down at last by law, but long before that it had been mortally wounded by the likes of Carl Laemmle and other independents who struck at two weaknesses in the Patents Company's constitution. First was its stubborn insistence that single reel shorts were the longest pictures that the moviegoer would sit through, and secondly that publicizing actors and actresses as "stars" would be bad for business.

A number of producers had actually produced "picture plays" of more than one reel length, but so adamant was the Patents Company about its one reel rule, that the producer's two or more reel picture would only be released one reel at a time. A "feature" film, according to Macgowan was defined as being at least five reels long.[15] One of the pioneers of this kind of film was an Italian studio, which in 1911 produced a five-reel film entitled *Dante's Inferno*, followed by *Quo Vadis*, which ran nine reels. Both films had successful runs in the United States. In 1913, Laemmle's Universal Film Company made *Traffic in Souls*, a six-reel exposé of white slavery; Griffith made a four-reel *Judith of Bethulia*, released in 1914. The public, given a good story, was quite willing to sit through six reels or more!

Laemmle's response to the second premise of the Patents Company was to turn Florence Lawrence and Mary Pickford, two well-liked but anonymous actresses, into famous personalities who drew devoted followers to films in which they starred.[16] He was the first to recognize the "box office" quality of popular performers. With the introduction of the "star" system and feature length pictures as the principal commodity of the studios, the essential structure of today's Hollywood was established.

Eastman and Labor

Labor/management conflict, often culminating in unbelievable brutality and bloodshed on both sides, had troubled the American industrial scene since the last third of the nineteenth century. Violence was most prevalent in the "dirty" industries—mining, smelting, steel making, meat packing, etc., however, organized labor was seen as a threat by industrialists in every sector of the economy.

As workers in the lowest wage groups were largely foreign-born or first generation Americans, union activities were generally perceived by management and the general public as well, as being "un-American," fomented by "foreigners" and "radicals." President McKinley's assassination in 1901 by Leon Czolgosz, a self-described "Anarchist," did nothing to allay such sentiments.[17] Eastman Kodak had been largely immune to labor strife, thanks undoubtedly to paying better than average wages and George Eastman's genuinely compassionate views of the wage earner's life.

As the company's earnings and earned surplus mounted, Eastman found innovative ways to distribute the money.[18] Early in 1911, Eastman presented a resolution to the Board, establishing a fund of $500,000 to be a benefit, accident, and pension fund for the employees. The money was to be taken out of surplus. Eastman said: "As the company accumulates age, we have got to be prepared to do something for men who have grown old in our service."[19]

The following year, Eastman declared a "dividend on wages" for all employees with five or more years service, two percent of all wages received by them during the previous five years. The payment of the dividend was to be accompanied by a note pointing out that it was being done because of an exceptionally prosperous year, but that it was not to be considered to committing the company to such action in the future. However, he did plan to continue the wage dividend, and it would be tied to the common stock dividend; if the common dividend went down, the wage dividend would go down, and vice-versa.

On April 4, 1919, Eastman announced his most innovative plan of all: an employee stock purchase plan. The mechanism in brief was to be as follows.

Eastman proposed to donate from his holdings, 10,000 shares of Eastman Kodak common stock to be offered at par to all wage earning and salaried employees who had completed two years of service as of January 1, 1918. Participants could purchase an amount of shares equal to two percent of their earnings, to a maximum of five years earnings.

The plan appears to have met with good acceptance; when in 1924 Eastman announced the last distribution of the remainder of his holdings, he pointed out that most of his "fellow employees" were then stockholders in the company.

Fig. 117. C.E. Kenneth Mees

Founding of Kodak Research Laboratories

During the brief reign of The Motion Picture Patents Company, Eastman Kodak Company had established a true research laboratory, the first in the United States photographic industry, and among the first of any United States industry. How this came about began with a chance event in 1909.

In that year, a young English scientist working in photographic chemistry, Dr. C. E. Kenneth Mees (Fig. 117), visited the United States as a consultant to the American Banknote Company, which was searching for a means to make photographic counterfeiting of bank notes as difficult as possible. While in the United States, Mees wrote to Eastman, asking for permission to visit the company. Eastman replied promptly, inviting Mees to visit, and arranged for him to tour Kodak Park.[20]

Mees (1882-1960), at the time just 27 years old, was managing director of an English manufacturer of dry plates and photographic filters. The son of a Wesleyan minister, Mees studied chemistry at University College in London under the renowned researcher and teacher, Sir William Ramsay. With Ramsay's guidance, Mees and a close friend and fellow student, Samuel E. Sheppard, received their doctoral degrees in the theory of the photographic process in 1906. Their theses and other papers they had written were published in 1907 as a book entitled *Investigations on the Theory of the Photographic Process*, which became a standard text on the subject.

The winter of 1911-1912 found Eastman on a tour of Europe, his itinerary including a visit to the giant Bayer chemical factory at Elberfeld, Germany. Despite the fact that Bayer had recently filed suits against Kodak, the Bayer executives honored Eastman with a formal luncheon. During the meal, one of his hosts remarked that Bayer found it necessary to employ several hundred research chemists, and inquired: "And how many do you have, Mr. Eastman?"[21] Eastman's reply is not on record, however on his return to London, he conferred with Thatcher Clarke, his technical liaison man in Europe, on the advisability of establishing a research laboratory and who might be qualified to organize and run such a laboratory. Clarke suggested Mees.

Eastman immediately telephoned Mees, asking him to come see him in London the next day. Mees advised that he was leaving that day to deliver a lecture in Hungary. Eastman said that he wanted to talk to him about coming to Rochester; Mees said that the meeting sounded more important than his lecture, wired Budapest his regrets, and went to see Eastman as requested. Eastman explained that he had in mind a laboratory to do pure research, which of course appealed immensely to Mees, for while he enjoyed his work at Wratten & Wainwright, Ltd., he would have much rather been doing research than managing a manufacturing company.

He had evidently discussed Eastman's offer with his partners so that he was able to respond to Eastman that he would come to Rochester on one condition, that Eastman would buy Wratten & Wainwright. Eastman said that would be all right, and terms were quickly agreed upon.

Mees arrived in Rochester in April of 1912 to lay out the building plans for the new laboratory. A completed three-story, steel frame, brick-faced building of 25,000 square feet was ready for occupancy by January 1913. A remarkable performance when it is considered that all of the individual laboratory spaces were piped for hot and cold water, distilled water, gas, compressed air and vacuum, as well as various electrical supplies.

In addition to pure research facilities, one section of the laboratory was designed as a small-scale plate and film-making factory, thus providing for testing of emulsions under production conditions, as well as serving as a production unit for specialty plates and films for which there was small demand. Eastman and Mees agreed that the primary objective of the laboratory would be basic research into the science of photography; however, it was understood that assistance would be given to any manufacturing problems as they arose and investigation of new materials or processes would be done as needed. It was also understood that the laboratory would not be expected to show any financial return for probably as long as ten years. This turned out to be remarkably prescient; exactly ten years later, the 16mm direct-reversal film system became the laboratory's first commercial product.[22]

Beginnings of Major Philanthropy

Eastman, as the largest shareholder in the company, saw his personal fortune growing almost exponentially and in 1912 made the first of a number of donations to the Massachusetts Institute of Technology. Eastman's interest in the Institute dated back to 1890 when young deLancey was hired, then Lovejoy, then Haste and others a few years later. The caliber of these men and the quality of the education they had received so impressed Eastman that he began studying the annual reports prepared by Dr. Richard C. Maclaurin, President of the Institute.

Early in 1912, at Eastman's initiative, a meeting was arranged at a Manhattan hotel, and over dinner, Maclaurin laid out his plans for a major expansion of the Institute. The two men found an immediate rapport; Eastman was impressed with Maclaurin's vision and enthusiasm, Maclaurin with Eastman's ready grasp of the problems facing the Institute and his evident willingness to contribute to bold solutions.

Eastman's initial gift, made within a week of his meeting with Maclaurin, was for $2.5 million, to be used for the construction of "suitable buildings on the new property that has been acquired by the Institute on Massachusetts Avenue, fronting on the Charles River Basin." Eastman laid down no conditions on the architecture, as he and Maclaurin had agreed on excluding any "extravagant architectural features" or "elaborate details." Eastman did ask that his identity be withheld, and for seven years the mysterious benefactor was known only as "Mr. Smith." The result of Eastman's gift is the magnificent group of Greek Revival buildings that stand today on the Cambridge banks of the Charles.[23]

The Company Goes to War

When the assassination of Archduke Franz Ferdinand of Austria at Sarajevo on June 28, 1914, plunged Europe into war, the fortunes of Eastman Kodak Company were almost immediately altered, and for all time. Within a month of the shooting, Europe was transformed into two warring camps: Austria and Germany on one side, and Serbia, Russia, France, Belgium and Great Britain on the other. As the German army stormed through Belgium and France, orders from Europe for Rochester's production dried up quickly. At the same time, as German submarines decimated Allied shipping, vital imports such as dyes, chemicals, and raw paper slowed to a trickle.

Eastman, unlike Henry Ford and some other titans of American industry, was almost from the beginning on the side of American intervention, or at least for active support of the Allies, i.e. Great Britain, France, and Belgium. He was thoroughly unhappy with President Woodrow Wilson's policy of neutrality, which he described as "weak and vacillating." He even campaigned actively for Charles Evans Hughes, who unsuccessfully opposed Wilson for re-election.

When the German submarine blockade of England began sinking American ships, Wilson finally had to recognize the inevitability of American intervention, and on April 6, 1917, the United States was formally declared at war with Germany.

Eastman immediately opened negotiations with the War and Navy Departments, offering the facilities of the Company to the war effort. One specific suggestion was that Eastman Kodak set up a school of aerial photography in Rochester to train men in the Signal Corps in this new technology. The government turned down his offer, but did ask for his help in designing an aerial mapping camera, and special emulsions for aerial photography.[24]

As war needs escalated, more and more of the company's regular production staples—film, paper, chemicals, and cameras—were going to the military. In addition, the company found itself recruited to produce binoculars, airplane gun sights, lenses for aerial photography, and trench periscopes. And one product that Kodak Park had been making on an experimental basis, cellulose acetate, turned out to have an important military application: the same "dope" that had been intended to make non-flammable film turned out to be just what the infant aircraft industry needed to coat the fabric wings of its aircraft.

Eventually the Signal Corps came back to Eastman's original suggestion, and early in 1918 the School for Aerial Photography was established with an objective of training one thousand men, in classes of 250.[25] In April 1918 the Air Corps sent a young lieutenant named Albert K. Chapman to Rochester to set up a special project in aerial photography. The Kodak people with whom Chapman came in contact were so impressed with his abilities that when the war was over, Chapman was offered a job. The job was heading up a newly created Development Department that had been suggested by Dr. Mees. The new department's mission would be to translate discoveries made by the Research Laboratories into commercial products or processes.

Eastman Kodak emerged from the war with an outstanding record of achievement in supplying the nation with an enormous amount of varied materials that could hardly been matched by any other supplier. From the beginning of the company's involvement in defense contracts, Eastman had stated his intention to make no profit on that business and at war's end returned a total of $335,000 to the government. But one piece of unfinished business hung over the company, and the first significant change in top management was put into effect.

Resolution of the 1915 Antitrust Judgment

Eastman Kodak's phenomenal growth over the years did not go unchallenged by either its competitors or the government. In 1912 the Federal Department of Justice and the Attorney General's office began looking into the affairs of the Rochester giant, by far the largest entity in the Motion Picture Patents Company.

It was Eastman Kodak's control of paper, dry plate and plate camera manufacturing, and its policy of requiring Eastman Kodak dealers to handle only Eastman products that drew attention. In August 1915, Judge John R. Hazel charged Eastman Kodak with intent to create a monopoly in the photographic industry. The verdict was appealed to the U.S. Supreme Court, and there the case languished for five years while Eastman lawyers sought to reach a negotiated settlement with the Justice Department.

Some of this delay was undoubtedly due to distractions to both sides by the war; at the same time, the attitude of the government and public opinion in general toward large successful corporations had changed considerably.

In January of 1921, sensing the changed political climate and calculating the probable costs of a lengthy trial, Eastman Kodak moved to withdraw its appeal. The court then issued a decree containing several stipulations. First, the company was to divest itself of the dry plate and dry plate camera manufacturers that it had acquired nearly two decades earlier. Since by this time, dry plates had been largely displaced by film, this was not a particularly onerous judgment. Next, Kodak was enjoined from requiring its dealers to sell Kodak products exclusively, at fixed prices.[26] Lastly, Kodak was prohibited from marketing its own private label film.

Thanks to Eastman Kodak's policy of generally denying access to its own history, the effect of the latter two stipulations of the decree on the company is difficult to determine. Seventy-two years later, the company filed a motion in federal court to lift both this decree and a second one issued in 1954. The latter required the company to cease selling amateur color film with processing included in the selling price.

On May 20, 1994, the court found in Kodak's favor, but the Justice Department appealed. The Appellate Court upheld the District Court, and finally, on August 1995, Justice announced it would make no further appeal. Kodak was at last free to compete on a more equal footing with competitors such as its arch rival Fuji Photo Film Co.[27]

As this is written, Kodak is still locked in a pot-kettle battle with Fuji, each side claiming to be blocked out of the others' home market. At the same time, Eastman Kodak is assuming a dominant position in photofinishing in this country.

Re-organization

Colonel Henry A. Strong, first believer in George Eastman's vision, and first backer of those ideas, died on July 26, 1919, just short of his eighty-first birthday. Well-to-do when he first met Eastman as one of the three principal holders of Eastman Kodak stock (Eastman and Walker were the other two) he became a very wealthy man.

Eastman turned 65 in 1919, and while far from ready to step down, he had given serious thought to the matter of his successor. With characteristic circumspection he commissioned the accounting firm of Price, Waterhouse to study the company's organization and make recommendations.

Not surprisingly, among their first suggestions was that Mr. Eastman delegate more responsibility to staff officers, and this recommendation was accepted at once. Five vice-presidents were created: legal, sales promotion, corporate attorney, photographic quality, and manufacturing. Stuber and Lovejoy filled the last two posts.[28]

A major recommendation was that the company break up its monolithic structure into a number of autonomous operating divisions, an idea that was popular in corporate thinking at the time. Kodak management viewed this proposal as quite inappropriate, primarily because it seemed perilously close to doing exactly what the government had been trying to do for years: break Eastman Kodak Company up into a number of small companies. Furthermore, the company felt that centralized control of the highly specialized knowledge of the photographic process was essential to successful operations. For these reasons, the idea of decentralization of the manufacturing organization was rejected.

The 16mm System

As related in Chapter 3, the idea of using a narrower than standard film for the amateur arose very early in the history of motion picture photography, such as the various 17.5mm systems offered around the turn of the century, and later Thomas Edison's 22mm Home Kinetoscope system of 1912.

In 1914 Frederick W. Barnes, manager of Kodak's Hawkeye Works, demonstrated for Dr. Mees a camera he had designed several years earlier to make use of short ends of commercial 35mm movie film. The film was run through the camera twice, exposing one half of the film each time. The camera could also serve as a projector by removing the back and adding a light source.[29]

Also witnessing the demonstration was John G. Capstaff (Fig. 118), another of Dr. Mees's recruits from Wrattan & Wainwright, where he had been in charge of filter production. John George Capstaff was born at Gateshead-on-Tyne, England, to a shipbuilding family.[30] Educated at Rutherford College and

Fig. 118. John G. Capstaff.

Armstrong College, Capstaff had planned on an engineering career, but when no jobs were forthcoming in that field, he found work with a leading photographer in Newcastle. There he proved to be a quick study and in a short while he opened his own studio. In 1912 his work came to the attention of Dr. Mees, who promptly hired him and placed him in charge of the photographic division at the Kodak Research Laboratories.[31]

Capstaff saw the possibilities of adapting the Barnes camera to form an economical motion picture system for the amateur. He borrowed the camera and began a long series of experiments. The film from the Barnes camera had been processed in the conventional way, i.e. it was developed as a negative from which a positive print was made on a separate piece of film, thus consuming two feet of film for every foot of projectable film. Capstaff was aware of a way around this wasteful procedure. While searching for a workable system of color photography, one of Mr. Eastman's long-standing goals, Capstaff had learned of a process described in 1900 by Professor Rodolfo Namias of Italy, called "direct positives by reversal."[32]

In this process, the exposed film is developed to a negative image, this image bleached out, leaving some unconverted silver halide grains. The film is then given a controlled second exposure and developed again, whereupon those previously unconverted silver halide grains now yield a positive image. The immediate saving of film recommended the process to Capstaff as ideal for amateur use.

Note the words "controlled second exposure" in the above; this was Capstaff's contribution. The process as described by Namias was far from commercially viable, as consistently good positives were difficult to obtain. Capstaff discovered that only by carefully monitoring the density of the first negative image, scene by scene, could satisfactory results be obtained.

Capstaff's work on this project was interrupted by the war, during which time he had served as an instructor at the Eastman Kodak School of Aerial Photography. By 1919 sufficient progress had been made to justify seeking Mr. Eastman's approval of a full-scale development program, which was granted. One thing was understood from the beginning, that only a system using acetate-based film would be acceptable for home use.

Next came the question of film and image size. Split 35 mm as a film size was unacceptable because of the potential danger of having split nitrate-base film get into amateur stock. With the considerable help of a laboratory technician named Harris B. Tuttle and others in the Kodak Research Laboratories, many experiments were run on varying image sizes. One happy yet unexpected result of the reversal process was the discovery that the average grain size in the reversal processed image was considerably smaller than in the conventional two-film system.[33]

With this phenomenon, it was determined that a picture area 10mm by 7.5mm could be satisfactorily projected on a screen as large as six feet by nine feet, adequate for most amateur usage. Adding 3mm on each side for perforations gave a film width of 16mm. Whether accidental or deliberate, the picture area chosen had the same "aspect ratio" (1.33 to 1) as what was then the "Academy Standard," meaning that commercial 35mm films could be readily reduction printed to 16mm stock.[34]

To design the first 16mm camera, Kodak hired a French designer who had reportedly worked on the 9.5mm Pathé Baby, Julien Tessier.[35] Tessier's design can be seen in U.S. Patent No. 1,572,252 , in which the aperture and focus controls were at the front of the camera, and the finder was arranged for waist level viewing (Fig. 119).

Before the camera was in production, however, the controls were moved to the rear, and the finder changed to eye-level, as shown in the famous photograph of Harris Tuttle cranking the camera (Fig. 120). When the battery drive was offered as an

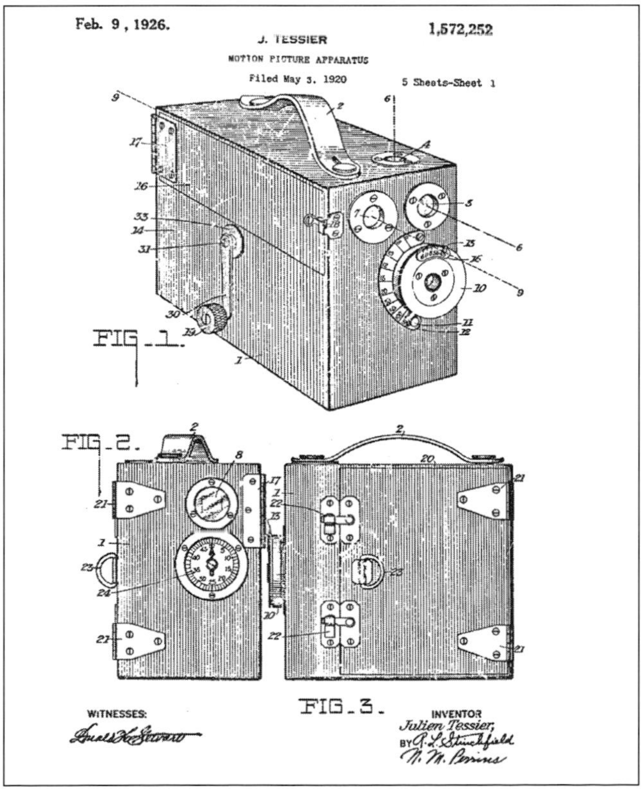

Fig. 119. Tessier's patent for the Ciné-Kodak.

Fig. 120. Harris Tuttle operating the Ciné-Kodak.

option early in 1924, the user could select direct eye-level viewing, or reflected (waist-level) viewing.

Despite having hired Tessier, the Development Department records show that a number of high-level Kodak executives took an active interest in the camera design, including Eastman, Mees, and Stuber. One of Mr. Eastman's suggestions that was adopted and retained on all subsequent Ciné-Kodak designs was a device to prevent closing the camera door until the gate and the sprocket idlers were in the closed position. On the other hand, his suggestion of a spring-motor drive was not adopted until the Model B was introduced in July 1925.[36]

Tessier's intention as stated in the patent was to design a camera which was compact, easy to load and operate, with sturdy construction, not likely to be easily damaged. These objectives were certainly met in the die-cast box-like construction, the large loading door, and the prominent and easy-to-read aperture and focus settings. The camera did have one drawback—being handcranked, it could not be hand-held, requiring to be mounted on a tripod for successful operation, just as did all professional cameras at that time.

Using a prototype camera, Capstaff and Tuttle tested the system under a variety of conditions, including a child's birthday party staged by Mrs. Harold Gleason, the wife of George Eastman's organist. This prototypical "home movie" featured two toddlers (one of whom was Mrs. Gleason's one-year-old son Charles), a bowl of jelly, a chocolate cake, and the family dog. Mrs. Gleason spread a tablecloth on her lawn, plunked the two children down on the cloth with the jelly and the cake. As Tuttle began to crank the Cine-Kodak, Charles conveyed a handful of jelly in the general direction of his mouth, the second little angel did a similar operation with the chocolate cake, at which point the dog joined the party and began licking the cake off the boy's face. This was a spontaneous variation of stock Hollywood "pie-in-the-face" slapstick, and the new camera and neophyte operator got it all on film.

A special showing of all the experimental takes was arranged for Eastman and Mees. The story goes that when the children's birthday party footage appeared on the screen, Eastman laughed as heartily as anyone, then turned to Mees and said "Okay, full steam ahead!"

A working camera was in operation by 1920, but the camera could not be marketed until a projector and processing equipment was perfected, which was to take nearly three years. Perfecting the processing equipment consumed many hours of Capstaff's and Tuttle's time. The reagents were corrosive, the timing of each stage critical if consistently good results were to be obtained. As noted in Chapter 3, Pathé launched its 9.5mm system in 1922 using a variation of the reversal process which was designed to enable the user to develop his own film, but Kodak considered it essential that processing be done under carefully controlled (laboratory) conditions.

In its final design, the Ciné-Kodak was a straight-sided die-cast aluminum box, 8-5/8" by 4-5/8" by 6", weighing 7-1/4 pounds. It took a 100-foot spool of film furnished in a steel canister, with leader and tail of black paper, permitting daylight loading. The entire left side opened for easy threading. A footage counter, eye-level finder, and aperture and focusing control of the f/3.5 lens were located at the rear of the camera. In an effort to insure that the customer got good results, the Ciné-Kodak was initially offered only as an outfit consisting of camera, projector, tripod, screen, priced at $335.[37] (See Fig. 121.)

The first public demonstration of the Ciné-Kodak system was given on January 8, 1923 by Dr. Mees at the East High School in Rochester. Harris Tuttle filmed the notable guests as they arrived, then while Dr. Mees lectured, the film was processed, and the results shown at the end of the lecture. The same lecture and demonstration was given on January 23, 1923, at the Franklin Institute in Philadelphia.

The Society of Motion Picture Engineers learned of Eastman's plans a few months later when Dr. Mees presented two papers, one on the new film and the second on the new camera and projector. In June the Company issued its *Trade Circular* to its dealer network, announcing the new system, describing how the consumer would be able to expose the film in the hand-cranked camera, have it processed in Rochester and returned for projection at home or at school on a Kodascope 30" by 40" screen.[38] Shipments of the new cameras and projectors to dealers also began in June 1923.

Both Bell & Howell and Victor Animatograph had been at this time experimenting with sub-standard width film and camera systems. Alexander

Fig. 121. The original Kodascope with reel enclosures.

Fig. 122. Gene Tunney, retired heavyweight boxing champion, posing with a Bell & Howell Model 75, ca.1932.

Victor had visited Rochester in 1920, inquiring about the availability of non-flammable film in 28mm gauge. Bell & Howell had started production of a 17.5mm system. On observing Kodak's achievement with the 16mm direct reversal system, both companies converted their plans to the 16mm format.

Despite the very substantial economy that the 16mm system offered over cameras using standard film, not all amateur moviemakers immediately chose the new gauge. As Coe points out, the arrival of two practical relatively low-cost systems (16mm and 9.5mm) coincided with the introduction of several small cameras using standard 35mm nitrate film, such as the French Sept, the Swiss Bol, and the ICA Kinamo from Germany.[39] These cameras in general cost about a third as much as either the Ciné-Kodak or Bell & Howell models; however, a finished film in 35mm cost over four times as much per minute of screen time because of the negative-plus-positive nature of standard film.[40]

Herbert C. McKay, in his 1924 book on motion picture photography for the amateur—one of the earliest books on the subject—devoted ten pages to the 16mm system and 35 pages to 28mm and 35mm

cameras.[41] Nevertheless, the introduction of the 16mm system attracted thousands of people to home movie making who would not otherwise have taken it up.

No better evidence of the emergence of this new market can there be than the founding in 1926 of the Amateur Cinema League—the first national organization with a monthly magazine devoted entirely to amateur filmmakers. The magazine, *Movie Makers*, carried illustrated stories of various and sundry royal persons, actors and actresses, politicians and other newsworthy figures of the day, carrying their personal movie camera or aiming it at each other (Fig. 122). Invariably it was a 16mm camera. Eastman Kodak, Bell & Howell, and Victor Animatograph were prominent advertisers.[42]

Home movies were not yet affordable to the broad market. The leisure class, however, seized on this new diversion with gusto. Before long, film-processing stations (Fig. 123) were being installed in major cities around the world and even on two of the famous Thomas Cook & Sons cruise ships.

The June 1923 Kodak Trade Circular announcement mentioned above also carried the promise of the establishment of a film rental library of "many hundred thousand feet of film suitable for Kodascope projection in the home." Dealers were cautioned that the rental of films would not be handled through its dealers, but rather through a new organization, Kodascope Libraries, Inc. (Fig. 124). Branches were established in New York City, Boston, Chicago, and San Francisco.

To head up this operation, Eastman Kodak hired away the head of the most successful film rental agency then in business, Pathé Exchange, Inc. Willard Beach Cook (1872-1952) was a civil engineer with a remarkable talent for marketing and management. In 1913 Cook had acquired the United States distribution rights to Pathé 28mm films and projectors and had energetically expanded his operations to include the production of cameras, projectors, and a commercial production agency for industrial and promotional films. Cook enthusiastically promoted the new gauge, and the Kodascope Libraries quickly outdistanced the competition in serving the home market. Cook remained as head of Kodascope Libraries until it closed as a Kodak subsidiary in 1939.

In May 1928 *American Photography* reported amateur film as the fastest growing branch of the motion pictures industry, with millions of feet of film being consumed each week and over 125,000 amateur cameras in use. Film libraries were multiplying and expanding their catalogs; rental of 16mm prints of Hollywood films was as popular then as video rentals are today. Eastman Kodak's annual report for 1929 reported that five new Ciné-Kodak processing plants were added during the year, making a total of 52 in service world-wide. Presumably in

Fig. 123. First continuous "tube" processor for 16mm film, installed at Eastman Kodak, Rochester in 1923.

Fig. 124. 1935 advertisement for Kodascope Libraries, Inc.

MOTION PICTURES FOR
HOME ENTERTAINMENT

KODAK
CINEGRAPHS

ADVENTURE ● NATURAL HISTORY
ANIMATED MODELS AND CARTOONS
WORLD WAR ● COMEDY ● TRAVEL
SPORT ● HISTORY ● GENERAL FILMS

Fig. 125. Advertisement for Kodak Cinegraphs

response to customer demand, about 1930 Kodak began as a separate operation, making "Kodak Cinegraphs," films to purchase, available at Kodak dealerships (Fig. 125).

Eastman Kodak had recognized the potential for commercial applications of 16mm even before the new gauge was announced to the public. Harris Tuttle shot many "firsts," including two surgical procedure films in 1921, time-and-motion study films the same year, and the first industrial film in 1922; the latter showed a pilot plant in operation making fireproof brick and building blocks.[43] The new gauge quickly drove 9.5mm, 17.5mm, and 28mm out of the amateur market, and more slowly but surely replaced 35mm in areas such as educational, industrial and military applications. The greatest boost to 16mm use in educational and training films came during World War II, as the services discovered how expeditiously training films could be made in the new gauge, and easily shipped and shown all over the world.

When the Kodak Research Laboratories were established in 1913, George Eastman gave Dr. Mees the understanding that the laboratory would not be expected to show any financial return for a number of years, and that about ten years of operation would probably be required before any results of financial importance to the company would be achieved.[44] in 1923, 16mm direct reversal safety film came on the market and became one of the most financially important products to be developed by the Laboratories, exactly fitting the expectations set forth ten years before.

First Color Movies for the Amateur

Capstaff's work in color photography did result in a two-color subtractive process that was the first to be given the name "Kodachrome." Introduced in 1915, it gave quite pleasing results in portraiture, but the narrow range of tones produced made it unsatisfactory for landscapes. Capstaff then turned his attention to a three-color additive process developed in France in 1922, and by 1928 was able to announce a new system called Kodacolor.[45]

Mr. Eastman was very pleased with the new system, and the public's reaction. Hiram Percy Maxim, founder of the Amateur Cinema League, was among the notables invited to the first public demonstration, held at George Eastman's home on July 28, 1928. Maxim described the experience in the September issue of *Movie Makers*:

Then they threw onto the screen a portrait of a woman's face. It was our first portrait of a living person. It struck us dumb, even the most loquacious. Silence fell but for the whir of the projector. Then a burst of applause. I have thought about that moment since. It was not the beauty of the lady. It was not because we wanted to be polite to Mr. Eastman, or to the lady. It was because of the startling effect of seeing living breathing flesh and blood on that screen. It was a real live woman, not a picture that we were seeing. It makes me wonder, if we were to throw onto the screen, in this fashion, the face of a loved one who had departed, could we endure it? Would it be too near to coming back from the grave to health, vigor and life? [46]

Color arrived at Kodak in 1928 in several ways, one of which was the result of hiring the American industrial designer, Walter Dorwin Teague. Teague (1883-1960) had become a successful advertising designer but had barely begun in product design when he was hired by Kodak to enliven the design of some of its cameras. One of his designs was the spectacular Vest Pocket Series III Camera, a metal and embossed leather folding camera which was available in five colors: Bluebird, Cockatoo, Jenny Wren, Red Breast, and Sea Gull. He subsequently worked with Kodak's ace product designer Joseph Mihalyi to style the revolutionary Super Kodak Six-20, the first camera with a coupled electric-eye for automatic exposure setting.

Teague's impact on Kodak's movie cameras was somewhat less dramatic, where "form follows function" was perhaps more rigorously observed than with still cameras. Ciné-Kodaks, heretofore like Henry Ford's cars coming only in black, in November 1928 were available in gray or brown. The following spring, the new smaller Model BB, came in black, blue, brown or gray. Kodak's 1928 annual report proudly displayed color photographs of these new colored cameras. It appears that the elegant Library Kodascope in its hand-rubbed walnut case and matching cabinet (Fig. 126) was also a Teague creation.[47]

Color had actually come to the company's annual report the year before; the 1927 report was such a radical departure from all previous reports as to make one wonder if they were issued by the same company. Up until 1926, Kodak's annual reports apparently reflected the relatively narrow ownership of the company at that time. The 1926 report is typical: it is just five pages long and contains the barest amount of information required by law. Included are a brief profit and loss statement and balance sheet, but no illustrations, no discussion of new products.

The 1927 report is 31 pages long, includes five pages of photographs of Kodak properties around the world, aerial views of the Camera Works, and the Kodak Office Building. There are colored bar charts and graphs of earnings and other financial data, a color print of a painting, and narratives of new products, industrial relations, and developments of 1927. The hiring of Teague and the dramatic makeover of the annual report suggests the presence of someone new on the sixteenth floor of 343 State Street, someone with a fresh outlook on public relations and marketing.[48]

Fig. 126. The Library Kodascope.

A Fortune Distributed

Eastman's gradual withdrawal from one-man leadership of the company began in 1919 with the appointment of the five vice-presidents and continued as Lovejoy demonstrated his executive abilities. Eastman grew comfortable with longer and longer absences, and once jokingly remarked that his ambition was to have just two vacations per year, each six months long.

His civic and philanthropic activities took an appreciable amount of time, but gave him great pleasure. As one example, when he reviewed the results of his leadership of the 1918 Rochester United War Fund Drive, which raised nearly $5 million, setting a record and during which he had relentlessly pressured other well-to-do citizens of Rochester, he said: "I never had more fun in working out anything in my life."[49]

Eastman's philanthropies, begun in earnest in 1912 with a $2.5 million pledge to the Massachusetts Institute of Technology, continued without abatement for the next dozen years. The University of Rochester, the associated School of Music, the School of Medicine and Dentistry, as well as The Massachusetts Institute of Technology were the principal beneficiaries of gifts totaling at least $50 million.

Eastman's identity as the "Mr. Smith" who had given millions to M.I.T. was finally revealed in 1919. In June of that year, Eastman wrote to Dr. Maclaurin that he was prepared to give the Institute, for endowment purposes, five thousand shares of Kodak common stock, provided the Institute would raise a like amount by December 31, 1919. The Institute was successful in matching Eastman's pledge, and on January 11, 1920, the Institute announced that "Mr. Smith" was George Eastman. His total gifts came to $11 million.

The Eastman School of Music, founded in 1919, was almost entirely Eastman's creation, and his interest extended to the smallest details—the architecture of the building, the staffing, even the proposed programming. He found it quite amusing that a person with no discernible musical ability should be directing the creation of one of the premier music schools in the country.

In 1924, after he had made gifts of Eastman Kodak stock totaling $15 million, it appeared that he had given away the balance of his fortune. Concerned that the distribution of such an amount of company stock would lead people to fear that the stock price would be driven down or that this signaled his immanent retirement, he wrote a long letter addressed to his "fellow employees," in which he explained that this distribution of stock represented "the last great block in existence, as the holdings of the other big owners, my old partners, Strong and Walker, have been distributed without disturbance of the market."

He also assured his employees that this action did not in any way indicate his intention to retire from the direction of the company.[50]

Nevertheless, the following year Eastman moved up to a newly created position, chairman of the board, and named Stuber to succeed him as president. At the same time, Lovejoy was named vice-president and general manager. Jenkins labels the Eastman and Stuber appointments as "honorific," with Lovejoy being the de facto chief executive of the company.

New Fields to Conquer

With the new management team in place and functioning to his satisfaction, Eastman felt free to take the first of the six-month vacations he had joked about. Travel had appealed to Eastman from his early days at the Rochester Savings Bank. So did camping. As his increasing wealth permitted, he travelled coast-to-coast and to Alaska, British Columbia, Labrador, and Panama.

1925 found him preparing for an extended tour of Africa. This was to be more than a sporting trip; Eastman was accompanied by Daniel Pomeroy of the American Museum of Natural History in New York, and Carl Akeley and his wife would join them in London. Akeley (1864-1926), inventor of the unique professional camera which bears his name, was a veteran of four previous trips to Africa, from which the huge collection of animals in the American Museum of Natural History was created.

Once in Africa, Eastman and party would meet up with the famed explorers, Martin and Osa Johnson. Martin Johnson (1884-1937), at this time 42 years old, was at least as well known as Akeley for his adventures with Jack London aboard the ill-fated *Snark* and his spectacular films of Solomon Island natives, such as *Captured by Cannibals*.[51] Osa Johnson, almost ten years younger than her husband, was a pretty, petite, and intrepid wife who had accompanied Martin on several South Sea voyages and could handle a rifle or an inquisitive headhunter with equal aplomb (Fig. 127).

The Johnson's first meeting with Eastman was not auspicious, according to Osa's account many years later. Returning from an African trip of their own sometime in 1923, the Johnsons secured an interview with Mr. Eastman, hoping to interest him in supporting a major study of the fauna of an area which at the time was largely unexplored, then Northern Rhodesia, now Zambia. Eastman listened politely to their story for a few minutes, then ended the interview with the remark that he made it a policy never to invest in private enterprises.

Crestfallen, the Johnsons took their leave and caught the next train back to New York. Before they had gone very far however, Martin decided that they had used the wrong approach, so he and Osa left the train at the next stop and returned to Rochester. Mrs. Johnson does not explain how they persuaded

Fig. 127. Osa and Martin Johnson with native camermen in Africa. Osa is embracing an Akeley, the two assistants have Universals, and Martin is behind a Bell & Howell Model 2709.

Miss Whitney, Eastman's long-time secretary, to give them another audience with her boss, but Eastman saw them again, and this time they convinced him that their mission was a truly scientific undertaking and not a moneymaking scheme. Eastman pledged $10,000 to them and gave permission to use his name to raise more money.[52]

By 1926 the Johnsons had a permanent base camp established in Zambia, where the Eastman party joined them. They would spend six months in East Africa hunting game with camera and gun. Most specimens were for the Museum, but on this and a second African trip, Eastman shot a number of specimens for his own collection. One such specimen was an elephant, whose head hung in the conservatory of Eastman's home for many years.[53]

Eastman kept careful notes of his safaris and published a book about the 1926 journey—*Chronicles of*

an African Trip. On his second visit, in 1928, he kept a record of the trip in a series of letters addressed to his secretary. The letters were actually intended to be copied and distributed to a close circle of friends at home. They were finally published in 1987—*Chronicles of a Second African Trip.*

This account makes disturbing reading for the present-day mind. There was no thought of conservation of African wildlife; Eastman and his party took specimens of species that were known to be nearly extinct even then. The native Africans provided all the manpower to carry freight, set up the camps, prepared and served the meals, tracked the game, carried the weapons (and even Eastman on one occasion), and butchered and skinnned the animals. The natives were seldom referred to by name; they were called "boys" or "witch doctors." Such were the mores of the times.

Eastman's second trip to Africa, in 1927/1928, was done in considerable style. A large, wood-burning river steamer was leased from Thomas Cook & Sons to carry the party up the Nile from Khartoum in Egypt to Rejaf, the last village accessible by boat, in an area where the Sudan, Uganda, and the then Belgian Congo come together. The steamer was fitted out to Eastman's specifications and included staterooms with private baths for the Eastman party, dining room, and observation deck. There was also a General Electric refrigerator on board to keep a generous supply of Australian butter sweet. The crew numbered 38 men, including three cooks, two waiters, and two cabin boys.[54]

The elaborate equipage and staffing notwithstanding, hunting elephants and rhinos was a strenuous and hazardous recreation for any man at age 74, yet Eastman performed well and showed remarkable endurance. He got his elephant, even though it took more than six slugs from his Westley-Richards .470 rifle to bring the animal down. On another occasion he was filming a rhino with his Ciné-Kodak Model B when the animal decided to charge (Fig. 128). Eastman calmly stood his ground, and, like a toreador, gracefully turned at the last moment to let the oncoming beast pass him by inches.[55] He was also an excellent camp cook (Fig.129). Osa Johnson's account of their first safari together mentions many instances of Eastman's skill at preparing puddings, pies, and breads, using his own preparations of what would today be termed "package mixes."

Eastman, who never married, enjoyed the company of attractive young women. At home in Rochester, he frequently entertained a circle of young Rochester matrons, and in Africa he found Osa Johnson to be particularly good company. His account of his second African trip is full of references to Osa, with rarely a mention of Martin, although Osa in her book recounts that the two men were on a friendly first-name basis. When Eastman started home at the end of his second safari, leaving the Johnsons in Africa, both Eastman and Osa were in tears. Eastman presented Osa with one of his prized Mannlicher rifles and promised to send her his electric refrigerator when they left the steamer. They were not to see each other again.

Eastman took movies of his trips that were shown to selected guests in this "theatre" on the third floor of his home (Fig. 130).

Fig. 128. Eastman and his white rhino, shot in Uganda on January 31, 1928.

Journey's End

Eastman found, with perhaps a touch of wonder, that the company seemed to run very well despite his long absences from 343 State Street. 1929 was a particularly active year. Kodak Park was expanded, and five new Ciné-Kodak processing plants were added, making a total of 52 in operation throughout the world.

In 1930, to celebrate the fiftieth anniversary of the company's founding, a massive promotional scheme was undertaken. A special No. 2 Hawkeye camera would be given away to every girl or boy whose twelfth birthday fell in that year. The camera was covered in tan reptile-grained paper, with a large gold-leafed seal applied to one side. Some 550,000 cameras were distributed, half a million in the United States, and fifty thousand in Canada (Fig. 131).

The stock market crash of October 1929 had little effect on Kodak, but the deep nation-wide depression

Fig. 129. Eastman blowing an ostrich egg at their Uganda campsite. Osa Johnson observes the process.

Fig. 130. Eastman's theatre, third floor of the George Eastman House, Rochester, presently the Director's office (without the moose).

Fig. 131. May 1930 advertisement for the Anniversary Kodak.

which followed for several years did eventually curtail sales substantially. Eastman's health seemed to follow the country's malaise; his visits to the new executive suite in the Kodak Tower became increasingly rare, and when he did come, his slow progress through the lobby was painful for friends to watch. By 1931 he rarely left the mansion at 900 East Avenue, except to be driven occasionally around Kodak Park.

On the morning of March 14, 1932, a group of intimates from the office were called to his home to witness the signing of a codicil to his will. His friends found him alert, even jocular, as he reminded Mrs. Hutchinson that the witnesses were to each receive a twenty-dollar gold piece for their services. Shortly after all had left his room, a shot was heard. Eastman had exercised his last act of control. His note read:

To my friends My work is done why wait? GE

Curiously, Ivar Kreuger, the "Swedish Match King," had committed suicide two days earlier, when his financial empire had collapsed in bankruptcy. Kodak executives quickly issued a statement reassuring the public that the manner of Eastman's death had no relation to the health of the company.

Eastman was a contemorary of several entrepreneurial giants: Thomas Edson, Harvey Firestone, and Henry Ford, among others. Firestone's home experiments with vulcanizing rubber are reminiscent of Eastman's kitchen emulsion laboratory. Eastman was more complex than any of those mentioned, his range of interests broader, his vision and his organizational ability decidedly suprior. To the public and casual acquaintances he was austere and reserved, to his intimates he was seen as kindly and not without a sense of humor.

His public generosity was legendary, yet he could be relentless in competition and sometimes in personal dealings. His treatment of Frank A. Brownell, who was responsible for many of Eastman Kodak's camera designs during the first two decades of the company, and whom Eastman himself once called "the greatest camera designer the world has known," at this distance seems shabby at best. And there are historians who feel that the Revernd Hannibal Goodwin created a flexible film base before Reichenbach, but was unjustly deprived of the benefits of his invention by the machinations of Eastman and his attorneys. To this observer, however, Goodwin's troubles seem to have stemmed in a good part from his own inexperience in patent litigation, plus some very bad advice from his patent attorney.

On the other side of the ledger, Eastman was farsighted and generous in treatment of his employees, initiating benefit programs which were generally well ahead of the times. His legacy to the world in general is indisputable: inventing and perfecting equipment which made photography available to the millions, and founding and building a multinational company which for more than a century has provided employment to thousands, and dividend income to other thousands.

5   The Eastman Kodak Company – Part II

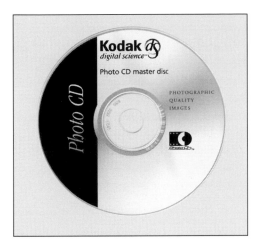

Kodak Photo CD

A New Chapter

With the passing of George Eastman, the company that bears his name entered a new chapter in its existence, so it has seemed fitting to divide this history accordingly. While the objectives and principles that Eastman established continued to guide the company for many years, there were inevitable changes in the company's character as the world around it changed. This chapter will recount the highlights of the company's course from 1932 to the present day, particularly as related to amateur motion picture technology.

Coping with the Depression

Despite his reduced involvement with management of the company and his own declining health, George Eastman had become seriously concerned with the potential effect of the great depression then gripping the nation on Kodak employees. Late in 1930 he directed his staff to implement a company-sponsored employee benefit plan. Eastman and Lovejoy had actually developed this plan some years before, but never put it in effect.[1]

The 1932 annual report noted that "conditions although bad in 1931 were much worse in 1932 . . . total volume of all operating companies declined about 20 percent, but substantial economies have been effected by salary and wage cuts."

Kodak also co-operated in a national "Share the Work" program, which consisted of reducing the workweek rather than laying off workers. The company had actually been following such a program for nearly ten years. In 1930, President Stuber was able to report that for the eight years from 1922 through 1929, the number of layoffs averaged only two percent of the total work force.

Perhaps indicative of Dr. Mees' strong position in Kodak's management hierarchy, the Kodak Research Laboratories were minimally affected by the great depression. In reply to a query from his counterpart at the Bell Telephone Laboratories, Mees reported that while KRL employees took a ten percent pay cut in 1932, as did all Kodak employees, the staffing of the Laboratories remained essentially constant throughout the depression.[2]

New Products for the Amateur Filmmaker

The decade leading up to World War II saw the introduction of two new products that were to have a profound effect on amateur motion picture making and the fortunes of Eastman Kodak. The first was a new amateur film gauge, promising the user movies at one quarter the film cost of 16mm, and the second was a brilliant, fool-proof color movie film.

As successful as 16mm was, particularly in semi-professional or non-theatrical fields, the cost of filming in 16mm kept amateur movie making from achieving the widespread popularity of still camera "snap shooting." A typical 16mm camera in the early 30's sold for over $100, and a roll of film cost $6, equivalent in year 2000 dollars to $1,080 and $65, respectively.[3]

A number of schemes to reduce the film cost had been attempted, as discussed in Chapter 3, none of which had proven very successful with the exception of 9.5mm. A truly novel approach to the problem made its appearance in 1930, from an unexpected quarter.

"Revolutionary New Movie Principle Cuts Cost of Taking Motion Pictures 75%. Astonishes Movie World!"

So read the headline of a double-page advertisement in the October 1930 issue of *Movie Makers*. The company was not Eastman Kodak, however, but one

heretofore unknown in photography: the Kodel Electric & Manufacturing Company, of Cincinnati, Ohio. The product was the Kemco HoMovie Camera, and it was indeed revolutionary.

The new camera and projector used standard 16mm film, but were designed to put four images in the space of one 16mm frame. This was accomplished by a film transport mechanism that gave the film transverse as well as longitudinal motion through the camera and of course through the projector as well. The resulting pattern of images has the elegant name boustrophedonic, from the Greek "as the ox plows." Since the film was perforated in the standard 16mm fashion, each image was exactly one quarter the size of the 16mm frame, or 3.5 mm by 4.8 mm.[4]

The camera, in a Bakelite body, measured 3-1/2" by 5" by 8", almost exactly the size of the Model B Ciné-Kodak, but slightly heavier. It took the standard Eastman Kodak 100-foot spool and came with a 15mm fixed focus, f/3.5 lens. The projector was equipped with a 50v, 250-watt lamp, and a single lever converted the film transport for standard 16mm travel and adjusted the lamp condenser focus to the full frame, for projecting conventional 16mm film (Fig. 132).

The Kemco outfit sold for $252.50—$90 for the camera, $150 for the projector, and $12.50 for a fold-

Fig. 132. The Kemco HoMovie Outfit.

ing screen. A 100-foot roll of Agfa film could be had for six dollars, including processing in those days. One Kemco ad cleverly pointed out that at those prices, by the time the user had shot 14 rolls of film, the equivalent in screen time of 56 rolls of conventional 16mm, the saving of 42 rolls of film would exactly equal the original cost of the outfit!

The man behind this remarkable system was a versatile inventor named Clarence E. Ogden (1891-1944). Ogden, born in Cincinnati, had at least 15 patents to his name between 1919 and 1932, most pertaining to storage battery chargers and AC to DC rectifiers. One obituary credits him with the invention of the Kuprox rectifier, which was widely used in the '20s and '30s as a DC source for radio receivers. He was also cited as the organizer in the '20s of the Cincinnati radio station WKRC, the first radio station in that area and one of the first in the country.[5]

Both the camera and the projector exhibited excellent workmanship. Ogden obviously expected a bright future for his invention; highly detailed instruction books were produced and many sophisticated accessories offered, such as a titling stand, editor, enlarging outfit, film album, and elegant HoMovie console. How many of these ingenious machines were ultimately produced is difficult to determine, but they are very rarely seen, leading one to believe that production was halted very soon after Eastman Kodak's announcement of its 8mm system.

Enter the Eight

The search for faster emulsions and finer grain film continued at Kodak Research Laboratories, and by 1928 it became evident that the 16mm gauge could probably be reduced even further. There was, however, another factor in the equation: the investment in all the machinery and apparatus designed to handle 16mm. A totally new gauge would perforce make all of that equipment useless in production of the new gauge. Would the savings in film cost justify the investment in new machinery? Not likely, since many costs of production were at most only marginally dependent on film size: handling, packaging, storage, and so on. However, if the existing machinery could be utilized for at least part of the manufacturing process, a new gauge could be produced to sell at a lower cost.

The answer harked back to the Barnes experimental camera, in which 35mm film was run through the camera twice, with one-half of the film exposed on each trip and the developed film then slit to 17.5mm. At that time however, such a scheme was deemed unacceptable, since it would permit unscrupulous persons to supply flammable film to the home user.

Now that safety film was available in 16mm, and all 16mm film was safety, the double run-through principle could be used, with no danger of flammable nitrate stock being substituted The user would be supplied 16mm safety film, which would be returned for processing as 16mm. This meant that raw film production and processing of exposed film could use existing equipment.

Thus it was that in 1930-1931 a camera was built in which a length of 16mm was run through exposing one half of the film; the film spools then reversed in position and the other half of the film exposed. After direct reversal processing as with 16mm, the film was slit in half and the two pieces spliced together. A 25-foot roll of film resulted in 50 feet of developed film, with images one quarter the size of the 16mm image. There would be only one row of perforations, but that was adequate for such narrow film.

The extremely small size of the image did require a film with very high resolving power and definition, which the Laboratories successfully produced. Some appreciation of the quality of the film may be gained when it is realized that to fill a 40" by 40" screen, the 8mm image is enlarged approximately 230 diameters (Fig. 133).

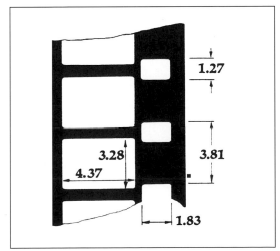

Fig. 133. Dimensions (in millimeters) of standard 8mm film.

Fig. 134. 1932 advertisement for the Ciné-Kodak Eight.

Fig. 135. Bell & Howell's Straight Eight, for pre-split 8mm film.

In July of 1932, the first amateur film, cameras, and projectors in the new format were ready. A double-page spread in the August issue of Movie Makers announced the new Ciné-Kodak 8 Model 20 at $29.50, the Kodascope 8 projector at $22.50, and a 25-foot roll of film for $2.25 (Fig. 134).

Acceptance of the New Gauge

The new system received "good press," at least in some quarters. Herbert C. McKay, pioneering writer on amateur cinematography, praised it highly, and then in apparent response to some unfavorable comments, recalled how just ten years earlier 16mm had been greeted with scorn as being little better than a plaything. The editors of *Movie Makers*, the official organ of the Amateur Cinema League, likened the advent of 8mm to that of inexpensive still cameras and roll film, when vast numbers of new photographers were born. They also observed that while this was not the first attempt to make amateur movies more affordable, this venture being backed by the largest photographic organization in the world stood a far better chance of succeeding.

Both the consumer and the competition reacted cautiously to the new gauge. Serious amateurs, who formed the backbone of the amateur film market at that time, were disinclined to switch to 8mm because the majority of that class were not particu-

larly concerned with economy.[6] Other 16mm manufacturers were wary of investing in new production machinery until the potential of the new system could be more accurately assessed.

Curiously, the next U.S. maker to advertise an 8mm camera was a firm making its debut in the movie machinery industry—the Stewart-Warner Co. of Chicago, primarily a manufacturer of automotive accessories. A June 1933 ad by Marshall Field & Co., Chicago's giant department store, offered the Stewart-Warner "Buddy 8" camera and projector at $29.50 for both. Another curiosity is that the Buddy 8 was an exact copy of the Keystone K-8, a camera not introduced by Keystone Camera Corporation until 1936, suggesting that Keystone took this as a way to test the market before committing their name and resources to the new gauge.

Bell & Howell, Kodak's strongest competitor, apparently hoping to create its own space in the marketplace and, always loath to ride on Kodak's coattails, in mid-1935 introduced the first camera designed to accept pre-split 8mm film, called the Filmo 127-A Straight Eight (Fig. 135). The camera was priced at $69, compared to Eastman Kodak's Model 20 at $29.50. Film for the camera was supplied to Bell & Howell by Eastman Kodak in 16mm width, which Bell & Howell split to 8mm and wound on special 30-foot reels.[7]

The first model of the Keystone K-8 mentioned above would accept either pre-split 8 or double 8. Later models would accept double 8 only. Revere Camera Corporation joined the pre-split parade in 1939 with a model called the Model C8 "Super 8mm." In December 1935, Bell & Howell abandoned single 8 and switched to double 8; the single 8 fad was over, except for one manufacturer. The longest lived single 8 system was introduced by the Universal Camera Corporation in 1936 with the UniveX Model A-8 Cine Camera, which remained on the market until 1946.

Usage of 8mm grew steadily in the first decade after its introduction. Writing a review of 1941, Dr. Walter Clark, F.R.P.S., of the Kodak Research Laboratories stated:

The 8mm and 16mm motion picture field had developed into an enormous industry by itself. Each year shows an increase in the number of amateur moviemakers and in the variety of equipment available to them. In 1941, the most interesting developments were a steady increase in the use of color and 8mm film and the introduction of a variety of devices intended to enable the amateur to approach the professional standard. [8]

Of the 23 films selected by The Amateur Cinema League in its annual competition for awards of excellence for the year 1940, almost half were filmed in 8mm. The League noted that this showing more than doubled 8mm's presence over the previous year and that for the first time an 8mm film won the top award.[9]

Camera design for 8mm film did not advance materially until production of amateur equipment was resumed after World War II. By the time Super 8 arrived in 1965, regular 8 cameras had reached a remarkable level of sophistication. Fully automatic exposure control came in 1957, with Bell & Howell's introduction of the Model 290. Zoom lenses for 8mm cameras were announced by Bell & Howell and Eastman Kodak in 1959. Reflex viewing appeared in 1961 and battery-driven cameras became common about the same time. Popular Photography's 1964 Directory listed five 8mm cameras selling for $400 or more, including models by Beaulieu, Paillard Bolex, and Ercsam, makers of the Camex Dual Reflex CR camera.

Never News as Big as This: Kodachrome!

Emblazoned on the cover of the May-June 1935 issue of *Ciné-Kodak News*, Kodak's little magazine for amateur moviemakers, was the above message announcing the arrival of a truly revolutionary product—Kodachrome film (Fig.136). The first fully successful amateur color movie film, Kodachrome had emerged from the Kodak Research Laboratories after nearly 15 years in gestation. Inside the magazine, an article by Dr. C.E.K. Mees, vice-president and director of research, explained the new process—how it

Fig. 136. Announcement of Kodachrome, 1935.

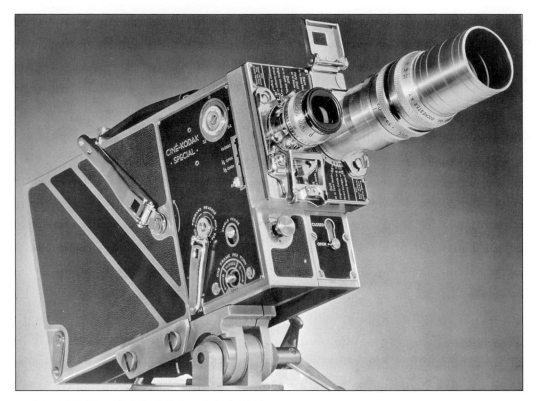

Fig. 137. The Ciné-Kodak Special of 1933.

worked, how it differed from the 1928 Kodacolor, and how easy it was for the amateur to use.[10]

As easy as it was to expose for good movies, the processing of the exposed film was extremely complex, requiring a number of carefully controlled steps which could only be performed satisfactorily with special machinery and carefully trained operatives. At first all processing was done at Rochester, but soon other processing stations were opened across the country. The full history of the development of Kodachrome is given in Chapter 8.

It is perhaps difficult for most of us today, surrounded as we are by color on the TV screen, at the movies, and in every magazine, to imagine what it was like when photography was almost always black and white and what it was like when this gorgeous new process became available to the inexpeienced amateur photographer. There had been color processes before, but none approached the naturalness and richness of the new film.

Even the professionals were awe-struck. Dr. Mees, certainly the scientist personified, was moved to say:

There is no need any longer for us to pretend that the world is monochrome and to represent the glorious colored world in which we live by a gray ghost on the screen.[11]

The public reaction to the new film was no less enthusiastic. By 1940, eight of the "Ten Best" amateur films submitted to the Amateur Cinema League's annual contest were filmed in Kodachrome.

At first available only as 16mm movie film, in 1936 Kodachrome became available as still film in 35mm and 828 Bantam sizes. It was an immediate success with photographers of every persuasion. Newspapers and magazines were particularly enthusiastic. Life and National Geographic were soon using Kodachrome for virtually all color photography.[12] It was a film that changed picture taking forever for the amateur and professional photographer alike.

New Hardware for the Amateur

New amateur equipment was often pictured in the company's annual reports, such as the Ciné-Kodak Special (Fig. 137), introduced in 1933. This remarkable camera incorporated many features generally only found on professional machines, such as detachable magazines, variable shutter, and reflex viewing. A two-lens turret accommodated any two of six lenses offered by Eastman Kodak, which included a 15mm f/2.7 wide angle, and a 6" telephoto. Each lens carried its own open frame finder, such as were supplied with the noted Model K Ciné-Kodak in 1930.

In addition, the Special was equipped with a reflex finder and ground glass screen showing the exact field and focus of the lens being used. A mask slot was also provided.[13] Film was carried in an external, removable magazine, available in 100-foot or 200-foot capacity. Each magazine contained film gate, spindles, pull-down mechanism, sprocket, and film meter. Another film meter on the camera registered the number of feet of film run or rewound. The camera could be spring motor driven, at continuously variable speeds from 8 to 64 frames per second, or hand cranked.

As might be expected, such a camera was not produced on an assembly line; it was fabricated in the Eastman Kodak Instrument Shop. If desired, individual specifications could be ordered. The company advertisements suggested that the customer discuss his requirements with the Kodak dealer and obtain a quotation. The camera could be furnished with the owner's name engraved on a special plate affixed to the front of the camera.

Notwithstanding the optimistic view of the potential market envisioned in the camera's advertising, Kodak management did not expect a runaway best seller. The initial production lot was scheduled at 500 units, but the camera was very quickly on back-order. It found precisely the market that Eastman Kodak had hoped for—very serious (and well-to-do) amateurs, and many users in medical, scientific, and industrial fields. The basic model with 100-foot magazine, f/1.9 lens, and a set of six masks was priced at $375, a very substantial sum for 1933, with the country in the grip of a severe depression. Nevertheless, an indication of the camera's basic "rightness" may be seen in the fact that it remained on the market until 1961, with just one modest design change in 1948.[14]

Despite the success of the elaborate "Special," Kodak did not lose sight of its fundamental marketing objective—to keep movie making accessible and affordable for the broadest possible market. Thus a 1937 advertisement headed "Who said 16mm movies are expensive?" announced the Ciné-Kodak Model E at the startlingly low price of $48.50, the least expensive 16mm camera Kodak ever marketed, less than half the cost of the "Magazine 16" camera which preceded it. A companion projector was offered at $59. Both machines were no-frills yet very

Fig. 138. 1937 advertisement for the Ciné-Kodak Model E.

serviceable, and many survive today, still in operating condition. An amusing note in the advertising for the unusually shaped camera was that it was designed to let the owner film even with his fedora firmly on his head (Fig. 138).

Arguably the most impressive looking piece of 16mm equipment ever to come off the Kodak drawing boards was the Sound Kodascope Special. Introduced in 1937, this optical sound projector was housed in a gleaming Art-Deco all-metal case and was avowedly designed to embody the utmost in projector design in every respect. It carried a retail price of approximately $800 and was not a big seller, nor was it expected to be.[15]

Some idea of the importance of the amateur motion picture market to Eastman Kodak's sales may be gathered from the fact that in 1939 more than 2,600 workers were employed in the manufacturing and processing of amateur motion picture products, not including a large number engaged in their distribution and sale. That figure represented approximately 10 percent of Kodak's total employment at the time.[16]

World War II

As noted earlier, the outbreak of World War I in 1914 found Eastman Kodak cut off from its normal sources of many essential supplies—raw photographic paper, glass, gelatin, and many chemicals. The steps taken at that time—finding domestic sources and making some materials in house—resulted in the company being totally independent of foreign sources when the clouds of war gathered again in 1939.

As with other manufacturers of photographic materials and equipment, but to a greater extent than most, Eastman Kodak's production capabilities were quickly adapted to the needs of national defense. The facilities for cameras and optical goods manufacture were readily converted to the manufacturing of military hardware. By 1940 some $35 million worth of contracts had been received for height finders for anti-aircraft guns, aiming circles, telescopes, and time fuses. The company also acted as subcontractor for other prime contractors, particularly in supplying optical components for prime contractors without facilities for such goods.

The company's extensive facilities for producing photo-sensitive materials, while meeting the heavy demand from the military for such material, were able to continue supplying civilian needs such as the motion picture industry, medical, industrial and office photography, and the publishing industry, whose needs might have been classified from "essential" to "important." The materials required for such production—cotton, spruce fiber, and silver—were, in the beginning at least, in good supply.

Amateur camera and projector production was halted almost immediately. Manufacturers such as Eastman Kodak and Bell & Howell urged their customers to take good care of their equipment and guard against its being stolen, since it would be generally impossible to replace. Eastman Kodak even asked the public to consider donating 8mm projectors to the United Service Organization or service camps, as most such locations were only equipped with 16mm projectors.

Curiously, amateur motion picture film continued to be advertised by Eastman Kodak and Agfa well into 1942, but later that year the War Production Board directed Kodak to cut its production of amateur film to 50 percent of 1941 levels and pro-

Fig. 139. Dr. Wesley T. Hanson.

fessional film to 75 percent of 1941 levels. Kodak exhorted its customers to save and return to dealers or Rochester "film reels, spools, film pack cases, retorts with spools, and aluminum canisters for 135 film."[17]

Not revealed until after the war was Eastman Kodak's involvement in the development and production of three weapons that played decisive roles in the Allied victory—the atomic bomb, the radio proximity fuse, and the explosive RDX.[18]

In 1943 General Leslie R. Groves requested that Eastman Kodak lend its expertise to a top-secret project—the development and production of the atomic bomb. General Groves was in command of the "Manhattan District," a military entity formed to carry out the atomic bomb project. The result was the transfer of several hundred chemists, physicists, engineers, and administrators from Rochester to either the E. O. Lawrence Laboratories in Berkeley, California, or to Oak Ridge, Tennessee. The two locations were code-named Shangri-La and Dogpatch.

Assigned to be manager of the analytical, service, and chemical control work of the Oak Ridge operation, where some 5,000 people were employed, was a young Ph. D. from the Kodak Research Laboratories, Wesley T. Hanson, Jr. (Fig. 139). Known affectionately as "Bunny," Dr. Hanson (1913-1987) was a child prodigy who had entered the University of Georgia at age 15 and received his doctorate in chemistry from the University of California at Berkeley at age 21.

Hanson returned to Rochester in 1945 and went back to research on color film. Frank W. Lovejoy had led the company since 1925, first as vice-president, then successively as general manager, president, and finally in 1941 as chairman of the board. Lovejoy died on September 16, 1945. He was eulogized as a quiet, unassuming man who led by encouragement and example.

RECONVERSION, LITIGATION 1946-1958
Back to Consumer Products

The end of the war found the public hungry for photographic products of every description. Since there had been no time devoted to new designs for almost four years, Eastman Kodak took the sensible step of resuming production of pre-war cameras, sometimes with some minor design improvement, or sometimes with merely a name change, such as the 1945 "Ciné-Kodak Magazine 16," which was identical to the 1936 "Magazine Ciné-Kodak."

By 1947, new and/or improved products for amateur photography were appearing in profusion; the 1948 annual report stated that more than 50 new

Fig. 140. Eastman Kodak's Television Recording Camera of 1947.

products and services were announced in the past year. Notable among the new products was what appears to have been Kodak's first interaction with television—the 1947 Television Recording Camera (Fig. 140), developed by Kodak in cooperation with the National Broadcasting Company studios at station WBNT and the Allen B. DuMont studio at station WABD. This 16mm camera, equipped with a 1,200-foot magazine permitting continuous recording of a half-hour program, recorded the TV broadcast by photographing the "monitor tube" in the studio.[19]

The films thus produced, called "kinescopes," could then be used for re-broadcasting by stations in other cities, supplementing the networking system of coaxial cables and radio relays then in use. These kinescopes also proved to be the only record of many of TV's pioneering programs, as tape recording would not be perfected for at least another decade. DuMont, where "The Honeymooners" was produced, had devised a camera, the Electrocam, that simultaneously produced a television signal and a 35mm film record.[20]

The first major post-war amateur motion picture product was the 1948 Ciné-Kodak Special II (Fig. 141), an upgrade of the 1933 Ciné-Kodak Special, with the turret face "angled" to accommodate the new longer Ciné-Kodak lenses without interference in the field of view. This sophisticated camera, with variable shutter, variable speed, hand-cranked or spring-motor drive, and interchangeable film magazines, was probably used by more professionals than amateurs, especially at its price of $893, with a 25mm f/1.9 lens.

Fig. 141. The Ciné-Kodak Special II.

An unusual application of the Ciné-Special II occurred in 1955 when the American Motors Corporation Building opened at Disneyland in Anaheim, California. In a circular theater 40 feet in diameter, without seats, the audience found itself surrounded by eleven 8 ft. by 11 ft. screens, set about eight feet off the floor. Behind the screens was a circular passageway, not open to the public, where eleven slide projectors, and eleven modified Eastman Kodak Model 25 16mm sound projectors were installed, all driven in synchronization by selsyn motors, each aimed at the screen opposite it.

The program begins with a voice explaining the projection system briefly, then launches into a clever "commercial": a series of slides showing various American Motors products, one at a time, until the audience is surrounded by pictures. The screen goes dark, the voice stops, and suddenly one screen comes alight with a title: "A Tour of the West."

All eyes turn to that screen, which perforce becomes the "front" of the theater. The remaining screens fill with images, now all moving. The audience finds itself as if in a moving vehicle with 360° windows. Ahead lies the road, and the viewer is on Wilshire Boulevard with traffic, houses, and palm trees going by on either side at breakneck pace, while to the rear is seen following traffic. Eventually Los Angeles is left behind, and the audience is on its way to Las Vegas. Arriving at a luxury hotel, viewers are taken poolside; the males in the audience risk serious neck injury trying to follow the "scenery" on both sides of the theater at once!

How was it filmed? Eleven Ciné-Specials mounted in a circle on a steel plate, with all drive shafts linked mechanically, tachometer monitored, and speed controlled from 8 to 24 frames per second. Most of the scenes were shot with the assembly mounted on top of a Nash Rambler, one of American Motors' cars of the period. The harrowing ride down Wilshire Boulevard was filmed at eight frames per second, with the Rambler being driven quite decorously. Projection at 24 frames per second gave the desired speeded up effect.[21]

One very significant post-war introduction was that of the 1951 Brownie Movie Camera (Fig. 142). This was a very simple 8mm camera, of stamped metal and molded plastic, designed to "bring snapshot ease and economy to the home movie field."[22]

Fig. 142. Sept. 1951 ad for the Brownie Movie camera.

Priced at $47.50 with a 13mm f/2.7 lens at introduction and soon reduced to $44.50, it was Eastman Kodak's least expensive movie camera since the Ciné-Kodak Model 25 of 1933, at one-half to one-third the price of any other Kodak 8mm camera then on the market. The choice of name is significant—it was expected to attract new customers from the millions of people who had never owned a movie camera, just as the Eastman/Brownell one-dollar Brownie did for the snapshooting public in 1900.[23]

The Ciné-Kodak K-100 (Fig. 143), introduced in 1955, was a professional-grade camera, featuring nylon gears, variable-pressure film gate, a Negator-type spring that gave an exceptionally long film run with constant speed, and provision for synchronous motor drive. This svelte 16mm camera embodied a novel marketing idea. It was designed, to quote Eastman Kodak's own literature: ". . . for those who don't want all of the advanced effects built into the incomparable Cine Special II camera, but who do want the very finest results from big-screen 16mm movies."[24]

The camera was sold with either an f/1.9 or f/1.4 Ektar lens and, in a departure from previous designs, separate "telescope" finders were provided for each

Fig. 143. The Ciné-Kodak K-100T with 3-lens turret.

lens. The price at introduction was $269 with the Ektar 25mm f/1.9 lens. One year later, the K-100T was introduced with a three-lens turret. It was Kodak's last 16mm camera that could be considered "amateur" and again found a market chiefly with professionals. The single-lens model was discontinued in 1964 and the turret model in 1973.

The Kodak Reflex Special 16mm Sound Camera, (Fig. 144) was introduced in October 1961. Designed for studio use for silent or single-system sound, it featured a synchronous motor drive, 400-foot film chambers, variable shutter, footage counter, three-lens turret with bayonet type, quick-release lens mounts. When equipped with a 25mm f1/4 Ciné-Ektar lens, the price was $1,895. Unfortunately, the camera was found to be noisier than its competitors and to have a maintenance problem, so was not widely accepted. It was discontinued in 1968, the last of Eastman Kodak's 16mm cameras.

Litigation

Every large corporation experiences litigation over its lifetime: civil or criminal; brought by government agencies, by competitors, by suppliers, by former employees, by customers. Some suits are trivial, some are serious, and many wind up costing one or both parties large amounts of money and time. Eastman Kodak was no exception and, due to its highly visible and dominant position in the photographic goods industry, may have experienced more than most companies of comparable size.

As described in Chapter 1, the first major action brought against the company was a suit filed by the

Fig. 144. The Kodak Reflex Special 16mm Sound Camera.

Goodwin Film and Camera Company in 1902, charging infringement of the 1898 patent issued to the Reverend Hannibal Goodwin for a flexible transparent film. This resulted in a 1914 verdict in favor of the plaintiff and the ultimate awarding of five million dollars to the Goodwin heirs.

Following an investigation begun by the Justice Department in 1912, a decision was handed down in 1915 charging the company with intent to monopolize the paper, dry plate, and plate camera markets and with violation of anti-trust statutes in its terms of sales to dealers. A negotiated settlement was reached in 1921. Details of this action and its resolution were covered in the previous chapter. Three of the more notorious later suits that seriously engaged Kodak are described below.

The 1954 Consent Decree

Amateur color films manufactured by Eastman Kodak, including 8mm and 16mm movie film, had been marketed since introduction with the processing charge included in the selling price. This practice

Fig. 145. The Pocket Instamatic Camera.

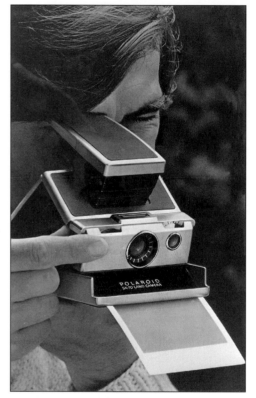

Fig. 146. Polaroid's SX-70 Instant Camera.

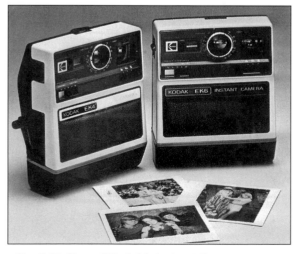

Fig. 147. Two of Kodak's Instant Cameras.

was established at least in part to insure the customer's satisfaction with his photographs, since the processing of color film, especially Kodachrome, was an extremely complex sequence of chemical operations that had to be conducted with the utmost care and precision, a task generally beyond the capability of the average commercial processing laboratory.

The government however saw the policy as a violation of anti-trust statutes and brought suit. After lengthy negotiations, Kodak agreed to a consent decree, issued on December 21, 1954, that required the company to:

Cease selling its amateur color film with the charge for processing included in the price, and to furnish to persons interested in processing in this country, licenses under its color film processing patents and certain other information and assistance relating to such processing.[25]

Kodak quickly converted the decree into a highway to the lucrative business of supplying equipment and chemicals to the processing industry. In the year following the decree, the company introduced a new line of inexpensive and uncomplicated color processing and printing equipment. Within a very few years there were hundreds of firms in the processing business, and Eastman Kodak was never required to divest itself of any processing facilities. The decree was finally lifted in 1995, giving Kodak a more level playing field on which to compete.

The Bell & Howell Suit

In January 1973, Bell & Howell sued Kodak over its 1971 introduction of the XL system of movie cameras and film and its 1972 launching of the Pocket Instamatic cameras for 110 size film. A Bell & Howell spokesperson said:

These films had been under secret development by Kodak, along with the cameras and projectors to use the film, for a number of years. As soon as Kodak introduces and begins promoting a new film and the equipment to go with it, equipment made by other manufacturers, who are not informed about the new film, and whose equipment cannot effectively use the new film, are placed at a substantial disadvantage.[26]

Bell & Howell had good reason to be concerned. Eastman Kodak's 1972 annual report stated that the new Instamatic cameras (Fig.145) were being ordered by dealers at a rate four times that at which the 1963 126 size film Instamatic cameras were ordered when they first came on the market, and over 70 million of those cameras were sold in the 60s.

This suit was settled remarkably quickly, by a court-approved agreement under which Kodak agreed to advance disclosure of any new film and cartridge format in amateur equipment, where such new formats could not be utilized by cameras and projectors already on the market. Such disclosure was not free however; any company that chose to participate in the program, including Bell & Howell, would be required to pay Kodak an initial fee of $10,000 for each disclosure and a royalty of one percent of sales during the 18 months following the introduction of equipment based on such disclosure. The program was to be available to Bell & Howell and other U. S. manufacturers for a period of six years.[27]

Kodak appears to have taken an entirely different stance with regard to the XL system and 110 film than it customarily had done with other innovations. Its plans for 16mm direct reversal film in 1923 were shared with its principal competitors, as were its plans for Super 8 in 1965.

The Polaroid Suit

By far the most costly suit against Kodak was brought by Polaroid Corporation in 1976, charging that Kodak's instant cameras and print film infringed on ten Polaroid patents, and seeking injunction and triple damages. Four of the patents cited related to Polaroid's SX-70 camera (Fig. 146), introduced in 1972, and six pertained to SX-70 film. While the subject of the suit had nothing to do with amateur motion pictures, the amazingly poor judgment on the part of Kodak's management and the staggering cost of the suit to the company makes it worth recording.

Kodak demonstrated its first instant cameras in April 1976 after seven years of effort to produce a system that would not infringe on Polaroid's chemical process patents nor mimic Polaroid's design features. Two cameras were introduced—the EK4 and the EK6 (Fig.147), which certainly did not look like the competitor's cameras and employed a processing system that one reviewer described as "founded on many ingenious variations of the Polaroid system" and "in many ways a technological mirror image of Polaroid's SX-70 system."[28]

At first, Polaroid appeared to take Kodak's challenge rather lightly, assuring its stockholders at the annual meeting that Polaroid executives were "in a considerable state of euphoria " after the Kodak products appeared, because they had feared that Kodak might have come up with a really brilliant design, but the reality was quite different. As might have been expected, Kodak introduced instant cameras that were sturdy, easy to hold and to use, with no non-essential niceties of design. And also as might have been expected they sold extremely well.

As sales of Kodak's instant cameras soared, Polaroid lost some of its insouciance. In an October 1976 interview Dr. Land was moved to say:

It seems to me that with an uncharacteristic lack of grace, they (Eastman Kodak) have combined some good but not quite finished chemical ideas with a number of techniques and devices that derive quite directly from our activities. [29]

Land also alluded to the fact that Kodak had been Polaroid's supplier of the negative component of their film for over a decade, and for other materials for a much longer period, which relationships might presumably be in jeopardy as a result of the lawsuit.

The trial that began in 1976 dragged on until 1982, and another three years elapsed before the court handed down a judgment. On October 11, 1985, it found that Kodak's PR-10 film and EK4 and EK6 instant cameras infringed on seven of Polaroid's patents. The court issued an injunction, effective January 9, 1986, prohibiting Kodak from further manufacture of such products. Kodak appealed the decision and moved for a stay of the injunction. This motion was denied, and the company immediately began the process of withdrawing from the instant photography business.

This included an act which Kodak termed "unique in industrial history," that of offering its customers the opportunity to exchange any Kodak instant camera for one share of Kodak stock, or one Kodak disc camera, or coupons good for $50 worth of Kodak products. Kodak had sold an estimated 16.5 million instant cameras by this time.[30]

Almost inevitably, one owner sought a lawyer[31] and a class-action suit was filed protesting Kodak's terms. The judge in the case then directed Kodak to withdraw its offer and enjoined the company from making any public statement about the matter until a court-approved settlement was formulated. This state of affairs understandably infuriated thousands of Kodak camera owners, who could neither get a rebate nor an explanation, despite Kodak having installed a special toll-free telephone number for just such calls.

In May 1988, a Cook County Circuit judge gave his blessing to a settlement, under which camera owners would receive between $50 and $70 in cash and coupons, depending on which models they had purchased of the 39 models Kodak had marketed. The original stock offer had been deemed too complicated, and the disc camera had been discontinued. The rebate program was not simple; owners had to call or write for a certificate, or clip one from advertisements that were placed in 100 major newspapers, then mail in the certificate with the camera nameplate.

Kodak had established a reserve of $193 million to pay for costs associated with its withdrawal from the instant camera business and, at the close of 1988, expected that the entire reserve fund would be consumed.[32]

Following the verdict in the trial to determining liability, which Kodak appealed unsuccessfully, the trial on the issue of damages was set for January 1989 in Boston. Polaroid submitted a calculation estimating its lost profits at somewhere between $4.2 billion and $5.7 billion and asked that that amount be trebled. Kodak labeled these claims "ludicrous" and "pure fantasy," citing Polaroid's internal documents to support its position and stated, "The analysis made by Polaroid would allow it to reap a windfall based on products it could not have built, sales it could not have made, prices it could not have received, and profit margins it could not have attained."[33]

Trial of the damage issues began on May 1, 1989, and concluded on November 20, 1989, with Polaroid asserting claims for damages of almost $14 billion, while Kodak countered that the figure should have been approximately $187 million. After various appeals by both sides, the court reduced the award to $873 million. Kodak's 1992 annual report stated that $888 million had been charged against 1990 earnings (which were $2.844 billion before taxes). Add to this the costs of the rebate program, and Kodak's costs for its venture into instant photography amounted to well over one billion dollars.

Divergent Trends - 1958 to 1981

In a special August 1958 issue devoted to photography, *Life* magazine noted that in the years 1948 to 1958 the United States photographic industry had grown by ten percent each year. Not surprisingly, Eastman Kodak's sales had followed the same curve, rising from $435 million in 1948 to just over one billion dollars in 1958. This remarkable trend would continue for Kodak, with sales reaching $10 billion in 1980. The spectacular growth of the photographic industry had two principal causes—the rise in disposable income and leisure time available to the general public in the years following World War II and the ever-widening applications of photographic processes into every area of human activity.

Amateur photography was the most visible of these expanding markets. The *Life* editors reported that there were more than 19,000 camera clubs, five national magazines devoted to photography, and countless newspaper columns offering advice and criticism, and that 2.2 billion amateur photographs would be taken in 1958.

In sharp contrast, the amateur motion picture market had reached a watershed in 1958, a level of unit sales that, except for an occasional brief rise, would never again be reached, and would fall to near extinction in 1981.[34] (See Fig.148.)

Why the Decline of Amateur Movie Making?

The conventional wisdom on the decline of home movies has it that the video camera ultimately knocked the film camera out of the market. However this does not explain the sharp drop from 1958 to 1964, since a popularly priced video camera did not arrive until the late 1970s.

Two studies undertaken by Bell & Howell in the early sixties offer some insights on the 1958-1964 decline. Those studies determined that approximately 20 percent of all U.S. households owned movie cameras and that this figure was unlikely to be improved. Among the reasons most frequently sited as deterrents to using a movie camera were the annoyance of the "double 8mm" spool that had to be removed and re-threaded after filming 25 feet, the need for those hot and glaring movie lights for indoor or night filming, and the difficulty of achieving good synchronized sound.

Despite the downward trend in sales of home movie equipment, Eastman Kodak continued to advance the technology of 8mm cameras. Automatic exposure control arrived in 1959, zoom lenses in 1960, reflex viewing in 1961, battery drive in 1962, and cassette loading in the same year.

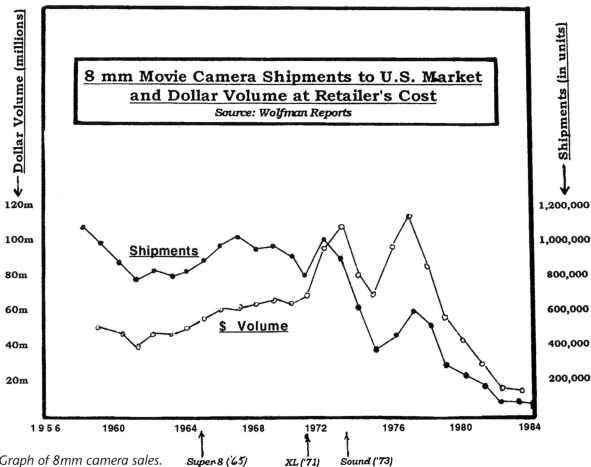

Fig. 148. Graph of 8mm camera sales.

1965 brought the announcement of the most significant advance in technology for the amateur since the introduction of Kodachrome film—Super 8, a new system consisting of a new film gauge, new cameras, and new projectors. The new system offered the user 50 percent more image area, larger and brighter projection, and drop-in cartridge loading that eliminated tedious threading and the possibility of double exposure.

The system was launched with a massive publicity campaign in all media, and the 1965 annual report stated that the sales of the new Instamatic movie cameras and projectors and the new film were exceeding the company's own estimates. Total industry 8mm and Super 8 camera shipments rose and remained at an elevated level for several years before starting a downward slide again.[35]

Regular 8mm was soon dropped by most other manufacturers. The 1969 Popular Photography Directory, published in 1968, listed one single-8 camera—the Bolsey, and one Japanese regular 8—the Jelco. By 1971 there were none.

1971 saw another brilliant Kodak development—XL, or existing light photography. With a combination of a faster film, rated at ASA 160 (Kodachrome II was ASA 25), plus a faster optical system in the camera, the user could get satisfactory exposure filming indoors in a room lit by a single 25-watt bulb. This eliminated the need for light bars, which were blinding and dangerous.

The XL system was well received by the public and the Wolfman Reports again showed a sharp upturn in sales of 8mm cameras. Again the upturn was brief. By 1973 shipments resumed their downward slide. Not even Kodak's introduction of Ektasound, a workable sound-on-film system for the amateur, could reverse the trend to lower unit sales. Dollar volume fell less severely due to the higher unit costs of the more sophisticated cameras.[36]

The Growth of Foreign Competition

The 1940 *Popular Photography* Directory Issue listed ten U.S. manufacturers offering 36 models of 8mm and 16mm cameras, and just three European manufacturers offering four models. By 1964 there were still just ten U. S. manufacturers, now offering 54 models, while the foreign contingent had grown to 28, offering 82 models of 8mm cameras alone. The biggest surge of foreign competitors had come in just two years, between 1959 and 1961, when the number of foreign suppliers had doubled from 13 to 26.

In 1964, the average domestic 8mm camera price stood at $152, while the foreign cameras averaged out at $200. This statistic taken alone is somewhat misleading, since the foreign models included nearly 30 models priced at $100 or under, while the U. S. manufacturers had only 12 in that range, eight of which were Eastman Kodak products. So Kodak, which did not particularly try to compete with such as Beaulieu, Bolex, Leica, and Pathé at the high end of the market, was even getting hammered at its traditional area, the mass market.

Eastman Kodak's Last Super 8 Product

A most interesting machine forming a bridge between film and video was announced in 1972 but did not appear on the market until 1975. Called the Supermatic VP-1 (Fig. 149), it was a player for showing Super 8 film through a standard TV set. The player, about the size of today's VCR, accepted Super 8 film on either standard reels or in the special Supermatic cassettes. An automatic threading system drew the film through the player continuously, without intermittent movement, past a "flying spot" scanning beam. The scanner converted the physical image to a radio frequency signal, which was fed to the UHF antenna terminal of the TV set where the image was displayed on the screen. Magnetic track sound film could also be played.

The machine had been originally planned for Eastman Kodak's Consumer Markets Division and was to have sold for about $500, but when it finally emerged from manufacturing, the price had escalated to three times that figure. The machine was then given to the Motion Picture and Audio Visual Division, to "fight the war against video in the newsroom." [37]

It was expected that it would permit small TV stations to use Super 8 film for newsreels, avoiding the higher cost of 16mm and video cameras that were then still heavy and quite expensive. Contemporary reviewers gave the machine generally favorable notices, although the $1,350 price tag put it out of reach of most amateurs. [38] When TV stations

complained that the VP-1 could not be synchronized with their systems and did not conform to Federal Communications Commission broadcast standards, Kodak developed the VP-X. This greatly improved model permitted direct broadcast or transmission over cable from Super 8 film. [39] While it was used briefly at a few small stations, improving video technology soon doomed both of these interesting machines.

A Dream Machine?

The VP-1 was the last Super 8 product to be marketed by Kodak. An even more unusual machine was conceived in the last days of that Super 8, but never reached the market. As we have seen, the early 1970s was a period of considerable turmoil in the amateur motion picture equipment field. Between 1968 and 1976, the average manufacturer's price to retailers for Super 8 cameras more than tripled, while the average retail price doubled, from $160 to $355. [40]

The consumer was confronted with a bewildering array of choices in price and complexity of equipment as one technological innovation after another appeared. Faced with such choices, many potential customers simply put off buying any camera for fear of finding their choice had become obsolete before they got it home.

The dismal state of Super 8 equipment sales in the late '70s prompted one Kodak product design engineer to begin a search for a movie system that would reverse the trend of the last 20 years, going back to the "Brownie principle," a simple, low-cost camera, and a projector or viewer. Donald O. Easterly was a young honors graduate of the Rochester Institute of Technology who began his career with Eastman Kodak as a co-operative student draftsman in 1955 and retired in 1986 as Manager of Consumer Products Design. Along the way he developed Super 8 movie systems, auto-focus Instamatic cameras and disc cameras, and collected 19 patents on photographic apparatus, as well as serving as a member of the Adjunct Faculty at Rochester Institute of Technology.

Using the 1974 Eastman Kodak Moviedeck Super 8 projector as a starting point, some models of which came equipped with a small fold-away rear projection screen, ample for viewing by two or three people, Easterly designed a projector/viewer not much larger than a paperback book. The small screen obviated the need to set up a conventional screen and darken the room and also meant a smaller projection lamp would be required, which would not need cooling, so space for the inevitably noisy fan would be saved. To further reduce its bulk, the viewer was designed just for the 50-foot spools on which the film was returned by the processor, studies having shown that most 8mm camera users seldom bothered to splice those 50-foot spools into longer lengths.

The heart of the viewer was a film transport mechanism for which Easterly received U. S. Patent No. 4,281,807 (Fig.150). Easterly's invention permitted a uni-directional motor to impart forward, reverse, or no motion to a film with a simple three-position slide control, with no gearing required.

The end result was a "personal viewer" which could be passed around the room, for viewing in broad daylight, just as with regular snapshots. The Industrial Design department came up with a lightweight camera, also of low cost, so that the entire camera/viewer package could be marketed at less than $100.

The system was so attractive it inspired the then manager of Consumer Products Engineering to describe it as "a real world-beater, an answer to all of the problems that our customers experienced." [41]

Kodak marketing executives were not impressed; they were possibly too concerned with other programs which were in the pipeline at the time and which were consuming large amounts of engineering time, such as Kodak's entry into the instant photography business, announced in 1976, and the disc system, announced in 1982. In the opinion of more than one Kodak engineer, a promising product that might have sustained Super 8 for a few more years was never given a chance to prove itself.

The Answer?

From all of the foregoing, it becomes clear that there is no single answer to the question of what caused the decline in home movies even before the home video camera became a practical alternative. Television programs pre-empted family viewing time; cost and complexity of equipment discouraged the new purchaser.

As the great majority of amateur filmers used the movie camera to record family history, the growing popularity of Kodachrome transparencies provided an alternate method that was easier to use, less costly,

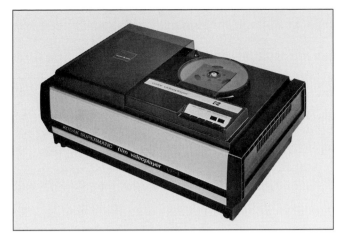

Fig. 149. The Kodak Supermatic VP-1.

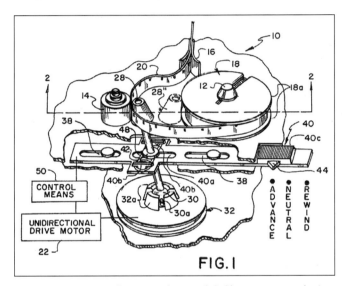

Fig. 150. Patent drawing of Easterly's film transport device.

and produced brilliant images which were easier to show and capable of "random access," a not insignificant advantage to a collection of slides versus a collection of reels of film.

The above factors depressed the entire industry, both foreign and domestic, while U.S. manufacturers suffered the added burden of foreign competition that, by 1968, accounted for approximately 17 percent of total United States sales dollars.

The Significance of Amateur Motion Pictures to Eastman Kodak Company

As specific market share figures were seldom published by any of the major manufacturers, the following analysis requires a number of assumptions, based on various scraps of information, as well as general statements made by one or more of these companies.

In 1968, the dollar volume of 8mm and Super 8

camera and projector sales to the U. S. market had reached $118.3 millions, made up of $54.6 million projector shipments and $63.7 million camera shipments. A 1968 study had shown that seven percent of all projector shipments to this market were imports. The percentage of imported cameras may be assumed to have been at least three times that figure. Thus:

Projectors: 7% of $54.6 million = $ 3.82 million
Cameras: 25% of $63.7 million = $15.93 million
Total Imports = $19.75 million

This leaves $98.6 million for the domestic producers. If we assume that the "big 3" accounted for 90% of that market, or $88.7 million, and further assume that their respective market shares were as follows: Bell & Howell—40%, Eastman Kodak—40%, and Keystone—20%; then Eastman Kodak's share of the market amounted to 40% of $88.7 million, or $35 million. As Kodak reported that in 1968 its total U. S. and Canadian Photographic Division sales were approximately $2.2 billion, the amateur motion picture business represented considerably less than two percent of the Division's sales.

Eastman Kodak's annual reports from 1965 on reflected the rollercoaster course of 8mm camera and projector sales from the advent of Super 8 until the curtain came down in 1981. As 1965 began, about 6.5 million 8mm cameras were in U. S. households. Over the next two years some two million Super 8 cameras were shipped to the U. S. market, almost half of them in 1967 alone.[42] This pulled the sales curve up to its highest point in seven years, and Eastman Kodak's amateur motion picture business entered a seven-year period of growth. The end of this period came at a surprising juncture.

1973 saw the introduction of the Ektasound system to general approval that however was quickly dampened by disastrously poor performance of the original Ektasound projectors. They were replaced the following year, and five new silent cameras, the XL300 series, were introduced, which sold very well.

This was the last cheerful note in what was to be the swan song for Kodak's amateur motion picture equipment business. Every report for the next four years noted "lower levels for amateur movie equipment," and even these remarks ceased in 1981. All Ektasound cameras were discontinued in January 1979; the XL line was stopped in 1981. The cameras which came off the last assembly line to operate were "Our Gang" XL 320s (Fig. 151). Unfortunately no one thought to save one for the Patent Department Museum.[43]

After Home Movies

For almost one hundred years Eastman Kodak pursued a remarkably constant course: the production of photographic products and the chemicals related thereto. At the same time, it relentlessly spent billions on research, resulting in a constant flow of new products to the market: new films, new chemicals, new applications for photography. At one time new products were rolling out the door at the rate of three or four per week. In 1978 the company reported that more than 30,000 products bearing the Eastman Kodak name were made and sold throughout the world.

Despite this plethora of goods, for many years Eastman Kodak's revenues came chiefly from three well-defined markets, in these approximate proportions: 30% consumer photographic products, 40% applied photography, including professional movie film, 20% chemicals and cellulose products, and 10% miscellaneous.

In 1988 the company made the largest acquisition in its history, its first in a field somewhat removed from its core businesses—the $5.1 billion purchase of Sterling Drug Incorporated. Sterling was a manufacturer of pharmaceuticals with a strong over-the-counter drug business. This acquisition was made during the tenure of Colby Chandler as chairman and CEO, but was reported to have been promoted by Kay R. Whitmore, then president (Fig. 152).

The rationale was that Eastman Kodak would provide Sterling with "an experienced, disciplined research capability and strong chemical background," while Sterling would provide Kodak with a ready-made international marketing and distribution network. Kodak had at this time a number of relatively minor products such as food colorings, medical diagnostic chemicals, agricultural and research chemicals, which with Sterling's product line would form a new entity called the Health group.

What was less apparent to the casual observer of this acquisition, but not to Wall Street analysts, was that coming after some large capital expenditures for Tennessee Eastman and Eastman Chemicals, the company's long-term debt had ballooned

Fig. 151. Eastman Kodak's last amateur camera—
the "Our Gang" XL-320.

Fig. 152. Colby H. Chandler (left) and Kay R.
Whitmore (right).

to over seven billion dollars, 100 times what it was in 1980.

Eastman Kodak's domination of the photographic film and paper business for so many years, with its dependable cash flow, had engendered a certain complacency in the entire organization. "It was a wonderful place to work," one long-time employee reported, "the pay was good, and you just figured you'd be there until you retired!"

But retirement came earlier than expected for some 12,000 employees, salaried and hourly, clerks and middle managers, secretaries and scientists, as management woke up in 1986 to the fact that the organization had grown fat. Net earnings had slipped severely for several years, despite a work force reduction in 1982. This time Whitmore struck firmly and a number of restructuring and cost reduction programs were put in place.

While Whitmore noted that 70 percent of the separated employees left voluntarily, as a family man with six children who was noted for his support of Rochester community affairs, these could not have been easy decisions to make. However, when Whitmore was advanced to CEO on the retirement of Colby Chandler in mid-1990, analysts expected him to be tougher in cost reduction efforts than Chandler had been, who was regarded as too paternalistic.[44]

Among the problems facing the new CEO were a depressed national economy, slowing sales of film

and paper as rival Fuji Film Co. lured customers with heavy promotions, aggressive pricing and a generally conceded quality product, plus an Information division, maker of copiers and printers, that was losing money. Again the medicine was to downsize the work force and to restructure, this time merging the Information systems groups into the Photographic groups for a newly created Imaging Group.

These measures bore fruit; 1992 net earnings surged to over three dollars per share against the dismal five cents of 1991. A number of peripheral businesses were sold off, with the proceeds applied to reducing the company's long-term debt. Whitmore remained bullish on the prospects for the Healthcare group, although the performance of Sterling Drug had been lackluster in the four years of Kodak ownership.

Wall Street was not satisfied, nor were some members of the board, although the latter was not apparent at the time. A severe critique of the company did appear in the financial press in the spring of 1992, in which several analysts were quoted as feeling that Kodak's restructuring and cost cutting had still not put the company back on the growth track; they called for still more severe measures.[45]

Another early retirement program was announced in mid-summer, with very generous benefits, and the response surprised even Kodak, particularly when a number of high-level people opted for early retirement. The package cost Kodak an average of $120,000 per retiree.[46]

In January 1993, Whitmore sent a three-page letter to all shareholders, in which he reiterated his confidence in the future of the Health Group, outlined a seven-point plan to improve the performance of the Imaging Group, stressing increased focus on a business strategy that "marries the best attributes of silver halide and electronic imaging technology." He also outlined a plan to have senior management work more closely with the board of directors.

Whitmore's program apparently did not impress the Kodak board, which at that time numbered 13, nine of whom were "outside directors," not Kodak employees. A special board meeting was called for July 23, 1993, at which the Committee on Directors asked Whitmore and the three other inside directors to leave the room, whereupon the remaining directors voted unanimously to replace Whitmore. Several directors subsequently spoke for publication, revealing that this action had been under consideration for several years.

Among others considered to replace Whitmore was John Sculley, chairman of Apple Computer, Inc., but the man ultimately chosen was another high profile executive, George M. C. Fisher (Fig. 153). Fisher had lately been responsible for pushing Motorola Inc. to the forefront of wireless electronic technology, thereby doubling that company's sales from $8 billion to $16 billion in his five years there as CEO.

Fisher arrived at Kodak in December 1993 and spent much of the ensuing year visiting Kodak installations around the globe, and meeting with major customers. With the insight thus gained, Fisher concluded that the company's future lay in imaging, and imaging only, but adapted for the information age. A banner printed in the 1994 annual report expressed his mindset most succinctly: "Our corporate vision is clear—our heritage has been and our future is to be the World Leader in Imaging."

At the same time, Fisher emphasized that the company could not prosper if film, its core business, did not prosper also. Imaging, by this time, was no longer accomplished solely with silver halides, and another statement of Fisher's was:

Photography is probably one of the most effective ways of capturing and distributing information. The key is to be able to use that information in digital form, as is

Fig. 153. George M.C. Fisher.

done with the Photo CD, then the world has no limits. I see Kodak sitting on this enormous capability for capturing and producing data that can go out over the communications networks.[47]

The Photo CD, announced by Kodak in September 1990, but not commercially available until 1992, was an offspring of the Digital Audio Disc music system introduced by Philips and Sony in the early 1980s, commonly known as the compact disc, or CD. The Photo CD formed a bridge between the traditional silver halide image and the electronic or digital technology, with the photographic image being transferred to the disc (Figs. 154, 155).

At first the system was designed to be simply for storing filmed images on a disc from which they could be played back through the user's TV set, but the technology soon advanced to making the CD a mechanism for storing 35mm negatives, when the film was brought in for development.

The transfer was to be accomplished by the photofinisher, who would require about $100,000 worth of equipment, including a Kodak film scanner that converted each picture into digital information, a Sun Microsytems computer workstation which could correct the image for color and density, and a disc writer with which to record the information on the compact disc. To provide some insight into the brilliance of this technology, ponder the fact that the pitch of the spiral track in which the information is stored is 1.6µm (1.6 millionths of a meter) and the length of the photographic information portion of the spiral track on a standard 12cm disc is about 5,378 meters, or 3.3 miles.[48]

Digital imaging soon took other forms notably as in the digital camera. As the name implies, the digital camera receives and stores the image electronically rather than chemically. The stored image can be viewed in the camera's viewing screen, copied to a disc, or fed directly to a computer and thence sent to any destination in the world via the Internet, for example. Digital print systems allow the customer to have a precious slide or photograph digitized and then have reprints or enlargements made. Digital imaging can be applied to moving images also, as the present spate of digitally animated films testifies.

And lastly there appeared in 1996 the Advanced Photo System, that Fisher characterized as "the most impressive, far-reaching achievement since the advent of color film."[49] The new system evolved from an idea born in the late 1980s whose greatest champion, insiders say, was Peter M. Palermo, then general manager of Kodak's Consumer Imaging group. Unhappy at the slumping sales in consumer photography, Palermo organized a study to determine what the public did and did not like about taking pictures.

The results of the study convinced Palermo's group that no mere refurbishing of existing products would work, but rather a whole new system of camera and film was needed. From here on, Kodak departed from a time-honored approach to such a project, namely, going it alone. Unlike its procedure with other technical innovations such as XL, Ektasound, and more recently, the ill-fated Disc camera, where Kodak worked in great secrecy and didn't disclose the new product until it was launched, this time Kodak actively sought partners.

Palermo visited a number of camera manufacturers and signed up Canon, Minolta, Nikon, and unbelievably, its erstwhile arch-enemy, Fuji! The joint development was announced in March 1992. Each company pledged millions of dollars to the project and, remarkably, Kodak's participation survived the wrenching problems that were facing top management at the time. Palermo elected to retire at the end of 1993, but before he left, managed to convince Fisher that the project should continue. All the venture partners agreed to share technological developments up to the point of individual

Fig. 154. Kodak Photo CD.

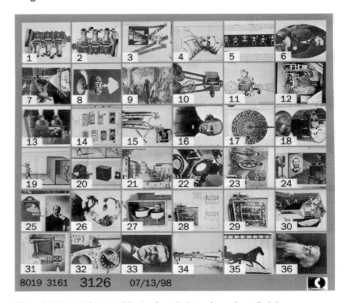

Fig. 155. A Photo CD Index Print showing 36 images stored on a Photo CD. Almost all the illustrations in this book were produced from photographic images transferred to Photo CDs and thence to Adobe Photoshop.

camera designs, but all agreed that the new film would be usable in all cameras manufactured by the consortium. Kodak would market its line under the name Advantix (Fig. 156).

The heart of the new system is a revolutionary film cassette from which no leader ever appears and which tells at a glance the state of the film--unexposed, partially exposed, fully exposed, or processed. The film itself carries a magnetic component on which the camera (some models) records information about the exposure of each frame. Among the many other features: three print sizes are available at any point in the roll and negatives are returned for storage in the cassette with an index print so a specific picture can be easily identified and reprinted.

With all these new weapons at his hand to do battle with the competition, Fisher, as he had promised to do, reorganized the company's operating divisions into eight business units, seven of which had "Imaging" in their title, serving seven different niches, Consumer Imaging, Health Imaging, etc. The eighth unit was charged with Customer Service.

As the new century arrived Kodak's image brightened somewhat. The Photo CD was succeeded by three products of greater sophistication. Kodak Picture CD, a CD ROM developed jointly by the chip manufacturer Intel, Inc. with software by Adobe Systems, Inc. carried its own software, permitting the user with a computer to perform basic manipulation of the images, stored at 1024 x 1536 pixels.[50] Kodak PhotoNet, developed in partnership with America Online, Inc., gave customers who were America Online subscribers the ability to send their pictures via email and the convenience of ordering reprints and other photo merchandise online. Kodak Picture Disk was an economy option with images stored at 400 x 600 pixels with viewing and emailing capability but without editing software.[51]

The Advanced Photo System finally gained acceptance, as evidenced by the giant retailer Wal-Mart adding APS developing to nearly one thousand of its one-hour photo labs.[52]

George Fisher stepped down as chief executive officer at the end of 1999 but agreed to remain as chairman until January 2001. Daniel A. Carp, a 29-year veteran, then president and chief operating officer, succeeded Fisher as chief executive officer.[53]

One rather ominous cloud had appeared on Kodak's horizon—electronic cinema (digital movies). Worldwide, 90 percent of all movies were using Kodak film, both as the initial imaging medium in studio cameras and in the thousands of release prints shipped to theatres all over the country.

The February 22, 1999 issue of the *New York Times* carried a story with this headline: "Coming Attractions—Digital Projectors Could Change Film Industry." The story pointed out how despite the impact of modern technology on many aspects of the motion picture industry, the role of film in making and

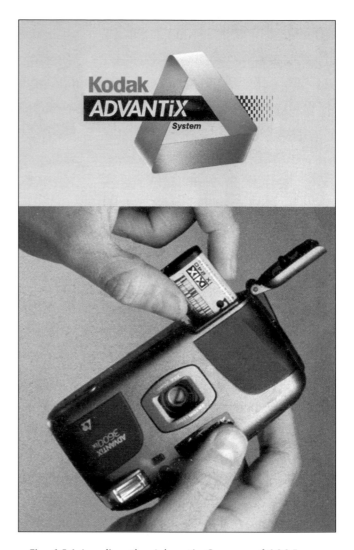

Fig. 156. Loading the Advantix Camera of 1995.

showing a movie had hardly changed from the earliest days. As the headline suggested, a new method, not only of projection, but also of distribution of films to theatres was at hand.

At present, film *cameras* still rule; no technology has appeared thus far that can surpass film in its ability to capture the nuances of tone, color, and contrast.[54] But once filming and editing are completed, instead of production of release prints, the images on the camera original will be converted to digital information, to be stored on discs or broadcast via satellite to the selected distributors. Within two years, it was predicted, movie theatres would begin installing the first generation of digital projectors.

Some questions remain unresolved. The new projectors were expected to cost up to $100,000 for each theatre. The studios on the other hand will have tremendous savings. How these costs and savings are to be equitably apportioned is not yet determined. Secondly, while digital transmission of data can be "enciphered," whether it can be made absolutely theft-proof is still under study.

Eastman Kodak stands to lose about one billion dollars worth of film sales per year should digital imaging totally supplant film, but Kodak does not see that as ending its association with the motion picture industry. In an address to the Society of Motion Picture and Television Engineers, Joerg Agin, president of Kodak's Entertainment Division, asserted that Kodak would survive and thrive by focusing on products and services that produce the best pictures, regardless of technology. He went on to say: "Digital and photochemical imaging will chase each other, challenge each other's superiority, and complement each other's capability." [55]

Digital imaging also struck at Kodak's core business: the still photographer using conventional Kodak film, processed to Kodak paper. A May 8, 2000 headline read: "Shutterbugs Ditch 35mm Gear for Digital Cameras, Computer Printers." The article pointed out that Kodak had launched its own line of digital cameras and despite having teamed up with Lexmark International to market a photo-quality ink-jet printer, many analysts felt that Kodak was lagging the competition in the printer race.[56]

The future was not always bright for George Eastman, so the Eastman Kodak Company may well prosper for another century, perhaps with products undreamed of today.

CODA

When I set out to write the conclusion to this chapter on the second part of Eastman Kodak's history, I began by looking for attributes of the company that would distinguish it from its 499 neighbors on industry's "social register"—but to my surprise, I had great difficulty in finding what I was looking for.

In the matter of longevity, while Kodak has paid cash dividends continuously since 1902, many companies can point to such a record going back to the nineteenth century. Its "total return" to stockholders (price appreciation of the stock with cash dividends reinvested) over the past five years is 11 percent, respectable but meager when compared with companies in biotechnology, computer services, or health care, to name a few. Its sales growth over the last 40 years really looks remarkable until plotted against the Consumer Price Index, whereupon it is seen that the two curves are practically collinear.

Then it came to me that I had been looking in the wrong books, that Eastman Kodak's greatest achievements are not to be measured solely in dollars, but also in the effect that the company's existence has had on the way America looks at itself, from the introduction of The Kodak Camera in 1888, through 16mm film in 1923, Kodachrome in 1935, down to the Oscar-winning film stocks it has supplied to Hollywood over many years.

Were all these gifts to be suddenly withdrawn, America would hardly recognize its world. Much as when it was briefly proposed, on Thomas Edison's death in 1932, that all electricity be turned off for one minute, we cannot imagine what our life would be like without the photographic industry which George Eastman and his company did so much to found and nurture for the last 116 years. Considered in this light, the company and its founder stand in a special pantheon of American heroes, alongside Thomas Edison, the Wright brothers, Henry Ford, Harvey Firestone, David Sarnoff, to name but a few.

The Bell and Howell Company

Early Bell & Howell 16mm projector.

Formidable Competitor

When Eastman Kodak introduced 16mm film in 1923, there were a few small companies manufacturing various kinds of amateur motion picture equipment, in a variety of designs and film gauges. Once the 16mm direct reversal system proved successful, a number of companies entered the market—some newcomers to the field, others well established concerns. Foremost among the latter group was Bell & Howell, whose story follows. Chapter 7 covers the second tier of competitors.

Beginnings of the Bell & Howell Company

The roots of the Bell & Howell Company are entwined with those of two other pioneering film industry figures in the Chicago area: Edward Hill Amet (1860-1948) (Fig. 157) and George K. Spoor (1871-1953) (Fig. 158). Amet was a bright young self-taught electrical engineer/consulting inventor, born in Philadelphia, raised in Chicago and practicing in Waukegan, Illinois. He received his first patent at the age of 17 for an improved telephone design. He is understood to have been an early customer at one of the several Kinetoscope parlors which opened in Chicago in 1894 who came away from the peepshow with the idea that the entertainment could be greatly improved if the pictures were projected on a screen.

Amet set to work on his idea in the machine shop of the Chicago Recording Scale Company in Waukegan, where his patented automatic railroad freight car weighing and recording scale was being manufactured. Apparently running low on funds, he approached George Spoor, a young train caller and part time theatrical impresario with operations in Chicago and Waukegan. Spoor saw the possibilities in Amet's ideas, and advanced a very modest sum which Amet said he needed to finish his projector. The completed machine, christened "The Amet Magniscope," made its first commercial appearance in 1895 using two discarded Edison Kinetoscope 35mm format films.[1] The Magniscope

Fig. 157. Edward H. Amet by his back yard "ocean set." Courtesy of Lake County (IL) Museum/Regional Historical Archives.

Fig. 158. George K. Spoor.

soon caught the attention of traveling exhibitors as it was hand-cranked and was not restricted to electricity for a light source. Over the next four or five years about 200 machines were sold through George Kleine in Chicago and John McAllister in New York.[2] (See Fig. 159.)

The Amet/Spoor partnership recognized the limitations of the projector business; their customer, the exhibitor, needed only one or perhaps a half-dozen projectors, but new films were needed every week.

Film production was the business to be in, and Amet set about obtaining the necessary equipment to become a movie producer. Unfortunately, very little is known about his equipment except that he constructed a camera he called the "Magnigraph" and that he also made perforating and printing machines. One of his mechanics at the Chicago Recording Scale Company, Nicolay Nelson, devised and patented a "Kinetographic Camera," but it would not have served Amet's purposes.[3]

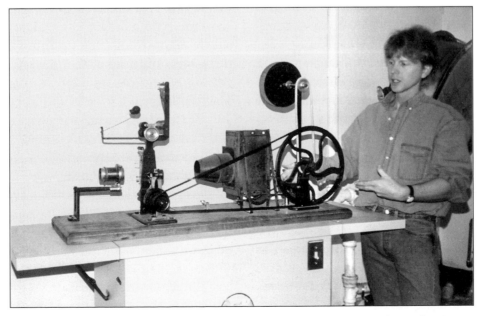

Fig. 159. Carey Williams, noted collector, with a Magniscope in his collection.

Amet was inventive and resourceful. Denied permission to go to Cuba to film the Spanish-American War, which had broken out with the sinking of the American battleship "Maine" in Havana Harbor on February 15, 1898, Amet proceeded to make war films based on newspaper accounts, by staging land battles in the Waukegan countryside using local "players." He built a "set" in his back yard to film *The Sinking of Cervera's Fleet* and several other naval battles. The set consisted of a 20-foot square pool, upon which were maneuvered 1/70th scale-model sheet metal ships, complete with firing guns, smoking funnels, and rippling flags. The ships rode waves generated by a wind machine; all of the apparatus was being driven electrically and controlled by an assistant while Amet worked the camera. The film went out to exhibitors, advertised as having been filmed from a dispatch boat six miles from the battle, using a telescopic lens. The deception was so good that the Spanish Government was reported to have bought a print for their naval archives at the time of Admiral Pascual Cervera's court martial.[4]

Despite the success of their joint venture, Amet lost interest in the motion picture business and sold almost all his equipment and films to a Philadelphia firm sometime after 1899. George Spoor kept one of the Magniscopes and soon, with an improved machine, the Kindrome invented by Donald Bell, he established a motion picture service extending from Syracuse, New York, to the West Coast. Spoor would go on to found the Essanay Film Manufacturing Company in Chicago (1907-1918) in partnership with G. M. "Broncho Billy" Anderson.

About 1896, Spoor began managing the famed Schiller Theater on Randolph Street, where he hired a young man named Bell as an usher.[5] Donald J. Bell (Fig. 160) was born in Jamestown, Ohio, in 1869, and came to Chicago in 1896. Nothing is known of his family, education, or previous employment, but he evidently had ambitions and talent beyond ushering. When Spoor replaced the Lumière Cinematographe in the Schiller projection booth with an Amet Magniscope, Bell talked his way into being promoted to assistant projectionist. Before long, he was also doing repair work on Spoor's projectors and filling in as projectionist at out-of-town theaters such as Waukegan and Syracuse, New York. At the latter location he operated a Kinodrome projector in the winter of 1899-1900.

Fig. 160. Donald J. Bell (left).

Bell had repair parts for Spoor's projectors made at the Crary Machine Works in Chicago. Here, in 1906, Bell met a young man named Bert Howell. Albert Summers Howell (Fig. 161) was born on a farm in Michigan in 1879 and moved with his family to Chicago in 1895.[6] Howell was bright, quiet and industrious. He put himself through high school at night while working as an apprentice mechanic at the Miehle Printing Press Co. After high school, he went on to get a degree in mechanical engineering, also at night, from the then Armour Institute, now the Illinois Institute of Technology. Sometime after getting his degree he went to work at the Crary Machine Works.

Mr. Crary, who described "Bert" Howell as a competent draftsman and skilled mechanic called Bell's attention to the young engineer. Bell's own words on their meeting are significant:

Bert's experience in my work set his ingenious and prolific mind to work and one day he referred a drawing to me which showed he was deeply interested in my line of work . . . a structure for which he had applied for a patent . . .[7]

The application Bell refers to presumably was one that Howell filed for on September 14, 1906, described as for "certain new and useful Improvements

Fig. 161. Albert S. Howell.

in Picture Exhibiting Machines . . ." and for which Patent No. 862,559 (Fig. 162) was granted on August 6, 1907. The patent makes five claims, all relating to means of adjusting the frame registration with the projector aperture. Films of that period were prone to uneven shrinkage or stretching, and if the film transport mechanism was not adjustable, very unsatisfactory projection would result. Significantly, the patent was assigned to Donald J. Bell.

Four months before Howell's patent application, on April 23, 1906, Bell filed an application for a patent, also for "certain new and useful Improvements in Moving-Picture Machines . . ." Bell's patent had just three claims, all describing two or more counter-rotating shutters of various openings. Bell's patent, No. 879,355 (Fig. 163), was issued on February 18, 1908.

The five drawing sheets accompanying the patent show a machine which bears very close resemblance to the "Kinodrome" (Fig. 164) now in

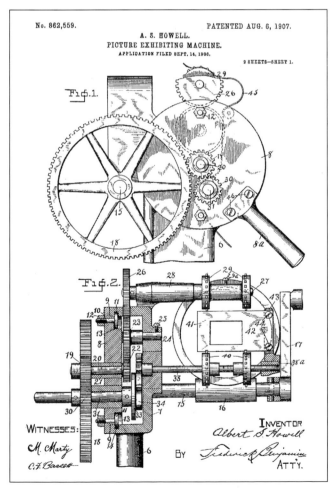

Fig. 162. Howell's patent for means of adjusting projector framing.

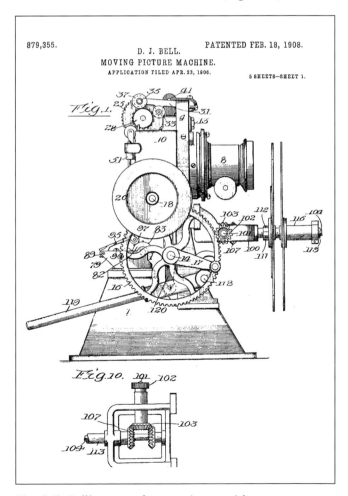

Fig. 163. Bell's patent for a projector with two counter-rotating shutters.

Fig. 164. Bell & Howell Kinodrome Projector.

Fig. 165. "Broncho Billy" Anderson.

the Bell & Howell Co. archives, also shown in Don Malkames' *S.M.P.T.E. Journal* article.[8]

The foregoing gives some insight as to how "Bell & Howell" came to be formed: both men were working independently at first, on improvements to the Kinodrome projector which George Spoor was marketing. Bell said later: "This display of talent by Mr. Howell convinced me that in order to avoid competition from his efforts it would be wise to establish a company wherein Mr. Howell would have a substantial interest."[9]

On February 17, 1907, the Bell and Howell Company was incorporated. The officers were: Donald J. Bell, chairman; A. S. Howell, secretary; and Marguerite V. Bell, vice-chairman. The incorporation papers listed the purposes of the company as follows: "To do general machine manufacturing, jobbing, leasing and repairing business."[10]

Interestingly enough, February 1907 is also the date that George Spoor and "Bronco Billy" Anderson (Fig. 165) formed their corporation—The Essanay Film Manufacturing Co. One may conclude that this was no mere coincidence, but a logical outcome of the respective interests of the men involved. George Spoor, entrepreneur and showman, saw the future in film production and distribution; Bell, entrepreneur and mechanically minded, saw the future in supplying the machinery. The result was the formation of two separate corporations.

For the first two years of its existence, the new Bell & Howell company did only jobbing and repairs. Its first actual product was a wooden-body, hand-cranked, 35mm camera, introduced in 1909 (Fig. 166). The camera featured internal wooden magazines, a fixed-pin shuttle movement covered by Patent No. 1,038,586 dated September 17, 1912. A distinctive feature of the camera was the metal lens board for interchangeablity of lenses, which also carried a viewfinder lens above the taking lens. Only eight of these cameras were produced, one of which was purchased by "Bronco Billy" Anderson of

Fig. 166 Bell & Howell's first camera, wood body, ca. 1909.

Essanay, believed to be the one now in the George Eastman House Museum.[11]

Albert Howell was probably the first cinemachinery builder to realize the importance of two precepts of technically successful motion pictures. First was the need for industry-wide dimensional standards. In the early days, each inventor was quite apt to design or utilize a film to suit his own convenience, so film width, image size and shape, and sprocket hole shape and spacing could and did vary widely. The second precept followed naturally from the first: utmost accuracy and "repeatability" of every operation that touched the film, from the raw stock in the camera, to the finished print in the theater projector. The camera must advance the film to the aperture in precise lengths and hold it there for a precise interval of time. Then the processed negative must pass through the printer with the same accuracy, with the positive raw stock in precise and continuous register with the negative. And lastly, the positive print must move through the projector with the same precision with which the negative moved through the camera.

Since all film movement in modern projectors is accomplished by means of sprocket holes in the film, it follows that the accuracy and uniformity of the perforating operation is the foundation for the success of the entire system. Bell & Howell's first perforator, designed by Albert Howell and introduced in 1910, surpassed all others on the market for accuracy and reliability. A measure of its success may be seen in a survey taken in 1942, which showed that 32 years after introduction of the first machine, over 90 percent of all professional film was being perforated on Bell & Howell perforators.[12]

The company's next product was a continuous contact printer, introduced in 1911. As in making a print of a still picture, the printer must bring the processed negative in contact with the unexposed print film, expose the two to light, then go on to the next picture, or frame. The continuous printer accomplishes this without stopping the film for each exposure. This requires that there be no slipping between the two films at any time. However, while both the negative and positive films start out with the same perforation pitch (.1870 inch is standard), the negative film undergoes a slight shrinking in processing, bringing its pitch to .1866 inch. To

accommodate this difference in length, Albert Howell designed his printer with a brilliant yet simple solution. Both films were carried past a curved exposure gate on a single sprocket, the negative on the inside, the positive on the outside. The diameter of the sprocket was nicely calculated so that the shorter negative took the inside, shorter path, while the longer positive traveled on the outside.

Howell's continuous printer replaced what were called "step printers" in which the films were stopped momentarily for the exposure cycle. These printers commonly operated at about 20 ft/min, while the Bell & Howell printer could run at 60 ft/min.[13]

With the four principal components of a 35mm system designed—perforator, camera, printer, and projector—Bell & Howell took the bold step of announcing to the trade that as a matter of company policy it would no longer sell or service any equipment that did not conform to the 35mm standard to which their printers and perforators were built. Coming from a company that had a virtual monopoly on the market for these machines and whose products were of unassailable quality, this policy played a major role in bringing the industry to the 35mm standard.

The year 1911 saw the introduction of one of the best-known products in Bell & Howell's history—the fabled Model 2709 camera (Fig. 167). Just two years had elapsed since the introduction of the short-

Fig. 167. The Model 2709 Bell & Howell Camera.

lived wood body camera, but the new camera was of totally different construction from its predecessor. The 2709 was of all-metal construction, with external top-mounted magazines which gave it its unique "Mickey Mouse ears" silhouette. Film transport was by a pilot-pin and shuttle mechanism, similar to that of the earlier camera but much improved. A single 32-tooth constant speed sprocket served for feed and take-up. Loading and threading was done through a left-hand door.

The camera was the first U.S.-made high-precision production camera and quickly became the camera of choice of professional cameramen and studios. Jesse Lasky, Charlie Chaplin, and Thomas Ince are among the famous names in the customer lists in the Bell & Howell archives. Martin and Osa Johnson, the explorers, carried two all over Africa in the twenties,[14] and Walt Disney used Camera Serial Number 50 to film Snow White and the Seven Dwarfs. Although the 2709 was in more or less regular production until 1958, the advent of sound in the mid-20s caused it to lose ground to the Mitchell and a few other cameras which could be more effectively silenced. Despite its long production life, a relatively small number of cameras was produced. The total is believed to be less than 1,500.[15] Due to its superb accuracy of registration, the camera is still in demand for animation and title work.

As movie production gradually shifted west to California, Bell was required to make frequent sales trips to the Coast, and his efforts were reflected in the company's books. By 1916, sales had grown to nearly $175,000, up from $60,000 in 1911. Possibly to relieve Howell of non-engineering tasks, Bell hired a bookkeeper named Joseph H. McNabb, who also functioned as general manager in Bell's absence (Fig. 168).

Returning from one trip in late 1917, Bell discovered that his acting general manager and his chief engineer had made some substantial changes in the company's operations. Perhaps goaded by some previous incident of perceived misbehavior, Bell summarily fired both McNabb and Howell. The firing did not take, however. The two men returned to Bell's office the next day with an ultimatum, "Sell us your share in the company, or we'll set up a competing one." After some negotiation, Bell agreed to sell his interest for $159,450 and left for New York, telling

Fig. 168. Joseph H. McNabb.

McNabb that he had bought "a milked cow."[16, 17]

The "milked cow" needed an infusion of "green," which came in the person of McNabb's father-in-law, Rufus J. Kittredge. Kittredge was the head of a well-known Chicago printing concern and brought to Bell & Howell a solid background in business management, as well as a substantial investment in cash. With Bell's departure, the company was re-organized, with Kittredge named president, Albert S. Howell, vice-president, and Joseph H. McNabb, treasurer. McNabb was elected president in 1923.[18]

Joseph Hector McNabb (1887-1949) was born in Canada. His working career began as a telegraph operator, after which he managed a small railroad in Nevada. He was auditor and chief statistician of the Chicago, Milwaukee, St. Paul & Pacific Railroad when Bell hired him. McNabb has been variously described as a man devoted to detail, a benevolent despot, and a little Napoleon. One former executive said of the McNabb tenure: "The Company was a dictatorship under the command of Joseph H. McNabb."[19]

Howell, by contrast, was quiet and unassuming. He managed by "walking around" and was seldom heard to issue a direct order. The man who succeeded him as chief engineer, Bruno Stechbart, said of him: "Where an ordinary engineer might think of five ways to do a job, Howell could think of ten, and four of them would be better than anyone else could come up with." Malcolm G. Townsley, who was vice president of Engineering from 1948 to 1962, said: "I consider him one of three or four geniuses that I have met in my career." [20] Howell was issued almost 150 patents and was one of three men to receive honorary life membership in the American Cinematographers Society, along with Thomas Edison and George Eastman. In 1949, he was elected Chairman of the Board of Bell & Howell, which was largely honorary, as he had little interest in management. He died on January 3, 1951, at the age of 72.

If, as someone once said, a great institution is but the lengthened shadow of one man, then Bell & Howell for a long time was largely the shadow of two men—McNabb and Howell. For over 40 years, the Company's growth and direction were shaped almost entirely by the personalities and intellects of these two men. Bell & Howell could not have come into being, nor produced the brilliant technical innovations it did, without Howell's mechanical genius; nor could it have survived and grown as it did without McNabb's managerial skill and force of personality. While markedly different in temperament, they worked together without strife. If there were disagreements, word of them never got beyond their respective office doors.

Such tight control by just two individuals did not always work to the Company's advantage; a new idea, if it did not originate with either Howell or McNabb was not apt to get a good reception. Malcolm Townsley described their management style as follows:

Engineering was secluded in a separate building, and contact from the Sales or Manufacturing group was prohibited. New products were worked out between McNabb and Howell. Tooling was designed and made by Engineering, and prototypes, drawings, tools, pricing decisions, and sales projections were delivered to Manufacturing and Sales in a meeting in McNabb's office.[21]

One new idea from "outside" which did get their attention was Eastman Kodak's plan for the 16mm direct reversal system. As related in Chapter 4, when McNabb and Howell visited Rochester in 1921 at Eastman's invitation for inspection of the new film, both men immediately recognized the technical and commercial superiority of the 16mm system over the 17.5 mm system they were working on. On their return to Chicago, they scrapped the 17.5mm program, which was almost ready for market.[22] (Fig. 169.)

Fig. 169. Bell & Howell's prototype 17.5mm camera and projector, ca. 1921.

McNabb not only recognized the potential of the amateur market, for which the 16mm system was designed, but he stood up to his father-in-law, Kittredge, who had urged Howell to devote his time to products for the professionals and expressed his preference to "stick to the line in which our name and reputation have been established."[23] Bert Howell's response to Eastman Kodak's new product was characteristically brilliant. Bell & Howell's 16mm camera, the "Filmo 70," leap-frogged the Rochester product. Howell's camera was lighter (4 lbs.-12 oz. vs. 7 lbs.-9 oz.), smaller, and spring-motor driven, meaning it could be hand-held, without the need of a tripod (Fig.170).

The Model 70 design was so successful that the basic mechanism and camera configuration was carried down through dozens of modifications and improvements over a period of 56 years. The movement of the Model 70, while not as mechanically sophisticated as the 2709, was manufactured to equally stringent tolerances. Intermittent motion (film advance) was provided by a cam-operated shuttle, working two pull-down fingers, and spring-loaded side guides. The camera head casting, which carries the lens seat, had a manufacturing tolerance of plus

*Fig. 170. Albert "Bert" Howell with his "Design 70,"
Bell & Howell's first 16mm camera*

*Fig. 171. Lt. George W. Goddard (later Brig. General
Goddard) famed champion of aerial
photography in World War II, shown here
using a 35mm Eyemo movie camera.*

or minus one-half-thousandth of an inch. This was to guarantee location of the lens with respect to the film plane. Such tolerances were achieved at a cost: high labor cost and low productivity. Bell & Howell boasted "World's Highest Quality . . . All the adaptability of Bell & Howell professional cameras costing up to $5,000."

In 1925, Bell & Howell brought out a 35mm version of the Model 70, called the Model 71, or Eyemo (Fig. 171). This camera was simply an enlarged version of the 70, with the body deepened and the film transport altered to accommodate the wider film. The silhouettes of the two cameras were identical and, in fact, several parts, including the door, were interchangeable.

The Eyemo quickly became the professional standard when a small, light weight, hand-held camera was needed. Every studio had at least one Eyemo in their camera department, and in one film, William Wellman's 1927 epic Wings, no less than 28 Eyemos were spotted around for one scene.[24] Despite its popularity, only about 12,000 cameras were produced.[25, 26]

The Filmosound Projector

The Filmosound was undoubtedly the most important single product made and sold by Bell & Howell over a forty-year period. It was certainly also the product that did the most to build world-wide

name recognition for Bell & Howell. (Everett F. Wagner, Vice-Chairman, Bell & Howell Co.)[27]

The next major product introduction after the Filmo in 1923 and the Eyemo in 1925 was Bell & Howell's first 16mm sound projector: the Filmosound, for optical sound-on-film, introduced in 1933. As a practical amateur sound-on-film camera did not exist at that time, the projector was designed for use with sound films that were reduction prints of commercial films. The projector, with its speaker in a separate case, was heavy, bulky and expensive; it was intended for the industrial and educational markets (Fig. 172).

And penetrate these markets it did, with

Fig. 172. Bell & Howell Filmosound Projector.

remarkable success. For several years after the projector's introduction, Bell & Howell's consumer magazine Filmo Topics featured regular sections headed "Motion Pictures in Industry," "Motion Pictures in Education," "Motion Pictures in Medicine" (with specific companies listed), and stories of repeat orders from organizations as diverse as The Union Carbide Corporation, Household Finance Corporation, the U.S. Navy, United Air Lines, Minneapolis Board of Education, etc.

With Christmas 1939 came an interesting change . . . the company announced a new Filmosound, "Styled for Talking Pictures in Your Home." The black leather-covered cases were replaced with handsome walnut "to be in harmony with the finest home furnishings." At a list price of $343, it would indeed have gone into none but the finest homes. For $57 more, the purchaser could rent any 12 sound film "programs," each for one-day rental within one year. The Filmosound Library catalog offered more than 1,700 titles, including Hollywood feature films, comedies and cartoons, newsreels, travel-adventure, sport and athletic films. For the children, there were "instructional" films.[28]

Bell & Howell dominated the market for many years, although Victor, Ampro, DeVry and others offered 16mm sound projectors. Eastman Kodak's Sound Kodascope Special, introduced in 1937, was priced at $800, which would not have placed it in many schools or churches. An article in the July 1948 issue of Fortune put Filmosound sales at 105,000 units to that date, more than the rest of the industry put together.

Arrival of 8mm Film and Cameras

1932 was a watershed year for the amateur motion picture industry with Eastman Kodak's introduction of 8mm film. As noted in Chapter 5, this was entirely an Eastman Kodak development, which Bell & Howell did not immediately follow. Instead, its Engineering Department made considerable effort to develop an alternate system using pre-split 8mm film, before conceding and bringing out a matching line of double 8mm equipment in 1935.

The new product was intended to open up an entirely new market for amateur motion picture equipment. Eastman Kodak ads featured their new camera at less than $30 and promised the customer: "Make movies for 10 cents a shot!" Home movies

would now be within the reach of thousands of moderate income families, and the "family record" was stressed as a principal venue for the new technology.

To compete successfully in this kind of market against Eastman Kodak, Bell & Howell needed to make radical organizational changes. Engineering had to design a low-cost, attractive product, still with quality and precision. Manufacturing had to abandon the old ways of individual craftsmanship, and gear up for high-volume production. And lastly, Marketing had to devise strategies for selling in a mass-market, in contrast to the elitist aura that had surrounded its 16mm business, with the camera usually shown in the hands of royalty, Hollywood or other.

It could not have been easy for management, i.e., McNabb, to commit the company resources to such sweeping changes for an unknown product, especially at the time of the great depression then gripping the country. But McNabb was equal to the task and, beyond turning the company in a new direction, instituted two far-sighted personnel policies. First, he arranged schedules so as to distribute the scarce workload among the employees, thus avoiding layoffs and keeping the work force intact. Secondly, of far greater long-range benefit, he instituted the sponsorship of promising college students in co-operative work/study programs.[29] Among those who began their careers with Bell & Howell under this program were: Malcolm W. Townsley in 1931, future vice-president of engineering, Carl Schreyer in 1935, future vice-president of marketing, and Charles H. Percy, future president and chairman.

War Time - A New Direction

As World War II worsened in Europe and America geared up for the inevitable, Bell & Howell found itself well positioned for production of military goods. Some years earlier, McNabb had purchased a large tract of land northwest of Chicago, in an area known as Lincolnwood. He had also foreseen the need to free the company from dependence on imported lenses and brought over from England the chief optical designer of Taylor, Taylor & Hobson, Ltd., to train Bell & Howell personnel in lens design and production. This was the London firm in which Bell & Howell had purchased a 51 percent interest in 1929 and which had been a major supplier of lenses.[30]

Contracts for military goods began to arrive in

1940, one of the first being for the familiar "GSAP," or gun sight aiming point camera. The Eyemo was drafted, and thousands were made for use by combat cameramen. By 1941, the company's facilities were inadequate for the demand. In April 1942, a contract was signed with the Defense Plants Corporation, whereby the company turned over the Lincolnwood plot to the DPC, who would build the plant, which Bell & Howell would operate, for the manufacture of military optical goods. Products included: gun sights, gun cameras, militarized civilian cameras, and 16mm sound projectors for training and entertaining troops. In a major break from its normal area of expertise, Bell & Howell won a "develop and build" contract for a "flight simulator." This complex of optics, mechanics, radio and ultrasonic technologies had a far-reaching effect on Bell & Howell, as it forced the company to hire engineers in the field of electronics, thus positioning the company to enter this burgeoning technology after the War.

Bell & Howell ranked itself as having "the largest engineering and research laboratory in the world, devoted exclusively to the development of motion picture and allied apparatus . . . and equipped with the machine tools and trained personnel necessary for such precision manufacturing."[31]

The man placed in charge of the Company's defense programs was Charles Harting Percy, who had joined the company as a management trainee in 1938. He was just 22 when he was given this major defense responsibility (Fig. 173).

The services desperately needed optical instruments of every description, and the contracts poured in. Bell & Howell sales doubled every year from 1941 to 1944. And on a sunny mild October afternoon of 1942, several thousand employees, subcontractors, and friends gathered in the parking lot of the Lincolnwood plant to watch President McNabb officially receive the Army-Navy "E" for "high achievement in the production of war equipment."[32]

The end of the war meant a sharp drop in sales for every defense contractor, and Bell & Howell was no exception. Nine million dollars in military contracts were canceled in 1945 alone. Nevertheless, the Company had grown by five-fold in sales since 1939, and if it was to continue to grow, more capital would be needed. Going public was the only answer. In the spring of 1945, Bell & Howell was chartered as a

Fig. 173. Charles H. Percy.

public corporation, with capitalization of $5,000,000 (up from $500,000) and the name officially changed from "Bell and Howell" to "Bell & Howell."

To say that Charles H. Percy's career with Bell & Howell was meteoric would for once not be hyperbole. Within five years of his graduation from the University of Chicago, he rose from management trainee to secretary of the Corporation, all the while serving three years as an officer in the Navy. When Joseph McNabb died on January 5, 1949, a letter McNabb had written in 1947 was opened and read to the board. In it, McNabb recommended Percy as his successor; needless to say, the board followed the recommendation.[33]

McNabb and Percy had some things in common; both men were highly organized, moralistic, and held similar religious convictions. Aside from those similarities; however, their personalities were decidedly different, and the organization would soon alter in consequence. Five days after McNabb's death, on January 5, 1949, a special meeting of the Board of Directors established an Executive Committee, charged with making recommendations on officers, salaries, borrowing, dividends, and general policy; all matters which had previously been handled by McNabb.[34] McNabb was a product of his times, as far as hiring practices. One former employee put it this way:

The policy for new hires in the Sales Department was: WASPS, middle class Protestants, (preferably Christian Scientists). The small foyer of the Larchmont Ave.

building had a "Science" literature rack. . . . No Jews were hired, but that was not exceptional in those years.[35]

When Percy became chief executive officer, there was not one black employee and very few women or other minorities in management positions. Shortly, Percy announced an "affirmative action" policy, long before any state or federal laws were on the books, and immediately implemented it by hiring an optical engineer who was black, and then actively recruiting for factory jobs from the black population of Chicago.[36]

Percy seems to have been consciously or unconsciously heading for his later public life almost as soon as he reached the top at Bell & Howell. At the end of his first year as CEO, he began a ceremony which was to become a tradition: a walking tour of the Chicago plant a few days before Christmas, later extended to other locations, during which Percy greeted each employee with a handshake and thanks for their loyalty and fine support. The tour was to take as long as four weeks some 12 years later.

Percy extended his visibility far beyond the factory walls, in contrast to McNabb, who after thirty-odd years as chief executive was hardly known outside the industry. One year after Percy's election to president, he was named by the United States Junior Chamber of Commerce as one of "Ten Outstanding Young Men of the Year," along with a young congressman named Gerald R. Ford.[37]

Despite McNabb's efforts at re-organizing the company when it embarked on the mass-market 8mm product, Percy felt the need for further strengthening, particularly in the area of dealer relations. Over a two-year period, he and top sales and marketing executives crisscrossed the country in a series of dealer meetings. Nearly 5,000 dealers were met personally at dinner meetings, where the company's merchandising plans for the future were shown.[38]

Bell & Howell's coverage of the 8mm market was extended to the low end of that market with the introduction in 1952 of the Wilshire and Monterey cameras, which were priced nearly 40 percent below the company's previously least expensive 8mm cameras. This ploy was clearly aimed at capturing some of this market from Eastman Kodak, Revere, and Keystone, all of whom had cameras in this price range or lower.

The 1950s were years of phenomenal growth in

Fig. 174. Assembling the Model 220.

the amateur motion picture industry, and Bell & Howell was the unquestioned leader in market share. Industry-wide shipments of 8mm cameras grew at the rate of 10 percent per year, and Bell & Howell made substantial additions to the Lincolnwood plant to accommodate this and expected future growth. Every annual report from 1952 on announced new products: the 1952 report was dominated by the Model 220 (Fig. 174), a simple camera with an exposure guide coupled to the lens aperture control, selling at $49.95, "the lowest prices in our Company history."

Other new products appeared, all making the amateur camera and projector easier to use, more versatile, more satisfactory. 1956 was a banner year; 12 new products reached the market, including the revolutionary 200EE, the world's first 16mm camera with automatic exposure control.[39] The following year this same automatic feature was applied to two 8mm cameras, again a first, and again prominently displayed throughout the annual report. How Bell & Howell went about the creation of its 8mm electric eye cameras provides an interesting example of Charles Percy's management style.

In the fall of 1956, as manufacturers of motion picture equipment were urging their dealers to stock up for the usual Christmas buying surge, Sam Briskin, president of the Revere Camera Company, sent a telegram to all dealers suggesting that they would be well advised not to lay in too many Bell & Howell 8mm cameras, because Revere was going to have an "electric eye" 8mm camera to introduce at the spring meeting of the Manufacturing Photographic Dealers and Finishers Association.

When Percy learned of Briskin's telegram, fearing a devastating effect on the sales of Bell & Howell's 8mm cameras if Briskin made good on his boast, he and Carl Schreyer quickly organized three separate teams of engineers and designers, each with the assignment to proceed at full speed to design an 8mm electric eye camera. The first team was drawn from the senior engineering staff, the second from men of intermediate experience, while the third was made up of brilliant but relatively inexperienced engineers and designers.

The senior group came up with a workable design, but one that would have taken a year and a half to bring to production and have been costly to manufacture. The intermediate group had not completed their design when the junior group presented a revolutionary design that nonetheless could be applied to an existing camera and thus put in production in a matter of months.[40]

The result was the Model 252EE,[41] later designated the Model 290, introduced at the Spring 1957 meeting of the MPFDA, and shipped to dealers later that year. The Model 290 was a great success, and it graced the cover of Bell & Howell's 1957 annual report. Sam Briskin did not have his camera ready for the MPFDA meeting, and in the opinion of some, Revere never recovered from this marketing defeat.[42, 43]

By 1958, the company reported that 82 percent of that year's sales were from products introduced since January 1, 1954. This dizzying growth phenomenon was recognized by the publishers of *Popular Photography* with the launching of a new publication in 1959: *Home Movie Making*, for which Bruce Downes, editor of *Popular Photography*, wrote an introduction which began as follows:

There never has been a phenomenon in the whole history of photography quite like the boom now boiling in home movies. Sales of 8mm cameras and projectors have been sensational. Each year sees new models, both domestic and foreign, entering a market that appears to have no saturation point.[44]

What was not immediately recognized amidst this euphoria was that the bull market for amateur motion picture cameras had reached its peak in 1958. That year, according to statistics gathered by Gus Wolfman of *Photo Dealer*, the total number of 8mm cameras shipped to the U. S. market reached 1,108,000 units. Shipments then began a slow decline of about six percent per year, for five years. The advent of Super 8 in 1965 reversed the trend temporarily, but the 1958 figure for U.S. shipments would never again be reached.[45]

Bell & Howell did not publicly acknowledge this situation until 1960, but even then, shareholders were reassured that despite a decline in total industry sales of all brands of 8mm movie equipment, the Photo Products Division had substantially increased its market share and ended the year in number one position in terms of consumer dollars spent for movie equipment.

Management's reaction to the 1958 leveling off was to initiate a market study to determine, if possible, why the market had peaked. The study concluded that between 15 to 17 percent of all U.S. households owned movie cameras or projectors, and that this appeared to be the "saturation point." The study also revealed that there were a number of factors which inhibited people from buying movie equipment.

Most frequently cited among those factors were: difficulty in determining correct exposure; need for lenses of different focal lengths; inconvenience of double 8 film; lack of sound recording capability; the need for harsh movie lights for indoor and night scenes; and lastly, cost. Most of these obstacles were eventually overcome by advancing technology, however by that time most of the market had been lost to the video camera.

A second study was undertaken in the mid-60s which concluded that the market for amateur motion picture equipment would never surpass 20 percent because of the inherent difficulty in making and showing movies, compared to taking snapshots. By this time, Bell & Howell had turned its attention to the European and Japanese markets which were growing and did eventually get close to the theoretical saturation point of 20 percent. The world market for 8mm, including Super 8, peaked at around 2.5 million units in the mid-1970s.[46]

Just as the market for 8mm cameras began its

decline, news came from NBC and CBS: both networks announced plans to build video-tape operations which would completely replace film for recording of television programs. The photographic press featured articles speculating on how soon a "video-tape camera" would be available for amateur use, with some pundits predicting that one could arrive within a decade. The message was not lost on Bell & Howell management; diversification away from consumer photo products, actually begun some years before, was to be aggressively pursued.

In the meantime, however, a pressing problem had to be addressed quickly; the Company's bottom line was bleeding from the badly under-utilized Lincolnwood plant. Built by the Defense Plants Corporation in 1943, turned back to Bell & Howell in 1946, it had been enlarged substantially since then in anticipation of continued growth in the amateur market. The decline of that market left large areas of the 730,000 square foot facility vacant.

One obvious way to increase Lincolnwood's work load was to sell more of its existing product. In the spring of 1959, the Company embarked on a revolutionary marketing adventure, through the hottest medium of the day—television. As might have been expected, a vehicle befitting the corporate image was chosen: sponsorship of public documentaries, a first for any photographic products manufacturer.

Bell & Howell called its new venture a civic duty, stating that a corporation bore a responsibility for public service. But to reassure the stock-holders that the expense was justified, it added:

The programs have been successful in demonstrating Bell & Howell products in action to an audience in higher-than-average education and income brackets, the best potential customers for our products.[47]

Not all of the programs were greeted with approbation; complaints were received from both ends of the political spectrum. As a result of one early program which told the story of a black man coping with discrimination, entitled "Walk in my Shoes," Bell & Howell's audio-visual dealer in Louisiana lost all his state-sponsored school business for 16mm projectors, overhead projectors, etc. For several years, Bell & Howell made up to the dealer his loss in gross margin, amounting to $50,000 or more per year.[48] In reference to another program which

Fig. 175. Peter G. Peterson.

dealt with a day at the Kennedy White House, one critic complained that the Presidency and the Administration had been "put up for auction, and sold to a Republican-dominated corporation." [49]

While this television venture bore the stamp of Percy's public vision, and while he inevitably took the heat of the accusations of sponsor interference with programming which followed, the company gave full credit for the conception and direction of the venture to the then Executive Vice President, Peter G. Peterson (Fig. 175).

Peter G. Peterson came to Bell & Howell from McCann-Erikson, Bell & Howell's advertising agency for many years. After graduating with honors from Northwestern University and post-graduate work at the University of Chicago, Peterson joined McCann-Erikson in 1953. He became general manager of their Chicago office in 1956. When it became evident that Chuck Percy had a political career in mind, the board began looking for his successor, and Peterson's work at McCann-Erikson on Bell & Howell's account made him a leading candidate. He joined Bell & Howell in 1958 as Executive Vice President and, three years later, not yet 40, was named President, as Percy moved up to Chairman and Chief Executive Officer.

Despite, or perhaps even because of, the television controversy, Bell & Howell increased its market share of the amateur movie equipment market, in the face of declining total industry sales. By the end of 1963, however, the company felt it necessary to warn stockholders that management saw no indication of any significant change in the downward trend in amateur motion picture equipment sales.[50]

Diversification

Between 1946 and 1960, Bell & Howell completed a number of acquisitions which in most cases were in totally new fields, giving the company a substantial presence in microfilming and office machinery. The first of these transactions came in 1946 with the purchase of the microfilm division of Pathé Manufacturing Company, which was particularly successful. In 1953, the company entered the rapidly growing tape recorder field with the purchase of the Three Dimension Company, a leading producer of slide projectors, stereo cameras, and tape recorders.

The following year, negotiations for the purchase of the DeVry Corporation were completed. DeVry was a major producer of JAN (Joint Army-Navy) 16mm sound motion picture projectors, with a number of contracts for supplying same to the United States Government. This would appear to have been the principal motivation behind this purchase; however, DeVry had one or more educational divisions, which were melded into Bell & Howell's diversification efforts.[51] The 1967 annual report listed the DeVry Institute of Technology as a division of Bell & Howell Schools.

In 1957, the Inserting and Mailing Machine Company was acquired, and in 1960 the largest acquisition was consummated with the merger of Bell & Howell and Consolidated Electrodynamics Corporation, a manufacturer of aviation and missile test equipment, electronic instrumentation and control systems. The 1960 annual report declared that the company could no longer be categorized as solely a photographic equipment maker, and the non-photographic elements of its business accounted for approximately one half of total sales, which stood at $114 million, nearly double the 1958 figure of $60 million.

Peterson became chief executive officer in 1963, and Percy resigned from the company in 1966 to devote full time to politics. He was elected to the United States Senate in 1967 and remained active in Republican politics and public service for many years.

In 1960, Bell & Howell entered into a joint venture with a major Japanese camera manufacturer, J. Osawa & Co., and established a factory in Japan. The first products were 16mm projectors formerly made by J. Arthur Rank in England, also 8mm cameras for markets other than North America. The 1945 contract with Rank was terminated in 1963, and most of Rank's production was transferred to Japan. All 8mm production of Lincolnwood was moved to Japan in 1969 and 1970.

The Japanese government at first limited Bell & Howell's ownership to 49 percent, but this was gradually permitted to increase to 90 percent as the Japanese became assured that Bell & Howell was not going to take over their domestic market. The name was eventually changed from Japan Ciné Equipment Manufacturing Co. to Bell & Howell Japan.

In 1963 Bell & Howell began negotiations with Polaroid Corporation for the manufacture of the Polaroid "Swinger," a very simple instant camera which was extremely popular for a few years, selling almost a million units in 1965 and three million the following year. The contract was profitable for Bell & Howell and absorbed large amounts of Lincolnwood overhead. Another product which helped keep Lincolnwood busy was an in-flight movie system which the Consolidated Electrodynamics division had developed for American Airlines' 707 Astrojets.

Bell & Howell's romance with Polaroid ran smoothly for several years, as production of the Swinger was succeeded by manufacture of the Colorpack II in 1969. In 1968 the two companies signed a contract under which Bell & Howell would design and build machinery for an instant movie system which Polaroid had invented the ill-fated Polavision system. Before any product came off the line however, one or both parties became very dissatisfied with the affair, with the result that in 1975 Bell & Howell sued Polaroid for breach of contract, asked for $15 million in damages, charging that Polaroid had refused to reimburse it for costs of $8.7 million.[52, 53] The suit was settled within a few months, with Polaroid purchasing inventories, tooling and other materials related to the Polavision system. Considering the market failure of Polavision, Polaroid may well have come to wish it had dropped the whole idea at that point.

The Arrival of Super 8

Along with the rest of the industry, Bell & Howell received notice sometime in 1963 of Eastman Kodak's intent to market a new 8mm format, Super 8: a film, camera, and projector system which promised the consumer greater image area, cartridge loading, and other benefits. Tooling up and preparing far the marketing of its own line of Super 8 cameras and projectors resulted in the largest development costs in the Company's history.[54]

Despite the introduction of Super 8, sales of 8mm products continued relatively flat until 1971, when Eastman Kodak introduced the revolutionary "XL" (for "existing light"), system of cameras and film, which greatly extended the range of lighting conditions under which filming could be done. The new system was enthusiastically received by the general public and resulted in a sharp upturn in the unit and dollar volume sales curves. Bell & Howell was not happy, however, as this time, in contrast to its development of Super 8, Eastman Kodak had not shared its plans with the industry. So the introduction of the new film and cameras caught the other manufacturers facing a highly popular product and having no product with which to compete. To make matters worse, less than a year later Eastman Kodak introduced a new still-photography camera and film, the fabulously successful 110-size film and "Pocket Instamatic" cameras, again without prior notice to the rest of the industry.

This was a circumstance to test the mettle of Bell & Howell's new leader, Donald N. Frey, (Fig. 176) who had arrived as a member of the board in late 1970 and, upon Peterson's departure to join President Nixon's cabinet, was elected Chairman and Chief Executive Officer.

Donald Nelson Frey was a brilliant young engineer, educated at the University of Michigan, where he received his Ph.D. in 1950, and subsequently taught chemical and metallurgical engineering. He had an illustrious career as one of Robert McNamara's "whiz kids" at the Ford Motor Company, which he joined in 1951. After various research, engineering and product planning posts, he was named Vice-President for product development in 1967. Leaving Ford for a brief stint as president of General Cable Company, he joined Bell & Howell in 1970.

Under Frey's direction, Bell & Howell, later

Fig. 176. Donald Nelson Frey.

joined by Berkey and GAF, brought suit against Eastman Kodak, charging the Rochester giant with trying to put its competitors out of business. The plaintiffs argued that Eastman Kodak, by its near-monopoly of film production, was controlling the "hardware" business of its competitors.

Bell & Howell asked the court to order Eastman Kodak to keep its competitors advised of expected changes in films so that they could begin to develop suitable cameras in a timely manner. Lost profits and triple damages were also sought.[55]

The suit was settled out of court some 18 months later. Under the terms of the settlement, Kodak agreed to a program under which Bell & Howell and others who chose to participate, could, on payment of a $10,000 fee for each new film or cartridge format involved, receive advance disclosure of the new product. In addition, each participant would pay Eastman Kodak a fee of up to one percent of sales during the 18 months following commercial introduction of amateur equipment based on such disclosures. It is believed that Eastman Kodak also made a cash settlement amounting to about $10 million.[56]

Bell & Howell ultimately brought out its own line of available light cameras in the fall of 1973, nearly two years after Kodak's introduction of the "XL" system.

In 1968, Bell & Howell introduced "Filmosound 8," a double-system Super 8 sound system, with sound recorded by a camera-linked tape recorder.

As is detailed in Chapter 11, none of the several similar double systems marketed at that time were commercially viable. It remained for Eastman Kodak to introduce in 1973, the first successful 8mm sound system, Ektasound, with sound recorded on pre-striped Super 8 film. Within two years, five other manufacturers including Bell & Howell were offering single-system Super 8 sound-on-film cameras.

Despite the addition of sound and low-light cameras and projectors to the product line, and despite fairly successful marketing arrangements made with Mamiya, Canon, and Beaulieu, Bell & Howell's Consumer Photo Products group as a whole ceased being profitable in 1974.[57] The Company put a bright face on the situation, its 1977 annual report alluding to "a strong and growing market for home movie equipment. . . ." For the industry as a whole, however, the outlook was not encouraging.

While 8mm movie camera shipments did recover in 1976 and 1977, the following year shipments were down 14 percent, the year after that, they were down a disastrous 50 percent to a mere 280,000 units, and sales would never recover.[58]

Peter G. Peterson had taken the helm just as the 8mm market had begun its downward slide in 1959, and he had vigorously followed the course of diversification away from amateur photo products begun by Percy. Inserting and mailing machinery, microfilming equipment, electronic instrumentation, and textbook publishing were among the diverse businesses acquired. Amateur movie equipment had accounted for no less than 80 percent of company profits in 1958;[59] by 1970, all "consumer products," which included home movie equipment, slide projectors, and still cameras, totaled just over 25 percent of sales.

Donald Frey continued the process of diversification, at the same time consolidating the Company's position in specialized business equipment, learning systems and materials, and instrumentation. He also presided at the largest divestiture in the Company's history, the sale of the Consumer Photo Products business.

The public record does not disclose precisely when Bell & Howell decided to rid itself of its oldest product line. As previously noted, the Consumer Photo Products business had ceased to be profitable

Fig. 177. Bell & Howell's Soundstar 1255 AF.

since 1974, yet the Company continued to turn out new models of cameras and projectors at a remarkable rate, while still holding on to its lead in market share. In the six-year period from 1974 through 1979, 21 new models of sound and silent movie cameras were introduced, including the 1979 automatic focusing Soundstar AF. At $499.95 it was the most expensive camera Bell & Howell ever marketed (Fig. 177).[60]

The 1979 annual report carried the news: on the last business day of the year, December 29, 1979, the sale of the Consumer Photo Products business to J. Osawa & Company, of Japan, was completed. Earlier in the year the company sold its rights to the Eyemo Design 71 35mm cameras and the Filmo Design 70 16mm cameras to Alan Gordon Enterprises of Hollywood, California.[61] Thus ended an illustrious 72-year career in the movie machine business, 56 of those years supplying the amateur cinematographer with some of the finest equipment available from any source. While Eastman Kodak dominated the amateur film market, largely because of its undeniable leadership in quality, product innovation and improvement, Bell & Howell was often the leader in these same attributes in the equipment field. The record includes: the first spring motor driven 16mm camera, the first 16mm camera with turret lenses, the first automatic exposure control cameras in both 8mm and 16mm. In 1980, an article in *Physics Today* ranked Bell & Howell seventh in the top 15 companies in "inventivity." "Bert" Howell would have been very proud.

Bell & Howell had been a remarkable company in many respects. Founded to serve the professional motion picture business, it did so with skill and profitability. When growth in that area faded, it shifted successfully to amateur motion picture machinery, in which field it quickly reached a dominant position. When that business showed weakness, the Company boldly explored and acquired new talents and new markets. Not all ventures were successful, but none of the failures seriously damaged the Company's basic strength. In 43 years as a publicly-held corporation, it maintained an almost unbroken record of profitability and dividend payment, while sales increased at a steady ten percent per year.

Bell & Howell was taken private in 1988, but in 1995 became a publicly-held corporation once more, with sales approaching the one billion dollar mark, in two areas, described as information access and mail processing. Information access includes the manufacture and marketing of systems to convert paper-based information into microfilm or electronic form and the subsequent distribution of that information to the consumer. The company's data collection is second in size only to the Library of Congress. The mail processing business includes high speed systems for the preparation and distribution of mail; it claims to be the world's largest manufacturer and supplier of such systems, and the U. S. Postal Service is one of its biggest customers.[62]

The roots of these two lines of business go back many years in the company's history. Bell & Howell's involvement with microfilming dates back to 1946, when it purchased the microfilm division of the Pathé Manufacturing Company. Mail handling was added to its repertoire when the Inserting and Mailing Machine Company was purchased in 1957. These were decidedly modest capital expenditures at the time; it is unlikely that anyone could have then envisioned that these two product lines would ultimately grow to form the two sturdy legs on which the Company now stands. While the Company's products today contain no vestige of its once core business, remarkably for this day and age, it has seen fit to retain its distinguished name.

Other Competitors

Fig. 178. Charles Pathé (right) with his director Ferdinand Zecca, ca. 1905.

The Second Tier

On April 3, 1952, the Development Department of Eastman Kodak Company filed a report entitled: "List of Manufacturers of 16mm and 8mm Cameras and Motion Picture Projectors." The sources for the report were given as the Card File in the Patent Museum and other sources. The report, listing no fewer than 140 names, is shown in Appendix 12. Obviously many changes have occurred since that report was prepared. However, it may serve to give an appreciation of the multiple firms that have been involved at one time or another in amateur motion picture machinery. This chapter will describe those companies, apart from the two major producers—Bell and Howell and Eastman Kodak—that played a significant role in the history of the industry. The companies are taken up in the chronological order in which they were founded. As stated in the Preface, my emphasis has been on the U.S. manufacturers. However, the products of two foreign concerns—Paillard Bolex and Pathé—have had sufficient presence in the U.S. market to warrant the inclusion of their histories.

The Pathé Companies

Charles Pathé (1863-1957) (Fig. 178) was one of three or four sons of a butcher of Vincennes, France. Following an apprenticeship in his father's shop, he left to seek his fortune in South America. After some time in Buenos Aires, where he found no fortune but contracted yellow fever, he returned to France early in 1894. Some of his biographers would have us believe that he brought back with him the first Kinetoscope to reach Europe, but it seems quite unlikely that such an apparatus would have reached Buenos Aires before it reached Paris.

What is certain is that shortly after his return young Pathé perceived that there might be a bright future in selling the latest Edison invention, the phonograph. The phonograph at that time was still something of a scientific curiosity, not as yet to be found in the home. Pathé envisioned it as suitable

Fig. 179. Exterior of Pathé factory at Vincennes, France, 1913.

Fig. 180. Interior of Pathé factory, believed to be women hand-coloring film.

for a carnival or festival, where for a few pennies the curious could hold a trumpet to their ear and hear the voice of Caruso, Angelina Patti, or a comic Irish minstrel.

To test his hypothesis, Pathé scraped together 1,000 francs to purchase one of the machines and, with his wife, set up a booth at a local festival in a suburb of Paris. Charging two sous for one "audition," the phonograph was an instant success, and Pathé resolved to become a distributor of phonographs to the itinerant showman trade.[1]

One problem arose at once; only authorized Edison dealers were permitted to sell Edison phonographs and no new dealers were needed in France. Pathé soon discovered that *copies* of the Edison machine were available in England, from two Greek merchants, the brothers Papastakyotenipoulos, who later called themselves "Les Frérès Mynas." These brothers were friends of Georgiades and Trajedis, who would later be responsible for producing Kinetoscope copies.

After some unpleasantness stirred up by the Edison forces, during which counterfeit machines were seized, Pathé became a distributor of both counterfeit Edison phonographs and Kinetoscope copies. The Kinetoscope copies, of course, were not subject to seizure since Edison had neglected to patent the Kinetoscope in Europe.

The brisk trade in Kinetoscopes did irritate Edison, and his man Gilmore choked off the supply of Kinetoscope films, restricting sales to just three films with each Kinetoscope sold. Without a ready source of films, Kinetoscopes would not sell, and

without a camera, films were hard to come by. Pathé met this challenge by engaging a sometime photographer and mechanic named Marie-Henri-Joseph Joly, who quite promptly turned out a workable camera, which was patented on August 26, 1896.[2]

Pathé and Joly soon had a falling out, something that seemed endemic to those early partnerships. Each went their separate way making films for the peepshow Kinetoscope, until the success of Lumière's Cinematographe rang down the curtain on the Kinetoscope, as we have seen in Chapter 2.

Pathé, now with two of his brothers brought into the firm, lost no time in producing films for the Lumière system and, in fact, soon eclipsed the Lumière firm. By 1902, Pathé Frérès and another Frenchman, the incomparable Méliès, were distributing films worldwide, while Lumière had almost ceased production.[3] By 1910, Pathé had created an empire encompassing every facet of motion picture making, even to making some of his own raw film stock.[4] His factories were turning out cameras, projectors, edited and processed films. The Pathé studios in Vincennes, a Paris suburb, churned out films that were distributed by Pathé distributors to Pathé-owned theatres (Figs. 179 and 180).

Pathé was Eastman Kodak's largest customer, a fact that also gave Eastman concern. In a December 1907 letter to his counsel, Eastman stated that shipments to Pathé were running at 60 million to 80 million feet per year.

In July of that year, Eastman had entertained Pathé in Rochester, evidently to encourage Pathé to join the group that was to become the Motion

Picture Patents Company. Pathé was indifferent to the idea at that time, for reasons that surfaced subsequently. Eastman prepared for a meeting with the European film industry in Paris in February 1908.[5]

Eastman hoped to establish an arrangement among all the European firms in the motion picture business along the lines of the agreement which had just been worked out in New York between Edison and the companies that would later comprise the Motion Picture Patents Company. This agreement gave Eastman a guaranteed market for his raw film and was supposed to prevent his customers from going elsewhere for film, but that did not always work, specifically in the case of Charles Pathé.

Pathé had written Edison some time in 1907 that he was using 45 miles of film per day. When Edison reported this number to Eastman, Eastman laughed and said "they did not buy that last year." Which could mean either that Pathé was exaggerating his consumption or that he was getting some film elsewhere, the latter being most likely.

Eastman had retained a very prominent French attorney as his counsel for the European meeting, Raymond Poincaré, later to become President of France during World War I. Poincaré advised Eastman that his plan for a European cartel would quite likely be considered in violation of French law. Eastman abandoned the plan and canceled the scheduled meeting.

Meanwhile, Pathé, who had initially refused to join either the Motion Picture Patents Company or the proposed European organization because it would open U.S. markets to his European competitors, was finally persuaded by Eastman that having all of his competitors playing by the same rules would help stabilize prices and further make it easier to put pressure on "dupers." Those were the bootleggers who rented films from the distributors then duplicated them and rented the duplicates to the exhibitors. Since this practice, which was fairly common, directly cut into the producers' profits, Pathé was soon convinced of the wisdom of Eastman's position and wired his U.S. subsidiary to sign the Motion Picture Patents Company agreement.

All of this peaceful accord with George Eastman hardly deterred Pathé in his quest to control all aspects of his business by seeking an alternate source for film. In this he was quite like Eastman himself, who surely understood Pathé's strategy and probably even admired him for it. Even when Pathé went so far as to "regenerate" film,[6] and package it in Kodak boxes, Eastman declined to take punitive action and simply waited for the inevitable quality problems with recycled film to force Pathé to abandon the practice.

As described in Chapter 4, Eastman Kodak had begun research on "non-inflammable" film base, or "NI" as he called it, as early as 1906. The results seemed so successful that by 1909 the company was ready to discontinue nitrate, and go entirely to acetate-based film.[7] However, the new film proved to be more susceptible to tearing and scratching. It met with such resistance from the film studios and exhibitors that Kodak was forced to abandon the product for commercial use in 1911.

Before that happened, however, as the largest supplier of film worldwide, Eastman's efforts with "NI" film were of great concern to the European film industry: how soon would it be introduced, how quickly would it supplant nitrate, what would it cost, etc. Not surprisingly, Charles Pathé took a bold defensive step; in 1912, the company announced the first complete "safety" system designed for the amateur, the 28mm film system as described in Chapter 3.

Pathé's first American subsidiary was established in 1904, and the Pathé Exchange, Inc., was incorporated December 24, 1914, in New York. The company was chartered for the manufacture and distribution, wholesaling and jobbing of motion pictures. Under the leadership of Willard Cook, the American subsidiary flourished.

Willard Beach Cook (1872-1952) who had acquired U.S. distribution rights for all Pathé motion picture products in 1913, was an 1892 civil engineering graduate of the University of Virginia, having been the first student to complete the three-year degree program in two years. After the Society of Motion Picture Engineers had accepted Alexander Victor's proposed 28mm Safety Standard in April 1918, Cook worked tirelessly to promote the use of the new safety film in public schools, with considerable success. By the end of the year, over 100 Pathéscope projectors were in use in New York public schools. The New Premier was advertised as "the only equipment approved by the Underwriters

Laboratories, Inc., for unrestricted use anywhere." [8]
A 1918 catalogue of films for sale or rental listed no
less than 935 titles, many of which were produced
for Cook by other studios.

Cook was determined to insure an ample supply of films for his projectors and expanded the
company's production facilities. By 1922 the company owned two factories in New Jersey for developing and printing, one in Bound Brook, the other
in Jersey City. The latter location also housed a studio that produced features, serials, comedy pictures,
Pathé News, cartoons, *Topics of the Day,* and educational films. A later catalogue entitled *Educational
Films for Classroom Use* was advertised as the *First
Text Book of Educational Films,* and described 575
subjects. [9]

Pathé News had a worldwide staff of over 400
cameramen and correspondents. Not surprisingly,
the company purchased its raw film from Pathé Cinema of France.

Despite the efforts of Alexander Victor, founder
of the Victor Animatograph Corporation, who was
largely responsible for the adoption of the 28mm
Safety Standard, and Willard Cook's success with
educational uses of the film, the fate of the 28mm
gauge was sealed when Eastman Kodak introduced
the 16mm direct reversal-safety film system. Film
in 28mm had never offered great economy of size
over 35mm and, being a positive/negative system,
was inherently more expensive than the direct-reversal 16mm film.

Eastman Kodak recognized Willard Cook's talents. When that company founded a new subsidiary, Kodascope Libraries, Inc., in 1924, Cook was
lured away from Pathé to run the new organization.
The Pathéscope Libraries were discontinued shortly
after the Kodascope Libraries were established. By
1932, however, Pathé had boarded the 16mm band-
wagon; an advertisement in the December 1932 issue of *Movie Makers* offered "Pathégrams," 16mm
short subjects, "Two complete stories on each 50 foot
reel." In the same issue, Willoughby offered a 9.5mm
Pathé package consisting of the Pathé Motocamera
and Pathé Model G projector with motor and super
reel attachment, a $129 value for just $37.50.

By the late 1920s, Pathé Frères' domination of
the European professional film markets had been
substantially weakened by the growing power of

Fig. 181. Alexander F. Victor.

Hollywood. In 1927 Charles Pathé and George
Eastman concluded an agreement merging Pathé
into Eastman Kodak. The union was described by
one observer as "a good marriage, one that began as
a marriage of expedience, but which quickly became
a marriage of sentiment—one that hurt neither
party." [10] Two organizations were formed for manufacturing and marketing: Kodak Limited for the British Commonwealth, and Kodak-Pathé for Western
Europe.

The "marriage" lasted until 1989 or 1990, when
the remnants of the Pathé company were sold to a
French shipping and communications company, The
Chargeurs Group. Charles Pathé lived to be 94.
George Sadoul, the film historian, visited the old
man near the end of his life and recalled that Pathé
kept repeating: "Oh the money I made with the cinema, M. Sadoul! What money I have made!" [11]

The Victor Animatograph Company

Alexander Ferdinand Victor (Fig. 181), the
founder of the Victor Animatograph Corporation,
was born in Bollnas, Sweden, a small town near the
Arctic Circle, on June 20, 1878. Victor showed an
aptitude for science at an early age, studying physics under the renowned Swedish scientist Solomon
Andree. At the age of 16, Victor attended a performance of a traveling magician, "The Great Stefanio,"
and was so entranced by what he saw that he decided then and there that this was the life for him.

"Boy runs away with the circus" is an oft-told
tale, but this was no ordinary boy. The Great Stefanio
evidently recognized something unusual about the

lad and took him on as an apprentice. Stefanio taught him sleight-of-hand and various tricks, while Victor was able to add some illusions to his mentor's repertoire.

While on a European tour with Stefanio in 1896, Victor attended an exhibition of Lumière's Cinematographe in Paris. What happened next is somewhat clouded by Victor's known propensity for embroidering his early years, but by his own account, he was so taken with what he had seen that he persuaded Lumière to sell him one of the projectors and some film. A brief showing of these films was added to Stephanio's program, which turned out to be very popular with their audiences.

Stephanio died suddenly while on tour in Cairo, Egypt, and Victor took over the show, now billing himself as "The Boy Wonder of Magic and Illusion." He carried the show and the Lumière projector throughout India and the Near East until 1900, when he came to the United States.

The trouble with the story so far is that Louis Lumière stated that none of his machines was sold until late 1897; also, as recounted earlier,[12] Lumière had refused an offer of 50,000 francs from the director of the Folies Bergères, after a showing in 1895. It seems highly unlikely that a young magician would have been any more successful. However, Shepard suggests that Victor may well have been able to buy one of the other machines that were being built at that time, such as those by Robert W. Paul.

According to one account,[13] Victor arrived in New York as a headliner and master magician, appearing at Tony Pastor's Fourteenth Street Music Hall, the premier Victorian house of the day. Ramsaye gives quite a different account, saying that Victor arrived in 1897, and that he set up a small theater in Newark, New Jersey, where he showed films using an Edison Projecting Kinetoscope. But Ramsaye credits Victor with what may have been a first: adding a live band to fill out the program.[14] This "added attraction" was only effective for a while, however. Attendance fell off for lack of new films of sufficient interest, and Victor's theater closed after a few months.

Undaunted, Victor set out to carry his magic and mystery show on the road. From 1901 to 1908, Victor fielded two companies of performers, appearing in small towns, while he added to his own repertoire

of magic tricks and illusions. At one point, Victor found himself booked into a brand new theater in Toledo, Ohio, where he was planning to perform a "disappearing lion" act. This required a trap door in the stage, in addition to one that was already there. The manager emphatically declined to have another hole cut in his stage. Victor equally emphatically insisted; the upshot was that the show was canceled and Victor moved his equipment to a nearby warehouse to wait until his next booking.

This was a fateful move; before the week was out, the warehouse burned to the ground, destroying all of the show's equipment. Somewhat surprisingly, given his energy and resourcefulness, Victor decided to quit show business and took a rather prosaic job selling hand-operated washing machines. He was employed by the Toledo office of the White Lily Washing Machine Company of Davenport, Iowa. Victor's inventive nature soon resurfaced, however, as he proceeded to design an electrically driven washing machine, which White Lily gladly marketed, paying Victor royalties for several years.

Washing machines were not uppermost on his mind, however, and in 1909 he had completed designs for three devices which he showed to White Lily's management. First was a motion picture machine, which he called the "Animato-Graph;" next, a machine to take and project color pictures; and lastly, a display machine which the local newspaper called "television."

What happened to the latter two machines is not evident, but Victor did construct a working model of the Animato-Graph. It so impressed the directors of the White Lily Company that they agreed to finance the manufacture of the machine, and the Victor Animato-Graph Company was established on April 1, 1910.[15]

The Animato-Graph was designed as an amateur motion picture system. From the patent drawing,[16] it appears that film was to be exposed and projected from a disc in a spiral arrangement, very much like the Urban Spirograph. The device was never marketed, however, as a number of operating shortcomings became apparent. Victor then turned his attention to another device called the Stereotrope,[17] (Fig. 182) in which a series of transparent pictures were arranged around the perimeter of a metal disc, 7-3/4" in diameter, quite reminiscent of

Fig. 182. Victor Stereotrope of 1914.

Fig. 183. The Viopticon lantern slide projector.

the machines of Uchatius and Anschutz. Victor provided two discs, one with 15 glass plates for showing still pictures, the other with 30 images of an animated cartoon.

The Stereotrope appeared to be marketable. Victor moved his fledging company, now consisting of Victor and three employees to a small frame house in Davenport, with machinery and furniture purchased from Victor's former employer, the White Lily Company. The Stereotrope was offered at $25.

About this time, Victor met a young stereo card salesman named Samuel Rose, who was stopping in a Davenport hotel. The story goes that Victor heard that there was a salesman in town who had just sold a batch of stereo cards to a one-eyed man. Victor figured anyone who could pull that off was just the man needed to sell Stereotropes and persuaded Rose to join the company.[18]

Samuel G. Rose (1888-1966), was born in North Dakota and went to high school in Sioux City, Iowa, where he was the high school reporter for the Sioux City Journal, under the sponsorship and tutelage of Jay N. "Ding" Darling, the famed cartoonist and conservationist. Rose graduated from the University of Nebraska and was planning to do graduate work at the University of Chicago when he stopped in Davenport.[19]

When sales of the Stereotrope proved disappointing, the young company launched another of Victor's inventions, a post-card projector, also selling at $25. Unfortunately, this opaque projector's utility suffered the same limitations that affected the

Stereotrope—the inadequacy of the incandescent lamps of the period. To solve this problem, Victor came up with still another invention, one that was to stand him in very good stead on several subsequent applications. This invention was a compact; five-ampere, self-centering arc lamp using two cored 6mm carbons.[20] It was the first truly portable light source with adequate illuminating power, compared to the bulky and dangerous gas lamps or the dim incandescent lamps then available.

The new lamp formed the basis for another invention, the Viopticon, (Fig. 183) introduced in 1912. This stereopticon had a cast aluminum body, 4-1/2" in diameter and 15" long, and weighed just 5 3/4 pounds. It took special Victor-designed slides measuring 2-1/4" by 2-3/4" in embossed cardboard frames. A box of 48 Viopticon slides weighed one and a half pounds; the same quantity of standard glass slides weighed nearly six pounds.

That same year Victor introduced the No. 1 Portable Stereopticon for standard 3-1/4" by 4" slides, also with the new arc lamp. This machine and subsequent models became extremely popular with lecturers in many fields, after the company created a library of slide sets for "illustrated lectures" on various religious, educational, or fraternal subjects. Slides were available in either standard of Viopticon sizes, black-and-white, or hand colored. Rose related, "We had a Davenport assembly line of 20 girls who painted those slides by hand."[21]

By 1921 Victor Animatograph Corporation had become the largest slide manufacturer in the United States, offering 300 different sets for rent and stocking twenty thousand different slides for sale.[22] Samuel Rose, in an interview many years later, recounted an unusual use for the stereopticons. "We sold thousands of these units to newspapers across the country to project election results on buildings across the street." 23

While the lantern slide and stereopticon business was flourishing, Victor had not abandoned his long-standing quest for means of making movies safely available to the individual, as essayed with the 1911 motion picture Stereotrope. In 1914 the company launched the Model 1 Animatograph, billed as "The First Professional Portable Motion Picture Machine" (Fig. 184). This was a projector for standard 35mm film, equipped with the Victor compact arc lamp, weighing just 25 pounds, and costing $125, including motion picture and stereopticon lenses, arc lamp and rheostat, extra reel and carrying case. When first introduced the projector used the Demeny beater movement for film advance, but this was replaced in 1915 with the Model 2 using a three-point Geneva movement.[24]

In the same 1962 interview, Rose remarked:

Both of us were hell-bent on putting motion pictures on a non-theatrical basis. We wanted to put movies in the hands of the church, the schools and the amateur. We fought for a broadened, educational use of this infant they called movies.

The Animatograph certainly addressed the problems of bulk and cost confronting the amateur wishing to show movies, but did nothing to alleviate the risks inherent in the use of nitrate film, and Victor was concerned with this. He would of course have been watching the arrival of Pathé's 28mm system and Edison's Home Kinetoscope in 1912. As Shepard suggests, the proliferation of incompatible home film gauges may have spurred him to launch the Animatograph. Other portable projectors were coming on the market. As they proliferated, the incidence of untrained operators using them in homes or schools and getting in trouble increased alarmingly.

Victor expressed his thoughts on this matter to the Society of Motion Picture Engineers in a brief but eloquently written paper, part of which read as follows:

The obvious thing to do—it seems to me—is not to meet the public demand, which results in an unhealthy condition; but to furnish the public with a product which meets its needs and creates a sound basis for the industry. Since standardization has produced a large library

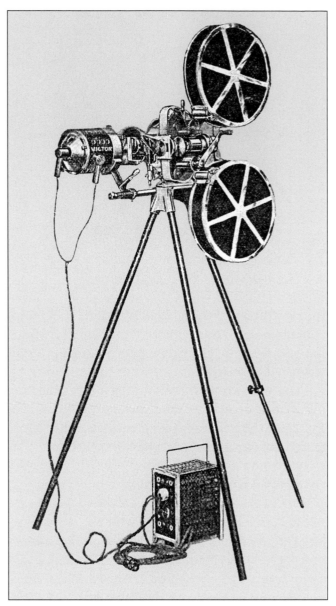

Fig. 184. Victor Animatograph Model 1, portable 35mm projector.

of inflammable film, why not create by the same means a library of non-inflammable film of suitable subjects and equal volume?

If all manufacturers of portable projectors were to combine and adopt a new standard for such machines, it would be but a short time before an enterprising industry would supply an adequate library of film. Since the number of existing film subjects suitable to portable projectors is so limited, it would seem quite practicable to arrange to have them reproduced on non-inflammable stock. The most apparent obstacle to this plan is this: If a new standard is established by this Society and accepted by manufacturers of portable projectors—who is to make the film?" 25

And that indeed proved to be a formidable obstacle. He was, after all, asking producers to create a product for which there might or might not be a demand, and for which there was almost no compatible equipment. It should be recalled that beginning in 1906, Eastman Kodak had striven to make an acceptable non-flammable film. It was introduced in late 1908, but complaints from exhibitors about its strength and resistance to wear caused Eastman Kodak to withdraw the film from commercial production in January 1911.

Victor concluded his paper by urging the Society to adopt a universal standard for approved non-flammable film, so that the products of all manufacturers would be interchangeable and that the term "Portable Projector" be added to the Society's nomenclature. Victor appended his own drawing of a suggested film configuration, which not surprisingly was identical to the Pathé 28mm system, except that Victor placed three perforations on each side per frame, which insured that the new film would run on either the Pathé projectors or the new standard.[26] Victor's arguments were persuasive, the Society adopted the new standard that same month as "Safety Standard Film" (Fig. 185).

In 1918, Victor introduced the Safety Cinema[27]

(Fig. 186), a projector built for his recommended 28mm film, and began a campaign to get producers to release films in the new gauge. His only ally in this struggle was Willard B. Cook, then the head of Pathéscope of America, Inc.

Cook and Pathé were glad to see another 28mm equipment producer, as it tended to reassure prospective customers that 28mm was a viable concept. Pathéscope and Victor expended substantial sums in lobbying state legislatures to modify existing fire laws and safety codes so that "safety film" would be exempt from the burdensome regulations put in place to protect the public from the hazards of nitrate film. A prime example of this was the "fireproof booth" that was required to surround any projector mechanism being used in a public place. Such a booth might weigh as much as 500 pounds and cost more than the projector it enclosed.

The war which had engulfed Europe since the assassination of Archduke Franz Ferdinand of Austria in 1914 finally touched American citizens, and Congress declared the United States to be at war with Germany on April 6, 1917. Victor Animatograph Corporation's contribution seems to have consisted chiefly of the production of stereopticon slide sets with patriotic or war-related themes, such as Belgium

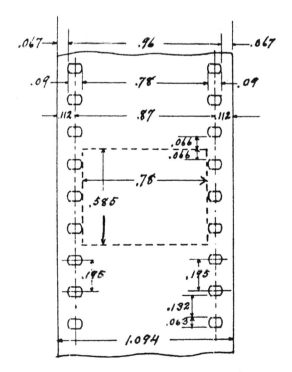

Fig. 185. Victor's proposed "Safety Standard," accepted by S.M.P.E. in 1918.

Fig. 186. Victor's "Safety Cinema" 28mm projector for the new Safety Standard Film.

The Downtrodden, Germany's Dream of Empire, even one entitled *Women's Part in Winning the War.*

Samuel Rose's 1963 paper on the history of the company makes only one reference to the war, citing it as the cause of the halt of the supply of imported Pathéscope 28mm projectors, which gave impetus to Victor's decision to produce the 28mm Safety Cinema projector, as noted above. Curiously, no patent for this machine appears in the list of U.S. patents issued to Victor, printed in Rose's paper.[28]

Victor had little or no success persuading the major studios to produce films in the new Safety Standard, even though the demand for non-theatrical films burgeoned after the war. The year 1918 saw the founding of a magazine called *Moving Picture Age—Reel and Slide Magazine,* which was designed specifically for the educational, industrial, and religious users of motion pictures.[29]

By 1920, the large format magazine had grown to 60 pages. A typical issue carried advertisements by no less than 12 producers or distributors offering films for non-theatrical use, in categories of agriculture, industry, scenic, science, and religion. Only two of these advertisers specifically stated that their films were on safety standard: Bray Studios and, of course, Victor Animatograph, or as the ad put it "Victor Safety Film Corporation." That ad claimed: "Five thousand subjects selected from the cream of the world's productions, now available for the school and church." Shepard relates that Victor persuaded George Kleine and Essanay to allow Victor to make and sell 28mm prints of their backlog of films, which may have been the source of these 5,000 subjects.

That the use of standard nitrate film was still preferred may be inferred from the fact that of the 11 advertisements for portable projectors, only one was for safety standard film: the Pathéscope. Victor did not advertise his projector at that time. The editorial content of Motion Picture Age left no doubt of the growing popularity of using films in schools and, at the same time, the lack of educational quality in most of the available films. Curiously, there was no editorial comment about safety considerations.

While the major producers did little to help Victor in his crusade for the production of non-theatrical films on safety stock, Eastman Kodak, ever ready to supply a new market, took full-page ads offering "Eastman Safety Film, Furnished in two widths, Pro-fessional Standard, 1-3/8 inches, and Safety Standard, 1-1/10 inches, Eastman Perforations."

By 1922, there was even an organization called The Associated Manufacturers of Safety Standard Films and Projectors, Inc., located at Suite 1421, 440 Fourth Avenue, New York City.

Among other considerations that made the producers reluctant to offer feature films in the Safety Standard gauge was the extra cost involved. Not only was the raw stock more expensive, but the distribution prints had to be made from the 35mm originals by a slow process called "step reduction printing," i.e., one frame at a time. This situation prompted Victor to produce one of his most important inventions: a printer in which any two films of dissimilar size could be run through the machine continuously at fairly high rates of speed. Victor set up a print reduction laboratory, but the demand did not materialize, and he finally decided to concede defeat rather than bankrupt the company. Victor did not apply for patents on his remarkable device, but gave it to the industry in the hopes that it would encourage the move to safety film for non-theatrical use. While the machine's intended use on 28mm did not develop, the printer gave valuable service some 15 years later when it was used to transfer 35mm sound tracks to 16mm print stock.[30]

There remained a large stock of 28mm films that the company had built up and, in the hope of creating a market for these films, Victor designed a very inexpensive projector named the Victor Home Cinema, its name indicating the target market. The machine, introduced about 1921, was hand-cranked, with side-by-side feed and take-up reels, and was constructed largely of stampings. The writer has never seen one of these machines, and it is believed that very few were produced.

A New Product From Eastman Kodak

Victor was at this time contemplating building a camera for home use, just as Bell & Howell was designing a 17.5mm camera and projector system, as related in Chapter 4. Harris Tuttle, the Kodak technician who played a substantial role in developing the 16mm system, relates that Victor wrote to Kodak in September 1920, inquiring if Kodak would make negative and positive 28mm film in safety stock for use with his 28mm camera.

Frank Lovejoy, then the number two man at

Kodak, wrote Victor and told him of Kodak's plans for 16mm direct reversal film, and invited him to come to Rochester to inspect the product. Tuttle recalls:

Mr. Victor came to Rochester—we showed him our 400 foot demonstration film. We offered him 28mm reversal film to test but (he) turned it down and said perhaps later when his 16mm camera was available he'd like to be able to receive a few rolls for testing his camera. Later we did, and I processed his tests.[31]

Tuttle went on to say that both Bell & Howell and Victor were told that Eastman Kodak would not be ready to supply 16mm film and processing until June 1, 1923. Both companies were urged not to announce their cameras before that time, so that customers would be assured of a film supply and processing after they bought cameras.

Victor may have managed to get a few cameras and projectors on the market before either Bell & Howell or Kodak,[32] and forever after, he boasted of having produced the first 16mm camera and projector, and if careless reporters then called him "the father of home movies," Victor was certainly not going to contradict them (Fig. 187).

Victor actually showed his camera and projector designs to the Society of Motion Picture Engineers as early as May of 1923. In a curious paper published in the *S.M.P.E. Transactions*, Victor praised the arrival of 16mm (without mentioning Eastman Kodak) while at the same time reminding his audience of his early efforts to produce low-cost home movie equipment. He then showed his designs, characterizing them as "the simplest camera and projector ever designed to satisfactorily take and show motion pictures." He then urged the Society to add another "Safety Standard," this time for 16mm.[33]

Victor's first 16mm camera was hand-cranked, as was the Ciné-Kodak, but was remarkably cheaper at $55 than either Kodak's or Bell & Howell's. It was a decidedly simple camera relative to either of its higher priced competitors, with a fixed-focus f/3.5 lens, Waterhouse stops in place of iris diaphragm,[34] and a simple folding sight. Victor records do not indicate how many were produced.

Fig. 187. Victor's advertisement in the Davenport (Iowa) Democrat, August 1923.

The Victor Ciné Projector was really little more than a toy. Of totally unique design, from the six-inch circular shutter enclosure out in front, to the two co-axial film reels at the rear, not forgetting the sewing machine bulb for projection, nor the film gate pressure spring which also served as a framing device; all bespoke Victor's efforts to get something on the market before anyone else and with a minimum of tooling-up cost. The first model was hand-cranked and listed at $45; somewhat later the Automatic Electric Model was offered at $60. Victor records show that about 400 of each projector model were produced.

Eastman Kodak had established a Patent Department early in the 1920s, one of whose functions was to acquire and evaluate competitor's products. The Department obtained, doubtless with more than usual curiosity, examples of the Victor products and put them through testing and evaluation.

The Kodak engineers found some points of Victor's designs to praise, but could not give them a good rating overall. The camera lens was described as being of poor quality, incapable of producing sharp pictures. Placement of the aperture ahead of the lens, a common practice in inexpensive cameras, was condemned as being further detrimental to image quality. The report on the projector stated:

The hand-driven projector produces a very poorly illuminated picture that is quite unsteady on the screen. There is objectionable flicker and the mechanism scratches the film so badly as to ruin it after passing through the machine two or three times.[35]

One of Victor's early customers was Thomas Willard, of the Willard Storage Battery Company. Quite understandably, Willard thought the camera should be battery-powered. He rigged up his camera with a battery compartment on the rear and fitted a small motor into the camera body to replace the hand-crank mechanism.

Willard then persuaded Victor to design and manufacture a battery-powered camera along these lines, which Victor did, calling it the Victor Ultra Ciné Camera (Fig. 188). The name was not totally pretentious; the camera design included an amazing variety of innovations, in addition to the battery drive. The f/3.5 lens focused from one foot to infinity, aperture adjustment still by Waterhouse stops; the Newtonian finder retracted into the cam-

Fig. 188. The Victor Ultra Ciné Camera.

era body, and could be set for eye- or waist-level viewing. The motor drive had speed control with a "correct speed" indicator window showing in the top of the camera, an exposed footage counter and a single frame lever. An external power supply socket for remote operation completed the accessories.

The battery, a six-volt, three-cell lead-acid wet cell, was contained in a two-inch extension on the rear of the camera. Unfortunately, the battery was not up to the task demanded of it; it discharged too quickly and had a tendency to leak. Only 80 of the cameras were produced,[36] priced at $140. They have markedly increased in value, however!

Bell & Howell's first 16mm camera, as noted in Chapter 4, was spring-motor driven, permitting it to be hand-held, thus much more convenient to use than the Ciné-Kodak. Victor soon countered with a spring-motor camera, the Victor Model 3 Ciné Camera, introduced in 1926. Instead of the side-by-side spool placement, the spools were placed one-over-one, as in Bell & Howell's Model 70. The Model 3 was quite sophisticated: an f/3.5 interchangeable lens in focusing mount, iris aperture, three speeds—half normal, normal, and four times normal; hand-crank drive option; telescopic finder with parallax adjustment; "plumb bob" in finder to avoid tilting the camera; [37] exposure calculator; unexposed film indicator. The Model 3 was introduced at $59.50 without lens, and was soon followed by the Model 4, equipped with a three-lens turret, also without lens, at $95.00. The Model 5 followed in 1930 with back-wind capability, at $147.50 (Fig. 189).

The period from 1930 to 1940 was a busy one

for the Victor design department, i.e. Victor himself, no less than 15 models of 16mm silent projectors were produced, and 23 models of sound projectors. Production runs were extremely short however, often less than 2,000 units, sometimes less than 500.

While the fortunes of the Victor Animatograph Corporation languished in the late 1930s and early 1940s, Victor himself appeared to be doing well. A 1939 interview by a Swedish journalist, published in a Stockholm paper, described Victor as follows:

It is exactly 60 years since Alexander Victor first saw daylight in a small Swedish village, but you can hardly believe it when you see the vigorous, youthful (man) in 1939. He looks more like a calm and friendly college professor than a successful business magnate and inventor who can afford to keep a whole floor on Park Avenue, a house in France, and a 3,000 acre farm in Canada, which by the way he hasn't visited in seven years.[38]

The first efforts at synchronized sound and film for the amateur generally consisted of some combination of projector and record turntable. Synchronization was to be achieved either by having one motor drive both mechanisms, as in the DeVry Cinetone, or separate motors kept in synchronization electrically as in the Vitaphone system of 1926.

Victor's first sound-on-disc projector, the Victor Animatophone of 1930 (Fig. 190) came with a surprising innovation. Victor stood the turntable on edge, with the tone arm moving vertically across the record. The arm was counterweighted and held against the record by a spring. The chief advantage of this arrangement seems to have been one of saving space; the machine came equipped with a 15-inch turntable, but had a "foot print" hardly bigger than a silent projector. Approximately 1,000 of these sound-on-disc machines were produced between 1930 and 1932.

As related in Chapter 11, sound-on-film for theatrical films came into general use in the years 1926 to 1928. The first 16mm sound-on-film projector was the "RCA-Victor Photophone Type PG-38," introduced in 1932, using an optical sound track.[39] Victor introduced his first sound-on-film projector, the Victor Model 12 Animatophone, the following year. According to Shepard, Victor avoided RCA-Victor patents by using a stationary sound drum and a free-

Fig. 189. Victor Ciné Camera Model 5.

Fig. 190. Rudy Vallee, the hugely popular singer of the 1930s, poses with his Victor Animatophone.

running, flywheel-loaded impedance or drag roller. The Model 12 was succeeded by several other models over the next five years, but sales were not impressive. Total sound-on-film projector production from 1933 to 1938 was approximately 5,000 units.

The hyphenated "RCA-Victor" name resulted from the merger in 1929 of Radio Corporation of America with the Victor Talking Machine Company, the latter company having no connection with Alexander Victor. The founder of the record company said he chose the name because it was short and had an upbeat sound.

However, that the Victor Animatograph Corporation and RCA-Victor were somehow related was a popular misconception that the cunning Victor did nothing to dispel. Quite the contrary, he invented a charming story that the founders of the phonograph company named the company in his honor after he had helped them solve some difficult problem with their machines! On another occasion he reportedly told an interviewer that it was his fox terrier Nipper that was the model for the famous trademark dog, with his head cocked by an old-fashioned gramophone. The latter fable was so patently impossible and so easily disproved that it makes Victor's audacity in fabricating such stories almost incredible.

Despite the plethora of models produced, the late 1930s were not kind to the Company. Bell & Howell had introduced its Filmosound line of 16mm sound-on-film projectors in 1933, which quickly dominated the market. Bell & Howell described the Filmosound as the most important single product in its history—formidable competition for the man from Davenport. A comparison of Bell & Howell's and Victor's earnings over a 10-year span gives a vivid picture of the relative strength of the two companies (Fig. 191).

Year	Bell & Howell	Victor Animatograph
1935	$ 66,564	$ 28,150
1936	463,307	11,338
1939	540,261	(23,488)
1941	319,500	46,500
1946	442,945	382,300

Source: Bell & Howell Annual Reports, Shepard paper on Victor.

Fig. 191. Comparison of Bell & Howell and Victor Earnings, 1935-1946.

Victor's decline in earnings in the late 1930s may have been in part due to the lingering effects of the great depression, exacerbated by Bell & Howell's phenomenal success with the Filmosound line. Both companies benefited from the widespread use of projectors by the military and industry. As Rose put it in that 1962 interview:

It took World War II though to prove the practicality of 16mm movies for all forms of education. The services

found the visual was more effective than the spoken word, and before long, our company—he one which started 16mm—was making 12,000 projectors a year.[40]

Rose went on to say that when the war ended, the Company organized to meet the tremendous expansion of the field of visual education. Under Rose's direction, sales offices or dealers were established in dozens of overseas locations.

Enter Curtiss-Wright

The program that Rose envisioned would obviously take a great deal of effort and money. By 1946, Victor and Rose had each put in 35 years with the Company; Victor was 68, Rose was 58. While both were in good health, perhaps the prospect of overhauling the company and going after increased capitalization seemed daunting. Certainly most of the load would have fallen on Rose's shoulders.

In any event, when the giant aircraft company Curtiss-Wright approached with an offer of $10 per share for all 150,000 outstanding shares of Victor Animatograph, it did not take long for the principals to accept. On July 9, 1946, Victor Animatograph became a division of Curtiss-Wright. Victor was to stay on as President and Director of Engineering while Rose became the Executive Vice President for Administration.

G. W. Vaughn, President of Curtiss-Wright, told reporters that his company was impressed with Victor's achievements in development of 16mm technology and looked forward to a broad expansion of the applications of that equipment in the fields of education, instruction, and home use. Rose told a reporter:

The purchase by Curtiss-Wright will usher in a still greater era of progress for our organization. The 16mm visual education industry that enjoyed a tremendous growth during the war because of its ability to train soldiers and war workers faster than under normal procedures, is now entering a new period of growth in education, in training and entertainment. Our pre-eminence in the field, combined with the additional resources at our disposal assures us of a generous share of that growth.[41]

It seems significant that while Vaughn of Curtiss-Wright mentioned "home use," Rose did not. It is unlikely that either Victor or Rose had serious thoughts of expanding their company's position in the amateur motion picture market at this time, which was marginal at best. They had elected not to venture into 8mm in 1932, while many other producers of 16mm equipment such as Keystone and Revere did so, nor had they made any significant improvements in their three models of 16mm cameras since they were introduced in the early 1930s.

Shepard does report that during the war Victor had designed a projector that could be used for stereoscopic projection of movies, or movies in color; However, nothing appears to have come of his efforts. Six months after the Curtiss-Wright buy-out, Victor retired and moved to Carmel, California. For a very brief time, the "adoption" of Victor by Curtiss-Wright seemed to be going well; on August 18, 1947, plans were announced for a large new plant to be built on the outskirts of Davenport to house Victor's expanded production. But before the year was out, Victor's sales had slumped dramatically, and Curtiss-Wright management was alarmed.

Vaughn and Rose, the latter now president of Victor, wanted to go after some of the markets that had been lucrative for Bell & Howell: slide and filmstrip projectors, cameras, and tape recorders. Such plans did not appeal to the majority stockholders of Curtiss-Wright, and Vaughn was ultimately forced into retirement.

With no money being expended in product development, Victor's sales fell even further and profits turned into losses. Sam Rose was replaced as general manager and retired. Curtiss-Wright went through a series of chief executives, and in December of 1950 the Victor plant was sold to Bendix Corporation. Victor employment had dropped from over 600 in 1946 to 265 persons at the time of the sale.

Victor's projector line had not been sold to Bendix and was bought by a Boston-based investment firm, the Whittemore-Eastern Corporation. Whatever their track record had been, this was not one of their successes. Less than six months after acquiring what was left of Victor, Whittemore-Eastern was seeking to unload. Learning of this, a small group of old and loyal Victor employees thought there was a chance of reviving the company and petitioned Sam Rose to lead the rescue.

On May 1, 1951, Rose and three others bought the machinery and equipment for the projector line and founded a new Victor Animatograph Corporation of Iowa. Without a physical plant to house the machinery, the new corporation finally settled on an old and respected manufacturer of professional theater projectors, the Motiograph Company of Chicago, in business since the turn of the century.

There followed five difficult years, with Victor personnel shuttling back and forth between Chicago and Davenport, trying to make a competitive product in what was a high-cost facility not really adapted to their product. They had no money for product development, nor for an engineering staff. With a sadly outmoded product line and entrenched competition such as Ampro, Bell & Howell, Eastman Kodak, and RCA, it was a losing battle.

In 1955, Rose and his partners began a search for someone to take over the struggling company, which led to talks with American Optical, Argus Camera, and Revere Camera Corporation. None of these companies could see sufficient potential in Victor's product line to justify its acquisition, and the search began anew for an alternate manufacturing facility.

The Kalart Corporation of Plainville, Connecticut, was a small manufacturer of photographic equipment with idle plant capacity. When the Victor partners approached Kalart about contract manufacturing, Kalart made a counter-proposal: they would buy Victor—lock, stock and barrel. This proposal seemed ideal to Rose; Kalart had the appropriate machinery, manufacturing know-how, capitalization, and urge to expand. When the negotiations were completed, Kalart agreed to purchase the Victor Animatograph Corporation for $194,000 and rename their company the Kalart/Victor Corporation. Rose and his partners had recovered their 1951 investment, and they had saved the Victor name, at least for a while.

Sam Rose retired shortly after the sale to Kalart, to his big gray Colonial home in Davenport, to which he had moved the massive desk from his days as chief executive of Victor Animatograph. He remained active in golf and civic affairs for the ten years that were left to him, but never ceased to regret the fiasco of the Curtiss-Wright take-over. If the Curtiss-Wright people only had had the vision— "By God," he told an interviewer, "we could have been big—bigger than Bell & Howell is today!" [42]

Alexander Victor's retirement was quite different—he had no family to retire to, having never married. His retirement home was on Pebble Beach, near Carmel, California, surrounded by wealthy Hollywood types, few of whom would have known who he was or what he did.

The old inventor had a childlike sense of humor that may have startled his neighbors; he once tied a horse to a parking meter and dared the local police to give it a parking ticket. On another occasion he suggested turning an elephant loose in California's Del Monte Forest to amuse the children.

The journalist George S. Bush visited Victor in 1958, and wrote the following account:

His mind full of technical and administrative matters, Victor works like a man possessed. He forgets to sleep. He forgets to eat. He forgets to get his hair cut. In his laboratory he usually sits at his desk, hunched over, a long cigarette holder in one hand, a chewed pencil in the other. Around him the large linoleum-floored room is crowded to the ceiling; bits of machinery are scattered here and there; stacks of motion picture reels climb up the walls; open crates are filled with the jumbled history of his career. Mixed in with old clothing are patent documents, scientific journals, honorary scrolls, letters from many people—among them Henry Ford, Theodore Roosevelt, Buffalo Bill, Charles Kettering, Mark Twain, John Barrymore, Sarah Bernhardt, Mary Pickford, Albert Einstein, Alva Roebuck, Red Skelton, Rudy Vallee, and the King of Sweden.

He rarely leaves his laboratory, even for the night. Often he slumps fully clothed on a cot for a few hours of sleep. Twice a day he crosses the street to Carmel's elegant Pine Inn for an eggnog. . . . He takes little advantage of the products he helped to create. He doesn't go to movies. He invites children in for magic shows in which he performs with trembling hands. His gruff voice softens and happy tears run down his cheeks when the youngsters laugh.[43]

Victor died on March 30, 1961. His will directed that the bulk of his estate, estimated to be about $150,000, be used to establish a foundation which would have as its purpose the promotion of birth control in undeveloped and over-populated nations, with the following explanation: "I assume people will come to realize that birth control is important to the welfare of all mankind. I believe such a realization may be present by 1975."

Victor appears to have been a decided agnostic. He further directed that should the trustees decide in 1975 that the foundation was no longer needed, the money "is to be given to charitable, scientific, literary or educational organizations which have birth control as their aim, but to no religious organizations."[44]

What exactly was Victor's legacy? With the exception of his continuous reduction printer, none of his motion picture inventions could be considered as major leaps forward; despite years of advertised claims, he had really nothing to do with the development of 16mm direct-reversal film, and Eastman Kodak's 16mm cameras and projectors were functioning months before Victor's were on the market. His great achievement was of course his hard-fought and ultimately successful campaign to force the industry to establish a safety standard film for non-theatrical use, and for this alone he deserves his place in the pantheon of motion picture pioneers. In 1964, the Society of Motion Picture and Television Engineers elected him to their Honor Roll, where he joined Eastman, Edison, Jenkins, and Albert Howell, among others.

The DeVry Corporation

Herman A. DeVry (Fig. 192), a producer and exhibitor of educational films founded the DeVry Corporation in 1913. The company's first product was a portable projector for standard (35 mm) film. While the company's principal markets continued to be in the educational and industrial fields, several interesting products were developed between 1926 and 1954 for the amateur motion picture maker.

Beginnings

Herman Adolf DeVry (1876-1941) was born in Germany and came to this country in 1885. His first job was as an attendant in a penny arcade in Kansas City. The proprietor of the arcade, a man named Guth, had brought over from Europe a Lumière Cinematographe, that DeVry learned to operate and with which he produced films for the arcade.[45] DeVry subsequently worked as a motion picture projectionist in Texas and Arizona. By 1899 he was, by his own account, assistant manager of a moving picture exhibition at the "Great American Exposition" in Omaha, Nebraska. The effect of this job on his life work he described as follows:

Fig. 192. Herman Adolf DeVry.

Fig. 193. DeVry Portable 35mm Projector.

Here I first noticed the intense interest of the public. I visioned the interest of children being taught by this method, and dreamed of the day when motion picture presentations correlating the text would be a reality in our schools. The idea grew with the years, and practically my entire efforts from then on were associated with motion pictures and equipment in one way or another. [46]

For the next ten years, DeVry crisscrossed the country working at a variety of jobs: traveling film exhibitor, electrical contractor, and builder of stage illusions for well-known magicians such as the Great Herrmann. During this time, he reportedly used a variety of projectors in addition to the Cinematographe: a Lubin, a Gaumont, and "the first Edison motion picture projector." [47] His experience with these projectors evidently spurred him to design a better machine:

About 1908 I constructed my first moving picture camera and made many of the scenes used later on in my feature travelogue picture of 1910. During my entire spare time I made plans for a really professional portable projector which would be practical for use by traveling salesmen and by schools. Such a projector was then non-existent. [48]

DeVry moved to Chicago in 1910, where he landed a job as cameraman with Watterson R. Rothacker. Rothacker, according to Ramsaye, was the first man to envision the use of motion pictures for industrial and advertising purposes and had just formed the Industrial Motion Picture Company for the production of such films. [49]

It is unclear how long DeVry worked for Rothacker, as Crakes reports that in 1912 DeVry was producing films that he sold to Pathé, Universal, Melies, and Eclipse. He also reportedly made and exhibited a "travel lecture film" at this time, *Around the World in 90 Minutes,* which included footage of his own—plus footage from other sources. Later that year he settled down to build the ideal projector which he had envisioned. His laboratory and workshop was in the basement of his home and, in 1913, the prototype was complete. Again in his own words, "It worked perfectly from the start, and I found a ready market, especially among the firms for which I had made industrial films."

Thus encouraged, DeVry formed the DeVry Corporation and set about making the projector in quantity, now called the Model E (Fig. 193). In 1915, DeVry moved his operations out of his basement into a factory building at 117 North Wells Street. While we may raise a skeptical eyebrow at the idea of the prototype working perfectly from the start, there can be no question about the success of the production model. The projector found considerable favor with schools, churches, and business firms. The construction was largely pressed steel, keeping the weight to a comfortable 20 pounds. Including

Fig. 194. The World's First In-Flight Movie? A DeVry portable projector set up in the cabin of the Aero-Marine Cruiser "Santa Maria" showing "Howdy Chicago!" while flying over the Chicago Pageant of Progress, 1921.

improved models, over 50,000 Type E projectors were ultimately sold.

By 1920, the projector business was sufficiently well established to justify a full-page advertisement in *Moving Picture Age*, which listed no less than 23 DeVry agents or distributors across the country. Two years later, the company advertised that it had invested $250,000 in special machinery, tools, and jigs to produce high precision projectors.

DeVry evidently maintained good relations with Rothacker and turned this relationship to good use. Chicago's 1921 Pageant of Progress featured a flying boat operating out of Lake Michigan, offering short sightseeing rides for selected patrons. A DeVry Model E projector was set up in the cabin and provided what was reported as the world's first in-flight movie. The film was a Rothacker film, *Howdy, Chicago!,* and the exhibition was arranged by Rothacker.[50] (See Fig. 194.)

The year of 1914 had marked the beginning of DeVry's second great endeavor: the establishment of an education branch of the company. The objective was, of course, to sell more motion picture projectors to the schools. The results at first were discouraging. In 1914 there were just not enough films available that educators would accept for showing to children. There were one-reel comedies that were innocuous enough to show as entertainment and some industrial films that had some educational value, but these were not plentiful enough to persuade any major school system to establish a regular program of motion picture use.

DeVry's response to this situation was to establish a production unit: DeVry School Films. With the help of a number of educators, a total of 86 reels of films were produced. It was a beginning. In 1925 a remarkable step was taken; the DeVry Summer School of Visual Instruction was opened. To this campus, hundreds of educators and religious leaders were invited yearly to learn the latest developments in the field and how to use films effectively. Herman DeVry bore all the expenses. The school and the concept were so effective that the project was eventually taken over by a group of educators and became the National Conference on Visual Education.

As observed in the preceding section on the Victor Animatograph Corporation, the early 1920s were years of foment in the "visual instruction" field. Educators and clergymen from every part of the country were clamoring for more and *better* films, for less expensive equipment, and to a lesser extent, for safer equipment. The major studios by and large ignored this potential market, being far too busy making lots of money turning out films that had mass-market appeal.

Alexander Victor's reaction to this impasse was to press for a new standard safety-film gauge and urge film producers to make films in that gauge. DeVry, however, resisted the idea of another standard. Given his large investment in standard gauge projectors and a substantial customer base of industrial firms so equipped, he decided to oppose the idea of a sub-standard gauge for his markets, but at the same time make a play for the home movie maker.

A 1927 advertisement carried the following headline: "If you give a movie camera—be sure it uses Standard Size Film."

There followed a side-by-side illustration of the two film widths, with the 16mm being labeled "off-standard," cannot be used for professional motion pictures," while the 35mm film was said to give "professional results." No mention was made of projection equipment.

The camera shown was the "DeVry Standard Automatic," DeVry's first camera for which there is clear documentation (Fig. 195). It appeared in 1926, a 35mm semi-professional camera generally known as "the lunch box," from its blocky shape and hasp-like fastenings. The camera took 100-foot spools of standard film, could be spring-driven or hand-cranked, and weighed 11 pounds.[51] The camera was advertised as being designed for amateurs but widely used by professionals for newsreels or even parts of feature films.

The second part of DeVry's plan appeared in a 1928 advertisement: "Bring the World to Your Liv-

Fig. 195. DeVry Standard Automatic Camera.

ing Room . . . with a DeVry home movie projector."

Illustrated was the first DeVry 16mm projector, the Type G, priced at $95. Thus DeVry was suggesting that the amateur *take* movies with a 35mm camera, but *show* his movies on a 16mm projector. How that was to be accomplished was never explained.

In December 1928, DeVry announced "Talking Movies for the Home—the first synchronized sound movie outfit for the amateur." The "DeVry Talking Movie Outfit" consisted of the Type G projector mounted on a common base with a 78 rpm turntable.[52]

1929 brought a radical move for DeVry: merger with the Q.R.S. Corporation, to form the QRS-DeVry Corporation, located at 333 N. Michigan Avenue, Chicago. The Q.R.S. Company of Chicago, founded circa 1902, was the world's largest producer of player piano rolls. Possibly because the piano roll business had peaked in 1926, the company cast about for another business, and in 1928 announced its entry into the home movie market with an unusual product, the Q.R.S. Combination Movie Camera and Projector. Less than one year later the two companies announced their merger.

Actually, as noted in Chapter 3, that combination of functions was not new, having been employed by a number of nineteenth century cameras. The Q.R.S. camera was remarkable however for its considerable bulk and weight, 6-1/4 pounds. The camera was equipped with a simple f/3.5 fixed-focus lens, a Waterhouse stop aperture control with settings for "bright," "gray," "dull," and "wide open." A trap door in the front of the camera gave access to the shutter that could be changed from the single-

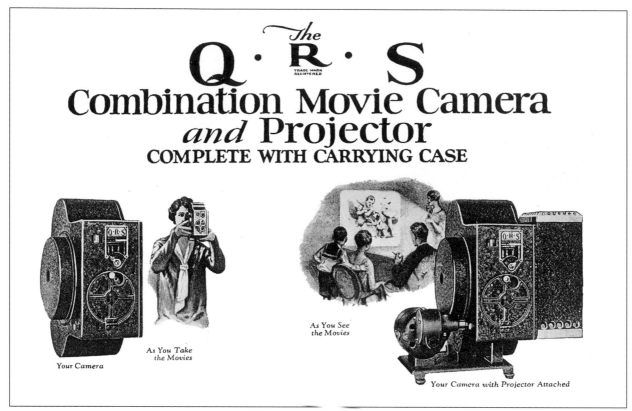

Fig. 196. QRS-DeVry Camera/Projector.

opening camera style to a three-bladed projector type, as required. To function as a projector, the camera was mounted on a stand holding the drive motor. A lamp house was then attached to the side door of the camera, which had an opening to admit the light beam to a 45° mirror in back of the film. The camera came in brown, green, or black, and with carrying case, the outfit sold for $98.50 (Fig. 196).

Curiously, none of the advertisements for the camera following the introductory one carry any reference to the convertibility feature nor showed the projector attachment. One might guess that few owners found the convertibility feature either convenient to use or satisfactory in end result. The camera alone sold for $39.50.[53]

Possibly prompted by the new management, DeVry finally made a serious effort to enter the 16mm market, a move he had resisted up until then. DeVry gave this rather patronizing explanation for the long delay:

The 16 mm films and lenses were being gradually improved so that it seemed possible that 16 mm might be of sufficiently good quality to be usable in the industrial and home fields.

A conventional 16mm projector was advertised in 1929 at $37.50, along with a "still projector" for $15, and a curious still camera in Bakelite case which took 40 exposures of 35 mm film on special cassettes.[54] The following year a conventional 16mm camera was introduced, the DeVry Model 47, at $47.50 with single lens, and the DeLuxe model with three-lens turret at $250. Possibly to compete with Eastman Kodak's "Kodatoy" projector which had appeared in 1930, QRS-DeVry brought out a line of inexpensively built 16mm projectors carrying the Q.R.S. name, starting at $6.50. "Kiddiefilms" were available in lengths of 10, 25, 50, and 100 feet, featuring Charlie Chaplin, Douglas Fairbanks, Tom Mix, Jack Dempsey, Admiral Byrd, Joan Crawford, Greta Garbo and others—at four cents per foot.

The last product known from the QRS-DeVry Corporation was a sound-on-film projector, which appeared early in 1931 and was advertised as the most compact portable sound-on-film projector on the market. It took standard 35mm film with optical sound track and, at $1,475, was built for the small theater owner, or manufacturers to show products, lecturers, educators and the like.

The curious alliance of the piano roll maker and

the dedicated motion picture man did not last long. The May 1931 issue of *Movie Makers* contained the following advertisement:

First Product of H. A. DeVry Laboratories:
The "H. A." DeVry Sound-on-Film Projector
Herman A. DeVry, Inc.
56 E. Wacker Drive, Chicago

And finally, the December 1931 issue of *Movie Makers* carried a letter from Joseph B. Kleckner, President of QRS-DeVry Corporation, which announced that the company had just undergone a compete reorganization, under which the 35mm and 16mm movie equipment business would soon be operating as a separate but wholly-owned subsidiary. A news item in the same issue of the magazine reported that H. A. DeVry had severed his connection with the company.

The brief liaison with Q.R.S. had little effect on Herman DeVry's energetic pursuit of his twin goals of dominating the educational film field, and carrying a broad line of non-theatrical motion picture equipment. In 1931, he and his two sons, Edward B. and William C., purchased a foundering school with an enrollment of 25 students and three employees. From this beginning arose the de Forest Technical Institute, named after the vacuum tube pioneer, with whom DeVry is reported to have worked at some time.

The QRS-DeVry Corporation, without the knowledge and leadership of DeVry, soon foundered and in November of 1932, Herman DeVry bought back the company. The Q.R.S. cameras were quickly discontinued and the company re-named Herman A. DeVry, Inc. The piano roll business was sold off to Max Fortlander, a former Q.R.S. employee, who renamed it the Imperial Industrial Co. and moved it to New York City.[55]

By 1938, speaking as founder and president of the DeVry Corporation, DeVry described the company's products as including: public address systems, theater projectors, 35mm and 16mm sound recording cameras, and stated that the DeVry line was complete for all projection needs of school, theatre or business firms. The company was also planning to compile a comprehensive library of sound films for classrooms (Fig. 197).

DeVry died in 1941, at age 65. His sons Edward and William, who had served as vice-presidents of the company, continued to run the school, which

Fig. 197. 1935 advertisement for DeVry products.

was renamed the DeVry Technical Institute in 1953. The following year Bell & Howell purchased the DeVry Corporation, stating in its annual report that the purchase "increased our ability to meet the needs of the military for JAN(Joint Army-Navy) 16mm sound motion picture projectors."

Bell & Howell purchased the DeVry Technical Institute in 1966. The 1967 Bell & Howell annual report indicated that the DeVry Institute of Technology was a division of Bell & Howell Schools and that it offered resident classes and home training courses in all areas of electronics, including automation, microcircuitry, instrumentation and control, and space, in addition to computer field engineering. At some time prior to 1987, Bell & Howell spun off DeVry, with most of the stock in the new entity held by the parent company.

In August 1987, the Keller Graduate School of Management, Inc., acquired the 85 percent of DeVry that was owned by Bell & Howell and the 15 percent that was publicly owned for about $182 million. The Keller organization was a closely held Chicago-based operator of business administration degree programs, founded in 1973.

Subsequent to the acquisition of DeVry Inc., Keller went public, the new corporation being named DeVry Inc., with the DeVry Institutes, Keller Graduate School of Management, and a unit called Corporate Educational Services operated as divisions. In 1994 DeVry Inc. was one of the largest publicly owned higher education companies in North America, with annual revenues of over $200 million.

Herman A. DeVry's name is carried on the Honor Roll of the Society of Motion Picture and Television Engineers, along with his contemporaries George Eastman, Lee de Forest, Albert Howell, and Alexander Victor.

The Companies Called "Keystone"

In June 1919, following the close of the World War, when the importation of German toys was at a low ebb, Edward M. Swartz, J. M. Weisman, and Benjamin Marks incorporated the Keystone Manufacturing Company and began the manufacture of the now famous line of Keystone steam shovel and truck toys. Originally occupying 2,000 square feet of area, this has grown until today more than 40,000 square feet are used in the production of metal, or so-called heavy-duty toys. A volume of about $50,000 in sales the first year has grown to $500,000 in ten years, and the company markets its products throughout the United States, Canada, Mexico, South America, Cuba, England, Australia, and the Philippines, while competition with Germany is keen, even with the 70 per cent tariff duty.

Mr. Swartz is president, Mr. Weisman, treasurer, and Mr. Marks, vice president, and I. Marks is secretary. The line of production has been enlarged to include not only steam shovels, with extensive arms and dump trucks, but also truck loaders, steam rollers, wrecking cars, mail trucks, U.S. army trucks, ambulances, chemical pump engines, water pump towers, fire trucks, aerial ladders, fire towers, mail planes, locomotives, freight cars, railroad wreckers, coaster trucks (sic), express vans, sprinkler tanks, moving vans and police patrols. [56, 57]

While the above account written in 1930 fails to mention it, Keystone Manufacturing Company had by that time added a new kind of toy to its product line. On October 17, 1919, Isidore Marks, listed as secretary in the above account, had filed for a "design patent" for a "Toy Motion Picture Machine," and a machine patent also for a moving picture machine, the first of a number of patents to be issued to Isidore Marks over the next 20 years.[58] (See Fig. 198.)

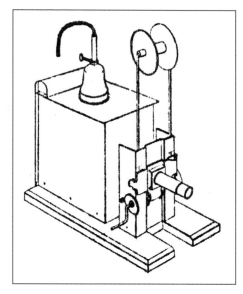

Fig. 198. Isodore Marks Design Patent of 1919.

The latter patent provides an insight into a marketing strategy employed by the fledging company. Possibly because of a perceived need to use a different marketing channel for motion picture projectors than that for toys; Keystone evidently arranged sales agreements with two other Boston retailers: Paramount Manufacturing Company and Warren Manufacturing Company. A 1921 advertisement by Paramount offered: "Six wonderful MOVIEGRAPH models priced from $3.00 to $25.00 postfree." Moviegraph was the name Keystone used for its projectors. The accompanying illustration clearly shows a Keystone Moviegraph, and the caption cites "U.S. Patent Nos. 55,107 and 1,345,793 (Fig. 199).

Keystone also sold through Sears Roebuck; a 1930-1931 catalogue carries an advertisement for a hand-cranked 16mm camera "at an unheard of low price of $10.98." The camera is not identified, but close inspection reveals it to be a Keystone Model C. By the following year, a spring motor driven 16mm camera had been added to the line, priced at $35. Among the features listed for the camera was an "audible footage signal."

One such device was invented by Arthur C. Hayden, a Brockton, Massachusetts inventor and manufacturer of motion picture accessories such as editors, projection stands, projector extension arms, etc. As his patent explained, an inexperienced camera operator often exposed too short a length of film for a proper scene length; an audible footage signal, that could be set for any desired length but was gen-

Fig. 199. A Keystone Moviegraph 35mm projector.

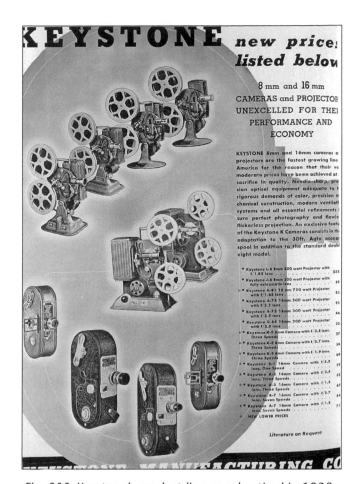

Fig. 200. Keystone's product line as advertised in 1938.

erally set for two feet, helped the camera operator know when sufficient film had been exposed, without having to try to count or examine the footage counter, if the camera was so equipped. Curiously, the patent drawing accompanying Hayden's patent shows a camera looking very much like the Bell & Howell Filmo.[59]

Isidore Marks also patented a sound footage indicator, filed some three years after Hayden's patent filing and of quite different construction.[60] Some Keystone cameras carry both patent numbers.

In common with Bell & Howell and others, Keystone did not immediately follow Eastman Kodak's 1932 introduction of 8mm with equipment for the new gauge. The first Keystone 8mm camera was introduced in late 1935. Hedging its bet on the ultimate acceptance of the new gauge, Keystone's ads cited an "exclusive feature," the camera's adaptability to the "single width Agfa economy spool," as well as the standard double-8 Eastman black-and-white or Kodachrome film. This duality feature was dropped before long, when single-8 film was abandoned by all manufacturers except Universal Camera Corporation.[61]

On the eve of World War II, Keystone's product line included three 16mm cameras, four 16mm silent projectors, one 8mm camera, and two 8mm projectors. In 1941, the company broke new ground with the only 8mm projector with a 750-watt lamp (Fig. 200).

Following the war, Keystone continued to pro-duce well-designed and well-finished cameras and projectors, incorporating innovations introduced by Bell & Howell and Eastman Kodak, generally at competitive prices. While obviously without the resources of its two bigger competitors, Keystone was serious about quality of product. In a 1959 interview, Edward M. Swartz, president, stated that the company had repair depots from coast to coast and operated a service program at a planned loss of $100,000 per year. [62]

An example of Keystone's keeping pace with advancing technology occurred in the introduction of automatic exposure control. As related in Chapter 9, Bell & Howell pioneered automatic exposure control, or "electric eye," cameras in 1957. Keystone had its KA-3 electric eye camera on the market the following year. By 1959, Keystone's K-4 DeLuxe, with three-lens turret and electric eye, was selling at $139.50, while Bell & Howell's 393E, basically the same camera, was listed at $169.95.

In 1958, Bell & Howell filed suits against Revere Camera, Wollensak Optical, and DeJur Ansco, claiming patent infringement on 8mm electric eye movie cameras. Notably absent from the list of defendants were Eastman Kodak and Keystone, both of which had devised their own single-vane automatic exposure control systems, which did not infringe on Bell & Howell's double-vane system.

Management of Keystone had been remarkably stable over its first 40 years; of the four original incorporators, three (Edward M. Swartz, Benjamin Marks, and Isidore Marks) continued in office, sometimes rotating jobs among themselves. Isidore Marks' name is not to be found after 1943, presumed deceased; Swartz and Benjamin Marks continued to direct the company until the early 1960s. In 1962, the officers were: Edward M. Swartz, president; Robert Berner, vice-president sales: Ted Roles, vice-president manufacturing; Robert French, engineering; Yale Greenberg, factory manager. The company name was now Keystone Camera Company.

The late 1950s and early 1960s saw radical changes in the amateur movie equipment market. The year 1958 was the high-water mark of 8mm camera shipments to the U.S. domestic market, declining every year after that; the Japanese and European competitors had moved in in force and a major U.S. producer had all but been removed from the field. Revere had been acquired by the 3M Company of Minneapolis, and its camera business left to wither.

The latter may be assumed to have had a positive effect on the remaining major producers, and in 1964, Keystone claimed to have 15 percent to 20 percent of the then 100 million dollar 8mm market.[63] In 1965, Keystone ran an advertisement which read: "Of the big 3 Keystone is the only Super-8 movie camera with power controlled zoom for as little as $119.95." A footnote explained that the big three were Keystone, Bell & Howell, and Kodak (Fig. 201).

At this time, the company's marketing strategy was to have three distinct price lines of cameras and projectors. Ranked in descending order of price, they were: 1. for the retail camera stores, 2. for the discounters, such as K-Mart, and 3. for the "premium" marketers. The chief competitor was always considered to be Bell & Howell, and while Eastman Kodak was not competitive in projectors, it was a strong competitor in cameras.[64]

An interesting marketing scheme was entered into with Trans World Airlines sometime in the late

Fig. 201. Keystone Super 8 camera, 1965.

1960s or early 1970s. TWA offered its "Getaway" cardholders a 14-day free trial of a complete Keystone Home Movie Outfit, consisting of Super 8 camera, dual gauge projector, screen, movie light, carrying case, film, etc., for $199.95, the retail value of which was at least $250.

The year 1966 was a momentous one for Keystone, Its officers, and its employees. Ben Berkey, founder of the photo-materials marketing giant, evidently thought he saw a tender morsel in the old-line Boston firm. Even though Keystone had been losing money, Berkey saw Keystone in a position to share in the anticipated upsurge of 8mm sales following Kodak's introduction of Super 8 in 1965. Edward M. Swartz, sole owner of the company and certainly nearing retirement age, facing the twin threats of Japanese competition and the steady growth of video camera technology, must have been relieved when Berkey made him an offer he couldn't refuse. The Keystone Camera Company was sold to Ben Berkey, for an estimated six million dollars.

The acquisition was not a gentle one—Berkey reportedly fired most of Keystone's salaried employees without warning. Then the expected boom in 8mm sales was short-lived. While Keystone broke even in 1966, conditions worsened in 1967 and Berkey decided to cut his losses. The Boston equipment and machinery was sold back to a partnership of former Keystone employees: Robert J. Swartz, Ted Roe, and Yale Greenberg. The partnership negotiated a ten-year lease on the land and buildings at Hallet Square and went into the business of high precision machining. The company retained the right to use "Keystone" in its name, as long as it did not use "camera." It is reported that the firm secured several large government contracts for machining artillery fuses.[65]

The Keystone camera business was continued in Clifton as a division of Berkey, under new management. The new line-up was: Sam Zausner, chief executive officer; Phil Rosen and Roy Beltzer, vice president of sales; Robert Markens, vice-president of finance; Gary Kaess, vice-president of engineering. Kaess had begun his career with Keystone as a summer intern while studying at Rensselaer Polytechnic Institute. Upon graduation in 1958, he joined Keystone as a design engineer, working on camera exposure control systems and self-threading mechanisms for movie projectors. Kaess left Keystone in 1962 for a one-year stint at Argus, then three years with Polaroid Corporation, where he designed the Polaroid ID-2 identification camera and the CU-5 close-up camera system. He rejoined Keystone in 1966 as chief engineer. Under Kaess' direction, the new Keystone engineering department was expanded. Many new product lines were launched, including among others, cartridge loading movie projectors, Super 8 cameras, movie editors, "instamatic" (126) cameras, instant cameras that accepted Polaroid film, and the first camera with built-in electronic flash—the Keystone Everflash.

The next change came in 1978, when Harvey Berkey, son of founder Benjamin Berkey and then president and chief operating officer of the firm, decided to go into business for himself. The Berkey firm had previously announced its intention to dispose of the Keystone division. This time Harvey Berkey, with the enthusiasm of youth, sprang forward to grasp the falling staff and hold high the Keystone banner once more. The sale price was $3.3 million, $1.8 million to be paid in cash, the balance over a ten-year period. The new company would also assume the division's liabilities of about $3.9 million, plus an unreported amount of contingent liabilities.[66]

On December 27, 1990, a brief news item appeared in *The Wall Street Journal*, reporting that the Keystone Camera Products Corporation of Clifton, New Jersey, was in a very serious financial condition. Struggling against fierce price-cutting by Asian competitors, the company had reported losses for five consecutive years. The chairman, Myron Berman, remained cautiously optimistic, the company having introduced in July two new camera models designed to hold down costs. Berman stated that profit margins on the new cameras should run 30 percent or more. The company was by this time making only still cameras, and was the last remaining U.S. maker of under-$50 cameras.[67]

Berman's efforts were to no avail; in April 1991, the assets, tooling, and brand names of Keystone were sold to Concord Camera Corporation of Avenel, New Jersey, a manufacturer and marketer of diversified lines of still cameras, including single use cameras, 110s, compact 35mm cameras with such fascinating attributes as date or message impression, underwater capability, red-eye prevention, choice of three fashion colors, and so on. The cameras can be supplied to dealers with the dealer's logo and/or message printed on camera and carton. Most of these cameras carry the Keystone name. Gary Kaess is at this writing vice-president of product development, with still more innovative products nearly ready for the market.[68]

Paillard-Bolex

Of the many European manufacturers of amateur ciné equipment, the Swiss firm of Paillard & Cie. (later Paillard-Bolex) undoubtedly had the most impact on the high end of the U.S. market. Its "H" series cameras, introduced in the mid-1930s became extremely popular with the serious amateur and offered the most vigorous competition to Bell & Howell.

The history of this company begins in the year 1814 when Moise Paillard of Geneva, Switzerland, founded a company to manufacture music boxes. The Paillard family carried on the business for more than three-quarters of a century, then joined forces with another well-known Swiss family, the Thorens. The new alliance added new products over the years—phonographs, phonograph motors, and radio receivers.[69]

Jacques Bolsey, Designing Genius

The Bolex name derives from a brilliant Russian-born engineer and designer known today as Jacques Bolsey (Fig. 202). Bolsey was born Yakob Bogopolsky in Kiev, Ukraine, on December 31, 1895. Bolsey's parents were well-to-do professionals—his father a pharmacist, his mother a concert pianist. Bolsey received a good education, and as a graduation present,

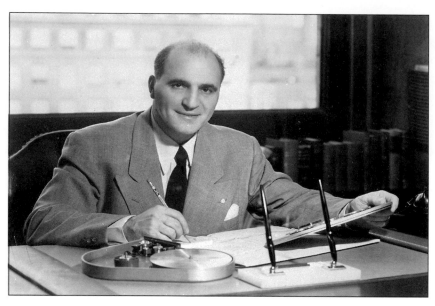

Fig. 202. Jacques Bolsey.

his parents sent him on a trip around the world.

In 1914, Bolsey was in Paris attending the Ecole des Beaux-Arts. When war broke out, he prudently moved to Switzerland, where he enrolled in the faculty of mediciné of the University at Geneva and in the Ecole des Beaux Arts. His artistic talents and energy were formidable even then; in order to support himself and his young family, he painted portraits of most of the faculty while at the University.[70]

Another side of his personality emerged in the early 1920s when he became a self-employed designer and engineer, specializing in photographic equipment. In 1916 Bolsey married Sima Tcherniak, to whom were born two sons, Raphael and Emil. After divorcing his first wife, he married his long-time secretary and assistant, Maria Nussbaumer, in 1946. They had one daughter, Carol Ann.

In 1923 with the backing of two Swiss financiers, Bolsey founded a company, Bol S.A. to exploit several patents he had obtained. The company's name changed to Bolex S.A. in 1925 and its first product was a 35mm motion picture camera for amateur use, called *Le Cinegraphe Bol* (Fig. 203). It was put on the market in 1924, and typically for those days, was designed to serve as projector and printer as well as camera. The camera was hand-cranked, but an optional spring-motor was available, quite similar to the spring-motor drive for the Pathé Baby camera. To function as a projector, accessory kits were available providing motor drive and the capability of projecting either 200-foot or 1,000-foot reels.

The arrival of 9.5mm and 16mm systems in 1923 had a depressing effect on the sales of cameras using standard size film, so Bolsey designed a line of 16mm cameras and projectors for this new gauge. These were: the Bol Auto Ciné Camera, Bol Auto Ciné Camera Model B, and Bol Auto Ciné Projector in two models, the second of which could project either 9.5mm or 16mm.[71] The cameras sold well, but not well enough to keep Bolex S.A. afloat. In 1930 Bolsey sold the company, including all patent rights, inventory, spare parts, accessories, and even the factory furniture to the Paillard Company. Bolsey accepted a five-year contract to stay on as a consulting engineer at the company's Saint Croix, Switzerland, works, where a design group was established.[72]

Paillard appears to have formed a U.S. subsidiary about this time, judging by a 1933 advertisement by the Bolex Company in *Movie Makers* (Fig. 204). The address given was 45 West 45th Street, New York City. Offered were a 9.5mm projector, a 16mm projector, and a combination machine that could show either gauge by a simple change of spindles, sprockets, and pressure plate. The single-gauge machine sold for $99, the dual gauge machine was just $10 more. The marketing pitch was: "9.5mm now leads all other film widths in size and economy," stating that four and one half minutes of screen time cost $5 in 16mm, $2 in 8mm, and a mere $1.25 in 9.5mm, due in part to the unique "stop title" feature of Pathé film.[73, 74]

Fig. 203. Le Cinegraphe Bol –
35mm, 1924.

The Swiss-Made Bolexes

In 1935, Paillard brought out the "H" series of 8mm and 16mm cameras, another product of Bolsey's genius. These retained the general shape of the Bolex Auto Ciné Model B, but otherwise were vastly improved. While Jacques Bolsey left Paillard at about this time, over the next 40 years the H series was destined to develop into one of the most sophisticated line of cameras ever made for amateur use.

The basic features of the H-16 at introduction were: capacity 100-foot daylight loading spools, D-shaped three-lens turret, camera speeds of 8, 16, 24, 32, 64 and single-frame, backwind capability, preview focusing through the top position of the lens turret, and footage counter. An external frame counter was available in 1941, eye-level focusing was added in 1949, the "Octameter" zoom type finder for eight focal length lenses came in 1951. In 1953, the Bolex became the first amateur camera to be equipped with a true variable-focus lens, when Paillard offered the SOM Berthiot Pan-Cinor f/2.8 20-60mm lens, at a price of £243.[75] (See Fig. 205.)

The early 1950s were a time of great activity in Hollywood to bring so-called "3D" movies to the public. Stereoscopic movies were first achieved in the early 1920s and attempted periodically every few years thereafter. The first stereo film using polarized light projection and Polaroid glasses for the audience was shown in England in 1951.

A number of stereoscopic films were shown in

Fig. 204. Bolex Model D Projector of 1933.

Fig. 205. Bolex H-16 with SOM Berthiot Pan Cinor f/2.8 20-60mm lens.

this country, beginning with *Bwana Devil* in 1952, followed by Warner Brothers' *House of Wax*, shown on April 10, 1953, accompanied by six-track stereophonic sound. The film was a great success. Other studios quickly followed suit, with over 60 films being shot in 3D in 1953.[76]

Fig. 206. Bolex H-16 equipped for stereo.

Bolex was the first to bring stereo movies to the amateur, with the Bolex Stereo System announced in November 1953, just in time for the Christmas shopping rush. The system's camera attachment consisted of two Kern-Paillard 5.3mm lenses mounted with 6cm separation (approximately 2-3/8 inches) with prisms, in a D-shaped holder which screwed into the turret and gave two half-width images on the film. The projector attachment projected the images through a pair of polarized filters. The system, complete with special film and two pairs of Polaroid glasses, was priced at $397.50. A stereo close-up attachment was available at $67.50 (Fig. 206).

The next major improvement to the H-16 came in 1956 with the introduction of reflex viewing, through the taking lens. This was accomplished with a flat prism set directly behind the lens, which deflected approximately 25 percent of the incoming light to the viewfinder. Cameras with this modification were designated RX models, not Rex, as is often supposed. The Rex nomenclature came in 1959 with the advent of the variable angle shutter.

At this point, the H-16 Bolex was almost the equal of the Eastman Kodak Ciné Special, except for one detail—its limited film capacity of 100-foot spools. The popularity of the advanced H-16s among serious amateurs and some professionals, despite the capacity limitation, was such that the Paillard service organization in Linden, New Jersey, instituted a program of modifying H cameras at customers'

request to accept 400-foot Mitchell magazines.[77] Finally, in 1967, Bolex introduced the H-16 Rex V, commencing with serial number 226,001, with a saddle-block on top of the body which would accept either a special 400-foot darkroom-loaded magazine, or 200-foot daylight-loading spools.[78]

Having established a foothold in the professional market and with amateur use of 16mm declining rapidly as Super 8 took over, Bolex decided to go head to head with Bell & Howell and Arriflex for a larger share of the professional 16mm market. Eastman Kodak had made one attempt in this direction with the short-lived Reflex Special (1961 to 1968) but had discontinued all other 16mm cameras by 1973.

The last H designs were introduced in 1968: models H-16 Pro and H-16 Pro 100. These cameras were designed for news and documentary filming and were self-blimped for magnetic sound-on-film recording or synchronous double-system sound. Bolex introduced a line of H cameras in 9.5mm somewhat later than 1935, but it is believed that these were never marketed in the United States.

The H-8, or 8mm camera line, was also introduced in 1935 and received most of the design improvements of the H-16s except that the H-8 reflex camera does not appear to have been marketed in the United States. Again, the Bolex H-8 was far and away the most expensive 8mm camera on the market, which is probably why so few of them appear in U.S. collections. In a 1956 survey by *Modern Photography*, of 22 camera models priced under $100, only one was a Bolex. It was a so-called "pocket" cameras. The H-8 series was discontinued in 1965 when Super 8 arrived; however, some specialty firms in this country and in Europe would convert certain of the H-8 models to double Super 8, for a substantial price.[79]

The first "pocket" 8mm Bolex was the L-8, (Fig. 207) introduced in 1942, beginning a series of 22 models that would be introduced over the next 20 years. The L-8 was simplicity exemplified: single running speed, single lens, simple viewfinder. Measuring 5" by 3" by 2", with an aluminum body entirely leather-covered except the edges which were polished, it had a pleasing appearance and a crisp, well-made feel. The advertising stressed that it shared the quality craftsmanship of the larger Bolex cameras.

Fig. 207. Bolex L-8.

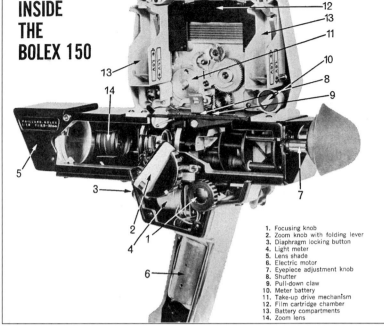

Fig. 208. Cut-away view of Bolex 150, Super 8.

The L-8 does not appear to have been marketed in the United States until 1948, at which time it was priced at $93.28, making it one of the most expensive standard 8mm cameras.

Numerous improvements were added throughout the 1950s, including twin- and triple-lens turrets, photoelectric cell exposure metering, and in 1957, a variable shutter. To meet the demand for a zoom lens, the "P" series of pocket cameras was introduced in 1961, which were fitted with zoom reflex Pan-Cinor lenses. The P-1 camera also featured a split-image rangefinder, reflex viewing through the camera body, and a through-the-lens metering system, with a retractable mirror in the light path. There was also a rewind crank, rewinding up to eight frames possible, sufficient for lap dissolves. At $330 it was not inexpensive, but one reviewer said it outperformed any other 8mm he had ever tested.[80] The last of the pocket series was the "K" series, which were made with a deeper camera body to accommodate an integral handgrip.

As noted, Bolex abandoned the H-8 series when Super 8 arrived in 1965, but was one of the few companies that did not immediately come on the market with a Super 8 camera. When it did, it was with a radically new design. Instead of conventional side-loading, the film chamber was located on top of the camera body, looking very much like a detachable magazine. This chamber also held the batteries for the motor drive and the exposure control meter. The first camera in the series was equipped with a Paillard f/1.9 8.5-30mm zoom lens; the second model, designated the Bolex 155 Macrozoom, could be focused from one inch to infinity, a feature that was made much of in the camera's advertising (Fig. 208).

In 1970, Paillard sold the Bolex division to Eumig, the Austrian camera manufacturer, which continued to produce cameras with the Bolex name while also having some cameras made in Japan by Chinon. Eumig had contracted with Polaroid Corporation to build the ill-fated Polavision cameras and projectors and had expanded capacity to meet the expected demand. When the Polavision system failed utterly in the market and Polaroid canceled its contracts, Eumig was forced into bankruptcy. This essentially spelled the end of both Bolex and Eumig as corporate entities; however, a few products bearing one or the other of those names continued to appear on the market for several years, as new owners took over what remained of the companies.[81]

Some time after Bolsey left Paillard, he joined forces with the Swiss firm of Pignons S. A., a watch and clock parts manufacturer interested in entering the photographic business. In 1939, the company started manufacturing a 35mm camera designed by Bolsey, named the Bolca Reflex, later renamed the Bolsey Reflex, still later the Alpa. The Alpa line was marketed by Pignons S.A. until the company ceased operations in 1991.

Jacques Bolsey, American Entrepreneur

Bolsey had long dreamed of some day immigrating to the United States. In 1925 he made an extended visit, traveling throughout the country and reinforcing his resolve to make the United States his eventual home. It is probable that he also visited Eastman Kodak and investigated the prospects for marketing his Cinegraphe Bol in the States.

As the menace of Hitler spread over Europe, Bolsey again made a well-timed move and, in 1939, sailed for America, taking up residence in New York City. Bolsey lost no time in finding ways to serve his adopted country, quickly becoming a consultant to the National Defense Research Committee, where his extensive knowledge of optics and optical manufacturing technology led to a number of contributions to the war effort.

Among his inventions was an automatic lens centering machine, which replaced a previous delicate and time-consuming hand-operation of making the optical and geometric axes of a lens coincident. In 1941 Bolsey formed Bolsey Laboratories, Inc., an organization for research, design, and development. The company did consulting engineering work for a number of companies, including Graflex Corporation, Argus, Inc., Sperry Gyroscope Company, and the Bulova Watch Company. Bolsey also did work for the Special Devices Division and Naval Ordnance Laboratory of the U.S. Navy.[82]

Bolsey's work for the military evidently did not prevent his thinking ahead to peacetime. In 1944 the Bolsey Corporation of America was established, which was to become the vehicle for Bolsey's entry into the American 35mm still camera market. The company's first product was the Bolsey Model B, introduced in 1947. This was a very compact and inexpensive camera, selling for under $60. Despite its small size, it was very well built and was accepted by all branches of the military. The camera sold well, but foreign competition and Bolsey's thin profit margin drove him out of this market after just a few years.

Fig. 209. The Bolsey 8.

Bolsey then turned his attention to the amateur motion picture field. In 1956 he introduced one of the most remarkable amateur movie cameras ever made. This was the Bolsey 8, billed as "the world's smallest movie camera," a claim which was undoubtedly justified at the time.[83] (See Fig. 209.) The stainless steel matte finished body measured 3-1/8" by 2-1/4" by 1-3/16". The lens was a Bolsey-Elgeet 10mm f/1.8, focusing from 0.1 foot to infinity, aperture settings from f/1.8 to f/22. The camera also claimed to be the only 8mm camera with a "variable speed shutter," which in actuality was a shutter with only one speed, but with an adjustable opening. The camera could be used as a still camera, in which mode the variable shutter gave "speeds" of 1/50th to 1/600th of a second. When the camera was nestled in its red silk-lined presentation case, it looked much like a piece of jewelry. It was said to have been a favorite of Jacqueline Kennedy.

Film for the camera was special pre-split single-8mm, provided in 25-foot factory-loaded magazines, either Kodachrome Daylight or Type A. An exposure guide was printed on the magazine that was visible through a window in the loading door of the camera. Exposed film was to be returned to a post office box in Cambridge, Massachusetts for processing.[84]

The first Bolsey 8 cameras were manufactured by a German firm named Saraber. However, Saraber's capitalization and manufacturing facilities were inadequate, with the result that many of the approximately 6,000 cameras shipped to the United States were defective and required repairs, which Bolsey had done in this country. When Saraber went bankrupt, Bolsey retrieved the tooling and parts inventory and turned the manufacture over to a small concern in White Plains, New York.

Salvaging the Bolsey 8 tooling proved unworkable, however. Bolsey turned to LeCoultre, the famed Swiss watch manufacturer, and persuaded that firm to retool and produce a new version of the camera, which was designated the Uniset, introduced in 1961. Possibly because of the expense of the variable angle shutter, that feature was dropped in the new model. The finder tube was molded plastic rather than steel. This camera is much less frequently seen than the Bolsey 8.

Ariel lists a fourth version, the Bolsey CIN S 8, introduced in 1963, the manufacturer still given as Bolsey Camera Corporation, although the camera body is marked "Swiss Made." This camera was equipped with automatic exposure control, a Schneider Kreuznach Xenar 10mm f/2.8 lens in focusing mount, and was covered in black pebble grain leather. Ariel gives the format as Super 8, which is obviously incorrect, not only for the year of manufacture, but also for the fact that the film cassette is marked "3M," which firm did not manufacture Super 8.[85]

Jacques Bolsey died suddenly on January 20, 1962, of a heart attack. His son, Emil, who had worked closely with his father for many years and who was a noted engineer in his own right, succeeded his father as president of the Bolsey Corporation. The company continued in business until 1963 or 1964.

Jacques Bolsey was a complex, many-faceted man: inventor, engineer, artist, humanitarian, businessman. He organized Switzerland's first amateur ciné club in Geneva and in 1935 presided at the foundation of the Federation Suisse des Cineastes Amateurs.[86] He was a long-standing member of the Society of Motion Picture and Television Engineers, the Society of Photographic Scientists and Engineers and, twice, was president of the Photographic Manufacturers and Dealers Association. Bolsey was the holder of more than 100 patents.

Despite his manifold engineering and business activities, he remained a devoted husband and father. His son Emil remembers him as an idealist, who conceived plans for an "ideal city," a planned community of a few thousand souls who would have ideal living and working conditions, going so far as selecting a site outside Los Angeles, for which elaborate plans and specifications were drawn.

The advent of World War II forestalled further work on this scheme, but a large mural of "Bolsey City" adorned his office wall for the rest of his life, and he never quite abandoned the dream. It is a pity that he did not live to see the coming of Super 8, there is no telling what other ingenious designs he might have achieved. Nevertheless, Jacques Bolsey's name is secure in the roster of outstanding camera designers of all time.

The Universal Camera Corporation

The story of the Universal Camera Corporation is essentially the story of three men: Otto W. Githens, entrepreneur, Jacob J. Shapiro, public relations expert, and George Kende, engineer and inventor. Otto Wolff Githens, (1894 - ?) was born in Philadelphia, grew up in Indianapolis, and while still in his twenties, founded an automobile financing company. When this venture failed, Githens moved to New York, where he became associated with another taxicab finance company. When this company fell victim to the great depression of the 1930s, Githens cast about for a new venture for his restless energies (Fig. 210).

A former business associate of his, Jacob J. Shapiro (1897- ?) was also seeking new employment, and the two men joined forces. Shapiro was a native New Yorker with considerable experience in sales and public relations and the man credited with having the basic idea that would lead them both to fame and fortune.[87] Shapiro believed that there was a market for a truly affordable amateur camera. Githens concurred.

Photography was a popular hobby in the 1930s, of course, but still largely a pastime of the fairly well-to-do. George Eastman had seen the possibilities of a mass market and offered a number of cameras priced under five dollars, including the No. 0 Brownie at just $1.50.

Otto Githens thought he could beat Eastman Kodak at their own game. A pack of cigarettes cost about 20 cents in those days, so a workable camera that cost no more than a couple packs of cigarettes

Fig. 210. Officials of Universal Camera Corp. Front row, l. to r., George Kende, Chief Engineer; Milton Shaw, Director; Otto Githens, President; Jacob Shapiro, Vice President; F.G. Klock, General Sales Manager.

should sell at least as well as Mr. Eastman's Brownie. A camera consumes film, another lucrative market. But how to compete with the established giants in film manufacturing and marketing? The fledgling entrepreneurs hit on a clever scheme; their camera would be designed to accept only film supplied by their company.

With these general objectives established, the Universal Camera Corporation was formed in 1932. But with no design or manufacturing experience in the background of the founders, an established concern with these capabilities was needed. One was found in the Norton Laboratories of Lockport, New York, a manufacturer of molded plastic parts. Githens and Shapiro visited Norton and persuaded a Norton vice-president, Carl H. Whitlock, to design and prepare to manufacture a small still camera which could be inexpensively manufactured in high volume, and which would only accept film on spools specifically designed for that camera.

When the camera design was complete, Githens and Shapiro inspected Whitlock's drawings, but without making any commitment to Whitlock, returned to their Manhattan offices, in all probability taking a set of the drawings with them. What kind of agreement between the two parties is not known, but it appears that Whitlock was a trusting soul and a poor businessman, as he had neither attempted to patent his designs nor insisted on a contract with his new customers.

Back in Manhattan, Githens and Shapiro looked about for a source of capital. With unerring discern-

ment, they caught the ear of one Philip Maslansky, the president of New York Merchandise Company, Inc., of 27-33 West Twenty-Third Street in Manhattan. This company, established in 1905, ran a flourishing business of jobbing and distributing the thousands of notion and novelty items with which the "5 & 10's" of those days were stocked. The fit between Universal's projected product line and New York Merchandise's expertise in merchandising and distribution was nearly perfect. Maslansky's firm advanced Universal one million dollars, the first of many cash advances it would make over the next 20 years.

In October 1933, Universal launched a camera called the UniveX Model A, patented by Otto W. Githens (Fig. 211). The camera, molded in gleaming General Electric's "Textolite," took six exposures on a special UniveX No. 00 film and sold for 39 cents; the film cost ten cents per spool. Despite the absurdly low price, the camera took surprisingly good pictures, at least by the unsophisticated standards of its target customers.

Public acceptance was immediate and enormous. Initial production was set at 500 cameras per day, but this was almost at once inadequate; within three years, 3 million cameras were sold.[88] The principal marketing channel was to sell the camera as a promotional premium or giveaway item, and this is where Universal's unique film spool paid off handsomely. The sale of a 39-cent camera returned very little to Universal, but the camera took good enough pictures to entice the owner to buy more film, which

Fig. 211. UniveX Model A.

could only be bought from Universal, and that was how the money came rolling in. By the end of 1937, over 22 million rolls of film had been sold.[89]

Meanwhile, Mr. Whitlock of Norton had completed the tooling for the camera he had expected Githens and Shapiro to approve, but had heard nothing from them. His dismay at the news of the introduction and runaway success of the UniveX may be imagined. Concluding that he had no legal recourse against his erstwhile friends, he decided that his only hope of recouping some of his investment was to get into production himself. He belatedly filed application for his design, after changing the spool slightly, so that Eastman Kodak could legally produce the spools, which they did for several years. In 1934, the Norton camera, looking very much like the UniveX Model A, was launched.

Githens immediately charged Norton with having copied his design and threatened suit for patent infringement. The patent examiner, finding Githens patent application pre-dating Whitlock's by eight months and further finding that Githens had been the first to "reduce the invention to actual practice," had really no choice but to award Githens the patents. Unfortunately, the general public never learned the true story behind this bit of skullduggery. Within the trade, however, Githens' and Shapiro's maneuvers were known; significantly, when a 1940 issue of *Modern Plastics* reviewed the history of molded plastic cameras, Norton Laboratories' camera was cited as "one of the earliest inexpensive miniature cameras . . . opening the floodgates for a surge of molded models to follow," while Universal was not mentioned at all.[90]

Universal went on to produce a line of inexpensive folding cameras, and the continued success of these products led the company to consider a new field: amateur motion pictures. A study done presumably around 1935 produced the information that while there were approximately 17 million amateur still cameras in use, only some 500,000 movie cameras were in amateur hands. The following table gives a partial insight into the reasons for those ownership statistics (Fig. 212).

Company	Camera	Projector	Total
Keystone	$27.95	$39.50	$67.45
Eastman Kokak	$22.50	$29.50	$52.00
Revere	$23.95	$59.50	$83.45
Bell & Howell	$49.50	$118.00	$167.50

Fig. 212. Retail 8mm Camera/Projector Prices 1936-1938.[91]

Again, Githens and Shapiro saw an opportunity. The capital outlay for the amateur wishing to take movies was four to five times that required for making still pictures. And as a later study would show,[92] cost was not the only impediment to the popularization of movie making. There was the widespread perception that motion picture equipment was not only costly, but cumbersome and complicated to use. So Githens and Shapiro had a new set of design parameters; a qualified designer was needed.

Githens and Shapiro again sought outside talent. An accomplished motion picture camera designer named Everett M. Porter was given a contract to design an inexpensive 8mm movie camera and projector. The target for the camera was "under $10." Porter was to be paid by a royalty payment on all sales of cameras and projectors of his design. Porter proceeded to design and construct a model of an 8mm camera which he believed would meet Universal's stated criteria, but before the camera went into production, another camera designer presented himself at the Universal offices.

The man was George Kende (1908-1988), a 27-year-old mechanical engineer with an impressive

Fig. 213. George Kende.

employment record (Fig. 213). Kende was born in Hungary but grew up in Canada, where he received his early education. After enrolling in college at Saskatchewan, he transferred to the University of California at Berkeley. Upon graduation, he went to work for De Forest Phono Films, and later for African Consolidated, Ltd. of South Africa. Returning to the States, he did work for Consolidated Film Industries of Fort Lee, New Jersey, and the research subsidiary of Warner Brothers Pictures of Long Island City, New York.[93] Seeing that background, Githens was eager to show Kende the new model that Porter had produced.

Kende's reaction must have come as a shock to Githens; after study of the model, Kende advised Githens that, in his opinion, Porter's design could never be manufactured for the target price of under ten dollars, largely because of the complexity of the mechanism. Githens thus found himself with a design engineer under contract whose designs were unworkable and with a would-be designer who seemed to know what he was doing. His first step was to hire Kende and put him to work designing an 8mm camera.

He then called in Porter for a meeting, the upshot of which was that Porter would do no further work for Universal, but his name would appear along with Githens' and Kende's on all patents relating to the first camera and projector designs (even though he had no part in them) and that he would be paid royalties under the original contract. These payments amounted to over $80,000 for the years 1936 to 1952. That Githens would have agreed to such a settlement that he must have realized would be costly suggests that Porter had a very well-drawn contract.

The Kende-designed camera, the UniveX Model A-8 Ciné Camera (Fig. 214), and the P-8 projector were introduced in September 1936. The camera, in a die-cast zinc alloy body, was extremely compact, measured just over 4" tall by 3-1/2" deep, and 1-1/2" wide, and weighed 24 ounces. The list price was $9.95, and the projector listed at $14.95.

After the stunning success in marketing their special private-brand film for the 39-cent UniveX Model A, Githens and Shapiro felt confident in taking the same strategy with their new movie camera, so the camera was designed to take only pre-split, single-8 film on special spools, only available from Universal. The film was supplied to Universal by Gevaert of Belgium and was packaged by Universal in 30-foot lengths in small metal cans, which were to be used to return the exposed film to the processing station. A slip inside the can warned the user against attempting any processing other than Universal, claiming to have "a highly technical, secret process known only to us." Film processing laboratories were opened in New York, Chicago, and Hollywood.

Universal began marketing on a modest scale, placing advertisements in a few selected magazines, yet the little camera caught the public fancy at once and orders quickly out ran Universal's ability to deliver. A planned $250,000 Christmas advertising campaign was postponed until the spring of 1937. In the first two years on the market, 250,000 of the Ciné 8s were sold and 175,000 projectors. There was no question that Universal had opened an entirely new market for home movie making.

Despite the "bargain basement" price of the camera, Universal offered the customer a variety of accessories, not elaborate, but generally quite serviceable. These included: a title stand, a so-called automatic titler, an editing attachment, splicers, screens, and an extinction-type exposure meter.

The 1939-1940 New York World's Fair drew exhibits by many photographic manufacturers;

Fig. 214. Universal's 1939 advertisement announcing the UniveX 8.

Eastman Kodak erected an entire building, and billed it as "The Greatest Photographic Show on Earth." Universal took space in the Communications Building, and exhibited two new ciné cameras. The Model B-8 featured a telescopic finder in place of the original folding-open frame finder. The Model C-8, promoted as the "World's Fair Ciné 8 Camera," had a built-in optical finder, simplified loading, and a self-locking hinged door. The new cameras ranged in price from $12.50 for the B-8 with an f/5.6 lens, to almost $50 for the C-8 with an f/1.9 lens. Ilex or Wollensak generally manufactured Universal's lenses, and this constituted important business for those two firms.

The Mercury

The popularity of the "candid" camera, led by the 1925 35mm Leica, gradually increased in the following decade, with a number of European small format cameras making their appearance in the United States. The first commercially successful American-made "candid" was the 1936 Argus A, manufactured by the International Radio Corporation (as it was then called) of Ann Arbor, Michigan.

By the end of 1936, some 42,000 imported candid cameras and 38,000 Argus 35s had been sold in this country for a sum approaching eight million dollars.[94] Such figures did not escape the notice of Githens and Shapiro. In 1937 George Kende was

Fig. 215. The UniveX Mercury.

directed to design an "affordable" 35mm camera which, in the Universal style, would accept only film marketed by Universal.

Kende's response was the Mercury (Fig. 215), a camera whose appearance was so unusual that it would be instantly recognizable amidst a sea of other 35's. What set this camera apart was the large rotary focal plane shutter, whose housing arose above the top deck like the sun coming up out of the Atlantic. To soften the effect of this anomaly, Kende inscribed both sides of the protrusion with a depth-of-field scale.

The shutter provided film speeds to 1/1000.[95] Its accuracy and reliability were so good that at least one observatory employed the Mercury shutter in a camera doing long-running studies of solar phenomena.[96]

The camera's picture format was "half frame," again facilitating Universal's marketing strategy of selling short lengths of film in large quantities. The film was supplied in either 18- or 36-exposure lengths, and was spooled on a special metal spool having a small gear on the bottom flange. When the film had been run through the camera, this spool then became the take-up spool, thus relieving the manufacturer of the task of loading a cassette or magazine.

Universal's manufacturing system was as unique as most of its cameras. Avoiding large capital investments, Githens and Shapiro contracted out almost all of their manufacturing operations to small specialty shops in the metropolitan area. The cast, stamped, or machined parts were shipped to

Universal's home factory at 28 West Twenty-Third Street for assembly.[97]

The one exception to this scheme was lens production. Initially, Universal imported lenses for the UniveX Model A and other early still cameras. When the Ciné-8 was launched, Universal decided to switch to domestic sources. Wollensak Optical and Ilex, both in Rochester, New York, became regular suppliers. When those companies could no longer keep up with Universal's burgeoning requirements, the company began to consider "vertical integration," i.e., making lenses in-house. In 1937 a study was begun on the technology of lens production. Two years later, Universal opened its own optical shop on one floor of the loft building on West Twenty-Third Street.

Here again George Kende was the leading figure in this endeavor, developing and introducing many innovative methods of lens production, which permitted unheard-of rates of production of high quality optics. These methods became of great importance when Universal secured a contract to supply binoculars for the U.S. and Allied armed forces. Production of military binoculars began on January 1, 1942. By war's end Universal was turning out 1,500 units per month, believed to be at least six times the combined production rate of all other American producing firms.

The wartime contracts came at a crucial moment in Universal's history. When Hitler's Wehrmacht overran Poland and threatened the Low Countries, Gevaert of Belgium was forced to suspend all shipments of film, leaving thousands of Universal's customers without film for their cameras. Dealers could not sell cameras for which there was not a reliable source of film. Universal's sales for 1940 fell 42 percent from the previous year. The company finished the year with a $125,000 deficit.[98]

The obvious solution to the unavailability of Universal's special film would be to design and introduce new cameras taking standard film, at the time still available from domestic suppliers. This is the course that Universal took, for both still and movie cameras.

Three new movie cameras were introduced in the summer of 1941, called the Cinemaster line, all three of which could accept either Universal's single 8 or standard double 8. This move also enabled the

UniveX moviemaker to shoot in Kodachrome, which had been available for other movie cameras since 1936.

The three models were the D-8 "Standard," an economy model with a half-inch Ilex Univar f/6.3 lens, selling for $15.95; the E-8 "Special" which incorporated an extinction meter, three filming speeds, and a variety of lenses; and the F-8 "Jewel." The latter was priced as top-of-the-line, but was simply the Model E with some chrome trim added. Before many of these models could be sold, Universal stopped all work on consumer products to convert entirely to production of binoculars for the Government.

Post-War

With the end of World War II and the military contracts, Universal sought the fastest way to get back into the civilian market. The course chosen was to resurrect pre-war models, with minimum tooling changes required. Typical of this strategy was the Cinemaster II Model G-8, which was essentially the pre-war F-8 with some very minor mechanical modifications, but a substantial price adjustment. While the F-8 was priced with an f/3.5 Universal lens at $32.50, the G-8 was priced at $51.90. Similar price advances were made in the projector line, with the result that Universal no longer held the substantial price advantage over its competitors that it had pre-war. Keystone, for one, marketed an 8mm line at almost exactly Universal's prices.

Universal's last movie camera was the Cinemaster H-8, introduced in January 1951, made for standard double 8 only. By this time, UniveX single-8 film stocks were exhausted, so there was no longer any need for the dual-8 capability that had been a feature of UniveX cameras since 1941. It is not known how many of these cameras were produced, but Repinski describes them as being "extremely rare."

The Cinemaster II line was introduced just as a series of misfortunes descended on Universal, starting with a C.I.O.[99] strike in August 1946 against New York Merchandise, Universal's landlord and parent company. While the strike was not directed against Universal, picketing and general harassment managed to disrupt Universal's operations to a considerable extent.

Of much greater impact was a strike against the area die-casting shops, shutting down one of Universal's major suppliers and halting shipments of all cameras and projectors. When the die-casters went back to work, Universal evidently rushed assembly operations attempting to catch up on outstanding dealer orders. This undoubtedly led to some malfunctioning products, a situation that was exacerbated by another problem that was not in the least Universal's fault.

Two of Universal's still-camera lines featured cameras with synthetic leather coverings on the camera bodies. Unbeknownst to Universal, the company supplying the adhesive for these coverings had changed the adhesive formula and failed to field-test it. It turned out that the new adhesive was unstable when heated, with the horrifying result that cameras that were exposed to any elevated temperatures in shipping, or in a display window, for example, were soon covered with oozing adhesive and curling "leather." Even though Universal quickly set up arrangements to clean and repair all the damaged cameras, the effect on customers, prospective customers, and dealers can well be imagined.

Adding to all of these problems was a serious miscalculation on Universal's part of the marketability of a radical miniature camera design launched in November 1949 called the Minute-16 (Fig. 216). This was an ultraminiature camera, perhaps conceived to compete with the German-made Minox or the several other ultraminiatures that were on the market at that time. It was designed for a daylight-loading cartridge of 16mm film, to take 14 exposures of 11mm by 14mm size.

Fig. 216. The Minute 16.

Unfortunately, several things conspired to produce a marketing disaster. First, the camera design included an erratic shutter, a mediocre lens, and a film advance that caused frequent jamming. Secondly, finding processing laboratories for the miniature negatives was not easy, as few processors were equipped for this size film. The Minute-16 was not George Kende's design, that gentleman having resigned from Universal in December of 1948.

The company had sunk over two million dollars in the development of the Minute-16, including several large bank loans, some secured by inventory of the new camera. When projected sales did not materialize and the loans came due, the company found itself in serious trouble. On June 24, 1952, Universal was declared bankrupt, and two bankruptcy sales were held in short order.

Curiously, a new Universal Camera Corporation, backed by two mysterious investors from Vermont, arose as a short-lived phoenix, with headquarters at 175 Fifth Avenue and a plant in North Adams, Massachusetts. Only one product emerged from this new corporation, the Universal Stere-All Camera, a stereo camera and the last product to bear the Universal name. The camera did not sell to expectations. On January 5, 1960, a public auction of all of Universal's equipment and machinery was held at the North Adams site, and the plant closed for good, with no forwarding address for Universal left at the post office.

Regardless what one may think of Universal's products or of the ethics of its principals, the fact remains that the UniveX Cine-8 induced many thousands to try taking movies who otherwise might never have thought to do so. More than a few now-sophisticated moviemakers will admit that their first movie camera was that little $9.95 machine and that it is remembered with affection.

The Revere Camera Company

Sam Briskin was a penniless Russian Jewish youth when he arrived in Chicago. His first job was repairing automobile radiators. Before long he owned the business and turned it into the nation's largest builder of replacement radiators for clients such as Sears Roebuck & Co. At a son's bar mitzvah, he observed a man taking movies and inquired how much he had paid for the camera. When told, he exclaimed "Hell, I can make a better cam-

Fig. 217. Sam Briskin.

era for less." And when he sold his camera company some years later, he pocketed $17 million dollars.[100] (See Fig. 217.)

The above capsule biography of Samuel Briskin was related to me by an executive of Bell & Howell Co., who had known Sam Briskin well. Until recently, that was almost all that was known of this brilliant entrepreneur and the two highly successful companies that he founded. Fortunately for historians, Briskin's son-in-law, Mr. Fred Pellar, graciously shared with the author his vivid memories of the Revere Camera Company, where he served from 1945 to 1960 as Vice-President, Production Manager, and Director of Purchasing.

Samuel Briskin was born in Russia about 1890, and while the date of his arrival in this country is uncertain, it is known that soon after his arrival he married Bessie Prosk. Their first two children died in infancy, circa 1918. There followed Rosalee in 1919, Philip in 1920, Jack in 1921, and Theodore in 1922.

Briskin's first job was in a scrap metal yard; he subsequently joined another man in a radiator repair business, soon bought out his partner, and founded the Excel Auto Radiator Company in 1920. This company, as noted above, became the leader in its field, supplying Sears Roebuck & Company, Montgomery Ward, and Western Auto. The company also made automobile heaters, household fans, and portable electric drills. With the main plant in Chicago, sub-assembly plants were established in Boston, Buffalo, Los Angeles, Minneapolis, and St. Louis.

By 1938, Sam Briskin was a millionaire with a thriving company, and three sons in their mid- to late-teens. Looking about for new fields to conquer, he founded the camera company, as related in the introductory anecdote. Another anecdote relates how the company got its name. During the depression, Briskin found it very difficult to get copper and brass for his radiator business. The only company that would extend him credit and metal was the Revere Copper Company. In gratitude for that help, Briskin named the camera company after his faithful supplier.

The Briskin sons quite literally took an active interest in the new camera company; Briskin gave them each a one-third interest, after keeping a five-percent interest for himself. He also continued the Excel Auto Radiator Company, with Fred Pellar in charge of operations, for another ten years; eventually tiring of it, he sold off the physical plant and absorbed the employees into Revere.

Revere's first product, introduced in 1939, was an unusual camera, the Revere "Super Eight," designed to take pre-split 8mm film, instead of the standard double 8mm format introduced by Eastman Kodak in 1932. Pre-split, or "single 8," enjoyed a brief popularity at this time, before being abandoned by all but Universal Camera Corporation.

The first listing of the Revere Camera Company in the Cook County Industrial Directory is for the year 1940. Theodore Briskin is listed as president, a surprising position for an 18-year old. The company address was given as 33 North LaSalle, Chicago.

The company was well established by 1940; a full-page advertisement in the May issue of *Popular Photography* listed branch offices in Philadelphia, Kansas City, Minneapolis, Los Angeles, and Dallas. The same ad showed that a conventional double-8 camera, the Model 88, had been added, as well as an 8mm silent projector. The Model 88 camera bore a very strong resemblance to the Bell & Howell "Companion" 8mm in design and construction, but was priced at $29.50, whereas the Companion sold for $49.50. The Revere projector was priced at $59.50, comparable to a contemporary Eastman Kodak pro-

jector, but half the price of Bell & Howell's lowest priced 8mm projector. Sam Briskin would appear to have made good on his boast.

As the country prepared for war in 1941, Revere's production machinery, as with other camera manufacturers, was well suited for military goods and defense-related products. The company became a major sub-contractor to defense contractors such as Grumman, Lear Aircraft, and Collins Radio. Products included wing actuators, screw machine parts, and small precision gears.

These contracts kept Revere 100 percent in government work for several years after hostilities ceased, during which time the company could not sell civilian goods. In 1948, Sam ordered the company to produce 25,000 8-mm cameras, and 25,000 8mm projectors. When the government finally released Revere later that year from its contracts, the company was able to flood its dealers with new cameras and projectors. At this time, four 8mm cameras were offered, ranging in price from $77.50 to $187.50, and four 16mm models were available, both lines included cameras with magazine loading and lens turret models (Fig. 218).

The post-war years were a period of rapid growth for Revere. The July 1948 issue of Fortune carried a story on Bell & Howell entitled "Elegant Bell & Howell." Within that story was the following passage:

Fig. 218. Revere Model 44 8mm.

The war has drastically altered the complexion of the motion-picture-equipment industry, and Bell & Howell may have to abandon its stately pace. Where there were less than half a dozen consequential producers before, there are now more than fifteen, and obstreperous Sam Briskin has given the old-time outfits a rude shock. His Revere Camera Co. is advertising like mad and flooding the market with low-priced, slick-looking, and entirely satisfactory cameras and projectors. If it continues its spectacular growth it may even displace Bell & Howell as the largest dollar volume producer. [101]

Earlier in the article, the authors listed Eastman Kodak, Ampro, Revere, and Keystone among Bell & Howell's major competitors, with good products and generally lower prices, but estimated that Bell & Howell outsold all but Revere and Keystone on a unit basis.

By 1952, according to a dated catalog of company products, Sam Briskin was Chairman of the Board, and the company was producing cameras, silent and sound projectors, electric drills, and tape recorders. The company occupied a large eight story main plant and office building, and four satellite plants.

A second eight-story building was subsequently added, with 20,000 square feet of space on each floor. Revere had almost totally integrated its production processes, making all major components except die-castings. The total plant included: optical shop, screw machine shop, plating and painting shop, punch press shop, and assembly shops for cameras, projectors, motors, amplifiers and tape recorders. At its heyday, Revere employed as many as 1,500 people (Fig. 219).

Fig. 219. The Revere Factory.

Sam was very proud of his operation. One of his friendly competitors related the following:

Sam was always inviting me over to see his latest acquisition: on one occasion, a lens grinding machine from Germany. He grinned at me "You people have to go through committees, have meetings, make studies; me, I see a machine I like, I buy it!" [102]

The "obstreperous" Sam Briskin may well have influenced Bell & Howell's marketing strategies, for in 1953 that company introduced 8mm cameras and projectors at prices 40 percent below any previous cameras in the company's history. The same year, Bell & Howell acquired the Three Dimension Company, whose product line included high quality tape recorders.

The latter move could not have escaped Sam Briskin's notice, who had been selling tape recorders since 1952 or possibly earlier. While Revere products were very well built, with solid construction, good finish and good style, Briskin may have felt that the Revere name still carried the stigma of Sam Briskin's humble beginnings. Perhaps it was simply a matter of controlling his sources—he had but one supplier of lenses; but in any event, in 1953 he took a major step—he purchased the Wollensak Optical Company of Rochester, New York. [103]

The purchase was effected in typical Briskin fashion. Sam's lawyer was a gentleman named Sam Rosenthal, who was on a ship bound for Europe one day when a cablegram was delivered to him. The cable was from Sam Briskin, advising Rosenthal that Briskin had just made a deal for the purchase of the Wollensak Optical Company and that Rosenthal was to return at once to Chicago to take care of the details. Aside from having had no prior knowledge of the Wollensak deal, Rosenthal's chagrin at having his trip interrupted may be imagined, but he reportedly took it all with equanimity. [104]

Wollensak Optical was founded in 1899, when Andrew and John Wollensak left the employ of the famed Bausch and Lomb Company to found a company to manufacture a line of high quality shutters to be sold at a reasonable price. In a short time the brothers added lenses to their product line, and in time the firm became a major supplier of high quality lenses and shutters for amateur and professional still cameras. Wollensak also sold lenses to many of the smaller motion picture equipment makers. [105] A

Fig. 220. Revere 16mm turret camera, Model 38.

Fig. 221. Revere DeLuxe Long Play Tape Recorder.

1968 catalogue listed over 750 stock lens designs, with focal lengths ranging from 3.4 millimeters to 330 inches (Fig. 220).

The takeover was entirely amicable; Revere financed a large-scale expansion and modernization of the Wollensak plant, including the installation of elevators. The product line of Fastax cameras was extended and a line of catadioptric lenses added. Ed Springer was president of Wollensak at that time.

The second part of Sam Briskin's strategy appeared in 1953, when a line of "Wollensak" 8 and 16mm cameras appeared—actually manufactured in Chicago by Revere, but carrying the Wollensak name. The 1953 *Popular Photography Directory* issue, which of course was prepared in late 1952, had listed 11 different Revere 8mm camera models, most of which had at least two lens options, presenting the buyer with 21 camera choices ranging in price from $50 to $168.

The 1954 *Directory*, prepared in 1953, listed the same 11 Revere models, plus four different "Wollensak" models. The latter were essentially duplicates of four Revere models in features, but carried prices from 20 percent to 50 percent higher than the equivalent Revere model. The same scheme was reportedly applied to tape recorders.

While 21 camera choices would seem to have covered the low-to-moderate price market, the introduction of equipment carrying the respected Wollensak name was intended to chip away at Bell & Howell's "elite" or upper-class market. Most people tend to believe that a higher-priced machine is a better machine, even without the salesman telling them so.

By 1960, Sam Briskin's health was failing—he was to die of cancer within a year. As noted in Chapter 5, the United States market for 8mm cameras had peaked in 1958, declining steadily at about 6 percent per year for the next five years. For these and possibly other reasons, Sam Briskin decided to sell Revere. The Minnesota Mining and Manufacturing Company was the buyer, and the price was variously reported to be $17 to $25 million.

Revere at this time was selling 150,000 tape recorders per year and was one of the 3M Tape Division's biggest customers.[106] (See Fig. 221.) The acquisition would seem to have been ideal; it gave 3M a ready-made entry into the booming tape recorder business, and the Wollensak lens and shutter expertise was just what 3M needed for its Microfilm Division.

In contrast to Revere's benevolent treatment of Wollensak, the purchase by 3M was traumatic for both Revere and the old-line Rochester firm. A series of events, some of them clearly mismanagement decisions by 3M and some beyond its control, brought about the eventual demise of both acquired companies. The 1960s saw the death of Wollensak's 8mm ciné lens business as integral optics were adopted by camera manufacturers. The same period as noted above saw the steady decline in the domestic 8mm camera market. As Wollensak sales flagged, 3M sent in its own management, but to no avail, and in 1969 Wollensak was sold to a venture capital group which moved the company to East Rochester and then shortly closed it down. A very limited line of simple Super 8 cameras was marketed by the Revere Division of 3M until about 1971.

The Wollensak name lives on: a Rochester entrepreneur purchased the name, engineering drawings, trademarks, and patents in 1975, after the Wollensak company had changed hands several times. Rudolph Novak had been an employee of Wollensak before leaving to found the Anson Instrument Corporation, manufacturers of optical equipment and photographic lenses. Novak, with a cadre of skilled optical craftsmen, was the right person to rescue the old company name. After the purchase, Novak changed the name of his company to Wollensak Optical Company; under which name it continues in business today, in a building that once belonged to the original Wollensak Company.[107]

The Briskin name lives on in a way. On one of my shelves of cameras is a pretty little 8mm magazine camera, possibly covered in real alligator hide, with a 13mm f/1.9 Wollensak lens. The name of the camera is The Briskin 8, "Manufactured by the Briskin Camera Corporation of Santa Monica, California." This company was the brainchild of Ted Briskin. Some time around 1950, Ted tired of life in Chicago, and moved to Hollywood. Reputed to have been extremely handsome, he met and married movie star and singer Betty Hutton, known as "the Blonde Bombshell," sold his interest in Revere back to the Company, and founded the Briskin Camera Company.

Unfortunately, neither the marriage nor the business survived for long; he and Ms. Hutton were divorced in 1952, the Briskin Camera Company went into bankruptcy, and Ted moved back to Chicago. None of the Briskins survive today.

Revere managed to hang on as a subsidiary of 3M into the early 1970s, by which time the Japanese invasion of the U.S. market had forced all domestic manufacturers but Bell & Howell and Eastman Kodak to close down or sell their camera businesses. It must be recorded that the 3M Company declares that all of its records pertaining to the Revere Camera Company acquisition have been destroyed, a sad commentary on the corporate sense of responsibility to history.[108] Such practice is all too common; much of America's industrial and corporate history is rapidly disappearing.

The amateur motion picture industry gave employment and enjoyment to thousands of people. For nearly three decades Sam Briskin's Revere Camera Company was a vigorous and respected member of that industry. Sam was quirky, aggressive, demanding, but withal likable and wise; his son-in-law worshipped him. No less than Charles Percy, chairman of Bell & Howell, valued his advice. It is a pleasure to place a small part of his life and achievements on the record.

16mm Kodachrome movie film.

Mr. Eastman's Dream

Possibly no other aspect of motion picture technology has spawned as many inventions as the effort to add color to the projected image. Brian Coe's incomparable book on the history of movie photography lists no less than 52 separate color processes devised between 1896 and 1935.[1]

Historically speaking, there are two distinct types of color processes: "additive," and "subtractive." An additive process is one in which there is no color in the film itself, but the desired colors are given to the projected image by interposing colored filters in the light path. A subtractive process is one in which the unwanted colors are removed from the light beam, usually by interposing filters that have selective absorption. All additive processes by their nature absorb more light than any subtractive process.

All modern films, i.e. Kodachrome, Ektachrome, Fujichrome, etc., are of the subtractive type, while the additive types were represented by Lumière's autochromes, the 1928 Kodacolor, and various other early movie color systems. All of the latter were characterized by having a rapacious appetite for light: both for exposure and for projection.

Most of the 52 processes described by Coe were but minor variants of the two basic processes, and many barely got past the conception state. Those that had some commercial success can all be placed in one of four types, as follows:

- Hand-colored, tinted, or toned, all additive.
- Bi-color additive, with external filters
- Mosaic or color screen, additive.
- Bi-color subtractive (principally Technicolor, four varieties).

This chapter will discuss the handful of processes that achieved a significant market, either in amateur or professional use.

Hand-Colored, Tinted, or Toned

Quite possibly the first exhibition of a color motion picture took place in London, on April 8, 1896. On that date, Robert W. Paul, the British inventor of the Theatrograph,[2] showed a brief color film entitled *Eastern Dance* at the Alhambra Theatre. The method of production was at once ridiculously simple in concept, and staggeringly laborious in execution—hand-coloring each frame. In an interview given shortly after the showing, Paul was quoted as follows:

Very nearly a thousand photographs go to form one picture; and so the immense difficulty of procuring coloured pictures will be apparent. The colours have to be very carefully chosen, and then every photograph has to be painted, with the aid of a magnifying glass, in identical tints. The photographs are about the size of a postage stamp and the work of colouring them occupies nearly three weeks—greatly increasing the cost of the exhibition, of course. But on the other hand, the coloured pictures give a remarkable fillip to the entertainment, and proved to be worth all the trouble and expense of preparation.[3]

As the Theatrograph was known to operate at 16 frames per second, *Eastern Dance* could have only lasted about one minute, nonetheless it was extremely popular, and Paul produced several other short colored films. It was reported in the press later that year that "Kinescopic (sic) images are being coloured by female labour at an average of forty shillings per hundred pictures."[4]

That hand coloring had certain risks was wittily noted by Henry Hopwood, writing in 1899:

Colouring is sometimes added; on this subject special words of caution are necessary. In an ordinary single lantern slide outline is of little moment, in a Living Picture it is everything. A spire of a church in the single view does not offend the eye if the colouring oversteps the proper outline, provided that the shape is rendered symmetrical. Far other in a Living Picture. The slightest variation between successive views gives rise to a continuous bulging and contraction which no respectable church would allow its steeple to indulge in.[5]

Pathé Frères appears to have been the next producer to essay colored pictures, using a stencil process that had been developed for coloring post cards. In this method, a number of prints were prepared, each of which would become a stencil, one for each color to be used. Each stencil film was passed through a viewing/cutting machine, along with a master print of the film, which was projected on a viewing screen. The operator moved a pointer over the image, outlining the areas in each frame to be colored, while a pantograph mechanism with a vibrating needle cut the stencil film. As many as 300 young women might be employed at this task.

A clear print was then mated with each stencil in turn and run through a dyeing machine, where dye was applied to the print through the holes in the stencil. This was repeated for each color.

Preparing the stencils was a slow and thus costly process, but once the stencil was made, prints could be run off at high speed. A minimum of 200 prints was required to make the process profitable. The resulting films were quite satisfactory, and the Pathéchrome process continued in use into the 1930s.

A somewhat related process was developed in the 1920s by Max Handschiegl and Alvin Wycoff in which, in effect, stencils were created photographically. This process, which does not seem to have received a name, was used in Cecil B. DeMille's 1917 film *Joan, The Woman* and in King Vidor's *Big Parade*, which ran for 96 weeks on Broadway in 1925 and grossed over $5,500,000.[6]

Many early films shot in black and white were given color by a process called tinting, in which segments of the positive print were dyed in a bath of color, chosen to fit either the mood, or to relate to a specific dramatic situation. A forest fire would turn the screen red, an approaching storm would be signaled by darkening skies, followed by a warm yellow glow as the sun reappeared.[7]

When optical sound arrived circa 1927, dyeing the film tended to obscure the optical sound track. To overcome the problem, Eastman Kodak Company introduced "Sonochrome," an assortment of colored stocks whose colors did not interfere with the optical sound track bearing such exotic names as *Inferno, Rose Dawn, Peach Blow,* etc. Use of such tinted stocks continued well into the 1960s.

"Toning" was a process known for years to still photographers, to give normally black or gray areas of a print a different color. Whereas tinting would affect only the light (i.e., silver-free) areas, the dark areas (i.e., with silver) could be given color by treatment with appropriate chemicals. An iron compound would yield a blue-green silver salt, a sulfur toner would produce a sepia tone, and uranium salts gave a reddish tone.

It was not uncommon for all of the foregoing techniques to be applied in a single film. One of the more spectacular applications of tinting and toning in one film was presented by Abel Gance in his 1927 over four-hour epic, *Napoleon*. In this film, Gance not only used tinting and toning at various points to enhance the military drama being played out on the screen, but also introduced a revolutionary three-screen process with which he anticipated Cinerama by 25 years.

The three-screen process as accomplished by Gance, involved filming with three cameras and projecting with three projectors on a triptych of screens. All three projectors could be projecting portions of the same scene, spread across three screens, or one could be projecting a principal scene on the center screen with supporting, but different, views on the flanking screens.

In the final scene of *Napoleon*, Gance projected a heroic close-up of Bonaparte on the center screen while his ragged but victorious troops marched by on either side. Gradually the left screen turned red, the center stayed white, the right screen turned blue, until the entire screen became the glorious tricolor of the French national flag. As the accompanying orchestra blared out the Marseilles, the audience, French of course, rose shouting and cheering in patriotic ecstasy.[8]

Bi-Color Additive Processes

True color cinematography could not reach the screen until emulsions were produced which would record a reasonably broad spectrum of colors. Early photosensitive materials were sensitive only to the shorter wavelengths: ultraviolet, violet, and blue. This meant that daguerreotypes, dry collodion plates, and gelatin silver bromide photographs would show little tonal difference between red and green objects.

In 1873, Dr. H. W. Vogel, a brilliant German photographic chemist, with the aid of a small spectrograph, discovered the power of various synthetic dyes to sensitize silver halides, a phenomenon he called optical sensitizing.[9] Other workers followed Dr. Vogel's lead, eventually resulting in films with sensitivity to all visible colors.

Sir Isaac Newton was the first scientist to observe in the mid-1600s that white light was composed of all colors; it was another 200 years before James Clerk Maxwell (1831-1879) the Scottish polymath, demonstrated the synthesis of colors by the use of colored filters. His description of his experiment is as follows:

Three photographs of a coloured ribbon taken through three coloured solutions, respectively, were introduced into the lantern, giving images representing the red, the green, and the blue parts separately, as they would be seen by Young's three sets of nerves, respectively. When these were superposed, a coloured image was seen, which, if the red and green images had been as fully photographed as the blue, would have been a truly coloured image of the ribbon. By finding photographic materials more sensitive to the less refrangible rays, the representation of the colours of objects might be greatly improved.[10]

His reference to "Young's three sets of nerves" is interesting; Thomas Young, (1773-1829) a British physician and scientist, was an infant prodigy who could read at age two and who had read through the Bible twice by the time he was four. Young was intensely interested in sense perception and vision. He was the first to propose that the retina might have separate sensors for the three primary colors.[11]

In 1899, two British workers, F. Marshall Lee and Edward R. Turner, obtained a patent for a camera fitted with a rotating filter wheel before the lens, having red, green, and blue filters. Each rotation of the filter wheel produced three adjacent frames, which recorded the proportions of these colors in the scene. The projector was equipped with three lenses, focused and aimed to the same point, and a segmented three-color filter wheel, so timed that while each frame was projected three times, the proper color segment was always in front of it (Fig. 222).

As ingenious as it sounds, the system did not perform very well and was never operated commercially. On the death of Turner, the patents were purchased by Charles Urban, who hired George Albert Smith, a British photographer and experimenter, to continue work on the idea. A breakthrough came in 1906 when either Urban or Smith discovered that quite satisfactory results could be had by simply using two colored filters, red and green. The system was dubbed Kinemacolor.

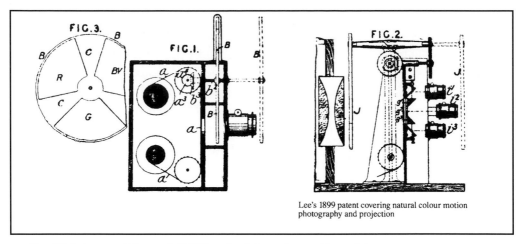

Fig. 222. Lee and Turner's 1899 patent for color motion pictures.

Ramsaye, whose classic 1925 history of the motion picture *A Million and One Nights*, is notorious for a certain cavalier attitude toward facts, relates that the two-color idea came to Urban while on a visit to Paris. According to Ramsaye, Urban was accosted by a street vendor on the Champs-Elyseé and bought two "naughty" French postcards. Both cards were transparent, one red and one green. Viewed separately they presented some innocuous scenery; when overlaid and held to the light, they revealed "not scenery, but *obscenery*."

The first public performance of the new process was a presentation to the Royal Society of the Arts, on December 9, 1908, and the first commercial showing was in February 1909 at the Palace Theatre in London.

The new system went from triumph to triumph. British newspapers gave it rave reviews, and showings were given at the Folies Bergères in Paris, the Berlin Winter Garden, and Madison Square Garden in New York in December 1909.

The most ambitious Kinemacolor undertaking was Urban's decision to film the visit of King George V and Queen Mary to India in 1911, where the King was installed as King-Emperor. For this project, Urban took six of his best cameramen and exposed nearly six hours worth of negative. Back in London, Urban had a reproduction of the Taj Mahal built as a set in the Scala Theatre and special music written to be performed by a 48-piece orchestra.

The opening performance, given in two parts, was a brilliant success, and Urban quickly put five road shows out in the country. For some reason,

possibly intervention of the infamous Motion Picture Patents Company, Kinemacolor was not successful in the United States.

The success of Kinemacolor inevitably led to imitators and innovators, including several revivals of the failed Lee-and-Turner system, some of which achieved modest success. However, all multilens and filter systems were burdened with the inescapable fact that the melding of the two or three separate images into one invariably led to some degree of color fringing, particularly around objects moving at high speed.

Two variants of the two-color additive process were made available to the amateur. The first, announced in 1928, was called Vitacolor and was the invention of Max B. Du Pont of Hollywood, California. The only description of this system known to this author is an account in the December 1928 issue of *Movie Makers*, and is a remarkable example of how to write several hundred words about a process apparently without having the slightest understanding of the topic. The only understandable statements in the entire article are that the system used filters and that it was available in 16mm as well as 35mm film.

The second process was announced in the July 1932 issue of *Filmo Topics*, Bell & Howell's consumer magazine, and was called "Morgana Color." Alternate frames were "photographed through complimentary color filters, and projected in the same manner." No other information is available on the process, but presumably it was similar to Kinemacolor. Perhaps the most interesting feature of the process is the fact that it was invented by a member of the British nobility, one Lady Juliet Williams, who revealed that the idea came to her on a visit to Hollywood and that she worked seven years to bring it to fruition. Bell & Howell made a special model of the Filmo, designated the Filmo AC, to incorporate the special mechanisms involved. It is not known if any examples of this camera exist (Figs. 223 and 224).

Mosaic or Color-Screen Processes

A system that avoided the use of multiple lenses (or used conventional lenses at least) or multiple frames, was devised by the Alsatian Albert Keller-Dorian in 1908 and made operational by Keller-Dorian's associate R. Berthon in 1922. The process began with the embossing of a series of fine cylindrical ridges, 22 per millimeter, running lengthwise on the back of the film support. The film was threaded into the camera with the ridges facing the lens, which was covered with a tri-color filter (Fig. 225).

The ridges, acting as lenses, create minute images of the tri-color filter on the emulsion. When the film has been reversal processed, a monochrome film results, but when threaded through the projector equipped with an identical tri-color filter, a color image appears on the screen.

The rights to the K-D-B process, as it was known, were purchased by Eastman Kodak in 1925 and a development program begun under the direction of J. G. Capstaff. The impetus for this program appears to have come from George Eastman himself. In a remarkable letter written while he was on his way to his first African safari in 1926, Eastman described to Frank W. Lovejoy, his second-in-command, a dream that he had had, in which C.E.K. Mees had come across a new full-color process of movie photography which could easily be used by amateurs. Eastman went on to describe the process, how the film was to be manufactured and marketed, and forecast enthusiastic reception by consumers, and a run on film, cameras, and projectors.[12]

Since all authorities assert that the company had acquired rights to the process the year before, this "dream" may just have been Eastman's way of impressing his management team of his strong desire to see the program come to fruition.

To make the process commercially viable, a number of obstacles had to be overcome, including the

Fig. 223. Bell & Howell Model 70 camera modified for the Morgana Color.

Fig. 224. Lady Juliet Williams.

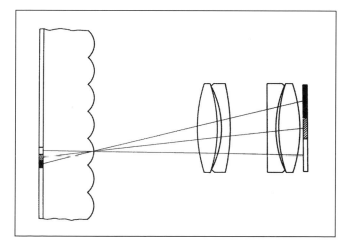
Fig. 225. Schematic showing the embossed film and tricolor filter in the Berthon process.

development of an emulsion which would be sensitive to red and green, a standardized embossing procedure, and the design of suitable optics, all of which were achieved in a remarkably short time.[13]

Kodacolor, as it was christened, was offered to the public in 1928. Mr. Eastman was so proud of the product and the company's achievement that he staged an elaborate party to celebrate the introduction. Invited to his mansion on East Avenue were Thomas Edison, General John J. "Black Jack" Pershing, Commander-in-Chief of the American Expeditionary Force of World War I, (a "Norman Schwartzkopf" of the day), Adolph Ochs, founder and publisher of The New York Times, and other notables of the time.

The guests were assembled in Eastman's rose garden, whose plants were in full flower, where a Ciné-Kodak Model B was loaded with the new film and passed among the guests, who were invited to try their hand at filming the colorful scene. After a sumptuous luncheon, the hastily developed film was shown to the company, to universal admiration of the remarkable fidelity of the colors. This gathering led to the oft-reproduced photo of George Eastman and Thomas Edison, both looking quite somber, apparently examining a professional camera and a length of 35mm film. What that had to do with the introduction of a 16mm color film is unknown.

Kodacolor film, when properly exposed and projected, produced very acceptable results and was on the market until displaced by the introduction of Kodachrome film in 1935. However, most amateurs continued to favor black and white.[14] This was probably due to two factors: the considerable loss of light incurred by the tri-color filter, which was quite dark, and the necessity of careful adjustment of the projector.

Exposure had to be made in full sunlight, with the lens wide open at f/1.7. Because of the non-circular construction of the color filter, a normal circular-aperture iris would decrease the edge bands disproportionately to the central band, so neutral density filters were provided for extremely bright situations. The projector had to be equipped with a special projecting lens and special condensing lens, each designed for the particular projector.

One further curious precaution had to be taken by the filmmaker using Kodacolor film. Since each batch of emulsion differed slightly in color sensitivity, a compensating, or ratio, diaphragm was enclosed with each roll of film. This diaphragm was designed to fit over the color filter and, with its peculiarly shaped opening, would mask each of the filter bands to compensate for the particular color response of the batch of film from which that roll came. The diaphragm was of course discarded once that roll of film was exposed.

Under Capstaff's direction, Eastman Kodak studied the application of the K-D-B process to 35mm and gave a demonstration to the Society of Motion Picture Engineers in 1936, but the process was never accepted commercially. Among other drawbacks, duplicates could only be made with great difficulty.[15]

Eastman Kodak's 1925 agreement with Keller-Dorian evidently called for Kodak to promote the use of the process in commercial cinematography. Despite Kodak's efforts in that direction, in 1948 the Keller-Dorian Color Film Corporation filed suit against Kodak, claiming the latter concern had failed to fulfill this obligation. The courts rejected the Keller-Dorian claims, and the suit was settled in Kodak's favor a few years later.

Technicolor

The first motion picture color process to achieve widespread and continual usage grew out of an association of two Massachusetts Institute of Technology graduates, Herbert T. Kalmus and Daniel F. Comstock. Both had gained their Ph.D. degrees, and Kalmus (1881-1963) had become an instructor in physics at that institution. Both men were interested in cinematography and photographic chemistry.[16] In 1913, they were joined by W. Burton Westcott in the formation of a consulting firm, Kalmus, Comstock and Westcott, organized to "provide research and development for industry."

The company's first product was a two-color additive system, centered around a camera developed by Comstock which could photograph a scene in two colors on two separate films simultaneously through one lens, by use of a prism. In projection, the two films were projected through one lens. The system was shown in operation to William D. Coolidge, a Boston lawyer, who was so impressed by the results that he advanced the young firm $10,000 to exploit their idea. It evidently seemed prudent to incorporate, so The Technicolor Motion

Picture Corporation was formed in 1915, named in honor of the alma mater of two of the founders.

After a year or so of refinement of the process and construction of what was undoubtedly the world's first, and perhaps only, traveling movie film laboratory, the partners were ready to produce their first film. The laboratory, built in a made-over railroad car, contained every piece of equipment necessary to process film: laboratory, darkrooms, fireproof safes, power plant, and offices. Behind the lab car was another special car to house the cast and crew.

In 1916, the company set off for Jacksonville, Florida, where the film, *The Gulf Between*, was to be shot. The production crew included Dr. Kalmus, his wife Natalie, Comstock, Westcott, and two new colleagues, J. A. Ball, cinematographer, and Professor E. J. Wall.

The film was finished in 1917 and shown privately in September, when it was adjudged to be superior to any other system then in use. There was one big problem—if the two films were not kept in perfect register, serious "fringing" would result. Nevertheless, Kalmus had great hopes for his process, and made arrangements to show the film one week each in several large cities. However, after "one terrible night in Buffalo" during which the films just could not be brought into register, the two-color additive process was abandoned.

The second process developed by Technicolor was a two-color subtractive process, which used a single-lens camera with a prism as before, but modified to advance the film two frames at a time. Thus two images were photographed simultaneously, one above the other, one through a red filter and one through a green filter. The negative was then printed on two separate positive films, one for each color, on film with a special thin base supplied by Eastman Kodak Company. The exposed prints were processed to form relief images on the gelatin layer and the silver removed. The two relief images were welded together in register, back-to-back, and the composite film floated over dye baths, red on one side, green on the other. Dr. Leonard T. Troland, Research Director for Technicolor, was largely responsible for this process.[17]

With a promising new process in hand, Technicolor needed financial help, which arrived in the person of Judge William Travers Jerome, a financier with connections. According to Jerome, he had been asked to investigate Technicolor and was so impressed with what he saw that he brought in Marcus Loew, Nicholas M. Schenck, and Joseph M. Schenck. At that time, Marcus Loew was head of Metro Pictures, soon to become MGM, Nicholas Schenck was Loew's second-in-command, while Joseph Schenck was doing very well as an independent producer, later to become chairman of 20th Century Fox.[18]

Marcus Loew committed Metro to produce a feature film named *The Toll of the Sea*, starring Anna May Wong, using the new Technicolor process. The movie was filmed in Hollywood, with the negatives being shipped back to Boston for processing. Technicolor had not then opened a lab in Hollywood. When eventually released in 1923, the picture grossed more than $250,000, of which Technicolor received approximately $160,000.[19]

The film was highly praised by the industry, including the actor Douglas Fairbanks, Sr., and others, which resulted in a contract being signed between Technicolor and Famous Players Lasky for a number of features, which ultimately included *Ben Hur* and *The Black Pirate*. The latter film scored high in audience reaction, press reviews and box office, but the new process brought some new problems.

Having emulsion coating on both sides caused the film to distort under the heat of projection, resulting in "cupping," which threw the picture out of focus and meant the projectionist had to keep adjusting the focus. Furthermore, the film tended to scratch readily, and the scratches were quite visible on the screen. All this meant that films were constantly being shipped back to Boston for repair and replacement films shipped to the distributors.

The problem was so severe that in 1925 one major distributor refused to take any more Technicolor prints, not only because of the quality problems, but also because Technicolor's film price was too high. Technicolor had managed to reduce its film cost considerably, which at one time was over 25 cents per foot, but the distributors wanted something in the neighborhood of eight cents. It was clear that a new process was needed.

In 1928, Technicolor introduced its third process, one known as "imbibition" or dye-transfer. In this process, the two prints were prepared as before, but instead of cementing the two films together, each film was made into a relief positive, which was then dyed either red or green and brought into contact with a third gelatin-coated film which would become the finished print. The gelatin of this print "imbibes" the dyes from the server print.

By 1929, all the major studios had lost their fear and distrust of sound, which in turn made them more receptive to the idea of color. Technicolor continued to turn out short subjects and "inserts" in Technicolor, and Paramount produced a feature length film, *Redskin*, in Technicolor. Not surprisingly, Warner Brothers, who had pioneered sound in feature-length films, was the first studio to make a major commitment to color, signing with Technicolor in 1928 for a series of 20 features, among them *On With The Show*, the first all-talking, all Technicolor feature-length film.

By this time Technicolor had modified its long-standing policy of total control of the process, to the extent of permitting the studios to rent the cameras, whereas heretofore Technicolor cameramen did all the filming. Developing and printing were still done only by Technicolor labs, which at first were only in Boston. By 1929, Technicolor had built a plant in Hollywood and one was planned for New York.

Technicolor continued to insist on "color control" of the production, always under the direction of Natalie Kalmus, Dr. Kalmus' wife.[20] This control extended to the color composition of sets, choice of materials and costumes, even to writing a color "score," for the picture, just as a musical score is written.

Just as it seemed that everything was blooming for Technicolor, the great depression finally caught up with the movie industry in the form of a sharp drop in motion picture theater attendance. This was quickly reflected in a drop in orders for Technicolor; its employment dropped from 1,200 with a payroll of $250,000 a month, to 230 employees and a payroll of $70,000 in mid-1931. The base price of Technicolor prints was reduced from 8-3/4 cents per foot to 7 cents per foot.

Research and development work continued; the two-color process was good, but three colors would be even better. By May of 1932, the first three-component camera had been built, as well as a portion of the laboratory equipped to handle three-color

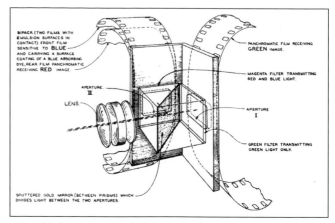

Fig. 226. Diagram of film and prism arrangement in three strip Technicolor Camera.

printing. The new system employed three films, two of which were made essentially as in the 1928 process, but sensitized for red and blue, while a third strip was added for green sensitivity. (Fig. 226)

Dr. Kalmus was delighted with the result; accuracy of color reproduction was greatly improved, and definition was markedly better. But selling it to the major studios did not prove easy. The camera was extremely bulky—practically useless for location shots and, of course, it consumed a great deal more film.

Walt Disney finally agreed to try the system for one of his Silly Symphonies, *Flowers and Trees*, released in 1932, followed by the classic *Three Little Pigs* in 1933. These films proved extremely popular, but the studios remained reluctant. Technicolor even managed to lower the base print price to 5-1/2 cents.

In 1935, Pioneer Pictures contracted with Technicolor for the first full-length feature to be filmed with the three-strip camera, *Becky Sharp*, directed by Rouben Mamoulian. Mamoulian's masterful handling of Technicolor in that picture undoubtedly encouraged other studios to consider Technicolor; by 1938 the company had contracts for some 40 feature-length films, from Warner Brothers, Selznick, 20th Century Fox, Loew's, Paramount, and Walt Disney (Fig. 227).

The most famous film produced by Technicolor's three-strip process was David O. Selznick's masterpiece *Gone With The Wind*, released in 1939. This film became the most printed Technicolor film in history and was the basis for Metro-Goldwyn-Mayer's spectacular achievement in blowing up the feature to a 70mm wide screen re-release in 1967.[21]

When Eastman Kodak Company introduced

Fig. 227. Three-strip Technicolor Camera.

Kodachrome film in 16mm in 1935, Technicolor realized that a successful single-strip process would inevitably displace the cumbersome three-strip process, so decided to join forces with Kodak in developing a 35mm version of Kodachrome for professional use. The result, announced in 1941, was Technicolor Monopack, a version of Kodachrome that allowed filming with any standard 35mm camera, while still maintaining Technicolor quality. Technicolor gradually lost its virtual monopoly of color movies after Kodak introduced Eastman color negative film in 1950. This technology formed the basis for a number of other color processes, such as Warnercolor, Color by de Luxe, Color by Consolidated, Metrocolor, Pathecolor, and so on.[22]

In 1947, the Department of Justice brought suit against Eastman Kodak and Technicolor charging them with forming a combination in restraint of trade under the Sherman and Clayton Acts. The suit against Kodak was dropped the following year when Kodak agreed to a consent decree, under which it would grant licenses permitting the licensees to process professional color motion picture film under certain Kodak patents.[23]

Kodachrome—Introduction

The best process for color motion pictures examined up to this point depended on creating three transparent films bearing the desired colors, in which the colors were imparted to the film by dyes either deposited or imbibed from an outside source. The three films then had to be superimposed, either physically or optically. The latter requirement resulted in the costly and cumbersome three-strip camera.

The ideal product would be to have the three emulsion layers in one film. Each emulsion would contain a substance sensitive to one of the three primary colors, which after exposure and treatment with a suitable developer would become a dye of the appropriate color. The result would be a single transparent film carrying the image of the scene in color, as photographed, with no filters required.

That was the challenge. While Technicolor was preparing to give Hollywood its beautiful three-color process with its amazing but ponderous three-strip camera, Eastman Kodak Company was preparing to give the amateur a small miracle: full color movies, taken with a camera that could be slipped in an overcoat pocket. That miracle was Kodachrome, and its story follows.

Background

The idea of a three-layered photograph consisting of three transparencies was proposed as early as 1868 by the French scientist Louis Ducos du Hauron, but neither suitable dyes nor emulsions existed at that time. In 1912, Rudolph Fischer of Germany obtained a patent for a multilayer color film incorporating substances that would produce dyes. Again, the required dye chemistry was not then available.[24]

The next advance in color photography came from an unexpected source. In 1921, George Eastman received a letter from Frank Damrosch, an acquaintance who was a brother of the celebrated conductor, Walter Damrosch, asking if Mr. Eastman would be interested in meeting two young men who were experimenting in color photography. Mr. Eastman met with the two men and admired their work, but apparently was not sufficiently impressed to suggest further meetings.

The two men were Leopold Mannes and Leopold Godowsky, Jr. Mannes was the son of violinist David Mannes and pianist Clara Damrosch Mannes. One of his uncles was Walter Damrosch, and another was Frank Damrosch who had written the letter to Eastman. Godowsky was the son of Leopold Godowsky, Sr., a respected concert pianist and composer.

Mannes and Godowsky were born within a few months of each other, in 1899 and 1900. They met at the Riverdale Country School in New York City, an upscale high school for children of the well-to-do. In addition to their common musical background, both were interested in photography. Their interest in color supposedly arose from seeing a movie short in color called *Our Navy*, which had been filmed in an early additive process.[25] The boys found the color pretty bad and, in blissful ignorance of the heroic efforts of dozens of scientists before them, decided they could make better color film.

Thanks to a remarkably indulgent teacher, they were given the keys to the school physics laboratory and actually managed to construct a two-lens camera which worked well enough to allow them to make a demonstration showing in one of " Roxy" Rothafel's theaters, Roxy being another friend of the family. The projectionist pointed out that it was almost impossible to keep the projector adjusted, and the young inventors shelved their interest in motion pictures for the time.

On graduation from high school, Mannes entered Harvard, where he majored in music and minored in physics. Godowsky went to the University of California at Berkeley, where he majored in physics and chemistry and played with the San Francisco Symphony. He later switched to the University of California in Los Angeles, where he played with the Los Angeles Symphony.

Back in New York after graduation, both men embarked on musical careers yet continued their photographic experiments together as time permitted. At first, they continued working with the additive process but soon concluded that it led nowhere. They turned to experiments with multilayered film. In 1921 they succeeded in photographing part of the solar spectrum on one of their two-layer plates, a feat that had eluded dozens of researchers up to that date. It was this point that Mannes' Uncle David saw their results and arranged the meeting with Eastman.

While that meeting came to naught, destiny was not to be denied. Another family friend, Robert W. Wood, head of the Experimental Physics Department at Johns Hopkins University, was impressed with their ingenuity. He wrote to Dr. Mees, describing the work that the young musicians were doing. This letter resulted in a meeting with Mees and a generous offer by Mees to supply the two men with some special emulsions made to their specifications. Having been cooking their own in one or the other's parent's kitchens, this must have truly seemed like manna from heaven (Fig. 228).

Fortune had more smiles. A rising young banker named Lewis Strauss, with the prestigious New York firm of Kuhn, Loeb & Company, heard of their experiments. He showed up at their home one day in 1922 and asked to see some of the new color plates. As it happened, none were at hand, but the two begged their visitor to wait while they completed some. The process took time, so between frantic trips to the kitchen/laboratory, the two entertained Strauss with some Beethoven sonatas. Said Godowsky later: "I don't think Strauss was much impressed with our music, but at least he liked our plates when we finally got them developed."[26] (See Fig. 229).

Strauss was certainly impressed; he returned to his firm and, shortly, Mannes and Godowsky were advanced $20,000 in loans to continue their work. On February 20, 1923, they filed their first patent application for a two-layered plate in which the color-forming developers were introduced through the emulsion by a carefully timed diffusion to a precise depth. The process was called controlled diffusion, and it represented a giant step toward the ultimate perfection of three-color photography. The chief problem remaining was to find color couplers that would not "wander" or migrate from one emulsion layer to another.

Incredibly, the two men managed to continue their experiments in chemistry *and* their careers in music. Mannes won a Pulitzer music scholarship in 1925 and, the following year, a Guggenheim fellowship to study composition in Rome. Godowsky, the violinist, set out on tour with his father, as his manager and accompanist.

By 1927, their continued experiments had led them to conclude that the color couplers should be introduced to each layer with the developing fluid by controlled diffusion. This would eliminate the problem of wandering couplers. Now the remain-

Fig. 228. Leopold Mannes (left) and Leopold Godowsky, Jr., (right) in their "laboratory."

Fig. 229. Godowsky at the violin, Mannes at the piano.

ing problem was to find sensitizing dyes that would not migrate.

Dr. Mees had been following their progress and came to realize that dye research being carried out by Leslie Brooker of the Kodak Research Laboratories could well provide the answer to the problems of the two young men. He arranged another meeting with them and made them an offer, in the form of a three-year contract: $30,000 up front to pay off the Kuhn, Loeb loans, $7,500 each per year in salary, and royalties on any patents taken out by the two prior to the agreement. Plus, of course, access to any relevant knowledge at KRL.

Curiously, it took Mannes and Godowsky several months to make up their minds, but on October 31, 1930, the contract was signed. Godowsky marked the occasion by proposing to Frances Gershwin, whom he had been courting for two years.

Their reception at KRL by the other researchers was something of a mixed bag. They were newcomers who had not "paid their dues" in long service, and they may even have been perceived as dilettantes, given their duality of careers. There is some evidence that they were thought to have been given more credit than they deserved, or at least that others did not receive the credit they merited. One former Research Laboratory employee put it this way: "Saying that Mannes and Godowsky invented Kodachrome is like saying the Wright brothers invented the 747."

One of their remarkable foibles was their practice of timing some of their darkroom experiments by whistling the last movement of Brahms' C-Mi-

nor Symphony, at the regular speed of two beats per second. Their explanation, which perhaps gives an insight to their attitude, was that they could not even use a luminous dial watch for fear of spoiling the negatives, but then said: "How could you go into all that with a scientist who never so much as heard of the C-Minor Symphony?"

Despite the melding of the Mannes and Godowsky talents with those of KRL, the end of their contract approached with an adequate color process still not perfected. The Great Depression of the 1930s had somewhat of a chilling effect on Kodak research, and Mannes and Godowsky began to feel that their chances of a contract renewal were very slim, unless they could come up with a product that would make money for the Company.

Dr. Mees did give them a one-year contract renewal, perhaps sensing that they were on to something, which they were. Thinking back to their experiments with motion picture film, they decided a two-color subtractive process that could be used for home movies was within the realm of possibility. They embarked on a crash program, sometimes working far into the night, and before their contract extension was up they had a working system. Management was delighted and approved it for production, but before it could actually be shipped, Mannes and Godowsky had perfected a three-color process that was far superior to the two-color one.

On April 15, 1935, Kodachrome film was announced to the world.[27] The product was first available as 16mm film, supplied in 100-foot spools, with an exposure index of ten. A double-page spread in

Movie Makers announced "One look will make you a Kodachrome fan. Never before full-color movies like this!" The ad emphasized that color movies could be taken with any 100-foot load 16mm camera, with any lens, without a filter, by simply using one diaphragm stop larger than that required for regular "pan" film, and could be projected on any 16mm projector. The film price was nine dollars, including processing.

The structure of the film was incredibly complex, five layers on top of the base, or support. The order was, from the top: a layer of blue-sensitive emulsion containing a yellow dye to trap all blue light, a layer of clear gelatin, a layer of blue-green sensitive, another clear gelatin layer, and finally a red-sensitive layer. Each layer was one to three microns[28] thick with an accuracy of plus or minus two percent. These layers had of course to be laid down in total darkness (Fig. 230).

The development process was equally complex: a series of developing, bleaching, re-exposing, second bleach, drying, spooling, for a total of 28 separate steps, all of which had to be carried out with the utmost precision. The processing program took three and one-half hours when first in place; over the years that was reduced to 36 minutes or less.[29] This lengthy processing time was not helped by Kodak's policy, in the early days, of re-processing a batch of film if it did not match the colors required by the customer as indicated by samples he or she submitted!

At introduction, Kodachrome was strictly a daylight film, but in April 1936, Kodachrome Movie Film (Type A) at Exposure Index 16, for exposure under photoflood lamps was announced. Movies could be made indoors without the use of a filter and with one quarter of the illumination previously required.[30] One month later Kodachrome was available spooled for 8mm cameras. In 1938 the process was considerably simplified, reducing the number of steps from 28 to 18. At the same time the color quality and stability were greatly improved.

Kodachrome was a transparency, or slide, film. In this form it became extremely popular, often cited as the single most important factor in the emergence and growth of 35mm photography. Commercial users were ecstatic: *National Geographic* photo-editor Louis Marden said: "The minute we saw this stuff

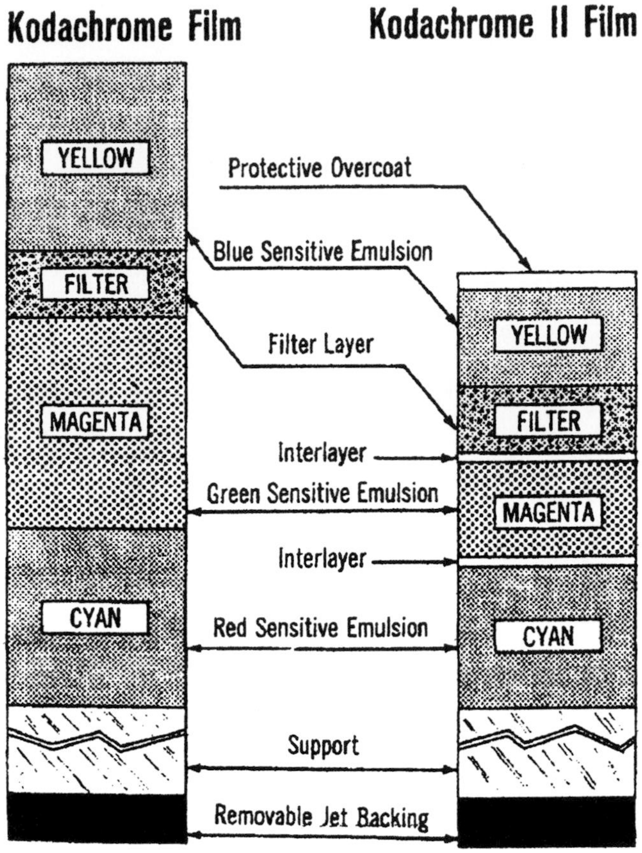

Fig. 230. Comparison of first Kodachrome and Kodachrome II.

projected we knew the millennium was here for magazine color reproduction. It had the possibility of almost infinite enlargement." [31]

Mannes and Godowsky left Eastman Kodak Company in 1939, but were retained as consultants. Mannes continued his musical career, while Godowsky set up a small laboratory in Connecticut and continued research in color photography. Mannes died in 1964, Godowsky in 1983. The Naylor Collection, now in Japan's National Museum of Photography, held many artifacts (including Godowsky's violin) and much correspondence documenting the work of these two men.

The year 1961 saw the first major change in Kodachrome in 25 years with the introduction of Kodachrome II. The new film had a speed of Daylight 25 instead of 10, Type A with photofloods was rated at 40 instead of 16. In addition, the film boasted less grain, lower contrast, and more saturated colors. As of year 2000, Kodachrome film is still solidly in the Eastman Kodak product line and still considered the finest in the world, the standard by which all other transparency films are measured.

Fig. 231. Edwin H. Land demonstrating the first Polaroid photograph to the Optical Society of America on February 21, 1947.

Polavision

No discussion of amateur movies in color would be complete without relating the sad story of one disastrous modern-day attempt at launching an additive color process. The date was April 26, 1977; the place was a warehouse in a Boston Massachusetts suburb called Needham. The warehouse had been temporarily converted to a theatre, to be the site of the fortieth annual meeting of the Polaroid Corporation. Drawn by a promise of an exciting new product, instant motion pictures, almost 3,000 stockholders and over 200 media people jammed the Needham building to learn of the next miracle from this high-flying company.

Dr. Edwin Herbert Land (1909-1991) (Fig. 231), Founder, Chairman, Chief Executive Officer, and Director of Research of the Polaroid Corporation, took the stage himself to demonstrate his latest product. Land explained that the new system, called Polavision, consisted of a lightweight camera, a cassette containing a revolutionary new film, and a "player." (See Fig. 232.) He then picked up the camera and proceeded to film a dancer clad in vivid col-

ors, performing on a brightly-lit stage. After two minutes or so of filming, Land opened the side of the camera, removed the cassette, and placed it in a slot in the top of the player. Land chatted easily with the audience for a few moments, accompanied by slight bumps and whirrings from the player. Suddenly the image of the dancer, in motion and color, appeared on the player screen. As a buzz ran through the audience, a triumphant grin appeared on Land's face. Quickly, several assistants moved among the crowd, inviting one and all to try their hands at this new technology, with no less than 20 special filming stages set up for the purpose.

The reaction of the audience was mixed; the demonstration was certainly impressive, particularly to those with enough knowledge of photography to appreciate the stunning technology that permitted instant, automatic development of a reversal color film entirely within the cassette. The less sophisticated were simply bemused. In the words of one Polaroid historian, "They had been shown a dog in a top hat walking on its hind legs, but they were not sure why." [32]

The financial reporters present were tougher; they quizzed Land on subjects such as: how much had been spent on development of Polavision, and what would be the effect on the Company's bottom line? And when Dr. Land, with fire in his eyes, struck back at these jackals nipping at his heels, his faithful stockholders rose as one and gave him a standing ovation!

The camera itself was unremarkable, resembling somewhat a Fuji Single 8 camera. The lens was f/1.8, 12.5-28mm manual zoom, through-the-lens

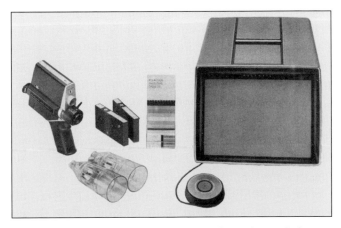

Fig. 232. Polavision Camera, cartridge, player, lights, remote control.

viewing, two focus positions for 6 to 15 feet, or 15 feet to infinity. The cassette, the heart of the system, was slightly larger than an audio cassette and contained about 42 feet of film, enough for two minutes and 40 seconds of viewing. It also contained a small pod of reagent, various spools and film guides, and was in effect a film processing machine in miniature. For some reason, Dr. Land insisted that the film, identical in width and perforation to Super 8, be called "tape," and the cassettes were labeled "Polaroid Phototape." (See Fig. 233.)

The "player" was about the size of a small portable TV set, but weighed 25 pounds. When the exposed cassette was inserted, two metal contacts closed a circuit and started the following sequence of events: first the player recognized an unexposed cassette and began rewinding. The first half-second of film movement unsealed the reagent chamber in the cassette, and a 10-micron layer of developer was laid down on the tape as it rewound. The rewind and coating process took about 20 seconds. When rewinding was complete, a notch in the tape changed the identification of the tape from "exposed" to "rerun." A 45-second delay allowed the processing reaction to complete, following which the tape was automatically played, then automatically re-wound and ejected, ready for removal or replay as the user chose (Fig. 234).

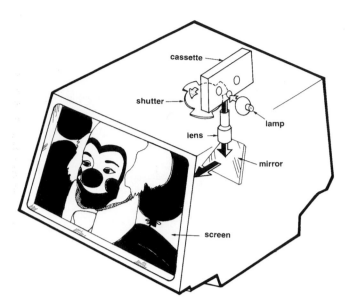

Fig. 234. Phantom view inside the Polavision player.

For reasons that are difficult to discern, Dr. Land had pursued an additive process for his instant movies and wound up with what he named Polavision. And like all its predecessors, Polavision required large amounts of light for exposure. The projected image, despite the special crossed-lenticular screen with which the player was equipped, could only be viewed satisfactorily by a few people, those sitting nearly in line with the screen.

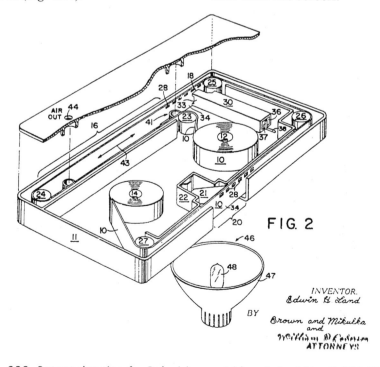

Fig. 233. Patent drawing for Polavision cartridge, Patent No. 3,709,588.

The reaction of professional critics was as to be expected. Tony Galluzzo, writing in the July 1977 issue of *Modern Photography*, pointed out the grainy image, the narrow viewing area, the short lengths of film, the fact that it was a silent system, when all amateur movie cameras of the time were sound.[33] And perhaps most telling of all: the vaunted "instant" feature was only a reality if you had that 25-pound player and a 110-volt outlet with you! Galluzzo closed his review saying, "I'll stick to my fine-grained, super-sharp Kodachrome movie film."

And the reaction of the buying public was the same. Barely six months after introduction at a suggested retail price of about $700, camera stores were discounting the outfit deeply. One store offered the camera and player for $525, plus a $50 refund on any old camera brought in! Six months later, they were widely offered at $350, somewhat below dealer's cost.

Despite this dismal reception, Polaroid kept pushing the product with incredible claims for its virtues and potential, using some of the most blatantly "non-truth in advertising" imaginable, in which the use of a "simulated picture" was ludicrous to anyone who had seen the actual performance. Finally, in the fall of 1979, the awful news came out; Polaroid was writing off $68 million in Polavision inventory, and Polavision was history.

How could a product with such obvious shortcomings get past the marketing executives of a multimillion dollar corporation? Part of the answer is that these people were ignored; Polavision was Land's baby, and he would not listen to any criticism of it. Then how could such a brilliant scientist be blind to the product's weaknesses? Perhaps all we can do is remember that Edison had his concrete houses, Ford had his Edsel, and Howard Hughes had his "Spruce Goose," Land was in good company!

CODA

Many readers will have noted the ongoing controversy between the "colorists" and the "anti-colorists," which has arisen since the practice of adding color to films originally shot in black-and-white. This practice began when owners of certain classic black and white films decided their marketability would be greatly improved by converting these films to color. The techniques for doing so have been greatly improved by recent advances in computer technology, but the results and the very idea have left many film-lovers in a state of rage.

To begin with, the anti-colorists maintain that black and white films and color films are two different genres—that the director chose one or the other as the vehicle for his vision just as carefully as he chose the actors, the sets, and the lighting. Further, it has been maintained that it is technically impossible to colorize a black-and-white film without destroying the relative light values that existed in the original scene; the lighting of any one scene for a color film being totally different from what it would be for shooting in black-and-white.[34]

Lastly, it may be of interest to read what Cecil B. DeMille once had to say about color photography, in a 1923 article entitled "The Chances of Color Photography in Moving Pictures."

Although it is probably only a matter of time before a process of producing naturally colored photographs will be perfected, I doubt seriously whether, when success in this endeavor is attained, it will revolutionize the motion picture industry. Partial success has already been achieved, but at present colored photographs, especially in the films, are not artistically perfect and their expense makes them impractical for general use. Even when these problems of experimenters and inventors have been overcome and color photography has been made economical and artistic, I believe it is a question whether the public will prefer colors to the black and white of the present day screen.[35]

DeMille of course was to change his mind; all but one of his last seven films, those made from 1940 to 1956, were in color.

Kodak Electric 8 Zoom Reflex Camera

Advancing Technology

With the exception of the introduction of 8mm in 1932, and magazine loading in 1940, the amateur movie camera changed very little in the two decades following the introduction of 16mm direct-reversal film in 1923. The proportion of U.S. households owning motion picture equipment remained relatively small. In the two decades following World War II, the number of users increased dramatically, as did the number of suppliers, now including Japanese as well as European firms. Vying for the mass market, manufacturers introduced one improvement after another, making the movie camera steadily more versatile, more portable, and easier to use successfully. By 1965, if the amateur's home movie still looked amateurish, it was not the fault of the equipment.[1]

Home Movies Come of Age

When United States "neutrality" from the conflict raging in Europe was shattered by the Japanese attack on Pearl Harbor on December 7, 1941, production of civilian photographic equipment came to an abrupt halt. Film production for civilian use had already been reduced in 1941 at the request of the Defense Department, as millions of feet were required for training films for all branches of the Services. Production of 16mm projectors was pushed; even so, the demand was so great that manufacturers asked their employees to turn in their personal projectors for use by the Armed Services. As noted in Chapters 5 and 6, both Eastman Kodak and Bell & Howell became important suppliers of highly technical military equipment, while production of amateur equipment ceased all together.

Fighting came to an end in Europe on May 8, 1945. At 8:15 a.m. on August 6, an atomic bomb was dropped on Hiroshima and, on August 9, another one on Nagasaki. Tokyo had been nearly leveled by conventional bombs on March 9 and 10. On September 2, 1945, Imperial Japan surrendered.

Viewing the photographs of the utter destruction of those cities, it is hard to conceive how a nation that had suffered that damage could, just 12 years later, be turning out cameras like the Canon, Fujica, Minolta, Yashica—cameras with quality of manufacture and level of operating features to challenge those of their Western competitors.

Of European camera manufacturers, the Germans were hardest hit, British and Austrian companies were only slightly damaged, and the facilities of Paillard-Bolex in Switzerland were unscathed. The British ciné manufactory was relatively small, and few pre-war British-made cameras found their way to American consumers, except for an occasional 16mm Ensign and the curious 9.5mm Midas combination camera/projector, manufactured by Camera-Projectors Ltd.

American amateur ciné technology was decidedly limited in the years prior to World War II, with only three 16mm cameras of any sophistication available, the Victor Model 5, the Bell & Howell 70 series and the much more elaborate Ciné-Special of Eastman Kodak. The European amateur had his choice of 16mm cameras among Agfa, Bolex, Ciné-Nizo, Ensign, Eumig, Siemens, and Zeiss Movikon. There was an even greater selection from the makers of 9.5mm equipment.

The 1940 *Popular Photography Directory Issue* listed, for 16mm cameras, eight U.S. manufacturers offering 23 models and two foreign companies offering two models. The U.S. models averaged $109 list price, the European, $318. Most of the smaller manufacturers of inexpensive 16mm cameras which had sprung up in the late 1920s had disappeared by 1940, many of them doubtless victims of the severe depression which gripped the country following the market crash of October 1929 and which lasted well into 1937. The typical U.S. 16mm camera was spring wound, either magazine or spool load, with a single lens, or at the high end, a Bell & Howell turret camera, or the Ciné Kodak Special.

For the 8mm filmmaker there were also four U.S. makers listed, with 11 models, and two foreign companies with two models. The U.S. models averaged $52 list price and, again, the European cameras averaged three times that figure. The technology did not differ substantially from that of the 16mm cameras.

The end of the war brought an almost immediate end to restrictions on production for civilian use, although it was to take some time for the pipelines to become filled. "Photo Fans Must Wait—no film until late 1945"—so read the *New York Daily News* of August 16, 1945. On June 1, 1946, Eastman Kodak resumed publication of *Ciné-Kodak News* after a lapse of nearly four years, with the slogan "It's time to take movies again!" The customer was urged to take his trusty "8" or "16" down from the shelf, give it a good inspection and cleaning, and load it up with color film. Color photography of favorite filming subjects was lavishly used in the publication to further encourage the amateur to shoot in color. For despite the introduction of Kodachrome in 1935, the 1942 introduction of Kodacolor prints, and the 1946 introduction of Ektachrome, as late as 1953 only 16 percent of amateur still pictures were on color stock. It might be assumed, however, that movie filmers were taking to color more rapidly than still photographers were, even if not as rapidly as Kodak had hoped.

Popular Photography resumed publication of its Directory issue in 1948. From this directory, it can be seen that, except for the emergence of the Revere Camera Company of Chicago, not many changes had occurred among suppliers of equipment. But substantial change had occurred in prices. By 1948, the average list price of a domestic 16mm camera had doubled, from $109 in 1941 to $222, and for the 8mm camera the figures increased from $52 to $119. Imported camera prices remained almost unchanged. As camera designs had changed very little during the war years, it may be inferred that the principle causes of the price increases were the increased costs of labor and materials.

This dramatic increase in camera prices was of concern to Eastman Kodak sales and marketing people. In 1951, as noted in Chapter 5, the company launched the Brownie Movie Camera at a list price of $47.50. The introductory price soon dropped to $43.50, less than 60 percent of its nearest competitor. Kodak advertised the camera widely, even in the prestigious and expensive *National Geographic*, in full color, emphasizing the simplicity of operation traditionally associated with the Brownie name. Sales soared; the Brownie Movie Camera became the first movie camera to record sales of over one million units in one year.

Over the years, the Brownie line stayed true to its *raison d'être*, eschewing such niceties as electric motor drive and zoom lenses; however, the 1956 annual report noted that there were models available priced from $29.95 to $79.50, the latter being for a three-lens turret model. When the designers in August 1958 launched a Brownie with a three-lens turret and an exposure meter, pushing the list price to $99.50, cooler heads soon prevailed. This cygnet among ducklings was quickly re-named "The Kodak Ciné Scopemeter." The lowest priced Brownie movie camera ever, and the last of the line, the Brownie Fun Saver, was announced in 1963 at $19.95 and survived until 1968.

Over the decade beginning in 1951-52, the number of manufacturers of amateur equipment would almost double, and the number of models offered increase threefold. During the same period, a chain of design improvements and innovations would raise the utility and versatility of the 8mm camera to rival the best of 16mm cameras. The story of those design changes follows.

Loading The Camera

Loading a movie camera with film has always been more complicated than loading a still camera, (if one ignores daguerrian or wet-plate cameras!) and designers have wrestled with the problem from the beginning of motion picture photography. The first U.S.-made camera to address this problem was the 1917 Movette, in which the film was supplied in a paper-wrapped metal magazine furnished by Kodak. The user had to extract a loop of film from the magazine and thread it over the camera sprockets and through the gate. The 9.5mm Pathé of 1923 and the Zeiss Kinamo S-10 eliminated sprockets, but still required the external loop of film. The first truly magazine-loading camera appears to have been the American 16mm Simplex-Pockette, manufactured by the International Projector Corporation and launched in 1931 (Fig. 235).

The camera was very compact and light; 1-1/4" thick and weighing less than 2-1/2 lbs. A rear door admitted the 50-foot steel magazine with its distinctive rounded end and spring, which served to insure that the film was pressed firmly in the gate when the door was closed. The magazines were designed and built by Eastman Kodak, licensed to IPC, and loaded with Eastman Kodak Safety film, either Pan-

Fig. 235. Simplex Pockette Camera.

Fig. 236. Bell & Howell Model 141.

chromatic or Supersensitive, and later Kodacolor. The purchase price included processing.

IPC must have encountered some piracy of its designs, judging by a full-page ad in *Movie Makers* for April 1934. The text put manufacturers, retailers and users on notice that IPC owned or had exclusive license to the patents relating to the Simplex Pockette camera and "proposes to enforce its rights against infringers in full accordance with the law."

Bell & Howell introduced its Design 121 in 1934, using the Simplex magazine. Meanwhile, Kodak had been working on an improved design and in January 1936 introduced its first magazine loading camera, the Magazine Ciné Kodak, with a re-designed 50-foot magazine. Bell & Howell adopted the new magazine for their Model 141 (Fig. 236), arguably one of the handsomest 16mm cameras that company ever produced, with its bright nickel fittings and gleaming black enamel trim done in Art Deco style.

Magazine loading came to 8mm in June 1940, with the introduction of the Magazine Ciné Kodak 8, Model 40. The magazine held 25 feet of double-8 film, so had to be turned over after the first side was exposed. DeJur, Keystone, and Revere added magazine models after the war.

Another approach to simplifying loading was launched by Kodak in 1962 with the Kodak Electric 8 Automatic Camera, which was also Kodak's first battery-powered camera. The film was the conventional 25-foot spool of double 8, but was loaded by the user into a molded plastic "Kodak Duex Cassette." (See Fig. 237). This operation still required some dexterity, as the film had to be threaded in the cassette from the feed spool, over the pressure plate and on to the take-up capstan. But once loaded, the cassette had merely to be turned over to expose the second side.

Bell & Howell countered with the "New Autoload Cartridge Loading Camera, Design 418," using a very similar container. The confusing nomenclature possibly arose from Kodak's desire to distinguish its new system from magazine loading, so called its system "cassette loading"; Bell & Howell, wishing to distance itself from Kodak, called its system "cartridge loading." Sears Roebuck marketed a "Cartridge Load" camera that appears to have been manufactured by Bell & Howell. Minolta also produced an 8mm cartridge loading system of the same type.

A third alternative loading system was introduced by Sekonic in 1963 with the "Simplomat," in which the entire film chamber and spring-motor drive was so mounted that it could be rotated 180 degrees within the frame of the camera. The film chamber was loaded with the conventional 25-foot spool and, after the first side had been exposed, the chamber was rotated and the second side exposed. This made for a rather cumbersome camera; the zoom model weighed four and one-half pounds.

Despite complaints by some users that magazine loading did not give a uniformly flat film plane, and occasional jamming of the magazines, the design was very popular with the smaller manufacturers particularly, as it greatly simplified camera production. Sprockets, film gate, and pressure plate were shifted to the magazine, which was supplied by Eastman

Fig. 237. Kodak Electric 8 with Duex Cassette.

Kodak, except for a very few minor brands such as the Irwin, where the manufacturer supplied its own make of magazine

While magazine loading was a boon for 8mm users, it was never as popular for 16mm cameras, principally because of its practical limit at 50 feet of film; 100 feet could not be pulled through the magazine successfully, which ruled it out for serious filmers who needed 100-foot loads. Magazine loading peaked around 1954, and then gradually dropped in popularity to a very minor market share in 1964, just before the arrival of Super 8 solved the loading problem for good.

Well, not quite; serious amateurs had been complaining for years about the inconvenience of the 50-foot load, particularly after sound cameras became available. Perhaps with an eye on potential television and commercial applications, both Paillard Bolex & Cie. and Beaulieu pressured Kodak for a larger sound cartridge. Action without sound could be cut almost anywhere, but talking subjects never seemed to limit their dialogue to the two minutes and 30 seconds allowed by the 50-foot cartridge at sound speed. The major problem confronting the camera designers was how to construct a film transport mechanism with sufficient strength to pull, say, 200 feet of film through the camera at a uniform speed.

Jasper S. Chandler joined the Kodak Research Laboratories in 1938 and retired in 1976 as senior research associate. In those 38 years Chandler made outstanding contributions in sound recording, film perforators and sprocket standards for 8mm, 16mm, and 35mm film, printers and Super 8 cartridge design. He was described informally by his colleagues as "the father of Super 8" because of his many contributions to all elements of that system. In particular, his experience with the Super 8 cartridge led him to perfect, after several years' efforts, a remarkable 200-foot cartridge announced in January 1975, together with the Kodak Supermatic Sound Camera.

The key element of Dr. Chandler's cartridge design was a unique spring known as the Negator spring that supplied almost constant torque to the relatively huge supply and take-up reels throughout the entire 200-foot run. Chandler also cannily designed the reel housing as an appendage on top of the standard 50-foot sound cartridge, so the existing sound camera designs could be adapted for the new cartridge by simply providing an opening in the top of the camera. Only the 50-foot "base" had to go inside the camera body.[2]

Cartridge Loading The Projector

Loading, or "threading" the projector, aside from setting up the screen, was probably one of the biggest deterrents to more general popularity of showing movies in the home. Curiously enough, one of the earliest amateur projectors made a brave attempt to simplify this chore, the 1927 Kodascope Model B (Fig. 238). This elegant projector was equipped with two spring-loaded film channels, which received the film from the drive sprocket, and guided it onto the take-up reel, thus becoming the first self-threading projector.

Another method to simplify threading was introduced in 1961 by Technicolor Products, Inc., a division of the color film company. The product was an 8mm projector about the size of a small table radio, which took special 50-foot factory-loaded cartridges. The projector had neither supply nor take-up reels; when the cartridge was inserted in the rear of the projector and the machine switched on, the film was automatically threaded and projected, and automatically rewound when the end was reached. Initially, film loading could only be done at time of processing, but a cartridge re-loading service was added later, as were larger cartridges, Super 8 and sound models. Thanks to the small size, lack of reels, and low voltage lamp, the original units sold for less than $100.

Fig. 238. Kodascope Model B.

The machines were not very popular with the home movie set. In a few years Technicolor switched its efforts to the audio visual markets, bringing out a broader line of projectors, including rear-projection models, and an extensive library of so-called "single concept" Super 8 cartridge three-minute films. A contemporary catalog listed over 450 titles, in such categories as Social Studies, High School Physics, Vocational Education, and Hygiene. The dealer cost for these "film loops" was $17.50 each; suggested retail was $24.95. Many of the original films were of British origin.

Fairchild Camera and Instrument Corporation followed a similar course in 1968 with a line of endless loop cartridge projectors taking 220 or 400-foot cartridges that gave 12 or 22 minutes of filming time.

Technicolor's success with its cartridge projectors led both Bell & Howell and Eastman Kodak to develop cartridge projectors, Kodak launching two models in 1969, one for 50-foot and one for 100-foot cartridges.[3] The following year a 400-foot cartridge and projector were introduced. All projectors could be quickly converted to reel loading, and all featured automatic rewind. Bell & Howell introduced its "Auto 8 Cassette" projector in 1970, which would accept 8mm or Super 8 loaded in special cassettes. The company announced that some unspecified "major manufacturers" had decided to adopt this system under license from Bell & Howell; however, it appears that nothing came of such licensing.

In the fall of 1973, Bell & Howell introduced a projector which combined the cartridge loading feature with a self-contained rear projection screen. The "Double Feature" projector accepted up to eight cassettes in a channel on top of the projector ready for projection. Operation began by pressing one button; cassettes automatically rewound after projection; depressing a second button advanced and started the next cassette.

The projector had a low profile and was covered with a dark acrylic cover when not in use. Bell & Howell's annual report for 1973 featured the projector on its cover and described it as the industry's first movie projector "designed as a permanent piece of furniture for living room, family room, or den."

Eastman Kodak introduced two unusual projectors in 1972, the Supermatic 60 and Supermatic 70. These projectors resembled tape recorders of the period, with the film running in the horizontal plane. They would accept everything from 50-foot reels to the 400-foot cartridge, silent or sound, and could project on a self-contained Ektalite screen, or direct to a conventional screen. The Model 60 could play only while the Model 70 could play and record. The machines received good press, stressing their versatility and ease of use. One lever controlled the motor and projection lamp, ran the film at 18 or 24 feet-per-second, still mode, and instant replay.[4]

Eastman Kodak encountered severe reliability problems with the cartridge designs, necessitating product recall and repair. As a consequence cartridge loading for the Ektasound projectors that were in process of design at this time was abandoned in favor of "slot" loading.[5] It may be assumed that Bell & Howell experienced similar reliability problems with cassette or cartridge loading—by 1977, out of 21 manufacturers, only Technicolor still offered cartridge loading.

Electric Drive

As related in Chapter 7, the first battery-driven amateur camera was undoubtedly the Victor Ultra Cine Camera, of which only a very few were manufactured. At about the same time Eastman Kodak, perhaps reacting to the Victor venture, or more likely feeling pressure from the spring motor-driven Bell & Howell Model 70, brought out in January 1924 a battery and motor attachment for the Model A Ciné-Kodak. The unit sold for $25 and was joined to the camera by removing the hand-crank handle and attaching with two screws. As the first models of the camera required the use of a tripod, they were equipped with an eye-level finder only.

When the battery-drive option permitted operation at waist level, a waist level finder was incorporated in the battery drive mechanism. And since the waist-level finder line-of-sight was no longer covered by the lens cover, the designers thoughtfully inscribed "Open Lens Cover" in the finder window. After an optional waist-level finder was built in to the camera, beginning with Serial No. 1266, the finder was eliminated from the motor drive. A battery-charging outfit was available. It is doubtful that the Ciné-Kodak battery drive was any more successful than the Willard/Victor, and in July 1925, Eastman Kodak introduced the spring-motor-driven Model B.[6]

The next battery-driven camera to appear was the 8mm Eumig C4, introduced in 1938. It sold for $55, just slightly above the average price of U.S. 8mm cameras at that time. Eumig continued to make battery-driven 8s through the 1950s, but no major U.S. manufacturer offered one until Eastman Kodak, as noted above, introduced the Kodak Electric 8 Automatic Camera in August 1962.[7] (See Fig. 237.) The camera was powered by four AA batteries and came with an f/1.6 lens, automatic exposure control, remote control outlet, and the aforementioned cassette loading. It listed at $99.50, substantially below the average price of 8mm cameras for that year, probably because so many were equipped with zoom lenses.

Electric drive burgeoned in 1963; Leendert Drukker, movie editor of *Popular Photography*, reporting on the 1963 M.P.D.F.A. Trade Show, counted 28 new 8mm cameras, 17 of which offered electric drive. He also noted that 17 of the new cameras also featured the new cadmium-sulfide cell "electric eye" for exposure control.[8]

Lens Design

The photographer seldom finds himself at exactly the right distance from his subject to achieve the image size that he wishes on the film. Standing on the rim of the famed Bingham Canyon Copper

Mine in Utah, for example, as he looks through the finder of his camera with a "normal" lens, he finds that he can only take in perhaps a third of the yawning two-mile wide pit before him (unless he pans), and a massive 250-ton truck at the bottom of the pit would be only an insignificant dot in the finder.

Since he can neither step back from the rim, nor fly like Peter Pan to the bottom, his dilemma can only be met by having lenses which will do these moves for him; or expressed another way, will change the size of the image, without moving the camera. This scenario brings us to the term "focal length," which is the technical but somewhat misleading term for the property of the lens that determines, for a given lens-to-subject distance, the size of the image. The rule is simple: image size varies directly with focal length—the longer the focal length, the larger the image, and vice-versa.

This is easily demonstrated with any two magnifiers with different focal lengths that might be found around the house. Try forming the image of your desk lamp, for example, on a white sheet of paper. Note the distance from lens to image, then try another lens, again focus, note the distance, and the size of the image.

At this point, it is worth remarking on what is considered a "normal" lens and how this designation came into being. In the earliest days of the movies, the action almost always took place on a set. These sets were typically just a drop, or a wall, with no sides. The camera needed to be far enough from the actors to avoid the distortion of foreshortening and yet not so far as to show the limits of the set. With these parameters, it was found that a lens of 50mm focal length nicely filled the 35mm frame and that became the standard for a "normal" lens. When 16mm film came along, half of 50mm, or 25mm, became the normal lens for 16mm cameras, and similarly, 12.5mm or 13mm was normal for 8mm film.

Going back to the filmer on the edge of the Bingham Canyon pit, it is evident that he needs two more lenses for his camera, one of short focal length (smaller image) to make the image of the wide pit small enough to fit the frame of his film, and for the distant machinery, a long focal-length lens, to make a large image. The short focal-length lens is called a "wide angle lens" but a long focal-length lens is generally called a "telephoto lens." When first developed, long focus lenses were actually as long as their focal length; advanced optical engineering shortened them to the compact design we know today as the telephoto lens.

This is where the cinematographer had an advantage over the still photographer. Since the size of the image on amateur film is relatively small, ciné camera lenses can be of short focal length and smaller in diameter than those for still cameras, thus making it feasible to mount all three lenses on the camera, in a turret.

The same configuration of lenses large enough to cover even a 35mm frame would result in a very awkward, unbalanced still camera, although such an arrangement was essayed with the Rectaflex Rotor in 1952, which was not a commercial success, undoubtedly because of its bulk. So still cameramen had to carry interchangeable lenses in their pockets or gadget bags until the zoom lens came along.

The idea of arranging multiple lenses on a turret for a motion picture camera seems to have come from the fertile mind of Albert S. Howell, when he produced the Design 2709 35mm professional camera, introduced in 1911 or 1912. As noted in Chapter 5, this camera, because of the extraordinary precision of its film-transport mechanism which gave rock-steady registration of each frame and thus rock-steady images on the screen, quickly became the favorite of studio cameramen and remained so for many years.

With the success of its professional camera, it is not surprising that Bell & Howell was the first company to offer the amateur the same convenience of turret lenses, which it did with its 16mm Design 70-C in 1927. Victor Animatograph followed suit with its Models 3, 4 and 5, beginning in 1928. Eastman Kodak's first turret camera was the very advanced Cine-Kodak Special, announced in 1933, which raised 16mm camera capabilities to an entirely new level. That some users wanted an even more versatile camera and were willing to pay for it is evidenced by the success of companies like Par Products of Hollywood that offered a four-lens turret for the Ciné-Special with integral viewfinder, "styled to harmonize with the Ciné-Special design," for $295.50, less finder objectives.[9] (See Fig. 239.)

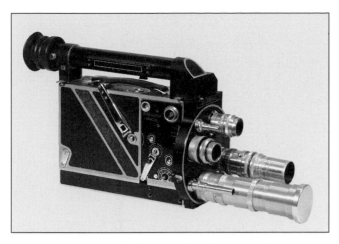

Fig. 239. Kodak Ciné Special with Par Products four-lens turret and telescope finder.

Fig. 240. Kodak Zoom 8 Automatic.

Zoom Lenses

While the turret gave the user a fairly quick selection of lenses, that speed came at the cost of added bulk, weight, and inevitably some interruption of filming. What was needed was a single lens that would take the place of three. Beginning in the early 1930s, lens designers such as Dr. Frank Back in the U.S. and Dr. H. Naumann in Germany developed lenses in which the focal length of the lens system could be changed by moving some of the individual elements, without changing the position of the image, i.e. the film plane.

To vary the focal length of the system, it is necessary that some of the elements move and some remain stationary, and there are two principal methods of doing this. In one system the image-forming elements remain stationary while the zooming elements move; in order to maintain focus, the front or focusing element moves slightly. This type of lens is called "mechanically compensated" or "reciprocally compensated." In the other system the zooming element remains stationary, while the other groups are moved. The latter system is somewhat less expensive to manufacture, but is not quite as accurate at all lens positions. It is known as "optically compensated." [10]

According to Auer, the first variable lens for amateur ciné cameras was the Transfokator, made by the Astro Co. of Berlin in 1936. This was not, strictly speaking, a variable focal-length lens, but an afocal telescopic attachment of 2X power clamped over the camera's fixed lens, thus giving a zoom range of 15 to 30mm. A similar lens, the Busch Vario-Glaukar 25 to 80mm varifocal lens was offered by the Berlin firm of Siemens & Halske, integrally installed on a Siemens 16mm camera. The date of this camera is uncertain. [11]

Designing a variable focal-length lens involves considerable balancing of conflicting objectives, and the quality of early efforts was greatly improved upon as the science of lens design became more sophisticated in the 1950s. In 1952, Paillard Bolex offered the Bolex C8 equipped with a Zoom Pan Cinor lens by SOM Berthiot of Paris, with an aperture of f/2.8, and a zoom range of 12.5 to 36mm. A coupled zoom finder was included.

The first U.S.-made 8mm camera with a zoom lens was introduced by Eastman Kodak in November 1959: the Kodak Zoom 8 Automatic, f/1.9, with a zoom range of 9 to 24mm (Fig. 240). The "automatic" in the name referred to its electric eye, which set the lens opening automatically, which will be discussed further on. The zoom lens, of the optically compensated type, was manually operated by sliding the lens barrel forward and had a range of 9 to 24mm.

Bell & Howell entered the lists a few months later with its "Zoomatic Model," also with manually operated zoom and automatic exposure control, but with several other features not found in its rival. Most apparent to the user was the zoom finder, which was coupled to the taking lens so that the user at all times saw the field that was being filmed. This feature, plus a focusing lens of the mechanically compensated type, a slow-motion option on the camera operating button, and manual exposure control option, added up to a camera of decidedly more versatility than the Eastman Kodak model, but at a correspondingly higher price—over $200 compared to $140 for the Kodak camera.

Reflex Viewing

Reflex viewing, which means viewing the scene to be photographed directly through the taking lens, represents the culmination of a long quest for a means to ensure that the camera is recording precisely the scene that the cinematographer wants on the film. Viewfinders on most early amateur ciné cameras were of the folding post-and-lens type, called a Newtonian finder, mounted on top of the camera, sometimes accompanied by a waist-level finder such as were common on still cameras.

When multiple lenses of differing focal lengths were introduced, more elaborate finders were needed and were generally of the telescope type, placed in the body of the camera or on one side, such as on the Bell & Howell Filmo cameras. This placement of the finder however, could produce "parallax error," the term for the fact that when the viewing lens is not co-axial with the taking lens, but set to one side or above, the viewer will not see exactly the same scene that the taking lens does. This error is generally negligible at distances over six feet, but becomes more significant as lens-to-subject distance decreases.

There are several methods of viewing the scene through the taking lens, the first and oldest being not reflex at all. This early method was to view and focus the scene as it was imaged on the film, or on a ground glass behind the film. This method, although common on early cameras such as the Moy, Debrie, Barker Brothers, etc., had several drawbacks. First, the image tended to be quite dim; it complicated construction of the camera, and finally the advent of opaque anti-halation backing on the film made the method totally unworkable.

There are three methods of achieving reflex viewing: use of a reciprocating mirror, a rotary mirror, and one or more beam splitters. The first of these methods to be applied to an amateur ciné camera was introduced in 1958 by Ercsam & Cie. of France, with its Camex Reflex, advertised as "the World's Only 8mm Single Lens Reflex." A small 45-degree mirror cemented to a guillotine-type shutter deflects the incoming light to a viewing tube or eyepiece

when the shutter is closed. This arrangement is expensive to construct and somewhat fragile, considering that the mirror must withstand reciprocation at 24 cycles per second, but has been successfully used in Beaulieu 16mm cameras.

Another approach is to use a rotating mirror that doubles as the shutter, the system used in Arriflex cameras. Besides being expensive, both mirror systems do produce some flickering of the viewing image, although chiefly noticeable at slow camera speeds.

In 1956, Bolex announced its Reflex models, which used the third system, a beam-splitting prism in the light path, which diverts some of the incoming light to the viewing system. The beam-splitter system is considerably cheaper to manufacture, and since there are no moving parts, it is less subject to damage or misalignment. As the beam-splitter diverts 20 percent to 30 percent of the light from the film, it robs the film of that much emulsion speed, and the finder image tends to be dim when the lens is stopped down to small apertures.

This is the system used in Bell & Howell's next entry in the technology sweepstakes: the Director Zoom Reflex Model 434, introduced in 1961. In this system the beam-splitter being placed ahead of the iris diaphragm diverts a portion of the incoming light to a second beam-splitter, while most of the light goes through the rear lens element to the film. The second beam-splitter sends most of its received light to the viewfinder, while a small portion goes to a cadmium sulfide (CdS) cell, the output of which goes to a galvanometer which actuates the diaphragm.

Focusing Systems

The earliest focusing system consisted of inscribed distance markings on the camera lens barrel; the user then measured or estimated the lens-to-subject distance and set the lens accordingly. This method left ample room for error on the part of either the user or the camera maker, and a more accurate method called critical focusing soon evolved.

Critical focusing is essentially the familiar method of focusing a view camera: the image is received on a ground glass placed at the film plane, which is inspected by the photographer from the rear of the camera. To accomplish this with a movie camera requires some modifications: the back of the film gate must be open and a viewing tube provided from the rear of the camera up to the rear of the gate. In the days before anti-halation backing, which made the film opaque, the photographer could focus on the film itself. This system was common on early professional cameras and was also used on the 1899 Birtac.

With the introduction of turret lenses, critical focusing was accomplished by rotating the taking lens to a position in front of a ground-glass screen located to one side of the film gate. There the image could be inspected from a top- or side-mounted window. This scheme was employed on many cameras, such as the Bell & Howell Filmo and the early Bolex H-16s.

Some cameras were equipped with rangefinder systems, which came in several varieties. The earliest produced two images, when these images were brought together, the distance was read off a scale and the lens set accordingly. With a coupled rangefinder, the action of bringing the images together automatically set the lens. Other rangefinders presented a split image in the form of a small circle in the center of the viewfinder image. The circle is brought over a vertical "edge" in the scene, the focus adjusted until the chosen edge goes unbroken across the circle. This can generally be done quite rapidly if there is a distinct edge in the scene.

A micro-prism rangefinder also consists of a small circle in the finder that is cross-hatched with a pattern of small prisms, which have the effect of magnifying any lack of focus. The lens is manipulated until the pattern within the circle shows least distortion. This system, while somewhat slower to operate, does not require a straight edge in the scene.

Exposure Control

Getting an acceptable exposure on movie film was a fairly simple matter in the days of black-and-white, relatively slow film and slow lenses. Most instruction books of the 1920s recognized four or five classes of subjects and a similar number of lighting conditions, giving a matrix of up to 25 combinations. It was then up to the operator to match the conditions confronting him with the table and select the indicated lens opening from the four or five available. Most cameras were provided with an exposure guide in the form of a plate affixed to the front of the camera, with light conditions marked

thereon. A pointer attached to the diaphragm control ring was then set at the existing conditions and the lens opening would be set appropriately.

This system was satisfactory as long as all the films available had the same speed, (at that time panchromatic black-and-white film with an exposure index of 40) but when faster black-and-white and slower Kodachrome came along in 1935 and cameras with variable frame rates became available, the old exposure guides were no longer usable. Eastman Kodak devised an interesting solution called the Ciné Kodak Universal Guide, which first appeared on the Ciné-Kodak Models 25 and 60, in 1933. Packed with every roll of Eastman Kodak film was a slip of silvered cardboard, printed with scale-of-light conditions for that film. This was slipped into a special frame on the side of the camera, which carried a moveable pointer wheel with a double-ended arrow. The user set one end of the arrow at the appropriate light conditions, and the other end indicated the lens opening. This simple device was used on 8mm Ciné-Kodaks well into the 1950s and even appeared on the elegant Ciné Special.

Another method of estimating the proper aperture setting was by the use of an exposure calculator. An early and quite elaborate example was Kaufmann's "Posographe," originating in France about 1923 (Fig. 241). The one illustrated was made specifically for the Pathé Baby, although they were also made for still cameras. A metal frame carried six pointers which could be set for various conditions, i.e.: month, hour, sky condition, nature of the subject and the surroundings, etc. The pointers were inter-connected by linkages arranged so that moving any one variable had its appropriate effect on the other pointers.

A much later exposure calculator was marketed by Eastman Kodak in 1947, in the form of a pocket-sized "Kodaguide," with two dials which gave exposures for color or black-and-white, indoors or out. It sold for 25 cents.

The earliest devices that attempted to actually measure the illumination of a scene were of the extinction type, in which the scene was viewed through a screen of graded density, carrying a series of letters or numbers. The highest number visible was then correlated to the proper aperture. Typical of this type was the Dremophot of the early 1930s, manufactured by Drem Products Ltd., of Great Britain (Fig. 242).

A considerably more precise measurement could be obtained if the illumination of the scene was compared to the brightness of a standard light source, in a device called a photometer. Bell & Howell made one, patented in 1924, in which the light source was a small bulb powered by a battery in the handle. A rheostat was built into the handle that was calibrated and marked with an aperture scale controlled the brightness of the bulb.

The application of the photoelectric effect to photography marked a major advance in exposure control. There are basically two kinds of photoelectric effect: one is the change in electrical resistance of certain materials when exposed to light, the other is the voltage generated by certain materials when exposed to light. The metal selenium exhibits both effects, and the very earliest photoelectric meters used the varying resistance property of selenium to measure light.

A number of meters were produced in Europe in the mid- to late-nineteenth century using the selenium cell, but the first such meter to be produced in commercial quantities was the Rhamstine Electrophot meter of 1931. Shortly thereafter, Weston began producing photoelectric exposure meters designed especially for amateur motion picture use, notably the rather massive Model 627 and the more compact Models 720 and 819. These meters all used the voltage generation property of the selenium cell, without auxiliary battery, and it is remarkable how many will be found still operable (Fig. 243).

As photoelectrical technology improved, meters were sized down until they could be conveniently clipped on to the camera. Eventually they were built in, with the meter needle visible in the viewfinder. It was only a matter of time until the aperture control was fitted with a pointer, also visible in the finder, and when the aperture pointer was lined up with the meter needle, the setting was correct. This was called the "match needle" system, available on many European cameras in the 1950s, such as the Eumig C3, the Nizo Heliomatic, and others. [12]

The first motion picture camera with fully automatic exposure control was the Bell & Howell Model 200EE, a 16mm magazine camera introduced in 1956. A selenium cell mounted under the lens fed

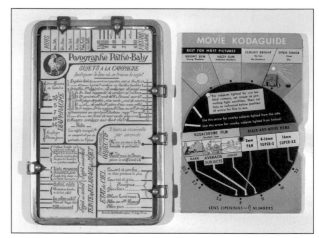

Fig. 241. Exposure guides, the Posographe (left) and Kodak Movie Guide (right).

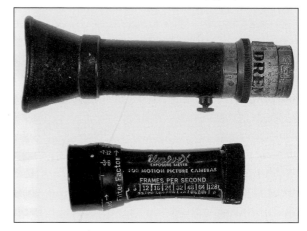

Fig. 242. Extinction meters, the Drem (top) and UniveX (bottom).

Fig. 243. Exposure meters: Norwood Director (top left), General Electric (top right), and Weston (bottom).

its voltage to a servomotor control that regulated the output of six Mallory mercury cells to a motor that operated the aperture blades. The instruction book said that the drain on the batteries was very low and that the six cells should last through 200 magazines of film. [13]

Within a year, Bell & Howell made another startling announcement. An October 1957 photo magazine editorialized "Bell & Howell's automatic-exposure Model 290 revolutionizes 8mm movie making." Bell & Howell's double-page ad proclaimed: "A camera that uses the energy of light to assure perfect exposures." (See Fig. 244.)

The camera was compact, all metal and spool-loading. A selenium cell with the familiar honeycomb diffuser mounted below the lens fed its voltage to a galvanometer also mounted on the lens board; the galvanometer shaft carried a pointer to show the aperture in a window and, at the same time, operated the aperture blades for the proper exposure. Since the output of a selenium cell varies with temperature, the designers included a compensating thermistor in the circuitry. There was also provision for manual override and a mask for the cell to provide for film speeds of either ASA 10 or ASA 16.[14]

The system was indeed revolutionary, but it had one limitation: the photoelectric cell had one angle of light acceptance, which was of course made to coincide with the camera lens, but when interchangeable lenses, converters, and zoom lenses came into use, the meter could not respond accurately. The answer, of course, was to place the meter behind the taking lens, so that it read only the light coming through the lens. This led to a profusion of designs, differing only slightly in principle.

An early example of behind-the-lens metering was the Camex CR offered by Ercsam in 1960, which company, as noted, pioneered reflex viewing with the Camex Reflex in 1956. The CR retained the mirror on an oscillating shutter, but the diverted beam was passed to a beam-splitter that divided the beam between a cadmium sulfide cell and the viewfinder. The CdS cell activated a galvanometer needle visible in the finder, for manual adjustment of the diaphragm. The system was thus termed semi-automatic exposure control. As the metering system was completely separate from the objective lens, interchangeable lenses could be used (Fig. 245).

Fig. 244. Bell & Howell Model 290.

The first U.S-made 8mm camera with full-time behind-the-lens metering was the Bell & Howell Director Reflex Zoom camera, introduced in 1961. The photocell received a diverted portion of the light passing through the taking lens, the balance of which went to the film. The cell was of the cadmium sulfide photo-resistive type, and power to operate the diaphragm was supplied by a 1.35v mercury battery. The camera was equipped with an Angenieux 9 to 36mm, f/1.8 powered zoom lens, and listed at $350 for the Model 434 (roll film) and $370 for the Model 444 (magazine) (Fig. 246).

The principal difference between this system and the semi-automatic system was that the output of the CdS cell operated the aperture blades automatically, without attention from the user. A film-speed knob on the camera added or subtracted resistance to the electrical circuit to adjust for the emulsion speed of the film being used.

This camera appeared in 1961. By the close of 1963, no less than 40 8mm cameras offering zoom lenses, fully automatic exposure control, and reflex viewing were on the market, ranging in price from under $80 for the Jelco Reflex 77 to $650 for the Bolex H8 Rex. Of these 40 models, not more than eight were of U.S. manufacture.

Effect on 16mm Camera Market

By 1964, the 8mm camera had reached a level of versatility and sophistication that had a profound effect on the fortunes of its parent, the 16mm camera. With the 8mm camera offering electric drive,

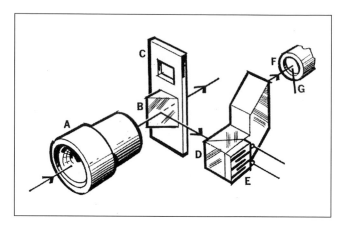

Fig. 245. Semi-automatic metering system for cameras with interchangeable lenses. (A) camera lens, (B) beamsplitter, (C) oscillating shutter, (D) second beamsplitter, (E) CdS cell, (F) viewfinder, (G) galvanometer needle.

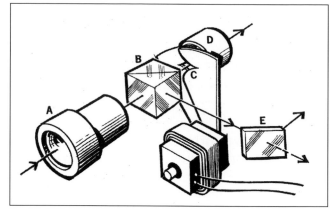

Fig. 246. Bell & Howell Director Reflex Zoom System. (A) camera lens, (B) first beamsplitter, (C) aperture blades, (D) second camera lens (E) second beamsplitter.

zoom lenses, automatic exposure control, reflex viewing and focusing—an instrument, in short, with many of the attributes of the professional camera, at an average list price of just 35 percent of that of a 16mm camera—more and more amateurs were turning to the narrower gauge.

Film cost, for which both purchase and processing cost vary directly as image area, weighed heavily in the equation, with 16mm film costing as much as three times 8mm cost for a given length of screen time. The result was a steady decline in the number of 16mm models offered, beginning in 1959 (Fig. 247).

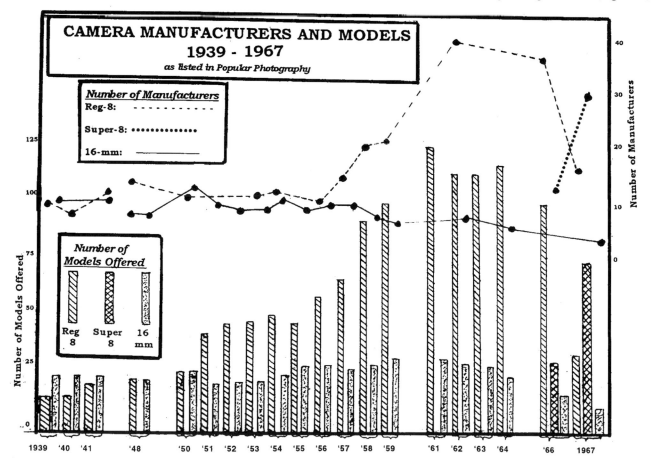

Fig. 247. Chart showing changes in camera manufacturers and models offered, 1939-1967.

The flight of the amateur to 8mm was somewhat offset by a steady growth in professional use of 16mm for sports reporting, spot news, and some documentaries.

The 20 years following World War II had seen almost every element of the amateur ciné camera undergo radical change; but in one area 8mm cameras had changed hardly at all. Except for the three makes of user-loaded cartridges as previously discussed, 8mm retained the time-consuming, error-prone chore of stopping filming after 25 feet, opening the camera, reversing the spools, and re-threading the film for the second 25 feet. But research had been going on at Eastman Kodak for several years on a new system which was to radically change the whole face of amateur technology: the Super 8 System.

Kodachrome II Super 8 movie cartridge.

8MM—Yearning to Be Heard

Standard 8mm, or "double eight" as it was sometimes called, introduced in 1932, persisted for nearly 30 years before serious proposals were advanced for changing the format. Firmly established in this country as the leading amateur gauge, even challenging 9.5mm in Europe, it had not as yet made substantial penetration of the commercial, industrial, or educational markets for several reasons. First, these markets required inexpensive, multiple prints, so-called "release prints," in color and sound. While Kodachrome came to 8mm in 1936, sound had only recently been applied to the small format, with barely acceptable performance.[1] Secondly, as films for those markets were shown, in general, to larger audiences than amateur movies, a larger and brighter screen image was needed.

Examining a piece of film, one sees that the width of the film must accommodate the picture, the sprocket holes, the sound track, and space at either edge for strength and positioning the film in the gate. Since the quality of both sound and picture extractable from the film is chiefly proportional to the area assigned to these functions, the designer's problem is to maximize the area (and thus width) given to these two functions, while giving the least possible width to the other functions.

As proposals for improving the 8mm format began to surface,[2] Eastman Kodak's Film Services Division was wrestling with the magazine problem. In 1961, Lawrence A. Ulmschneider, one of the Division's engineers and an expert on injection molding, proposed making a disposable plastic magazine, but as that still permitted the public to put the magazines in wrong, double expose, or half expose, Kodak management vetoed the idea. Instead, Dr. J. S. Chandler of the Kodak Research Laboratories, after a thorough study of all existing and proposed film formats, decided the only solution lay in an entirely new approach: pre-split, single-width 8mm film.

An additional incentive to revitalize the standard 8mm format could well have been the sharp drop in U. S. 8mm camera sales, as noted in Chapter 5; from a high of 1,108,000 units in 1959 to 787,000 in 1961. In *Kodak Dealer News* for July 1963, Ken Stuart, Kodak's director of market research, stated that unit sales of 8mm cameras and projectors had declined every year since 1959. Stuart postulated three reasons: many people still felt that taking movies was more difficult than taking still pictures, most people thought that movies were expensive, and some dealers had a tendency to oversell more advanced and thus higher-priced features than the customer really needed, or wanted. How these factors were met by Super 8 will be examined further on, but Kodak's marketing people must have felt that a system that would banish the old 25-foot run and the magazine turn-over, and give a bigger, brighter image, would give the 8mm camera market a much needed boost.

A New Format Proposed

Kodak's approach to a new format was made public in a paper presented on April 30, 1962, at the Society of Motion Picture and Television Engineers Convention in Los Angeles.[3] In this paper, C. J. Staud, then Director, Kodak Research Laboratories, and W. T. Hanson, Jr., Assistant Director, carefully reviewed the parameters mentioned above, as well as perforation pitch and aspect ratio, and the necessity for balancing the sometimes conflicting demands of these functions. A most important consideration in any proposal to change of format was the desirability of keeping the new format compatible with reduction printing from 16mm originals, considered to be the method yielding the best quality of sound color release prints.

Beginning with the basic premise that greater image area was an absolute necessity, Staud and Hanson looked first at the most obvious element in the standard 8mm format: the perforations, which were the same size and shape as those used in 16mm film. A reduction of no less than 50 percent of the width of the perforation was deemed feasible without requiring any more than a narrower pull-down claw. Similarly, the 8mm frame line (the space between adjacent frames) was narrowed. With these two changes, Staud and Hanson declared that a 50 percent increase in picture area was possible. They did acknowledge that this would change the perforation pitch, making the proposed format incompatible with existing projection equipment. The new pitch however would still be within acceptable limits for reduction printing from 16mm originals, and would leave sufficient room for a sound track.

On the question of sound, their work had persuaded Staud and Hanson that optimum sound quality would be achieved with magnetic, rather than optical (i.e. photographic), sound recording. While a magnetic system was somewhat more expensive, they were convinced that continuing research and experimentation would eventually lower this differential.

Staud and Hanson's conclusions were not universally accepted. For example, J. A. Maurer, an ardent advocate of optical sound who had proposed an 8mm film with optical sound track in 1961, now proposed still another format using film 8.75mm wide, with optical track which could be slit from 35mm film.[4] There is no evidence that this proposal ever received serious consideration.

The prospect of any new format that would be incompatible with existing 8mm equipment, particularly projectors, was distressing to many in the industry. Writing in *Popular Photography* of February 1963, Leendert Drukker deplored the fact that new standards were being considered when regular 8mm standards had just been ratified by the industry and stated that there was no room for two parallel miniature movie formats. He also warned "the latest barrage of proposals and counter-proposals will inevitably upset 8mm's progress as a mass communications medium." This despite the fact that he had been assured a few months earlier by Dr. Staud as follows:

It appears to us that for many years to come the current format will continues to be used, both in the professional and amateur field, and that equipment such as the Kodak 8mm sound projectors should continue to prove useful for many years in the future.[5]

Notwithstanding Dr. Staud's assurances on the future of standard 8mm, Kodak was proceeding at full speed with the development of a new format that would completely supplant the old 8mm format.

The New System Unveiled

Almost exactly two years after the Staud/Hanson paper, on April 17, 1964, Evan A. Edwards of Kodak's Film Services Division, read a paper at an SMPTE Technical Conference in Los Angeles entitled "Format Factors Affecting 8mm Sound Print Quality." [6] Despite the undramatic title, the paper, co-authored by Edwards and Dr. J.S. Chandler (Fig. 248) of the Kodak Research Laboratories, revealed that Eastman Kodak was now positioned to take the revolutionary step merely suggested in the Staud/Hanson paper and launch a totally new format which would be incompatible with the 30-year-old standard 8mm. Detailed engineering drawings of the proposed film and drive sprockets were shown, as well as the results of extensive projection life tests.

In the discussion that followed, the authors were questioned closely about the impact of the new format on the five million amateurs who owned standard 8mm equipment, and secondly on the probable date of introduction of the new format. In answer to the first question, Edwards and Chandler emphasized that the format being proposed was aimed specifically at the commercial, industrial and educational markets, where there was relatively little 8mm equipment in use, and that if it were generally accepted in these fields, then in all probability equipment for the amateur market would follow suit. On the second question, they declined to give a specific answer, possibly on the instructions of their marketing people; the actual introduction of the new format came just one year later.[7] (See Fig. 249.)

Publicity "Beat"– Shades of 1923!

The general public received its first look at the revolutionary system sometime in May of 1965, when the June issue of *Popular Photography* hit the stands, with a stunning cover showing a very futuristic-looking projector and several cameras. The copy read in part: "New Concept In Movies—Super 8—A Bell & Howell Super 8 Camera And Projector Grow Before Your Eyes" but not a word about Kodak. Inside, a 7-page story by Leonard Lipton began:

For the first time in the history of any major photographic magazine, a major photographic manufacturer has opened the doors to its shops, laboratories, production lines, and conference rooms so that the readers of Popular Photography might see how a new product is born. [8] (See Fig. 250.)

Fig. 248. J.S. Chandler.

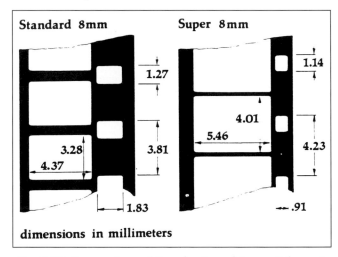

Fig. 249. Comparison of Regular 8 and Super 8 formats.

The "major photographic manufacturer" was Bell & Howell, and a reader could have easily missed the two casual mentions of the name of the company that developed this revolutionary system. He would have also looked in vain for any advertisement of a Kodak movie camera in this issue, which, for a company that regularly took several pages, was nothing short of astounding.

This peculiar situation was a bizarre reprise of some events that took place in 1923 when Alexander Victor, contrary to a solemn agreement with Eastman Kodak, jumped the gun with the announcement of his 16mm camera some two months before the agreed-upon release date. Then forever afterwards Victor claimed priority in bringing the 16mm system to the public. This time the culprit was Bell & Howell. Whether the coup was entirely deliberate or a failure in communication is not known, but the end result was the same: Eastman Kodak's carefully planned introductory publicity was upstaged by an arch-rival in the amateur ciné equipment business.

As it had in the past with other innovations, Kodak made its plans for a new format available for a price to other camera manufacturers in pure self-interest. The more Super 8 cameras in the public's hands, the more Super 8 film would be consumed, and Eastman Kodak enjoyed a dominant share of the amateur film market.

Once Kodak management was convinced that the Super 8 format would be a viable and profitable product, an invitation went out to all camera manufacturers to attend an informational meeting in Rochester. There they were shown the startling new features of the system; the 50-foot drop-in-loading cartridge; the automatic daylight filter setting, the 50 percent greater projected image area. They were also presumably given some insight into the engineering and manufacturing problems that would be involved to tool up for this new product.

Not all manufacturers were willing or able to make the investment; many adopted a "wait-and-see" attitude. Bell & Howell marketing executives, however, were quick to appreciate the potential of the new system, and resolved from the first meeting to have cameras and projectors on the market at least as quickly as Kodak and sooner, if at all possible. Engineering and manufacturing staffs were given this goal as top priority.[9]

Kodak, meanwhile, had planned a June 1965 release date. If the June issue of *Popular Photography* hadn't somehow slipped out in May, all would have been well. Kodak's then vice-president of marketing, (later chairman), Gerald B. Zornow, was not amused; harsh words were exchanged with *Popular Photography's* publisher, threats of withdrawing advertising were made, but the damage, if any except to pride, was done.[10]

On June 6, 1965, Kodak's announcement came. The company unleashed what it described as the biggest movie marketing-assistance program in Kodak history, beginning with six full minutes of network television commercials on Disney's *Wonderful World of Color*, and 20 more minutes of network ads later in June. The same month saw multi-page spreads in *LIFE, LOOK, Saturday Evening*

Post, TIME, and *The New Yorker*. Over 200 daily newspapers carried 1,000-line ads, and dealers had fountains of display materials available to them with their first order on the factory.

Some aspects of this bravura assault on the amateur market makes one wonder why Kodak maintained as late as 1963 that the new format was aimed at "educational, commercial and industrial applications." The targeted market for the new product seems unquestionably to have been the amateur filmer, beginning with the Instamatic name itself, thus tying the product in the public's mind with the hugely successful Instamatic still cameras, which sold over ten million units in the first two years on the market. And with Walt Disney as salesman for the vast TV audience, Kodak chose a handsome little blond four-year old called "Speedy Loadum" to demonstrate the product to retailers, in *Kodak Dealer News* for July-August 1965. The message was: Super 8 cameras are "FUN" and "EASY TO USE!"

Behind the Scenes at Bell & Howell

While Bell & Howell did not reveal all of its secrets to Leonard Lipton for the *Popular Photography* article, at least the names of principal designers were given, as well as a general idea of the creative process.

Bell & Howell management set a goal of two cameras, code-named "Bluejays," and four projectors code-named "Pointers." Four design teams were assigned to the project: an industrial design team headed up by Robert Smith, a camera design team under David MacMillan, a projector design team under George Krtous, and an optical design team under the direction of Dr. Arthur Cox.

The industrial design team's task was to come up with as many fresh ideas for the external appearance of both camera and projector as possible. From their sketches, wooden mock-ups of the most promising designs were made, and many of these appeared in the cover illustration (Fig. 250).

The camera design team, again selecting the most promising of the mock-ups, set about to design "the most comfortable, easy-to-handle (camera) . . . that should be usable without a pistol grip." An impartial observer, holding a Design 431 in hand today might well ask "What happened?"—as the heavy, blocky camera, with its operating button way up on top of the body is quite difficult to operate

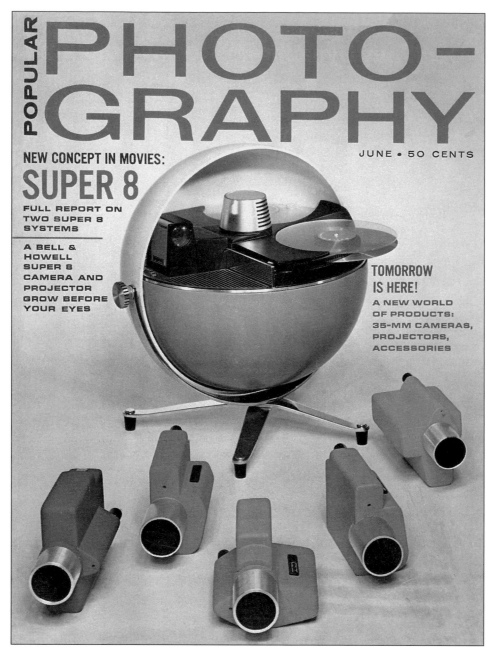

Fig. 250. Popular Photography cover, June 1965.

for a person with small to average hands, yet is totally saved if the detachable pistol grip is used.

Dr. Cox's optical design team utilized what was then the relatively new technique of computer-aided lens design, known as optical transfer functions, or OTF. This enabled the designers to create lens designs in hours, which might have taken years by human computation. The end result was a zoom lens with comparable zoom range to the old style lens with one-fifth of the volume.[11]

The automatic exposure control system was described as a closed-loop feedback system and, from a schematic shown in the article, appeared very similar to Matzkin's Type No. 3 in the placement of the beamsplitters, aperture blades, and use of a moving mirror.[12] Designing such systems was nothing new to Bell & Howell, of course, since the first 16mm camera with automatic exposure control in 1956, the first 8mm system in 1957, and the first through-the-lens electric eye camera in 1962 were all Bell & Howell innovations.

One problem remained; as faster and faster films were introduced, ever smaller apertures were required for very bright light situations. Very small apertures, however, cause diffraction of the light rays passing through the aperture, resulting in a fuzzy image. This is particularly a problem with lenses of short focal length, such as are typically found on 8mm cameras.

Bell & Howell's approach to the problem was to place a small opaque dot on the center of the lens element directly behind the aperture blades. When the blades are wide open, the dot has an insignificant effect on the amount of light passed; however, as the aperture blades close down, the dot occupies a larger proportion of the open area. With this device, the Bluejay lens could be stopped down to an effective aperture of f/64.

The final Bluejay cameras, designated Models 430 and 431, were equipped with f/1.9, 11-35mm zoom lenses in focusing mounts, reflex viewing, automatic exposure control, and battery drive. The Model 430, with manual zoom, was priced at $159.95; the Model 431 featured power zoom, and was priced at $219.95 (Fig. 251).

The motion picture projector was just as vital to the amateur movie enthusiast as his camera—even more so, since if he didn't own a camera, he could still enjoy purchased or rented films if he owned a projector. As noted in a previous chapter, during the first two decades of the century, movie projectors were decidedly more common in the home than movie cameras.

One of the principal challenges facing the projector design team was to punch as much light through the new 50 percent larger frame as possible. Three major lamp manufacturers were consulted who came up with three new high-efficiency lamps. The new lamps, coupled with increased cooling at the film gate, resulted in a series of projectors that gave from 100 percent to over 200 percent greater screen lumens than the standard 8mm projector.

Bell & Howell introduced four projectors, all of which featured so-called "automatic reel-to-reel loading," i.e., self-threading of the film from the first film sprocket to the take-up reel. This design was not an unmixed blessing; when a cobble did occur, it was much more difficult to remove the film than with the old open film-path design. It is interesting to note that Bell & Howell retained the all-gear drive of feed and take-up spindles, which it pioneered back in the 1930s. It is also interesting that Bell & Howell did not offer a dual-8 projector at this time.

Fig. 251. Bell & Howell Model 431, with power zoom lens.

Behind The Scenes At Eastman Kodak

Six months elapsed before Eastman Kodak's turn came for a story similar to the Bell & Howell scoop; an article by James S. Forney in the December 1965 issue of *Popular Photography* focused chiefly on the design of the cartridge. Again, fortunately for the historian, the names of the protagonists were given. Kodak's camera design team was led by Vernon H. Jungjohann, the optical design group by Clair Smith, and the projector specialists team by Morris E. Brown.[13]

Designing The Cartridge

Evan A. Edwards and Lloyd Sugden (Fig. 252) had the responsibility for cartridge design. Edwards was a specialist in molded parts, having worked on the Instamatic 126 cartridge (1963), the Pocket Instamatic 110 cartridge (1972), and held numerous patents on injection molding, molded products, and injection molding machines.[14]

The first problem in designing a new cartridge to replace the old magazine was to accommodate twice the length of film. Keeping the one-over-one arrangement as in the Duex cassette design, for example, would have necessitated a long thin cartridge that would be prone to distortion in handling. The

Fig. 252. Evan Edwards(left) and Llyod Sugden
(right) of Eastman Kodak.

answer lay in a co-axial design, with the supply spool side-by-side with the take-up spool. This yielded the boxy and extremely sturdy final design.

Another major consideration in designing the new cartridge was to achieve absolutely smooth transit of the entire 50-foot length of film through the cartridge, essential for steadiness of the film image. To study the dynamics of the film transit, Edward's group constructed a "dynamometer camera." This ingenious device continuously measured and recorded the force required to move each frame through the film gate. The pull-down claw, just a quarter-inch thick, was equipped with a strain gauge. Thus force/displacement graphs could be plotted over a wide range of temperatures and humidity levels. It was soon discovered that there were a number of delicate mechanical adjustments required to guarantee uniform progress of the film, and some elegant solutions to all the problems were eventually found.

The film advance through the gate was actually accomplished by "push down;" the claw engaging the film two frames above the aperture. This arrangement was necessitated by self-threading projectors, which require the claw to be located above the aperture. If the projector uses the same perforation that was used by the camera, then any slight variation in the perforation process will not affect the steadiness of the projected image.[15]

The final cartridge design was an assembly of six injection-molded parts, each of different composition depending on their function, and one phosphor bronze spring, bearing on the pressure plate, all manufactured to extremely close tolerances. To avoid the film plane positioning inaccuracies to which previous magazine designs were subject, the new cartridge had a spring-loaded pressure plate behind the film. When the cartridge was inserted in the camera, that plate pushed the film into the camera's film gate where three locator studs arrested the pressure plate and film in precise position relative to the optical system.

The cartridge had two other functions; by means of notches on the front edge, it told the camera what speed of film it contained, and whether or not a Type A filter was needed. On top of all this, the cartridge had to be nearly indestructible under the worst conditions that might be encountered in its life from Kodak Park to the consumer, then to the processor, and yet be readily opened by the processing laboratory.

Designing The Camera

Designing a camera for a mass market is a complex task, of which the interior mechanism is of course an essential part, but not the whole job. The camera body must have eye-appeal, be comfortable to hold, easy to operate, and sturdy. And above all, the final design must be capable of mass production at a cost that will permit a modest selling price and still leave a margin for profit.

The Kodak camera design team was headed up by David Babcock, chief of the Development Department, working with Senior Engineer William Martin, Richard Olson of the Industrial Design Department, and Donald O. Easterly.[16] The first working prototype camera was whittled out of wood by Dick Olson, to which Easterly added parts from one of Kodak Park's cartridge dynamometers. The camera actually took pictures and, when suitably "dressed up" and demonstrated to management, received the go-ahead signal from Marketing.

Directed to produce designs for a full line of cameras using the new film and cartridge, from inexpensive to a full-featured zoom lens model, the team spent countless hours over drawing board and model bench. To meet the low-end cost targets, Olson and Easterly designed a camera body using glass-reinforced plastic for structural and exterior parts. Kodak marketing executives were not comfortable with a plastic body for the high-end camera, so Olson and Easterly designed a die-cast metal body for the camera that would become the M-6 model. One of the "blue sky" models which Olson devised was the so-called "binocular format," which was considered extreme at the time but eventually became the model for the 1971 XL camera.

The cameras were initially designed to load in the conventional manner on the left side, an arrangement which arose from the necessity for spring-motor driven cameras to have the winding handle on the right side, convenient for the right hand. Just as the prototype was ready for tooling, the designers realized that with the surge in popularity of battery-operated cameras, a spring-driven model would probably not be needed, and that the camera might as well be designed for right-hand loading. The change was made, to the considerable annoyance of the cartridge design team at Kodak Park, where thousands of cartridges were being turned out for testing. As Easterly pointed out, with today's computer-aided design technology, making mirror images of drawings is child's play; in those days it meant many hours of drafting board time.[17]

Large scale testing of the cameras and cartridges was considered imperative. While cartridges were tested at Kodak Park, the Apparatus Division made over 100 trial cameras that were given to employees to test on weekends. Over 300,000 cartridges and 15 million feet of film were tested before the system was released to the public.

The Product

The end product, as far as the purchaser was concerned, was the Kodak Instamatic Movie Camera, and its film, a 50-foot load of Kodachrome II Super 8 film in a chunky black plastic cartridge, called a Kodapak. As the ads trumpeted, all you had to do was open the box the cartridge came in, open the camera, drop in the cartridge, close the camera, and shoot. There were three camera models, labeled M2, M4, and M6 Instamatics, and they promised to do for the movie maker what the cartridge-loaded Instamatic camera had done for the still camera shooter (Fig. 253).

All three models featured drop-in loading, electric motor drive, automatic Type A filter positioning keyed to the specific film in the cartridge, snap-in slot for a movie light, auto footage indicator. The M2 had an f/1.8 fixed focus lens; the M4 added automatic exposure control; while the top-of-the-line

Fig. 253. Kodak's Instamatic Model M6 camera, M-70 projector at rear.

M6 sported a 12 to 36mm zoom lens and reflex through-the-lens viewing. Prices were $46.50, $69.50, and $174.50. As the new film could only be projected on a projector designed for it, Kodak introduced six Instamatic movie projectors, one of which could project either Super 8 or regular 8mm.

A comparison of these models with Bell & Howell's introductory models is illustrative of the marketing strategy of the two companies. Kodak's most expensive model, the M-6, was exactly equal in features and price to Bell & Howell's lower priced, manual zoom Model 430, but while Bell & Howell offered a power-zoom model at almost 40 percent more, Kodak offered two simpler models at roughly one-half and one-third the price of the M-6.

On The Bandwagon

Bell & Howell, Kodak's biggest competitor in amateur movie apparatus, as we have seen, was one of the first domestic producers to get on the market with both Super 8 cameras and projectors.

Curiously, only one company advertised a Super 8 product in the June 1965 "breakthrough" issue of *Popular Photography;* Eumig presented its Mark S 8mm sound projector, which was available in either standard 8 or "the all-new Super 8." However, under new product information, a dozen manufacturers were listed as either offering, or about to introduce at least two dozen Super 8 products. And by December, when the 1966 Directory was published, there were 13 manufacturers offering 30 different Super 8 models. Of these 13 companies, seven were U.S., the balance were foreign.

Single 8—Sincere Flattery?

Kodak's announcement of Super 8 coincided with the announcement of another "new" format, or more accurately, a duplication of the Super 8 format on a different film base; Fuji Photo Film Company's Single 8. The format was identical to Eastman Kodak's Super 8 down to every last dimension.[18] The film itself, however, was polyester-based, rather than the acetate-based Kodak film. As polyester has a higher tensile strength than cellulose triacetate, Fuji was able to use a base approximately two-thirds the thickness of Kodak's film.[19]

This permitted the Fuji engineers to design a considerably smaller cartridge. The diameter of a 50-foot coil of polyester being two-thirds or less than a coil of acetate, the designers could revert to the over-and-under configuration that was used back in 1923, when Pathé introduced the 9.5mm Pathé Baby camera. In fact, you can almost slip a Pathéx cartridge into the Fujica camera! Also like the Pathéx cartridge, the Single 8 cartridge did not contain the pressure plate, which was mounted in the camera. A length of film extended from the cartridge and was inserted in the film gate/pressure plate assembly in the camera.

This configuration led to another benefit: backwind capability. The somewhat convoluted film path in the Super 8 cartridge ruled out backwinding. Other features of the Single 8 cartridge mimicked the Super 8 cartridge: notches in the back to automatically adjust the camera's automatic exposure control system for the proper film speed, and positioning of a Type A filter if needed.

Fuji launched the new system with two new cameras, and two projectors—one silent and one sound. The low-end camera, the Fujica P1, (Fig. 254) was battery operated, single speed, f/1.8 lens with fixed focus, automatic exposure control by CdS cell and mercury battery, and was listed at $79.95. The Z-1 featured a 9.5-29mm f/1.6 focusing zoom lens, 18 and 24fps camera speeds, manual over-ride of the automatic exposure control system, and was listed at $159.50.

Fig. 254. The Fujica P-1 Single 8 camera and cartridge.

Initially, Fuji announced that some 15 manufacturers were considering the Single 8 format, and at Photokina 1966 Single 8 models were shown by Canon, Elmo, Konica and Yashica, as well as Fuji. However, in the 1973 *Popular Photography* directory, only Fuji was shown as supplying Single 8 equipment.

Super 8—How Successful Was It?

There is some evidence that both Eastman Kodak and Bell & Howell were surprised at how well the new format caught on with the buying public and how quickly it displaced standard 8mm in the home market. Within two years of the introduction of Super 8, the number of standard 8mm camera models offered on the U.S. market by all manufacturers dropped from a high in 1964 of 117, to a mere 38 in the 1967 directories. Kodak itself discontinued all but one standard 8 camera by the end of 1966, the Brownie "Fun Saver," which was discontinued in November 1968.

A Bell & Howell *Dealer Bulletin* of October 1965 advised dealers that:

Orders for Super 8 equipment have far exceeded our expectations. Super 8 has received a very enthusiastic reception from both dealers and the public. We are struggling to catch up with your orders, please be patient, you can be sure we will do everything we can to fill your orders as quickly as possible.

Even allowing for marketing professionals' innate optimism, it seems probable that Kodak's publicity blitz had paid off. Curiously, there is little evidence of strong marketing efforts by Kodak's competitors during the months immediately following Kodak's introduction of Super 8; in fact while Kodak continued to advertise, none of the other domestic manufacturers took ad space in the popular photography magazines, yet foreign manufacturers advertised their Super 8 products quite heavily. The same *Dealer Bulletin* reported another interesting phenomenon: 1965 was a very strong year for standard 8mm sales, particularly projectors. This was almost entirely due to the "dumping" of standard 8mm equipment by dealers who realized that these stocks would be increasingly difficult to sell as Super 8 took over the market.[20]

There were some discordant voices, however. Some 8mm users, thinking no doubt of past experience with 8mm magazines, were quick to point out the potential for trouble with the pressure plate being located in the film cartridge rather than in the camera and the possibility of film jamming in the cartridge. Neither of these fears was realized; the cartridge designers had done their work carefully. Millions of Super 8 users seemed to be quite satisfied with the sharpness of their films. Jamming or any other malfunctions due to the cartridge were extremely rare.

Not all manufacturers were happy; Paillard was reported to have been undecided about entering the Super 8 market and published a list of arguments against abandoning the standard 8mm format. Most of these alleged shortcomings were familiar: the pressure plate in the cartridge, the incapability of backwind, and the fact that only Kodachrome II Type A was available in the cartridge. Paillard was also thought to have been waiting to bring out a Super 8 Bolex for professional use, taking film in 100-foot lengths or more, but was stymied until Kodak provided Kodachrome II in these lengths.[21]

Eastman Kodak did offer Kodachrome II A, Kodachrome II Daylight, and Tri-X black and white reversal film in "double Super 8," 16mm film with Super 8 perforations on both edges, which was handled as with standard 8mm, run through the camera twice, and split and spliced after processing. At least one European manufacturer seized on this format and produced the Pathé DS-8/BTL, which at $844.50 with an Angenieux f/1.9 8mm-64mm lens was obviously not aimed at the amateur market.

Another very versatile and very expensive Super 8 camera was the Beaulieu S2008 introduced in 1966 that, while still loading with the Kodapak Super 8 cartridge, featured interchangeable C-mount lenses, multiple filming speeds, frame and footage counters, and variable shutter. The S2008 had a list price of $695.

By June 1969, four years after the introduction of Super 8, Eastman Kodak had brought out 18 camera models, or better than four per year. The average model life was 2-1/2 years, and the cameras seemed to fill every conceivable level of sophistication and price niche, from the palm-sized 1967 Model M12, which at $29.95 had a lens and a shutter and very little else, to the 1968 Model M9 at $229.50, with an f/1.8 9.5 to 45mm power zoom lens, focusing to four feet, four filming speeds, backlight compensation, remote control socket, etc. Other U.S. manufacturers such as Keystone, Revere, and DeJur followed this "saturation" strategy to some degree, while European manufacturers tended to limit their offerings to two or three models.

Actual sales figures are impossible to obtain, for several reasons. First, ever fearful of charges of monopoly, Eastman Kodak made sure that market share and film and camera sales figures were known only in the highest levels of management. Finally, as a result of a painful lawsuit, Kodak installed a "Records Retention Schedule" that imposed stringent limits on the length of time that records could be retained, so that in all likelihood sales figures for 15 or 20 years ago have long since been shredded.

One year after Super 8's introduction, according to a story in *U.S. Camera*, a large segment of the photographic industry was asking whether Super 8 was a big boom or a big bust. Again, the supposed problem areas were the familiar ones, the pressure pad matter, the need for more camera speeds, and in general, the need for more sophisticated features.[22]

But two years after introduction, these obstacles had either been shown to be no problems after all, in the case of the pressure plate, or had been overcome by the rapid introduction of the features that were deemed to be lacking on the first anniversary. By 1968 there were no more standard 8mm cameras listed in the *Popular Photography* Directory.

By 1972, writer and cinematographer Donald Sutherland was moved to write that Super 8 was following the trail blazed by 16mm – taking steps out of the amateur market into the hands of professionals. The great economy of Super 8 film over 16mm, plus the light weight and affordability of Super 8 equipment, made the system very attractive to film schools for student use, to corporations for research or process analysis, sales training or sales promotion, and to medical and dental schools for training films.

Sutherland further pointed out that the single most important factor keeping Super 8 from making further inroads into the professional area was the lack of certain film stocks that professional use demanded, particularly a low-contrast film for making duplicate prints. Furthermore, at that time at least, there were few if any laboratories offering such services as edge numbering, "timing" of a release print,[23] adding "opticals": fades, dissolves, wipes, split-screen effects, etc.[24]

However, a new Super 8 film had been launched the previous year, Ektachrome 160, another triumph for the Kodak Research Laboratories and another shackle struck from the amateur filmmaker's hands: motion pictures in full color by available light!

Eastman Kodak, for its development of the Super 8 format, became the first "outsider" to receive the Bell & Howell Company's Albert S. Howell Award, named after the inventive genius and cofounder of that company, for "distinguished technical achievement in photography."

Super 8 Today

In 1998 Eastman Kodak inaugurated a Super 8 section in its Professional Motion Imaging Web Site. Information is offered under headings such as Products, History, Processing, Ordering and Tips. Clicking the mouse on Tips brought up an article headlined "Will Kodak Discontinue Super 8 Film?"

The first paragraph of the article contained this statement: "It is our intention to continue to offer Super 8 film products to the marketplace just as long as there is a 'reasonable market demand' for these films." There follows a statement that the continued manufacture of certain products, specifically sound striped Super 8 film and Ektachrome Super 8 film, is rendered impractical by "current governmental regulations for Health and Safety." This situation, coupled with a continuing downward trend in sales of these products has led the Company to discontinue their production."

The internet article concludes with a table listing four products that continue to be available: Kodachrome, Ektachrome, Plus-X-Reversal (black and white), and Tri-X-Reversal (black and white).

Despite the ubiquity of the home video camera and its undeniable technical virtuosity, Super 8 retains a small but devoted following. According to a 1994 directory, there were then over 600 undergraduate and graduate schools in the United States offering courses in film and video; of these approximately two thirds were listed as having Super 8 equipment. As noted in Chapter 13, there is a unique organization devoted to the culture of this 34-year-old medium, the International Center for 8mm Film, directed by Toni Treadway. The organizations's journal provides information on sources of film and processing, used hardware, equipment repair, and notices of festivals. Treadway sees the future of 8mm film in this light:

The affordability, portability, convenience, beauty and image permanence of real movies continues to attract discerning artists to small gauge film, despite the ease of digital video camcorders. The roster of working filmmakers today whose careers include movies in 8mm or Super 8 is stunning: not just the generation of Stephen Speilberg, Spike Lee, Gus Van Sant, Rick Linklater, but the emerging directors like Jem Cohen, Matthew Harrison, Kelly Reichardt, and a host of experimental film artists not yet widely known. So here we are in year 2000 still shooting 8mm film. How much longer? As long as filmmakers buy it. Film is a compelling medium that sings a beautiful song on any screen.[25]

11   Existing Light, Then Sound

Kodak XL camera.

Kodak Ektasound Camera

PART ONE

Perfecting Existing Light Cinematography
A Case Study of Corporate Research

From the days when Edison mounted his "Black Maria" studio on wheels to follow the sun, filmmakers have ever longed for light and more light. Not for the cinematographer the easy solution of a time exposure in poor light conditions; the inexorable, if intermittent, march of movie film past the lens meant bright sunlight, if available, and if not, row upon row of hissing arc lamps.

The amateur filmmaker faced the same problem. Kodachrome, with its brilliant life-like colors, was welcomed with open cameras. However with a film speed of ASA 10, compared with ASA 100 or better for many black-and-white films available at the time, outdoor filming in color required either full sunlight or a fast lens, and fast lenses for movie cameras were expensive. Indoor filming could be done after a fashion with high-wattage flood lights, but the glare was extremely unpleasant for the subject, and resulted in much squinting and grimacing at the camera

Eastman Kodak and Ansco were for a long time in a technological race to develop new films, in which Ansco held the lead in the late 1930s and early 1940s. Ansco's panchromatic films were faster and finer grained than were Eastman's.[1]

Kodak took the lead, however, in 1961 with the announcement of Kodachrome II, with an ASA of 25, available in 8 and 16mm. The 16mm filmmaker had fast emulsions since 1956, when Ansco introduced Anscochrome Daylight, rated ASA 32, and Anscochrome Tungsten, which could be push-processed at ASA 125.

Faster Kodachrome was not an unmixed blessing. Amateur movie camera lenses did not function well at apertures of f/16 or below, which would be called for with fast film in a very bright light situation. Very small apertures tend to degrade the sharpness of the image because of an effect called "diffraction losses."

215

One Kodak scientist who became concerned with this problem was a research chemist named Donald Gorman. Sometimes described by his colleagues as "an ingenious loner," Gorman actually fought management over its proposal to set the new Kodachrome speed at ASA 50.

To convince management of the problems such a speed would entail for the customer, Gorman made a demonstration film showing the actual loss of sharpness in 8mm images, as apertures were reduced from f/5.6 to f/22. Faced with this evidence, management scaled back its demand for Kodachrome II speed to ASA 25.[2] (See Fig. 255.)

Gorman's demonstration led others at Kodak to explore the next seemingly obvious remedy. If smaller apertures were not feasible, why not decrease exposure time? This could readily be accomplished with any camera having a "variable shutter," i.e., one in which the open portion of the shutter could be varied from totally closed to as much as 280° open. Normal opening for most cameras was 165°.

The experimenters soon discovered that decreasing the shutter opening led to an entirely different, but equally unacceptable result: the so-called "stroboscoping," or "animation effect." When the shutter-open period was of considerably less duration than the closed period, an object in motion, particularly one crossing at 90° to the camera, would appear to move in jumps. Even though individual frames were sharper, the overall effect on the observer was of jittery motion.

At this point, management lost interest in the effect of high film speed on the amateur filmmaker; millions of still camera users would be delighted with Kodachrome at ASA 25, or faster if it could be had. Gorman, however, was still concerned with the customer and how he or she would handle this problem.

His next step illustrates how the inventive mind works. Faced with the inescapable fact that decreasing exposure times gave unacceptable results, Gorman did an about-face. What would be the effect of *increasing* the shutter opening beyond the conventional 165°? Would a larger open sector produce even smoother motion? An increased open sector led to another problem, however: less dark time for the camera pull-down mechanism to work. What was needed was a camera with extremely fast pull-

Fig. 255. Don Gorman, holding the XL camera and photographed by his friend and co-worker Pete Chiesa.

down, such as that used in most projectors. Projectors use a quite different shutter.

The typical projector shutter has three dark blades, the extra blades being used to increase the "flicker rate" to a point where it is not visible to the eye (Fig. 256). Film pull-down is accomplished during the passage of one of the three blades, in 60° of shutter rotation. At that point, one of Gorman's colleagues remembered the ill-fated Wittnauer Cine-Twin, a curious camera-projector combination that had appeared in 1957, and disappeared soon after (Fig. 257).

Manufactured by the Longines-Wittnauer Company, the watchmaking concern, the Cine-Twin was

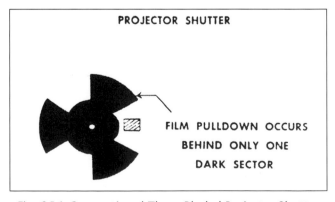

PROJECTOR SHUTTER

FILM PULLDOWN OCCURS BEHIND ONLY ONE DARK SECTOR

Fig. 256. Conventional Three-Bladed Projector Shutter.

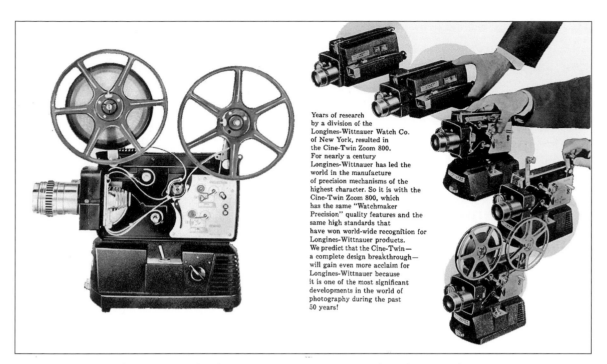

Years of research by a division of the Longines-Wittnauer Watch Co. of New York, resulted in the Cine-Twin Zoom 800. For nearly a century Longines-Wittnauer has led the world in the manufacture of precision mechanisms of the highest character. So it is with the Cine-Twin Zoom 800, which has the same "Watchmaker Precision" quality features and the same high standards that have won world-wide recognition for Longines-Wittnauer products. We predict that the Cine-Twin— a complete design breakthrough— will gain even more acclaim for Longines-Wittnauer because it is one of the most significant developments in the world of photography during the past 50 years!

Fig. 257. 1957 advertisement for the Wittnauer Cine-Twin combined camera/projector.

really not as revolutionary as the advertising would have had one believe. Cameras that could double as projectors had been produced as early as the Birtac of 1898, or the Lumière Cinematograph, and many others since. The Cine-Twin design was clever, which is not surprising when one realizes that it was the work of John Oxberry, designer of the famed animation stand that bears his name.[3]

The Cine-Twin was essentially a moving picture camera with a number of projector mechanisms packed into the camera body, such as reel arms and light source, but ingeniously arranged to shift easily from camera to projector mode. The shutter was constructed as two concentric shutters, the inner section for projection consisting of three 60° blades and three 60° open sectors: the outer section, or camera shutter with one dark and one open sector, each 180°. When the reel arms are raised, the axis of the shutter is shifted horizontally, to bring the projector shutter into position (Fig. 258).

Gorman found a Cine-Twin in the Kodak Patent Department Museum and quickly realized that this combined camera/projector would be ideal for his experiments. After a lengthy search of Rochester camera stores, one was eventually discovered in a jewelry store.[4] The camera was stripped of its projector mechanisms and the shutter modified by cutting away the outer sector and two of the 60° blades,

creating a 300° open sector, leaving the remaining 60° closed sector for pull-down.

Using the modified camera whose 300° shutter gave an exposure time of 1/19th second, and a carefully selected standard camera with a conventional 165° shutter giving a 1/35th second exposure,[5] Gorman made two comparison films. These were shown to a number of Kodak people, many of whom were trained observers of motion picture projection. To everyone's surprise, including Gorman's, even though the observers were told that they were seeing 1/19th versus 1/35th exposures, almost none of the observers could tell the difference.

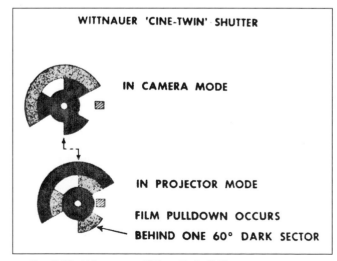

WITTNAUER 'CINE-TWIN' SHUTTER

IN CAMERA MODE

IN PROJECTOR MODE

FILM PULLDOWN OCCURS BEHIND ONE 60° DARK SECTOR

Fig. 258. Wittnauer "Cine-Twin" Shutter.

The significance of this demonstration was that conventional cameras could be operated at one full stop larger than their rating. Or put another way, film rated at ASA 25 in a conventional camera could now be rated at ASA 50 in this modified Cine-Twin. And since there was an old saying around the Research Laboratories that film speed evolved by one stop after every ten years of research, this was a bonanza for the Emulsion Department.

All of this led Gorman to wonder what could be accomplished with the fastest 8mm lens available, which was determined to be the f/0.9 13mm Switar made by Kern-Paillard. A very expensive lens retailing at $189, it gave an additional two stops of speed.

Development work on Kodachrome X had just been completed, (early 1962) with a rating of ASA 64, but the film was not available in 8mm. Gorman managed to spool some for his 8mm experimental cameras and now had a camera and film which enabled him to film in extremely low-light situations. As Gorman described one episode:

[I filmed] a person lighting a cigarette, then finally just the glow of the cigarette as the smoker extinguished the match, then as he took a hefty drag, it looked as if he had a railroad flare in his mouth!

Gorman then decided to find out what more could be gained with even faster films, such as Ektachrome films at ASA 125 ASA 160.[6] In the course of such experiments, a curious phenomenon was encountered.

Using fast films, wide open shutters, and fast lenses, it is possible to photograph a scene, apparently correctly exposed by the meter, which will not look "normal" when projected on the screen. The answer is that the meter tries to produce all pictures with the same brightness when projected, with the result that a candle-lit scene looks as bright as the same room lit by normal household lighting. But of course a candle-lit scene should look like candlelight, so it appears that there is a point below which exposure should not be increased, if the scene is to look right Gorman determined that this point was in the six foot-candle range, and named it TEMS, or Terminal Exposure Modulated Scene.

This elegant designation was actually given in a joking manner. As Gorman himself admits, the expression would be more understandable if the word "Brightness" were added, but "TEMSB" made an unpronounceable acronym, and TEMS has remained in the literature.

High Level Encouragement

While Gorman was exploring the limits of high-speed films, other entities in the company were working on another project; an entirely new format for 8mm: Super 8. Inevitably, not everyone who learned of Gorman's one-man existing light crusade was sympathetic. One critic described available light movies as "a pipe dream that exists only in the Research Laboratories and on the top floor of Kodak Office." As Gorman expressed it, "the chippers were turned loose, to chip away at every turn." This reaction from other departments may have been due to some extent to Gorman's uncompromising, even abrasive, manner in pursuing his ideas in the face of criticism, as well as simple jealousy engendered by his knack for getting the attention of top management.

Some time before, Gorman had done some innovative work with Kodachrome and subminiature cameras, which had caught the eye of Dr. Albert K. Chapman, then chairman of the board and chief executive officer of the company. Chapman was greatly impressed with Gorman's work and had arranged for him to present his achievement to a number of groups throughout the company. This boost from the top had generated some resentment in other departments, which Gorman had learned to ignore.

Thus when Dr. Chapman inquired, on one of his periodic visits to the Research Laboratories, "What are you up to, Mr. Gorman?"—Gorman happily informed Chapman of his experiments with existing light and showed one of his demonstration films. Chapman was immediately taken with the implications of the project and indicated that he would give it his full support.

Evidence of this support was not long in coming; in 1964, Gorman was given a full-time assistant, Peter P. Chiesa (Fig. 259), a research worker in the Emulsion Research Division, and an accomplished photographer. Chiesa later described how it came about:

I was shooting a lot of pictures for my own enjoyment, using up my year's allotment of film by February,[7] when someone said 'Why don't you talk to Don Gorman,

Fig. 259. Peter P. Chiesa.

he always has lots of film.' And of course Don did have lots, because of the work he was doing he was always asking people to try various kinds of experimental film. Don was also interested in stereo, and when he heard that I was doing stereo, and interested in shooting film, it was a natural that we would pair up. I started spending all my spare time with him. I was actually assigned to work on high-temperature color processing, but evenings and weekends I was bootlegging experiments for Don. Finally one day, they asked me if I would be interested in working with Dr. Gorman. That was a dream come true for me, finally getting to work in photography. . . .We worked together—it was almost like he was Alexander Graham Bell, and I was Watson, you know? [8]

With management approval of the project, other departments were assigned the many design problems that would have to be solved before the experimental existing-light camera could become a commercial reality. Some of these problems were: design a new wide-aperture, short focal length lens (i.e. universal focus) that could be produced at a cost suitable for a mass-market camera, design a viewfinder that would work at very low light levels, design a new film that would work under all lights sources that the filmmaker might encounter in everyday life, design a quieter shutter, then design a faster film to make up for the shorter exposure that the new shutter would impose, and lastly, solve the original problem of how to accommodate very bright light levels.

With other design teams working on these problems, Gorman and Chiesa were free to continue exploring the capabilities of the experimental camera. They scoured the country for more Wittnauer Cine-Twins, more Switar lenses, and constructed a number of cameras that they loaned to all and sundry who were interested in experiencing existing-light cinematography. Without exception, every volunteer was converted to enthusiastic endorsement of "XL" and the end of "movie-light misery."

At this point, Gorman and Chiesa began applying what they had learned about camera design to one of Kodak's most successful 16mm cameras, the Cine Kodak K-100. Introduced in 1955, this camera took 100-foot loads and had an exceptionally strong mainspring, called the "Negator," which permitted a 40-foot film run without rewinding. This freed the cameraman from the trailing cord of an electric drive and yet permitted a long-enough run for most scenes. This and other features made the camera popular with professionals such as doctors, engineers, etc.

The camera also had a most unusual film-advance mechanism. An orbital-groove cam mounted on the shutter imparted the in-and-out motions and speed of the pull-down claw. This meant that a K-100 could be converted to XL photography by simply replacing one part, the modified shutter. This arrangement was ideal for Gorman and Chiesa's objective of converting the K-100 to XL photography. A variety of new shutters were constructed with shutter openings ranging from 3° to 240°. The 240° opening proved to be the most satisfactory. When the camera was fitted with an Angenieux f/0.9 lens, and loaded with Ektachrome 160, the K-100 was capable of filming under the most extreme conditions. [9]

So successful were these efforts, and so confident were Gorman and Chiesa of the great benefit to be offered to the professional user of the K-100, that Chiesa prepared a presentation to be made at a 1967 Society of Motion Picture and Television Engineers conference. At the last minute, however, permission was rescinded; Kodak sales people decided that such a presentation might tip their hand as to the Super 8 XL system, which at that time was not ready to launch.

A Brand New Camera

The unveiling finally came on August 4, 1971, at the 70th annual meeting of the corporation, held in Flemington, New Jersey. President Gerald Zornow showed the assembled stockholders and newsmen a movie filmed by candlelight. Two camera models were shown: the XL33 with a fixed-focus, f/1.2 9mm lens, and the XL55 with a focusing f/1.2 9 to 21mm zoom lens (Fig. 260). These lenses were a compromise from the f/0.9 Switars that Gorman had worked with, as it had proven too expensive to produce a lens any faster than f/1.2. The lenses carried the respected Ektar name heretofore reserved primarily for lenses on industrial or professional equipment. Kodak stated that these Ektar lenses were among the best it had ever produced for Super 8 equipment.

Both cameras had a unique shape: the film chamber filled a vertical space in the center of the body, while the battery compartment on one side and the viewfinder tube on the other formed "wings" by which the camera was grasped, much as you would a pair of binoculars.

The final design of the shutter provided an open sector of 230°, which, operating at 18 frames per second gave an exposure time of 1/28 of a second. This was also a compromise, as the 260° shutter once contemplated proved too noisy.

Fig. 260. The Kodak XL camera.

To compensate for the loss of light from the smaller shutter opening, the film designers increased the new film to ASA160 rating. It had been hoped that the new Ektachrome could be made usable under daylight or artificial lighting without a filter, but this goal was not achieved until later, so the camera was equipped with an optional filter.[10]

In the interest of getting the greatest amount of light to the film, neither camera employed reflex viewing nor metering, as reflex systems generally consumed 15 percent to 20 percent of the incoming light. The automatic exposure control system was designed to deliver the utmost light possible to the film in low light conditions (Fig. 261). To this end, the designers departed from the single-vane aper-

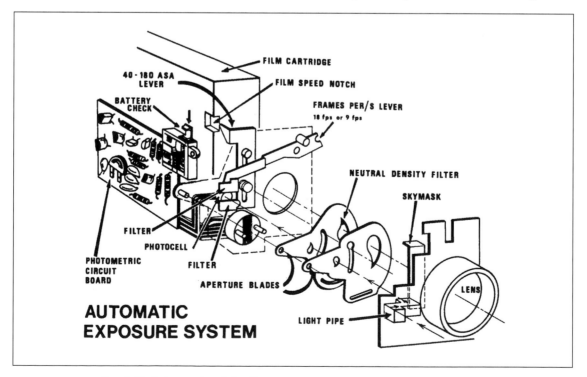

Fig. 261. Schematic of the XL automatic exposure system.

ture control system conventionally used on "popular priced" cameras and designed a more expensive two-vane system. This obviated the need for the "compensating mask" necessary with the single-vane system, which, since it is permanently in the light path, robs the film of some light even when the aperture is wide open.[11]

Finally, to answer the problem which had started Gorman on his voyage of discovery in the first place, which was how to handle extremely bright light conditions, the designers installed a new type of evaporated-metal neutral-density filter which swung into place when the camera meter called for it.

Public Reaction

The photographic press gave the XL system very good reviews. There was a consensus that the new cameras were easy and fun to use, that they permitted filming under many low-light situations other than just in the home, and that they were ideal for the casual filmer. But with these words of praise, there was also the message that the cameras were not very sophisticated and would probably not satisfy the "serious" filmmaker. The rather limited telephoto end of the zoom lens range was cited, for example; but in the same breath it was conceded that most filming around the home would be done at close or medium distances, for which the 9-21mm range was fine. But wasn't the first assessment exactly what Kodak had always intended for its cameras? "You press the button, we do the rest."—that famous phrase fitted the XL cameras perfectly.[12]

The marketplace reacted accordingly; after some big TV promotions featuring John Forsythe and Dick Van Dyke, Kodak found itself flooded with dealer orders. A Kodak executive, in a March 1972 interview, stated: "By last Christmas, we were shipping them by the thousands, but that still wasn't fast enough. Even now we are still trying to fill orders we received last November."[13]

Somewhat surprisingly, there was not an immediate rush by other manufacturers to adopt the new technology. At Photokina '73, the giant photographic trade show held annually in Germany, only a handful of models featured the XL 230° shutter, ultra-fast lens, etc. However, many cameras had their automatic exposure control systems upgraded to accommodate ASA 160 films. By 1974, eight other manufacturers listed one or more XL models in their product lines.

One of these manufacturers was Bell & Howell, who, as recounted in Chapter 5, had brought suit against Eastman Kodak, charging the Rochester firm, with attempting to put its competitors out of business. As one reporter stated:

Bell & Howell, smarting under the twin Kodak coups of the XL low light Super 8 movie cameras and films, plus the Kodak Pocket Instamatic cameras and films, has filed an action against the jolly yellow giant under the antitrust laws.[14]

Bell & Howell based its suit on the premise that since Eastman Kodak held a dominant position in the film market, by introducing a totally new film system and equipment system to go with it without prior notice to its competitors, the company gained an unfair advantage. Bell & Howell sought to have Kodak either advise its competitors sufficiently far in advance to permit them to introduce compatible equipment, or have Kodak divest itself of its camera and projector business. The suit was settled in 1974, with Kodak signing a disclosure agreement and making a cash payment. Bell & Howell introduced its own line of XL cameras in 1973. Within a few more years, existing light cameras had become the rule and "standard" cameras were the exception.

Don Gorman was disappointed that he was not allowed to stay with the XL camera until it was ready for market, but within the company at least he was recognized as the inventor of "XL." Dr. L. J. Thomas, senior vice-president and director of the Kodak Research Laboratories, hailed Gorman as "typical of the lone inventor, tenaciously pursuing solutions to a set of problems—still one of the most successful approaches to new product development."[15] Thomas likened Gorman's work to that leading to xerography and instant photography.

PART TWO
Sound for the Amateur
History of Sound Recording

The first efforts to add sound to professional motion pictures were not for the purpose of adding dialog, which was actually considered superfluous. Music on the other hand, could be used in two ways; first on the set to assist the actors in portraying emotions and moods and secondly to accompany the film in projection, to convey these same emotions and moods to the audience. Many filmmakers resisted the idea of actors speaking. Edward W. Kellogg, consulting engineer, in a paper dated May 5, 1954, wrote: "Throughout the long history of the efforts to add sound, the success of the silent movie was the greatest obstacle to commercialization of talking pictures." [16]

The first man to claim to have synchronized speech with action was William Kennedy Laurie Dickson, Thomas Edison's sometime assistant. Dickson, some years after the fact, claimed to have shown his boss a short film after Edison's return from a European trip on October 6, 1889, in which Dickson was shown walking forward, tipping his hat and saying: "Good morning, Mr. Edison, glad to see you back. Hope you like the Kinetophone." [17] Unfortunately, this account apparently was an "invention" itself; Edison was later to deny that it ever happened.

It is unlikely that Edison ever achieved true synchronization of the Kinetoscope with his phonograph, although a number of "Kinetophones" were constructed. A phonograph mechanism was installed in the base of the Kinetoscope. Two rubber ear-tubes led up to the front of the machine, allowing the viewer to listen to a musical accompaniment to such films as: *Fairies Dance, Jolly Darkies, Buck and Wing*, etc.[18]

Edison, whose cylinder phonograph was completed in 1877 and improved upon by Alexander Graham Bell among others, had of course achieved recording of sound by itself. Edison had succeeded in converting sound wave signals into mechanical analogs, i.e. grooves in a wax cylinder that in turn could be reconverted to audible sound waves, thus reproducing, within limits, the original signal. The limits were substantial, as anyone knows who has listened to an old Edison machine; the mechanical transformations involved were just not capable of reproducing the total range of human speech frequencies.

Furthermore, a considerable loss of energy occurred in the original recording and the mechanical reproduction, meaning that the speaker or singer had to practically bellow into a huge horn—acceptable for a Caruso, but most inappropriate for more delicate voices. Various schemes were devised for mechanical amplification, such as the one in which a delicately balanced valve, actuated by the record's stylus, controlled the flow of compressed air through a resonant pipe. With such devices, satisfactory volume could be obtained for audiences as large as several thousand people. Here again, frequency response was relatively poor.[19]

Alexander Graham Bell discovered a way to convert sound wave signals into electrical impulses, which could be transmitted over wires to a distant receiver, there to be reconverted to mechanical impulses of a diaphragm, and thence to sound waves. Today we recognize these devices as microphones and loudspeakers. Bell was deeply interested in the mechanical reproduction of sound, spurred on by a most personal reason. Bell, the son and grandson of Scottish educators who were authorities on phonetics and defective speech, had become professor of vocal physiology at Boston University in 1872.[20] One of his students was a pretty, vivacious young woman, ten years Bell's junior, who had been stone deaf from age five. Mabel Hubbard and Alexander fell in love, and Bell redoubled his efforts to find a way to convey speech to the deaf.[21]

Electrical Recording

As noted above, the mechanical recording of sound required large amounts of energy, as did the reproduction, both of which processes are described as "acoustic." A better method of amplification of the signal was needed, and it came with the use of electrical energy.

The Western Electric Company, the manufacturing arm of the Bell Telephone Company, was the first to commercialize electromechanical recording and reproducing of sound. Bell had begun serious study of speech sounds, their transmission, and the recording of both speech and music as early as 1912. These efforts were so successful that in 1925 both leading phonograph companies, Columbia and Victor, took licenses from Western Electric Company to use the recording methods and apparatus developed by that company.[22]

In that same year, Western Electric gave a demonstration of the apparatus to several motion picture company executives, but only Samuel Warner of Warner Brothers was impressed. Warner conferred with his brother and arranged for further tests, using the Warner Brothers studio in Brooklyn. The brothers were impressed with the results of these tests and, in April 1926, the Vitaphone Corporation was founded, with Samuel L. Warner as president.

The Vitaphone camera and the recording turntable were driven by synchronous motors, which gave excellent synchronization. The Vitaphone projector could be any silent projector, which would be fitted with a Western Electric-designed turntable, connected to the projector drive by gearing. The records were 16 inches in diameter, and ran at 33-1/3 rpm, giving sufficient recording time for a 1000 foot reel of film.[23] (See Fig. 262.)

On August 6, 1926, Vitaphone presented its first sound picture, *Don Juan*, starring John Barrymore and Mary Astor. The dialogue was not heard, however, the principal sound being a synchronized musical score. There was a brief speech by Will Hays, introducing the Vitaphone as an innovation that would revolutionize the cinema. It is doubtful that many of the "experts" who heard Hay's speech took much stock in his prophecy, but of course the public was to prove him absolutely correct.[24]

Warner Brothers followed *Don Juan* with *The Jazz Singer* in 1927, which featured the Broadway musical star Al Jolson doing his famous blackface songs. What really made the picture, however, was when Jolson ad-libbed his trademark "you ain't heard nuttin' yet."

The picture was an immediate success, and this sent shock waves throughout the industry. Converting silent studios and silent theaters to sound would be an enormously expensive undertaking, to say nothing of the effect that this new genre would have on the overseas markets. Silent films were cast in a universal language: mime. Actors conveyed emotions and thoughts by facial expressions and body language, but with talkies, "everyone in the films spoke American."[25]

The sound-on-disc system gave quite acceptable sound quality but had several drawbacks, chief among them the difficulty of restoring synchronization in the event of film breakage or a stuck needle. In addition, the heavy 16-inch records were easily broken or cracked and were expensive to ship.

Sound-On-Film

While the sound-on-disk technology was evolving, parallel research on recording sound directly on the film was being carried on by a number of workers. The idea of recording sound photographically occurred to Alexander Graham Bell in the early 1880s. He established a laboratory in Washington,

Fig. 262. First model Simplex 35mm professional projector with early Western Electric turntable sound system.

D.C., employing his cousin Chichester Bell, a chemist, and a skilled technician named Charles Sumner Tainter. On May 4, 1886, the three men received U.S. Patent No. 341,213 entitled "Transmitting and Recording Sounds by Radiant Energy."

The machine shown in the patent drawings bore little resemblance to any sound-recording mechanism known then or since. Light from a steady source, in this case a heliostat (a clock-work device which can track the sun and is used to study solar flares, print photographic plates, etc.) was directed through a stationary glass plate, then through a slit and a lens, to a circular rotating sensitized disk. Just above the point where the light beam passed through the stationary plate, a small nozzle mounted in a sounding board introduced a flow of opaque liquid. Sound waves directed against the sounding board caused waves in the flow of liquid across the light beam, thus modulating the beam as it fell on the photographic disk.[26]

While a number of European workers did inter-

223

esting work in this field, only the work of three Americans who made major contributions to the optical recording of sound will be treated here.

Joseph Tykocinski-Tykociner was born in Poland in 1867, immigrated to the United States in 1885, where he found work in the electrical industry. In 1900 he returned to Poland and acquired sufficient technical education to enable him to become Chief Engineer and Manager of Research of the British Marconi Company. He pioneered in short-wave radio and served several years in technical positions with the Imperial Russian Government. When the Bolshevik revolution came, Tykociner escaped to Poland, where he organized its first wireless communication system.

In 1920, he returned permanently to the United States and became first Research Professor of Electrical Engineering at the University of Illinois. It is thought that Professor Tykociner had first become intrigued with the idea of capturing sound on film nearly a quarter century before, when he saw a motion picture in New York City, presumably an Edison Kinetoscope.

Tykociner's first experiments were with a manometric flame, which he attempted to photograph on film as a variable density track. A manometric flame is one in which the flame height, and thus the light emitted, is modulated by varying the pressure of the gas which is feeding the flame. If the gas

flow is led through a chamber of which one wall is a flexible diaphragm, sound waves striking the diaphragm will modulate the flame. Tykociner's early efforts to reproduce recorded sound were hampered by the poor sensitivity of the selenium cell he was using at that time and the lack of amplifying devices.

At the University Tykociner found the time and resources to pursue the experiments begun so long before. Both a sensitive photoelectric cell and vacuum tube amplifiers were available, and his progress was rapid. On June 29, 1922, before the Urbana (Illinois) Section of the American Institute of Electrical Engineers, Professor Tykociner, standing modestly behind a laboratory bench crowded with cameras, projectors, cables and other paraphernalia, turned to an assistant, and signaled for the room lights to be dimmed (Fig. 263).

A modified Simplex projector shot a beam of light across the room to a screen, where the image of a woman appeared, holding a bell. In a clear voice, the woman announced "I will ring the bell," which she did, the sound of the bell startling the assembled engineers. "Did you hear it?" she inquired. With that, Professor Tykociner turned off the projector and the room lights came back on. A few frightening moments of silence ensued, then the hall exploded in applause and cheers. Professor Tykociner had just presented the first successful demonstration of a workable sound-on-film motion picture system.[27]

Fig. 263. Professor Tyckociner at his laboratory bench; the equipment, left to right: Bell & Howell 2709 camera with top-mounted sound-recording sound recording camera, reverse-megaphone carbon-grain telephone transmitter used as a microphone, mercury vapor lamp with sound-modulation amplifier, Simplex projector with top-mounted sound recording aparatus with Kunz photocell. (Photograph courtesy of University of Illinois Archives, RS 39/2/20.)

Fig. 264. Theodore W. Case, a portrait in later years.

As Tykociner was happily receiving the plaudits of his peers in Urbana, a few hundred miles to the east in a privately built laboratory on the grounds of an imposing estate in Auburn, New York, two men were nearing completion of a nearly identical course of improvisation and discovery.

The Auburn Inventor

Theodore W. Case (Fig. 264), scion of one of the wealthiest clans of Auburn, New York, graduated from Yale in 1911. His father, a millionaire electrical engineer and inventor, set his son up in a combined laboratory, tool-and-die shop, and recording studio, built in a converted coach barn and greenhouse on the family estate, where Case began a search for a means of recording sound on film.[28] (See Fig. 265.)

After five years of solo effort, Case was joined in 1916 by Earle I. Sponable, a chemist from Cornell University. Working within an annual budget of $100,000 provided by Case's father, the two men had their first notable success with a light-sensitive vacuum tube that Case had developed for the U.S. Navy as part of an infrared communications system. This tube was christened the "Thalofide Cell." (See Fig. 266.) The sensitive substance was a thallium/oxygen/sulfur compound, most sensitive in the infrared end of the spectrum. They also developed a cold-cathode glow lamp, called the "Aeolite," (Fig. 267) whose light emission varied with the impressed voltage.

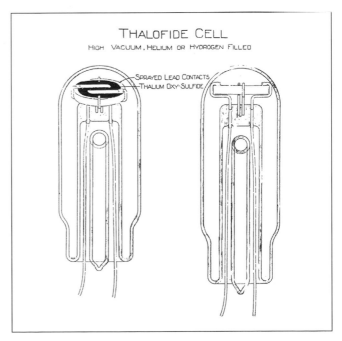

Fig. 265. Theodore Case, taking home movies with a Ciné-Kodak.

Fig. 266. A Thalofide cell, as constructed at the Case Research Laboratory, Inc.

225

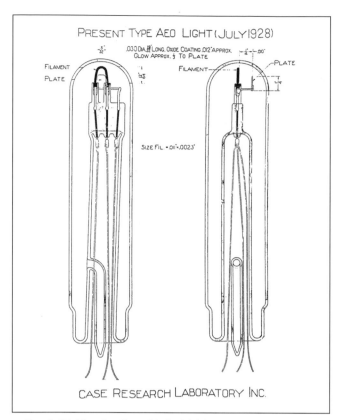

Fig. 267. The Aeolite of July 1928.

Fig. 268. Lee de Forest, holding an example of his Audion, standing by a modified Bell & Howell 2709.

An optical sound recording and playback system requires, first, a sound-to-voltage-to-light transducing device in the camera, i.e., a microphone to modulate the conversion of sound waves to voltage that is fed to a lamp whose light output varies with voltage, in this case the "Aeolite" mentioned above, the light output being imprinted on the film. Then for projection, the optical sound track on the film is "read" by the Thalofide cell, which converts the light signal to voltage that is fed to a speaker, the signal emerging once again as sound.

By this time, Case had met another inventor/ researcher, Lee de Forest (Fig. 268), a fellow Yale alumnus with a solid record of accomplishments, including improvements on Marconi's wireless signal transmission and, more importantly, the invention in 1906 of the triode. A triode is a vacuum tube with three electrodes; a diode is one with two electrodes and, while it is never so designated, an ordinary light bulb could be properly called a "monode," since it has but one electrode. There are two wires going in, of course, but they simply form a coil, which functions electrically as one.

Thomas Edison, in the course of his work in developing a workable light bulb, discovered that particles of carbon from the heated carbon filament were being carried over to the inside of the bulb, and that if a second wire, or electrode, were inserted in the bulb and given a positive charge, a current of electricity would flow from the filament to the positive electrode. Edison could see no immediate use for this phenomenon, but in his methodical way, he filed for and received a patent for the device. While Edison had no idea what caused this effect, the existence of electrons not having been posited at this time, he did astutely note that the effect could be used to measure the flow of an electric current. The phenomenon has quite justifiably been named the "Edison effect."

In 1906, Lee de Forest was a frustrated man; a failed marriage and unpleasant divorce had left him emotionally distraught. This was followed by a stunning defeat in a lawsuit that destroyed a wireless telegraph company he had founded, and required him to pay heavy damages to a man de Forest believed had stolen his invention. Despite this sea of troubles, de Forest began searching for a new method of generating and detecting radio frequency waves.

In the literature of the field, de Forest found a description of Edison's diode, plus the report of an improvement made by a British scientist, Sir John Fleming. Fleming's discovery was that if an alternating current were supplied to the filament, a direct current flowed from the other electrode, now known as "the plate." Fleming thus had discovered what would now be called a half-wave rectifier.[29]

De Forest took several of Fleming's "valves," (the British term for radio tubes) and tried introducing a third electrode, placed between the filament and the plate, which he called a "grid." He then discovered that if a positive voltage was applied to the grid, the current from the plate increased exponentially. He had thus created an amplifier of such power that the feeblest currents pulled from radio signals in the air could be amplified thousands of times, sufficient to fill an amphitheater with sound. De Forest called his device the "Audion." [30]

The Audion seemed to de Forest to be just what he needed to re-establish himself in the world of wireless telegraphy, and he continued to experiment in this field for several years. In 1913 a group of businessmen approached him with the proposition that he develop his Audion for the purpose of adding sound to motion pictures. While the offer never came to anything, it turned de Forest's attention away from wireless telegraphy toward motion pictures and led to his meeting with Case.

The two men soon formed a working relationship in which Case provided most of the technological innovations, while de Forest enthusiastically pursued the commercial applications of their combined efforts. De Forest purchased a number of Thalofide cells from Case, which he used in a sound-on-film system he called "Phonofilm." His first recording modulator was a glow lamp of his own invention which he called a Photion. It was not sufficiently sensitive, however, and he soon called on Case for improvements. Case's response was the Aeolight and, with this technology, de Forest's "Phonofilm" became commercially viable. [31]

"Phonofilm" was demonstrated to the press on March 13, 1923, and in 1925 a number of short demonstration films were produced. De Forest formed the Phonofilm Corporation, with himself as president, and installed the system in a number of theaters. Despite this seeming success, none of the major Hollywood studios showed much interest in talking pictures. De Forest's debts mounted and his relationship with Case deteriorated, as the latter began to realize that de Forest was not about to acknowledge Case's contributions to the success of Phonofilm, such as it was. Finally in 1926 he decided to sever relations with de Forest by selling all his sound movie patents to William Fox, the head of Fox Film Corporation. The sale price was estimated to have been about $1.5 million, which Case generously shared with Sponable and several assistants. [32]

William Fox organized Fox Movietone News to utilize Case's technology and began regular releases of sound newsreels in the fall of 1927. Feature film production began the following year. [33] (See Fig. 269.)

In summary, viable commercial sound-on-film

Fig. 269. Fox Movietone News crew filming Sunrise in 1927 at their West Coast studio, the first feature-length film with a soundtrack. The Case AEOlite, used to record sound, can be seen projecting from the Wall camera. Manufactured in Syracuse, New York.

movies were made possible by three inventions: de Forest's Audion provided the necessary amplification of the sound-to-voltage signal; Case's Aeolight provided the voltage-modulated light source, and Case's Thalofide cell provided the light-modulated voltage which turned the signal back into sound.

Magnetic Recording

Magnetic recording of sound was first accomplished by the Danish engineer Valdemar Poulson in 1898. In 1904 he received a patent on a device which he called the Telegraphone. An iron wire or tape was passed through an electromagnetic field that was modulated by a sound-generated current, thus imprinting the signal on the wire. The wire would then be passed through another magnetic field which "read" the signal as a current to reproduce the original sound. Wire was soon replaced by flexible tape, carrying a stripe of magnetic powder. The method was improved upon by various workers but did not receive serious attention until research by RCA, Bell, the Armour Research Foundation, and others developed special iron powders with the proper magnetic and physical properties.[34]

The developments and publications of Marvin Camras of the Armour Research Foundation in 1947 aroused much interest and experimentation. By 1952 most Hollywood studios were recording sound on magnetic tape. Since many prints of professional films are needed for distribution to the theaters, and since duplication by optical printing is faster and cheaper than duplicating the film *and* the magnetic tape, studios routinely made the original recording on magnetic tape, then converted the sound track to optical for the master prints.

Sound for the Home—Sound on Disk

The home screen may have uttered its first words in 1912, when the American Photophone appeared on the market. This ingenious device consisted of a small disk phonograph with a projector mounted on a shelf at the rear; the phonograph horn's axis was coincident with the optical axis of the projector, the projected beam passing through an opening at the rear of the horn. The phonograph motor was fitted with an extension shaft that drove the projector.[35]

The next amateur outfit to provide sound, of which there is record, was the DeVry Cine-Tone projector of 1928 (Fig. 270). The Cine-Tone consisted

Fig. 270. DeVry Cine-tone 16mm projector.

of a 16mm projector of conventional design mounted on a common base with a 78-rpm turntable. A rigid shaft extended from the projector drive to the turntable. Films and matching records were sold as sets, with the film having a marked starting frame and the record a matching starting dot. The output of an electric pick-up was fed to the owner's radio or a suitable loudspeaker. The manufacturer advised that: "regular releases of talking and singing movie films will be issued each month. These will include dramas, recitations and songs by well-known actors, singers, and orchestras." Some titles were: *"I Wanna be Loved by You"* with Helen Kane (The Betty Boop Girl) doing the lyrics; *"Doin' the Racoon,"* with George Olsen, *"Cohen on the Telephone"* with Julius Tannen; etc. The machine listed at $250.[36]

The DeVry machine set the pattern for a flood of similar projector/turn-table machines that followed in a year or two: the Tone-O-Graph Jr. marketed by Willoughby's, the Cine-Voice from Hollywood Film Enterprises, the Filmophone and Filmophone Radio by Bell & Howell, and the Animatophone by Victor Animatograph Corp. The Bell & Howell offering, as might have been expected, was the most elaborate; the projector and turntable being housed in an imposing radio cabinet. The Victor Animatophone Model 5, introduced in 1930, was of unusual design, with the turntable and record mounted in a vertical position. The tone arm was balanced on a vertical support and the pick-up held against the record by spring pressure. It was designed to take the professional 16-inch records. This projector is shown in Fig. 187, in Chapter 7.

Since the average amateur could not readily produce his own "talkies," a substantial source of professionally made films with accompanying records was essential if the home talkie machines were to appeal to the public. Bell & Howell, for one, stepped up to the plate; an article in *Filmo Topics* for October 1931 announced: "Sound Films Now Plentiful in 16mm." The article went on to say that the Bell & Howell Film Library had over 230 16mm sound subjects in stock, with the expectation of approximately 25 releases monthly for the next 12 months. The films were reduction prints from 35mm originals, while the disks were identical to the professional ones. Among the producers were Pathé, Universal, and Ufa, the latter a producer of educational films.

The films were stocked by Filmo dealers, at prices ranging from $30 to $60 per 400-foot reel; subjects included: Hoot Gibson in *Long, Long Trail*, six reels; *Hooked*, Grantland Rice narrating salt and fresh water fishing, one reel; and *Red Hot Rhythm*, a nine-reel feature on New York's Tin Pan Alley, "portraying the struggles and joys, heartbreaks and triumphs of the song writers."

Advanced amateurs soon began to wonder when they might be able to produce their own talkies; but Russell Holslag, technical consultant to the Amateur Cinema League, was skeptical. Writing in the July 1930 issue of *Movie Makers*, he voiced as his opinion, "the average amateur has barely learned how to use his present silent camera—he had best master that before he attempts sound movies."

Nevertheless, many serious amateurs found it possible to fashion their own sound accompaniment for their films, generally consisting of background music, sound effects, or narration, none of which required absolute synchronization. The popular photography magazines regularly carried articles explaining how the amateur could build a dual-turntable set-up, whereby easy "cueing" of multiple records could be accomplished; or how to link projector and turntable to keep them in synchronization.

Some amateur apparatus reached remarkable levels of sophistication, such as one described by Herbert C. McKay in a 1934 article in *Movie Makers*. McKay advised the amateur how he might cut his own records:

Using the new pre-grooved records in compound or aluminum, almost any electric phonograph may be used by feeding the microphone into the amplifier, and leading the amplifier output to the pickup which then acts as the cutting head.

For successful playback, it was necessary to build an elaborate commutator-synchronizer, which fitted over the turntable spindle and kept the projector running at the same relative speed as the turntable. While the author suggested that the amateur build his own synchronizer, such units were available commercially.[37]

The Cine-Kodak Model A, with its rectangular lines and sturdy die-cast aluminum body, lent itself to many amateur modifications. An extreme example, perhaps, was described in the February 1943 issue of *American Cinematographer*. Raymond L. Maker explained how he built his own sound-on-film camera with which he successfully filmed a feature-length Western in Kodachrome, complete with dialog and sound effects. He used a Model A as the foundation, and constructed a "light valve" from a rebuilt RCA phonograph pick-up. The completed camera weighed 60 pounds.

Up until 1947 all commercially produced sound-on-disk projectors were made for 16mm film, as that was the only gauge for which films with accompanying records were available. In 1946, the Calvin Corporation, under the direction of Lloyd Thompson, secured an arrangement with Castle Films, a well-known distributor of professional films for the amateur market, to supply Calvin with suitable films with sound accompaniment. Thompson then designed an 8mm system, using a Kodascope 8-33 projector, combined with a commercial turntable, amplifier, and speaker, all fitted in one case. The turntable ran at 78 rpm for home records and 33-1/3 rpm for the Castle films, which were chiefly prints made at the conventional sound speed of 24 frames-per-second. Since the projector was designed to operate at 16 frames-per-second, Thompson had to devise a skip-frame printer to convert the Castle films to 16 frames-per-second. Despite the slight error in synchronization which resulted, the system performed quite well. Approximately 1,000 of these units were produced and marketed by Continental Products Corporation, a Calvin subsidiary.[38]

The Calvin Corporation was founded in 1931

by Forrest Calvin, his wife Betty, and Lloyd Thompson to produce 16mm films for industry. The company's talents were drafted for the war effort in the early 1940s and millions of feet of 16mm film were turned out for the U.S. Navy and for training of defense plant workers. As an outgrowth of its commercial business, the company developed the lightweight projectors mentioned above.[39] The company also worked closely with Eastman Kodak and Bell & Howell on the development and testing of numerous mechanical and chemical innovations for commercial motion picture processing.

Sound-On-Film, Optical

The first 16mm projector for sound-on-film produced in the United States appears to have been the RCA-Victor "Photophone 16mm, Type PG-38," introduced in 1932.[40] Other manufacturers quickly brought machines to market, including the Bell & Howell Filmosound of 1932. Designed for the educational and industrial markets, it accepted 16mm optical sound films, generally produced as reduction prints from commercial feature films, as well as documentaries and instructional films. List price at introduction, with f/1.5 lens and 750 watt lamp was over $500. Subsequent models came down in price, as Bell & Howell sought to include the well-to-do amateur in the market.[41]

Perhaps the most elegant, and certainly one of the rarer amateur sound projectors, was the Sound Kodascope Special introduced in 1937 (Fig. 271). Enclosed in a sparkling, silver-finished, all-metal case, when closed the projector was the epitome of 1930's Art Deco design. The exterior bears the unmistakable stamp of Walter Dorwin Teague, the famed industrial designer hired by Eastman Kodak in the 1920s to give new life to Kodak's all-black boxes and folders. Teague was responsible for the appearance of such classic cameras as the Vanity Kodak Ensemble, the Beau Brownie, and the Super Kodak Six-20.

The Sound Kodascope Special mechanism was also unique, incorporating an oil-immersed intermittent typical of professional theater projectors and a take-up spool mounted at right angles to its conventional position. The latter feature permitted the projector to accommodate 1600-foot reels without having the take-up arms extend out over the edge of the projector support.

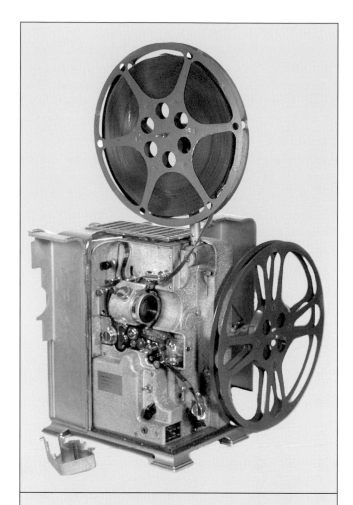

Fig. 271. Sound Kodascope Special shown open and ready to operate (above) and closed (below).

Fig. 272. Apollo Projector.

The projector was first manufactured at the Hawkeye Works of Eastman Kodak and the story goes that Mr. Eastman had ordered its development "to keep the boys busy" during the depression; however, the Company's 1937 annual report stated that it was designed as a deliberate effort to produce the finest possible machine in the sound-projection field, surpassing all previous efforts. As might be imagined, it was very expensive to manufacture and carried a price tag of $775, more than double the average price of all other sound projectors then on the market. The projector was discontinued in 1942 and it is estimated that not more than 500 and possibly as few as 350 units were produced.[42]

The year 1941 saw the introduction of a more conventional line of sound Kodascopes—a total of five models, most of which were intended for the educational or industrial markets. Among these was the FS-10N, which was widely used by the armed forces.

The Calvin Corporation produced the first popularly-priced 16mm sound-on-film projector, called the "Movie Mite," introduced in 1940 at $150. The projector, much smaller and lighter than any other on the market at that time, was designed to be carried by salesmen as a demonstration tool. Its manu-

facture was licensed under RCA and Western Electric patents.[43]

Another very economical and unusual projector was the "Apollo," manufactured by Excel Products Company of Chicago and introduced in 1948 (Fig. 272). Manufacturing cost was lowered by supplying the projector without a speaker. The sound output was played through the user's radio by means of a transmitter incorporated in the projector's amplifier; an "antenna" wire leading from the projector was to be laid in front of the radio and the radio dial set at "64," a spot on the dial generally only used by low-power local stations. In place of the normal incandescent "exciter" lamp, the designers placed a small length of Nichrome wire that sent an infrared beam to scan the optical sound track. The theory was that this wire would not burn out as frequently as small bulbs did in those days. The receptor cell, being sensitive to infrared, might have been a reincarnation of Case's Thalofide cell. The Apollo Sound P-76 sold for $129.50, without case.[44]

Sound-on-Film Cameras

The first amateur camera permitting direct recording of sound-on-film was the 16mm RCA-Victor camera, announced in 1933, but not available until 1935 (Fig. 273). The first model was designed to record the cameraman's voice as he held the camera up to his eye. Sound waves entering through a

Fig. 273. The RCA-Victor 16mm sound-on-film camera of 1935.

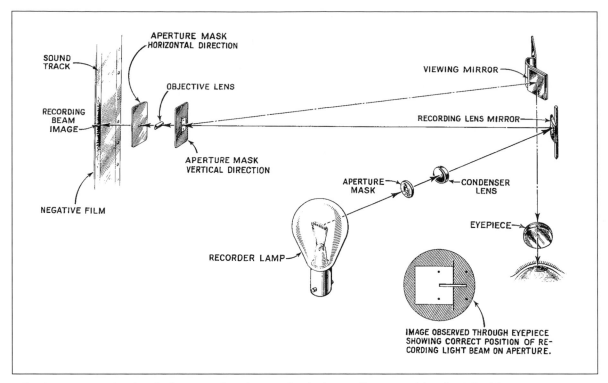

Fig. 274. Instruction book diagram showing method of recording sound by the RCA-Victor camera.

grille on the side of the camera acted on a suspended mirror, which reflected a beam of light from a small light bulb to the film, to produce a sound track (Fig. 274). A later model was equipped for a remote microphone. The list price in 1938 for a camera with an f/3.5 lens was $250. It is not believed to have been very successful.[45]

Other optical sound-on-film cameras appeared after World War II, such as Berndt-Bach, Inc.'s Auricon Cine-Voice at $695 (Fig. 275), and the Morton SoundMaster at $645, both appearing in the early 1950s.

World War II had put a hold on amateur camera design and development, but at the same time had vastly increased the public's familiarity with 16mm cameras and projectors. Millions of service men and women sat through hours of training films, civilians watched films on civil defense, defense plant workers were trained or exhorted to greater efforts through films. The projectors were 16mm optical sound machines made by Ampro, Bell & Howell, Calvin Corporation, Eastman Kodak, DeVry, Victor Animatograph, and others. The effect of this expanding market on Bell & Howell has been discussed in Chapter 6.

Magnetic Recording for the Amateur

As mentioned above, the Armour Research Foundation had been working on the development of magnetic sound tracks for 8mm, 16mm and 35mm film. In 1949, Sterling Kemp, Director of the Magnetic Recording Division of the Foundation, announced that patents had been received for methods of applying magnetic sound tracks to film and for designs of magnetic recorders and projectors. It was also announced that Eastman Kodak would immediately begin to use the Foundation's patents to produce pre-striped film, as well as adding magnetic stripe to customers' old silent films. Eastman Kodak was also reported to have begun the design of a magnetic sound projector. Ampro Corporation, Bell & Howell, and Revere Camera Company were also developing projectors with built-in magnetic sound capability.[46]

The RCA-1000 sound projector introduced in late 1951 has been cited as the first 16mm projector to offer both optical and magnetic sound capability, although it is not clear that this machine was aimed at the amateur market.[47] The following year Bell & Howell introduced the 16mm Filmosound "202" projector, also for optical or magnetic sound,

Why Not Own the Best?

-DADDY!

Shoot your own 16mm
TALKING PICTURES IN COLOR!

For home movies of theatrical quality, try
the new "Cine-Voice" 16mm Sound-On-Film
Camera. Shoot full-color or black & white.
Now you can enjoy your own High-Fidelity
Talking Pictures!

Auricon "Cine-Voice" 16mm Camera

$695.00 with a 30-day money-back
guarantee. You must be satisfied.

*Fig. 275. 1950s advertisement for the Auricon
Cine-Voice camera by Berndt-Bach.*

Fig. 276. A typical Filmosound projector of the 1950s.

*Another Bell & Howell engineering first...
magnetic sound on double-perforated film
...makes sound movies cost even less!*

*Fig. 277. Post-filming sound striping was offered for
double perforated film.*

advertised as "the greatest motion picture development since talking pictures." (See Fig. 276.)

Copywriter's hyperbole aside, the amateur could
at last add sound to his home movies quickly, easily
and cheaply, whether black-and-white or color, original or duplicate. Even optical sound prints could
have a magnetic stripe added, without harming the
original track. "Soundstripe" service was available
at 3-1/2 cents per foot at facilities in Chicago or
Hollywood. Even the user's double perforated 16mm

silent film could have a magnetic stripe added, as
shown in a Bell & Howell advertisement of November 1952 (Fig. 277).

At the same time, Bell & Howell announced a
new 70DL camera designed to take single-perforated
film, with a sound-speed setting among its seven
speed choices. The camera listed at $365 and the
projector at $699, which meant that less expensive
alternate sound systems would remain popular for
some time to come.

Eastman Kodak brought out a magnetic-optical
projector in 1956—the MK-4, at $795; Bell &
Howell's comparable model was then $734. By this
time magnetic sound-on-film projectors were available from Ampro, DeVry, Forway, Revere, Siemens
& Halske, and Victor Animatograph Corp.

233

Among the alternate systems were those based on a tape recorder and the user's own silent projector, kept in synchronization by a "synchronizer." Typical of such outfits was the "MOVIEVOX," complete with synchronizer, microphone, amplifier, wire recorder, speaker, and cords, all for just $225.

The magnetic/optical projectors facilitated "post-production" work—that is, the addition of sound after the film had been shot and edited. This of course precluded having truly synchronized sound, such as for speech. To accomplish the latter, two systems existed: single-system and double-system.

Single-system sound recording means recording the sound on the same film at the same time the photographic record is being made. This system has the advantage of simplicity; only one machine is involved and one piece of film. The film is exposed, processed, and returned to the maker with sound perfectly and permanently synchronized.

Single-system also has a major drawback: the near impossibility of editing. Any cut made in the film cuts both picture and sound, but not corresponding pieces. Because the film must move continuously and smoothly over the sound head, the sound head must be placed at some distance from the camera aperture, where the film is moving intermittently. The usual "separation" for 16mm film is 24 frames ahead of the film gate. From this it can be seen why editing single-system sound is next to impossible.

Double system, as its name implies, means making the picture record on one piece of film and the sound record on another piece of film (if optical) or piece of tape (if magnetic). The camera and recorder must of course be kept in perfect synchronization, which can be accomplished simply by driving both with the same motor connected by a flexible shaft or, more conveniently, driving each by its own synchronous motor.

As tape recorders became smaller and less expensive, amateurs were encouraged to build their own synchronized systems, with the guidance of expert amateurs such as George W. Cushman. Cushman, who was an amateur only in the sense that his filming was done purely for pleasure, was a professional writer who produced articles on all aspects of amateur filming for many of the popular photography magazines, as well as several books.

Typical of his books was one published in 1958, which, among other things, described how to convert any silent projector to sound and how to build a synchronous camera/recorder system [48]

Magnetic Sound for 8mm

The first U.S.-made magnetic 8mm sound-on-film projector, the Movie-Sound-8, was introduced in 1952 by the Movie Mite Corporation, a subsidiary of the Calvin Corporation. (Not to be confused with the 1946 8mm sound-on-disc projector also called "Movie-Sound-8.")

There were two obstacles to quality sound recording on 8mm film. First, the area available for the sound stripe was limited and, secondly, the speed of the film past the magnetic sound heads was insufficient for good sound fidelity. By 1959 advances in magnetic sound technology had produced magnetic material with greater sensitivity, permitting a narrower stripe; furthermore, advanced magnetic heads had been designed which could give good fidelity even at the low travel speed of 8mm film. The first of the new generation of 8mm sound projectors was the Elite 8, a product of the Norwegian firm of Norske Smalfilm Apparater a.d., introduced in this country in 1959.[49]

Several other European 8mm sound projectors were introduced in 1960, and an exceptional machine came from Eastman Kodak, the Kodak Sound 8 projector (Fig. 278), designed by R. J. Roman, J. M. Moriarty, and R. B. Johnson of Eastman Kodak's Research Laboratories. Among the innovations which set the projector apart from its predecessors were: 1) the heads made of Alfenol, an alloy of aluminum and iron developed by the Navy, with superior magnetic properties and yet extremely hard; 2) deriving from the Alfenol properties, a 20-mil head width operating on a 30-mil stripe minimized edge distortions, and a gap setting of just .001," for maximum frequency response: 3) a special flywheel which gave excellent speed uniformity; and 4) a speed control which achieved full speed in less than one second. The projector gave acceptable frequency response at silent speed of 16 frames per second and excellent response at sound speed of 24 frames per second. [50, 51]

The Kodak Sound 8 projector was hailed as not only a great boon for the amateur but was expected to find wide use in professional applications such as

Fig. 278. Kodak Sound 8 Projector of 1960.

educational and industrial films. *American Cinematographer*, the professional's magazine, ran a two-part series on the development of the projector. The article pointed out that while there was a small saving in the use of 8mm over 16mm, the difference was unlikely to be enough to justify a switch for those with a large investment in 16mm cameras, projectors, and recording equipment.[52] This turned out to be an accurate assessment; 8mm sound film found very little professional use.

Also in 1960, Eastman Kodak announced "Sonotrack Coating," its trade name for the addition of a magnetic stripe to 8mm Kodachrome film, either at the time of processing or to previously-processed film.[53]

A single-system sound camera for the amateur was first achieved by the RCA Victor camera of 1935 mentioned above and, in 1960 by the Fairchild Camera and Instrument Corporation, with the introduction of the Fairchild Cinephonic 8 (Fig. 279). This was a sturdy camera weighing 4-1/2 pounds in a die-cast aluminum body, driven by a built-in rechargeable Nicad 12-volt battery, which also drove the

Fig. 279. The Fairchild Cinephonic 8mm sound-on-film camera.

Fig. 280. Fairchild Cinephonic projector.

built-in transistorized amplifier. Ansco Corporation supplied a special 25-mil pre-striped double 8 film rated at ASA 12, in 50-foot rolls. The companion projector took 400-foot reels, and provided editing, playback and erasing capability (Fig. 280). The camera, with a 13mm f/1.8 fixed focus lens was priced at $239.50, the projector at $249.50.[54]

The introductory model was faulted for providing only a single lens and for the lack of recording level indicator; in 1963 a new model with a 10 to 30mm focusing zoom lens, and reflex viewing was introduced, with a $100 price increase. Despite favorable reviews in the popular press and reports of successful commercial use by station KPHO-TV in Phoenix, the camera had operational problems and the line was discontinued about 1965. A larger model intended for industrial use, with 200-foot magazines was introduced at that time and was on the market for a few years.[55] As improving tape recorder technology led to more compact units, considerable effort was made to achieve workable double-system recording that would be portable enough for amateur use.

A system developed by Michael Deangelo of Flushing, New York, in 1959 bears examination for its anticipation by nearly ten years of the much better-known "Filmosound 8" system brought to market by Bell & Howell in 1968. Deangelo's system, which he called "Synchro-Sound," consisted of: a camera containing a pulse-generator coupled to the film drive, a cable connecting the camera to a tape recorder, a two-tracked tape, and a microphone cabled to the recorder. In operation, the pulses gen-erated by the camera traveled to one track of the tape; the sound signal from the microphone was recorded on the other track of the tape. To edit, the tape was treated with a dye that converted the pulse impressions to black dashes, clearly visible against the brown tape. With a pulse for every frame, it was a relatively simple matter to remove and insert equivalent lengths of film and sound tape.

In projection, the speed of the projector was controlled by the pulse marks on the control track of the tape, thus ensuring that picture and sound were always in synchronization. Deangelo actually proposed furnishing and installing the necessary control equipment on the customer's own camera, recorder, and projector, at a cost ranging from $300 to $500, depending on the customer's particular equipment. It is not known how "Synchro-Sound" fared in the market place; it does not appear in any subsequent product directories.[56]

Very little advance in amateur sound technology took place until November 1968, when Bell & Howell announced: "HOME MOVIES THAT TALK, The Most Significant Development in Home Movies in Forty Years." (An amazing dismissal of 8mm, Kodachrome, and Super 8!). The product was the "Filmosound 8" system, consisting of a camera, tape recorder, and projector. The Filmosound camera contained two mechanisms that distinguished it from a silent camera. The first was a signal lamp located behind the film gate which, when the camera film drive was started, flashed a spot on the edge of the film. The second mechanism was a pulse generator that emitted an electric pulse for each frame of film.

In operation, at the start of each scene the camera flashed the starting spot on the edge of the film, the pulse generator sent its signal through a cable to the tape recorder, which as in the Deangelo system, had a bi-track tape, one track for the audio signal, the other for the synchronizing pulse signal.

When the developed film was run through the projector, the starting spot signaled the recorder to start, while the synchronizing pulses on the film were sent to the recorder, where the recorder compared the projector's speed with the previously recorded speed and signaled any necessary adjustment back to the projector.[57]

Despite initially favorable reviews, the

Filmosound system had operational problems and did not attract the buying public; Bell & Howell dropped the line within a year or two. One authority has maintained that Bell & Howell went to this double system because of their inability to furnish magnetic striped film in a rapid-loading, foolproof cartridge.[58]

Double-system Super 8 sound did appeal to the professional, non-Hollywood filmmakers, however. The potential savings in the use of Super 8 over 16mm were too great to be ignored. In 1971 the Massachusetts Institute of Technology awarded documentary filmmaker Richard Leacock a grant of $300,000 to develop a complete Super 8 synchronous sound system. The Leacock system, completed in 1972, was based on the use of "full coat" Super 8 magnetic film as the sound medium and crystal-controlled cameras and recorders.

"Full coat Super 8" was simply sprocketed film which was coated on its entire surface, in place of the conventional unsprocketed cassette tape. "Crystal control" meant the installation of high frequency oscillators and receivers in both camera and recorder, which eliminated the need for cables between the two machines. The Leacock system also included sophisticated editors and mixers, bringing the price of a complete system to $6,000 and more.[59]

While such systems were out of reach of the average amateur, they did bring Super 8 sound to a professional level and into considerable use for documentary, industrial, and TV news production.

Breakthrough For Super 8

The sound system for the average home filmmaker came in 1973, with Eastman Kodak's announcement of Ektasound. The system consisted of a new Super 8 sound cartridge, containing 50 feet of pre-striped Super 8 film, a choice of two new sound cameras, and two new projectors. The sound cartridge was just six-tenths-inch longer than the silent Super 8 cartridge, allowing room for a loop sensor, recording head, capstan and pressure roller. The capstan motor was electronically controlled to carry the film past the recording head at 18 frames per second. As in silent super 8 cameras, film advance was by "push down," two frames above the aperture. Six AA batteries carried in the camera handle supplied power. Two camera models were offered: the Ektasound 130 with a 9mm f/1.9 lens at

Fig. 281. Kodak Ektasound Camera, Model 180.

$189.50, and the Ektasound 140 with 9-21mm zoom lens at $274.50 (Fig. 281).

As noted in Chapter 10, the Super 8 format had been designed for sound, i.e., there was a space for a 30-mil magnetic sound stripe opposite the perforations, as well as a balance stripe between the opposite edge and the perforations. This configuration had two benefits: the balance stripe gave greater film flatness in the projector gate, and moving the sound stripe away from the perforations gave greater sound fidelity. The perforated edge of the film tended to distort slightly from a true curve as it passed over the sound drum, producing "reading" errors in both optical and magnetic sound systems.[60]

The Ektasound projectors were of a radically new design, resembling a tape recorder turned up on its front side (Fig. 282). The 400-foot reels were placed on either side of the film transport and lens. By means of a pivoted mirror, projection could be either to the back or the front of the projector. The Ektasound 235, for play only, listed at $219.50; the Ektasound 245 offered play and record, at $279. The new cartridges were $4.95 for Kodachrome II and $5.70 for Ektachrome 160.

Public reaction to Kodak's new product line was guarded; while it certainly appeared to be precisely what the amateur had long been looking for, other

Fig. 282. Ektasound projector, with cover in place.

camera manufacturers adopted a wait-and-see attitude. As a result of a suit filed by Bell & Howell and others in 1973, Eastman Kodak did offer the new technology to its competitors, for a price. A number of manufacturers were reported to have paid the $5,000 fee to examine the system; a number did not, preferring to wait for the buying public's reaction. Some expressed doubt about sound-on-film for amateur cameras, the problems of recording "selective" sound and the difficulty of editing.[61]

That the new system was a gamble on Kodak's part was expressed by Tony Galluzzo, movie editor for *Modern Photography*:

After countless brave but futile attempts to market synchronized home movie sound by Fairchild, by Bell & Howell, and by Synchronex, Kodak has finally come forth with their very own.[62]

Bell & Howell was one of the first to take the gamble along with Kodak and launch a camera to use the new Kodak Ektasound cartridge. Its 1974 annual report announced that the company had "moved into the sound home movie market." with the introduction of the Filmosonic XL super 8 sound movie camera. Other manufacturers followed suit, particularly the Japanese. By January 1976, one independent filmmaker and writer on amateur movies reported on 18 different sound-on-film Super 8 camera models, ranging in price from about $200 for the Ektasound 130 to $2,000 plus for the Beaulieu 5008S.[63] (See Fig. 283).

Eastman Kodak reported that consumer reaction to the Ektasound products was "gratifying." The

Fig. 283. Marcel Beaulieu cradles his masterpiece, the Beaulieu 5008S.

1973 Annual Report carried this wistful remark:

One potential plus for the quality of home movies: scenes tend to be longer and less fragmented as home cinematographers seek to capture meaningful segments of conversation or music.

The Ektasound 130 was obviously the "bare bones" camera for the amateur who wished to put a timid toe in the water, while the elegant Beaulieu sported, among other features, an f/1.2 6 to 80mm Angenieux lens in focusing mount, macro focus to 26", multi-speed power zoom, through-the lens fully automatic exposure control, reflex finder, ground glass focusing, rechargeable Nicad battery, and provision for single, double, single/double combined sound systems. The Beaulieu was widely acknowledged to be the most advanced Super 8 sound camera produced up to that time (Fig. 284).

As noted in Chapter 9, Eastman Kodak in 1975 introduced a newly designed 200-foot cartridge and the Supermatic 200 camera that accepted either the standard 50-foot sound cartridge or the 200-foot cartridge. The Supermatic 200, while providing the filmmaker with up to 10 minutes of filming time without reloading, did not offer many of the features that had become almost standard in silent cam-

Fig. 284. Close-up of the camera in Fig. 283.

eras: reflex viewing and metering, greater zoom range, power zooming, etc. The first fully featured camera to accept the 200-foot cartridge came from Japan, the Sankyo XL61-200S introduced early in 1978. Also appearing that year were two 200-foot models from Elmo.

While there appears to have been no comment from Kodak, various reasons were reported for the three-year delay between Kodak's introduction of the cartridge and its adoption by other manufacturers—one was that the first production runs of the cartridge revealed design problems which had to be corrected before other manufacturers could be given specifications which would enable them to design their cameras.

By the close of 1978, there were 16 manufacturers offering over 70 models of Super 8 sound cameras, almost all of which were XL, ranging in price from $200 to over $2,000. Bell & Howell and Eastman Kodak were the only two U.S. manufacturers, and the former company's cameras were manufactured in Japan. Eastman Kodak's last introduced camera was the Ektasound 260.

The vast diversity of models and range of prices illustrated two significant trends: first, the high average cost of Super 8 sound cameras, compared to silent cameras, meant the near-abandonment of the mass market that had long been the backbone of Eastman Kodak's business. The average price of six Kodak XL cameras in 1974 was $179; the average price of four Ektasounds in 1975 was $328, an 80 percent increase. By 1978, only one silent camera was available under $200 and only one sound camera at less than $300.

In January of 1979, Eastman Kodak announced the discontinuance of all Ektasound cameras; the last "XL" cameras were discontinued in June 1981. Bell & Howell closed its Consumer Division in 1979, and by December 1982, not a single movie camera advertisement appeared in *Popular Photography*. The American amateur motion picture industry was history.[64]

The Coming of Video and Its Influence on Home Movies

JVC-VHS Format System, 1978

A New Medium

The term "television" is generally understood to encompass the recording, storage, transmission and display of images by electronic means. The video camera, or camcorder, the device that has all but displaced the use of film by the amateur, is another manifestation of television technology. The lightweight camcorder is a marvel of engineering, combining as it does all the elements enumerated above except transmission. The development of this instrument is reminiscent of the evolution of the hand-held calculator. The computing capability of today's pocket calculator, costing perhaps $25, duplicates the power of a room-size computer of 30 years ago that cost thousands of dollars. Similarly, today's camcorder sells for far less than the cost of the lens alone for a 1950s studio TV camera.

How It All Began

As photography is founded on the chemical reaction of certain salts on exposure to light, so does television rest on two phenomena involving light, electricity, and matter. First, certain substances, such as the metal selenium, give off electrons when exposed to light; secondly, certain other substances, known as phosphors, give off photons of light when struck by electrons. These reactions were chiefly scientific curiosities when discovered in the early nineteenth century; they led dozens of experimenters, working with these and other phenomena for nearly three quarters of a century, to bring us television as we know it today.

A sensitized photographic plate or film is essentially a mosaic of thousands of silver halide grains, waiting to be acted upon by light when the camera shutter is opened. Now imagine that in place of the halide grains are grains of selenium, each grain having a wire attached to collect the emitted electrons. Imagine these wires leading to an array of tiny light bulbs, arranged in the same spatial configuration as the selenium grains in the receiving plate.

Now let a pattern of light and shadow fall upon the plate—the result will be thousands of electrical signals coming over those wires, one from each selenium grain. The strength of each signal will be proportional to the amount of light received by each selenium grain. As each lightbulb lights up according to the signal it receives, the pattern of light and shadow that fell on the first array of selenium cells will be duplicated on the array of lightbulbs.

Just such a scheme was proposed in 1875 by a Bostonian named G. R. Carey, though he recognized the problem presented by the impossible bulk of the number of wires that would be required and the number of bulbs. To eliminate the need for wires and bulbs, Carey proposed, rather than trying to deal with the thousands of picture elements all at once, to "scan" the mosaic of electric signals coming from the receiving plate, using a detector moving in a spiral path, picking up each elemental signal in a time- and space-defined sequence. These signals could then be transmitted to a receiving machine equipped with a synchronously spiraling lamp; it would emit a burst of light for each signal received and thus reproduce the original pattern of light. Carey's scheme was never constructed but his ideas were incorporated in several early experimental systems.

The German scientist Paul Nipkow in 1884 proposed replacing Carey's mosaic of receiving cells with a small image (actually the size and shape of the standard 35mm motion picture frame) which would be scanned by a 20-inch disk carrying a spiral of 60 small holes, each admitting light from the image to a selenium cell. The disk was to operate at 1200 rpm, which would mean the frame would be scanned with 60 lines, in 1/20th of a second.

Nipkow's scheme was theoretically sound, but three factors made the proposed system impossible at that time. These were: the slow response time of the selenium cell, the lack of a means of amplifying the small voltages produced by the cell, and the lack of light bulbs with easily and rapidly controlled brilliance.

It would be more than 30 years before all of these obstacles were overcome. Fast and sensitive photoelectric cells were not available until 1913; de Forest perfected his Audion, or triode amplifier, in 1906 and D. McFarlan Moore of General Electric produced a satisfactory neon lamp in 1917.

Fig.285. John Logie Baird's experimental television.

Interestingly, none other than C. Francis Jenkins, one-time partner with Thomas Armat in the development of a successful motion picture projector in 1895, was one of two experimenters who, in 1925, eventually produced and demonstrated the first electrical transmission of a television image using the Nipkow disk. The other experimenter was the Englishman J. L. Baird, who accomplished the same result independently and simultaneously with Jenkins (Fig. 285).

The transmitted image was quite coarse; as noted, the Nipkow system utilized just 60 scanning lines and, since the current United States standard is 525 lines, the relative quality of Jenkins' image may be imagined.

The one device chiefly responsible for the modern television camera and receiver is the cathode ray tube, the origins of which go back to the British physicist Sir William Crookes, who first discovered rays being emitted from the cathode of a vacuum tube in 1875. A German scientist, Karl F. Braun, in 1897 discovered that the rays that had been shown to be a stream of electrons could be directed by electromagnetic or electrostatic fields.

A cathode ray tube, or CRT (Fig. 286), in its simplest form consists of an evacuated tube having a cathode (A) at one end, one or more anodes coils (B), electrostatic deflection plates (C), and a sensitized screen (D) at the other end. This screen may be designed to convert incident light to voltage, or to convert impinging electrons to light.

For operation as a camera, the tube is constructed to convert incident light to voltage. The image to be televised is focused on the screen, where the light

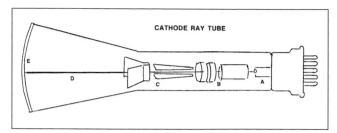

Fig. 286. Simplified diagram of cathode ray tube:
a) cathode, b) anodes, c) electrostatic plates,
d) electron beam, e) sensitized screen.

rays cause the screen to acquire a pattern of electrostatic charges. The electron beam coming from the cathode is made to "scan" the screen by the influence of the plates (C), or coils (D). The scanning beam converts the pattern of charges to a series of electrical signals that can then be stored on magnetic tape or transmitted to another location for conversion back to a visual image.

For operation as a receiver, the tube is constructed for the second mode of operation. In this case, the electrical signals received from the transmitter, or camera, are applied to the anodes to modulate the electron beam. At the same time, the beam of the receiving CRT scans its screen exactly as the camera beam had screened the image. The screen of the receiving CRT now emits light in a pattern exactly duplicating the pattern received by the camera tube.

The early operating CRTs were massive; one designed by C. J. Davisson of the Bell Telephone Laboratories and used in the first transmission of television signals over the coaxial cable from New York to Philadelphia in 1937 was approximately five feet long.

As popular and scientific interest in the perfection of television grew, more talent on both sides of the Atlantic and Pacific was brought to bear on the problems of the new technology. Camera tubes shrank dramatically in size, from a 1939 "iconoscope," approximately 8 inches in diameter at the face, to the "image-orthicon" of 1946, with a 3-inch diameter face, to the 1953 "vidicon," approximately 1 inch in diameter.

The above tubes were all for black-and-white television; when the demand for color became imperative about 1956, cameras then needed three tubes, one for each color, and sometimes a fourth tube for the "luminance" signal. The body of an early broad-

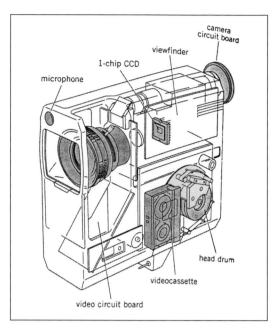

Fig. 287. Charge-coupled device installed in Sony's prototype camcorder CCD-M8U, 1980.

cast color camera was described as being 52" long by 34" wide by 40" tall and requiring four strapping men to maneuver it on location shooting.[1] Again, advancing technology soon reduced the bulk of both studio and location cameras, particularly with the introduction of tubes using lead oxide as the light-sensitive material, called "Plumbicons," and the arrival of charge-coupled devices (CCDs). (See Fig. 287.)

CCD refers to solid-state, light-sensitive devices that may typically contain several hundred thousand light-sensitive spots or cells called "pixels" (for picture elements). The CCD is smaller and lighter than a tube, requires less power, will not be "burned" by too much light, and is much less prone to blurring of the image if the image or the camera is moving too quickly.[2] As everyone knows who watches television news, the modern color TV camera is easily carried over the cameraman's shoulder.

First Effects

The first impact of "video" on the home movie industry was not from the video cassette recorder, nor the camcorder, but from network television, and the first segment of the industry affected was the film rental business.[3] The September 1951 issue of *Photographic Trade News* reported on a survey of photographic retailers that had film rental departments. For the purposes of the study, the stores were divided into two sections, those in areas with TV reception and those without. Information was sought on film rentals and sales of home-projection equipment. While there was wide disparity in the amount of gain or loss reported in each section, three out of four stores in areas with TV competition reported losses in film rental business ranging from "slight" to "90 percent," while three out of four stores in areas without TV showed gains. This of course was years before the first video rental became available.

The spread of television receivers throughout the country was dramatic: one source reported that there were four million receivers in U.S. homes in 1949, 81 million by 1969, and 150 million by 1979.[4] In contrast, shipments of 8mm projectors declined by 34 percent between 1968 and 1979.[5]

The intrusion of the TV set into the American living room inevitably pushed the movie projector further back in the closet. Screening home movies was almost unavoidably an evening activity, given the need to darken the room. In the 1950s, except for afternoon programs for the children, television viewing was an evening activity also. While the image quality of even a standard 8mm family movie was superior to that of the early TV, and was quite apt to be in color while TV was still black and white, the entertainment quotient was decidedly inferior. It became increasingly difficult to lure the neighbors over to watch "Our Trip to Niagara Falls" if they were planning to watch Milton Berle (a comedian who became known as "Mr. Television) or Edward R. Morrow (the dean of TV newsmen in the 1950s).

The video tape recorder was the child of television. The essence of television is the conversion by the television camera of the viewed image into a series of electronic signals that are then transmitted through the ether to the customer's television set, where the signals are re-converted to a visual image. In the beginning, all of this happened in "real time;" Every television show in the early days was "live."

Various schemes for recording the TV signal were devised, including those using film, as in the Kinescope camera mentioned in Chapter 5. However, the difference in frame rate between the television camera and the film camera, plus optical losses, made film recording systems less than satisfactory. The first major advance in television recording came in 1951 when the Electronics Division of Bing Crosby Enterprises gave its first demonstration of a video tape recorder, in black and white.[6] In 1956, Ampex marketed its Ampex VR-1000 recorder for television sta-

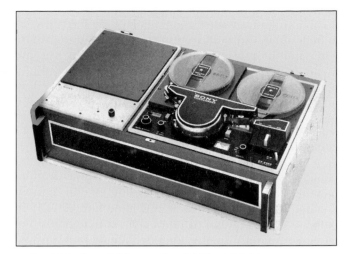

Fig. 288. Sony Videocorder 2000 of 1966.

tions, recording picture and sound on 2 inch tape. It was approximately the size of a large kitchen range and carried a price of $45,000.

While tape had quality problems of its own, it did have the substantial advantage of instant playback—no waiting for film development.

The first video tape recorder that could possibly be considered as suitable for amateur use was announced by Sony in March 1965 (Fig. 288). The Videocorder 2000, for recording a video transmission using half-inch tape running at 7-1/2 inches per second, It weighed 30 pounds and was priced at $500. An optional camera was available to record live action, price not given. The following year Sony showed the first color home videotape recorder.[7]

From then on the course got crowded. Within a year of Sony's announcement, Ampex, Concord, Panasonic, Roberts Electronics, and Shibaden announced video tape recorders, at varying prices. In November of 1966, Sony announced that in a few months it would market a three-piece video outfit consisting of camera, recorder, and battery pack. On top of the camera was mounted a one-inch cathode ray tube monitor. The total weight was to be 21-1/2 pounds and the price was $1,000.

In 1971, Sony again led the field by being the first to break away from reel-to-reel handling of the tape, with the announcement of a video cassette system. The cassette, slightly larger than the familiar audiocassette, held one hour of color TV, with two audio tracks for stereo or bilingual programs, and could play through any color TV. The price for one cassette was a hefty $30.

In 1973, a five-page article appeared in a national magazine comparing tape and film for the amateur, authored by an experienced filmmaker. His conclusion was that film was still superior to tape in every respect except cost of the medium. Otherwise, for tape the initial investment was much higher, the equipment was heavier to carry around, more susceptible to down-time, more difficult to edit, and the results were in black and white to boot.[8]

Such particulars did not deter everyone, to be sure. One award-winning amateur filmmaker—J. Joseph deCourcelle, a Fellow of the Photographic Society of America (FPSA)—began his career in 1928 with a hand-cranked 16mm camera. He worked in 8mm for 17 years and then used a Bach-Auricon Ciné-Voice 16mm sound-on-film camera. In 1975 deCourcelle took the video plunge. He bought a Sony Model AVC-3400 camera, a Sony AV-3400 video recorder, and a monitor. His first attempts were shot in a dimly lit basement game room. When the resulting tape turned out to be perfectly exposed, he never looked back; it was tape from then on.[9]

Of course Mr. deCourcelle was not a typical amateur, but he was typical of a small segment of the amateur market. He was a typical "technology junkie," one of those intrepid and generally well-heeled amateurs who has to have the latest gadget regardless of cost. Market analysts who happened to query the deCourcelles of the world tended to make errors on their estimates of market demand for new technology.[10]

For the next several years there appeared a confusion of incompatible systems that fought for leadership, but by 1978 these had been reduced to four half-inch tape formats. In this case, "format" means the manner in which the television signal is recorded on the tape. These systems were: Betamax, pioneered by Sony, VHS advanced by Japan's Victor Company and parent Matsushita, Quasar also by Matsushita, and V-Cord II backed by Sanyo and Toshiba. The latter two concerns were soon to go to VHS and Beta, respectively, which became the dominant formats.[11] These two have survived to the present day, although VHS has all but entirely supplanted Betamax. (See Fig. 289)

There was another recording system—the video disk—was first seen several years previously but had not received a great deal of attention up to this point.

Fig. 289. The 1978 Akai video camera with separate tape recorder, here being tested for Modern Photography by Tony Galluzzo.

A video disk is produced in a manner quite similar to that by which an audio compact disk (CD) is produced. The television signal modulates a laser beam focused on the surface of a spinning disk of metal, creating a series of "pit" or "no pit" signals analogous to the TV signal. As with the audio record process, a master disk is first made, from which thousands of plastic disks can be pressed very inexpensively.

The video disk had the great advantage of low price, it could be "random accessed," and it was less susceptible to damage. But it could not be created at home, giving video disks just the pre-recorded market. After some years in the financial doldrums, RCA in 1981 launched a $20 million promotional campaign for its new $500 disk player. Magnavox had introduced Magnavision two years earlier, and a joint venture of GE/Matsushita/JVC introduced another disk system in 1982. The technology evolved into the fabulously successful compact disc systems of year 2000.

What the home movie maker had been eagerly awaiting seemed to be at hand in the fall of 1981 when rumors surfaced that Sony and Eastman Kodak were planning to team up to produce a combined videocassette recorder and camera. The proposed joint venture did not materialize, nor did the combined camera/recorder, but the threatened entrance of the Rochester giant may have resonated in other boardrooms. In 1982, several major photographic companies, including Canon, Minolta, Olympus, and Pentax, entered the market with new camera and recorder designs. Many cameras featured zoom lenses, auto exposure, color balance, and electronic viewfinders. Prices for a color camera ranged from $860 to $2,150, and for a VCR, $875 to $1,295.[12]

By May 1983 there were no less than 18 manufacturers offering 42 models of video cameras. Prices ranged from $559 for the model QC-50 from Sharp, to $1,995 for Hitachi's VK-C2000. Weights ranged from just under three pounds to seven pounds, with most running about five pounds.[13]

At last came a breakthrough at a news conference in New York City on January 4, 1984, Eastman Kodak Company announced and demonstrated the Kodavision System, becoming the first company to commit to the long-awaited 8mm tape format and to combine the functions of camera and recorder in one compact package. Two camera models were shown, the Kodavision 2200 and the auto-focus model, the Kodavision 2400. Both cameras weighed about 5 pounds, and accepted either 60- or 90-minute 8mm videocassettes, which were slightly smaller than a standard audiocassette (Figs. 290 and 291).

The cameras had a 7 to 42mm f/1.2 power zoom lens focusing to four feet, with "macro" option at wide-angle setting. The image tube was a newly developed 1-1/3" Newvicon. The model 2200 was

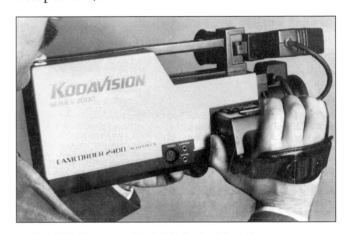

Fig. 290. Eastman Kodak's Kodavision Camera.

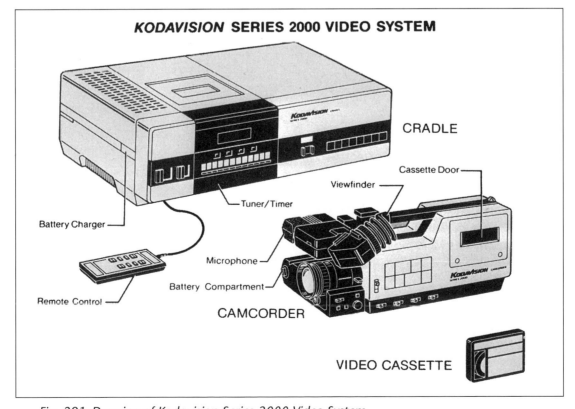

Fig. 291. Drawing of Kodavision Series 2000 Video System.

priced at $1,599, the 2400 at $1,899. The cameras were manufactured by Matsushita and the tapes by TDK. Included with each camera was a storage cradle that provided means to play back and transfer recordings to a TV set, recharging for the camera battery, and an optional timer/tuner that converted the cradle into a full-featured videotape recorder.[14]

The major video manufacturers had met in January of 1982 and issued a statement that agreement had been reached on a standard for one-piece camera/recorders—one hour tape, 8mm wide. The word "camcorder" had more-or-less officially entered the English language.

Following Kodak's announcement, RCA showed a prototype camcorder manufactured by Hitachi, Polaroid demonstrated a camcorder, and General Electric announced that it would soon market an 8mm machine.

A groundbreaking entry into the 8mm race came at the 1985 Consumer Electronics Show when Sony unveiled its Mini-8 camcorder, formally the CCD-M8U and known commercially as the "Handycam" (Fig. 292). The initials CCD stood for "charge-coupled device," described above. This device permitted a much more compact design of the camcorder and spelled the end for all those using image tubes, including Kodak's Kodavision.

Almost exactly three years from Eastman Kodak's entry into the 8mm video camera field, rumors began to surface that the Rochester company was about to withdraw from this 300 million dollar a year market. Observers noted that Kodak had not introduced a new 8mm model since September 1985, nor had the company done much advertising of the line in the most recent. A Kodak spokesman denied that the company was planning to discontinue the 8mm camera, but admitted that the product was "coming slowly."[15]

The rumors proved to be true, however; the Kodavision camera that even Kodak insiders described as "clunky" and outclassed by its Japanese rivals had been quietly discontinued in 1986. But the 8mm cassette format that Eastman Kodak had pioneered would quickly become the standard for the amateur camcorder.[16]

As noted in Chapter 5, 8mm amateur movie camera and film sales had reached a plateau in the late 1950s and then began a decline in the early

Fig. 292. Sony's Camcorder Video 8 CCD-M8U, or "Handycam."

1970s, long before the video camera became a home-consumer item. Among the reasons cited for this decline were the inconvenience of the 25-foot spool loading system, the need for hot, hazardous movie lights for indoor filming, and the difficulty of obtaining synchronized sound.

Ironically, just as camera and film manufacturers, led by Eastman Kodak, met these challenges, home video systems were being perfected. There were some at Eastman Kodak who believed that the company abandoned Super 8 too quickly—that there were developments in progress in Engineering which, if backed by management, might have extended the life of the medium for another few years.

But the appeal of the video camera was irresistible to many; again, as with 16mm in 1923, the early video cameras found their market among the well-to-do. In 1978, a dozen models of color video cameras were available at prices ranging from $800 to $1495.[17] These prices were not so far from those of the top-of-the-line Super 8 sound cameras; the almost negligible cost of tape versus film was an added attraction.

And as video cameras became more affordable, "home movie" makers increasingly switched to video. Video offered significant advantages—almost unlimited footage without stopping to reload, effortless recording of synchronized sound, easy and immediate playback on a TV set without having to darken the room and set up a projector and screen, and the elimination of the cost and bother of film processing.

By 1981, the sale of Super 8 cameras had dropped to about 200,000 units per year, from 600,000 in 1977, while video camera shipments had risen to 200,000. By late 1984, an estimated one million units were in use.[18]

Unfortunately, these tempting features of the video camera led to excesses in its use that were unheard of with a film camera. No longer restricted to 25 feet of 8mm film before flipping the spools over, or 50 feet of Super 8 that forced the filmer to give some thought to scene length, now the camera could run on and on. At one film school beginning students are deliberately limited to 30-minute tapes for their student projects, the faculty having learned that without this restriction beginners tend to tape much more footage than they can edit in a reasonable time.

Nor was this freedom lost on the working cameraman. One professional reports:

When broadcast news photographers traded in their Bell & Howell 70DR cameras, which held a 100-foot spool yielding about three minutes of footage, for the new three quarter inch U-Matic portables (cameras), which recorded 20 minutes on tape, they thought they had died and gone to heaven.[19]

By the year 2000 the amateur videographer had a marvelously broad range of fine instruments to choose from. A 2000 Buyer's Guide listed no fewer than 86 models in five formats—digital, 8mm, Hi8, VHS, and VHS-C. The digital camera, as its name implies, records the image as digital data on tape, while the others record the images as analog data on tape. Among the features available were autofocus on all models. Most models offered audio and video input, audio dub, character generation, connection to a home computer, image stabilization, and color LCD monitor.

Manufacturers's suggested retail prices for the digital cameras ranged from just under $1,000 to $4,000; tape camera prices ran from $300 to $1,600.

Editing digital or analog tape was a very different process than with film. With the advent of the flying erase head, simple editing with a VCR was possible for those willing to spend the effort. For greater control and accuracy, software was available (at a price) to permit editing through a computer which, in the words of one writer, was still "a pain." Cited were the huge amounts of data to be collected, organized, and recorded, the requirement for lots of computer memory, and the need to work with frame-rate accuracy at the level of 1/30th of a second.

Despite their sophistication and complex engineering, the cameras were generally easy to use and hundreds of former filmmakers, finding 8mm or Super 8 film increasingly difficult to obtain and process, happily switched to video. This rejuvenated many of the local, national, and international amateur movie clubs that are described in Chapter 14.

One question remains: home movies taken 75 years ago, if they have had even marginally decent storage, are still viewable. Whether this will be true of digital movies in 2075 remains to be seen. There is solid evidence that many of the early tapes are seriously degraded. As one film-to-video transfer professional put it:

Those who switched from film to video have discovered that while their sensibly stored black and white and Kodachrome images of their grandparents' activities of the 1930s and 40s are projectable today (or transferable to video) in arresting contrast and unfaded color, their VHS images of their own children from the 1970s and 80s can be viewed only through a blizzard of static and degraded color as the oxide leaves the tape. There seems to be reason for keeping at least one movie camera loaded with Kodachrome film.[20]

With the growing awareness by archivists of the value of amateur films and videos, it may be that more attention will be given to preserving this successor media to film.

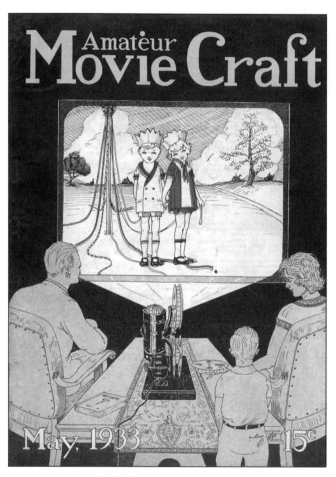

Amateur Movie Craft *magazine, May, 1933.*

A Treasure Lode of Information

The literature on amateur motion picture photography that I have examined for this book falls into three general classes: books and periodicals devoted entirely to the subject; portions of general photographic periodicals; and manufacturers' literature including sales catalogs, instruction manuals, and corporate annual reports. The search has been for two kinds of information: the history of amateur motion picture technology and the nature of the information and guidance offered to the amateur filmmaker.

I have endeavored to identify and describe the more significant sources as listed above, but with a few exceptions, I have not included periodicals or books that were written primarily for film students or advanced filmmakers.

The popular photographic periodicals have been the greatest source of information in both of the areas mentioned above; in fact, this book could not have been written without constant reference to a personal collection of these magazines spanning nearly 60 years.

Books for the Amateur

Less than five years after motion pictures became a commercial reality, a wonderful book on the history of the new art appeared: *Living Pictures: Their History, Photo Production and Practical Working,* by Henry V. Hopwood, published in London in 1899. Despite its cumbersome title, the book is a pleasure to read; Hopwood does not avoid technical descriptions, but his style is down-to-earth and graced with humor and gentle irony. Take for example his comments on the "Lapiposcope," one of the dozens of pieces of apparatus with strange names that had emerged at that time:

Under the somewhat gruesome title is hidden the instrument whose working principles were described in connection with Figure 132. That the inventor's name is Lapipe may be an explanation; it can hardly be an excuse. Fancy the dreadful compounds which might be evolved were this example generally followed.

While there were not many machines that could be described as amateur at that time, Hopwood's lucid coverage of pre-cinema, as well as the earliest successful machines, and the fact that we are reading the comments of a contemporary of so many of these historically significant machines makes the book well worth reading. It can be found as an Arno Press Reprint Edition of the *1970 Literature of Cinema Series*.[1]

Another British book worth examining is *Practical Cinematography and Its Applications*, by Frederick A. Talbot, published in London in 1913, 258 pages, illustrated. The preface states that the volume was written with the express purpose of "assisting the amateur who is attracted towards Cinematography." Among the many illustrations not otherwise readily accessible are several showing Professor Marey's work, the high-speed camera of Lucien Bull,[2] and four excellent views of the Aeroscope camera. Built in 1911 by the Polish inventor, Kasimir Proszynski, the Aeroscope was probably the world's first motor-driven camera, powered by a compressed air motor, fed by tanks within the camera.

The Cinema Handbook, published in 1921, written by Austin C. Lescaboura, when he was managing editor of *Scientific American,* may be the first movie-making manual written for the non-professional. It was truly a handbook: 500 pages just 3-1/2" by 5-1/4", packed with chapters on the hardware, planning and filming the amateur "photo play," with most emphasis on the hardware and mechanics of production.

Lescaboura proposed eight steps to a successful production:

1. A Good Plot
2. A Written Scenario
3. A Capable Director
4. Selecting the Cast
5. Proper Makeup
6. Continuity
7. The Hand of the Artist—camera angles, close-ups, etc.
8. The Importance of Editing

The total orientation of the Handbook toward the production of amateur dramas is noteworthy, in that it illustrates the almost unwritten rule of the early

Fig. 293. Herbert C. McKay, ca. 1918, with the Actograph 17.5mm camera.

days that the proper thing to do with this new but expensive toy was to mimic Hollywood and produce "photo plays."

Herbert C. McKay (Fig. 293) was born in Terre Haute, Indiana, on April 8, 1895, to Isaac Newton McKay and Keziah Brown McKay. His formal education seems to have been limited to three years at Indiana State Normal School. After a stint as a bacteriologist at Camp Taylor, Kentucky, during World War I, he became a cinematographer. In 1924 Falk Publishing Company published his first book, *Professional Cinematography*. This was followed in the same year by *Motion Picture Photography for the Amateur*.

In 1925, McKay was elected Associate of the Royal Photographic Society of Great Britain and was appointed dean of the New York Institute of Photography, a position he held until 1936. During this time he published a spate of books including: *The Photo Era Reference Book of Photography and Cinematography, Photographic Technology, The Voice of the Films,* and *A Course in Photographic Journalism.* He also found time to serve as technical editor of *Minicam,* department editor for natural color in *Camera,* and motion picture editor for *American Photography.*

McKay's career took an interesting turn in 1928 when, apparently on his own initiative, he wrote to the National Broadcasting Company, proposing a program to be called Adventures in Photography, which would include:

Real life adventures of famous photographers such as Steichen, Margaret Bourke-White, John Craig, and prominent persons who have used or made a hobby of photography, such as Gordon MacCreagh, the explorer-author; Jay Hyde Barnum, the famous magazine artist; Paul Draper, the internationally known ballet-tap artist; and those who use photography in their daily work such as Roy Chapman Andrews, Raymond Ditmars, and many scientists, criminologists, and businessmen who would appear on this series regularly with other guests of the same type.

McKay's idea was accepted and he became the first person to put photography on the air, with lectures over WEAF in 1928. His program, under different titles, was heard over WJZ, New York, and WHN (1010 on the dial).[3]

McKay's *Motion Picture Photography for the Amateur* appears to be the first of its kind to arrive after the introduction of the 16mm system by Eastman Kodak. McKay devoted several pages to that film and cameras made for its use: the Ciné-Kodak, the Victor, and the Bell & Howell Filmo. He remarked about the Filmo: "I believe it will be a long time before this camera is surpassed," a most prescient observation. Curiously, however, the first camera he described was the ill-fated Vitalux, which I have described in Chapter 3. Also included in his chapter on amateur equipment were the Pathéscope 28mm camera, the Sept, and the Ica Kinamo.

The inclusion of the latter two cameras, made for standard film, is clear evidence that despite the arrival of the safety film system, many amateurs stayed with standard film. McKay gave as one reason for this the fact that amateur-filmed news events could be readily sold to newsreel production companies for the standard one dollar per foot of accepted film.

McKay also included a chapter on "news and topical cameras," and another on "professional cameras," all using standard 35mm nitrate film. News cameras included the Home DeFranne, the Wilart News camera, the Universal, and the Ernemann. The professional cameras included the Pathé Studio Camera, the Wilart, the Debrie and the Bell & Howell 2709, with considerable detail given on the workings of these cameras. The cost of a complete Bell &

Howell with lenses was given as between $3,000 and $3,500, equivalent to $28,000 to $32,000 in year 2000 dollars.

McKay's book was just 200 pages long. While all the principle aspects of movie making were covered, the treatment of all topics was necessarily brief. Nonetheless, his training and experience as a professional cinematographer is evident in his writing. The book was listed as being used as a supplementary text at the New York Institute of Photography, where McKay served as dean.

A second book for the amateur by McKay appeared in 1928, entitled *Amateur Movie Making*. This was a greatly expanded version of the 1924 book, being over 300 pages long, with great detail on every subject. More than 250 pages were devoted to the mechanics of making a movie, including home processing of reversal film, how to tint and tone,[4] and even a section explaining the advantages of using the negative-positive film system, contributed by a representative of the DuPont-Pathé Film Manufacturing Company. The balance of the book consisted of special instructions on how to produce "record films," nature study and scientific films, etc. The book's illustrations and 17 pages of advertising in the back of the book give a wonderful glimpse of the equipment available to the amateur at the time.

McKay tends to be didactic, opinionated, and to have curious views on what constitutes art. Some idea of his cultural orientation is apparent in these phrases selected from the introduction to his book.

And by the way, by art is meant not that jargon of empty phrases, not that inane and insane daubing which is known as the modern school, but those concrete expressions of intangible emotions to which the soul of the common man—and woman—respond. . . . We must learn that the motion picture has no inherent relation to any form of dramatic art . . . not until the amateur has become so familiar with the work . . . will the true value of the motion picture be disclosed to the world.

For the amateur who sought simply information on the tools of the trade, a compact little paperback appeared in 1935 entitled *Movie Making Made Easy*, by William J. Shannon, author of *Home Movie Gadgets Any Amateur Can Make,* and at least six other titles. This approach was popular and the book went through 11 printings up to 1939.

In 1940, the Amateur Cinema League brought out *A Guide to Making Better Movies;* no author is listed. Perhaps the most unusual feature of this book is its stated scope. The opening chapter explains that there are three general categories of movies: theatrical movies, primarily for entertainment; personal movies, i.e. family records, vacations, special events, etc.; and special-purpose movies, including religious, business, ethnology, etc. The word "documentary" seems not to have been in use at that time.

The authors make the rather dubious assertion that the techniques for each of the above types of film are different. The chapter concludes with the declaration that the book will not cover theatrical films, plus the curious statement: "The number of personal and special purpose filmers is so large that their particular needs deserve definite response, which this book tries to give."

How To Make Good Movies, a 200-plus page book published by Eastman Kodak Company made its appearance in 1938 (Fig. 294). As might be expected, the illustrations all feature Eastman Kodak equipment but otherwise it offers guidance on every aspect of amateur movie making in a very clear if somewhat chatty, informal style.

The book begins by introducing the reader to a young couple who have evidently been making some home movies, but are about to embark on a voyage of discovery through the pages of this book. The wife plays the role of gentle questioner to her somewhat dim-witted but genial husband. She is given to remarks like:

"Filters! I'm afraid this is going to be so much Greek to me!"

While he exclaims:

"Well I'll be hanged! And I thought you could only make color movies in bright sunlight!"

Not surprisingly, the generous photographic illustrations are of excellent quality. George Eastman was once asked to approve a proposed sales brochure that had no illustrations. Eastman returned it with the brusque note "Our business is photography— use some!"

There is a decided emphasis on "family" movies, although space is given to the importance of having a plan, having your movie tell a story, how to insure continuity, etc. Under the heading "Play Making," the editors assert that most owners are not at all interested in using their cameras for subjects other than purely personal films of family and

Fig. 294. A scene from How to Make Good Movies, by Eastman Kodak.

friends, but that there is a small and determined faction of movie makers whose goal is to make theatrical films with all the professionalism at their command. They admit that this book will not be of much help to that group. Then follows this statement:

So we will not stray far from the theory that most cinematographers are not interested in the complex phases of cinematography.

This perspective on the amateur filmmaker by Eastman Kodak, the largest player in the field at that time, was undoubtedly grounded in reality, but is perhaps part of the evidence from which one observer concludes that there has been "a systematic stripping of the democratic, participatory, and public potential of amateur film and its marginalization within the much more privatized, isolated, and denuded domains of the nuclear family."[5]

How to Make Good Movies (after 1958, *How to Make Good Home Movies)* was printed on glossy stock, in hard covers, and sold for $2. Its initial press run of 10,000 copies was quickly sold out. The book is estimated to have sold close to 100,000 copies before it ceased publication in the late 1960s. Its companion book for the still photographer, *How to Make Good Pictures,* cost 50 cents and was reputedly the largest selling photography book ever published. Eastman Kodak published *How to Make Good Sound Movies* in the 1970s and, at about the same time, a 16mm sound film, *Basic Movie Making,* was available from the Eastman Kodak Audio-Visual Services Library. Guidance films were produced at least as early as 1933, as attested by a 400-foot 16mm silent film in author's collection entitled "Using the Ciné Kodak Special."

No other manufacturer that I am aware of has produced a "how to" book, although several have permitted the use of their corporate name on privately written and produced booklets. The Chilton Company produced the *Modern Camera Guide Series* in the 1950s, with booklets on Bell & Howell, Bolex, Canon, Keystone, Revere, and other movie cameras. As a rule, these books were straightforward instruction manuals for particular hardware without philosophizing on the art of the movie, so they have not been included in this overview.

Editing Your Home Movies by George W. Cushman appeared in 1957, followed by *Sound For Your Color Movies* in 1958 by the same author (Fig. 295). These

Fig. 295. George W. Cushman.

small paperbacks were part of a series published in the 1950s by Camera Craft Publishing Company of San Francisco. George Cushman was an authority on amateur cinematography and a prolific writer, author of seven books and hundreds of articles on movie making, the latter appearing in photographic and movie magazines all over the world. He was also a driving force in amateur moviemakers associations, as related in Chapter 14. The Camera Craft series included *Lens Technique for Color Movie Magic,* by Glen H. Turner, an outstanding filmmaker whose career is also described in Chapter 15.

The great strides in amateur camera technology that occurred following the advent of Super 8, such as existing light capability, and sound-on-film, led to increased use of Super 8 by the serious amateur, the film student, and even professional users. This in turn led to the publication of a number of books aimed at these more sophisticated users.

One of the first of this genre was *Guide to Filmmaking,* by Edward Pincus, New American Library, 1969. Pincus, who taught film at the Massachusetts Institute of Technology, addressed his book to "filmmakers," by which he meant people "who wished to use motion picture film to achieve some conceptual whole, . . . ranging from a well-done home movie to a full length feature film."

Pincus' book covered only the technical aspects of filmmaking and considered standard

8mm, Super 8 and 16mm formats with, as he declared, deliberate emphasis on 16mm.

Personal Filmmaking, by James Piper, Reston Publishing Co., 1975, was an unusual treatment in that it was written specifically for use in general education programs in high schools and colleges. Piper at the time was an instructor in English and Film at Fresno City College in Fresno, California. Piper emphasized what could be done with readily available and affordable equipment, either standard 8, Super 8, or Single 8. His style is personal, user-friendly. Over two-thirds of the book is devoted to the creative side of filmmaking, thoroughly illustrated, including frames and script excerpts from students' films.

In 1975 the first book devoted exclusively to the Super 8 system appeared, *The Super 8 Book,* authored by Lenny Lipton, long-time *Popular Photography* editor. This is a *tour de force* on the technology of the Super 8 format and all the equipment associated with it. The book is 300-plus pages long, divided into seven sections: Format, Cameras, Sound, Processing and Striping, Prints, and Projection. There are over 200 drawings, photographs and charts or tables, and there is a carefully prepared index. At $6.95 in paperback, the book was an excellent buy. Lipton also authored *Independent Filmmaking,* and has produced a number of Super 8 films.

Myron A. Matzkin, Senior Editor at *Modern Photography,* published *The Super 8 Film Makers Handbook,* Amphoto, Garden City, New York, in 1977.

Handbook of Super 8 Production, by Mark Mikolas and Gunther Hoos, United Business Publications, 1978, is an exhaustive treatise on the mechanics of Super 8 filmmaking. While the authors declare it to have been written for users at every level of interest, the book includes detailed descriptions of the most advanced technology of the time, including top-of-the-line cameras, projectors and editors, many of which were in professional use. An interesting feature of the book is the inclusion of a number of "guest essays" by some noted authorities such as Tom Hope of Hope Reports Inc., established filmmakers such as Elinor Stecker-Orel, later an editor at *Popular Photography*, and Fred Paskiewicz, writer and cinematographer of *The Retaliator,* a one and one half hour Super 8 feature film.

At the time of publication, Gunther Hoos was president of Super8 Sound, Inc. of Cambridge,

Fig. 296. Toni Treadway and Robert P. Brodsky.

Massachusetts, manufacturers of highly sophisticated Super 8 recording, editing, and projection equipment. He was on the staff of the Rockland Children's Psychiatric Hospital, NY, as a media instructor. Mark Mikolas was an educator, computer operator, psychiatric social worker and was a colleague of Hoos at the Rockland Hospital. The two men pioneered the production of Super 8 films of hospital patients, which were subsequently used at other hospitals as diagnostic and training tools.

In 1983, an unusual book appeared, entitled *Super 8 in the Video Age—Using Amateur Movie Film Today,* by Robert P. Brodsky and Toni Treadway (Fig. 296). This is a book for the serious filmmaker, whether amateur or accomplished independent, and therein lies its originality. To begin with, the authors are passionately devoted to the proposition that every independent filmmaker should be able to bring his message to an audience, large or small, and that the Super 8 system is the ideal medium for many people who would otherwise be excluded by one or more attributes of the so-called professional venues: 16mm, 35mm, or professional video.

Yet the authors recognize the limitations of Super 8 and carefully point out when the small gauge should not be used. Examples are usage by someone hoping for a career in the film or television industry, or when a grant or other funding is sought. However, in their view there are a number of filmmaking circumstances where Super 8 is the ideal medium. These circumstances are spelled out and illustrated by a unique approach. They suggest that a Super 8 film can be produced by any of four "Systems," ranging in complexity from "System Zero," where the filmmaker uses the simplest equipment readily available—new or used—and does not attempt synchronized sound, up to "System Four," in which the film is created in Super 8, using the best equipment available for film and audio, and then transferred to 16mm, 35mm, or video in expectation of exhibition on network television or at media centers. The authors leaven their instructions with pithy accounts of personal experiences in film production.

In addition to well-written passages on filmmaking fundamentals, a substantial portion of the book is devoted to sophisticated techniques and practices that will only be of interest to those working in System 4, such as four-track sound recording, selecting a transfer studio, obtaining rights and releases, etc. In the 1994 third edition, the authors report that a number of revisions were required, due to the substantial changes in availability of film stocks, equipment, and processing facilities since the 1983 edition.

Brodsky and Treadway were independent filmmakers who began their partnership in 1975, doing documentary work for the nation's Bicentennial, some of which they produced in Super 8. They also began writing a Super 8 column for the magazine *The Independent*; a film and video monthly published by the Association for Independent Video and Filmmakers in New York City. Searching for first rate film-to-video studios led them to establish their own studio in 1981. As their skills were honed, they began conducting technical workshops nationwide, for which they received support from the National Endowment for the Arts. This led to the formation in 1983 of the International Center for 8mm Film (Toni Treadway, President), an organization dedicated to the support of 8mm film users with workshops and technical assistance and a newsletter. This effort was also supported by the NEA and by the Massachusetts Cultural Council.[6]

Giles Musitano, a London-based filmmaker and specialist in the professional application of Super 8, has authored the latest book on filming with sub-standard film, The Super 8 Guide, now in its fourth edition. Musitano describes his book as follows:

The Super 8 Guide is the only book consolidating all the information relevant to the current use of Super 8 by both amateur and professional users, including equipment guides, interviews, special features on alternative shooting methods, and post-production, a comprehensive international contact list for all the products, services and resources related to Super 8, and an insight into how the new digital technology available can be merged with the Super 8 format to enhance the medium to a new level of versatility.

Musitano, who has a background in post-production work, also teaches practical courses for Super 8 users at various film workshops and is a prolific and passionate writer on his subject.[7]

Photographic Periodicals

Periodicals for the amateur photographer have an ancient and honorable lineage, both in this country and abroad. It will be remembered that George Eastman was an avid reader of such literature when he first became interested in photography, while the art was still in its infancy.

Anthony's Photographic Bulletin, for example, founded in 1870, published by E. & H. T. Anthony, catered almost exclusively to amateurs, and survived well into the twentieth century. It was eventually absorbed by *American Photography.*

To *Photo Era,* a monthly established in 1898 in Wolfeboro, New Hampshire, goes the honor of carrying the first regular amateur motion picture department, beginning in December 1922 and edited by Herbert C. McKay. The department continued under McKay until *Photo Era* was merged with *American Photography* in 1926, where a Cine Amateur Department was established under Karl A. Barleben, Jr., Associate of the Royal Photographic Society, also later dean of the New York Institute of Photography. Barleben was its regular editor until May 1932, when McKay returned and took over the column.

The Cine Amateur Department disappeared in 1939. Shortly thereafter the magazine was merged with *Popular Photography,* one of several competitive publications by then. The first of these was *Movie Makers,* the official organ of the Amateur Cinema League, launched in December 1926.

The first issue, 40 pages of slick copy and photographs, set the tone of the magazine for many years to come. Today's reader might well decide "elitist" was an appropriate word to describe the tone: a full page photograph of Mrs. Harry S. New, wife of the postmaster general, filming six be-hatted ladies at a Washington lawn party, including Mrs. Calvin Coolidge, wife of the President of the United States. "Celebrities-as-movie makers" was a common feature of the magazine for many years. The arrival of 8mm in 1932 tended to democratize the typical user.

The editorial content of the early issues was on the whole low-key, even light-hearted. Most contributors seemed at pains to encourage the reader to enjoy the new hobby while following certain basic principles that would attempt to minimize technical and mechanical errors.

Physically the magazine was very attractive, particularly for the first 15 years or so, when the brightly colored covers were reminiscent of the John Held, Jr. style of illustration.[8] (See Fig. 297.) The magazine's

Fig. 297. Movie Makers, June 1933.

generous size, 9" x 12", allowed for easy-to-read type, large illustrations, and plenty of white space. Among early contributors were such as Joseph H. McNabb, president of Bell & Howell, and Harris Tuttle of Eastman Kodak. In fact Tuttle turned in so many articles he submitted many of them under various pen names.[9]

Equipment manufacturers loved the magazine; Eastman Kodak was a steady and lavish advertiser. In the June 1935 issue, for example, Kodak took the double-page centerfold to blazon the news of Kodachrome film (in a black-and-white ad!) and the inside back cover to promote the Ciné-Kodak Special. In the same issue were full-page ads by RCA for their sound-on-film camera and projector, Victor Animatograph, International Projector Corp. for the Simplex Pockette, Ampro, DeVry, and Dufaycolor. Agfa Ansco had a two-page spread for their black-and-white fine-grain Plenachrome film.

When the Amateur Cinema League was merged into the Photographic Society of America in 1954, Movie Makers ceased publishing.

Home Movies, a monthly published by Ver Halen Publications, Hollywood, was first issued in 1934. It proclaimed itself as America's only magazine devoted exclusively to 8mm and 16mm movies. The format was 9" by 12", and issues generally ran 30 to 40 pages. The editorial content was largely of the basic "how to" topics, such as lighting, plotting, editing, etc., but there was a small section headed "Professional 16mm Section," which carried stories of interest to TV and documentary filmmakers. Lars Moen, once dean of the New York Institute of Photography, was technical editor in 1950. The magazine was published into the 1960s.

Popular Photography made its appearance in May 1937, just six months after *Life* magazine introduced a new era in photojournalism. Those who can remember the tremendous enthusiasm that greeted that pioneering magazine of photographs might well wonder if Messrs. Ziff and Davis, publishers of *Popular Photography,* were inspired by the success of *Life.*

The first issue was described some years later by Bruce Downes, then editor and publisher, as follows:

The first issue, with its daring four-color cover—the first ever used on a photographic magazine—was an immediate sell-out. It wasn't very pretty, the layouts were

Fig. 298. Leendert Drukker.

messy, the pictures by today's standards were corny, but it was healthy and alive . . .[10]

The first anniversary issue was 123 pages long and contained 18 articles on general photography with titles such as "How Kodachrome Works," and "Take it in Color," by Ivan Dmitri, and one entitled "The ABC of Home Movie Making." Downes, in the editorial quoted above, gave a slight nod towards amateur movies, remarking that the introduction of Kodachrome in 1935 had given home movies their first real boom. Nevertheless, home movies received scant attention for the first several years of the magazine's existence.

It was not until 1942 that a regular Amateur Movie Section appeared, with no regular authors, and not until 1960 that the magazine created the post of movie editor. The first person to hold that position was Charles R. Reynolds who had been writing a section called "Creating With Film" since the early 1950s. In January 1960 Reynolds was named movie editor and Leendert Drukker joined the magazine as assistant editor. The latter's first piece was entitled "What's New in Editors," purely coincidence, I'm sure (Fig. 298).

For quite a few years Reynolds and Drukker ran parallel columns, Reynolds' titled as above, while Drukker's was called "Methods and Materials." Drukker had an engineer's grasp of the mechanics of cameras and projectors and an obvious fondness for that area. In a reminiscence written a number of years after his retirement, he recalled with great accuracy the construction details and foibles of cameras that had appeared 30 years before.[11]

Fig. 299. Elinor Stecker-Orel.

Fig. 300. Tony Galluzzo.

Reynolds' column, as the name indicates, generally treated the creative and esthetic aspects of film-making, frequently suggesting specific Hollywood films as subjects for the amateur to study for plot development, pacing, establishment of mood, and so on.

This division of labor eventually changed as Reynolds went on to become picture editor and Drukker became a senior editor, writing about video when that appeared. The movie section was given the curious title of "Audio Visual Playback." Lenny Lipton was movie editor in the 1960s. Elinor Stecker, who had been freelancing for the magazine on film-making and audio-visual, joined the staff when Drukker retired in 1985. Ms. Stecker (later Mrs. Stecker-Orel), with experience in professional Super 8, wrote on Super 8 and video, became senior editor in 1990, then went on a contributing basis when the magazine downsized the staff in 1994 (Fig. 299).

At the top of the masthead for nearly 20 years was Bruce Downes (1899-1966). Downes died of a stroke in Pusan, Korea, while on a State Department tour of the Far East, lecturing on photography. William Ziff, president of Ziff-Davis Publishing Company, eulogized Downes as "a disciplined and delightful man, intensely committed to the better-

ment of the whole spectrum of photography, from high art to family album."

Modern Photography, or *Minicam Photography* as it was called then, was also launched in 1937. The publisher was Photography Publishing Corporation of New York, later Billboard Publications. Augustus Wolfman was editor-in-chief. Myron Matzkin, later senior editor, was the first regular writer on amateur ciné, although he did not receive the title of movie editor until the early 1960s.

Matzkin was succeeded in 1970 by Tony Galluzzo, a filmmaker and producer in 16mm, who had a background in newspaper and magazine journalism, including film reviewing (Fig. 300). Galluzzo also was strong on technology and wrote many excellent pieces explaining the new technological developments in a clear and engaging style. Beginning with the November 1980 issue, the magazine ran a six-month series of special sections entitled "Video Today," one of the most comprehensive treatments of the new medium to appear at the time. Galluzzo left *Modern Photography* in 1989 and went on to write on video for *Shutterbug,*[12] *Popular Photography*, *Video Maker*, and several other publications.

Modern Photography's size, makeup, and editorial content were very similar to those of *Popular*

Photography, and was second in circulation, with more than 600,000 readers. The magazine ceased publishing in 1989. Its subscription list and trademarks were bought by *Popular Photography* in 1991.[13]

U. S. Camera began life in 1935 as an annual compendium of news of the photographic world, produced by the U. S. Camera Publishing Company. Tom Maloney was publisher/founder, and his longtime friend, Edward Steichen was editor. Edward E. "Ed" Hannigan joined in the late 1940s as managing editor, rising to executive director at the time of his retirement from the magazine in the mid-1960s. The annual evolved into a quarterly in 1938 and a bi-monthly in 1939. When wartime restrictions on coated printing paper eased, the magazine became a monthly.

As with its two competitors, *U.S. Camera's* primary audience was of course still photographers; just 15-18 percent of its readers were estimated to own 8mm or 16mm equipment.[14] The early issues carried occasional pieces on movie making, and in the early 1950s a movie section was initiated. One of the first writers for that section was James W. Moore, who had been an editor at *Movie Makers* until that publication closed.

U. S. Camera saw itself as a "how to" magazine, featuring top-name photographers, as well as a leader in giving up-and-coming photographers an opportunity to be published in a nationally circulated magazine. It also sponsored a major annual photo competition, in which as many as 40,000 entries were received. The magazine reached a circulation of 260,000 by 1963, ranking it after *Popular Photography* and *Modern Photography*.[15] The U. S. Camera Publishing Company was sold to American Express Company in 1969.

One publication with perhaps the shortest life span on record was *Home Movie Making,* launched in late 1958 by the publishers of *Popular Photography*. It was billed as "The World's First Yearbook Devoted to Amateur Movie Making." The first issue cost one dollar, was 150 pages long, and carried 33 articles on various aspects of filmmaking. The 1960 annual appeared in late 1959 and despite selling almost 100,000 copies, it was the final issue.[16]

Better Movie Making, later *Better Home Movie Making* was first issued in 1959 as a bi-monthly. The last issue was the March/April issue of 1966. It was aimed primarily at professional and semi-professional users, *Filmmakers' Newsletter* appeared in November 1967. Founded by H. Whitney Bailey, publisher and editor-in-chief, Suni Wallow was the international editor. The magazine ceased publication in early 1982.

Petersen's Photographic Magazine was introduced in May 1972, published by the Petersen Publishing Company of Los Angeles. Paul R. Farber was editor, Karen Sue Geller, managing editor, and David B. Brooks, feature editor. Among its contributing editors were Ben Helprin and Kalton C. Lahue. Lahue wrote a number of books on films and co-authored, along with Joe A. Bailey, *Glass, Brass, and Chrome*, a definitive history of the American 35mm camera.

The editorial content *of Petersen's* was hardly distinguishable from the other popular photography magazines. The magazine had only about 100 pages, half the number of its competitors. There was considerably less advertising, partly because it would not take mail-order advertising. This was applauded by some readers, who deplored the "commercialization" of the other publications. Revenues suffered, however, and this practice was abandoned after a year or two. When the magazine first appeared, the opening editorial declared that two objectives of the magazine would be to seek out and present the work of relatively unknown photographers and to find, encourage, and develop new talent in the field of photographic writing.[17]

As one of a "Basic Series" of how-to books, in 1973 the company published *Petersen's Guide to Movie Making,* by David MacLoud and the editors of *Photographic Magazine*. This was an 80-page soft-cover book in magazine format, intended, as stated in an introduction, to lead the amateur movie camera owner away from making "movie snapshots" into making movies. The editors did a remarkable job, covering the history of amateur motion picture equipment, its selection and operation, sound filming, planning, scripting, and of course editing, all accompanied with excellent illustrations. The book sold for two dollars.

With the arrival of Eastman Kodak's existing light system in 1971 and workable single-system sound in 1973, Super 8 cameras had reached the technical capability of many professional cameras. Twenty-nine manufacturers from all over the industrial world seized on these American achievements and came on the market with dozens of models, ranging in price from Kodak's Instamatic M-22 at $35 to Pathé's Electronic DS8 at $2,155. Filmmakers at every level, from the casual shooter to the professional independent filmmaker, could find equipment to match their needs and budget. No less than 90 film schools across the country specialized in Super 8.

The time was ripe for a special publication to cater to this phenomenon. In February 1972 a group of young filmmakers and writers, headed by Paul M. Sheptow, founded PMS Publishing Company with editorial offices in New York City. Their publication was *Super8Filmaker;* the editor was Mimi Gold, and contributing editors included such well-known names as Lenny Lipton and Elinor Stecker, while Donald Sutherland was a frequent contributor (Fig. 301).

Super8Filmaker was by and for the young, "age of Aquarius" crowd—no Wall Street tycoon filming his trip to Europe nor dad shooting baby's first footsteps. The readers were presumed to be serious and avant-garde, pushing the envelope on the new medium. A 1977 photo of the staff shows no one apparently over 35. Upscale equipment was advertised and discussed. By 1976 the enterprise had moved to

Fig. 301. Super8Filmaker, August 1975.

San Francisco, which milieu undoubtedly better suited its editorial staff and readership. Yet on careful examination one sees that the advice offered the reader was not so very different from that given in the older magazines. The filmmaker was still encouraged to title, to watch for continuity, to plan before filming, and so on. The magazine was renamed *Moving Images* in late 1981 and ceased publishing in mid-1982.[18]

Company Publications

One of the earliest publications devoted to the amateur cinematographer was established by the Eastman Kodak Company in June 1924, just a few months after the introduction of the 16mm direct reversal system. Entitled *The Ciné Kodak News*, it was a slim four pages long for the first several years, expanding to 12 in February of 1930, with slick two-color covers (Fig. 302).

The editorial content consisted chiefly of references to the Ciné Kodak and how to use it, but also contained suggestions on lighting, making titles, unusual picture-making opportunities, and so on. There were also usually two or three letters from subscribers. One remarkable example was from a

Fig. 302. The Ciné-Kodak News, July-August 1932.

gentleman who, while claiming never to have used even a still camera before, reported on a round-the-world trip during which he shot 38 reels of film with his Ciné Kodak and returned with "3,790 feet of good pictures with which I am delighted." One wonders how his audience felt about that assessment.

Filmo Topics (Fig. 303), published by Bell & Howell, first appeared in 1925 and was published monthly through 1932. At that time publication abruptly dropped to three issues per year, a change possibly related to the fact that that year saw Bell & Howell post its first loss in company history. As the

company's financial health improved, the number of issues rose to as high as six per year. However, publication ceased with the Christmas issue of 1943.

The Bolex Reporter, which billed itself as "America's Leading Movie Magazine," appears to have been launched in 1951, initially as a quarterly. It was published by Paillard Inc. in New York City at 35 cents per copy and distributed by Bolex franchised dealers. It was a high quality, sophisticated production, with contributors such as Weegee, the notorious New York City news photographer, Ernst Wildi, and other prominent names in photography.

Fig. 303. Filmo Topics, October 1931.

As might be expected, each publication extolled the virtues of the company's products, announced new models and accessories, answered readers' inquiries, and carried the usual array of "how to" articles on planning, camera handling, lighting, splicing, editing, and so on. There were however, distinct differences in the editorial slant of each magazine.

Up until the arrival of 8mm film in 1932, which reduced the cost of film screen time by two-thirds that of 16mm, amateur cinematography was a fairly expensive hobby, principally indulged in by the upper middle class. This was quite evident even in the *Ciné-Kodak News*. The users were typically shown at such pastimes as attending a college football game, playing golf, or viewing a yachting regatta. In one issue of *Filmo Topics*, a U.S. senator, a film star, a Navy commander, and a Swedish prince were shown squinting through the finders of their favorite Filmos.

After 1932, the *Ciné-Kodak News* emphasized that everyone could afford movie making. Bell & Howell, as noted in Chapter 6, also aimed its 8mm cameras at a mass market.

Filmo Topics tended to be more technically oriented than *Ciné-Kodak News*, perhaps assuming that its readers, being better heeled than the users of Brand X, were also more technically sophisticated. A series of articles called "Facts about Film" ran to 18 installments, beginning with the January 1930 issue. Included were chapters entitled "The Essentials of the Filmo Camera," "What is a Nine-to-One Movement?," "A Look Inside the Filmo 75," and "Making Filmo Projection Lamps." The articles were carefully written and did not play down to the reader. The insights thus given into the design considerations and manufacturing methods of cameras, lenses, lamps, and projectors that would be difficult to find elsewhere. Another excellent series on lens design and selection ran for five installments in the 1937 and 1938 issues.

Delightful nuggets of information turn up unexpectedly in all these publications. How else would we know the dramatic demise of the Tacoma Narrows Bridge, which waltzed itself to death in a windstorm one fall day in 1940? It was caught on film by two Filmo-wielding amateurs! The Summer 1941 issue of *Filmo Topics* shows the two men in action,

along with several dramatic stills from their 16mm Kodachrome film, which was bought by Universal Newsreel, enlarged to 35mm black-and-white, and released to theatres all over the world.

While the amateur had a variety of periodicals to scan for information and ideas, and several organizations to which to belong, for the professional cinematographer there was but one organization and one publication. The American Society of Cinematographers, founded on January 8, 1919, was open by invitation only, to directors of photography and others "whose achievements in that field entitle them to membership."[19] The Society established its journal, *The American Cinematographer*, in 1920.

The magazine's content was not so very different from that of the "popular" magazines. There were "how to" and "how this was done" articles and ads for equipment and services. The difference was that the "how to" article might be "The Traveling Matte Process for Making Composite Motion Pictures" or "Professional Titling with an Animation Stand." The "how-this-was-done" piece was "Filming 'The Alamo' in Todd-AO."

Many of these articles could be of value to the amateur. While the specific hardware described was of course beyond the reach of all but the most affluent amateur, the techniques used by the professionals could often be adapted in some modest form by the home filmmaker. A youngster's four-wheel wagon could substitute for a motorized studio dolly costing thousands of dollars. The magazine occasionally took note of developments in amateur equipment, particularly if the innovation appeared to have potential professional application. A two-part story on the Eastman Kodak Sound-8 projector of 1960 was a good example, although in this case the anticipated entry of 8mm sound into professional use never materialized.[20]

Technology—Accurately Reported?

The early books on amateur cinematography did a reasonably good job of describing the relatively simple equipment of the years up through the early 1930s. As cameras and projectors grew more complex, the newly founded popular photography magazines rose to the occasion with greatly expanded treatment of the new mechanisms. When an important new technology was announced, the magazines generally produced detailed, well-illustrated explanations, providing the reader with information otherwise only available from highly technical publications such as the *Journal of the Society of Motion Picture and Television Engineers*. *Popular Photography*'s coverage of Super 8 in its June 1965 issue, or *Modern Photography*'s multi-part series on video beginning in 1981, are good examples.

Manufacturers routinely supplied the publishers with information packets on new products, from which product news reports were written. If the editors deemed the product of sufficient import, a sample model would be obtained and a performance report written, based on field trials by the movie editor, or in some cases, based on results of tests in the magazine's own testing laboratories.

Starting in 1939 *Popular Photography* began publishing an annual Directory Issue which listed, for every manufacturer that supplied the necessary data, every model in that manufacturer's current product list, with description and price. The description included all essential features such as film gauge, type of loading, capacity, camera speeds, motive power, lens equipment, exposure control, and any optional features.

From the pages of these annual directory issues it is possible to trace the product history of all the leading manufacturers, from 1939 to the early 1980s, by which time almost all the U.S. manufacturers had gone out of the amateur movie business.

Were the product reviews honest and objective? The answer would seem to be—not entirely. A noted scholar and writer on amateur movies has accused the amateur photography magazines of enjoying "incestuous relationships" with American camera and film manufacturers; the implication is that any advertiser's products would always receive favorable reviews, regardless of quality of the product.[21] One editor responded:

Editorial and advertising tried to keep very much apart. (We) did not accept articles placed by public relations people. Reviews of equipment were fair, although sometimes when negative comments were made, they were tempered so they didn't seem quite so bad.

Sometimes "being fair" bordered on being blind. As an example, when that strange hybrid camera/projector from the Longines Wittnauer Company came on the market in 1957, two of the three leading magazines greeted the Wittnauer Ciné-Twin with glowing reviews. "This revolutionary camera/projector must be seen to be appreciated, but even then it seems too good to be true."[22] "Sensational is the only word—a fantastic electric drive camera beautifully styled and well constructed—at an amazing low price."[23]

Modern Photography, while describing the machine as the first successful attempt to combine camera and projector, did at least point out that the camera was extremely heavy, double the weight of a normal 8mm camera and, further, that the camera was useless as a projector as long as there was film in it.

What none of the reviewers seemed to notice, or perhaps ignored, was the fact that the system's utility was severely limited; besides the camera's limitation as noted above, the combination's supposed mobility was illusory; the projector was still tied to a source of 110-volt current. The market quickly discovered these shortcomings, and the Ciné Twin disappeared after a few seasons.

Popular Photography was the first to comment on Polavision, that remarkable system of instant movies announced by Dr. Edwin Land at his company's annual meeting on April 26, 1977. In the June 1977 issue, Leendert Drukker reported on his attendance at that historic meeting, with a brief description of the equipment and a restrained, but significant commentary on the Polavision image. Drukker noted that the image showed "some grain" at close-in viewing and was highly directional, a sort of euphemism for "You had better be directly in front of the screen." He also noted that editing was "impractical," which might have been better described as "extremely difficult," or "next to impossible."

Eight months later, in its February 1978 issue, *Popular Photography* ran two more articles on Polavision, one by Don Leavitt, one by Drukker. Leavitt's piece can only be described as "puffery." It reads as if copied verbatim from a Polaroid Company handout. Drukker this time gave a sober, detailed description of the camera, the film (Dr. Land called it tape), and the player. Again he pointed out the drawbacks to the system and flatly declared that it was not in the same league with Super 8 Kodachrome. Finally in May 1979, Drukker reported the system only marginally improved and chided Polavision for its blatantly false images shown in its

TV commercials. The print ads used the same images, but did at least, in fine print, say "simulated picture."

Modern Photography's Tony Galluzzo also attended the Polaroid meeting and reported on Polavision in the July 1977 issue. Galluzzo noted exactly the same limitations as did Drukker, but was a bit blunter. In a follow-up review eight months later, Galluzzo found little or no improvement in the quality of the image. He also pointed out the much higher cost per minute of viewing time for the Polavision system, $3.98 versus $2.30 for Kodachrome 40.[24]

Thus two of the most respected writers on amateur motion picture technology wrote objective, accurate reviews of a new motion picture system, carefully describing its achievements and its shortcomings. Can we fault them for not declaring that the new system was doomed to commercial failure, if indeed they did think so? Hardly, when Dr. Land himself could not be so persuaded by his own staff, many of whom had grave doubts about the system.

In Summary

Reading through nearly 60 years of photography publications, looking for the "presence" of the amateur filmmaker, one is struck by several curious things. First is the almost total absence of letters to the editor from this segment of the readership. Assuming the beginning filmmaker encountered just as many problems as the snapshooter, the only conclusion is that the editors just decided such letters were not of broad enough interest.

Secondly, the appearance in the movie columns of the same admonitions over and over again, year after year, from the 1930s through the '70s. "Plan your films . . . tell a story . . . don't pan too much . . . watch the lighting . . . edit, edit, edit!" There could be no clearer proof that the secret of good movie making lay in the mind behind the camera and had little to do with the camera itself.

To this observer, the amateur filmmaker was well served by the literature of the times. Periodicals furnished timely accounts of new products, generally well-written pieces on every aspect of filming, within the space limitations of a monthly publication. The writers achieved a reasonable balance between hardware and brainware—an analysis of over 100 articles on movies written between 1951 and 1978 showed 60 percent discussed the mechanics of filmmaking and 40 percent dealt with the creative processes. True, most writers strove to guide their readers in the paths of professionalism, not an unworthy objective, despite the negative reaction that word engenders in certain quarters.

14

Amateur Organizations

Hiram Percy Maxim

The Rise of Amateur Ciné Clubs

The name and founding date of the first amateur ciné club seems lost to history. However, it is likely that such clubs would not have appeared until amateur equipment became relatively inexpensive, say after World War I, when cameras like the Movette, the Actograph, and the Sept became available. One writer asserts that:

The first amateur ciné club in Britain was started at Cambridge University in 1923, to be followed in 1925 by the first film society, which met in a cinema in Regent Street, London, (and) included many of the intelligentsia of the day.[1]

Eastman Kodak's 1923 introduction of 16mm direct reversal film, the first practical and affordable amateur movie system, gave considerable impetus to the formation of cinema clubs. According to one report, by 1928 there were estimated to be nearly a half million amateur moviemakers in the United States. Amateur movie clubs had been established in Great Britain, France, Australia, New Zealand, Japan, and Siam (as Thailand was then known). The latter club reported that it was sponsored by the King and Queen, who had graciously provided the club with a palace for its meeting place. The King's son, H. R. H. Prince Purachatra, was president.

One early American club of which there is record was the Motion Picture Club of the Oranges (New Jersey), described as "a body of some twenty youngsters just out of high school." Its first production was titled *Love by Proxy*, which was shown to an audience of 600 persons at the East Orange Women's Club (Fig. 304). It was reported that most outdoor scenes were filmed "on the grounds of Mr. and Mrs. Everet Colby's estate." Interior scenes were at the Braidburn Country Club, and the Lackawanna Railroad was persuaded to have the Chicago Limited make a special stop for one location shot. These are interesting clues to the social standing of the members of this pioneering club.[2]

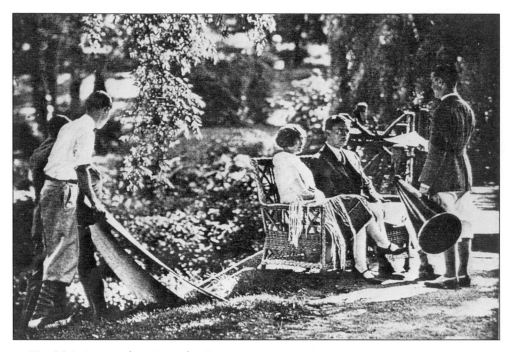

Fig. 304. A scene from Love by Proxy.

Every major American city was home to one or more clubs; Chicago even had a club just for devotees of the 9.5mm gauge. Few of these clubs survived past the peak years of amateur camera sales in the late 1950s. One notable exception was the Metropolitan Motion Picture Club of New York City, which celebrated its 27th "Gala Night" at Hunter College in Manhattan on June 7, 1960, indicating its organization in 1933. This affair was attended by 1,600 people who viewed 13 films, one of which had won a silver medal at the Cannes Film Festival.[3]

The Washington, D.C., Society of Amateur Cinematographers, founded in 1937, is now incorporated as The Washington Society of Film and Video Makers, Inc. The Washington club holds monthly meetings from September through May. Each meet-

Fig. 305. The organizational meeting of the Amateur Cinema League, Biltmore Hotel, New York City, July 28, 1926.

ing is normally devoted to some particular aspect of the filmmaking process. The discussion is led by a member with particular skills in a given area or by an invited guest speaker. There is also usually a screening of one or more members' films, followed by "constructive criticism." The club conducts its own film competition with judging by a panel of non-member experts in the field of communication arts. A monthly bulletin is published.

The Society maintains affiliation with the American Chapter of the International Amateur Cinematographers, a British organization, and its successor, the Society of Amateur Cinematographers, and the Photographic Society of America. Club members have garnered numerous awards in film festivals and competitions. At its peak, the Society membership stood at over 100 paid members, recent years have seen a falling off in membership, and a general decline in interest. Almost all "filming" is now in video, with one member still working in 16mm.[4]

Larger Organizations

The first national organization in this country for amateur moviemakers was The Amateur Cinema League, founded in 1926. On July 28th of that year, about 50 amateur ciné enthusiasts gathered for a formal dinner at the Biltmore Hotel in New York City, to plan such an organization (Fig. 305). Hiram Percy Maxim, president of the Maxim Silencer Company and the man behind the whole idea, was elected president, and Colonel Roy W. Winton, a lately retired U.S. Army officer was named executive director.

Among those present were Joseph H. McNabb, president of the Bell & Howell Company, Lewis B. Jones, a vice-president of the Eastman Kodak Company, and Alexander Victor, president of the Victor Animatograph Corporation.

Other notables who did not attend, but sent greetings included Arthur Brisbane, columnist of the *New York Times*, T. A. Willard, president of the Willard Storage Battery Company, Mme. Galli-Curci, the legendary opera diva, Carl Laemmle, head of Universal Studios, Jesse Lasky of Paramount Pictures, and Will Hays, powerful head of the notorious Motion Picture Producers and Distributors of America, commonly known as the Hays Office, the regulatory agency which set the moral standards of Hollywood for over 30 years. Mr. Lasky expressed the hope that "from these enthusiastic young amateurs the motion

Fig. 306. Hiram Percy Maxim working on his silencer.

picture industry may possibly recruit valuable additions to its acting and directorial forces." Mr. Hays admitted to being an avid amateur motion picture maker of his son, while Carl Laemmle looked for interested amateurs to stimulate moving picture theatre attendance.

Hiram Percy Maxim (1869-1936) (Fig. 306) was born in Brooklyn, New York, into a family of inventors. His father was Sir Hiram Stevens Maxim, who rose from boyhood on a Maine farm to become a prolific inventor of devices ranging from an automatic mousetrap to improved incandescent lamp filaments. He removed to England in 1880, where he developed a vastly improved machine gun and an early smokeless powder, both of which inventions were adopted by the British armed services. In recognition of his service, having become a naturalized British subject, he was knighted by Queen Victoria in 1901.[5]

The younger Maxim graduated from Massachusetts Institute of Technology and apparently inherited his father's talents. Among his inventions were many electrical devices, gas and electrically powered engines for automobiles for the Pope Manufacturing Company, in 1899 the leading U. S. manufacturer of "motor carriages." His most well known invention was of course the Maxim silencer, a device for reducing the muzzle noise from rifles and handguns. Maxim had a lively curiosity about many things; among his enthusiasms, in addition to amateur movies, was the then-new phenomenon of radio, which led him to found the American Radio Relay League, an organization of "ham" operators which is still in existence.

The stated objectives of the Amateur Cinema League were:

- to publish a monthly magazine, (named at first *The Amateur Movie Maker*, later just *Movie Makers)*;

- to increase the pleasure of making home motion pictures by aiding amateurs to originate and produce their own plays;

- to promote amateur cinematography as a national sport; and

- to maintain home motion picture making on an amateur basis." [6]

The league was organized to provide service to individual amateur filmmakers. It exercised no control over amateur organizations, although it did encourage the formation of such clubs, offered advice on rules, etc., and published such news of the clubs' activities as was submitted. The League also offered free advice on members' films sent in for examination and suggestions. From this service in 1930 came the idea of selecting the ten best films received during the year and singling them out for recognition in *Movie Makers*.

Film Contests and Festivals

Film contests for amateurs have been around from the earliest days of amateur cinematography, often sponsored by film or equipment manufacturers such as Eastman Kodak, Bell & Howell, Ansco, or publications such as *U. S. Camera*. These contests tended to be sporadic, coming and going after a few years. Film contests generally did not include a public showing of the winning films at a specific time and place, although winning films were sometimes made available on request to groups or organizations.

Amateur film festivals, on the other hand, were patterned after the professional ones such as those at Cannes, Venice, and Oberhausen. The prize-winning films were presented to the public in a program often lasting two or three days.

One of the earliest film festivals on record began in 1930 at Columbia University, under the direction of Duncan MacD. Little, instructor in film and the American officer of a British organization

called the Institute of Amateur Cinematographers. [7] From modest beginnings, the annual affair, called the International Amateur Movie Show, attracted 335 people to its 1938 meeting, with films submitted from the United States, Japan, England, Canada, and many other countries. [8]

Also established in 1930, as mentioned above, was the Ten Best competition conducted by the Amateur Cinema League. In addition to the Ten Best, the judges selected up to 15 films for Honorable Mention. A brief description of all winning films and their makers was published in *Movie Makers*. In 1937 the children of Hiram Percy Maxim established a memorial award in his name, which was thereafter bestowed on one of the ten best which the judges deemed the best of the best. The award consisted of a check for $100 plus a replica of the memorial sculpture kept in the League headquarters in New York. The judges were the editorial staff of *Movie Makers*.

The Amateur Cinema League experienced financial difficulties in 1954. Publication of *Movie Makers* ceased, and the League's membership was taken over by the Motion Picture Division of the Photographic Society of America, a large organization of individual photographers, camera clubs, photographic dealers, and industrial members, founded in 1935. The Photographic Society of America continued the Ten Best competition until 1962, when the name was changed to the American International Film Festival, with screenings of the winners held at the Society's annual meetings.

When interest in the festival flagged, the Society discontinued it in 1990, whereupon a group led by George Cushman withdrew from the Society for the express purpose of continuing the festival. [9] Cushman formed the American Motion Picture Society, "dedicated to assisting the serious motion picture enthusiast in all phases of motion picture production." There is a curious vagueness in both the name of the new society and the term "serious motion picture enthusiast," which undoubtedly stemmed from Cushman's aversion to the word "amateur." This is evident in his translation of the name of the European organization known as UNICA, or Union Internationale du Cinema Amateur, which he rendered as "Union Internationale du Cinema Non-Professionnel." While Cushman's organization was clearly for the amateur, he was determined not to use that word, feeling it had such distasteful connotations in the mind of the general public.

Cushman's principal goal in forming the American Motion Picture Society was to continue the traditional Ten Best competition begun in 1930 by the Amateur Cinema League. To this end, Cushman organized an alliance of several western amateur movie clubs and began a Ten Best of the West competition, then arranged with several other groups, including the Society for Amateur Video and Ciné, of New York, and the Society of Canadian Ciné Amateurs, to participate in a competition with the rather grandiose title of the American International Film and Video Festival.

Cushman also began publishing a bi-monthly newsletter, which he named *Movie Makers* to emphasize the continuity of the contests with the original ones. The newsletter carries brief items on new equipment and technology for film and video, essays on technique, full reports on the American Motion Picture Society's festival results, and a calendar of other festivals.[10]

Cushman's efforts were remarkably successful; the 1995 festival attracted 254 entries from all over the United States and nine foreign countries. Interestingly, 97 percent of the submissions were on videotape, which could indicate multiple submissions by the filmmaker, while not excluding the possibility that many were made from film originals. It should be noted that these competitions were not festivals in the usual sense of the term, in that they did not have two- or three-day showings to which the general public was invited.

An outstanding festival based in Rochester, New York, has the beguiling title "Movies on a Shoestring" or MOAS. Organized in 1959 by a group of local independent filmmakers looking for an audience, the first showing of just 16 films was held at the Rochester Public Library. The next year a film from Canada was accepted and the screening was moved to the Dryden Theatre at the George Eastman House where 300 people attended.

By 1964, the festival had become fully international, with films being received from all over the United States and several foreign countries. The following year, in recognition of its international

stature, a more dignified name was felt desirable. The function became the Rochester International Movie Film Festival. It became a charter member of the International Association of Amateur Film Festivals, when that organization was formed in 1966.

The mechanics of producing a festival are formidable. An all-volunteer MOAS staff fills 24 administrative and production positions. Shortly after a festival is concluded, invitations are mailed to past participants and film schools. Entries are received December through February. Most submissions are on VHS, even from people who work in film. Preliminary judging is done in meetings of the MOAS volunteers as the entries come in. Each member critiques each film on artistic and technical merit in writing, which is followed by an often lively discussion and a "keep or reject" vote. Surviving films, usually about 40 percent of the entries, are held for final judging in March, a marathon weekend effort that selects the best works. A s many as possible are fitted in to the Festival's screen time. Awards of Honorable Mention are given to some of those that did not make the cut, and critique comments are included in the letter accompanying the returned films to the filmmakers, a feature much appreciated by the recipients.

Submissions come in from a broad spectrum of occupations and expertise; the only stipulation being that the film must not exceed 30 minutes in length. This adroitly and effectively bars "commercial" efforts while leaving the door open for films made for the filmmaker's pleasure or artistic pursuit. A brief sampling of recent entry forms yielded: a video artist/writer/performer, a marketing executive, a graduate of The University of Southern California Film School, a self-taught New York University student, and one who listed himself as an "executive producer." None of these entries made the final cut, but some received Certificates of Merit.

All films selected for screening receive the organization's trophy, a small sculptured rendition of a tied shoelace. Honorable Mention Certificates are awarded, as well as Certificates of Merit (the latter for works that did not pass the preliminary judging but which had some feature worthy of recognition.)

For the 1999 festival, 140 entries were received from 24 states, plus entries from Australia, Austria, Canada, Czech Republic, England, Finland, Germany,

Republic of Ireland, Spain, Switzerland, and Yugoslavia. Of the 140 entries, 58 films and videos made it to the final judging, of which 32 were shown at the festival. The program has recently grown to five different showings, four evenings and a Saturday matinee, and is working toward a full week of presentations. Not satisfied with seeing five months work culminate in just a few nights of festival showings, MOAS decided in 1972 to extend the festival by obtaining prints from the filmmakers for a lending library called "The Best of the Fest" now containing over 200 films and videos.

It was not until 1983 that Movies on a Shoestring accepted a video entry, but by 1999, 14 of the 32 selected entries were on video. Eleven were on 16mm, and five of the films shown were on 35mm. Surprisingly, none were on Super 8. The last Super 8 film that was accepted for showing was submitted in 1990.

A recent arrival on the festival scene, with its first meeting in Rochester, New York, in 1993, is the Rochester Lesbian and Gay Film and Video Festival. At the 1994 meeting, films were shown coming from as far away as New Zealand.[11]

At one time there were dozens of festivals catering to 8mm and Super 8 filmmakers, but at this writing, there is just one juried festival limited exclusively to films which originate on Super 8 film or 8mm video. This is the United States Super 8 Film/Video Festival, held annually at Rutgers University, New Brunswick, New Jersey, under the auspices of the Rutgers Film Co-op, New Jersey Media Arts Center, and sponsored by that organization and Eastman Kodak Company.

This festival was founded in 1989 by Albert G. Nigrin, a lecturer on film at Rutgers' Program in Cinema Studies and an accomplished filmmaker, whose objective is to encourage the use of 8mm film for all genres: animation, documentary, experimental, fictional, narrative, etc. Nigrin's first show consisted of five films by Man Ray shown to just 30 people. With each successive festival the program was broadened to include old, mainstream, avant garde, and cult classics. Entries are received from all over the United States and Canada, from which approximately a dozen prize-winners are selected, who share $1,200 in cash and prizes. The winning films are exhibited over a two-day program at Rutgers University. The 1996 festival ran from September 6 to November 26, screened over 30 films and was expected to draw over 15,000 viewers.

Four touring programs are constructed of selections from Festival winners of the past four years, and are exhibited at many media art centers, film festivals, and universities, including: the World Festival of Video in Brussels, Belgium, the Visual Studies Workshop in Rochester, New York, the Boston School of the Museum of Fine Arts, the Melbourne Super 8 Festival in Australia, and many others.

Among the finalists in the 1996 Festival were the following films, as described by the filmmakers:

A Day in the Life of a Bull-Dyke (1995)

> Shawna Dempsey, Lorri Millan, Winnipeg, Canada. 11 min. Super 8 + 3/4" video. A fictionalized lesbian history of a big-boned butcher who finds passion and purpose. Both the public and the private lives of this "strange animal" are documented with the same mix of reverence and glee found in the educational exposés *Bull-Dyke* mocks.

NYC Symphony (1995)

> Reynold Isto, Brooklyn, New York. 10 min. Super 8 + 3/4" video. Utilizing documentary narrative and experimental tactics, *NYC Symphony* is a personal view of New York City at the end of the millennium. It is an ambient film symphony in the tradition of the 1920s city films.

Fat of the Land (1995)

> Niki Cousino, Sarah Lewison, Julie Konop, Florence Dore, Gina Todos, San Francisco, CA/New Brunswick, New Jersey. 55 min. Hi8 + 3/4" video. In this kitchen-grease-powered road movie, five women tour America fueling up on the waste fat their fellow travelers have left behind. From New York to San Francisco, the women careen across the nation stopping at "greasy spoons" and asking for leftover frying oil to fuel their vehicle. Through interviews and chance encounters, the video sardonically critiques the stranglehold petroleum has on our economy while investigating one fuel for the future—vegetable oil.

It would be impractical to attempt to list every film festival in this country; the ones described above constitute a representative sample. Similarly, I have not attempted to list or describe the European amateur film festivals. George Cushman admitted to having a list of over 500 festivals world-wide for "independent and non-commercial film and video makers." [12]

Are Movie Clubs Worth Joining?

This question was posed by the editors of *Popular Photography* in 1961 and was answered pro and con by two experienced amateur filmmakers: E. Louise Gnerich, then president of the Metropolitan Motion Picture Club of New York, Inc., and Ed Corley, an independent filmmaker of some renown.

Mrs. Gnerich, not surprisingly, took the positive position. From the viewpoint of an obviously gregarious and upbeat personality, she found nothing but good in the companionship and mutual admiration of results that apparently prevailed at the meetings of her club:

What's wrong with admiring each other's work well done? I say this is a splendid attitude. It makes everybody happy and creates harmony. Contests in clubs also make for good sportsmanship, for in an atmosphere of mutual respect for ability petty jealousy will be crushed by the general conspicuous good fellowship among members.

Ironically, these statements constitute an innocent but telling indictment of the club mentality. Mrs. Gnerich seems to be saying that creation of harmony and good sportsmanship is high among the objectives of a club. She does add that learning how to use the camera and maintain it, and lighting, exposures, lenses, etc., are benefits of club membership, but there is no mention of what might be learned about film content, or creativity.

On the other side, Mr. Corley pulled no punches, declaring that the average ciné club was:

Run by a passel of old foops . . . whose leadership was indifferent, opposed to or ignorant of what the young filmmaker wants to do, (who wants to) say something, not simply record a trip to Disneyland or capture for the ages the kids acting out a cute little story about Goldilocks and the Three Bears.

The judging of films in club-sponsored competition was frequently tainted by club politics, in Corley's view, and generally resulted in the exclusion of experimental films or films that did not conform to the accepted norms of camera technique. He concluded his argument with this exhortation: "If you want to make good films, go out and make them—the various film festivals will provide you with something of an audience." [13]

The Photographic Society of America (PSA) itself came under severe criticism the following year, when Jacob Deschin, a well-known photographer and writer for *Popular Photography* wrote a column entitled "What's Wrong With the PSA?" His answer was— "practically everything," which he detailed as follows:

An organization of salon-oriented escapists, worshipers of technique for its own sake, and hobby riders of the trite, the bloodless emotion, and the pretty-pretty sentiment. Of the exhilarating progress in attitudes and approaches toward the photographic medium that has been evident all around it in the course of the nearly three decades of its existence, little has penetrated the Society. It stands today an island more barren than ever in a world of widening exploration and discovery of individual potential. [14]

Deschin was a still photographer, and of course his polemic was aimed at the still photography groups in the PSA, but it is reasonable to assume that many of the attitudes of the still photography hierarchy carried over to the Motion Picture Division of the PSA.

Ten years later a prominent member of the Motion Picture Division had this to say:

Practically the only thing one hears or learns in an amateur movie club deals with technique—never with content. You can master lap dissolves, fades, and all the other techniques and you will still be a woeful movie maker if you haven't realized that they are only the tools . . . which you may use to express your creative abilities. If you haven't stimulated your creative juices, you are simply playing around with an expensive toy to satisfy your own egotistical needs. [15]

Perhaps the really good filmmakers are born that way.

15

Some Home Movies

A Sampling of the Product

If you have made it this far in the book, you will have read almost all there is to say about the technology of making a movie at home, and along the way have had occasional glimpses of some films and the people who made them. This chapter will describe a sampling of home movies and their makers taken from a large body of films made between 1930 and 1954, a smaller sample of films made between 1971 and 1997, and a few very unusual films.

As observed previously, users of amateur motion picture equipment came in many gradations of intent, ambition, and skill. Not all users of amateur equipment can fairly be described as amateurs. The classic definition of an amateur in any field of endeavor is, of course, "one who performs (any activity) for the love of it." In my view, this excludes avant garde or experimental filmmakers, who may very well make films for the love of it, but at the same time fully intend to see their efforts bring some financial return if at all possible. Additionally, most avant gardistes and/or experimental filmmakers have had some professional training.[1]

Some who started as amateurs became proficient enough to have their works accepted for commercial use, as was the case with some of the filmmakers whose films are described in this chapter. Their commercial films are so identified. My definition of a home movie is then: one made on an amateur film gauge with what is generally accepted as amateur equipment, not intended for commercial distribution.

Family Archives

By far the great majority of users purchased equipment with the express purpose of making a family record. And millions of people made these records. But the results more often than not were shoeboxes full of 50-foot reels of unedited film. Many of these films were screened only once or twice and soon the film, camera, and projector were relegated to a closet shelf. This is evidenced by the number of amateur cameras and projectors dating from as far back as the 1920s that can be found in pristine condition, many in the original boxes.

Sadly, few family record films survive; children grow up and move away, families dissolve. More recently, video has moved in to displace film entirely. The cameras and projectors have been discarded, or wound up in yard sales or thrift shops. Rarely, some films have come into the hands of persons with an appreciation of their worth, and some very perceptive essays have been written on the home movie,[2] and some films have been made from home movies, such as *Family Album* (1986), by Alan Berliner. [3, 4]

Award Winners

There does exist however a record of approximately 1,000 amateur films made between 1930 and 1979. These are the films that were submitted to the Amateur Cinema League and its succeeding organization, the Motion Picture Division of the Photographic Society of America, and chosen for an award, as described in the previous chapter. While under the auspices of the Amateur Cinema League, the winning films were described in considerable detail in the League's journal, *Movie Makers;* under the Photographic Society, the reporting of award-winning films was so abbreviated as to preclude inclusion of those films in the following study. However a sample of the work of several California filmmakers working between 1975 and 1997 has been included.

The data from 1930 to 1954 covers nearly 500 films and yields for each film: length, gauge, color or black and white, kind of sound if any, and a precis of the film. From these 500 films a sample of over 200 films has been analyzed for type of film, and from which some general trends are posited. In addition, the achievements of a number of outstanding filmmakers are described.

The League at first made no attempt to distinguish between films made by amateurs and those submitted by professionals or semi-professionals. In 1931, a 3,000-foot 35mm film, *The Eyes of Science,* by J. S. Watson Jr., and Melville Weber, was accepted and named one of the year's top ten. Dr. James Sibley Watson, Jr. (ca. 1900-1987) was an independently wealthy radiologist of Rochester who was fascinated by film. He made some of the first x-ray motion pictures and made two avant-garde films: *Lot in Sodom* and *The Fall of the House of Usher*—using a pioneer-

ing optical printer for special effects. Melville Weber was his assistant.[5]

In 1936 the League recognized the inequities in its system and created two classes of films, one for filmers who received no compensation for their films, and a "Special Class" for those who did. Compensation was understood to include proceeds from sale or rental of the film, regardless of the intent at the time of the film's making. This class was eventually dropped and only purely amateur efforts were accepted.

Missing Footage

It could be argued that films produced by members of The Amateur Cinema League and submitted for competition are not representative of amateur movies as a whole. This is undoubtedly true on two counts: first, on the premise that people who took the trouble to join an organization would be more serious about their movie making than the average owner of a movie camera, plus the fact that films to be submitted in competition are going to be more carefully planned and executed than the impromptu "Wait till I get my camera!" kind of film.

Second, given the relatively high cost of film and equipment compared to other forms of home entertainment such as listening to the radio or playing the phonograph, most filmmakers for the first decade of 16mm's existence were generally well-to-do. Their films betrayed their background: records of foreign travel, Ivy League football games, "photo plays" staged at the local country club, and very occasionally, simple family record films. A quality camera and projector outfit in 1930 cost about $300 or $3,000 in year 2000 dollars. It was not until the 8mm system became available in 1932, cutting the cost of filming by 75 percent, that the ranks of filmmakers were opened to people of modest means.[6]

What has been lost by omitting the more typical "home movie" from this study and from film archives in general? The happy-go-lucky, sometimes funny, sometimes boring, truly intimate, unpretentious family film. Enough examples survive to show that we probably have lost a great deal of entertaining and even historically valuable footage. As an example, my collection of amateur footage includes approximately 4,000 feet of16mm film shot between 1926 and 1931 by one Louis Latham Clarke. Some research revealed that Louis Latham Clarke was the fourth and last of a family of New York bankers. Mr. Clarke's father traced his ancestry back to Charlemagne and Henry I of England; his mother was a descendant of a signer of the Declaration of Independence.

The Clarke films were generally well shot, well-exposed, and carefully titled by Eastman Kodak. They follow the family's activities at their palatial summer home on the Jersey shore, vacations in Europe, cruises on the family yacht, the butler helping Mrs. Clarke into the limousine, and officiating at a rocket launch in the front yard. How these films came to rest in an antique shop on Manhattan's Second Avenue is unknown. So while this survey is not a survey of *all* amateur films, it does provide a fairly detailed look at an important segment of such films.

Advances in Technology

The period covered by this study, 1930 to 1953, saw the United States struggle through a devastating depression and the agonies of World War II and Korea. The same period saw the introduction of two innovations in amateur film technology that had more effect on home movie making than either the depression or the war: the introduction of the 8mm system in 1932 and Kodachrome film in 1935.

When first introduced, the 16mm camera was largely a plaything for the well-to-do and, to a limited extent, a new tool for scientific, medical, and industrial work. The unquestionably upper class makeup of the Amateur Cinema League can be no better illustrated than by quoting two editorials from *Movie Makers*. The first appeared in the June 1932 issue in which the editor, giving a nod to the dismal state of the economy, suggested that it was time for everyone to make certain adjustments and sacrifices, to do "double duty":

The general sales manager is his own assistant . . . the woman whose superintendance of her husband's establishment would normally be limited to conference with the housekeeper now deals directly with the service group. . . . Pleasure cars and business cars are merged in the same piece of equipment. . . . The country place will be [leased] for the winter, and a similar arrangement made for the city apartment in the summer. [7]

The editor then went on to suggest that the prudent movie amateur would make his vacation do double duty by preserving it on film, for a second of third enjoyment at a later time. This suggestion

came at a time when thousands of men were out of work, selling apples on the street, and standing in bread lines.

The second editorial appeared after 8mm was announced in August 1932, when the country seemed to be pulling out of the depression. It had this to say about the arrival of the new gauge:

Wealth cannot make better movies than modest competence, and by now, the earlier restriction of movie making to monied amateurs has been removed. The field is now open to almost everybody that has a job—and more people are going to have jobs. [8]

The new gauge was expected to stimulate more people to try "home movies" even at a time when disposable income for the average household was decidedly limited.

The general public reacted cautiously, however, as noted in Chapter 5, and the "serious amateur" even more cautiously. An 8mm film did not appear among the Amateur Cinema League's winners until 1935, when one film in the new gauge shared the stage with 20 16mm films. The narrow gauge did not achieve a substantial presence until 1940, when nearly half of the top films were in 8mm. After Pearl Harbor, December 1941, 16mm was only available to the military, where great quantities were needed for training films. By 1945 16mm had resumed its dominant position.

Entries with Color

The June 1935 issue of Movie Makers carried a long article on the newly introduced Kodachrome film by Harris Tuttle, Eastman's public relations man for amateur film since 16mm was introduced in 1923. Tuttle explained some of the fine points of using Kodachrome to best advantage. Eastman Kodak wanted everyone to be successful with the new product.

Available at first only as 16mm movie film, Kodachrome had a much more dramatic effect on amateur movies than the introduction of 8mm. Kodacolor, the curious process introduced in 1928 that projected an image in color from black-and-white film, occasionally appeared in the lists of prize-winning films. Even more rarely Dufay Color won a prize. But Kodachrome roared ahead of black-and-white film, Kodacolor, and Dufay Color. One-third of the prizewinners in 1935 and three quarters of them in 1938 were in Kodachrome. The percetange would have been 100 percent in 1947 had there not been one entry in Agfacolor, a Kodachrome look-alike, which received an honorable mention.

Entries with Sound

One writer has said that there were only two classes of amateurs—the serious ones, those that edited *and added sound to their films,* and those that did not. That may sound a bit arbitrary, but until Eastman Kodak made sound-on-film inexpensive and simple, the addition of sound to a film took considerable effort, if it was to be done at all well.

The really successful addition of sound to a silent film required, first, a willingness to learn how to manipulate some tricky mechanical equipment such as record turntables, wire or tape recorders, and second, a discriminating ear, to match the sound esthetically to the image on the screen. Relatively few amateurs had such gifts or cared to invest the time and effort to acquire the necessary skills.

As discussed in Chapter 11, the earliest method of providing a sound accompaniment to home movies was by use of phonograph records, either with professionally recorded music and/or sound effects or with such sounds recorded by the filmmaker himself. Beginning in 1934, "sound-on-disc," as it was referred to, was increasingly present on the award-winning films. The disc system gradually gave way to sound on tape or wire and, eventually, to sound-on-film. The latter made its first appearance among the winners in 1937; however, the film so selected was professionally made, but permitted in the competition at the time.

Types of Amateur Films

The amateur or home moviemaker made movies of almost as many types as did Hollywood, plus one that Hollywood never made—the family record. The films in this study fall into five types, although it is often problematical as to how to classify a specific film as it may have had characteristics of several types. In the following lists, the five types I have settled on are, in order of their frequency of appearance. documentary, travel, drama, experimental, and family record.

The documentary was the odds-on favorite of the Amateur Cinema League members, consistently outnumbering the other four types of films, generally by a factor of two. The travel film was the second most popular, making up 23 percent of the

selected films. The difference between documentary and travel and was sometimes hard to define. Dramas took third place, with 22 percent of the films falling in that category.

Family record and experimental films tied at five percent each. For the experimental category, one has to consider the mores of the times; now one is as likely to find "gangsta rap" among the popular songs of the day as to find scratching, painting, burning of film, deliberate distortions of viewpoint; none of these radical techniques was even dreamed of years ago, or if so was never submitted to the contest. Thus the examples listed, as unremarkable as they appear in year 2000, were at least considered out of the ordinary at the time of their making. Out of the 25 or so films selected each year for recognition, there were seldom more than one or two in this category, and often none at all.

In the January 1926 issue of *Movie Makers,* Hiram Percy Maxim, founder of the Amateur Cinema League, offered the following selection of films from his personal library to exchange with other filmmakers. The descriptions as given are his: *Fishing Trip,* a canoe trip through the Moose River Country from Jackman, Maine; *Development of An Old Farmhouse into a Country Home,* a record of an old house in Lyme, Connecticut; *Mag the Hag,* a very funny example of early attempts at amateur photo plays; *Field Day, 1925 at Dobbs Field,* a day at the Master's School, Dobbs Ferry, New York.[9]

Here, five examples of each type have been selected for illustration. The initials following each description are:

HPM Hiram Percy Maxim Award, inaugurated in 1937, means the film was selected as the best of the Ten Best

TB One of the Ten Best

HM Honorable Mention.

The quoted comments are the judges' remarks.

DOCUMENTARY:

The Tombs of the Nobles (1931) (TB)
By John Riggs Hansen of Washington, DC
400 feet, 16mm, black and white

Mr. Hansen photographed hundreds of tomb paintings in Egypt, relying on reflected natural light by placing and manipulating sheets and mirrors in the cramped spaces available to him. The judges termed it "a technical triumph over seemingly insuperable photographic odds."

Fishers of Grande Anse (1935) (TB)

By Leslie P. Thatcher, Toronto, Canada
300 feet, 16mm, black and white

"A study of the highest order, with impeccable photography showing the primitive ways of men and women who live from the sea."

Humming Birds (1940) (TB)

By E. R. Hoff, Freeport, Illinois
400 feet, 16mm, Kodachrome

"A revelation of incredible patience—you will know more about the ways of this nearly invisible aerial dynamo than you believed possible."

The Inside Story of the Outside Cover (HM)

By George E. Valentine, Glenbrook, Connecticut
400 feet, 8mm, Kodachrome, with narration

"If you have a certain admiration for the technical skill that goes into (making four color engraving plates) that admiration is likely to be heightened by Mr. Valentine's step by step story of this process . . . a real technical achievement because of the conditions under which it had to be made."

Canadian High Adventure (1953) (TB)

By Jerry Moore, Denver, Colorado
600 feet, 16mm, color not indicated
With optical sound on film

A study of mountain climbing. "The film presents an amazing variety of camera angles. Mr. Moore is obviously a competent climber as well as cameraman."

TRAVEL

Italy (1931) (TB)

By Stephen F. Voorhees, New York City
400 feet, 16mm, black and white

This film is arguably as much documentary as travel, as the judges observed that it had "a natural and easy continuity, jogging amiably through Venice and its environs, pausing for a bit of incidental human interest." It was also a professional study of architectural details that Mr. Voorhees brought home for future use. Mr. Voorhees was a managing partner in the firm then known as Voorhees, Gmelin and Walker, which was founded in 1885. The firm, known today as HLW International LLP, is rated as one of the oldest continuously operating design firms in this country.

Bermuda, the Floating Gardens (1935) (HM)

By Konstantin T. Kostich, Long Island City, New York
400 feet, 16mm, Kodachrome

"Setting forth the many tourist attractions of the islands, with high levels of color results."

Holiday in Dixie (1940) (TB)

By Morton H. Read, Springfield, Massachusetts
1200 feet, 8mm, Kodachrome
With music, sound, and narrative

From Washington, D.C. to the deep South "a Yankee from Massachusetts has so well understood the essence of the Old South— Southern hats should come off to him."

New England Autumn (1947) (TB)

By Hamilton H. Jones, Buffalo, New York
475 feet, 16mm Kodachrome
With music, sound effects on disc, and narrative

"Hamilton H. Jones has again shown his marvelous ability to combine beautiful movies and fine music on the double turntable into a cinematic whole." (See Fig. 307.)

The Enchanted Isles (1953) (TB)

By Alfred T. Bartlett, Brisbane, Queensland, Australia
750 feet, 16mm, Kodachrome with sound on tape

"Bartlett has painted all the elements (of the Great Barrier Reef, Whitsunday Group) in large lush compositions and with observant attention to the minutiae of vibrant life around him."

DRAMAS

Hearts of the Golden West (1931) (TB)

By Theodore Huff, Englewood, New Jersey
1200 feet, 16mm, black and white

A light-hearted spoof of Hollywood westerns, performed entirely by youngsters under 13. The producer made use of all the cinematic clichés, including the dance hall with balcony, a fight to the finish, and a moral conclusion.

Children Grow Up (1935) (TB)

By Charles J. Carbonaro, New York, New York
1200 feet, 16mm, black and white

A social treatise on family life offered in dramatic form, showing "intelligent use of parallel action, sound photographic ability . . . capably directed."

The Will and the Way (1940) (HPM)
By Chester Glassley of Dallas, Texas
200 feet, 8mm, Kodachrome, with music on disc

The simple story of a young pregnant wife who pleads to be attended by a prominent but expensive obstetrician; the husband gamely submits to various indignities to accumulate the necessary cash; the good-hearted doctor returns the partial payment marking the bill paid in full, in tribute to the husband's heroism. Mr. Glassley handled this potentially mawkish plot with restraint and skill. The judges noted excellent editing, brilliantly executed montage sequences, and dubbed the filmmaker "Chester *Capra* Glassley."

The surprising epilogue to the film's award: Glassley wrote to his idol, the renowned director Frank Capra *(Mr. Deeds Goes to Town* (1936) and *Mr. Smith Goes to Washington* (1939), thanking the director for being his inspiration and role model. Capra replied with an invitation to visit him "and bring your film, I want the Academy to see it." Three days later, in the main projection room of Paramount Studios, *The Will and the Way* became the first 8mm film ever formally presented to the Academy of Motion Picture Arts and Sciences.

While the Earth Remaineth (1945) (HPM)
By Frank E. Gunnell, Staten Island, New York
900 feet, 16mm, Kodachrome, with music on disc

This film was based on the 8th chapter, 22nd verse of Genesis, in which the flood having abated, the Lord promises that He will never again visit such destruction on the earth. Gunnell produced a film interpretation of this story, actually going back to the first chapter of Genesis. Using appropriate clips, Gunnell suggested the "darkness on the face to the deep (with) sequences of geysers, boiling springs of mud . . . the creation of heaven, earth and oceans." Appropriately for such a weighty theme, Gunnell scored his film with selections from Beethoven's Pastoral Symphony, Schuman's Third Symphony, and other works of similar stature.

Concerto (1953) (TB)
By Warren Doremus, Rochester, New York
325 feet, 16mm, black and white, with sound on disc

"A sensitive and touching story of young love, done with such warmth that the observer cannot help being caught up in the current of emotions that fill the film." [10]

Experimental

Traum in Karneval (1931) (TB)
By Dr. Max Goldschmidt of Vienna, Austria, with
    the assistance of Richard Teschner
1000 feet, 35mm

The only experimental film to place among that year's Ten Best, it was also the only 35mm film so honored. The film was described as "a distinctly new technique in ciné puppet drama . . . working with puppets controlled entirely from below the line of camera sight. The camera moved freely from near shot to close-up . . . inserted scenes from real life (served) only to heighten the cinematic illusion." Tribute was also given to the mastery of Richard Teschner, eminent European puppeteer.

Christmas Nuts (1935) (TB)
By Paul Braun and Howard Goodman, Baltimore, Maryland
400 feet, 16mm, Kodachrome, with sound on film

"Ambitious and well carried out experiment in filming puppets in color."

An Anaesthetic Fantasy (1940) (HM)
By Ernest Kremer, Flushing, New York
275 feet, 8mm, Kodachrome, with music on disc

"The nightmare of a dental patient under laughing gas. Clever trick camera work, dissolves, and stop motion, accompanied by unusual records played on a dual turntable outfit."

Fantasy in Toyland (1947) (HM)
By Charles H. Benjamin, Brooklyn, New York
400 feet, 16mm, Kodachrome

"Using animated puppets worked from below stage level, filmed frame by frame by remotely controlled camera, Benjamin takes a curious dog through an adventure to save a fabulous female canine in distress."

Candy Capers (1953) (HM)
By Roy M. Fulmer, Jr., Livingston, New Jersey
100 feet, 8mm, Kodachrome, with sound on tape

"A gay little dance fantasy in animation, using lollipops, wafers and other familiar childhood sweets, Fulmer makes a bit of confection that is a delight to the eye and ear."

FAMILY RECORD

A Christmas at Home (1935) (TB)
By Edmund Zacher II, of West Hartford, Conn.
550 feet, 16mm, Kodacolor, with sound on disc

Despite the all-too-familiar subject matter, the reviewers found that Mr. Zacher handled his chosen theme with consummate skill, including multiple exposures as opening and closing sequences, as well as achieving excellent results in predominately interior scenes with Kodacolor, no easy assignment. The judges said the film "glows with all the warmth and color associated with the season." It was also the last Kodacolor film to receive an award, before Kodachrome succeeded that process.

Santa Passes Out (1938) (TB)
By John Martin, Leek, England
400 feet, 16mm, Kodachrome

"A series of unusually fine child studies makes this film outstanding, and the utterly spontaneous character of most of this material carries the story forward."

Magic Stairway (1947) (TB)
400 feet, 8mm, Kodachrome
By Margaret and Harlan M. Webber, Schenectady,
      New York

The Webbers wove a lively and natural movie of their son and daughter working through a potentially unhappy Christmas to a joyful ending "making this film far above the average family film."

Bless This House (1950) (HM)
By Grace Lindner, Kenmore, New York
40 feet, 8mm, Kodachrome, with music on disc

"A brief film designed as a trailer for home use rarely possesses the quality of general audience appeal. Grace Lindner may be justly proud of having achieved this elusive element."

A Look at Some Multiple Winners

Hamilton H. Jones of Buffalo, New York, won his first Ten Best award in 1932, with *Canadian Capers,* described by the judges as "a superlatively good vacation picture—containing several magnificent examples of sequencing—one of the best railroad film studies ever made." After adding some footage and doing some further editing, Jones resubmitted the film the following year as *Under the Maple Leaf.* This time he received an honorable mention, in spite of a comment from the judges that his editing and cutting still left room for improvement.

Not one to abandon a promising vein, Jones returned in 1937 with *Western Holiday,* a 2,500-foot 16mm Kodachrome film with musical and sound effects scoring from double turntables. This time Jones garnered the top honors, becoming the first contestant to receive the Hiram Percy Maxim Award. The remarks on his film included these words:

Here Kodachrome caught the first rosy glow (of a sunrise) on the cold blue snow . . . which blossomed into a chromatic crown of jewels. Jones, in the highly intelligent cutting of his train sequences, gave the student of continuity another of these thrills. Those who are charmed by double turntable accompaniment will recognize the perfection with which an almost impossibly difficult feat of lip synchronization with record scoring has been achieved. [11]

From a small photograph, it appears that Jones built his own turntable phonographic apparatus into a suitcase (Fig. 307). Mr. Jones was described as a paid lecturer on the vacation advantages of the Dominion of Canada. The film appeared to be a promotional piece for the Canadian National Railways, taking the viewer on a rail journey from Victoria, British Columbia across the Canadian Rockies to the eastern seaboard. Since Jones did not receive any compensation directly for the film, the film was accepted in the non-commercial class. By 1947 Jones had been made a Fellow of the Amateur Cinema League and was still working in color and sound. As noted above, his entry that year, *New England Autumn,* captured another Ten Best.

Ralph E. Gray of Mexico City, Mexico, won his first Ten Best award in 1937 for an 800-foot, 16mm Kodachrome documentary, *Primitive Patzcuaro,* that portrayed the life of the Tarascan Indians in a remote and rarely visited section of Mexico. The December issue of *Movie Makers* carried an article by Gray entitled *Mexican Movie Diplomacies,* a subject on which he was obviously well qualified to write. The following year Mr. Gray doubled his efforts and submitted a 1600-foot Kodachrome film *Mexican Fiestas* that "ranged the length and breadth of Mexico to record with amazing vitality the thrilling ceremonies of a people at play . . . an authentic documentation of religious and quasi-religious holiday customs, both pagan and Christian." The film received the Hiram Percy Maxim award for 1938.

Fig. 307. Hamilton Jones' turntables.

Fig. 308. Glen Turner.

Fig. 309. Glen Turner filming a "set."

In 1943, now living in San Antonio, Texas, Mr. Gray won a Ten Best for *Paracutin,* again in 1945 for *Arts and Crafts in Mexico,* 1600 feet, Kodachrome, and in 1946, his *Typical Times in the Tropics* gave him his second Hiram Percy Maxim Award.

Springville, Utah is a quiet town about 50 miles south of Salt Lake City off State Route 15, just east of Utah Lake. It was the home of a remarkable amateur filmmaker, Glen H. Turner. (Fig. 308 and Fig. 309.) Mr. Turner burst on the amateur scene in 1949 with a deceptively simple film entitled *One Summer Day,* 350 feet, 8mm Kodachrome, with music and sound effects recorded on wire. As his first submission to the League contest, it won him the Hiram Percy Maxim Award. Describing it, the judges said:

Neither the lead title nor the unpretentious opening scenes—as a small boy is seen building a crude toy boat—prepares the spectator for the pure enchantment of this film. For, almost unrealized even as it happens, the film melts with incredible smoothness from live action into animation and make-believe. Highly imaginative camera handling, technical skill, and a keen sense of cinematic values make this an outstanding example of personal filming. Glenn Turner has added a new dimension to amateur filming with this simple story so superbly told.

The following year Turner was among the top ten with *The Barrier,* an 800-foot 16mm Kodachrome with music, sound effects, and narration on wire. This was an adventure film, with a wandering western horseman, hostile Indians, and a thrilling escape over rough terrain.

In 1951, Turner's entry was *In Fancy Free,* 600 feet, 16mm Kodachrome, with sound on wire. The judges described the film as a direct descendent of *One Summer Day,* his 1949 Maxim Award winner, which in a narrow sense it was. Both films were cinematic depictions of fantasy, but the fantasy in the 1949 film was playful, while the fantasy of *In Fancy Free* was tragic.

In Fancy Free opens with a girl in her teens who is daydreaming of life as a ballet dancer. Scenes of ballet and other activities appear. Then in a brief and shocking climax, we realize that the girl will never become a dancer, that she is in fact a paraplegic.

This somber scenario was relieved by an original and brilliant score written for the film and recorded by the orchestra of Brigham Young University, where Turner was an assistant professor of art. University dance students performed the dance sequences. It is not recorded how other contestants felt about such collaboration, but the judges warned those who might be inclined to cry "unfair," that "Great art is created by the mind and heart of the artist—not by the hands of those who help him."[12]

Glen H. Turner was born on March 11, 1918, in Monroe, Utah. Upon graduation from Brigham Young University in Provo, Utah in 1939, he became an instructor in art at the University, and then a full professor on obtaining his master's degree in 1947. Turner became a member of the Amateur Cinema League in 1949 by joining a local camera club of just 12 couples, which met monthly and had annual meetings where public showings of the member's slides and films were held.

Turner's first camera was an 8mm Bell & Howell Sportster, with which he filmed his 1949 *One Summer Day*. He later moved up to 16mm. Eventually he added a Ciné-Kodak Special, a Bell & Howell 70DA, a Bolex, and still later Canon and Chinon Super 8 cameras.

As his skill increased, Turner looked for wider horizons. Being free when classes at the University suspended for the summer, he approached the Union Pacific Railroad, showed them some of his work and was hired as staff cinematographer for the railroad, a position he held for five summers. His work caught the attention of two advertising agencies in Salt Lake City, for whom he was soon filming television commercials. He also did a documentary for Brigham Young University on the Hopi, Navajo, and Ute Indians, which was shown on public television quite regularly for several years.

Turner could also write well. In addition to contributing over two dozen articles for various photographic magazines, including the professional *American Cinematographer,* he authored a small book on lenses published by Camera Craft and two data books for Eastman Kodak Company, one on magnetic sound recording, and one on titling and animation. Turner retired in 1980, but remained active in the Amateur Cinema League and its successor, the Photographic Society of America, often being called on to speak at their annual conventions. He died on December 3, 1993.[13]

Frank E. Gunnell (Fig. 310) was an elementary school teacher on Staten Island who loved to travel.

Fig. 310. Frank Gunnell.

He and his wife were among the first owners of a classic Airstream travel trailer, and when school was out they set out to explore the country and record their travels with a movie camera.

Gunnell's first winning film was *Adirondack Adventure,* 1935, 400 feet 16mm black and white. The film was a family record relating the adventures of the Gunnell's very young son in a camp in the mountains. The judges found the photography "a joy to behold" and acknowledged that the subject matter was one of the most difficult for the amateur to handle successfully. It received a Ten Best award.

Over the next ten years Gunnell garnered four more Ten Bests. In 1945 his most ambitious undertaking was *While the Earth Remaineth*, which has been described above. Gunnell's 1947 Ten Best winner, *Bryce Canyon Trails*, 700 feet, 16mm, Kodachrome, with sound-on-disc and narration, was described by the judges as "breathtaking camera work . . . enhanced by touches such as the darting antics of a chipmunk and a running gag about the hungry cameraman whose equipment cases also carry edibles."

The year 1948 marked the end of Gunnell's career in amateur movie making. His entry that year and his last Ten Best winner was *The Salmon—River of No Return*, 2000 feet, 16mm Kodachrome with music on disc and narrative. With his productions, Gunnell had accumulated seven Ten Bests, five Honorable Mentions, and one Maxim Award. Only two other contestants in this group had won as many.

Gunnell's nephew, Albert A. Gunnell, remembers with great pleasure the screenings of his uncle's films when he returned from vacation. Gunnell's ex-

Fig. 311. Jack Ruddell.

pertise was recognized in his school system. He was ultimately transferred from teaching and promoted to the Film Division of the New York City Department of Education. Frank Gunnell died on April 16, 1997. His films were donated to the social center of a mobile home park near Flagstaff, Arizona.

Perhaps the most remarkable record of all is that of a Canadian engineer/administrator, Jack Ruddell of Toronto (Fig. 311). Ruddell's first movie camera was a little Ciné-Kodak Magazine 8, which he took with him on a summer vacation in 1950. By the time he retired from active filming some 40 years later, he had produced dozens of award-winning films seen by thousands of people in Canada, the United States, Europe, and Japan. In fact he became so accomplished that many of his films found commercial outlets.

Ruddell was also an avid gardener. Not long after making his first movie he decided to attempt time-lapse photography of the blooming of flowers. The Magazine 8 was traded for a Bolex H-8, for its single-frame capability. With his own design of a variable rate timer, he made the first time-lapse film of flowers ever made in Canada. His accomplishment was aired on Canadian Television in 1952.

The following year Ruddell switched to 16mm, with a Bolex H-16 so that he could record sound. The result was *Prelude to Spring* (1957), 536 feet, 16mm Kodachrome, with magnetic sound on film.

This was also a time-lapse study of opening flowers, synchronized frame by frame with the music of the ballet *Swan Lake*. The film took four years to complete and was submitted to the 1957 competition, by this time under the aegis of the Photographic Society of America, where it was named one of the year's Ten Best. It went on to win major awards in Canadian, British, German, Italian, and Japanese competitions. Ruddell told me in 1997 that when he stopped sending it out to competitions it had won ten awards in seven countries.

After two more Ten Bests in 1959 and 1960, Ruddell entered a documentary, *Disneyland* (1963) 575 feet, 16mm Kodachrome with magnetic sound-on-film. This film took the top honor, or the Gold Medal in the PSA contest, plus top awards from Canadian and Australian competitions. Ruddell's second Gold Medal came just two years later with *The Settlers*, (1965) 1,000 feet, 16mm Kodachrome with optical sound-on-film. This ambitious film took three years to complete, used amateur actors recruited from his circle of friends, and told the story of two pioneering settlers on an Ontario farm about 1835, with all the attendant trials, failures, and successes. This film won two awards in Canada, two in England, and one each in Switzerland, Australia, and South Africa.

Having entered *The Settlers* in amateur competitions all over the world, Ruddell in 1977 offered it to Coronet Films, an American film distributor who kept it in stock for about seven years and paid the filmmaker a modest royalty on each print sold. This was actually not Ruddell's first venture into commercialism; beginning in 1957 he found a number of ways to make his hobby help pay its way. Well-made films of resorts or lodges could be exchanged for accommodations; travelogues could be traded for free travel or could be rented out as television programs.

In 1965 Ruddell, now vice-chairman of the Motion Picture Division of the PSA, was asked to conduct a group of PSA cinematographers on a six-week world tour, stopping in Holland, Turkey, Iran, India, Kashmir, Nepal, Thailand, Hong Kong, and Japan. Ruddell made a feature length film of the tour that was widely shown.

Having acquired a taste for world travel, Mr. and Mrs. Ruddell organized and conducted a group tour of East Africa's game parks and of Morocco, which resulted in a film which was traded to Alitalia for two free tickets good for any place on the line's system. And after retiring from Canada Packers, the Ruddells set off on a ten-week filming tour of Rome, India, Sri Lanka, Singapore, Bali, Australia, and New Zealand, all on the Alitalia passes. The films made of Singapore and New Zealand were accepted by a distributor for Canadian and American distribution. The film made in Bali was entered in the 1986 PSA competition and won Jack his last Gold Medal. Ruddell's most recent film is *Sri-Lanka* (1992), 865 feet, 16mm Kodachrome, with magnetic sound-on-film—a documentary on this beautiful island before its troubles began.

With such a background, Ruddell has been very much in demand as a speaker. Between 1958 and 1982 he delivered 47 lectures, illustrated with films, to organizations ranging from the University of Toronto to the Kodak Camera Club (Rochester) on subjects from time-lapse photography to wedding photography. Ruddell has also authored numerous articles on various aspects of cinematography, which have appeared in *Bolex Reporter, The PSA Journal, Popular Photography*, and other publications.

What the Amateur Cinema League began as the rather humble Ten Best Competition in 1930 evolved under the aegis of the Motion Picture Division of the Photographic Society of America into the American International Film Festival. In 1979 that organization elected to hold a 50th Anniversary Festival. The chairman of the 50th Anniversary Festival Committee was George W. Cushman. The Festival Program listed the Ten Best winners for each annual competition beginning in 1930. The program also noted that only five filmmakers had won the sweepstakes award twice, that only four persons had placed two films in the Top Ten in one year, and that only three had won as many as seven Top Ten awards. Jack Ruddell's name appeared in all three of those special niches. The Program also noted that a Special Award was to be presented at the Festival: "All Time Festival Champion." The recipient? Jack Ruddell.

It would be nice to report that most of Jack Ruddell's films are available for study; however, at this writing only the whereabouts of a few of the films is known. Twelve films are in the library of the

Fig. 312. Marion Gleason.

Society of Canadian Cine Amateurs, and some are in the Toronto Movie and Video Club Library.

It's Not Only for Men

Despite Eastman Kodak's best efforts and, to some extent, that of other manufacturers to encourage women to use the movie camera, most early amateur filmers were men. Beginning almost as soon as the 16mm system was introduced, Eastman Kodak advertisements frequently showed women, generally young, aiming a movie camera, generally at a child or children. Actually, one of the first persons other than Eastman Kodak engineers or research people to use the Ciné-Kodak was Marion N. Gleason, wife of Harold Gleason, George Eastman's organist (Fig. 312).

When the newly developed 16mm camera was ready for field testing, Mrs. Gleason was recruited to be a filmer. In her own words, "They wanted someone who knew nothing about movies, to be sure that anyone could operate the camera. I was terrified." Unfortunately it is unknown if any of Mrs.

Gleason's filmmaking efforts survive.

Gleason later produced a much more elaborate film entitled *Fly Low Jack and the Game* (1927), which is available at the George Eastman House for research purposes. Gleason went on to write articles on amateur filmmaking including several for *Movie Makers*, later served as publicist for the George Eastman House, and then as an editor of publications at the Strong Memorial Hospital at the University of Rochester. [14]

"It's Not Only For Men" was the title of a full-page article in the Souvenir Program for the Golden Anniversary Film Festival of the Photographic Society of America—Motion Picture Division, held in Hartford, Connecticut on October 5, 1979. The article noted that the festival was only three years old when Elizabeth Rearick, a student at Columbia University, made a film entitled *Glimpses of Rural Hungary*. She entered in the 1933 festival and that won a Ten Best award. The film was circulated for many years by the University of Colorado. The article went on to chronicle all the women who had won Ten Best Awards from 1933 to 1971, 25 in all, many of whom won more than once.

Esther S. Cooke, of Albany, New York (Fig. 313), began her string of winners in 1950, with *Next-door Neighbor*, a 400 foot 8mm Kodachrome travel film on Mexico, with music on disc, which the judges said showed "a fine talent for blending human interest with purely scenic passages . . . (and) diligent research, able organization and skillful editing." [15]

In 1954 Mrs. Cooke scored again with another travel film, *Het is Lente in Holland*; the following year, her *Corpus Cristi Day in Hallstatt* won the top award, a gold medal that replaced the Maxim award. Her films *The Swiss Scene* (1956), *Bruges the Beautiful* (1958) and *In Old Rothenburg* (1959) were each in the top ten for those years.

"Cooke's Tour with a Movie Camera" was the title of the lead article for the movie section of the May 1960 issue of *Popular Photography*, with the subtitle: "A top amateur producer of travelogues offers practical advice." It was of course, written by Esther Cooke and, besides being very well written, bespoke the author's obvious experience. A sidebar article by the usually negative Charles Reynolds was unstinting in praise of Cooke's achievements, noting that her 1958 film *Bruges the Beautiful* won a silver medal

Fig. 313. Esther Cooke.

at the Cannes, France, *Festival International du Film Amateur* in 1960, a ceremony which Ms. Cooke was able to attend.

Dolores Lawler of Kenosha, Wisconsin, and her husband Timothy M. Lawler (Fig. 314) won their first Ten Best in 1950 with a 200-foot 16mm Kodachrome film, *Isle of the Dead*, described as a cinematic tone poem, combining the "famed Boecklin painting," music from Rachmaninoff, with scenes from Yellowstone National Park and the Bad Lands. In 1952 their film *Duck Soup* won the top award, and this husband and wife team placed again in the top ten in 1957, 1962, and 1963.

As previously noted, the Amateur Cinema League accepted some films for which the maker had received compensation, but limited the number so accepted and placed them in a separate category, named "Special Class." In the 1945 competition just one Special Class film was recognized, and it was

Fig. 314. Timothy M. and Dolores Lawler.

indeed special. Entitled *Meshes of the Afternoon*, 500 feet, 16mm black-and-white, it was submitted by Maya Deren and Alexander Hammid. It received an Honorable Mention.

The judges described it as:

Experimental in nature and exciting in its cinematic development. Although one sees on the screen the familiar backgrounds and impedimenta of physical existence, the events which transpire among them portray a subjective feeling rather than objective incident. Ms. Deren's creative use of her camera to suggest these emotions blazes new and stimulating trails in pure cinematography.[16]

Meshes of the Afternoon went on to greater fame than the staff of *Movie Makers* could have dreamed. It was the first production of Deren, a brilliant young woman whose tragically brief career produced just a handful of films and articles, yet whose work is considered by many to have had the greatest influence up to that time on the serious amateur or independent filmmaker.

Maya Deren (1919-1961) (Fig. 315) was born in the city of Kiev, Ukraine, in 1919 and immigrated with her parents to the United States in 1922. Her father was a psychiatrist at a Syracuse mental hospital. Deren studied journalism at Syracuse University and later received a B.A. from New York University. Deren was a person of great enthusiasms, among them poetry and modern dance, which led her to join Katherine Dunham, then the leading exponent of modern dance. Dunham introduced her to a well-known professional filmmaker named Alexander Hammid (originally Hammerschied), whom she married in 1942.

Their first film was *Meshes of the Afternoon*, which according to Sitney[17] they shot in two and a half weeks in their home, using the simplest of 16mm equipment. Sitney is somewhat ambivalent as to which of the two partners contributed the most to the film, pointing out that the camera work was almost entirely Hammid's, but also observing that none of Hammid's subsequent films (they divorced shortly after *Meshes* was completed) resembled this first film in any way.

When Deren submitted *Meshes of the Afternoon* to the Amateur Cinema League, she also submitted her second film, *At Land* (1944) and an excellent article entitled "Efficient or Effective?" which explained the reasons for many of the techniques

Fig. 315. *Maya Deren.*

employed in the two films. The manuscript editor, in his monthly column on what filmmakers were doing, was quite frank in his reaction to Deren's films, admitting that after two viewings of each film he still had no clear idea what either film was about, but "they excite us tremendously!"

Deren's response is worth repeating:

My husband and I have been primarily concerned with the use of cinematic technique to create the feelings which a human being experiences about an incident, rather than simply to record the incident.

This explanation was amply borne out by the "Efficient or Effective?" article, which quite lucidly explains how the emotional content of a simple action can be dramatically altered by such things as the choice of camera angle or field of view. It is instructive to read her article before and after viewing the two films.

Deren's appearance among the filmmakers of the Amateur Cinema League was rather as if a Maori maiden wandered into a Scarsdale Garden Club lawn party. For one brief moment, the avant garde and the ultra conservatives crossed paths and, one may suspect, with little lasting effect on either party.

Some Recent Filmmakers

As mentioned in the previous chapter, after the Amateur Cinema League was dissolved into the Photographic Society of America in 1954, a number of amateur movie clubs sprang up on the West Coast, perhaps not surprisingly, given the beneficent climate and the proximity of Hollywood. Some of these organizations, their acronyms and the awards they offered are: Southern California Association of Amateur Movie Clubs, SCAAMC, Top 8 and Sweep-

Fig. 316. Walter Haskell.

stakes; Society of Amateur Videographers and Cinematographers, SAVAC; Ten Best of the West, TBW, Ten Best; and Society of Canadian Cine Amateurs, SCCA. Four filmmakers who are members of one or more of these organizations were asked to submit resumes of their filming careers to this author, and their responses are here recorded.

Walter Haskell, business executive, historian, world traveler, and film and video maker was born in Los Angeles in 1909 (Fig. 316). He graduated from the University of Southern California in 1933 with a B.S. in Business Administration. Haskell's filmmaking career began when his first daughter was born in 1944. His first camera was a Bell & Howell Sportster 8mm. Like thousands of other dads, Haskell filmed family affairs, birthdays, and vacations. And also as happened to thousands of other dads, filmmaking eventually palled; for 25 years the Haskell family record was preserved on slides, so much simpler to take with good results and to show.

Haskell's interest in filming returned in 1969, when he and wife Janet embarked on an extended trip to Europe. The Sportster went along, but when the Haskells reached Switzerland the little 8mm was retired, replaced by a brand new Bolex Super 8. This European trip marked the first of their world-ranging jaunts that accelerated when Walter retired from The Southern California Gas Company in 1975. For the next ten years, the Bolex Super 8 was kept busy filming journeys through Canada, the British Isles, China, Japan, and New Zealand, as well as the United States.

On returning from their first European tour, the Haskells joined the Southwest 8mm Club of Los Angeles, where Walter learned how to add sound to his films. They soon won awards at various California amateur film festivals. All films were in Super 8 Kodachrome, with magnetic sound track added. Some of his films were:

China Today—Xian (1980), 20 minutes. This documentary was filmed at Xian, deep in the interior of China where in 1974 archaeologists uncovered the long-hidden army of clay warriors who had stood in serried ranks for centuries guarding the tomb of some long-dead emperor. The film won a Ten Best and a Top 8.

Silk Road Series (1983). This series of four 20-minute films begins in the far northern mountains of China in the city of Urumqi, head of the fabled ancient "Silk Road," or trade route, opened by Marco Polo and for centuries China's only opening to the western world. Haskell, like all foreigners, was an object of curiosity. The first film in the series, *People of Urumqi*, won a bronze medal from PSA.

Flying Scotsman Series (1984). Three 15- to 20-minute films trace the Haskell journey from London to Edinburgh on the 1923 classic train, *The Flying Scotsman*, pulled by a steam locomotive. Their journey took them past the Isle of Skye, the Kyle (fjord) of Localish, and other beautiful spots of Scotland. The film won SCAAMC Sweepstakes and a PSA bronze medal.

Whose Side Are You On? (1985), 300 feet. This little film documents the friendly rivalry between Canada and the United States as to which country provides the most beautiful view of Niagara Falls. Haskell showed admirable impartiality, with his film displaying the best of both sides of this well-known tourist attraction. The film won a bronze from PSA-International and a Top 8 from SCAAMC.

On retirement, Haskell became active in several California historical societies, eventually becoming president of the California Conference of Historical

Societies. This interest led to no less than 34 films on the history of different California locales, ranging from Eureka in the north, through Death Valley to sunny San Luis Obispo. A sample of these films follows:

Freeman Mansion—Last Days (1971), 20 minutes. This film documents the demolition of this 1889 mansion, home of Daniel Freeman, owner of the 25,000 acre Rancho Centinela and founder of the town of Inglewood. Important parts of the structure, such as cabinetry, paneling doors, and hardware were saved and built in to the Walter Haskell Heritage Center on the Centinela Adobe Property.

Eureka—Carson Mansion (1980), 15 minutes. This shows a visit to the Carson Mansion, a large Victorian home, deemed the best of its type, home of a lumber and shipping magnate. The house is normally closed to the public; Haskell received permission to film the luxurious interior.

Weaverville (1984), 20 minutes. This documentary visits the Gold Stamp Mill and Joss House, or Chinese religious center, erected by the Chinese immigrants who provided most of the labor to build California's first railroads and later migrated to the gold fields.

Haskell was also active in the Historical Society of Centinela Valley, where as president he led a fund raising for a small museum-heritage center which building was later named the Walter Haskell Heritage Center. In 1989 Haskell became interested in video and quickly became adept at this medium. In 1998 he completed a 31-minute documentary video production *A Birthplace Reborn,* depicting the reconstruction of the Centinela Adobe structure after extensive earthquake damage in 1991. This film required weekly visits to the site over a period of eleven months. This talented filmmaker has created a body of work that is obviously an historical treasure for the state of California, and he has had a greatly satisfying time in so doing.

Howard Lindenmeyer was born in Terry, a little town in eastern Montana, and was brought up on a large cattle ranch, the Kempton Ranch and Cattle Company, where his father was the "ramrod" or foreman. Howard was a cowboy in every respect. He learned about the history of eastern Montana through actual experience and listening to tales of the town from the days of Lewis and Clark until the present time. Lindenmeyer's films include:

New Zealand—Land of Maori Mythology (1976), 16mm Kodachrome, 18 minutes, narrative sound on film. Lindenmeyer captures the colorful Maori folklore that co-exists with modern day New Zealand civilization, all against the background of this beautiful land of contrasts. The film won the PSA Gold Medal, Best Documentary and Best Editing.

Home Town (1978), 8mm Kodachrome, 24 minutes, narrative sound on film. Lindenmeyer uses his first-hand experience as a cowboy to document the history of his hometown as it grew from a pioneer settlement to a thriving community (population 639 in 1992). The film closes with scenes of the Prairie County Rodeo, held every year on the Fourth of July.

Rodeo Cowboys (1983), 8mm Kodachrome, 12 minutes, with sound on tape. This film shows branding time at a working ranch and compares this with the excitement of a present-day small town rodeo.

Rubbish to Riches (1986), 16mm Kodachrome, 12-minute narrative. This film documents the waste collection and disposal system of the City of Los Angeles. It begins with a dramatic shot of six bulldozers at work on a landfill, continues with the story of how recyclable materials are recovered, burnables are fed to boilers to produce electricity, and the remainder taken to a landfill where any gas produced is collected and sold to the local gas company. This film won the PSA Gold Medal and Best Documentary.

The Dominguez Story (1984), 16mm Kodachrome, 14 minutes. This film documents the history of the Dominguez family who received the first royal grant of land in Southern California, 75,000 acres given by the King of Spain, circa 1770. From this beginning the Dominguez family fortunes were thenceforth entwined with the development of Greater Los Angeles, through ten generations. Lindenmeyer's account of this dynasty's history won the Best Independent Film Trophy at the Canadian International Film Festival in 1984.

Lindenmeyer is currently president of the Los Angeles Cinema Club and chairman of the Club's Video Workshop, a Fellow of the Photographic Society of America, Motion Picture Division, and holds the title of Master Degree in the Society of Amateur Videographers and Cinematographers.

Dicie Ann (Vander Molen) Sizemore of Torrance,

California, is a second-generation filmmaker. Her parents were founding and life-long members of the Kalamazoo (Michigan) Movie Club. Sizemore and her brother grew up partaking of all club activities including appearances in club and parental film productions. When just ten years old, Sizemore began taking still photographs and continued with photographic courses in high school and college. Her first film, *Stop Over*, was made while she was attending Western Michigan University, using her father's 1966 Bauer Super 8 camera.

Upon graduation, Sizemore moved to California, began working for American Airlines, and in 1972 married Ken Sizemore, a Pacific Telephone Company employee whose hobby was scuba diving. Before long, Ken Sizemore combined their hobbies and became a skilled underwater cinematographer. The Sizemores joined the Los Angeles 8mm Movie Club in 1978 and have been club officers and award winners ever since.

Stop Over (1967), Super 8 Kodachrome, 10 minutes, music on tape. This delightful short tells the story of two young strangers who arrive at a large railroad station on different trains bound for different destinations. While waiting for their respective trains, they furtively eye each other, each wanting to speak but not until the girl is boarding her train do their eyes meet. They both smile wistfully, thinking what might have been. The Michigan Council of Amateur Movie Makers named it one of the top films of 1967.

The Ordeal (1979), Super 8 Kodachrome, 10 minutes, sound-on-film music. Ken relaxes on the couch until Patches the cat shares some of her fleas with him. The ordeal comes when Ken puts on a jacket and catcher's mask to give Patches a bath in the sink. There is a happy ending with cat and master relaxing on the couch again. Awards: LA 8—1979 Top Film, Sweepstakes, Sound Award; TBW—Top Ten; SCAAMC—1980 Top Eight.

Friends (1979), Super 8 Kodachrome, 15 minutes, sound-on-film narration and music. A young girl is startled and embarrassed when she meets a deaf girl, but she decides to learn sign language so they can communicate. They become best friends over a fun summer. Awards: LA 8 1979 Top Film and Sister Club Award.

An Introduction to Another World (1981), Super 8 Kodachrome, 18 minutes, sound-on-film narration and music. This an action documentary gives the basics of the exciting sport of scuba diving. The underwater footage was taken around Catalina Island, California. Awards: LA 8—1981 Sister Club Contest, First Place; Top of LA 8; Sweepstakes Award. TBW—1981 Top Ten; Sound Award. SCAAMC—1982 Best Documentary; Sweepstakes. PSA—1983 Ten Best; Silver Medal.

Taking the Plunge (1988), Super 8 Kodachrome, 15 minutes, sound on film. A young couple gets in over their heads as Ken Sizemore films their underwater wedding. The guests showered the happy couple with periwinkles. LA 8—1983 Top of LA8; SCAAMC—1990 Top 7 Award; Best Scenario. TBW—1990 Top Ten; PSA—1990 Bronze Medal; Second Place Documentary.

Mackinac Island, that historic bit of land that lies between Michigan's upper and lower peninsulas, has been the subject of thousands of amateur vacation films, including a number made by Dicie Sizemore's father from 1937 to the late 1960s. A few years ago the Mackinac State Park Commission began seeking amateur footage to be used in an exhibit at the Park Museum on the island. When Sizemore learned of this, she sent in a video copy of 23 minutes of her father's footage that included several of their vacation trips to the Island. The Sizemores could not attend the grand opening of the exhibit to learn whether or not their footage had been used, but on a visit several months later, Sizemore was delighted to learn that she and her brother are now part of a permanent museum exhibit.

Dicie Sizemore does most of the above-water filming, using a Nikon R10 Super for silent footage and a Canon 1014XL for sound. She also writes scripts and narration and does most of the post-production work of editing, titling, sound/music selection and recording. Ken Sizemore shoots underwater footage with his Eumig Nautica, narrates many of the films, and is the principal actor in most of the films that this husband and wife team has produced. In 1991 they reluctantly began shooting in Super VHS video with a JVC GR-S505 camera, which Dicie Sizemore explains was done primarily because of the high cost of film. They would have much preferred to stay with film for the superior image quality, but felt compelled to "follow the crowd."

Stan Whitsitt was born in Illinois, grew up on a farm in Indiana, and came to California in 1940 to work for Lockheed Aircraft Corporation. After service in World War II with the Field Artillery and the Paratroops, Whitsitt began making films in 1951, about the time he married and started a family. The Whitsitts have a son and a daughter. The children's journey from babyhood on was faithfully documented on regular 8mm film, starting with a DeJur 8 and ending with Bolex H-8 Rex. With the children grown, Whitsitt moved away from family films, switched to 16mm with a Bolex H-16 Rex, joined the Lockheed Employees Movie Club, and began making serious films.

On retiring from Lockheed, closing a 32-year career with that organization, Whitsitt began extensive travels to Africa, Central and South America, the Galapagos Islands, as well as North America from Alaska to Florida. The Bolex was kept busy. Including some made in his own back yard, over 60 films were produced, a great many of them won awards in the various competitions held in California by the organizations previously described.

Asked for his favorite, Whitsitt suggests that his most popular film is *A Bird Named Fred,* filmed twice—first in 1980 on 8mm Kodachrome and again in 1985 on 16mm Kodachrome (3 minutes, magnetic sound on film). Filmed in 8mm, this backyard study of an uncooperative bird giving the filmmaker a hard time and vice-versa, won a Silver Medal and Humorous Film Award at the PSA International Festival in Denver in 1978. After receiving many requests to show the film, Whitsitt re-shot it in 16mm, in which form it was shown in Canada, England, and Australia. The film continued to win awards. Other Whitsitt films include:

The Water's Edge (1984), 16mm Kodachrome, 13 minutes, magnetic sound on film. This nature film chronicles the amazing variety of life that manifests itself on the banks of the Kwai River in Botswana in the course of one day. It received a Ten Best in 1983, a PSA Silver in 1984, and a Cinematography Award from CIAFF in 1992.

Wind, Fire and Sky (1982), 16mm Kodachrome, 9 minutes, magnetic sound on film. Shot at an an-nual hot-air balloon festival in Albuquerque, New Mexico, the film captures the pageantry and mystique of this colorful sport. Not entirely satisfied with his footage from the first meet, Whitsitt returned the following year, took his camera aloft, and added balloon-to-balloon views of these spectacular machines. The film was a Top 8 in SCAAMC in 1984 and Best Film at SAVAC in 1991.

Canal Zone (1985), 16mm Kodachrome, 18 minutes, magnetic sound on film. Whitsitt shows that there is much more to Panama than the Canal, taking the viewer up the Mogue River to visit the Choco Indians and to the San Blas Islands to observe the colorful Cuna Indians, who have preserved their pre-Columbian culture and tribal governments.

Song of Baja (1983), 16mm Kodachrome, 30 minutes, magnetic sound on film. A natural history expedition to San Ignacio Lagoon in Baja California observes the Gray Whales wintering there. Stops were made at the islands of Todos Santos, San Benito, Cedros, and San Martin, where elephant seals, California sea lions, wild burros, harbor seals, and osprey were filmed.

Whitsitt is also a talented writer, with an autobiography and a book of verse to his credit, as well as numerous articles on movie making for the *PSA Journal, SAVAC Movie News, Western Photography,* and others. He has edited the newsletter of the Lockheed Employees Movie Club for eight years, garnering several editorial awards during his tenure.

By his own words, Whitsitt is somewhat of an anomaly among amateur filmers, not only still shooting film while all around him have gone over to video, but also shooting in 16mm. "Ninety-nine percent of my contemporaries have switched to video, but I cannot reconcile myself to expending all the effort and money to make a film in a format that provides such a lousy image."[18] Happily he is still working, having completed two films in 1997; *Ding,* a nature film shot in the Ding Darling Wildlife Refuge in Fort Meyers, Florida, and *Wing,* an aviation documentary which chronicles the history, resurrection, and flight of the only extant example of a Northrup Model N9M "flying wing" aircraft.

FILMS OF THE JAPANESE INTERNMENT
Prologue

The United States involvement in World War II began on the morning of December 7, 1941. The news reached North America by radio:

The Japanese have this morning launched a massive bombing attack on our naval installation at Pearl Harbor—seven battleships sunk or destroyed, 1200 servicemen dead.

The attack came even as Japan's Ambassador Kichisaburo Nomura was meeting in Washington with Secretary of State Cordell Hull, ostensibly seeking to negotiate a peaceful settlement to the differences between the two nations, yet it was quite evident that Nomura had known that the attack was to take place. This duplicity, together with the harrowing scenes of destruction at Pearl Harbor, inflamed many Americans into hate and distrust of anything Japanese, not just of that nation's leaders but everyone of Japanese descent or appearance.

Fifty Years of Immigration

On the West Coast, particularly in California with its large population of people with Japanese heritage, this animus found fertile ground in which to grow. Japanese immigration had begun before the turn of the nineteenth century, and by 1908 135,000 Japanese had arrived, most as laborers or farmers. Many Japanese farmers settled on land that white farmers had spurned as unworkable, but by dint of great effort and determination the Japanese had turned it into productive land, often out-producing the whites. In 1940 the average value per acre for all farms in Washington, Oregon, and California was $37.94; for Japanese farms the figure was $279.

Despite their substantial presence in California and other areas of the United States, Japanese Americans prior to World War II were almost never featured in news stories, movies, or other media, except for occasional villainous roles. Fortunately, a number of home movies taken by some early Japanese settlers in this country have been collected and restored by Robert A. Nakamura, a Los Angeles filmmaker. The collection is available on a 31-minute videotape produced by Karen L. Ishizuka, Senior Curator of the Japanese American Museum in Los Angeles, and narrated by George Takei. Ishizuka wrote the following descriptions of these film makers:

Setsuo Aratani immigrated to San Francisco in the early 1900s at age 22 and farmed in Santa Maria. He became one of the first to pack vegetables in ice and ship them to neighboring states by train. Aratani bought his first movie camera from a traveling salesman in the mid 1920s. From that time on he enjoyed filming what meant most to him—his family, his business, and his love of sports. His films include footage of the Keio University baseball and judo teams in action.

Naokichi Hashizume made his living as a gardener but at heart he was an artist. When the first amateur movie camera became available to the public, Hashizume embraced the new art form with enthusiasm. Now he could use his creativity to make moving pictures to send back to Japan to show what life in America was like. He filmed his family and friends as well as the streets and scenes of his adopted city of Los Angeles. His films reveal a delightful suburban family, with pretty, laughing children dancing, eating ice cream, and mugging for the camera.

Hiromi Inouye ran a small dry cleaning business in Los Angeles. However in the growing Japanese American community he was better known as a favorite teacher at the Japanese Language School. Inouye taught hundreds of second generation Japanese Americans the language of their parents—and with the language, the values and essence of the Japanese immigrant world. Inouye also caught a rare visit of Japanese royalty.

Masahachi Nakata was an adventurous and intrepid entrepreneur. He mined for gold in Alaska, pioneered the frozen pea business, and ventured into oyster seeding before beginning his successful lumber exporting business. His collection, dating back to 1925, is among the earliest home movies. He made films of his family. He also filmed a documentary of the burgeoning economy of the Pacific Northwest. This is a remarkable film for its excellent scenes of a sawmill operation, from the lumberjacks poling the logs in the millpond to the loading of the finished timbers. Among his other documentaries are a 1920 Independence Day parade in Seattle, fishing for sea urchins, and a seaside clam roast.

Kurakichi Nishikawa and his wife Yone were sharecroppers. Following the enactment of the Alien Land Law of 1913 in California, Japanese immigrants were forbidden to purchase land, so the Nishikawas worked land that belonged to others and made it prosper. In 1935 their harvest yielded an unprecedented 2,000 bags of onions per day. Proud of their hard work and accomplishments, Nishikawa had this film taken to send to their oldest daughter who was in Japan. The backbreaking work of harvesting acres of onions by hand is well documented.

Reverend Sensho Sasaki was a 25th-generation Jodo Shinsu Buddhist priest. Sasaki was an avid home movie buff who approached his hobby with the passion and care of a professional. Because he served throughout California and Washington for almost half a century, he was in a key position to document the growing Japanese American community from the 1920s until his death in 1972. Sasaki's films of football and baseball games and a wedding are among the most carefully filmed of the collection.

George Keiichiro Sayano came to America in 1920 at the age of 16. He worked at and then owned the Nanka Seimen Company in Little Tokyo, Los Angeles. Sayano was a serious amateur photographer who even showed his work publicly. Like most fathers, he bought his first movie camera to record his growing children. His home movies reflect the affection and warmth he felt for his family, friends, and community.

Back to 1942

As Japanese forces swept through the Pacific, capturing Guam, Hong Kong, Manila, and Singapore, fears mounted of a possible invasion attempt on the West Coast. U.S. military reaction was to propose evacuation of all Japanese from "strategic areas" such as airports, naval bases, and power plants. Finally on February 19, 1942, President Roosevelt signed Executive Order No. 9066, giving the military the authority to remove enemy aliens and anyone else suspected of disloyalty. On March 2, Lieutenant General John L. DeWitt, Commander of the Western Defense, announced that all Japanese, regardless of citizenship, would be evacuated from the entire West Coast and placed in relocation centers, or internment camps.

Ten permanent internment camps were established, two each in California, Arizona, and Arkansas, and one each in Idaho, Wyoming, Utah, and Colorado. The Canadian government also succumbed to xenophobia and relocated 26,000 of its citizens.

Thus began the story of one of the most incredibly flagrant violations of the civil rights of Ameri-

can citizens, second only to the treatment of African Americans. Within the next three months more than 120,000 men, women, and children were uprooted from their homes and shipped off to hastily built camps, almost all located in areas of miserable climate. For the next four years that is where they lived—in America's gulags, surrounded by barbed wire, the bounds patrolled by armed soldiers with orders to shoot anyone attempting to escape.

While not all camps were the same, a description of Manzanar, in the high desert of astern California may suffice. Manzanar was modeled after an Army base designed to house single men. It was one mile square and contained 856 barracks made of wood and tarpaper, each 20 feet wide and 120 feet long. Each barrack was divided into "rooms" 16 feet by 20 feet, supposedly to accommodate a family of up to eight, but in many cases total strangers were forced into this intimacy. Each room was furnished with one hanging bulb, an oil stove, one cot, a mattress, and two blankets per person. Food preparation and sanitary facilities were equally primitive, and bouts of sickness were common.

A remarkable record of this disgraceful saga exists, thanks largely to the efforts of Karen L. Ishizuka and her husband, Robert A. Nakamura, an accomplished filmmaker. Together they located and collected many feet of home movies taken by inmates of the camps. From this collection they have produced a 40-minute video entitled *Something Strong Within*.[19]

The films cover at least five of the camps. One might expect to find in them some documentation of the deplorable living conditions. But such scenes are almost totally absent, aside from some vivid footage of bitter winter storms buffeting the inmates. Even that circumstance had its lighter moments as young men and women gleefully pelted each other with snowballs. There are many scenes of the work it took to live—women preparing food, washing dishes, and sewing clothes, and men and women chopping firewood and carrying water. There are many scenes of recreation—baseball games, judo matches, Boy Scout parades, and even art classes. Through it all, whether at work or play, everyone looks cheerful and smiling, as if life were wonderful. One is also impressed at how neat and carefully dressed are both men and women. How the women kept so fresh looking is a mystery, yet their appearance must have contributed greatly to the general morale. Some comments from Dave Tatsuno, a home movie maker, are very revealing:

Despite the loneliness and despair that enveloped us, we made the best we could with the situation. I hope when you look at these you see the spirit of the people; people trying to reconstruct a community despite overwhelming obstacles. This, I feel, is the essence of these home movies.

Epilogue

In January 1945 the United States Supreme Court ruled that the detention camps were unconstitutional. By the end of that year most internees had been released. A scattering of groups urged some form of compensation, including the American Friends Service Committee, the American Civil Liberties Union, the American Socialist Party, and the Workers Defense League. In 1948 President Truman signed the Japanese Evacuation Claims Act, but a relatively trifling amount has been paid to date. Manzanar became a National Park Service Historic Site in 1992, with a plaque and two or three small structures standing forlornly in the desert.

A Happier Documentary

A very different documentary of life in the United States filmed by a Japanese has been described by Dr. Jeffrey Ruoff in his paper "Forty Days Across America—Kiyooka Eiichi's 1927 Travelogues." Kiyooka was a young Japanese of good family who had been sent to the United States to study. Upon graduation from Cornell University, he purchased a Ciné-Kokak and a Model T Ford and with two friends set out for California, filming their adventures as they crossed the country.[20]

MOST NOTABLE AMATEUR FILM EVER MADE?

Over the 75 years that amateurs had access to a motion picture camera, a few remarkable films have been made documenting an historic event that was unattended by a professional. Undoubtedly the most historically significant amateur film footage ever made was the 26 seconds of 8mm film that captured the assassination of President John F. Kennedy on November 22, 1963.

Many thousands of words have been written about that fateful day in Dallas, but only one worker has researched and documented every photographic record that is known to have been made—that is

Fig 317. Bell & Howell 414PD.

author and archivist Richard B. Trask whose 1994 book, *Pictures of the Pain—Photography and the Assassination of President Kennedy,* has been one of my principal sources for the account that follows.

On that sunny November morning, the President had flown to Dallas to speak at a luncheon at the Trade Mart. Hundreds of friendly Texans lined the route that the Presidential motorcade would take from the airport through downtown Dallas. Among the spectators at Dealey Plaza was Abraham Zapruder, a Russian-born clothing manufacturer who had brought along his Bell & Howell 414PD 8mm movie camera (Fig. 317). The Director Duo Power Zoom 414PD, to give it its full name, was one of the better new 8mm cameras that Bell & Howell had introduced the previous year. It featured fully automatic exposure control with dual electric eye, a 9-27mm power zoom f1.8 Varimat lens with wide-angle and telephoto control buttons on top of the camera, and single-frame, normal and slow motion camera speeds.

Zapruder's camera was loaded with Kodachrome II. The first 25 feet of the spool had been exposed a few days earlier and the spool turned over. A careful man, Zapruder tested the camera by filming a few seconds of his receptionist, who was standing nearby. Then as the first sounds of the approaching motorcade reached Zapruder he climbed up on a nearby concrete pedestal that gave him an excellent view over the "grassy knoll" that would figure so largely in the "conspiracy theories" that arose after the assassination.

When the lead motorcycles of the Dallas Police came into view, Zapruder, with the zoom lens set at telephoto, aimed the camera at them and ran off about seven seconds of film before he realized that the President was not yet in view. Then as the big blue Lincoln convertible appeared, Zapruder began filming again and did not stop until the terrible action was over. He panned slowly as the limousine bearing the President, Mrs. Kennedy, Texas Gover-

nor John B. Connally and Mrs. Connally passed along Elm Street at about 11 miles per hour. Zapruder, as later examination of the film seemed to indicate, jumped slightly as the first rifle shot echoed through the Plaza. After the second shot, Zapruder recounted later, he saw the President lean over and grab himself. For a moment Zapruder thought he was playing. Then came the third and final shot; Zapruder described it this way:

I saw his head open up and blood and everything came out . . . then I started yelling, they killed him, they killed him . . . and I was still shooting the pictures until

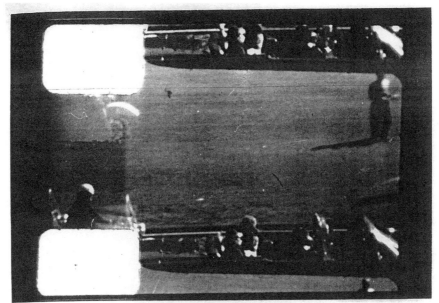

ZAPRUDER FILM—FRAME 327

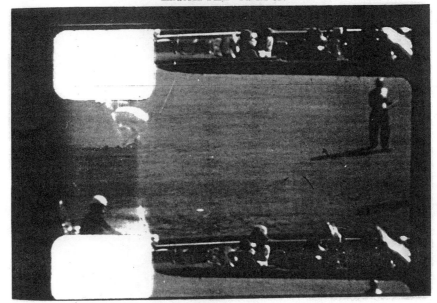

ZAPRUDER FILM—FRAME 328

Fig. 318. Frames 327 and 328 of the Zapruder film.

he got under the underpass . . . I don't even know how I did it. (See Fig. 318.)

When Zapruder stopped filming, 26 seconds had elapsed, 476 frames of Kodachrome II film had been exposed, and the most complete photographic record of that terrible event had been made. Every one of those 476 frames was destined to be examined and re-examined by hundreds of people.

What Happened To The Zapruder Film

As the President's limousine sped off to Parkland Hospital, Zapruder hurried back to his office, still crying, "They killed him. They killed him." Back in the office Zapruder locked the camera in the office safe, refused demands by Dallas police to turn over the film, and had his secretary call the Sheriff and the Secret Service. Shortly, Forrest Sorrels, Agent in Charge of the Dallas Office of the Secret Service arrived along with a reporter for the *Dallas Morning News*. Sorrels asked if they could view the film, to which Zapruder agreed, and the search began for a lab to process the film. The *Dallas Morning News* lab could not do it, nor could its television lab because those labs were equipped only for Ektachrome film. Finally a call to Eastman Kodak's Dallas lab produced an affirmative answer.

After the film was processed, it was projected while in the 16mm format, to check for any processing problems, of which there were none. At this point Zapruder asked for duplicates. The lab people explained that the film could only be duplicated if kept in the 16mm format and printed on Kodachrome Duplicating Film, but none of this film in the double-8 perforation form was on hand. The solution was to give Zapruder his original film plus three rolls of unexposed Type A film and direct him to the Jamieson Film Company, a custom lab in Dallas. At Jamieson, while Zapruder watched, three duplicates of the original film were made. Zapruder took his original and the three exposed but undeveloped rolls back to the Kodak lab where they were processed and slit. About 15 members of the Kodak lab watched as a print was projected. Zapruder noticed that he jumped slightly when the shots were heard.

Zapruder gave two of the copies to Agent Sorrels with the understanding that they were for official use only and were not to be given to the media. Sorrels flew one copy to Washington for further duplication.

One of the first national news media representatives to contact Zapruder was the Los Angeles regional editor for *Life* magazine, Richard B. Stolley. Stolley quickly discovered that while Zapruder was still very upset by what he had seen and filmed, he was fully aware of the film's potential value to him and his family, and that he was determined to get as much for it as possible. The result was that Zapruder was offered and accepted (after some negotiation) $50,000 for the print rights only. Stolley left for Time/Life's offices in Chicago with the original and one copy of the film. When *Life* magazine's top management saw the film they quickly decided that it must at least attempt to purchase all rights to it, and Stolley was sent back to Dallas to negotiate with Zapruder.

Monday morning found Zapruder, Stolley, and Sam Passman, Zapruder's lawyer, closeted in Passman's office. After four hours of gentlemanly negotiation a deal was struck. In essence the agreement called for Zapruder to sell his original and his one remaining first-generation copy of the film, together with all of his rights, title, and interest, whether domestic, foreign, newsreel, television, motion picture or otherwise. For this Zapruder or his heirs would receive $150,000, paid in six $25,000 installments over five years. Included in the agreement was wording in which Time, Inc., agreed to "present said film to the public in a manner consonant with good taste and dignity."

With this prize in their pocket the editors of *Life* literally stopped the presses on the November issue, tearing apart thousands of already printed copies to insert a total of 37 pages of photographs, essays, and editorial comment relating to the Dallas story. Included were the subsequent shooting of Lee Harvey Oswald, Kennedy's assassin, and 31 frames of the Zapruder film. The demand for this issue, which hit the newsstands on November 26, 1963, was the greatest in the magazine's history.

On November 29 President Johnson issued an executive order creating a special commission to investigate the assassination of President Kennedy. U.S. Supreme Court Justice Earl Warren was named chairman. Included in the mass of data submitted to the commission was the Zapruder film, although not the original nor even a first generation copy. Later the chief of *Life*'s photographic laboratory projected the original for the Commission and then provided the Commission with 35mm transparencies of frames 171 through 334 from the original. These proved to be clearer and to give more detail than the second or subsequent generation films.

Film archivists will shudder at *Pictures of the Pain* author Richard Trask's description of the insults to which the priceless original film was subjected after it left Zapruder's camera. When the Warren Commission report was made public it was discovered that the original film had been broken. A poorly done splice had been made, spoiling adjacent frames, so that a total of a total of six frames were damaged or missing, fortunately none in the critical areas. It was also discovered that during *Life*'s possession, the cardinal rule of film archiving had been frequently ignored, in permitting the original to be used for viewing rather than a copy.

After the Commission report became available in September 1964, a number of people examined copies of the film and came forward with wildly conflicting theories of who had fired the shots, where they had come from, how many there were, and so on. *Life* came under severe criticism for its virtual sequestering of the film and eventually decided to divest itself of the problem. At first they considered donating the film to the National Archives. However, that was impossible under the terms of the 1963 agreement with Zapruder, who had died in 1970. The arrangement that was finally agreed to was to transfer the original film and its copyright to Abraham Zapruder's heirs—daughter Myrna Hauser, son Henry Zapruder, and widow Lillian. Later, at the request of the family, the National Archive provided "courtesy storage" of the film, although no public access was permitted.

In August 1997 following three public hearings, the Government, under the provisions of the 1992 John F. Kennedy Assassination Records Collection Act, took possession of the Zapruder film. Compensation to Zapruder's heirs was to be established by August 1, 1998. The Government's offers did not meet the Zapruder family's demands of $18 million, so both parties agreed to mandatory arbitration to be completed by June 1999, with a ceiling of $30 million.

Missing the June deadline, the panel of three arbitrators noted that putting a value on the film "proved most difficult." In the end, the majority of the panel settled on a value of $16 million for the film, not including the copyright, which remained with the Zapruder family.[21] The arbitrators' decision was reached on July 19, 1999, but was not announced until August 3, out of sensitivity for the Kennedy family in view of the accidental death of John F. Kennedy Jr. just three days before.

What Happened to the Zapruder Camera?

Zapruder once remarked that after the shooting he could not even pick up the camera without an emotional reaction, yet when Bell & Howell suggested that they would like the camera for their archives and offered to exchange it for a new model, he accepted and turned it over to them.

The camera itself did not attract the attention of the FBI until December 1993, when they realized that to use the film for accurate time/distance analysis it was necessary to know the running speed of the camera. The camera was borrowed from Bell & Howell. A series of tests showed the camera speed, while varying slightly over a 60-second run, held very closely to 18.3 frames per second over the 26-second run of Zapruder's film. The camera was returned to Bell & Howell, who kept it for a few years then, prompted by the contentions of one particularly vociferous "conspiracy theorist," Harold Weisberg, ran tests of its own. Peter G. Peterson, President of Bell & Howell at the time, stated "Our tests would appear to corroborate the FBI testimony before the Warren commission that the average speed at which the film passed through the camera was at 18.3 fps." Bell & Howell turned the camera over to the National Archives on December 7, 1966.[22]

The Warren Commission Report did little to satisfy the public's curiosity about the whole tragic affair, nor did it quiet the suspicions of the many un-official investigators who were extremely suspicious of every government agency involved in the investigation of the assassination. After years of clamor for release of the records of these various agencies, Congress passed the JFK Assassination Records Collection Act of 1992 mentioned above, mandating the gathering and opening of all records concerned with the death of the President. Congress also established the Assassination Records Review Board (ARRB), whose purpose was to re-examine for release the records that the agencies still regarded as too sensitive to be open to the public. The Act also

Fig. 319. Roland J. Zavada.

required all government agencies to search for such records in their possession and place them in the National Archives. There are now more than four million pages of records open to the public on the subject.

In 1996 the ARRB asked for the cooperation of Eastman Kodak Company in a study of the photographic evidence and initiated the first known authenticity study of the Zapruder film. A major objective of this study was to investigate the so-called "anomalies" present on the Zapruder film. Roland J. Zavada (Fig. 319), retired Standards Director for Imaging Technologies, Eastman Kodak Company, was asked to assist in this study because of his extensive experience as a product engineer on reversal

motion picture film and the fact that he was a member of the teams that developed the Super 8 system. After an approximately one-year study, his report was submitted to the ARRB on September 24, 1998. It is from that report that most of the following account has been prepared.

To determine the precise cause of the anomalies, Zavada sought and received the cooperation of many Bell & Howell engineers who had shared in the design of the Director Series cameras. Zavada then literally dissected several 414PDs and studied every element of the camera's design, including optical system, exposure control, film transport, film gate, and spring motor drive.

The Bell & Howell 414PD camera, in common with most 8mm cameras, advances the film by means of a claw that moves through a cutout slot in the film gate adjacent to the image-forming aperture area, to engage the sprocket holes in the film (Fig. 320). Under certain circumstances of camera and lens design, light from part of the scene being photographed will reach the film area between the perforations through this slot and, consequently, expose an image in this area, beyond the normal frame area. This image, however, can be considerably modified by other camera-generated phenomena, causing the image in this area to look quite different from the primary image area.

These "anomalies" were what led some examiners of the film to conclude that the film had been tampered with. Zavada ultimately determined that there were five different image anomalies present

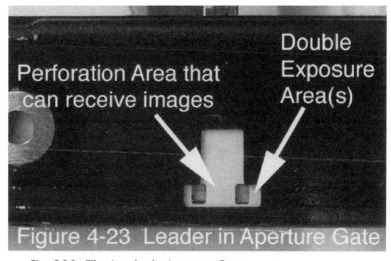

Fig. 320. Film Leader in Aperture Gate.

in the Zapruder film, as follows:

1. Claw shadow. This is a darker area in the image between the perforations, caused by the claw traveling upwards during the exposure time, thus cutting off some light in that area. This is clearly seen in Fig. 318—the dark rectangular area between the perforations.

2. Conversely, on occasion light reflected off the claw may cause a light streak between the perforations in the perforation area. This phenomenon is slightly visible in Fig. 318 as a light streak just above the inner edge of the bottom perforation.

3. Multiple exposure areas. Because the cut-out area for the pull-down claw is longer than the distance between perforations, the area immediately above and below the perforation is exposed twice. These appear as images between the perforations and occur because the *exit window* of the Varimat lens, i.e. the area imaged by the lens, at the telephoto setting is sufficiently large to cover the perforation area of the film.

4. Ghost images. These turn out to be images of real objects that were exposed twice because of the conditions mentioned above. A "ghost image" of the motorcycle policeman is visible in Fig. 318.

5. First frame overexposure. This appears to be a relatively minor problem occasionally found in 8mm cameras from various manufacturers.

Zavada's exhaustive analysis demonstrated beyond a reasonable doubt that all of the "image anomalies," thought in some quarters to be evidence of image tampering, were clearly the result of the image capture (optical and mechanical) characteristics of the Zapruder camera.

It is difficult to appreciate just how remarkable Zapruder's performance was—to keep filming as that dreadful sequence unrolled before his eyes. Even if we have seen the film, we are too far removed from the reality of what it must have been like to have been behind the camera. One seasoned professional there on assignment froze at the critical moment and did not capture the fatal shot. Five other amateurs with movie cameras and two professional movie cameramen were known to have been present, yet none of their results came remotely close to providing the information that is contained in Zapruder's film. And still the film has not closed the door on speculation. Ironically, Richard Trask, the man who has studied the total photographic evidence as perhaps no other individual has, closes his chapter on Zapruder with the revelation that the film has not shown him "exactly what happened or who did it."

LOOKING BACK
What Were "Home Movies" Really Like?

When Hiram Percy Maxim wrote the first editorial in the first issue of the journal of the Amateur Cinema League in December 1926, he envisioned amateur cinematography becoming:

> . . . a means of communicating a new form of knowledge to our fellow beings, be they where they may upon the earth's surface. An amateur cinematographer in the tropics may convey to an amateur in a cold country precisely what life in the tropics is, and convey to him exact knowledge that is not only vital, but cannot possibly be conveyed in any other way. The professional cinema cannot do this in the perfect way that the amateur cinema can. Professional pictures must appeal to mass interest and mass interest does not always embrace the things that ought to be known. On the other hand, the amateur has no necessity for appealing to mass interest. He is free to reproduce and record any action his fancy or the fancy of a friend may dictate.

Maxim went on to state that such "great possibilities" could not be realized without organization, as in the Amateur Cinema League, whereupon: "Organization will place the cinema amateurs of the world in communication with each other at once, and all that the entire world possesses is available to each one of us."[23]

To what extent Maxim's lofty vision has materialized over the past three-quarters of a century is debatable, but a remarkable collection of essays written in 1986 offers some insight. In that year, Toni Treadway, director of a special project of The International Center for 8mm Film and Video (as it was then known) asked ten Super 8 filmmakers from the United States and several foreign countries to write a brief statement on the situation of Super 8 in their country at that time. With the aid of a grant from the Massachusetts Council on the Arts and Humanities, the essays were collected and published in a monograph entitled *Foreign Correspondence—The International Super 8 Phenomenon*.[24]

It should be understood that by 1986 Super 8 was swiftly being displaced by the video camera for the average "home movie" maker, but was still the medium of choice for the distinctly different amateurs who thought of themselves as "independent film makers."

One theme is common in almost all the essays. In a remarkable echo of Maxim's 1926 editorial, the 1985 essayists stressed the freedom the amateur filmmaker (Super 8 user) enjoyed compared to the commercial filmmaker. This included the total control of subject matter and execution, plus having no need to appeal to a wide audience. There was also agreement that the independent Super 8 filmmaker was best equipped to tell truths about his country that would otherwise be ignored or suppressed by the professional.

A somewhat related theme was expressed in several essays—the independent's view of the establishment (i.e. commercial filmmakers, the professional media, etc.) as the enemy, or at least something evil. Willie Varela, a self-taught independent from Texas said "Super 8 provides the greatest potential for talking back to the media." James Irwin, a writer and film artist in San Francisco, warned that "technology is initiated by businessmen out to make a profit, designed by technicians earning wages, and purchased by consumers who were not consulted in the design." Just what threat this posed to the independent is not made clear, nor what Irwin would have done for a camera if it weren't for those "businessmen and technicians." Alfonso Dagron of Bolivia lamented that when "industry" discovered cinema, it lost its freedom by conforming to commercial interests.

The anthropologist Richard Chalfen, in his 1975 paper "Cinema Naïveté: A Study of Home Moviemaking as Visual Communication," [25] states as the objective of the essay, "to show that a particular arrangement that would otherwise be ignored or suppressed by commercial filmmakers" of "events" and "components" distinguish and isolate a unique genre of film called "home movies." To accomplish this objective, Chalfen consulted an unspecified number of "How To" manuals, viewed some 9,000 feet of films shown in the homes of the filmmakers, and interviewed 40 home movie viewers.

To begin, Chalfen posits that all home movies can be put in five categories. But then actually describes just three categories of home movies and two uses of home movies. The three categories he lists are in his words:

1) the "artistic" home movies produced by members of the New American Cinema, which may be understood as a kind of Dadaist reaction to Hollywood and to stereotypic Hollywood film products; 2) native-generated films such as Worth and Adair's Navaho-made films (1972) or Chalfen's socio-documentary films made by groups of Philadelphia teenagers (1974); and 3) home movies made mostly by middle-class amateurs for family use only.

The other two categories he suggests are the use of actual home movie footage in commercial films and the use of home movie style in commercial films, such as in *Up the Sandbox,* filmed in 1972. The rest of Chalfen's article consists of an analysis of a selection of films falling in category 3 above.

Chalfen's conclusions were, first, that hardly any of his observed filmmakers paid any attention at all to the warnings, prescriptions, and directions set forth in the "How To" manuals. His other conclusions, as nearly as can be determined from the academic jargon, were: 1) most home movies picture the same set of circumstances and cast of characters; 2) most home movie makers do not exploit the full capability of their equipment, or as he puts it: "de-emphasize the manipulative potential of the recording technology," and c) home movies do not document a reality of everyday life—commonplace behavior, mundane activities, and everyday happenings do not get recorded. The latter statement is particularly difficult to understand, since the very banality of the average home movie is supposed by many to be its most defining characteristic.

The general tenor of Chalfen's conclusions, coupled with his characterization of the category that he selected, would suggest that he saw no films by serious amateurs such as described earlier in this chapter.

In the fall of 1986, possibly the first group discussion of home movies and amateur filmmaking was organized by Patricia Erens, who was at that time Associate Professor in the Department of Communication Arts and Sciences at Rosary College, River Forest, Illinois, and editor of the *Journal of Film and Video,* the quarterly journal of the University Film and Video Association. Professor Erens called upon

11 scholars of various disciplines in the field to submit their ruminations on, and assessments of, home movies for inclusion in a special issue of the *Journal*.[26]

Included were three independent filmmakers, seven identified as professors of film, communications or video art, one professor of anthropology, and one retired engineer (myself). My assignment was to briefly describe the development of amateur motion picture equipment.

Professor Erens evidently gave the invitees considerable liberty of approach to the subject, with the result that it is nearly impossible to summarize their findings. In the belief that this seminal examination of the structure and significance of home movies is pertinent to the purposes of this book, a précis of each contribution is presented as follows:

Michelle Citron, then Associate Professor in the Department of Radio-Television-Film at Northeastern University in Boston, chose to describe her inheritance and examination of a large collection of family home movies filmed by her father some 25 years earlier. Using slow motion projection and step-printing to duplicate and repeat film sequences, Citron discovered hitherto unobserved expressions of emotion and feelings between family members, including anger, hostility, frustration, and love. Citron notes that her father, as well as filming birthday parties and other festive events, also filmed private domestic moments—cleaning house, cooking, and doing dishes. This illustrates one contradiction to Chalfen's comment on "mundane behavior" noted above.

One independent filmmaker, Lance Bird of Five Points, Indiana, in the process of making his documentary *The World of Tomorrow* (1984), discovered that there existed hundreds of amateur film clubs. On being invited to attend a meeting of one such club, he was amazed to discover the generally high quality of the members' films as well as the dedication of these amateurs to making good films. One film in particular stood out for exceptional cinematographic skill. The filmmaker was a New York City bus driver, known only to us as Ray, and his film was about the 1939 World's Fair. Ray had made the 45-minute, 16mm color film over the period of two years that the Fair was open. Working strictly as an unauthorized amateur, paying admission each time he visited the Fair, often ducking or bribing guards,

Ray laboriously sought out the best vantage point from which to shoot each attraction. During evenings at home, he edited his shots and worked out a sound accompaniment using recorded vintage music of the 1920s and a twin turntable set-up, cueing in as many as 25 or 30 sound "bites," including the memorable melody "Sidewalks of New York" which the Fair vehicles played in lieu of horns. Later on, Ray invested in a sound projector that permitted him to record his musical accompaniment onto sound-striped film.

Bird states that he was never able to persuade Ray to let him use Ray's film in Bird's documentary, nor even to permit it to be shown on TV. Sadly, the ultimate fate of this classic is unknown.

Fred Camper, another independent filmmaker and writer on film, took as the primary goal of his article the assertion of the need of an archive of home movies in which all types and manner of home movies would be collected and preserved, where scholars could go about the work of studying and evaluation. Among Camper's other observations were that the frequency of interaction between subject and camera, and the technical gaffes that the amateur is prone to, tend to destroy the "illusionist grip" on the audience that professional films usually achieve.

Camper also noted that the widening popularity of home video will eventually drive out the *film* home movie, largely because of the forced time formulation of the 3-minute roll of film. Camper closed his piece with this paragraph:

The home movie is a form of cinema unlike any other. Its varied forms have different effects and implications than the narrative feature, the documentary, and the commercial travelogue. Its presence in our culture has been strong since the 1930s and pervasive in recent decades. Film historians should cease their worship of commercial narrative and open their eyes to "see" all the varieties of our medium.

Richard Chalfen contributed two papers. The first was entitled "Media Myopia and Genre-Centrism: The Case of Home Movies." Its purpose was "to clarify the social and cultural values that ordinary people put on pictorial products of their own indigenous folk culture." Chalfen studied seven guidebooks and discovered what he had observed before, that most home movie makers ignored the recommendations of the guidebooks. He then selected and quoted two paragraphs from one book[27] and proceeded to deny, ridicule, and contradict every sentence in those two paragraphs. His conclusions—guide books tend to mock naïve movie makers, and authors of guide books want readers to adopt attitudes, techniques, and conventions familiar to professional filmmaking.

Chalfen's second paper is entitled "The Home Movie in a World of Reports—An Anthropological Appreciation," and his introduction is: "My objective here is to comment on the cultural significance of home movies and home movie making as a communicative enterprise." His conclusions are somewhat obscure, but this paragraph near the end of the piece may provide some clues:

It follows, logically, that ordered collections of home mode imagery are repeatedly telling the same "stories" according to some master scenario. The metaphoric use of "story" is based on the pictorial rendering and unfolding of an interpretation of experienced daily life and a "punctuation" of special experiences. In both literal and figurative senses, we may now speculate on the existence of a visual narrative style, developed to deliver culturally significant tales and myths about ourselves to ourselves.

Chuck Kleinhans is presently Director of Graduate Studies, Radio/Television/Film at Northwestern University in Evanston, Illinois, with professional experience in Super 8 and 1/2-inch VHS video. For his essay, "Aunt Alice's Home Movies," he reviewed a sizeable collection of home movies and videos made by his aunt over a period of more than 30 years. Stating at the outset his possible bias, he observed that his aunt was at times a typical "snapshooter" and at other times a talented filmmaker who strove for originality. Admitting that many of her films were typical family record films that would interest only those who could share in recognition of the individuals and locales shown in the films, Kleinhans discovered at least two films that broke away from the "home movie" cliché. One of these was *Christmas 1953* a film that begins conventionally enough with Alice hanging decorations but soon segues into a fantasy in which Santa appears and dolls and other toys come to life. Reality returns with Dad reading a Christmas story. *Return of the Jetai* (August 1981), filmed in Super 8 with synch sound, was produced by Alice, with the family children taking the roles of the characters in the Star Wars film and supplying the "hardware" (Star Wars toys). Not having seen the film, Alice's title was her transliteration of the children's pronunciation of Jedi. Kleinhans attributes the charm of this film to the contrast between the elaborate special effects and lavish production values of the original film with the obvious fun and satisfaction that the children had in making do with what was available.

Kleinhans uses this film to challenge the notion held by "many intellectuals and social commentators" (his words) that the products of mass culture somehow limit the imagination and creativeness of the amateur filmmaker. The essay concludes with a brief section entitled "Women's Hobby Art," in which he postulates that as with Aunt Alice, "women are often the historians of domestic space and activity." If he meant that women were often the filmmakers of home movies, such is not born out by the evidence in popular journals. While Marion Gleason has the honor of filming the first 16mm movie, from that day on the popular magazines continually lamented that more women did not get involved in making home movies.

John Kuiper, Director of Film Collections at George Eastman House in 1986, commented on the lack of data on the history of promotional material for amateur film and equipment produced by the manufacturers during the 1920s. As examples of the desirable materials of this kind, Kuiper cites two films: *Picnic Party*, described in Chapter 4, and *Flowers for Rosie*, shown at the press party when the 16mm system was introduced. A third film, *Fly Low Jack and the Game*, was written and directed by Marion Gleason and filmed by Harris B. Tuttle and Allan H. Mogenson. *Picnic Party* and *Fly Low Jack and the Game* are available for study at the George Eastman House but *Flowers for Rosie* has apparently been lost.

Professor Erens contributed two essays to the monograph. The first consisted of a thoughtful analysis of the Galler Family Movies, taken over a 12-year period—July 21, 1935 to July 21, 1948—in 12 segments. Each segment was taken on the birthday of Jerry Galler, the youngest of the family. Charles Galler, the father, was almost always the filmer, mother Florence was the leading lady, and older sister Dolores was the budding starlet.

Erens notes that the films were remarkably consistent in execution and content. Subjects were almost always aware of the camera and, while the usual "amateur" shortcomings were evident, the level of skill improved over the years. The settings were also consistent—summer at the country home, arrival of the birthday cake, pleasant meals, and other happy occasions.

In summary, the Galler family films epitomized many of the cliches of home movies, such as uneven cinematography and recording of only leisure times, yet they faithfully recorded the ideologies of the times, including gender and generational roles in family life.

Professor Erens' second essay is a brief discussion of how various professional filmmakers have incorporated either genuine home movie footage or pseudo-home movies, i.e. footage shot by professionals with deliberate errors such as jump cuts, over- or under-exposure, erratic camera movement, etc. Such footage is almost always used to evoke some past generally happy, innocent period in a character's life. Erens notes that Martin Scorcese made extensive use of "home movies" in *Raging Bull* (1980).

Maureen Turim, Associate Professor in the Cinema Department of the State University of New York and Binghamton, took as her subject the feminist avant-garde. Not surprisingly, Professor Turim began with Maya Deren and her film *Meshes of the Afternoon* and followed with an analysis of four other films by women. I will not attempt to describe these films except to say that all were filmed by women, were largely about women, and in "avant garde" style, i.e. more unconventional and daring (with nude scenes) than would be found in most home movies, especially those filmed by *pater familias*.

The longest article in Erens' collection was contributed by Patricia R. Zimmermann, then Assistant Professor in the Department of Cinema and Photography at Ithaca College, New York. Professor Zimmermann's essay, "The Amateur, The Avant-Garde, and Ideologies of Art," is best described by her introductory paragraph:

In this essay, I would like to tease out the intersections between commercial filmmaking codes and structures, the avant-garde, notions of the social ideologies of art as both resistance and cooptation, and the accessibility of amateur camera designs. These correspondences and contradictions are significant both theoretically and historically, since they suggest that resistance to aesthetic norms and conventions is not located solely on a formal level, but on the material level of accessibility to the means of media production. This confluence of ideas on the social utility of art within capitalist societies, on alternative filmmaking, and technological access that marginal cinemas—such as amateurism or the avant-garde—weave together a series of discourses at specific historical junctures.

Zimmermann is also the author of the first full-length study of home movies: *Reel Families—A Social History of Amateur Film*, published in 1995. This book, that began as Zimmermann's doctoral dissertation, is an ambitious study of the origins of amateur film and the interaction of this medium with the popular literature on the subject, the film and equipment manufacturers, and professional filmmaking, i.e. Hollywood. In Zimmermann's view, those last-named entities deliberately operated to trivialize home movies, stifling all efforts of the amateur filmmaker to produce anything other than banal family records. The following excerpt from Zimmermann's Preface illustrates the above observation:

From 1897 to 1962 amateur film discourse incrementally relocated amateur filmmaking within a romanticized vision of the bourgeois nuclear family, thereby amputating its more resistant economic and political potential for critique. [28]

CODA

So what were home movies really like? From all of the foregoing it is evident that "home movies" were marvelously varied in content, in execution, and in their significance as social and historical documents. Fortunately, their value has come to be recognized, as witness the number of archives now in existence (See Appendix 1). Doug Hubley, one of the foremost archivists of amateur film, put it this way:

Moving image preservationists are now acting on the fact that finding a place for amateur film is essential for its future as historical documentation. Scholars, archivists, and administrators have started this effort late in amateur film's long history. The reward is in the frames themselves, as the intimate joys, fantasies, and community acts of American life come to life. [29]

Fig. 321. Harry Gross with T. F. "Jack" Naylor.

Rembrandt's Brushes

Quite a few years ago, while attending a symposium on photographic history, the stranger seated next to me inquired as to my field of interest. When I explained that I collected movie cameras, he replied with a barely disguised sneer that he could understand people collecting old masters, but he could not understand why anyone would collect Rembrandt's brushes! Of course my table mate may well have been deliberately trying to get a rise out of me, but his remark does represent the attitude some people have toward motion picture cameras, particularly amateur ones. Curiously, the same people will rhapsodize over a still camera that belonged to Ansel Adams. Yet isn't that precisely equivalent to Rembrandt's brush?

Fortunately, this attitude is changing, with classic professional cameras and some rare amateur equipment regularly commanding four-figure amounts at auction. Collecting motion picture equipment is an interesting, rewarding field because so little has been done compared to collecting of still cameras. Of persons interested in photographic history, perhaps one out of 100 has any interest in motion picture equipment. This means more opportunities for original research, for building an uncommon collection without spending a fortune, and for having less competition for the available collectible pieces.

Why Collect Now?

A good reason for starting a collection now is that many of the people who designed the equipment are still with us and can help document the history behind a particular instrument. In the case of amateur equipment, the situation is particularly critical; many valuable artifacts are being discarded because the general public doesn't recognize their historical importance.

A quality movie camera, even an amateur camera, is a remarkable engineering achievement, considerably more complex than most still cameras. The study of the evolution of movie camera design should appeal to anyone with an engineering or scientific bent. A well-designed movie camera can be aesthetically pleasing: witness the sleek yet functional lines of the Bell & Howell 200T, which won the Society of Motion Picture Art Directors Design Award in 1951, or the gleaming brass and mahogany beauty of a 1909 Moy & Bastie studio camera.

And of course collecting puts you in touch with other collectors scattered around the world, which can lead to some valuable friendships, as well as broadening your outlook. There are camera collectors' societies in several states and provinces, as well as many foreign countries. It is well to join the nearest one to you, not just for the pleasure and value of attending interesting meetings and taking a table at their shows, but also getting your wants known to other people who frequent camera shows, antique stores, flea markets, and so on.

Lastly, some item in your collection might be of great interest to a local film archive. Films in some long-obsolete gauge are of limited value if they cannot be viewed or projected. Your 11mm Vitak or 22mm Edison Home Kinetoscope, if in working condition of course, could prove of great value to the archivist.

Settling on an Objective

Collectors rarely begin their collection with a long-term objective in mind; nor is there any pressing need to establish such an objective at the outset. One begins by picking up an item that appeals for one reason or another, then other pieces with a similar appeal are acquired. Eventually there will come a time when the realization dawns that a lot of unrelated pieces have been accumulated, are taking up exhibit or storage space, and will sooner or later have to be disposed of. When this happens it is time to give some thought to what is the real objective of the collection.

For the history-minded, tracing the evolution of the movie camera from Kircher's magic lantern to a modern Arriflex is one avenue. Others might be collecting one fine example of cameras in every film gauge, following the addition of sound to movies, assembling all the motion picture products of Eastman Kodak or some other manufacturer, and so on. Your collection will be of much greater value and of interest to others if it has a clearly developed theme.

Do not worry if your first chosen objective turns out to be unrealistic. The folly of buying every 8mm camera you can afford will soon become apparent when your collection outgrows your display and/or storage space. Your overgrown collection can be modified and trimmed to retain just the significant items in your new grand plan.

Another advantage to a plan is that it will help you concentrate on learning all you can about your now-defined specialty. It is wise to learn all one can about the field before making any major acquisitions. You don't want to spend a lot of money for a piece and find out later that it is not uncommon and that you have paid too much for it.

Where to Begin?

The history of motion picture technology, most experts agree, begins with the invention of the magic lantern. You may not have considered including magic lanterns and other pre-cinema artifacts in your collection, but such items can add a great deal to its appeal to the general public as well as to fellow collectors.

As your collection and your knowledge grow, unless you are a very unusual person, you are going to become a showman. Half the fun of collecting is showing your collection to others, and if you want people to be interested you must think like a showman or a salesperson. Your display should be eye-catching, and yes, intellectually appealing, not just to another ciné collector, but to persons who may know absolutely nothing about motion picture technology. You should have a "spiel" prepared, so that you can explain your collection in a rational fashion and draw your visitor into your world, so to speak, so that he will feel your enthusiasm and understand why you collect what you do.

Young people in particular who may have little interest in the mechanisms of a motion picture camera or projector will, almost without fail, be enchanted by their first experience of spinning a phenakistoscope. This simple device together with a few magic lantern slides make a painless way to get across the basic phenomena that make motion pictures possible.

Original pre-cinema items are of course relatively rare and expensive; however modern reproductions are readily available at places like museum gift shops and will serve the purpose admirably.[1] These will include thaumatropes, flip books, phenakistoscopes, zoetropes, and possibly other devices. Be on the lookout for modern twentieth century variations of these artifacts that have been produced as children's toys; they may be made by Mattel but they were inspired by Plateau or Reynaud!

Where to Look

Amateur motion picture equipment can appear in many places, now that it is no longer in general use. In his pioneering book *Collecting Photographica,*[2] George Gilbert mentions 18 different venues for discovering photographica, from your own or relatives' attics to photographic fairs.

Examining the record of my collection, I find that most of the pieces were acquired at camera trade shows. Other sources are flea markets, thrift shops, and antique shops. I distinguish between the latter two because the price of a given camera in an antique shop will generally be anywhere from twice to five times the price for an identical camera in a thrift shop.

Those sources account for 75 to 80 percent of my collection. The remainder, consisting largely of my most prized specimens, came from being part of a network. By this I mean that news that the piece was available came from a fellow collector, a dealer, or some total stranger who was referred to me by one of the foregoing, or from one of the several local collecting societies to which I belong.

About Condition

Generally speaking, a camera in poor condition with worn finish and/or missing parts may be worth as little as one-half or less of the same camera in perfect condition. Some collectors spurn anything but cameras in perfect condition. If it is a very rare camera it may be worth having in your collection even if its condition is second-rate. I have more often regretted *not* having bought the rather sad-looking specimen than I regret having bought something less than perfect.

Naturally every collector would like to have every item to be in the finest condition possible, and some do have collections in which every piece is in near-mint condition. How closely one comes to this ideal is primarily a function of the size of one's purse, but it is also a function of time and luck. The time element is obvious—the longer you are at it, the more shows you attend, the greater the odds of finding a rare piece. Luck is when someone walks into a show with just the piece you are looking for, or you persuade your long-suffering spouse to go to one more yard sale with the same result.

The answer to whether or not you should buy a piece in less than perfect condition depends on several factors—rarity of course, the extent of the damage, the possibility of restoration, and your own set of values. You may not have the time or inclination to do repairs, and getting others to do it can be quite expensive. Here there is no substitute for experience. Until you have a good feeling for what is rare and in what condition these rare and important pieces are generally found, it is probably best not to buy pieces with damage or missing parts.

That being said, I must add that *you should never pass up a rare camera because a part or parts are missing!* If you are sure of the identification and the authenticity of the piece, try to get the price down to a level where buying or having the missing part made will still keep your investment within reason. Here again, experience counts. This means going to every trade show that you can and keeping records of what dealers are asking for the model you want. If you can't attend a major auction of ciné equipment, at least buy the catalog so that you will receive the list of prices realized.

The first Edison Home Kinetoscope that I ever saw was at a large New England trade show, and it looked complete and beautiful. I knew what it was, having read about it in the Matthews and Tarkington article in Fielding's *A Technoligical History of Motion Pictures and Television*, listed below under "Guides." The price seemed reasonable and I was ready to buy, until the dealer pointed out that the arc lamp was missing, which explained the modest price. My ardor cooled somewhat, but fortunately some small voice said "Buy it!" and I did.

On the second day of the show I was showing off my prize to a friend, who said "Do you know that so-and-so in the next room has one on his table? It doesn't look as good as yours, but . . ." Before he could finish the sentence I was on my way, and-you guessed it—this one was in poor condition but the arc lamp was intact! So I went home with one complete Edison Home Kinetoscope and some spare parts that later turned out to be very valuable.

About Prices

There is a saying in the front of Jim McKeown's *Price Guide*, known as McKeown's Law, to the effect that the price of an antique camera depends on the mood of the buyer and seller at the time of the transaction. Within limits, there is a lot of truth in this adage. An example of a "mood situation" might be when the show is almost over. The seller has had a slow day and now he would rather knock something off the price than pack the piece again. The other side of the coin is that the buyer may be thinking that there won't be another show for six months, and if he doesn't buy this one he may never see another.

Price guides will not satisfy everyone. Some readers will insist that the values given are too low; others will equally vehemently declare they are all inflated. The McKeowns have arrived at their prices through a painstaking gathering of data supplied by many specialists in the field and through the careful monitoring of world-wide sales and auctions.

Prices asked at tag sales, flea markets, etc., may be greatly below the range shown in McKeown's *Guide* if the seller has no idea what is being offered; it may just as possibly be outrageously higher, also because of ignorance on the part of the seller.

Two other sayings are quoted in the *Guide*. The first says: "If you pass up the chance to buy a camera you really want, you will never have that chance again." The second is: "If you buy a camera because you know you will never have the chance again, a better example of the same camera will be offered to you a week later at a much lower price."

These are of course variations of a sort on Murphy's Law, and we know they are given with tongue firmly planted in cheek. But in my experience the first adage is more often true than the second. I can think of at least a half-dozen important items in my collection that gave me considerable pause when they were offered, partly because of their price but also because I was not sure of their rarity or significance. Fortunately I bit the bullet and bought them. In the 20 years or so since, I have yet to see another example of any of them offered for sale. On the other hand, I can remember only one instance of the second adage being in operation. When it happened, I simply bought the second beauty and eventually sold the first specimen.

Protecting Your Investment

Most amateur cameras and projectors are really quite sturdy. In fact many machines that left the factory 50 or even 75 years ago have come down to us in remarkably good shape. Of course it must be granted that this is often due to the fact that their original owner may have only used them half a dozen times, then put them back in their original cases. There they remained, reasonably protected for all those years.

The above not withstanding, wood, metal, and leather are not indestructible. A relatively short exposure to unfavorable conditions can result in considerable harm. Most of us cannot readily duplicate the ideal conditions that museum curators demand, but that should not discourage anyone from coming as close to archival conditions as possible. Ideal conditions are: humidity kept between 15 and 45 percent; temperature, the cooler the better; and both parameters kept as constant as possible. And of course, protection from fire and theft.

Fortunately these are conditions that also suit most humans, including ciné collectors, so "living quarters conditions" are not bad for your precious wood and leather cameras. The only fly in that ointment is that the collection soon competes for space with the human residents of the home, but that is a problem that all collector must solve for themselves.

To Insure or Not?

You cannot insure your collection against loss due to improper storage conditions but you can insure it against loss from fire or theft. The question remains: should you have such insurance? Insurance can be very expensive and, under certain circumstances, may not be justified. A very few collectors who have extraordinary collections do not insure at all, relying on elaborate security and environmental control systems for protection.

If you are not in that rarefied class, but your collection does include a number of valuable pieces, the insurance company will require an appraisal by a certified appraiser, which can be expensive. To minimize the appraisal fee you might consider having only the most valuable pieces appraised and insured under a special coverage policy or rider, while the remainder of the collection is insured under the personal property coverage of your homeowners policy. Note that the aggregate loss on *all* your personal property is usually limited to 50 percent of your dwelling loss limit, so unless you are living with a huge collection in a one-room shack, you should be all right.

The above comments are mere suggestions; you should consult with your insurance agent for your specific needs.

Exactly What Do I Have?

Do you really know the value of your collection? If you did have a loss, is the inventory shown in your insurance policy up to date? If you needed to know quickly how many 16mm Bell & Howell cameras you have, could you answer without going through a physical check? Could a stranger examining two or three seemingly identical cameras in your showcase find a record that would explain the differences?

If you can't answer yes to all those questions, then you need a carefully constructed inventory of your collection. What constitutes a well-designed inventory depends to a large extent on what uses you may find for the list. Make, model, film gauge, year of manufacture, serial number, lenses, accessories, date purchased, and seller, should be included in any list. Since the first use may be for insurance purposes, the purchase price and estimated value or appraised value are essential. Properly designed, and especially if carried in your computer, the inventory can easily be converted to serve as a sales list. For the latter use, you would probably include more physical description than would be required for insurance purposes.

The list of all the items in your collection, including cameras, projectors, auxiliary lenses, other accessories and attachments, instruction books, manuals, catalogs, etc., is just one part of a workable inventory. The other part is what ties a specific item to a specific entry in the inventory—an identifying mark on the camera or whatever. Small sticky labels can be unobtrusive, especially if placed inside the camera. While you will, of course, have recorded any serial number, it is wise to use an identifying label also; serial numbers, especially on Ciné-Kodaks, are often difficult to find.

Your catalog form should have space for recording any interesting historical data pertaining to the item, such as a famous previous owner, the fact that this model was the same one that Zapruder used to film the assassination of John F. Kennedy in Dallas, how few were made, and so on. If this information is too voluminous it could be placed in a separate record, and so noted on the catalog entry.

Guides to Collecting

The first book on collecting photographica that included motion picture equipment was written by Harry I. Gross of Eugene, Oregon. Entitled *Antique and Classic Cameras*, it was published in 1965 by Amphoto in New York and simultaneously in Toronto by Ambassador Books, Ltd. The book's 192 pages range over every aspect of photography, from the camera obscura to the Kodak Ektra, from daguerreotypes to Land's Polaroid, with good photos on every page. There are, surprisingly, a number of motion picture items shown, including a 1909 Ernemann, the original Ciné Kodak, the Edison Home Kinetoscope, and others.

Obviously the treatment of each item is neccessarily brief and, sad to say, not always accurate. Nevertheless, we owe Harry Gross our thanks, for his book stimulated many others to write about collecting and played a significant role in the growth of interest in collecting photographica (Fig. 321).

Next came *Histoire de la Camera Ciné Amateur*, by Michel Auer and Michèle Ory. This coffee-table-sized book is a detailed history of the evolution of amateur ciné, including sections on pre-cinema, early cinema, and on through 35mm, 16mm, 9.5mm, 8mm, sound, color, and 3D. The text is in French, but the illustrations are self-explanatory. Published in 1979 and now out of print, it may be available through specialty dealers.

Brian Coe, curator of the Kodak Museum at Harrow in England, published *The History of Movie Photography* in 1981. In addition to being an excellent reference book on the history of professional movie photography, it includes a brief but very well illustrated chapter on amateur motion picture history.

Undoubtedly the most complete guide to sub-standard gauge cameras and projectors, magic lanterns, and some optical toys is *Ariel's Cinematographic Register*, in four volumes, published in 1989. The text is all in German, with details of year of manufacture, cost, film gauge, film capacity, lens equipment, exposure controls, motive power, description of camera finish, and so forth. With some practice and the help of an included glossary, the technical details are not difficult to translate. In addition, each camera or projector is shown in a large, clear oblique view, as well as smaller views of the camera shown front, rear, side, and open. Over 1,100 items are covered, including data that will not be found elsewhere.

Well known to still camera collectors is *McKeown's Price Guide to Antique and Classic Cameras*, published by James and Joan McKeown. The *Guide* has for several years now included a section on movie cameras and projectors that, while not a comprehensive coverage of all collectible movie machinery, is at this writing the only price guide for such equipment.

The best history of amateur film gauges is contained in *A Technological History of Motion Pictures and Television*, an anthology of articles from the *Journal of the Society of Motion Picture and Television Engineers*, edited by Professor Raymond Fielding, published by the University of California Press (1967). This invaluable book also includes many excellent articles on the history of motion picture technology, many authored by the pioneers themselves.

An authoritative history of pre-cinema and cinema is a slender volume entitled *Dates and Sources*, by Franz Paul Liesegang, translated and edited by Herman Hecht and published by the Magic Lantern Society of Great Britain in 1986. This is a chronological account with illustrations of the inventions and their improvements that led to modern motion picture technology, from Kircher's 1646 book *Ars Magna Lucis et Umbrae* to a 1922 entry for "Talking Pictures." The entries are brief but, as the title of the book indicates, original literature sources are given, for the infinite benefit of the serious researcher.

And Don't Forget Film

You are almost bound to come across, or be offered, film as you search for movie equipment—cans of 16mm home movies from the 1920s and 30s, reels of 8mm commercially produced "shorts," or even big 1,000 foot cans of 35mm prints. Should you buy? Beware of the latter—the films may be nitrate, not something to be casual about. However, you might just have something really special, as I did one time—nine reels of *The Redman*, a 1929 film that the George Eastman House was delighted to get, and I was delighted to get out of my garage.

On the other hand, 16mm films are safe to have around and can be very informative and entertaining, even if you have no idea of who the people are in the film. The 16mm films taken in the 1920s are quite apt to be fascinating glimpses into lives of the well-to-do, the people that could afford the 16mm system at that time. At the other end of the social spectrum, 8mm home movies also can make worthwhile viewing. While the filming may not be as expert, the subjects may be more down to earth and the acting more spontaneous.

If you have no interest in keeping a film that comes your way, but the subject matter of the film is interesting and the film itself appears to be well made, you might want to consider donating it to one of the many film archives that do collect amateur gauge films within their field of interest. See Appendix 1 for a listing of such archives.

The Last Word

Amassing a significant collection of historic photographic equipment or photographs is somewhat akin to taking a journey. Earlier in this chapter we talked about the desirability of making plans for the journey by having an objective, intended to give guidance along the way. As every human journey has an ending, a plan for that part of the journey is just as necessary as the plan for the beginning and may even be more difficult to formulate. Briefly, it must answer the question: "What is to be done with my collection when I am gone?"

If you have not made a decision on that question and communicated it to your heirs, you may be leaving them with a serious and vexing problem—unless of course someone in the family is ready and willing to take on the collection, understands its value, and is prepared to give it the attention that it will require. Curiously, this willingness does not seem to happen very often, particularly with specialized collections such as technological artifacts.

Your family will undoubtedly try to do what they think you might have wanted, such as keeping the collection intact, possibly to be sold to a museum, for example. They will soon discover that very few museums have an interest in this kind of material, even as a gift. This is not to say that some small regional museum or historical society would not be grateful for a donation of some pieces that were manufactured locally, or used by some famous native son, or had other local significance.

If your collection was a sizeable one with a number of very desirable pieces, your passing will not escape the notice of the collecting fraternity, including dealers, who will soon be calling on the family to inquire about purchasing a part or all of the collection. The latter not very likely. Most dealers will only be interested in the major pieces that can be re-sold quickly. They will be reluctant to take on a lot of smaller pieces for which the demand is limited and their profit necessarily small. If your heirs insist on an all-or-nothing sale, the dealer will heavily discount the less desirable items.

The highest return can probably be realized by selling the collection through the mail, but this is the method that will take the most time and effort. It assumes that you have left an inventory that includes an estimated market value for each piece, and that your heirs are willing to write the advertisements, answer the resulting inquiries, and pack and ship the goods—not a scheme to be undertaken lightly.

A much simpler and faster method which I have seen used successfully is to have your heirs arrange with your own collecting society to conduct an auction of your collection for a pre-agreed commission. This presupposes that the auction will be well publicized and be held in or near a major metropolitan area to attract the largest audience possible. This method has the advantage of benefiting your society with a donation, which should be tax-deductible.

Auctioning the collection through a commercial auction house is another alternative, although the house's commission will be sizeable.

The new millennium has brought the Internet, perhaps the best potential market of all for buying and selling collectables. Auction sites, as well as sites dedicated to specific equipment, offer a huge potential market for goods of all kinds, including photographic materials.

There are undoubtedly other means of passing on your collection which may occur to you and which you will wish to discuss with your executor, heirs, family, or whomever will have the responsibility. When a method has been agreed upon, including a back-up or second choice in the event the first proves unworkable, the plan should be reduced to writing and copies given to all concerned, including one filed with your will.

In building your collection, you have done a service to generations to come. When you have done all you can to hand it on in good condition, with your knowledge also passed on, you can sleep easier—you have been a good curator and custodian!

No discussion of collecting photographica would be complete without mention of the Naylor Collection. Thurman F. "Jack" Naylor (Fig. 321), of Chestnut Hill, Massachusetts, is undoubtedly the world's foremost collector of photographica and a leading authority on photographic history. In 1994 the Naylor Collection, started in the 1960s, was purchased by the Japanese government to form the basis of a Museum of Photography established in Yokohama. To the great relief of the collecting fraternity, Naylor has rebuilt his collection, thereby once again rescuing and conserving the invaluable artifacts of photographic history.

The second Naylor collection, started in 1994, has more than 26,000 items of photographic history. It is the largest such collection in the world. Included are rare pre-cinema and early cinema equipment, still cameras, and more than 2,000 daguerreotypes. The collection is displayed in a 4,000 square foot private museum near Boston. Jack is generous with his time, frequently opening the museum to classes of college level students and others, as well as many national and international visitors.

FOOTNOTES FOR ALL CHAPTERS IN THIS BOOK

Complete descriptions of all books cited are given in the Bibliography.

FOOTNOTES – CHAPTER ONE

1 These concepts are discussed but not well explained in Michael Chanan's book, *The Dream That Kicks.*

2 Athanasius Kircher, Ars Magna Lucis et Umbrae (1645), as referenced by Franz Paul Leisegang, *Dates and Sources.*

3 Leisegang.

4 Georges Sadoul, *L'Invention du Cinema, 1832-1897.*

5 C.W. Ceram, *Archaeology of the Cinema.*

6 Richard Balzer, *Optical Amusements.*

7 Alan D. Kattelle, "The Marcy Sciopticon," *Journal of the Photographic Historical Society of New England,* March/April 1983.

8 Sadoul. (D'Arcy actually observed and attempted to measure "critical fusion frequency." (See Note 1 above.)

9 Brian Coe, *The History of Movie Photography.*

10 Isaac Azimov, *Azimov's Biographical Encyclopedia.*

11 Ceram illustrates a disc which may be readily copied for a homemade phenakistoscope.

12 Henry V. Hopwood, *Living Pictures Their History.*

13 Ceram, p. 71.

14 Josef Maria Eder, *History of Photography,* p. 499.

15 Sadoul is excellent on Reynaud's productions.

16 Coe, *The History.*

17 Beaumont Newhall, *The History of Photography.*

18 Today the site of a huge Kodak Pathé factory producing photographic film, paper and chemicals.

19 Eder, p. 194.

20 Ibid.

21 A number of dioramas were created in the United States, one of which opened in Boston's South End in 1884 as the Cyclorama, showing "The Battle of Gettysburg." Two great "Gettysburgs" survive, one at Gettysburg and one in Atlanta. Christopher Rawlence, *The Missing Reel.*

22 Excepting only Great Britain.

23 Eder.

24 Brian Coe, *The Birth of Photography,* p. 28.

25 It is a curious fact that, up until that time, there was not one contribution to the science of photography by an American listed in any of the most comprehensive histories of the subject.

26 Carl W. Ackerman, *George Eastman,* p. 28.

27 Reese V. Jenkins, *Images and Enterprise.*

28 Leon Warnerke, "A New Departure in Photography," *British Journal of Photography,* 18 September, 1885.

29 Frank B. Mehlenbacher, "Frank A. Brownell: Mr. Eastman's Camera Maker," Image, *Journal of the International Museum of Photography,* Rochester, N.Y., June 1983, and personal communication from Mr. Mehlenbacher to the author.

30 Eastman and Strong's partnership, formed in January 1881, was called The Eastman Dry Plate Company; on October 1, 1884, it became The Eastman Dry Plate & Film Company; and on December 4, 1889, The Eastman Company. On May 23, 1892, it was incorporated as the Eastman Kodak Company of New York.

31 Eastman explained the origin of the word Kodak when he was required to do so by the British Patent Office. He wrote:

This is not a foreign name or word; it was constructed by me to serve a definite purpose. It has the following merits as a trade-mark word: First, it is short. Second, it is not capable of mis-pronunciation. Third, It does not resemble anything in the art and cannot be associated with anything in the art except the Kodak.

32 Jenkins.

FOOTNOTES – CHAPTER TWO

1 Robert Taft, *Photography and the American Scene.*

2 U.S. Pat. 31,357, February 5, 1861.

3 H. Mark Gosser, *Selected Attempts.*

4 Homer Croy, *How Motion Pictures are Made.*

5 Martin Quigley, Jr., *Magic Shadows.*

6 Hopwood, *Living Pictures.*

7 He was born Edward Muggeridge; he reputedly changed it to what he believed was the original Anglo-Saxon spelling.

8 Gordon Hendricks, *Eadweard Muybridge.*

9 Georges Sadoul, *L'Invention du Cinéma;* see also Auer, *Histoire etc.* for excellent illustrations.

10 For a brilliant new look at the work of Marey and Muybridge, see Marta Braun, *Picturing Time—The Work of Etienne-Jules Marey.*

11 Ramsaye, p. 85.

12 Marey, *Le Mouvement,* as quoted by Liesegang.

13 Hopwood, p. 82.

14 Ibid., p. 144.

15 Braun, p. 224.

16 Barnes, *The Beginnings of the Cinema in England.*

[17] Christopher Rawlence, *The Missing Reel: The Untold Story of the Lost Inventor of Moving Pictures.* This is the definitive and brilliant work on LePrince, which provided most of the information presented here.

[18] U.S. Patent No. 376,247; application filed November 2, 1886; issued January 10, 1888.

[19] Gordon Hendricks, *The Edison Motion Picture Myth.*

[20] Ronald W. Clark, *Edison, The Man Who Made the Future.*

[21] A caveat was a brief outline of a patent to be filed; if another patent for a similar idea was submitted within one year, the original inventor had three months to file his complete specification. Edison filed four motion picture caveats between October 17, 1888, and November 2, 1889.

[22] Both Edison and Dickson later claimed that their experiments with motion pictures began in 1887; Hendricks' research convinced him the date should be 1888.

[23] Clark.

[24] W.K.L. Dickson, *A Brief History of the Kinetograph, the Kinetoscope, and the Kineto-Phonograph.*

[25] Rawlence.

[26] Clark.

[27] Hendricks, *The Edison Motion Picture Myth.*

[28] Hendricks, *The Kinetoscope.*

[29] Hendricks states that 973 Kinetoscopes had been manufactured by December 8, 1899, but while serial numbers up to 1026 are in existence, A. R. Phillips, Jr. believes that very very few were manufactured after the 1899 date. Next to Hendricks, no one knows more about the Edison Kinetoscope than the historian and craftsman Ray Phillips of Studio City, California. Phillips has constructed over 16 meticulously accurate working replicas of the Kinetoscope for museums and private collectors all over the world. He believes that not more than 12 original Kinetoscopes still exist; nine of the regular Kinetoscopes and three of the Kinetophones, those in which a phonograph had been installed. Personal communication to the author, February 19, 1998.

[30] Ibid. Hendricks quotes extensively from contemporary news stories, none of which suggest anything but a genuine fight.

[31] Dickson, *A Brief History, etc.*

[32] Terry Ramsaye, *A Million and One Nights.* Ramsaye says this fight was filmed on the roof of Madison Square Garden, with Dickson "officiating."

[33] Edison opened an iron mine in central New Jersey in the early 1890s which was to consume $2,000,000 of his capital and several years of his and Dickson's time before the project, a scheme to magnetically concentrate iron ore was abandoned.

[34] The Viviscope is described in Chapter 1.

[35] G. W. Bitzer, *Billy Bitzer His Story,* p. 22, gives this as the number of cards; the dimensions are from an example in the author's collection.

[36] Hendricks states that this scene is of the Pennsylvania Railroad, not a view of the Empire State Express, as it is sometimes identified.

[37] Gordon Hendricks, *Beginnings of the Biograph.* Hendricks quotes both Bitzer's and Casler's description of the projector.

[38] Bitzer.

[39] Gerald Mast, *A Short History of the Movies.*

[40] Thomas Armat, "My Part in the Development of the Motion Picture Projector," Raymond Fielding, *A Technological History of Motion Pictures and Television.*

[41] U.S. Patent No. 5212,562, filed March 28, 1893, issued June 19, 1894.

[42] U.S. Patent No. 536,569, filed November 24, 1894, issued March 26, 1895.

[43] Jenkins claimed years later that it was successful, but proof of his assertion has never been produced.

[44] U.S. Patent No. 586,953, filed August 25, 1895, issued July 20, 1897.

[45] Patent Office Interference No. 18,032.

[46] Amet's story is related in Chapter 5.

[47] U. S. Patent No. 673,992, issued May 14, 1901.

[48] Ramsaye quotes this letter at length on page 224.

[49] I have been unable to find the source of *Kaiser Whilhelm,* but suspect it was a Birt Acres film.

[50] Armat eventually formed his own company and successfully sued Edison for patent infringement. Despite this, he became an enthusiastic member of the Motion Picture Patents Company. His views on the virtues of that organization are recounted in his memoir entitled *My Part in the Development of the Motion Picture Projector.*

[51] Ramsaye, p. 147 et seq.

[52] John Barnes, *The Beginnings of the Cinema in England.*

[53] Robert Paul resigned from the industry prior to 1910.

[54] Liesegang, *Dates and Sources,* p. 60.

[55] Brian Coe, *The History of Movie Photography*. This showing would seem to predate both Paul's first in England and the Lathams'.

[56] Sadoul, p. 238.

[57] Kenneth Macgowan, *Behind the Scree*. Macgowan says when Lumière refused Méliès, he fabricated one himself from parts ordered from Robert W. Paul in London.

[58] Ramsaye, p. 263.

FOOTNOTES – CHAPTER 3

[1] John Barnes, *The Beginnings of the Cinema in England*.

[2] Brian Coe, *The History of Movie Photography*.

[3] Dr. Mees provided another view of this figure in his 1955 farewell address: a 1900 survey in London established that £1-0 was sufficient to support a small family for one week at the poverty line.

[4] The East Anglian Film Archive reported in 1998 that at least 14 variations of 17.5mm film had been identified. Geoff Clarke, AMIA Newsletter.

[5] Michel Auer and Michèle Ory, *Histoire de la caméra ciné amateur*.

[6] Ibid.

[7] James Cornwall, "The History of the Ernemann Company and its Cameras," Proceedings of First Western Photohistory Symposium, May 16, 1980, University of California at Riverside.

[8] In an article entitled "The First Thirty Years," Crawford wrote in part: "Excellent as these machines would seem to have been, I can still find no record of any attempt to market or distribute them here. It is safe to say also, that they probably had only a limited commercial success in England."

[9] Ben Singer, "Early Home Cinema and the Edison Home Projecting Kinetoscope," *Film History*, Volume 2, pages 37-69, 1988.

[10] Crawford states that the Vitak was designed for 17.5mm film but examination of several examples including one in my collection show that they were actually made for 11mm film. Regarding the Duplex projector, Crawford describes the film as having 2 round perforations on each edge, which was repeated by Matthews in his 1955 S.M.P.T.E. article. However some correspondence between Matthews and one C. H. Carleton, a former employee of the Duplex Corporation, and some film samples recently discovered in the George Eastman House archives by Rita Belda confirms that the film was actually center-perforated.

[11] Brummit, p. 110. This is the only reference to an Ikonoscope camera that I have ever seen.

[12] An advertisement in *Wilson's Magazine* for December 1913 lists Schneider as a manufacturer of cameras, projectors, printers, polishers, tripods, menders, etc.

[13] Crawford, "The First Thirty Years," *Movie Makers*, December 1930.

[14] Singer.

[15] Herbert C. McKay, *Amateur Movie Making*.

[16] William Stull, "Forty Eight Years of Home Movies," *American Cinematographer*, February 1943.

[17] Catalog collection, George Eastman House.

[18] U.S. Patent No. 1,291,865 for combined camera/projector, issued 1919.

[19] Herbert C. McKay, *Motion Picture Photography for the Amateur*.

[20] Jason Schneider, "The Camera Collector," *Modern Photography*, July 1976.

[21] Amet's Magniscope is described in Chapter 6.

[22] Auer, *Histoire*, has an excellent photograph of this machine, p. 57.

[23] David H. Shepard, *Victor Animatograph Company*. This is the definitive work on the life of Alexander Victor.

[24] Samuel G. Rose, "Alexander Victor–Motion Picture Pioneer," *Journal of S.M.P.T.E.*, Vol. 72, August 1963.

[25] Victor received U.S. Patent No. 976,954 on November 10, 1910, for the projector.

[26] More information on Kinemacolor will be found in Chapter 8.

[27] Pete Ariel, *Cinematographic Register, No. ACR 840*. This reference is a facsimile reproduction of the Spirograph sales brochure.

[28] C. Francis Jenkins, "The Discrola" Trans. of S. M. P. E., No. 16, May 1923.

[29] Sadoul says: "High born men of France opened a passage through women and young girls with blows of their canes."

[30] David Robinson, *History of World Cinema*.

[31] Mees, *From Dry Plates to Ektachrome Film*.

[32] Coe, *The History of Movie Photography*.

[33] More information on this company is included in Chapters 4 and 7.

[34] William B. Kruse, "Willard Beach Cook, Pioneer Distributor of Narrow Gauge Safety Films and Equipment," *Journal of S.M.P.T.E.*, Volume 73, July 1964. Kruse was Archivist with the National Education Association. This paper with its references is an excellent source of information on the genesis of film libraries.

35 Invented by the German physical chemist of that name, a small rod of rare earth oxides can be heated to incandescence by comparatively little current. See *Encyclopedia Brittanica,* 11th Ed., Vol. 16. An example exists in the IMP-GEH archives.

36 Author's collection.

37 Singer, "Early Home Cinema, etc."

38 Nevins, Allan. *Ford—The Times, the Man, the Company.* Chas. Scribner & Sons, New York, 1954, page 527.

39 In the author's experience with one machine, the baby-arc functioned flawlessly.

40 Ronald W. Clark, *Edison, the Man Who Made the Future,* pp. 214-215.

41 A handwritten record in the George Eastman archives states that the Movette was designed by F. L. Hough of Chicago; trade mark registered March 23, 1920, by Movette, Inc., Rochester, New York.

42 The report of an undated test of a Movette camera by Eastman Kodak personnel cites jamming of the film and six-week delay in return of film from processing. IMP-GEH archives.

43 Matthews and Tarkington indicate that it used 17.5mm safety film.

44 When Schlicker filed for the Kinetograph in 1918 he was a German citizen living in New York City; in 1919 when he filed for a film container patent he was a U.S. citizen living in Milwaukee, and he assigned half of his patent to John R. Freuler.

45 One in the author's collection; one reported to belong to a collector in Connecticut

46 A 1927 Pathex catalog in the author's collection lists over 400 titles in 21 categories, including films of Harold Lloyd, Stan Laurel, Will Rogers, *Our Gang,* Grantland Rice, and others.

47 Auer, *Histoire.*

48 Louis J. J. Didée, "Memories of the Early History of 9.5mm," *Journal of S.M.P.T.E.,* Vol. 75, pages 1181-1183, December 1966.

FOOTNOTES – CHAPTER 4

1 Kent, a leading Rochester photographer, was one of four local businessmen, acquaintances of Eastman and Strong, who invested varying amounts in the company.

2 Jenkins, p. 180.

3 Brummit, p. 66.

4 Ackerman quotes a letter in which Eastman offered Stuber a salary of $30 per week plus one percent on net receipts of plate sales. Ackerman says three other key employees had similar contracts. It would be interesting to know how long such arrangements were maintained.

5 Jenkins, p. 181 et.seq.

6 The exception was Thomas J. Hargrave, a young Rochester attorney who started part-time with Eastman Kodak in 1927, went full-time in 1934, and moved up from Secretary to President in 1941.

7 Rose R. Stuber, *William G. Stuber—A Biography,* Privately printed, 1951.

8 Jenkins, Table 12.1, p. 279.

9 In June 1900 Eastman Kodak advised its dealers that Kodak ads were running in media with combined circulation of over 6,000,000 copies per issue, not just with one insertion, but most with every issue. Ackerman, p. 170.

10 Ramsaye, p. 427.

11 Gerald Mast, *A Short History of the Movies,* Macmillan, New York, 1986, page 43.

12 Jenkins, p. 289 et. seq.

13 Jenkins, p. 290.

14 Macgowan, *Behind the Screen,* p.137.

15 Macgowan, p. 155 et. seq.

16 Ephraim Katz, The Film Encyclopedia, p. 677.

17 In contemporary accounts, the word took an initial capital, as in this excerpt from a Sept. 7, 1901, news story on Czolgosz: "While acknowledging himself an Anarchist, he does not state to which branch of the organization he belongs." Loyalty and Security in a Democratic State, N.Y. Times-Arno Press, Richard Rovere, Editor, New York, 1979.

18 Between 1910 and 1920, dividends on common stock averaged almost $8 million per year; earned surplus averaged $5.4 million per year.

19 Ackerman, p. 234.

20 Mees recounted later that Mr. Eastman "talked to me for half an hour about American football, which was something in which I had no interest whatever."

21 Brummit, p. 208.

22 Mees, op. cit., p. 50.

23 See Ackerman for details of Eastman's donations, p. 324 et seq.

24 Brummit describes (p. 250) a camera that was operated by small propellers placed in the slipstream of the plane, making the camera so noisy it was dubbed "Whistling Jim." The Government ordered 200.

25 Brummit, p. 252.

26 Brummit, p. 278.

27 "Kodak is Freed From Restraints on Marketing." *The Wall Street Journal,* November 8, 1995.

28 Jenkins, p. 328.

29 Matthews and Tarkington, p. 130.

30 Capstaff's birth date is given by Tuttle and Matthews as February 24, 1897; however, as this would make him barely 15 when he went to work for Mees, the year 1887 seems much more likely.

31 *75 Years, etc.*, p.11.

32 Eder, p. 700.

33 Since large grains react faster than small ones, a higher percentage of them are bleached out after the first exposure; the final image thus contains relatively more small grains.

34 "Aspect ratio" is the ratio of the width of the image to its height; 1" to 3/4" was chosen by Edison and was standard for many years until the advent of various wide screen formats.

35 Harris Tuttle, "The Emergence of Practical Home Movies," Lecture delivered to The Photographic Historical Society, Rochester, New York, October, 1973.

36 D.F. Lyman, "Historical Notes on the Development of Amateur Motion Pictures," April 26, 1948. This is an extremely detailed 36-page report on the genesis of 16mm and 8mm camera and film systems at Eastman Kodak Company. It carries the following notation at the top of the first page: "Prepared for Messrs. Donovan, Leisure, Newton, Lambard and Irving." The report describes the different departments of the Kodak organization that were involved, the systems of paperwork: approval cards, Development Department Cards, meeting and conference reports, etc. As the designated recipient is quite obviously a law firm, it is reasonable to assume that the report was requested by that firm because of an existing or anticipated legal challenge to the Company.

A second document entitled "The Part Played by the Eastman Kodak Company in the Development of Amateur Motion Pictures" carries neither date nor signature, but may have been a somewhat earlier report from which the 1948 document drew much of its information. Both documents are in the George Eastman House Archives.

37 Eastman Kodak Company Trade Circular, Vol. XXIV, No. 6.

38 Eastman Kodak Company Trade Circular, Vol. XXIV, No. 6.

39 Coe, p. 168.

40 McKay, *Motion Picture Photography for the Amateur*, gives the cost per foot of finished 35mm film in 1924 as follows: negative stock—four cents, development—one cent, positive stock—two cents, processing and printing—three cents, total for 1,000 feet or 16 minutes of screen time, $6.25 per minute. The new 16mm direct reversal film cost six dollars for a 100-foot roll including processing, or $1.50 per minute of screen time.

41 Ibid.

42 Chapter 14 describes the founding of The Amateur Cinema League.

43 Harris Tuttle, "Some Notes on the Early Reversal Processing . . ."

44 Mees, *From Dry Plates to Ektachrome Film.*

45 This process is fully described in Chapter 8.

46 *Movie Makers*, September 1928, as quoted in *75 Years, etc.*

47 A 1930 advertisement for the Library Kodascope states that it was "created by a world-famous designer."

48 That person was Marion B. Folsom, at the time Assistant to the President (Mr. Eastman) and later a director of the company. "A Great Man," Marion B. Folsom, University of Rochester Library Bulletin, Vol. XXVI, No. 3, Spring 1971.

49 Ackerman, p. 316.

50 "Six Million More from Mr. Eastman," University of Rochester Alumni Review, 1924.

51 London was a best-selling author when he and his wife and Martin Johnson attempted to circumnavigate the globe.

52 Osa Johnson, *I Married Adventure*, pp. 266-270.

53 The original head eventually succumbed to rot and insects. It has been replaced with a fiberglass replica.

54 George Eastman, *Chronicles of a Second African Trip.*

55 Johnson, p. 298.

FOOTNOTES – CHAPTER 5

1 Brummit, p. 319.

2 *Journey: 75 Years of Kodak Research.*

3 U.S. Dept. of Labor, Bureau of Labor Statistics, Urban Consumer Price Index.

4 Standard 8mm is 3.28mm by 4.37mm.

5 Ogden's obituary in the *Cincinnati Times-Star* of March 27, 1944, relates that he was "a great friend" of Thomas Edison, who once invited Ogden to join the inventor's staff; however, the Edison archivists have been unable to corroborate this story.

6 Surviving home movies that can be dated from the 1920s and 1930s almost invariably indicate that their makers were comfortably upper middle class or better, economically.

[7] Bell & Howell archives. A Bell & Howell 8mm engineering model in my collection is dated 5-28-32, indicating that Bell & Howell was aware of Kodak's plans for 8mm before it was formally announced.

[8] Walter Clark, *"A Review of 1941."*

[9] "The Maxim Memorial Award." Movie Makers, December 1940.

[10] The name "Kodachrome" was first used by Dr. Capstaff for an entirely different two-color process he developed in 1915. It had limited success as a transparency film. Capstaff later experimented with the same process for professional movie film; however, it was eclipsed by the arrival of Technicolor's three-color process about 1932. Mees, *From Dry Plates to Ektachrome Film.*

[11] *Journey*, p. 55.

[12] *Journey*, p. 53.

[13] Masks, as the name implies, were used to block off portions of the film, permitting double exposures, vignetting, and many special effects.

[14] In 1948 the lens turret face was angled to permit mounting the new longer lenses without having them show up in the field of view.

[15] See Chapter 11 for details on this projector.

[16] Annual Report, 1939.

[17] A news item in *Popular Photography* for March 1945 reported: "The use of 16mm film for home movies has been cut to a minimum, from the average peacetime rate of 6,500,000 per quarter to the current rate of 1,000,000 linear feet per quarter, the War Production Board announced."

[18] Annual Report, 1945.

[19] "Television Recording Camera Developed by Eastman Kodak," *American Cinematographer,* December 1947.

[20] Richard Kozarski, personal communication to the author.

[21] *Popular Photography*, December 1955.

[22] Kodak Annual Report, 1951.

[23] Dealers must have encountered some resistance even at the introduction price, since by August of 1951 the camera was advertised at $44.50, in January 1952 at $43.30, and by December 1952 at $42.50.

[24] *Kodak Movie News,* March/April 1955.

[25] Kodak Annual Report, 1954.

[26] *Chicago Tribune*, January 5, 1973.

[27] "Suit Against Kodak is Won by Bell & Howell." *Chicago Tribune,* July 9, 1974.

[28] Victor K. McIlheny, "Kodak and Polaroid: Color Systems Differ." *New York Times*, April 23, 1976.

[29] As reported in the *Stamford Advocate,* Stamford, Connecticut, October 19, 1976.

[30] Kodak Annual Report, 1985.

[31] Joyce and William D. Samson were the first names on the plaintiff's list.

[32] "Kodak Settles Suit by Owners of 'Instants.'" *Wall Street Journal*, May 17, 1988.

[33] "Polaroid Seeks Patent Damages of $5.7 Billion." *Wall Street Journal,* February 22, 1988

[34] *The Wolfman Reports*. Gus Wolfman was executive editor of *Photo Dealer* where annual reports of amateur movie equipment sales were first published until 1969, after which Wolfman left *Photo Dealer* and continued the reports under his own name. This information supplied by Thomas W. Hope of Hope Reports, Inc.

[35] See Chapter 10 for the story of Super 8's genesis and introduction.

[36] See Chapter 11 for the story of the XL system and Ekatasound.

[37] Dr. Joe A. Bailey, Personal communication to the author. July 1993.

[38] Dealer's "low net" price for 3-99 units was $945. Eastman Kodak Co. records.

[39] Mikolas & Hoos, *Handbook of Super 8 Production.*

[40] All data calculated from Wolfman Reports and *Popular Photography Directory* issues.

[41] Name withheld, at his request.

[42] Eastman Kodak Annual Report, 1965.

[43] David A. Gibson, personal communication to the author, February 18,1987.

[44] Hilary Appelman, "Kodak President, Company's Future in Focus." Associated Press news story, April 1991.

[45] Joan E. Rigdon, "Kodak's Changes Produce Plenty of Heat, Little Light." *Wall Street Journal*, April 8, 1992.

[46] In addition to full health and dental care for life, plus bridge payment equal to retirees' Social Security payments thru age 62, those who retired in 1991 received up to a year's salary.

[47] Annual Report, 1993.

[48] Dennis Howe, "PhotoCD—Music for Your Eyes." *Optics and Photonics News*, February 1993.

[49] Annual Report, 1995.

[50] Alec Klein, "Kodak Is Rolling Out Digital Photo Processing on CD-ROM Disks, *Wall Street Journal,* Feb. 9, 1999.

51 "Put Your Pictures on Your PC," Eastman Kodak promotional brochure picked up at CVS drugstore.

52 Laura Johannes, "For New Film a Brighter Picture," *Wall Street Journal*, May 5, 1998.

53 Alec Klein, "Shutter Snaps on Fisher's Leadership," *Wall Street Journal*, June 10, 1999.

54 J.F. Dupont, "Film and the Future of Imaging," *Journal of S.M.P.T.E.*, October 1999. A lucid explanation of the superiority of film.

55 Ben Rand, "Kodak vows to survive, thrive in the dawn of digital movies." *Rochester Democrat and Chronicle*, November 23, 1999.

56 Alec Klein, *Wall Street Journal*, May 8, 2000.

FOOTNOTES – CHAPTER 6

1 Kirk Kekatos, "Edward Hill Amet—Inventor," *By Daylight*, The Chicago Photographic Collector Society, Winter 1993.

2 George K. Spoor, letter to Ray Brian, May 1, 1948.

3 Nelson received U.S. Patent 594,094 on November 23, 1897, for a camera taking a spiral of pictures on a glass plate. Seventy years later, when DeMaas of 3M Company received U.S. Patent 3,381,086 on April 30, 1968, for "Production of television signals from photographic disc recordings," the new patent referred to Nelson's patent.

4 Kekatos, op. cit..

5 Donald J. Bell, "A Letter From Donald Bell."

6 Jack Fay Robinson, *Bell & Howell—A 75 Year History*, p.17.

7 Bell, op. cit.

8 Donald Malkames stated, "This was the first projector to accomplish framing by revolving the intermittent, and employ counter-revolving shutters; both of which mechanisms are employed on projectors of today." "Early Projector Mechanisms," *Journal of S.M.P.T.E.*, Oct. 1957.

9 Bell, op. cit.

10 Robinson, op. cit., p.16.

11 Morgan Wesson, personal note to author. An example in the author's collection, with no serial number, is sheathed in zinc and has metal magazines.

12 Laurence J. Roberts, "Cameras and Systems," A History of Contributions from the Bell & Howell Company, Part I, *Journal S.M.P.T.E.*, October 1982.

13 Ibid., p. 937.

14 Johnson, Osa, "I Married Adventure."

15 Roberts, p.938.

16 Ibid.

17 Thomas J. Rappel: "Bell's niece states that Bell died with little money, lost in poor investments." Mr. Rappel, retired vice-president of Bell & Howell, kindly provided me with this and other information on Bell & Howell's history.

18 Robinson.

19 Malcolm G. Townsley, personal communication to the author.

20 Ibid.

21 Ibid.

22 Robinson, op. cit.

23 Ibid.

24 Kevin Brownlow, *The Parade's Gone By*, p. 201.

25 "Elegant Bell & Howell," *Fortune*, July 1948.

26 Roberts reports that the first Eyemo was sold to P.K. Wrigley, the chewing gum magnate.

27 E.F. Wagner, letter to J. F. Robinson, Sept. 25, 1981.

28 *Filmo Topics*, Christmas 1939 issue.

29 Wagner.

30 Robinson, p. 57.

31 Ibid.

32 *Filmo Topics*, Christmas 1942 issue.

33 Robinson, p. 78.

34 Ibid, p. 81.

35 Thomas D. Hardwick, letter to author, Jan. 25, 1986.

36 Charles H. Percy, letter to J.F. Robinson, Dec. 14, 1981.

37 Ibid.

38 Bell & Howell Annual Report, 1950.

39 This camera is described in Chapter 9.

40 Percy.

41 Details of this camera are given in Chapter 9.

42 Rappel, personal communication to the author,

43 When Revere and others did bring out electric eye cameras, Bell & Howell sued them all for patent infringement.

44 *Home Movie Making*, Ziff-Davis Publishing Co., 1959.

45 1969 Wolfman Report, *Modern Photography*.

46 Rappel.

47 Annual Report, 1959.

48 Rappel, personal communication to the author.

49 Robinson, op.cit. For a detailed treatment of these broadcasts and the controversy surrounding them, see Patricia Zimmermann's *Reel Families*.

50 Annual Report, 1963.

[51] Annual Report, 1954.

[52] *Chicago Tribune*, June 3, 1975.

[53] For a somewhat different account of this incident, see Peter C. Wensberg's *Land's Polaroid*, p. 225.

[54] Annual Report, 1965.

[55] *Chicago Tribune*, Jan. 25, 1973.

[56] Rappel.

[57] Rappel.

[58] *Modern Photography*, 1984-85 Wolfman Report.

[59] Peterson, letter to J.F. Robinson, Nov. 24, 1981.

[60] Annual Report 1979, and *Popular Photography Directory and Buying Guide*, 1980.

[61] As of this writing, the company is still marketing those two lines of equipment.

[62] Annual Report, 1995.

FOOTNOTES – CHAPTER 7

[1] Charles Musser, *High Class Moving Pictures*.

[2] Georges Sadoul, *L'Invention du Cinema*, Editions Denoel, p. 178.

[3] Gerald Mast, *A Short History of the Movies*.

[4] Wyatt Brummit, "George Eastman of Kodak," p. 305.

[5] Ackerman, p. 212 et.seq.

[6] "Regenerated film" was used film from which the emulsion was stripped and new emulsion applied. It was not considered top quality and was generally only used for titles.

[7] Raymond Fielding, *A Technological History*, p. 130.

[8] W. F. Kruse, "Willard Beach Cook, Pioneer Distributor," *Journal S.M.P.T.E.*, Vol. 73, July 1964.

[9] *Motion Picture Age*, July 1922.

[10] Brummit, p. 305-6.

[11] David Robinson, "Something to Crow About," *London Times*, November 23, 1994.

[12] Chapter 2, p. 50.

[13] David H. Shepard, *The Victor Animatograph Company and the Genesis of Non-Theatrical Film*. Privately printed © 1975, University of Iowa Library.

[14] Ramsaye, p 349.

[15] Samuel G. Rose, "Alexander Victor—Motion Picture Pioneer," *Journal S.M.P.T.E.*, Vol. 72, August 1963.

[16] U.S. Patent No. 976,954, November 29, 1910.

[17] U.S. Patent No. 1,096,873, May 19, 1914.

[18] This anecdote, reported by Shepard, was confirmed by Rose in an interview many years later.

[19] Rose obituary, *Quad City Times*, March 25, 1966.

[20] U.S. Patent No. 1,062,622, May 27,1913

[21] Wundram, "He Met a Magician and from it Came a Great Industry," Davenport Times-Democrat, November 11, 1962.

[22] Shepard.

[23] Wundram.

[24] Rose.

[25] Alexander F. Victor, "The Portable Projector."

[26] Shepard, *Journal S.M.P.T.E.*, Volume 6, April 1918.

[27] A 1918 price list from United Projector & Film Company of Buffalo, New York, lists the projector with carrying case at $250, without case $240.

[28] The nameplate on the Safety Cinema in the author's collection says "Patented," but no patent number is present.

[29] Class Publications, Inc., Publishers, 418 S. Market Street, Chicago, Illinois.

[30] Shepard.

[31] H. B. Tuttle, Sr., personal communication to the author, June 21, 1985.

[32] Shepard reports that Victor worked "twenty and thirty hours at a stretch."

[33] A. F. Victor, "The Motion Picture—A Practical Feature of the Home," Transactions, *S.M.P.T.E.*, Vol.16, May 1923. Unfortunately Victor's drawings were not reproduced with this article.

[34] A thin metal plate with holes of various sizes which can be indexed into the light path, common on early still cameras.

[35] Shepard.

[36] Statement of Samuel Rose to Edward K. Kaprelian, related to author.

[37] U.S. Patent No. 1,885,269, application filed December 1, 1927, issued April 26, 1932.

[38] Einar Thulin, "Bollnaspojken som uppfann Smallfilmen," *Stockholms-Tidningen*, January 31,1939. Translation by Helge Thelander.

[39] *American Photography*, December 1932.

[40] Wundram.

[41] *Davenport Democrat*, July 9, 1946.

[42] Wundram.

[43] George S. Bush, "The Great Mr. Victor," *American Mercury*, July 1958.

[44] James Arpy, article in *Quad City Times*, April 6, 1961.

[45] Dr. C. R. Crakes, "Herman A. DeVry: A Brief Saga of a Great American Inventor and Educational Pioneer." Publisher and date unknown.

[46] Herman A. DeVry, "I Visioned the Interests of Children," *American Cinematographer*, June 1938.

47 Crakes' words, presumably meaning the 1896 Vitascope.

48 DeVry.

49 Ramsaye relates that Rothacker obtained financing for his company from Carl Laemmle in return for naming the company as he did, the first initials of which are IMP. Laemmle was then head of the Independent Motion Picture Company, also known as "IMP," which was embroiled with the infamous Motion Picture Patents Company. In event of legal trouble, Laemmle reasoned he could switch his operations to the Industrial Motion Picture Company and keep them out of reach of the Patent Company's bailiffs.

50 *Moving Picture Age*, September 1921. The editor's comments were prescient: "it is by no means difficult to look ahead a brief period to the time when the novelty (of flying) will have been dissipated and moving pictures will be the normal recourse for whiling away hours in the clouds."

51 U.S. Patent No. 1,758,221, application filed October 21, 1925, issued May 13, 1930.

52 See Chapter 11 for details on this machine.

53 Advertisement, *The Saturday Evening Post*, August, 1928.

54 *McKeown's Price Guide to Antique and Classic Cameras*, 1995-1996 Edition.

55 Harvey N. Roehl, *Player Piano Treasury*, Vestal Press, 1961.

56 O.L. Stone, *History of Massachusetts Industries*, 1930.

57 Original Keystone toys are today eagerly sought after by toy collectors.

58 Design Patent No. 55,107, May 4, 1920; U.S. Patent No. 1,345,793.

59 U.S. Patent No. 1,722,088, issued July 23, 1929.

60 U.S. Patent No. 1.841,748, issued January 19,1932.

61 The Keystone 8mm camera was unique in having pin-registry of the film in the gate and was smaller than the Kodak. The design was patented by Lewis H. Moomaw of Wilmette, Illinois, who had six camera patents, some of which were sold to Eastman Kodak and Bell & Howell.

62 Mel Hosnsky, "Keystone Head Sees Expanding Movie Market as Firm Celebrates 40th Year" *Photographic Trade News*, April 27, 1959.

63 Donald White, "A New Debut for Keystone Co." *Boston Globe*, November 9, 1967.

64 Alan Barnett, personal communication to the author, April 1995.

65 Barnett.

66 "Son of Berkey Photo Founder to Leave Firm, Buy Keystone Division." *Wall Street Journal*, June 28, 1978.

67 *Wall Street Journal*, December 27, 1990.

68 The author is extremely indebted to Mr. Gary Kaess for almost all information on Keystone after 1966.

69 Gerald McKee, *The Home Cinema*, Gerrards Cross, Bucks. SL989Y, England, 1989.

70 Ms. Carole Bolsey, personal communication, February 3, 1996.

71 Andrew Alden, *A Bolex History*, self-published, 1993.

72 Emil Bolsey, personal communication, August 3, 1996.

73 Bolex Company, New York Advertisement for the Model D projector. *Movie Makers*, February 1933.

74 Pathé films were provided with notches at each title frame, which held that frame stationary for a second or so, thus four or five frames could do the work of four feet of film for a conventional title.

75 Alden, op. cit., points out that this was about the price of a family sedan at the time.

76 Coe, op. cit.

77 Chris Lydle, "A Barrel of Bolexes," *Shutterbug Ads*, Aug.-Nov. 1978.

78 An indication of the high regard in which the Bolex cameras were held is given in the fact that a brisk business flourished briefly in converting some H-8 cameras to take 100-foot rolls of double Super 8, thus freeing the filmmaker from the limits of the three-minute Super 8 cartridge while utilizing all the versatility of the Bolex camera. The cost of conversion ran from $150 to $275 depending on choice of artisan and model of camera to be converted. Tony Galluzzo, "Movie Making," *Modern Photography*, December 1973.

79 Toni Galluzzo, "Movie Making," *Modern Photography*, December 1973.

80 Leendert Drukker, "Bolex Zoom Reflex P-1 Test Report," *Popular Photography*, January 1962.

81 For details of these ownership changes, see Alden's book, p. 3.

82 Bolsey family records, courtesy of Emil Bolsey.

83 Eric Berndt, designer of the Auricon sound camera, built a camera for 3mm film in the late 60s, but it was never marketed. *Sixteen Frames*, Vol. 3, No. 3, Winter 1990.

84 The instruction book with an example in my collection gives the company name and address as Bolsey-Delmonico, Long Island City, New York.

85 *Ariel Cinematographic Register*, No. 325.

86 Roland Cosandey, La Suisse Romande Entre Deux Guerres.

87 Cynthia A. Repinski, *The UniveX Story*, Centennial Photo Service, 1991. Unless footnoted otherwise, most of the information on Universal has come from Miss Repinski's exhaustive study of that company.

88 Kalton C. Lahue and Joe A. Bailey, *Glass, Brass, and Chrome*, p. 166.

89 Morris Moses, "A Short Legend in American Camera History—The Universal Camera Corporation," *Antique Trader Weekly,* December 1980.

90 Repinski.

91 *Popular Photography Price Guide*, 1936, and contemporary advertisements.

92 See Chapter 5, page 15.

93 Moses, Morris G., "The Legacy of George Kende," *Shutterbug Ads*, July 1989

94 Lahue and Bailey.

95 A 1939 model briefly marketed had a top speed of 1/1500.

96 Harvard's Observatory at Climax, Colorado. See Repinski, p. 72 et seq.

97 Morris Moses, "The Universal Camera Company," *The New England Journal of Photographic History.* March/April 1983.

98 Repinski, p. 112.

99 The initials stand for "Congress of Industrial Organizations," the powerful amalgamation of trade unions organized in 1935 by John L. Lewis, president of the United Mine Workers.

100 Carl Schreyer, personal communication to the author, March 1994.

101 As an example of Revere's competitive pricing, the 1948 *Popular Photography Directory Issue* shows Bell & Howell's Filmo Tri-Lens 8 listed at $134.55; Revere offered the Model 99 with three-lens turret and comparable lenses at $110.

102 Schreyer.

103 Robert Herden, "What Ever Happened to Wollensak?" Paper presented to the Photographic Historical Society, November 1994. I am indebted to Mr. Herden for much information on Revere's purchase of Wollensak.

104 Herden.

105 Rudolf Kingslake, "The Rochester Camera and Lens Companies" Paper presented to the Photographic Historical Society, Rochester, New York, March 1974.

106 Pellar.

107 Vicki Brown, news story in the *Rochester Democrat and Chronicle*, May 1, 1975.

108 Diana Ryan, 3M Company, personal communication to the author, September 1994.

FOOTNOTES – CHAPTER 8

1 Brian Coe, *The History of Movie Photography.*

2 See Chapter. 2, page 22 et seq.

3 John Barnes, *The Beginnings of the Cinema in England*, p. 114.

4 The reader may make his own speculations as to what this amounted to per "female" per day.

5 Henry V. Hopwood, *Living Pictures - Their History.*

6 Coe, *The History*, p. 114.

7 Amateur 16mm projectors of the 1930s were sometimes equipped with a three-color filter wheel in front of the lens to permit the amateur to get the same effect.

8 Kevin Brownlow, *Napoleon-Abel Gance's Classic Film.*

9 Eder, *History of Photography*, p. 458.

10 Ibid. p. 641.

11 Azimov, *Biographical Encyclopedia.*

12 Brummit, *George Eastman of Kodak.*

13 Not to be confused with the color print film of the same name introduced in 1942.

14 Mees, *From Dry Plates to Ektachrome Film.*

15 Tuttle, "The Father of Home Movies," *PSA Journal*, July 1952.

16 Kalmus attracted considerable attention at one point for having allegedly discovered a cure for lupus through the use of ultraviolet rays. Undated news clipping, perhaps circa 1910.

17 "Color in the Motion Picture," *American Cinematographer,* January 1969.

18 In a 1929 newspaper interview, Jerome stated that he and his friends initially advanced $40,000, and continued to finance the company for eight years, investing a total of nearly four million dollars.

19 H. T. Kalmus, "Adventures in Cinemaland," *Journal of SMPTE*, December, 1938. Vol. 31.

20 This arrangement continued even after the couple divorced in 1944, for the second time.

21 *American Cinematographer*, November 1967.

22 Coe, op. cit., p. 139.

23 Kodak annual reports, 1947 and 1948.

24 Mees, op cit.

25 Coe, p. 127, says the film was the product of William Van Doren Kelly, founder of Prizma, Inc.

26 *Journey; 75 Years*, author not identified in the publication.

27 The name was taken from an entirely different process developed by Capstaff in 1915. Brian Coe gives a good history and description of the process in his *History*, pp. 126-7.

28 Equivalent to 4 to 12 ten-thousandths of an inch.

29 Eastman Kodak Company publication NS385227EXP, 1985.

30 As of year 2000, this film is still in production.

31 *Journey; 75 Years*.

32 Peter C. Wensberg, *Land's Polaroid*.

33 Dr. Land demonstrated a "unique and ingenious stereo audio system" at the Company's 1979 Annual meeting, using a full-width unsprocketed sound tape co-wound with the picture tape and played by a magnetic head module attached t the silent player. Described as "experimental," it is not believed to have ever reached the market. Reported by Leendert Drukker in *Popular Photography*, July 1979.

34 Daniel Guenzel, Director, MorningStar Film Productions Ltd., Milwaukee, Wisconsin, letter to the *Wall Street Journal*, January 12, 1987.

35 *American Photography*, January 1923.

FOOTNOTES – CHAPTER 9

1 A 1952 study done by Bell & Howell determined that only six percent of U.S. households owned movie equipment; a 1960 study by Bell & Howell set the figure at 5 to17 percent.

2 J. S. Chandler, and Hugh R. McNair, U. S. Patent No. 3,949,952 issued April 13, 1976. See Chapter 11 for more on the Supermatic camera.

3 Joe A. Bailey, personal communication to the author.

4 Tony Galluzzo, *Modern Photography*, August 1972.

5 Donald O. Easterly, personal communication to the author. In a "slot loading"or self-threading projector, the film leader is inserted in a slot where it is picked up by pressure rollers and carried to the film gate and feed claw.

6 A letter dated July 9, 1923, from Eastman Kodak Rochester Development Department, advised Kodak Ltd., London, that: "As an additional accessory for (the Cine-Kodak) we will supply a walking stick, the handle of which is removable and the lower part provided with a screw that fits the tripod socket on the Cine-Kodak. The walking stick can then be used as a support for the camera when it is motor driven."

7 The DeMornay-Budd Automatic Eight electric-drive 8mm magazine camera was listed in the 1948 *Popular Photography Directory*, and nowhere thereafter.

8 *Popular Photography*, June 1963.

9 Par Products Corp. advertisement, *Popular Photography*, May 1950.

10 Rudolf Kingslake, *Lenses in Photography*.

11 Michel Auer in *L'Histoire de la camera ciné amateur* states that the Transfocator was first, however *Ariel's Cinematographic Register* lists the Siemens camera as appearing in 1933.

12 The Eumig C2, a 9.5mm camera introduced in 1935, was possibly the first camera with built-in meter. See "An early automatic small-film camera," *Journal SMPTE*, May 1966, pp 508.

13 Two special commemorative models of the 200EE were produced with gold-plated metal parts. One was presented to (then) Princess Elizabeth of England and the other was placed in the Bell & Howell archives. The latter camera has disappeared and cannot be accounted for.

14 In 1958 Bell & Howell filed suits claiming infringements of patents for 8mm electric eye cameras against Revere, DeJur Ansco and Wollensak. Bell & Howell1958 Annual Report.

FOOTNOTES – CHAPTER 10

1 R. B. Rawls, "8mm Sound Film - A Professional News Medium for Television," *Journal S.M.P.T.E.* August 1962, pp. 575-577.

2 John Flory, "The Challenge of 8mm Sound Film," *Journal of S.M.P.T.E.*, August 1961, pp. 581-585. A thorough discussion of the problems confronting full utilization.

3 J. C. Staud and W.T. Hanson, Jr., "Some Aspects of 8mm Sound Color Print Quality," *Journal of S.M.P.T.E.*, August 1962.

4 John A. Maurer, discussion on above paper.

5 Drukker, quoting Dr. Staud, Methods and Materials, *Popular Photography*, October 1962.

6 E. A. Edwards and J. S. Chandler, "Format Factors Affecting 8mm Sound Print Quality," *Journal of S.M.P.T.E.*, July 1964.

7 Two of Edwards' questioners were from Columbia Pictures and Universal Studios, whose interest may be explained by the following item which appeared in Drukker's column in *Popular Photography* for September 1962: "Columbia Pictures Corporation is reported to be busily printing 8mm sound copies from its vast film library, duplicating 35mm films shot at 21fps to 18fps, 8mm."

8 Leonard Lipton, "The Evolution of the Bluejays" and "Evolution of the Pointers," *Popular Photography*, June 1965.

9 Carl Schreyer, personal communication to the author, October 1992.

10 Leonard Lipton, personal communication to the author, October 1992.

11 Bell & Howell's Design 414PD, the last standard 8mm camera made before Super 8, carried a Bell & Howell f/1.8 9 to 27mm zoom lens which measured 60mm long by 53mm in diameter; the Design 430 lens was f/1.9, 11 to 35mm zoom, and measured 23mm long by 36mm in diameter.

12 See Chapter 9, under Exposure Control.

13 James S. Forney, "Inside Super 8 - How it was Developed at Eastman Kodak," *Popular Photography*, December 1965.

14 It was not uncommon for management to assign "back-up" design teams within engineering and research staffs to insure that all useful ideas were being explored. In this case Dr. Chandler's design for the 50-foot cartridge was not chosen for the introductory Super 8 models, however his design did form the basis for his subsequent successful design of the 200-foot cartridge, introduced in 1975. Dr. Chandler, personal communication to the author, April 1993.

15 Donald O. Easterly, personal communication to the author, December 1993.

16 See Chapter 5 for more of Easterly's achievements.

17 So strong was the left-side loading convention that Kodak's first battery operated camera, the Kodak Electric 8 Automatic Camera still loaded on the left side.

18 When Fuji first revealed its Single 8 design, Evan Edwards of Eastman Kodak recognized Fuji's drawing as his own. Edwards, personal communication to the author, November 1992.

19 The Fuji film base was polyester terephthalate, while the Kodachrome II base was cellulose acetopropionate. Wallace Hanson, "Fujichrome RT50,," *Popular Photography*, June 1967.

20 Bell & Howell annual report, 1965.

21 "Behind the Scenes," *Modern Photography*, November 1965.

22 Ralph Miller, "Third Look at a Two-Year Old," *U.S. Camera*, August 1967.

23 "Timing" is the laboratory process of making corrections to the release print to compensate for under- or over-exposure of the original.

24 Donald Sutherland, "Who Needs 16mm?" *Popular Photography*, June 1972.

25 Toni Treadway, email to author, April 10, 2000.

FOOTNOTES – CHAPTER 11

1 William S. Allen, Vice President, Eastman Kodak, retired. Interview, November 14, 1991.

2 A great deal of the information in this section was provided by Donald Gorman from his personal notes, kindly made available to the author.

3 In his patent, Oxberry referenced "1,536,347 May 1925 Lovejoy." This patent covered a combination camera/projector with a dual-function shutter, and was issued to Frank W. Lovejoy, who died in 1945 in office as Chairman, Eastman Kodak Company.

4 Longines, being primarily a watch-making concern at that time, misguidedly elected to distribute the camera through jewelry stores, a gambit which may have contributed to the limited success of the venture.

5 At 16 frames per second, a 300° shutter gives (1/16 x 300/360)=1/19th sec.; a 165° shutter, (1/16 x 165/360)=1/35th sec.

6 Peter P. Chiesa and Donald Gorman, "An Historical Review of the Development of an Existing Light System of Motion Picture Photography." *Proceedings of the Rochester Chapter of the Society of Motion Picture and Television Engineers, 1971-1972.* Much of the information in this section has come from this paper.

7 Chiesa's department, as did others in Kodak Research, gave its employees an annual film allotment; Chiesa said his amounted to about $15 worth. Author's interview with Chiesa, May 1990.

8 Ibid.

9 Chiesa, letter to author, July 5, 1988.

10 Ektachrome Type G, usable under all conditions without filter, was introduced in 1973, but proved to entail processing problems and was subsequently withdrawn.

11 Eastman Kodak advertisement, *Modern Photography*, May 1973, p. 76.

12 David MacLoud, "Kodak's XL Movie System," *Peterson's Photographic*, May 1972.

13 Charles Resler, General Manager Consumer Markets Division, interview in *Business Week*, March 18, 1972.

14 "Behind The Scenes," *Modern Photography*, June 1973.

15 Leo J. Thomas, "Available Light Movies—An Individual Inventor Made It Happen," *Research Management*, November 1980, The Industrial Research Institute.

16 Edward W. Kellogg, "History of Sound Motion Pictures" *Journal of S.M.P.T.E.*, Vol. 64 June 1955.

For Hollywood's reaction, see David Robinson's *The History of World Cinema*, p.155 et seq.

[17] W. K. L. Dickson and Antonia Dickson, *History of the Kinetograph*.

[18] Gordon Hendricks, *The Kinetoscope*, p.118 et seq. Hendricks states that only 45 Kinetophones were made and sold.

[19] Brian Coe, *The History of Movie Photography*, p. 94.

[20] *Encyclopedia Britannica*, 11th Ed., Vol. 3, p. 684.

[21] Bell and Hubbard did eventually marry.

[22] Kellogg.

[23] Ibid.

[24] David Robinson, *History of World Cinema*.

[25] Ibid., p. 162.

[26] Kellogg.

[27] Paul Doering, Lecture given at George Eastman House, 1994.

[28] Joseph E. Aiken, "Technical Notes and Reminiscences on the Presentation of Tykociner's Sound Picture Contributions," *Journal S.M.P.T.E*, August 1958, Vol. 67.

[29] Isaac Asimov, *Biographical Encyclopedia of Science and Technology*. Asimov gives a very succinct description of the respective discoveries of Edison, Fleming, and de Forest. See also Thomas S. W. Lewis, *Empire of the Air—The Men Who Made Radio*. This is an excellent story of the careers of Lee de Forest, Edwin Armstrong, and David Sarnoff.

[30] Kellogg.

[31] Coe.

[32] Reed Johnson, "Faded Image," *Rochester Times-Union*, Sept 12, 1989. This article has provided most of the information on Theodore Case's life and achievements. The Case Research Laboratory Museum in Auburn, New York has been restored and is open to visitors.

[33] Coe, p. 105.

[34] Wire recorders were capable of excellent fidelity and were quite successful for a number of years.

[35] John Minnis, "Early Talking Picture Systems Before 1914," manuscript in author's collection, no date.

[36] Author's collection.

[37] Herbert C. McKay was a former Hollywood cameraman and a prolific writer on motion pictures for the amateur. See Chap. 13 for further details.

[38] Hedden, William D. and Curtis, Kenneth B., "Early 8mm Sound Developments," *Journal of S.M.P.T.E.*, Vol. 70, August 1961.

[39] Ibid.

[40] This description is from *American Photography*, December 1932.

[41] *Filmo Topics*, Christmas Issue, 1938.

[42] David A. Gibson, letter to author, May 16, 1985.

[43] *Kansas City Star*, November 10, 1940.

[44] Author's collection.

[45] Coe.

[46] Sterling Kemp, "Magnetic Sound for 8-16mm Movies," *U.S. Camera*, December 1947 (?).

[47] Coe.

[48] George W. Cushman, "Sound For Your Color Movies," *Camera Craft*, 1958.

[49] Leendert Drukker, "Synchronized Sound for 8mm," *Popular Photography*, May 1959.

[50] Drukker, "Now Professional Sound for 8mm." *Popular Photography*, May 1960.

[51] R. J. Roman, J. M. Moriarty, and R. E. Johnson, "A New 8mm Magnetic Projector," *Journal of S.M.P.T.E.*, Vol. 69, December 1960.

[52] John Forbes, "8mm Comes of Age," *American Cinematographer*, October/November 1960.

[53] *Popular Photography*, August 1960, page 104.

[54] The Fairchild camera was invented by Lowell A. Wilkins and Henry S. Kane, both of Chicago, Illinois. U.S. Patent No. 2,910,911, November 3, 1959.

[55] Drukker, "Breakthrough in 8mm Sound," *Popular Photography*, April 1960.

[56] Drukker, "Synchro-Sound System," *Popular Photography*, March 1959.

[57] Harvey Fondiller, "It's Here—Instant Lip Sync for Super 8," *Popular Photography*, November 1968.

[58] Lenny Lipton, *The Super 8 Book*, 1975, p.113.

[59] Robert O. Doyle, "Double System Super 8," *Photomethods*, April 1975. This is an excellent treatise by the leading expert in the field. Dr. Doyle, a Harvard-trained astrophysicist who worked on the National Aeronautics and Space Adminstration's Skylab missions, was at the time president of Super8 Sound, Inc. of Cambridge, Massachusetts, manufacturers of sound systems for Super 8 film, including the Leacock system.

[60] Jasper S. Chandler, letter to the author, March 17, 1993.

[61] "Behind the Scenes," *Modern Photography*, October 1973.

62 Tony Galluzzo, "Sync Sound Movies Anyone? - Kodak Takes the Gamble," *Modern Photography*, October 1973.

63 Donald. Sutherland, "Shopper's Guide to Sound-on-Film Super 8 Cameras," *Popular Photography*, January 1976.

64 Except for certain emulsions of Super 8 film still being offered by Eastman Kodak, as noted at the conclusion of Chapter 10.

FOOTNOTES – CHAPTER 12

1 Paul R. Beck, Director of Engineering, Emerson College. Letter to the author, February 17, 1998.

2 Michael F. Tompsett of Bell Telephone Laboratories received a patent in 1978 for his charge-coupled device.

3 Network television only covered the East and Midwest until September 4, 1951, when the AT&T microwave-relay system spanning the continent was opened.

4 Francis Wheen, *Television, A History*, Century Publishing, London, 1985.

5 Wolfman Reports, 1975-76.

6 Albert Abramson, "A Short History of Television Recording," *Journal of S.M.P.T.E.*, February, 1955.

7 *Popular Photography*, March 1965.

8 Donald Sutherland, "Video Tape vs. Super 8." *Popular Photography*, September 1973.

9 Joseph J. deCourcelle, "Venture into Video," *Photographic Society of America Journal*, September 1975.

10 Andrew Pollack, "The Perils of Consumer Electronics," *New York Times*, March 22, 1981.

11 Tony Galluzzo, "Home Video Moves In," *Modern Photography*, August 1978.

12 Peggy Sealfon, "The Coming Age of Electronic Movie Making," *New York Times*, October 10, 1982.

13 Dawn Gordon, "Complete Guide to Video Cameras" *Popular Mechanics*, May 1983.

14 Arthur Goldsmith, "An Electronic Rebirth of Home Movies," *Popular Photography*, March 1984.

15 Clare Ansberry, "Analysts Speculate Kodak Leaving 8mm Video Market," *Wall Street Journal*, January 29, 1987.

16 A retired Kodak employee advised me that shortly after the CCD cameras appeared, the Company called in all unsold Kodavision cameras from its dealers, gathered them into a pile, and crushed them with a heavy truck.

17 *Popular Science*, November 1978.

18 Arthur Goldsmith, "Photons and Electrons," *Popular Photography*, September 1984.

19 Paul R. Beck, Director of Engineering, Emerson College, Boston. Letter to author.

20 Bob Brodsky, letter to the author, February 9, 2000.

FOOTNOTES– CHAPTER 13

1 Also in this series, *Animated Photography—The ABC of the Cinematograph*, by Cecil M. Hepworth, has a brief section on the Birtac and the Biokam.

2 At that time assistant director of the Marey Institute.

3 Maurice Greeson, Mr. McKay's grandson, kindly provided much of the information on Mr. McKay's life.

4 See Chapter 8 for the difference of these two processes.

5 Patricia R. Zimmermann, *Reel Families, A Social History of Amateur Film*, Indiana Univ. Press, 1995, page iv.

6 Toni Treadway, *B&T's Little Film Notebook*, P.O. Box 335, Rowley, MA 01969. Website: www.littlefilm.org

7 Giles Musitano, *The Super 8 Guide—Traditional & Emerging Media for the Small-Guage Film-Maker*, Focal Press, London.

87 John Held Jr. (1889-1958) was renowned for his drawings of flappers and hip-flasked college boys who epitomized the "roaring twenties" on the covers of popular magazines of the day.

9 Tuttle, personal communication to the author.

10 Bruce Downes, "A Quarter Century of Photography," *Popular Photography*, May 1962.

11 Drukker, personal communication to the author, October 30, 1992.

12 Founded in 1971 by Glenn E. Patch as *Shutterbug Ads*, a magazine for camera collectors. Today *Shutterbug Ads* today is a general interest photographic magazine.

13 *Modern Photography*'s circulation in 1979 was over 600,000, according to the publisher.

14 Edward Hannigan, personal communication.

15 Tony Galluzzo, personal communication.

16 Drukker, personal communication.

17 Editorial, *Petersen's Photographic Magazine*, June 1974.

18 H. Benner Hoeper, personal communication.

19 *American Cinematographer*, September 1960.

20 John Forbes, "8mm Comes of Age," *American Cinematographer*, September-November, 1960.

[21] Zimmermann, *Reel Families.*

[22] John Durniak, "The Wittnauer Ciné-Twin, A Revolutionary Camera/Projector," *Popular Photography*, November 1957.

[23] "The Wittnauer Ciné Twin," *U.S. Camera*, October 1957.

[24] Tony Galluzzo, "Polavision Revisited," *Modern Photography*, March 1978.

FOOTNOTES – CHAPTER 14

[1] John Chittock, "From Home Movies to Home Video," *The Story of Popular Photography*, Colin Ford, Editor, Trafalgar Square Publisher, Pomfret, Vermont, 1988.

[2] *Amateur Movie Makers*, October 1926.

[3] Charles Reynolds, "Creating With Film," *Popular Photography*, July 1960. The film title was *Boop*, 16mm animated black-and-white, shot by Mr. and Mrs. Grain.

[4] Most of the information on the Washington society has been provided by Mr. H. Benner Hoeper, past president of the Society.

[5] One of Sir Hiram Stevens' less successful inventions was a steam engine driven airplane. Incredibly, it achieved airborne status for a very brief period. *Encyclopedia Britannica*, 11th ed., 1911, Vols. 10 and 17.

[6] This curious statement may have been related to a perceived threat at that time by the professional projectionists' union to require a union projectionist to show movies in the home.

[7] This organization was in existence as late as 1959, according to a news item in *U.S. Camera*, May 1959.

[8] News item, Bell & Howell's *Filmo Topics,* Summer 1937 and Christmas 1937.

[9] The writer on film referred to in Chapter 12.

[10] Cushman died on February 4, 1996. Mr. Howard Lewis succeeded him as editor.

[11] All of the information on the Rochester-based festivals has been received through the courtesy of James E. Dierks, historian, grants coordinator, and master of ceremonies of *Movies on A Shoestring.*

[12] *Movie Makers*, Vol. 3, No. 5, September/October 1993.

[13] "Are Movie Clubs Worth Joining?" *Popular Photography,* November 1961.

[14] Jacob Deschin, "What's Wrong With the PSA?" *Popular Photography*, January 1962.

[15] Stuart M. Dabbs, "Let's React Today," *PSA Journal,* September 1972.

FOOTNOTES – CHAPTER 15

[1] Of the 39 filmmakers listed in the 1997 Festival Program of the Rochester International Independent Film Festival, all but six had either attended some kind of film school or were working professionally in film or video.

[2] *The Journal of Film and Video*, Volume 38, No. 3-4, 1986, a double issue with 15 articles, chiefly on the sociology of home movies.

[3] This one-hour film, constructed entirely from clips of home movies, with narration and musical background added, was selected for the 1987 Whitney Museum of Art Biennial Exhibition and was a grand prize winner at the San Francisco International Film Festival.

[4] See also "Recycled Images—The Art and Politics of Found Footage Films," by William C. Wees, *Anthology Film Archives,* New York 1993.

[5] Philip Condax, Curator of Technology, George Eastman House, personal communication, 1993.

[6] A television producer in New York City once called to ask if I had any home movie footage that was shot by people living in Chinatown or Little Italy in the 1930s! She didn't seem to accept my explanation that using a movie camera was not a hobby of the residents of those areas at that time.

[7] *Movie Makers*, June 1932.

[8] *Movie Makers*, October 1932.

[9] *Amateur Movie Makers*, Vol. 1, No. 1, January 1926.

[10] Warren Doremus is a retired Rochester television personality and founding member of the Rochester International Independent Film Festival.

[11] "The Ten Best," *Movie Makers*, December 1937. Jones' account of the making of Western Holiday can be found in *Movie Makers* for January 1938.

[12] *Movie Makers*, December 1951.

[13] Much of the biographical information on Turner has been graciously provided by Mrs. Glen H. Turner, his widow.

[14] John Kuiper, "A Note on Research in Progress, etc." *Journal of Film and Video,* Summer/Fall, 1986.

[15] *Movie Makers*, December 1950.

[16] *Movie Makers*, December 1945.

[17] P. Adams Sitney, *Visionary Film.* This work is my principal source for information on Deren and her films.

[18] Stan Whitsett, personal communication to the author, January 14, 1998.

[19] *Something Strong Within*, a film by Robert A. Nakamura. (40 minutes, B&W and color footage) Japanese American National Museum, Los Angeles, 1994.

[20] Jeffrey K. Ruoff "Forty Days Across America— Kiyooka Eichi's 1927 Travelogues" Film History, Volume 4, pp 237-256, 1990. Dr. Ruoff, now professor of film and video at Middlebury College, Middlebury, Vermont, learned of the existence of Kiyooka's films in 1989. Dr. Ruoff was able to borrow Kiyooka's 30-minute film and had it transferred to one-inch video tape. He was also able to interview Prof. Kiyooka when the latter visited this country in 1989. From the interview and study of Kiyooka's film, Dr. Ruoff has constructed a delightful account of a most unusual film that sheds light on many aspects of American life in the days of the Model T, as well as the reaction of a young Japanese to this country and its mores.

[21] Ellen Joan Pollock, "Film of JFK's Assassination Gets Price Tag of $16 Million," *Wall Street Journal,* August 4, 1999.

[22] Curiously, Zapruder, when first asked about his filming speed, reportedly replied that his camera was "set to take normal speed movies at 24 frames per second." Although he later amended this remark, the erroneous figure was seized upon by critics of the Commission's report as evidence of manipulation by the FBI. Those who believed that more than one gunman was involved postulated that the FBI used the slower camera speed figure to make it seem possible for one gunman to get off three shots in the allotted time. Of course Zapruder was wrong, the camera could not and did not operate at 24 frames per second, and it was shown that a practiced shooter could get off three shots in the time that elapsed, as shown by Zapruder's film.

[23] *Amateur Movie Makers,* Vol. 1, No. 1, December 1926.

[24] Copyright 1986, International Center for 8mm Film and Video.

[25] Richard Chalfen, "Cinema Naiveté: A Study of Home Movie Making as Visual Communication." *Studies in the Anthropology of Visual Communication,* 2:2 (1975): 87-103.

[26] Journal of Film and Video, Volume 38, Number 3-4, Summer-Fall 1986.

[27] *How to Make Exciting Home Movies & Stop Boring Your Friends and Relatives*. Ed and Dodi Schultz. (Title page missing from my copy!)

[28] Patricia R. Zimmermann, *Reel Families—A Social History of Amateur Film*, Indiana Press, 1995.

[29] Doug Hubley, "Amateur Film: What Really Matters?" *Moving Image Review*. Northeast Historic Film, Winter 1999.

FOOTNOTES – CHAPTER 16

[1] Optical Toys, P. O. Box 23, Putney VT 05346 carries an assortment of toys, some replicas of the originals.

[2] George Gilbert, *Collecting Photographica*, Hawthorn/Dutton 1976.

BIBLIOGRAPHY

Ackerman, Carl W., *George Eastman*, Houghton Mifflin, 1930. Authorized and edited by Eastman himself, this work treats its subject very gently.

Alden, Andrew, *A Bolex History*, cameras, projectors, etc. Self-published, West Yorks, England, 1992.

Amateur Cinema League, *Guide to Making Better Movies*, NY 1940.

Ariel, Pete, *Cinematographic Register*, Deutsches Filmmuseum, Frankfurt Am Main, 1989. Four volume set, loose-leaf, pictures and text (German) on 1,120 items of pre-cinema, magic lanterns, and amateur and professional motion picture cameras and projectors, with great detail on year of origin, cost, and technical specifications. Invaluable to the serious collector.

Auer, Michel and Michele Ory, *Histoire de la Camera Cine Amateur*. Les Editions de l'Amateur, Paris, 1979. Narration and good photos.

Azimov, Isaac, *Azimov's Biographical Encyclopedia of Science and Technology*, Doubleday & Co. 1964. Biographies from Aristotle to John Glenn.

Bailey, Joe A. See Lahue and Bailey.

Balzer, Richard, *Optical Amusements: Magic Lanterns and Other Transforming Images*. Self-published, 1987. Excellent source of illustrations of lanterns and slides.

Barnes, John, *The Beginnings of the Cinema in England*. David and Charles, London, 1981.

Bennet, Colin, *Handbook of Kenematography*. London, 1911.

Bitzer, G.W., *Billy Bitzer His Story*. Farrar, Strauss and Giroux, NY 1973. Memoirs of Griffith's clever cameraman.

Brayer, Elizabeth, *George Eastman A Biography*. Johns Hopkins University Press, Baltimore, 1996. Massive (637 pages). First biography of Eastman since Ackerman's. Marvelously detailed personal history of the man and his friends, frequently shedding light on the technical history of the company.

Braun, Marta, *Picturing Time—The Work of Etienne-Jules Marey*. University of Chicago Press, 1992. Consummate work of scholarship on this seminal figure in the photography of motion.

Brodsky, Robert P. and Toni Treadway, *Super 8 in the Video Age-Using Amateur Movie Film Today*. Brodsky & Treadway, 1983.

Brownlow, Kevin, *Napoleon—Abel Gance's Classic Film*. A.A. Knopf, New York, 1983.

Brownlow, Kevin, *The Parade's Gone By*. A. A. Knopf, Inc. Ballantine Books, NY 1968. Fascinating interviews with all the great names of silent films; stars, directors, producers and cameramen. Illus.

Brummit, Wyatt, *George Eastman of Kodak*. Unpublished manuscript by a Kodak veteran who was assigned the task, ca.1960. No t.o.c., no index.

Ceram, C.W., *Archaeology of the Cinema*. Harcourt Brace & Word, ca. 1940? Good material about pre- and early cinema, excellent illustrations, bibliography. A classic.

Chanan, Michael, *The Dream That Kicks The Prehistory and Early Years of Cinema in Britain*, Second Edition. Routledge, London 1996. 293 pages with no illustrations! The jacket says "a fascinating account of the rich but hitherto hidden history of the origins of film."

Clark, Ronald W., *Edison, the Man Who Made the Future*. G.P. Putnam & Sons., New York 1977.

Clarke, Charles G., *Professional Cinematography*. The American Society of Cinematographers, Hollywook, California, 1964.

Coe, Brian, *The Birth of Photography*. Taplinger Publishing, New York, 1977.

Coe, Brian, *The History of Movie Photography*. Ash & Grant, London 1981. Important book, large format, well illustrated.

Cook, Olive, *Movement in Two Dimensions*. London, 2963. Illustrated history of pre-cinema.

Croy, Homer, *How Motion Pictures are Made*, Harper & Bros. New York, 1918.

Cushman, George W., *Sound for Your Color Movies*, Camera Craft Publishing Co. San Francisco, 1958.

Dickson, W.K.L. and Antonia Dickson, *History of the Kinetograph, Kinetoscope and Kinetophonograph,* Ayer Company, Salem NH, reprint edition 1984.

Eastman, George, *Chronicles of a Second African Trip,* The Friends of the Eastman University of Rochester Libraries, Rochester, NY 1987.

Eastman Kodak Company, *How to Make Good Movies,* Rochester, NY 1938.

Eastman Kodak Company, *Journey: 75 Years of Kodak Research,* Rochester, NY 1989. Informal biographies of many of the significant men and women of Kodak Research Labs.

Eastman Kodak Company, *How to Make Good Sound Movies,* Rochester, New York, 197? (exact year not known).

Eder, Joseph Maria, *History of Photography,* Dover 1972. Massive volume, heavy on technology to 1932.

Encyclopedia Britannica, *A Dictionary of Arts, Sciences, Literature and General Information.* Eleventh Edition, 29 volumes, 1910–1911. A delightful source of information on technology as it was then   photography, photometry, photochemistry and celestial photography occupy fifty pages.

Fielding, Raymond, *A Technological History of Motion Pictures and Television.* An anthology from the pages of the Journal of the Society of Motion Picture and Television Engineers. Edited and with an introduction by Raymond Fielding. University of California Press, Berkeley, California, 1967. Includes the Matthews and Tarkington "Early History of Amateur Motion Picture Film" as well as many others of historical interest.

Ford, John, editor, *The Story of Popular Photography,* Trafalgar Square Publishing, North Pomfret, Vermont, 1988. Chapters by various British authorities.

Galluzzo, Tony, Home Video Movies—*How to Get the Most From Your Camcorder and VCR.* Compute! Publications, Inc., Greensboro, North Carolina, 1987.

Gilbert, George, *Collecting Photographica.* Hawthorn/Dutton, New York, 1976.

Gosser, H. Mark, *Selected Attempts at Stereoscopic Motion Pictures and Their Relationship to the Development of Motion Picture Technology, 1852-1903.* Arno Press, 1977.

Gross, Harry I., *Antique and Classic Cameras.* Amphoto, New York, 1965. A pioneering book, with some errors.

Guide to Making Better Movies, Amateur Cinema League. New York, 1940.

Hendricks, Gordon, *Beginnings of the Biograph,* The Beginnings of American Film, New York, 1964. This and the two following volumes are very important sources on their subjects, thoroughly researched, heavily footnoted.

Hendricks, Gordon, *The Edison Motion Picture Myth,* The Beginnings of American Film, New York, 1961.

Hendricks, Gordon, *The Kinetoscope, The Beginnings of American Film,* New York, 1966.

Hendricks, Gordon, *Eadweard Muybridge—The Father of the Motion Picture,* Grossman, New York, 1975.

Hepworth, Cecil M., *Animated Photography—The ABC of the Cinematograph.* 1900, Reprint edition by Arno Press, 1970.

Hopkins, Albert A., *Magic—Stage Illusions and Scientific Diversions, Including Trick Photography,* 1897, Arno Press, Reprint 1977.

Hopwood, Henry V., *Living Pictures Their History, Photo Production and Practical Working,* 1899 Reprint edition by Arno Press, 1970.

Jenkins, Reese V., *Images and Enterprise, Technology and the American Photographic Industry, 1839 to 1925.* Johns Hopkins University Press. Detailed, scholarly work.

Johnson, Osa, *I Married Adventure.* J. B. Lippincott, 1940. 376 pages of the Johnsons' classic African adventures. Amusing, informative, good photographs.

Katz, Ephraim, *The Film Encyclopedia,* Putnam & Sons, NY 1979. Bios of actors, directors, etc.

Kingslake, Rudolf, *Lenses in Photography.* A. S. Barnes & Co., New York, Rev. ed. 1963. By the dean of lens design.

Kircher, Athanasius, *Ars Magna Lucis et Umbrae.* Rome, 1646, Second Edition, Amsterdam, 1671, as referenced by Liesegang.

Lahue, Kalton C. and Joe A. Bailey, *Glass, Brass, & Chrome: The American 35mm Miniature Camera.* University of Oklahoma Press, Norman, 1972.

Lescaboura, Austin C., *The Cinema Handbook*. Scientific American Publishing Co., New York, 1921.

Lewis, Thomas S. W., *Empire of the Air—The Men Who Made Radio*. Harper Collins, 1991. Excellent story of the careers of deForest, Armstrong, and Sarnoff.

Liesegang, Franz Paul, *Dates and Sources*. First printing in 1926, 1986, ed. by the Magic Lantern Society of Great Britain. The latter work has furnished much of the information on the eighteenth century works.

Lipton, Lenny, *The Super 8 Book*. Straight Arrow Books, San Francisco, 1975.

MacGowan, Kenneth, *Behind the Screen*. Delacorte Press, New York, 1965.

Marey, Etienne Jules, *Le Mouvement*. Paris, 1894. As cited by Liesegang.

Mast, Gerald, *A Short History of the Movies*, Macmillan, New York, 1986.

Matzkin, Myron A., *The Super 8 Film Makers Handbook*. Amphoto, Garden City, 1977.

McKay, Herbert C., *Amateur Movie Making*. Falk Publishing, New York, 1928.

McKay, Herbert C., *Motion Picture Photography for the Amateur*. Falk Publishing, New York, 1924.

McKee, Gerald, *The Home Cinema: Classic Home Movie Projectors 1922-1940*. Gerald McKee, Gerrards Cross, Bucks., England, 1989.

McKeown, James M. and Joan C., *Price Guide to Antique and Classic Cameras*. Centennial Photo Service, Grantsburg, Wisconsin, 1995-1996 edition. Unique and indispensable illustrated catalog of over 7,000 items.

Mees, C.E. Kenneth, *From Dry Plates to Ektachrome Film, A Story of Photographic Research*. Ziff-Davis Publishing Company, New York, 1961.

Mikolas, Mark, and Gunther Hoos, *Handbook of Super 8 Production*, United Business Publications, 1978.

Musser, Charles, *High Class Moving Pictures: Lyman Howe and the Forgotten Era of Traveling Exhibitors*. 1880-1920., Princeton University Press, 1991.

Newhall, Beaumont, *The History of Photography*. The Museum of Modern Art, 1949.

Pincus, Edward, *Guide to Filmmaking*. New American Library, 1969.

Pintoff, Ernest, *The Complete Guide to American Film Schools and Cinema and Television Courses*. Penquin Books, New York, 1994.

Piper, James, *Personal Filmmaking*. Reston Publishing Co., 1975.

Quigley, Martin Jr., *Magic Shadows: The Story of the Origin of Motion Pictures*. Quigley Publishing Co., New York, 1960.

Ramsaye, Terry, *A Million and One Nights*. Simon & Schuster, NY, 1926. A contemporay of many of the pioneers, Ramsaye spins a tale perhaps biased and embellished a source of facts (?) to be found nowhere else.

Rawlence, Christopher, *The Missing Reel*. Atheneum Macmillan New York, 1990. A unique, thoroughly researched story of the mysterious Augustin Aime LePrince.

Remise, Jac, Pascal Remise, and Regis Van DeWalle, *Magie Lumineuse*. Balland, Paris, 1979. Large (10" x 13"), marvelously illustrated history of pre-cinema amusements.

Repinski, Cynthia A., *The Univex Story*. Centennial Photo Service, Grantsburg, Wisconsin, 1991.

Robinson, David, *History of World Cinema*, Stein & Day, 1973.

Robinson, Jack Fay, *Bell & Howell Company—A 75 Year History, Bell & Howell Company*. Chicago, 1982. An "approved" history.

Roehl, Harvey N., *Player Piano Treasury*. Vestal Press, 1961.

Rose, Samuel G., "Alexander Victor—Motion Picture Pioneer," *Journal S.M.P.T. E.*, August 1963.

Sadoul, Georges, *L'Invention du Cinema* 1832-1897. Editions de Noel, Paris, 1945.

Shannon, William J., *Movie Making Made Easy*. Moorfield & Shannon, Nutley NJ 1934.

Sitney, P. Adams, *Visionary Film: The American Avant-Garde 1943-1978*. Oxford University Press, Second Edition, 1979.

Stone, O. L., *History of Massachusetts Industries*. 1930 Edition.

Stuber, Rose R., *William G. Stuber—A Biography*. Privately printed in an edition of 165 copies, 1941.

Taft, Robert, *Photography and the American Scene*. Dover Publications, 1964.

Talbot, Frederick A., *Practical Cinematography and its Applications*. London, 1913.

Trask, Richard, *Pictures of the Pain—Photography and the Assassination of President Kennedy*. Yeoman Press, Danvers, Massachusetts, 1994. Monumental study of every photographic record of the assassination, with excellent coverage of Abraham Zapruder's filming.

Wensberg, Peter C., *Land's Polaroid, A Company and the Man Who Invented It*. Houghton Mifflin Company, Boston 1987. An insider's sympathetic view.

Wheen, Francis, *Television, A History*. Century Publishing, London, 1985.

Zimmermann, Patricia R., *Reel Families –A Social History of Amateur Film*. Indiana University Press, 1995.

PICTURE CREDITS

Picture Credits.

The following abbreviations have been used:

AR	*Ariel's Cinematographic Register*	**VA**	Victor Animatograph Co.
BH	Bell & Howell Company	**J75**	*Journey: 75 Years of Kodak Research*
CC	Ceram, *Archaeology of the Cinema*	**KA**	Author's Collection
CB	Coe, Bryan, *The Birth of Photography*	**MB**	Maison Balland
CH	Coe, Bryan, *The History of the Movies*	**MOJ**	Martin & Osa Johnson Safari Museum
CM	The Cayuga Museum	**PB**	Paillard Bolex Co.
EKC	Eastman Kodak Co	**RB**	Robinson, *Bell & Howell Co.*
FL	Liesegang, *Dates & Sources*	**RM**	Ramsaye, *A Million and One Nights*
GEH	George Eastman House	**RV**	Revere Camera Co.

Numbers shown are Figure Numbers. Refer to the Bibliography for a full description of the source.

Chapter 1

1, 2, 10, 21, 22, 24 **FL**; 3, 4, 5, 6, 9 **MB**; 7, 8, 11, 12,13, 14, **KA**; 15, 16, 17, 23, 30, **CC**; 18 Hopwood, *Living Pictures*; 19 Science Museum, London; 27, 29, 36, **CB**; 28 Gernshiem Collection, University of Texas, Austin; 31, 33 Jenkins, *Images and Enterprise*; 34 *Rochester Democrat & Chronicle*; 37 *Image*, **GEH**, Vol. 26, No 2, June 1983; 32 Bayerische National-museum, Munich; 35 **J75**; 38 **EKC**.

Chapter 2

40, 73, Croy; 41, 42, 44 Hendricks; 43, 45, 48, 50, 51, 82, 83 **CC**; 46, 79 **CH**; 47, 49, 52 Poyet; 53, 54, 55 **GEH**; 68, Hopkins; 56, 60 Clark; 57, 61, 62, 63, 64, 70, 71, 74, 75, 78 Ramsaye; 58, 67 Edison National Historic Site; 65, 66, 81 *Scientific American*; 69 Bitzer; 72 **KA**; 76 Alan B. Cotter; 77 Kirk Bauer; 80, **AR**.

Chapter 3

84, 87, 88, 89, 98 **AR**; 85 Barnes; 86 Hopwood; 90 Fred Spira Collection; 91, 92, 93, 94, 99, 100, 101, 102, 106, 107, 108 Courtesy of Mrs. Jesse Walker Griggs; 109, 110 **KA**; 96 *American Photography*, August 1923; 97 *Camera Craft*, April 1913; 104 Edison National Historic Site; 105 *American Boy*, April 1917.

Chapter 4

112, 117, 118, 119 **J75**; 113 **EKC**; 115 Edison National Historic Site; 116 **RM**; 120, 123, 126, 130, **EKC**; 121 **KA**; 122 *Movie Makers*, February 1932; 127,129, **MOJ**; 128 Eastman, *Chronicles of A Second African Trip*.

Chapter 5

132, 151 **KA**; 134, 136, 137, 138, 140, 141, 142, 143, 145, 147, 149, 152, 153, 156 **EKC**; 135 **BH**; 139 **J75**; 146 Polaroid Corporation.

Chapter 6

158, 165 Chicago Historical Society; 164, 167, 169, 171, 172 **BH**; 159 Kirk Kekatos; 160, 161,168, 170, 173, 175, 176 **RB**; 166 **KA**; 174 Bell & Howell Annual Report, 1952; 177 Bell & Howell Annual Report, 1978.

Chapter 7

178 **CC**; 179, 180 Pathé Frères Catalog, 1913; 181, 184, 185, 186, 189 **VA**; 182, 187 Rose, Samuel G., "Alexander Victor..." *Journal SMPTE;* August 1963; 188, 195, 203 **AR**; 190 *Movie Makers*, December 1931; 192 *American Cinematographer*, June 1938; 193,194 *Moving Picture Age,* January 1920, September 1921; 204, 206, 207, 208 **PB**; 210, 211, 213, 215, 216 Repinski, Cynthia, *The Univex Story;* 217 The Briskin Family; 218, 219, 220, 221 **RV**.

Chapter 8

222 **FL**; 223 **BH**; 224 *Filmo Topics,* June-July 1932; 225, 226 Mees, From Dry Plates . . . ; 227 **CH**; 228, 229 **J75**; 230 *U.S. Camera,* May 1961; 231 Wensberg, *Land's Polaroid;* 232, 234 Polaroid Corporation.

Chapter 9

236, 239, 240, 241, 242, 243 **KA**; 237 **AR**; 238 **EKC**; 244 **BH**; 245, 246 Sherman/Matzkin, *Modern Photography*, November 1963.

Chapter 10

248, 249, 253 **EKC**; 251 **BH**; 252 photo by Leonard Lipton, *Popular Photography,* December 1965; 254 Fuji Film Corporation.

Chapter 11

255 **J75**; 256, 270, 271, 272, 273 **KA**; 259 Mrs. Peter Chiesa; 260, 278, 280, 281, 282 **EKC**; 261, Petersen's Guide to Movie Making, 1973; 262 Wohleber "How the Movies Learned to Talk," *American Heritage of Invention and Technology*; 264 – 269 Case Research Lab Museum, Cayuga, NY; 274 RCA Victor Corporation; 276, 277 **BH**; 279, 280, Fairchild Camera and Instrument Corporation; 283, 284 Cinema Beaulieu Div. of Hervic Corp.

Chapter 12

285 Cavendish, *New Illustrated Scientific & Invention Encylcopedia;* 286 **KA**; 287, 288, 292 Sony Corporation; 290, 291 **EKC**.

Chapter 13

293 Maurice Greeson; 294 **EKC**; 295 Tom Cushman.

Chapter 14

304, 305 *Movie Makers,* December 1926, Vol. 1, No. 1; 306 The Maxim Family.

Chapter 15

307 Movie Makers, January 1935; 308, 309 The Turner Family; 310 The Gunnell Family; 312 Charles N. Gleason; 313, 314 Amateur Cinema League 50th Anniversary Program; 315 Anthology Film Archives; 317 **BH**; 318 Warren Commission Report, Exhibit 885; 320 Roland J. Zavada, "Report to the Assassination Review Board," Figure 4-23.

Chapter 16

321 T.F. Naylor.

APPENDIX 1 – ARCHIVES OF AMATEUR FILMS – A SURVEY

A survey of archives of amateur film was undertaken in mid-1997. Questionnaires were eventually mailed to 27 archives including two in Europe, two in Canada, and the rest in the United States. Numerous follow-ups were required and after 12 months, 22 replies were received. A summary of the replies by question follows.

Question No. 1

Approximately what percentage of your film archive is amateur footage? If possible please estimate the number of feet in 8mm, Super 8, 16mm and video.

Of the 17 that reported percentages, 10 reported 5 percent or less, two reported 10 percent, four reported 20 percent to 30 percent, and 2 reported 50 percent to 75 percent.

From the 10 respondents that gave estimated amounts, a total of 4,543,000 feet of amateur film, all gauges, was reported. By far the greatest amount of film, probably 80 percent or more is in 16mm.

Question No. 2

Are you actively seeking amateur footage?

There were thirteen unqualified "Yes" answers, three qualified "Yes", and six clear "No." Of the six negative answers, only one offered an explanation, which was that while they were deeply interested in films about a certain cultural group, they would not want it advertised "for fear of being flooded with useless material." In one or two cases the objectives of the archive make it unlikely that amateur film would be of appropriate content.

Question No. 3

Do you specialize in a particular genre of amateur film?

Here the answers were generally predictable from the name of the archive, except that it might not be immediately apparent that the National Archives at College Park, Maryland accept only visual records that "are appropriate for preservation by the Government as evidence of its organization, function, policies, decisions, procedures, and transactions."

A major non-regional archive gives priority to amateur films made prior to 1928. The state archives understandably give first priority to films made by residents of the state, and of state or regional significance. One interesting response was "We prefer films made by cinema clubs, as their films tend to be of better quality."

Question No. 4

What are your criteria for accepting amateur films?

Almost all respondents put relevance to their mission as first criterion; the second most mentioned was good production quality. Less often cited were copyright or other use restrictions and physical condition of the film. In general, the larger the archive, the more detailed are the collecting policies. The Operational Policies of the Human Studies Archives of the Smithsonian Institution and those of Northeast Historic Film, each having holdings of 1,400,000 feet, are examples of detailed, formal policy statements. Northeast Historic Film re-packages and sells some of its acquired footage, and its policy manual is here reproduced by permission.

Question No. 5

In general, do you feel that more effort should be made to preserve amateur films?

This was the only question on which there was absolute unanimity. Specific answers were informative; two respondents stressed the need to educate the public about the importance of preserving amateur films. One archivist stated: "Our amateur collections contain the best documentation of the fishing industry, depression era, logging, construction, and recreation that we have. I see these amateur collections as giving us a vision of our recent past, documenting the everyday social structures of our lives, not the ones presented to us by the entertainment, industrial or news type collections."

Another interesting response to this question was: "A particular problem are the people who come into a town, advertise for home films, give a showing at a local theater, then give the films to the local historical society, who generally have no idea of how to conserve them."

One respondent suggested that more scholarly articles should employ amateur footage as primary source material.

Question No. 6

Please describe the accessibility of your archives to the public or qualified researchers.

The replies to this question ranged from "practically none at present" to "open, no restrictions," with the majority describing a distinctly limited public access, chiefly because of staffing problems. Not surprisingly, the larger the archive the more structured are access regulations, however these archives appear better equipped to handle sophisticated research tools such as lap-tops, scanners, data transmission, etc.

Some archives charge a user fee, generally the larger ones, citing the cost of preservation and staffing. One archive reported that their catalogue is "slowly going on the Internet." Again, the response of Northeast Historic Film is quoted with their permission: "See website www.acadia.net/oldfilm for access. Free to researchers at archives. Reference copies also sent out."

Archives Responding

Alaska Moving Image Preservation Association, Anchorage
Amateur Athletic Foundation, Ziffren Sports Center, Los Angeles
Andy Warhol Foundation, New York City
Archives of Ontario Library, Toronto
Center for the Study of Southern Culture, University, Mississippi
Chicago Historical Society, Illinois
East Anglian Film Archive, Norwich, England
George Eastman House, Rochester, New York
Japanese American National Museum, Los Angeles
Long Beach Museum of Art, California
Minnesota Historical Society, St. Paul
National Archives at College Park, Maryland
National Archives of Canada, Ottawa

National Center for Jewish Film, Brandeis University
National Center for Film and Video Preservation, Los Angeles
National Museum of Natural History (Smithsonian)
Nebraska State Historical Society, Lincoln
Northeast Historic Film, Bucksport, Maine
Oregon Historical Society, Portland
State Historical Society of North Dakota, Bismark
State Historical Society of Wisconsin, Madison
University of California at San Diego

Summary – Overall

As an overall summary, all respondents stressed the value of home movies as historical documents. All agreed that more effort should be made to preserve amateur footage. Almost all replies indicate that the costs of preservation, storage, cataloging, and staffing lead either to severely limited access for the general public or highly structured access procedures.

Some conclusions that might be drawn from this limited survey are:

1. Greater effort must be made to educate the public as to the value of amateur footage.

2. More scholarly study should be made of known archives of amateur film.

3. More funding should be sought for regional archives.

Two archives have particularly significant amounts of amateur footage: Northeast Historic Film, in Bucksport, Maine, has nearly 1.5 million feet in all gauges, reportedly the largest such archive in North America. The National Museum of Natural History in Washington, D.C., has almost the same amount. Both are actively seeking amateur footage that meets their specific criteria.

Some film festivals retain copies of selected entries, which are then made available to groups, or are included in touring programs to other festivals, media art centers and universities. The Rochester International Independent Film Festival, better known as "Movies on a Shoestring," has preserved copies of selected films from its festivals since 1972.

APPENDIX 2: CHRONOLOGY OF AMATEUR MOTION PICTURE FILMS PRODUCED BY EASTMAN KODAK

Note: Figures in parentheses are American Standards Association (ASA) film speed ratings: (daylight/tungsten). The character "a" signifies "with appropriate filter."

1923 June
16mm reversal film on cellulose acetate (safety) base. (10/?)

1928 August
16mm Kodacolor, black and white film with embossed base, requiring tri-color filters on camera and projector.

1931 June
Cine-Kodak Super Sensitive Panchromatic film.

1932 March
New Supersensitive Kodacolor film.

1932 July
Cine-Kodak Eight Panchromatic film. (8/5)

1934 May
New Cine-Kodak 16mm, emulsion more sensitive to color values, speed amply sufficient for ordinary work indoors and out, less expensive.

1935 April
Cine-Kodak Kodachrome Safety Film, full color in the film. (8/3a)

1936 April
Cine-Kodak Kodachrome Safety Film, Type A, made for use with photoflood lamps. (8a/12)

1936 May
Cine-Kodak Eight Kodachrome film.

1936 September
Regular outdoor Kodachrome film for both 8mm and 16mm increased in speed

1936 October
Type A Kodachrome available in 8mm.

1938 November
Cine-Kodak Super-XX Panchromatic Safety film Twice as fast as 1931 film. "Take pictures in pouring rain, in woods, after dark. Indoors at f/1.9 with 2 50 watt bulbs placed 3 feet from subject." (100/64)

1939 April
Cine-Kodak Super-X Panchromatic. Slightly higher contrast, less graininess, better definition. (32/24)

1939 August
Cine-Kodak Eight Panchromatic Film.

1941 February
"Safety positive film (16mm perforated for Cine-Kodak Eight camera) is available. In addition to clear base, the following tints are also available – fire-light, sunshine, purple haze, inferno."

1948 March
Announced Kodak Reversal Panchromatic safety film for 8mm and 16mm with blue-dyed anti-halation backing. In July, film names changed to Kodak Super-X blue film (40/32) or Super-XX blue base film (100/80).

1952 June
Kodak Sonotrack coating announced for processed single-perforated 16mm film.

1953 June
25-foot magazines of 8mm Kodak Super-X blue base reversal film (Ciné-Kodak film without processing) and 8mm C-P color film (Kodachrome film without processing) is available. (Magazines painted an olive color to distinguish them from film that can be processed by Kodak.)

Ciné-Kodak Tri-X C-P reversal film announced. 16mm film with a speed approximately 50 percent higher than Super-XX film, with medium graininess. (Commercial, industrial, athletic uses where adverse lighting condition frequently encountered. (200/160)

1955 June
Ciné-Kodak Tri-X C-P reversal film available. (High speed and improved suitability for processing in Independent 16mm processing laboratories.)

1958

Names of all Cine-Kodak films changed:

Kodachrome film, daylight type, 8mm, becomes Kodachrome movie film, daylight type, 8mm

Ciné-Kodak fine grain positive film, 8mm, becomes Kodak fine grain positive movie film, 8mm.

1960   May

Kodak Processing Laboratory in Rochester ready to provide Kodak 8mm Sonotrack coating service. (Stripe is applied to processed 8mm movie film between perforations and film edge, for magnetic sound track.

1960   July

Kodak announces Kodachrome 8mm or 16mm duplicates, plus Sonotrack coating service.

1961   February

Kodachrome II film (2-1/2 times faster, less graininess, improved color rendition, reduction in contrast allows greater subject brightness range; 8mm and 16mm, Daylight type (25/6a) and Type A (25a/40).

1965   May

Super 8 film, a new gauge of Kodachrome II film, 8mm wide yet with 50 percent larger picture area. Supplied in 50 ft. cartridge. Processing available at all U. S. labs. Duplicates available from Rochester only. Sonotrack also available for original or duplicates.

1968 Apr. Kodak Plus-X reversal film 7276 and Kodak Tri-X reversal film 7278, available in 50-foot Super 8 cartridges. (Previously only available on special order.)

1965   June

Double Super 8 films, Kodachrome II, Plus-X and Tri-X available on special order.

1969

Kodak projection cartridge A (Super 8, 50-foot) and Kodak projection cartridge B (Super 8, 100-foot) available.

1970   June

Protective clear 16-inch leader and 7-inch trailer added to Super 8 cartridges for Kodachrome II movie film, Type A, (KA464).

1971   August

Ektachrome 160, a new Super 8 film, with speed of ASA 160, enables filming indoors without movie lights: "movies by candlelight." Called "XL" for "existing light." (100a/160)

1973

Ektasound System announced, cameras taking special Ektasound Super 8 cartridge.

Note: Most of above information was excerpted from Eastman Kodak Company News Release CP77100469NR, estimated to have been released circa November 1971. Text in quotation marks has been copied verbatim (more or less) from that document. Prior to 1971 Kodak did not show film speeds. Those shown were obtained from Popular Photography Directory issues. A retired Eastman Kodak engineer advised that for decades Kodak refused to publish any speed value for its films or to acknowledge the validity or usefulness of those published by others, probably for doubt of the reliability of older speed value systems.

–Martin Scott, e-mail to author, August 31, 1999.

Film Width in mm	FILM NAME	TYPE	EXPOSURE INDEX ASA or equivalent — Day	Tung.	LENGTHS in FEET AND PACKING (D.L.=Daylight Loading; Mag.=Magazines; B=Bulk; L.P.=Laboratory Packed)	SPECIAL CHARACTERISTICS, FEATURES, AND USES
	AGFA-GEVAERT, INC.					
8	Agfachrome CT 13 S	Color	16		25 ft., 100 ft. D.L.	Fine-grain, very thin emulsion
8	Agfachrome CT 17S	Color	25(a)	40	25 ft., 100 ft. D.L.	Fine-grain, very thin emulsion
	BOLSEY KII					
Sgl. 8	Daylight Type	Color	25		25 ft. D.L. magazine for Bolsey 8 camera	
Sgl. 8	Type A	Color		40	As above.	
	CINEPHONIC *Dist., Fairchild Industrial Products*					
Dbl. 8	Cinephonic, Type A	Color	10(a)	12	50 ft. D.L. rolls	Balanced for 3200 K photoflood
Dbl. 8	Cinephonic B&W	Pan	100	120	50 ft. D.L. rolls	
	COLORCADE *Dist., Chemtrol Corp.*					
Dbl. 8	Colorcade	Color	10	10(a)	50 ft. D.L.	
Dbl. 8	Colorcade	Color	10(a)	16	50 ft. D.L.	
	DU PONT					
16	928 A "Superior" 4 (negative)	Pan	320	250	100 ft., 200, 400 D.L.; 400, 600, 1,200 ft. L.P.	Highly sensitive, for low light levels
35	928 B "Superior" 4 (negative)	Pan	320	250	100 D.L.; 200, 400, 1000 ft. L.P.	Same as above
16	910 A (Neg. or Rev.)	Pan	50(b)	32(b)	100, 200 D.L.; 400, 1,200 ft. L.P.	Fine grain, wide latitude, medium speed
16	930 A Rapid Reversal	Pan	32	25	100, 200, 400 D.L.; 400, 600, 1,200 ft. L.P.	Fine grain, wide latitude; for rapid reversal
16	931 A High Speed Rapid Reversal	Pan	64(b)	50(b)	100, 200, 400 D.L.; 400, 600, 1,200 ft. L.P.	Especially for extra-rapid high-temperature processing
35	931 B High Speed Rapid Reversal	Pan	80	64	100 D.L.; 400, 1000 L.P.	Especially for extra-rapid high-temperature processing
16	936 A Superior 2 (negative)	Pan	160(b)	125	100, 200, 380, 400, 1000 ft. D.L.; 400, 600, 1,200 ft. L.P.	Very fine grain, medium speed, wide latitude
35	936 B Superior 2 (negative)	Pan	80	125	100, 200, 380, 400, 1000 L.P.	Same as above.
16	131 "Gronar" High Speed (Neg. or Rev.)	Pan	160(b)	100	100, 200, 400, 1000 L.P.	Especially for rapid high-temperature processing
35	136 "Gronar" Superior Fine Grain Negative	Pan	80	64	125 ft. D.L.; 250, 500, 1,250 ft. L.P.	Fine-grain, medium-speed, wide latitude
16	136 "Gronar" Superior Negative	Pan	125	100	125, 230, 450 ft. D.L.; 500, 1,250 ft. L.P.	Same as above.
35	140 "Gronar" High Contrast Negative	Pan	125	100	125, 250, 500, 1,250 ft. L.P.	High-contrast, fine-grain
16	140 "Gronar" High Contrast Negative	Pan	80	64	125, 250, 450 ft. D.L.; 500, 1,250 ft. L.P.	Same as above.
16 & 35	937 "Superior" 3 Negative	Pan	250	200	16-mm: 100, 200, 380, 400 ft. D.L.; 400, 1,200 L.P. 35-mm: 100 ft. D.L.; 200, 400, 1,000 ft. L.P.	For professional motion picture and television production; high-speed
	DYNACHROME					
Dbl. 8	Dynachrome 25	Color	25	12(a)	25 ft. D.L. rolls	Reversal, fine grain
Dbl. 8	Dynachrome 40	Color	25(a)	40	25 ft. D.L. rolls	Reversal, fine grain
16	Natural Color, Daylight Type	Color	10(a)	5(a)	25 ft. D.L. rolls	Reversal
Dbl. 8	Natural Color, Type A	Color	40	16	25 ft. D.L. rolls	Reversal
Super 8	Dynachrome Super 8	Color			50-ft. continuous cartridge	
	ESO-S					
16	Durachrome	Color	25	40	100 ft. D.L., 200 ft. B	
Super 8	Durachrome	Color	25	40	25 ft. D.L., 200 ft. B	
Dbl. 8	Durachrome	Color	10	16	100-ft.; 50-ft. mag.	
16	Miracle Color	Color	25(a)	40	25-ft. mag.; 25-ft. D.L.; 100-ft. H-8 Bolex	High-resolution, fine grain
Super 8	Miracle Color	Color	25	40	25-ft. cassette	High-resolution, fine grain
16	Deluxe Sepia	Pan	40	25	100-ft. D.L.	Has characteristic sepia color when finished
Dbl. 8	Deluxe Sepia	Pan	40	25	25-ft. D.L.	
16	Miracle Hi-Speed	Pan	250	200	100-ft. D.L.; 50-ft. mag.	High sensitivity
Dbl. 8	Miracle Hi-Speed	Pan	250	200	25-ft. D.L.; 25-ft. mag.	

335

APPENDIX 3 – 1967 SURVEY OF AMATEUR FILM MANUFACTURERS

continued on next page

Format	Product	Type	Speed	Sizes	Notes
Super 8	Super 8 Miracle Hi-Speed	Pan	250 / 200	25-ft. mag.	High sensitivity
Super 8	4-S High Speed	Pan	800	100 ft. D.L.; 50-ft. mag.	Recommended for very poor light conditions
Dbl. 8	4-S High-Speed	Pan	800	100 ft. and 200 ft. D.L. sound and sil. perf. 50 ft. 16-mm mags, and	
16	4-S Hi-Speed	Pan	800	100 ft., 400 ft. B	
16	Super Panchro	Pan	40 / 25	25-ft. mag.	All-purpose
Dbl. 8	Super Panchro	Pan	40 / 25	25-ft. mag.	
Sgl. 8	Super Panchro	Pan	40 / 25		
8 & 16	Standard	Ortho	20	8-mm: 25 ft. D.L.; 16-mm: 100 ft. D.L.; 8-16-& mm mag.	For outdoors
& 16	Hi-Speed Color	Color	125	8-mm: 25-ft. D.L.; 16-mm: 100-ft. D.L.; 50-ft. mag.	For available-light conditions
& 16	Triple Speed	Pan	1600	8-mm: 25-ft. mag.; 16-mm: 100-ft. D.L., 50-ft. mag.	For low-light situations.
Super 8	Triple Speed	Pan	1600		
Dbl. 8	Economy Plus	Ortho	5 / 5	25-ft. mag.	Fine-grain.
16	Economy Plus	Ortho	5 / 5	25-ft. D.L.	
Dbl. 8	F-G Positive	Ortho	5 / 2	100-ft. D.L.	Suitable for negative or reversal processing; no anti-halation backing.
16	F-G Positive	Ortho	5 / 2		
Dbl. 8	Hi-Speed Sepia	Pan	250 / 200	25-ft. mag.	Sepia color; for low-light situations.
Super 8	Hi-Speed Sepia	Pan	250 / 200		
16	Hi-Speed Sepia	Pan	250 / 200	100-ft. D.L.; 50-ft. mag.	
Dbl. 8	Pioneer Color	Color	40 / 100	100-ft. D.L.; B	
16	Pioneer Color	Color	40 / 100	200-ft. B	

FOTOCHROME

Format	Product	Type	Speed	Sizes	Notes
Dbl. 8	Fotochrome	Color	16 / 24	25-ft. spool load.	

GENERAL ANILINE & FILM CORP.

Format	Product	Type	Speed	Sizes	Notes
16	Anscochrome D/50	Color	50 / 20(a)	100 ft. D.L. rolls; 400, 1,200 ft. B	Wide latitude, fine-grain
16	Anscochrome D 100	Color	100 / 40(a)	50 ft. D.L. rolls; 50 ft. Mag.	Processing at 80 F. High-speed.
16	Anscochrome T 100	Color	64(a) / 100	100 ft. D.L. rolls; 50 ft. Mag.	Same as above.
16	Anscochrome D 200	Color	200 / 80(a)	100 ft. D.L. rolls; 50 ft. Mag.	Same as above.
Dbl. 8	Moviechrome Daylight	Color	20 / 10(a)	25 ft. rolls	High-speed, fine grain.
Dbl. 8	Moviechrome, Type A	Color	10(a) / 16	25 ft. rolls	High-speed, fine grain.

ILFORD, INC.

Format	Product	Type	Speed	Sizes	Notes
16 & 35	Ilford Pan F Negative Cine Film (s)	Pan	50	100 ft. D.L. and B	Very fine grain; medium speed
16 & 35	Ilford FP3 Negative Cine Film Series 2 (s)	Pan	125	100 ft. D.L. and B	Fast fine grain, medium contrast
16 & 35	Ilford HP3 Negative Cine Film (s)	Pan	400	100 ft. D.L. and B	High-speed
16 & 35	Ilford HPS Negative Cine Film (s)	Pan	800	100 ft. D.L. and B	High-speed

KIN-O-LUX

Format	Product	Type	Speed	Sizes	Notes
16	Kin-O-Lux T-V (Rev.) (s)	Pan	64 / 50	100, 200-ft. D.L. Rolls; 400, 1200 ft. B	Medium speed
16	New Gold Seal (s)	Pan	200 / 160	100, 200 ft. D.L. Rolls; 400, 1200 ft. B	Use under poor light or tungsten
Dbl. 8	Kin-O-Lux T-V (Rev.)	Pan	64 / 50	25, 100 ft. D.L. Rolls	Medium speed; fine-grain
Dbl. 8	New Gold Seal	Pan	200 / 160	25, 100 ft. D.L. Rolls	Use under poor light or tungsten

KODAK

Format	Product	Type	Speed	Sizes	Notes
16	Kodachrome II, Daylight Type	Color	25 / 12(a)	100, 200-ft. D.L. rolls; 50-ft. mag.	
16	Kodachrome II, Type A (Photoflood)	Color	25(a) / 40	Same as above.	
Dbl. 8	Kodachrome II, Daylight Type	Color	25 / 12(a)	25, 100 ft. D.L. rolls; 25 ft. mag.	
Dbl. 8	Kodachrome II, Type A (Photoflood)	Color	25(a) / 40	Same as above.	
Super 8	Kodachrome II, Type A	Color	40 / 40	50 ft. in super 8 movie cartridge.	
16	Plus-X Reversal (s)	Pan	50 / 40	100, 200 ft. camera spools; 400, 1200 ft. on core; 50 ft. mag.	Medium speed; reversal
16	Tri-X Reversal (s)	Pan	200 / 160	100, 200 ft. D.L. rolls; 400, 1,300 ft. on core and 50 ft. magazine.	Extra high speed; wide exposure and development latitude; reversal
16	Double-X Negative (s)	Pan	250 / 200	100, 200 ft. D.L. rolls.	Medium high speed; negative
16	Tri-X Negative (s)	Pan	320 / 250	100, 200 ft. D.L. rolls.	Same as above; negative
16	Plus-X Negative (s)	Pan	80 / 64	100, 200 ft. D.L. rolls.	Medium speed; negative
16	Fine Grain Positive	Bl. Sens.	2	100, 200 ft. on core.	For printing from negatives, title making
Dbl. 8	Fine Grain Positive	Bl. Sens.	2	100 ft. on core.	For printing from negatives, title making

PERFECT PHOTO, INC.

Format	Product	Type	Speed	Sizes	Notes
Dbl. 8	Perfect 8 Hi-Speed	Color	25 / 40	25-ft. D.L. rolls.	

PERUTZ

Dist., Burleigh Brooks

Format	Product	Type	Speed	Sizes	Notes
Dbl. 8	Perutz Perkine U15	Pan	25 / 16	25-ft. D.L.	Reversal
Dbl. 8	Perutz Perkine U21	Pan	100 / 80	25-ft. D.L.	Reversal
Dbl. 8	Perutz Perkine U27	Pan	400 / 320	25-ft. D.L.	Reversal

APPENDIX 3 – 1967 SURVEY OF AMATEUR FILM MANUFACTURERS

Film Width in mm	FILM NAME	TYPE	EXPOSURE INDEX ASA or equivalent — Day	EXPOSURE INDEX ASA or equivalent — Tung.	LENGTHS in FEET AND PACKING (D.L.=Daylight Loading; Mag.=Magazines; B=Bulk; L.P.=Laboratory Packed)	SPECIAL CHARACTERISTICS, FEATURES, AND USES
SEARS						
8	Sears Color 7270, Daylight	Color	25		25 ft. D.L. rolls	
8	Sears Color 7271 Indoor Type A	Color	25(a)	40	25 ft. D.L. rolls	Sound tracking available
SUPERIOR BULK FILM CO.						
Dbl. 8	Superior Color, Daylight Type	Color	10	3	25 ft. D.L.	Subtractive dyed image type; screenless
16	Superior Color, Daylight Type	Color	10	3	100 ft. D.L.; 50 ft. Mag.	Same as above
16	Superior Color, Tungsten Type A	Color	10(a)	16	25 ft. D.L.	Subtractive dyed image type
Dbl. 8	Superior Color, Tungsten Type A	Color	10(a)	16	100 ft. D.L.; 50 ft. Mag.	Same as above
16	Speed XX	Pan	200	200	25 ft. D.L.; 200, 400, 1000 ft. B	Fine grain, soft contrast. Hardened emulsion for high speed processing at high temperatures. For home processing
Dbl. 8	Speed XX (s)	Pan	200	200	100 ft. D.L.; 50 ft. Mag.; 200, 400, 1000 ft. B	Same as above
16	Superior 40	Pan	32	20	25 ft. D.L.; 200, 400, 1000 ft. B	Fine grain, wide latitude, non-halo base, good contrast; for home processing
Dbl. 8	Superior 40 (s)	Pan	32	20	100 ft. D.L.; 50 ft. Mag.; 200, 400, 1000 ft. B	Same as above
16	Superpanex 64	Pan	64	40	25 ft. D.L.; 200, 400, 1000 ft. B	Fine grain, wide latitude; good contrast. Specially hardened emulsion for processing at high remperatures
Dbl. 8	Superpanex 64	Pan	64	40	100 ft. D.L.; 50 ft. Mag.; 200, 400, 1000 ft. B	Same as above
16	Super 500 (s)	Pan	650	500	100 ft. D.L.; 50 ft. Mag.	Gray non-halo base; fine grain considering speed; wide latitude
Dbl. 8	Super 500	Pan	650	500	25 ft. D.L.; 100 ft. B	Same as above
16	Eastman Tri-X Reversal	Pan	200	160	100 ft. D.L.; 200, 400, 1200 ft. B	Wide exposure and development latitude. For home processing
Dbl. 8	Eastman Tri-X Reversal	Pan	200	160	25 ft. D.L.; 200, 400, 1000 ft. B	Same as above
16	Plus	Ortho	16	3	100 ft. D.L.; 50 ft. Mag.; 200, 400, 1000 ft. B	Extreme fine grain; medium latitude; blue non-halo base; high contrast for copying. Can be processed under red safe light
Dbl. 8	Plus (s)	Ortho	16	3	400, 1200 ft. B	Same as above
16	Positive	Bl. Sens.	5		400, 1200 ft. B	Fine grain release positive for printing. Can be reversed. Clear base
Dbl. 8	Positive (s)	Bl. Sens.	5		8-mm: 25, 100 ft. D.L.; 16-mm: 100 ft. D.L.; both 100, 200, 400, 1200 ft. B	Same as above
Dbl. 8 & 16	Superior 36	Pan	325	250	8-mm: 25, 100 ft. D.L.; 16-mm: 100 ft. D.L.; both 100, 200, 400, 1200 ft. B	Reversal-type; high-speed; opaque backing
Dbl. 8 & 16	Superior 30	Pan	80	64	100 ft. roll	Reversal-type; medium-speed; fine-grain; opaque backing
VAR-I-PAN *Dist., Supreme Photo Products*						
16	Var-I-Pan	Pan	50	32	100 ft. roll	Reversal
WESTERN CINE SERVICE						
Dbl. 8 & 16	Ektachrome ER Type B	Color	80(a)	125	25 ft. D.L. Mag.; 16 mm: 100 ft. D.L.	Reversal type
16	Plus-X Reversal	Pan	50	32	25, 100 ft. D.L. rolls; 25 ft. Mag.; 400, 1200 ft. B	Same as above
Dbl. 8	Plus X Reversal (s)	Pan	50	32	50, 100 ft. D.L. rolls; 400, 1200 ft. B	Same as above
16	Tri-X Reversal	Pan	200	160	25, 100 ft. D.L. rolls; 25 ft. Mag.; 400, 1200 ft. B	Same as above
Dbl. 8	Tri-X Reversal (s)	Pan	200	160	50, 100 ft. D.L. rolls; 400, 1200 ft. B	Same as above
Dbl. 8 & 16	Superspeed	Pan	600	500	8-mm: 25, 100 ft. D.L.; 16-mm: 100-ft. D.L.	Reversal type; also available in prestriped magnetic

NOTES:

*Free processing on D.L. and magazines only.
(a) With filter recommended by the manufacturer.
(b) As reversal film

(n) Not recommended for use with this illumination.
(s) Also available perforated one edge for sound, rolls only.
(w) Trial exposure on white card with no lettering.

Bell & Howell 8mm Cameras

MODEL NO.	DESCRIPTION	PRICE	YEAR
127-A	For special "FILMOPAN" single 8mm film in 30 ft. spool, 8-32 fps "STRAIGHT EIGHT"	$69 with f/2.5 lens	1935
127-B	Same as above, except 16-64 fps		1936
134-A	For 25 ft. spool of regular double 8, single lens		1936
134-E	Similar, with 8-16-24-32 fps	$80 with f/2.5 lens	1938
134-F	Same except 16-32-48-64 fps	$85 with f/2.5 lens	1938
134-G	Same except for lens	$55 with f/3.5 lens	1938
134-H	Same as 134-G except with 16-32-48-64 fps	$60	1938
Aristocrat	Similar to all above except with 3-lens turret, each lens has separate finder lens	$140 with f/2.5 lens	1940
Companion	Similar to above except 8-16-24-32 and single lens only	$49.50 with f/3.5 lens	1940
Sportster	Same as Companion except lens	$75 with f/2.5 lens	1940
Tri-Lens 8	Similar to Aristocrat, 3-lens turret 16-32-48-64 fps	$134.55	1948
Auto 8	Magazine load, two-lens turret, each lens has finder lens	$253.90	1948
134-W	Roll-load, exposure guide, dial footage indicator, 8-16-24-32 fps	$79.95 with f/2.5 lens	1952
Tri-Lens 8	(134-TA) 3-lens turret, with matching finders	$129.95 with f/2.5 lens	1952
172-A	(Explorer) Very similar to Auto 8 Magazine load	$164.95 with f/2.5 lens	1952
172-B	(Voyager) Same as above except single lens	$134.95	1952
220 Wilshire	Roll load, 16 fps, single frame, "Sun Dial" exposure guide	$49.95 with f/2.5 lens	1954
252 Monterey	Similar to above	$59.95 with f/2.3 lens	1954
172-C	Magazine load, 2-lens turret	$159.95 with f/2.5 lens	1954
252-B	Monterey Deluxe - Similar to 252 A Monterey, except with f 1.9 lens		1957

Note: In 1957 and 1958 both the Monterey and Monterey Deluxe were available as part of matched sets. One set included camera, sheath case, filter holder 2-1/2 x telephoto attachment and retaining ring, light bar and 2 lamps - $89.95. The other set included camera, projector, sheath case, bar light, and 2 lamps, 50 ft. cartoon - $137.

252 TA	Roll loading, 3-lens turret with wide angle and telephoto converters	$99.95 with f/1.9 lens	1958
290 A	Roll loading, with electric eye exposure control, or manual	$169.95 with f/1.9 lens	1958
290 B	Same as above, except no manual control	$149.95	1958
390 391 392 393	Same as above but with f/2.3 lens Same as above but with f/1.9 lens Same as above but with f/1.8 lens Same as above but with 3-lens turret	$99.95 $119.95 $129.95 $159.95	1959
319 Sun Dial	Roll-loading, "Sun Dial" exposure guide, clip-on exposure meter	$49.95 with f/1.9 lens	1960
323 Sun Dial	Similar to above but with f/2.3 lens	$44.95	1960
333	Similar to 319 but with 3-lens turret, with converters	$79.95	1960
220MM	(Sunometer) – Roll load, f/2.5 lens detachable exposure meter	$39.95	1961
Director 410	Roll load, tri-lens turret, automatic exposure control, 16 and 48 fps with one button	$199.95	1961

Bell & Howell 8mm Cameras (continued)

MODEL NO.	DESCRIPTION	PRICE	YEAR
Director 414	Zoomatic – Similar to 410 except with 9-27mm f/1.8 zoom lens	$209.95	1961
Director 414P Duo Power	Zoomatic – Similar to 414 but with motor powered zoom, WA and TELE buttons on top of housing	$239.95	1961
Director 420	Similar to 410 but loads with 8mm magazine	$199.95	1961
Director 424	Zoomatic – Similar to 414 but magazine load	$229.95	1961
Director 424P	Zoomatic Duo-Power – Similar to 424 but with motor-powered zoom	$259.95	1961
310	Roll load, fixed focus 9-27 mm zoom lens, automatic exposure control	$109.95 with f/2.3 lens	1962
312 314	Similar to 310 but with f/1.8 zoom lens Similar to 312, with focusing mount	$129.95 $169.95	1962
Director 434	Reflex Zoom – Roll load, 9-36 mm f/1.8 zoom lens, reflex finder with ground glass for thru-the-lens light readings, automatic exposure control, power zoom	$349.95	1962
Director 444	Reflex Zoom – Similar to 434, but loads 8mm magazine	$369.95	1962
Director 414PD	Roll load, 9-27mm f/1.8 zoom lens, fully automatic exposure control, power or manual zoom, dual electric eye	$219.95	1963
Reflex 416	Optronic Eye – Similar to 414 PD but electric eye is behind the shutter	$249.95	1963
Canon Motor Zoom 8 EEE	Roll load, 10-40 mm Canon f/1.7 zoom lens, auto exposure control	$269.95	1963
Autoload 305	Takes user-loaded regular 8mm cartridge, automatic exposure control, reflex viewing	$89.95 with f/1.6 lens	1965
315 315PZ	Autoload – Same as 305 but with 9-29mm f/1.8 zoom Autoload – Same as 305 but with folding pistol grip	$119.95 $149.95	1965
417CP	Autoload – Same cartridge load, f/1.8 power zoom lens, auto exposure, control with back light compensation	$199.95	1965
418	Autoload – Cartridge load, 9-27 mm f/1.8 zoom lens, thru-the-lens metering for auto exposure control	$249.95	1965
Cine Canonet 8	Roll loading, 10-25mm Canon f/1.8 zoom lens, auto exposure control, electric drive	$149.50	1965

Bell & Howell Super 8 Cameras

430	11-35 mm f/1.9 zoom lens auto exposure control by thru-the-lens metering, reflex view finder, battery drive	$160	1965
431	Similar to 430, but with 18 and 36 fps, power zoom	$220	1965
432	9-45 mm f/1.9 zoom lens, power zoom and focus, movie light mount	$269.90	1967
Autoload 306	15 mm f/1.9 lens, auto thru-the-lens exposure control, spring motor 18 fps speed	$79.95	1968
Autoload 311	Similar to 306 but with 11-35 mm f/1.9 zoom lens	$109.95	1968
Autoload 440	11-35 mm power zoom lens, auto exposure control, reflex view finder, folding grip	$149.95	1968
Autoload 372	14 mm f/2.8 universal focus lens, auto exposure control, electric camera drive	$49.95	1970
Autoload 374	Similar to 372 but with 12.5-25 mm zoom lens, FOCUS-MATIC setting device	$79.95	1970
Autoload 376	Similar to above, but with f/2.3 lens	$44.95	1960
Autoload 379	Similar to 376 but with f/1.9 3:1 zoom lens	$119.95	1971

Bell & Howell Super 8 Cameras (continued)

MODEL NO.	DESCRIPTION	PRICE	YEAR
Filmosound Autoload 375 SG	Synchronizied for sound with FILMOSOUND tape recorder. 12.5-25mm f/2.8 lens, fully auto exposure control, electric film drive, with grip. Focus Matic distance measuring system	$99.95	1971
376 SG	Autoload – Similar to 375 but with power zoom	$119.95	1971
379 SG	Autoload – Similar to 375 but lens is 11-22mm, focus from 3 feet	$129.95	1971
Autoload 433	Similar to 375 except 9-45mm f/1.8 lens, 18-36 fps camera speeds auto exposure with manual override	$199.95	1971
436	Provides lip-synchronous sound when used with special portable cassette tape recorder and projector. 11-35mm f/1.9 zoom lens, push-button automatic distance measurement, auto exposure control, reflex viewing, electric drive	$129.95 for camera $99.95 cassette recorder $179.95 projector	1971
Filmosound Autoload 442	Similar to 436, but has fully automatic focusing from 5 ft., 18-32 fps, treadle control for zooming	$159.95	1971
491-F	12.5-25mm f/2.8 lens, auto exposure control, reflex finder, trigonometric focusing with reading transferred to lens, electric drive	$89.95	1973
492F 493F	Similar to 491F but power zoom Similar to 491F but lens is 11-33mm	$104.95 $119.95	1973
493SF	Similar to 491F but can be used with FILMOSOUND RECORDER	$129.95	1973
670XL	Existing light camera, 8.8mm f/1.2 universal focus lens, auto exposure control for ASA film speeds 25 to 160, low-light indicator, electric drive	$130.00	1974
671XL	8.5-24mm f/1.3 zoom lens, auto exposure control, other wise same as 670XL	$194.95	1975
673XL 674XL	Similar to 671XL but power zoom Similar to 673XL but with back-light contrast control	$234.95 $239.95	1975
Autoload 1216	Built-in Filmosound 8 capability for sound filming use. Filmosound tape recorder and projector. 8.5-51mm f/1.9 lens, 2-speed power zoom, Focus Matic, auto exposure control	$259.95	1975
Autoload 1218	Automatically keyed type A filter, 7.5-60mm f/1.8 macro-zoom lens, 2-speed power zoom, auto exposre control, reflex finder dual-beam dichroic focusing electric drive	$224.95	1976
2103XL	8.5-24mm f/1.2 lens, manual zoom, auto exposure control trigonometric gauge focusing, electric drive	$169.96	1978
2123XL	Similar to 2103XL but has single speed power zoom, back light compensation, range finder prism focusing	$209.95	1978
2143XL	Similar to 2103XL but with 2-speed power zoom, manual fades, manual exposure control	$224.95	1978
2146XL	7-45mm f/1.2 zoom, macro-focus to 1.2 inches, 2- speed power zoom, push button fades, automatic thru-the-lens exposure control, reflex finder, provision for remote control, etc., etc.	$289.95	1978
Filmosonic 1230XL	8:5-24mm f/1.3 zoom lens, auto exposure control, reflex finder accepts magazine striped or silent film, electric drive	$319.95	1978
Filmosonic 1235XL	Similar to 1230XL but lens has manual and power zoom, signal light on front	$359.95	1978
Filmosonic 1236XL	8.5-24mm f/1.3 focusing lens, autoexposure control, provision for on-camera shotgun microphone, omni-directional microphone, monitoring earphone	$379.95	1978

Bell & Howell Super 8 Cameras (continued)

MODEL NO.	DESCRIPTION	PRICE	YEAR
Filmosonic 1238XL	Similar to above but lens is 7.5-60mm f/1.8, 2-speed power zoom	$389.95	1978
1227XI Filmosound	7-45mm f/1.2 lens, macro focus single speed power zoom, auto exposure control, reflex finder	$489.95	1978
1237XL Filmosound	Similar to above, but lens has 2 speed power zoom	$499.95	1978
Soundstar	8.5-24mm f/1.3 lens, auto exposure control, reflex viewing, ALC sound level selector	$299.95	1979
Soundstar 4	8.5-34mm f/1.3 lens, power zoom, macro capability, auto exposure control, 18-24 fps speeds	$409.95	1979
2144XL	Similar to 2103XL but with 2-speed power zoom	$279.95	1979
1225AF Soundstar	8.5-24mm f/1.3 power zoom lens similar to previous Soundstars except has "Autofocus" automatic focusing feature	$639.95	1979
Soundstar XL	Fixed focus f/1.3 zoom lens, reflex finder, auto level control	$299.95	1979

Bell & Howell 16mm Cameras

MODEL NO.	DESCRIPTION	PRICE	YEAR
Film 70-A	Spring-motor drive, single lens, 8-16 fps		1923
70-C	3-lens "spider" turret 8-16-32 fps		1927-28
"Field Model"	Compact oval shape, 100 ft. capacity single lens		1928 - ?
75	As above, but with embossed design cover in 3 colors	$65.00	1928
70-D	Similar to 70-C, but with compact turret	$192 with f/2.7 fixed focus lens	1929
70-DA	Same as 70-D, with critical focus	$233	1930
70-E	Similar to 70D, with 8-16-24-64 fps	$185 with f/1.5 lens $150 with f/3.5 lens	1933
121-A	Magazine camera, using 50 ft. Simplex magazine, 16-24 fps, eye and waist level finders	$85 with f/2.7 lens	1934
70-F	3-lens turret, electric motor drive, 200 ft. or 400 ft. external magazines		1936
141-A	Magazine camera, using 50 ft. Eastman magazine, single lens, 8-32 fps		1937
141-B	Same as above, except 16-64 fps		1937
Auto Load	For 50 ft. magazine, brown crinkle finish with leather panels, 8-16-24-32 fps	$131.20 with f/2.7 lens	1942?
Auto Master	Same as above, except 3-lens turret head, 16-24-32-48-64 fps	$216.55 with f/2.7 lens	1942?
Auto Load Speedster	Same as Auto Load except 16-24-32-48-64 fps	$147.20 with f/1.9 lens	1942?
70-J Specialist	100 ft. capacity or 400 ft. magazines, 204° shutter, 1/30 second shutter speed, spring motor or hand crank, and electric motor drive, 4-lens turret, ground glass focusing, shift-over focus, 8-12-16-24-32-48-64 fps	$2,643.00	1948
200 Auto Load	Magazine load, 1/43 second shutter, 12 ft. run.	$189.95 with f/2.5 lens	1952
200-T	Same as above except has 2-lens turret	$234.95	1952
70-DL	Roll-load, 100 ft. capacity, 204° shutter 8-12-16-24-32-48-64 fps, 3- lens turret, with matching finders, on side-mounted drum. Single or double perforated film	$341.50	1952-1955

Bell & Howell 16mm Cameras (continued)

MODEL NO.	DESCRIPTION	PRICE	YEAR
70-H	Roll-load, 100 ft. normal cap, optional 200 ft. and 400 ft. external magazines, 1/28 second shutter, Veeder footage counter, critical focusing, adapted for single perforated sound film, 3-lens turret.	$675.50	1952-1955
70-S	100 ft. capacity, single or double perforated, adaptable to 400 ft. magazine.	$365.50 with f/1.9 lens	1952-1955
200-EE Electric Eye	16mm silent, magazine load, automatic exposure control, auto-exposure warning device	$299.95 with 20mm, focusing f/1.9 lens	1957
200-S Auto Load	Magazine load, 20mm Sunomatic f/2.5 lens, fixed focus, exposure guide, 16-24-32-48-64 fps	$174.95 $199.95with f/1.9 lens	1957
200-T Twin Auto Load	As above except has 2-lens turret	$219.95	1957
70-DR	Roll load, hand crank, or spring motor, coupled finder lens turret	$361.50	1957
70-SR	High-speed 128 frames per second only. Adapted for sound, 400 ft. magazines	$534 with f/1.9 lens	1957
200 TA Automaster	Similar to 200-T except has 3-lens turret	$284.95 with f/2.5 lens	1963
200 T25 200 T19 200 T95	Magazine load, 2-lens turret Similar to 200 T25, with f/1.9 lens Similar to 200 T25, with f/0.95 lens	$239.95 with f/2.5 lens $264.95 $407.50	1963
70-HR	3-lens gear-coupled turret, roll load, normal 100 ft. load, adapted for 200 ft. and 40 ft. external magazines, 7 camera speeds, critical focus, motor drive or hand crank	$700 with f/1.9 lens $895 with f/0.95 lens	1963
70-SR	Similar to above except with spring motor or electric drive	$585 with f/1.9 lens $735 with f/0.95 lens	1963
240 EE	Roll load, 20mm Super Comat f/1.9 lens, fully automatic exposure control	$349.95	1963
240 T25	Roll load, 2-lens turret, spring motor drive, automatic exposure control	$239.95 with f/2.5 lens	1963
240 T19 240 Z	Same as above, but with f/1.9 focusing lens Same as T25 but with 17-68mm zoom lens	$264.95 $640	

APPENDIX 5 – CHRONOLOGY OF BOLEX-H CAMERAS 1935-1975
(DATES ARE APPROXIMATE)

MAJOR MODIFICATION	MODEL	H-16 CAMERAS		H-8 CAMERAS	
		YEAR	SERIAL NO.	YEAR	SERIAL NO.
Introduction of Camera	H-16	1935	7,500	1935	10,000
Addition of External Frame Counter		1941	15,000	1941	15,000
Built-in Frame Counter	H-16 Leader	1947	33,191	1947	33,191
Addition of Eye Level Focus View Finder	H-16 Standard	1949	50,000	1949	50,000
Addition of Octameter View Finder	H-16 De Luxe	1950	55,000	1950	55,000
Built-in Filter Slot	H-16 Supreme	1954	94201		
Introduction of Zoom Lenses (First in United States)		1954		1954	
Introduction of Stereo System		1954		1954	
New Registration Claw, Pressure Pad		1955	100,401	1955	97,801
New Style Turret		1956	121,401	1956	121,801
Introduction of Bolex H-16 Reflex	H-16 Reflex	1956	116,001		
Introduction of Anamorphic Lenses		1957			
Introduction of Bolex T	H-16 T	1958	148,000	1958	148,000
Introduction of Bolex M	H-16M	1958	153,000		
Introduction of Rex-1 (Variable Shutter 145°)	H-16 Rex-1	1959	162,306	1962	189,901
Rex-2 New VF (Variable Shutter 130°)	H-16 Rex-2	1963	195,801	1963	198,591
Rex-3 Built-in Ease	H-16 Rex-3	1963	202,501		
Introduction of Automatic Zoom Lens		1963			
Introduction of Bolex S	H-16-S	1965	203,301	1963	203,301
Rex-4 1:1 Ratio Shaft	H-16 Rex-4	1965	210,601	1965	212,401
Rex-5 400 ft. Magazine, Clapper	H-16 Rex-5	1967	226,001	END OF STANDARD 8mm	
SBM Bayonet Mount, 400 ft. Magazine	H-16 SBM	1971	300,001		
SB Bayonet Mount 100 ft. Capacity	H-16 S8	1971	300,201		
H-16 EBM Built-in Electric Motor	H-16 EBM	1971	300,401		
H-16 EL Built-in Electric Motor, Exposure Meter	H-16 EL	1975	310,001		

APPENDIX 6: EASTMAN KODAK AMATEUR MOTION PICTURE EQUIPMENT 1923-1981

KODAK 16MM MOVIE CAMERAS - 1923-1973

Author's Note: Beginning with the 1923 introduction of the Ciné-Kodak 16mm camera, all Eastman Kodak camera names began with "Ciné-Kodak followed by additional nomenclature, until 1947. On cameras introduced after 1947, the accent was dropped. Beginning in 1957, "Cine Kodak" was replaced by "Kodak Cine," and finally, in 1959 the word Cine was dropped.

CAMERA NAME	FROM	TO	FRAMES/SEC.	LENS	LIST PRICE
Ciné-Kodak Outfit – Consisted of	June 1923		Hand Cranked		
Cine-Kodak Camera	Note: Itrems listed separately in January, 1924.				$125
Kodascope and Splicer	Motor Drive, January 1924 for Ciné-Kodak with serial number under 1266 was available with top finder, May 1924 . . . $25				$160
Tripod					$25
Screen					$25
Total for Outfit					$335
Ciné-Kodak Camera	June 1923	1930	Hand Cranked	Kodak Anastigmat 25mm f/3.5	$125
50 or 100 ft. reels Note: Letter "K" added to Serial Number October 1929	Feb. 1926	1930		Kodak Anastigmat 25mm f/1.9	$200
Ciné-Kodak Model B Camera (black)	July 1925	June 1931	16	20mm, f/6.5	$70
50 or 100 ft. reel	April 1926	June 1931		20mm, f/3.5	$100
	June 1927	June 1931		25mm, f/1.9	$150
(gray, brown)	Nov. 1928	June 1931		25mm, f/1.9	$175
Ciné-Kodak Model BB Camera (black, blue, brown, gray) 50 ft. only	April 1929	May 1932	8, 16	25mm f/1.9	$140
(black only)	April 1929	May 1932		20mm f/3.5	$75
Ciné-Kodak Model K camera (black, blue, brown, gray)	July 1930	March 1935	8, 16	25mm, f/3.5	$110
	July 1930	May 1946		25mm, f/1.9	$150
Ciné-Kodak Model M Camera	July 1930	Feb. 1934	16	20mm, f/3.5	$75
Ciné-Kodak Special Camera	April 1933	July 1948	8, 16, 32, 64, single frame	25mm, f/1.9	$375
(Turret threaded one side)	Oct. 1937	Aug. 1946		25mm, f/1.9	$465
(Turret threaded two sides)	Oct. 1937	Aug. 1946		(Without lens)	$425
Ciné-Kodak Special II Camera	Aug. 1948	March 1961	8, 16, 24, 32, 64, single frame	25mm, f/1.4	$893
	Dec. 1948	March 1961		25mm, f/1.9	$750
Magazine Ciné-Kodak Camera	Jan. 1936	Oct. 1937	8, 16, 64	25mm, f/1.9	$125
	Oct. 1937	Sept. 1945 Name change	16, 32, 64		
		Note on camera speeds from May 1944 instruction manual: There are five models of the Magazine Ciné-Kodak. The motor of each model is capable of running at three different speeds. These models have speeds of: 8-16-24 16-24-64 24-32-48 16-24-48 16-32-64			

KODAK 16MM MOVIE CAMERAS - 1923-1973 (Continued)

CAMERA NAME	FROM	TO	FRAMES/SEC.	LENS	LIST PRICE
Name change to: Ciné-Kodak Magazine 16 Camera	Sept. 1945	Dec. 1950	16, 32, 64		
	Note on camera speeds from April. 1949 instruction manual. These speeds can be changed to any other three speeds from 8 to 64 provided both the 8 and 64 speeds are not included.				
Magazine Cine-Kodak Sixteen-10A Camera	Feb. 1942	Sept.1945 Name change	8, 16, 24	25mm, f/1.9	$120
Name change to: Ciné-Kodak Magazine 16A Camera	Sept. 1945	Dec. 1950	8, 16, 24		
Ciné-Kodak Model E Camera	Jan. 1937	Feb. 1946	16, 32, 64	10mm, f/3.5	$48.50
	June 1940	Feb. 1946		25mm, f/1.9	$67.50
Ciné-Kodak Royal Magazine Camera	Nov. 1950	Nov. 1967	16, 24, 64, &	25mm, f/1.9	$192.50
	July 1951	July 1954	single frame	25mm, f/2.8	$166.50
Ciné-Kodak K-100 Camera, Single Lens	Mar. 1955	Sept. 1964	16,24, 32, 48, 64, & single frame	25mm, f/1.4	$369
Cine-Kodak K-100 Camera, Turret model	March 1956	Aug. 1973	16, 24, 32, 48, 64, single	25mm f/1.9	$315 last price $725
	March 1956	Aug. 1973	Same	25mm f/1.4	415
Kodak Reflex Special Camera, 16mm for silent film or single system magnetic sound. Includes camera mechanism, Kodak Synchronous Motor Drive, Model 1 (60 cycle), 25mm, f/1.4 Kodak Cinc Ekton lcns, Kodak 400-foot film chamber, Kodak mounting bracket for matte box, Kodak mounting bracket for director-type flnder, carrying handle, and S Mount template.	Oct. 1961	June 1968	Variable 8 to 64 depending on motor drive supplied	Many available from 10mm to 150mm, Type R mount	$1,895

Accessories for Separate Sale:
  Kodak 400-foot Film Chamber
  Kodak 200-foot Film Chamber
  Kodak Compartment Case
  Kodak Magnetic Sound System, Model 1
    (without installation)
					$250
					$395
					$39.50
					$900

KODAK 16MM SILENT PROJECTORS

PROJECTOR NAME AND MODEL	FROM	TO	LAMP USED WATT VOLT	CURRENT LAMP (ASA)	MAXIMUM REEL SIZE	PRICE AT INTRODUCTION
Kodascope Projector	June 1923	Dec. 1925	50W 14V T-8 med. screw	N.A.	400 ft.	$160
	April 1924	Jan. 1926	200W 50V T-10 med. screw	N.A.	400 ft.	$180
			200 watt lamphouse also available to convert 56W projectors			$30
	July 1924	Jan. 1926	200W 50V T-10 med. screw	N.A.	400 ft.	$180
			Available with special rheostat for 210-250 Volt			
	July 1924	Jan. 1926	165W 30V T-10 med. screw - For use on 32 Volt systems			$180

KODAK 16MM SILENT PROJECTORS (Continued)

PROJECTOR NAME AND MODEL	FROM	TO	LAMP USED WATT VOLT	CURRENT LAMP (ASA)	MAXIMUM REEL SIZE	PRICE AT INTRODUCTION
KODASCOPE Projector Model A (change of name with introduction of Model C	Feb. 1926	July 1928	200 W 50V T-10 med. screw	N.A. (CSK)	400 ft.	$180
	Feb. 1926	July 1928	165W 30V T-10 med. screw	N.A.	400 ft.	$180
			For use on 32V systems			
KODASCOPE Projector Model A Series K (for use with KODACOLOR film	Aug. 1928	Oct. 1929	N.A.	N.A.	400 ft.	$180
	Nov. 1929	1934	300W 120V	CYK* or CXY*	400 ft.	$180
			*Requires rewiring of lamp socket to bypass the resistor			
	Earlier KODASCOPE Model A Series K Projectors could be converted to use 250W lamp by parts kit for $40					$40
KODASCOPE Projector Model B	Nov. 1927	Aug. 1928	200W 50V	CST (SDV)	400 ft.	$300
			T-10 med. pref.			
			200W 120V	CVS/CVX*		
			300W 120V	CXK* or CXY*P		
			*Requires rewiring of lamp			
KODASCOPE Projector Model B Series K (KODACOLOR Models Serial no. preceded by letter K)	Aug. 1928	Oct. 1928	200W 50V	As above	400 ft.	$300
	Black finish		T-10 med. pref.			
	Nov. 1928	Oct. 1929	250W 50V	CXK* or CXY*P	400 ft.	$275
	Bronze finish		T-10 med. pref. *Requires rewiring of lamp			
	Nov. 1929	Dec. 1932	300W 120V			
	Bronze finish					
	Earlier models could be altered at the factory or branch to use 205W lamp					$40
Library KODASCOPE Projector This is a KODASCOPE B in a walnut case provided with translucent screen for rear projection with 1-inch lens or direct projection with 2-inch lens. Prism to reverse image for rear projection available Nov. 1929.	May 1929	Oct. 1929	200W 50V	CVS/CVX*	400 ft.	$300
			T-10 med. pref.	200W 120V		
				CXK* or CXY*P		
				300W 120V		
	Nov. 1929	Dec. 1932	250W 50V	As above	400 ft.	$300
			T-10 med. pref. *Requires rewiring of lamp socket to bypass the resistor P - Preferred subsitute lamp			
	(Author's note: Also available, at $150, was a matching walnut storage cabinet with room for 26 400-foot reels and editing and splicing equipment. The top of the cabinet could be rotated through 360 degrees.)					
KODASCOPE Projector Model C This was a hand-cranked model only.	Feb. 1926	April 1933	100W 30V	100T	400 ft.	$60
			T- 8-1/2 med. pref.	8-1/2 8 microscope lamp		
	July 1926	April 1933	100W 30V	N.A.	400 ft.	$60
			T- 8-1/2 med. pref.	For 32V systems		
			Beginning Jan. 1928 above models were supplied with motor rewind.			
	Jan. 1928	April 1933	72W 6V	CPR	400 ft.	$60
			T-10 med. pref.	18 Amp 6V		

KODAK 16MM SILENT PROJECTORS (Continued)

PROJECTOR NAME AND MODEL	FROM	TO	LAMP USED WATT VOLT	CURRENT LAMP (ASA)	MAXIMUM REEL SIZE	PRICE AT INTRODUCTION
Eastman Business KODASCOPE Projector	Sept. 1928	May 1935	100W 120V T- 8-1/2 med. pref.	100T 8-1/2 8 microscope lamp	400 ft.	$90
	This is a KODASCOPE Model C in a carrying case provided with a 5-1/2 x 7 inch translucent screen on one end for rear projection. It was also available in a hand-cranked model for use on 6 volts.					
Cine-Kodak Enlarger	Dec. 1928	1933	100W 120V T- 8-1/2 med. pref.	100T 8-1/2 8 microscope lamp		$75
	This looks like a KODASCOPE Model C but has no claw mechanism. film was hand-cranked until the desired frame was reached. The frame was printed onto 4 x 5 inch sheet film with a 3 x 4 inch image size and the negative was then contact printed onto paper. This was a darkroom device for use by photofinishers.					
KODATOY Projector AC Model	Oct. 1930	Oct. 1932	21-21 cp 6-8V	32-32cp 6-8V	100 ft.	$12 with 8-1/2 silvered screen
			#1110 auto - #1000 from antique auto parts dealers			
	Jan. 1931 - motor available for 115 V 60Hz AC					$6.50
	April 1931	Oct. 1932	Same	Same		$18.50 with motor
KODATOY Projector Universal Model AC or DC	May 1931	Oct. 1932	50W 120V	CDS/CDX	100 ft.	$15 without motor
			100W 120V	100W 120V		$25 with motor
	Note: Hand-cranked models were supplied until stock was exhausted, Nov. 1934					
KODASCOPE Projector Model K	July 1931	Feb. 1933	260W 52V T-10 med. pref.	N.A.	400 ft.	$160
KODASCOPE Projector Model K-50	Feb. 1933	Mar. 1935	500W 100V or 500W 120V T-10 med. pref.	CZX/DAB	400 ft.	$175
	Will be necessary to rewire socket on models originally supplied with 100V lamp in order to bypass lamp resistor					
	1934	1940	Conversion Kit offered to change K-50 into K-75			$35
KODASCOPE Projector Model K-75	Feb. 1933	Mar. 1935	750W 100V T-12 med. pref.	DDB*	400 ft.	$200
	*Requires rewiring lamp socket to bypass lamp resistor.					
KODASCOPE Projector Model R	We believes that this was a Model K, factory reqorked to take 750W lamp.					
KODASCOPE Projector Model D	April 1933	Mar. 1936	400W 115V T-10 med. pref.	CZX/DAB 500W 115V	400 ft.	$62
			300W 115V T-10 med. pref.	CXK 300W 115V		
KODASCOPE Projector Model L	Nov. 1934	Sept. 1938	400W 120V T-10 pref.	N.A. - Use 500W	400 ft.	$184-$202.85 Depending on lens and lamp supplied.
			500W 120V T-10 med. pref.	CZX/DAB		
			750W 120V T-12 med. pref.	DDB		

KODAK 16MM SILENT PROJECTORS (Continued)

PROJECTOR NAME AND MODEL	FROM	TO	LAMP USED WATT VOLT	CURRENT LAMP (ASA)	MAXIMUM REEL SIZE	PRICE AT INTRODUCTION
KODASCOPE Projector Model E Model E Projector could be converted to Model EE at factory or branch for $5.50	Mar. 1936	Mar. 1937	100W 120V T-10 pref.	N.A. Use 500W	400 ft.	$54.50-$61.85 Depending on lens and lamp supplied
			500W 120V T-10 med. pref.	CZX/DAB		
			750 W 120V T-12 med. pref.	DDB		
KODASCOPE Projector Model EE	Feb. 1937	April 1939	Same as E	Same as E	400 ft.	$59.25-75.10 Depending on lens and lamp supplied
	May 1937	April 1939	72W 6V T-10 med. pref.	CPR 18 Amp 6	400 ft.	$63 without lens
			For use on 6 volt system			
	May 1937	April 1939	200W 25V T-10 med. pref. or 300W 30V T-10 med. pref. Available 6/40	N.A. (CRS)	400 ft.	$58 without lens
			For use on 32 volt system			
KODASCOPE Projector MODEL EE Series II	April 1939	Oct. 1941	Same as Model EE		400 ft.	Same
KODASCOPE Projector MODEL G	Mar. 1938	April 1939	400W 120V T-12 med. pref.	N.A. Use 500W	400 ft.	$10.75-130.10 Depending on lens and lamp supplied
			500W 120V T-12 med. pref.	CZX/DAB		
			750W 120 V T-12 med. pref.	CZX/DAB		
KODASCOPE Projector MODEL G Series II	April 1939	Oct. 1941	Same as G	Same as G	400 ft.	Same as G
Repeater KODASCOPE Projector, Model G Series II	July 1940	July 1945	Same as G	Same as G	400 ft.	$162.65-$177.95 Depending on lens and lamp supplied
KODASCOPE Sixteen-10 Projector	Dec. 1941	Feb. 1952	750W 120V T-12 med. pref.	DDB	400 ft.	$90
			1000W 120V T-12 med. pref.	DFD		
KODASCOPE Sixteen-10R Projector (with remote reversing switch)	Sept 1950	Oct. 1952	Same	Same	400 ft.	$185
KODASCOPE Sixteen-20 Projector	April 1945	July 1950	500W 120V T-10 med. pref.	CZX/DAB	400 ft.	$174.50
			750W 120V T-12 med. pref.	DDB		
			1000W 120V T-12 med. pref.	DFD		
KODASCOPE Analyst	1953	1956	750W 110V		400 ft.	$295
KODASCOPE Royal Similar to Analyst but smaller and lighter, without remote reversing switch	1953	1956			400 ft.	$245

KODAK 16MM PORTABLE SOUND PROJECTORS

PROJECTOR NAME AND MODEL	DATE SUPPLIED	LAMP	REEL CAPACITY	LENS	PRICE
Sound KODASCOPE Special Aluminum die-cast case	1937	400-750W	1600 ft.	EKC 2 inch f/1.6 3 inch and 4 inch available	$800
Sound KODASCOPE FS-10N	1948	750W	2000 ft.	2 inch f/1.6 coated	$500 with single speaker $565 with twin speakers
KODASCOPE Pageant Sound Projector Model 1 (8 inch speaker, 7 watt amplifier)	1951	750 or 1000 W	2000 ft.	2 inch f/1.6 coated 1 inch, 1-1/2 inch, and 4 inch available	$375
KODASCOPE Pageant Model AV-071	1954	Has Plus-40 shutter for 40 percent greater illumination than Model 1. Sound speed only.			$375
KODASCOPE Pageant Models	1954	These projectors were similar to the Model 1 except with larger speakers for larger auditoriums.		AV-151-S	$440
				AV-151-SE	$440
				AV-151	$495
KODASCOPE Pageant 154-S	1957	750 or 1000W	For Optical Sound		$469
KODASCOPE Pageant MK4	1957	Similar to 154-S but for Magnetic and Optical Sound and Magnetic Sound Recording			$795
KODASCOPE Pageant 8K5 (Magnetic Sound, Projection Only)	1958	750 or 1000W	2000 ft.	2 inch f/1.6	$429

KODAK 16MM SOUND PROJECTORS - NOT PORTABLE - FOR AUDITORIUM USE

PROJECTOR NAME AND MODEL	FROM	TO	WATT VOLT	LAMP	LENS AND SPEAKERS	PRICE
Eastman 16mm Projector Model 25	Mar. 1950	July 1957	Tungsten 1000W 115V base up T-12	DGS DEC DAS	2 inch f/1.5 projection Ektar lens 25W amplifier Altec-Lansing Model 500 speakers	$3675
			Arc - 46 Amp carbon - Manufactured by Stron Electric Co.			$4570
Eastman 16mm Projector Model 25B	July 1957	April 1964	Tungsten	DGS DEC DAS	2 inch f/1.5 projection Ektar lens 30W amplifier Altec-Lansing Model 500 speakers	$5250
			Arc - 46 Amp carbon			$6750
Eastman 16mm Projector Model 25C	April 1964	May 1965	Tungsten	DGS DEC DAS	Without lens or speakers	$8345
			Arc - 46 Amp carbon			$8370
Eastman 16mm Projector Model 30C (replaces 25C Arc Model	May 1965	Oct 1967	Arc 46 Amp carbon Manufactured by Strong Electric Co.		Without lens of speakers	$8895

KODAK CONTINUOUS TELEVISION PROJECTORS FOR 16MM FILM

PROJECTOR NAME AND MODEL	DATES SUPPLIED	WATT VOLT	LAMP	LENS
Eastman Continous Television Projector Model 300 (for use with flying-spot scanners)	Ca.1955?	No projection lamp. Exciter: BSK		3 inch f/1.6 Projection Ektar lens with diaphragm
Eastman Continuous Television Projector Model 350 (for projection into a TV camera using a Vidicon tube)	Ca. 1961-1963?	750W 115V base up T-12 DEC (Exciter: BSK, BVL)	DEC DGS DAS	Same
Eastman Continuous Television Projector Model 400 (for projection into a TV camera using a Vidicon tube)	Ca. 1963?	Same	Same	Same

KODAK 8MM MOVIE CAMERAS, 1932-1966

CAMERA NAME AND MODEL	FROM	TO	FRAMES PER SEC.	LENS	LIST PRICE
Ciné-Kodak Eight - Model 20	July 1932	Jan. 1946	16	f/3.5 lens	$29.50
Ciné-Kodak Eight - Model 60	Oct. 1932	March 1947	16	f/1.9 lens	$79.50
Ciné--Kodak Eight - Model 25	July 1933	Nov. 1946	16	f/2.7 lens	$45.00
Magazine Ciné-Kodak Eight - Model 90	June 1940		16-24-32-64	f/1.9 lens	$97.50
Ciné-Kodak Magazine 8 Name changed July 1946		Dec. 1955		f/1.9 lens	$147.50
		May 1952		f/2.7 lens	$127.50
Magazine Ciné-Kodak Eight, Model 90A	Aug.1941		8-16-24-32	f/1.9 lens	$101.50
Ciné-Kodak Magazine 8A Name changed July 1946		March 1948		f/1.9 lens	$148.06
Ciné-Kodak Reliant camera, spool	April 1949	July 1954	16-24-32-48	13mm, f/2.7 lens	$89.00
	Oct. 1949	July 1954		13mm, f/1.9 lens	$97.50
Ciné-Kodak Medallion 8 camera Magazine	Sept. 1956	July 1958	16-24-32-48	Fixed focus 13mm, f/1.9 lens	$129.50
	Oct. 1955	July 1958		13mm, f/1.9 lens	$144.50
Kodak Medallion 8 Movie camera, f/1.9 Change in name only	March 1957	June 1959		13mm, f/1.9 Fixed focus	$99.50
Kodak Medallion 8 Movie camera, Turret f/1.9	March 1957	Dec. 1959	16,24,32,48	9mm 13mm 24mm lenses	$149.50
Kodak Cine Scopemeter camera, Turret f/1.9 Prevlously offered as Brownie Turret Movie Camera, Scopesight f/1.9 (8/58)	Dec. 1958	Deb. 1962	16	6.5mm 13mm 24mm	$99.50
Kodak Cine Automatic camera, f/1.9	April 1959	June 1960	16	13mm f/1.9 lens	$92.50
Kodak Cine Automatic Turret camera, f/1.9	April 1959	Feb. 1963	16	6.5mm 13mm 24mm lenses	$124.50
Kodak Zoom 8 camera (Automatic f/1.9)	Nov. 1959	Feb. 1962	16	9mm to 24mm f/1.9	$139.50
Kodak Zoom 8 Reflex camera (Automatic f/1.9) October 1961; name changed to: Kodak Zoom 8 Reflex camera	Sept. 1960	Feb. 1962	16	8.5mm to 24mm f/l.9	$189.50
Kodak Zoom 8 (Automatic f/1.9) Model 2	Sept. 1960	Feb. 1962	16	9mm to 24mm f/1.9	$139.50
Kodak Automatic 8 Movie camera	Mar. 1961	May 1964	16	13mm f/1.6 lens	$49.95
Kodak Zoom 8 Automatic camera	Aug. 1961	Apr. 1965	16	9mm to 25mm f/1.6 lens	$109.50
Kodak Zoom 8 Reflex camera, Model 2	Dec. 1961	Jan. 1964	16	8.5mm to 25mm f/1.9 lens	$214.50
Kodak 8 Movie camera f/1.9	Mar. 1962	Apr. 1965	16	13mm f/1.9 lens	$34.50
Kodak Electric 8 Automatic camera (Uses Kodak Duex 8 Cassette)	Aug. 1962	July 1965	16	13mm, f/1.6 lens	$99.50
Kodak Electric 8 Zoom camera (Uses Kodak Duex 8 Cassette)	April 1963	July 1965	16	9mm to 27mm, f/1.6 lens	$149.50
Kodak Electric 8 Zoom Reflex camera (Uses Kodak Duex 8 Cassette)	March 1964	Juy, 1965	16	6.5mm to 52mm, f/1.8 lens	$295
Kodak Escort 8	March 1964	April 1966	16	13fmm, f/1.6 lens	$54.50
Kodak Escort 8 Zoom	March 1964	Dec. 1966	16	9mm to 27mm f/1.6 lens	$99.50

HAWKEYE MOVIE CAMERAS (FOR PREMIUM MARKET)

CAMERA NAME	FROM	TO	FRAMES PER SEC.	LENS	LIST PRICE
Hawkeye 8 (8mm) Movie Camera	Apr. 1962	Mar. 1968	16	f/2.3, 13mm	
Hawkeye Instamatic Movie Camera Super-8)	Mar. 1967	Nov. 1970	18	f/2.7, 14mm	
Hawkeye Instamatic Movie Camera (Super-8) Model B	Oct. 1969	July 1975	18	f/2.7, 14mm	

BROWNIE MOVIE CAMERAS - 1951-1973
(All have 16 fps speed only)

CAMERA NAME	FROM	TO	FRAMES PER SEC.	LENS	LIST PRICE
Brownie Movie Camera	Feb. 1951	Mar. 1956	16	13mm f/2.7	$47.50
	Aug. 1953	Mar. 1956		13mm f/1.9	$49.50
Brownie Movie Camera Turret f/1.9	Oct. 1955	May 1963		9mm, 13mm, 24mm f/1.9	$79.50
Brownie Movie Camera f/1.9 lens (Model 2)	Mar. 1956	Aug. 1959		13mm f/1.9	$44.50
Special model: white & gold Brownie Movie Camera in Kodak Movie Camera Gift Kit	Mar. 1958	June 1959	Designed as a wedding present	13mm f/1.9	$44.95
Improved Model 2 re-introduced	Mar. 1960	Sept. 1962		13mm f/1.9	$34.50
Brownie Movie Camera f/2.3 lens (Model 2)	Mar. 1956	Sept. 1960		13mm f/2.3	$37.50
Brownie Movie Camera f/2.7 lens (Model 2)	Mar. 1956	Apr. 1958		13mm, f/2.7	$29.95
Brownie Movie Camera Turret f/2.3	Mar. 1958	June 1959		9mm, 13mm, 24mm f/2.3	$59.50
Brownie Movie Camera Scopesight f/1.9 (Exposure Meter Model)	Sept. 1958	Aug. 1959		13mm f/1.9	$79.50
Brownie Turret Movie Camera Scopesight f:1.9 (Exposure Meter Model Name changed Dec. 1958 to Kodak Cine Scopemeter camera, turret f/1.9	Aug. 1958	Feb. 1962		6.5mm, 13mm, 24mm	$99.50
Brownie Automatic Movie Camera f/2.3	Apr. 1959	Feb. 1962		13mm, f/2.3 lens	$74.50
Brownie Movie camera f/1.9 lens (Model 3)	Apr. 1959	Mar. 1962		13mm, f/1.9ns	$44.50
Brownie 8 Movie camera, f/2.7	Apr. 1960	Nov. 1962		13mm, f/2.7 lens	$24.50
Brownie Fun Saver Movie Camera	Sept. 1963	Nov. 1968		13mm, f/2.7 lens	$19.95

KODAK SUPER 8 MOVIE CAMERAS 1965-1981

CAMERA NAME	FROM	TO	FRAMES PER SEC.	LENS	LIST PRICE
Kodak Instamatic M2 Movie camera Two-tone charcoal and black finish introduced in April 1966	May 1965	Mar. 1968	18	13mm f/1.8	$46.50
Kodak Instamatic M4 Movie camera Two-tone charcoal and black finish introduced in April 1966	May 1965	May 1967	18	13mm f/1.8	69.50
Kodak Instamatic M6 Movie camera Two-tone grey and black	May 1965	Sept. 1966	18, SF	12mm to 36mm f/1.8	174.50
Kodak Instamatic M6 Movie camera All black finish	Aug. 1966	July 1968	18, SF	12mm to 36mm f/1.8	159.50
Kodak Instamatic M5 Movie camera Pistol grip added October 1966	Mar. 1966	May 1968	18	13mm to 28mm f/1.9	$119.50
Kodak Instamatic M8 Movie camera	Aug. 1966	Dec. 1968	9, 18, 24, 32, SF	9.5mm to 45mm f/1.8	$224.50
Kodak Instamatic M12 Movie camera	Mar. 1967	Aug. 1969	18	14mm f/2.7	$29.95
Kodak Instamatic M14 Movie camera	Mar. 1967	Aug. 1969	18	14mm f/2.7	$49.50
KODAK Instamatic M16 Movie camera	Mar. 1967	Aug. 1969	18	13mm f/1.8	$59.50
KODAK Instamatic M18 Movie camera	Mar. 1967	July 1969	18	13mm to 28mm f/2.7	$79.50
KODAK Instamatic M20 Movie camera	May 1968	Aug. 1969	18	13mm to 28mm f/1.9	$99.50
KODAK Instamatic M7 Movie camera	Aug. 1968	Mar. 1971	18, SF	12mm to 36mm f/1.8	$169.50
KODAK Instamatic M9 Movie camera	Aug. 1968	Mar. 1971	12,18, 24, 32, SF	9.5mm to 45mm f/1.8	$229.50
KODAK Instamatic M22 Movie camera Improved model: End-of-film indicator in the viewfinder	June1969 July 1971	May 1972 Jan. 1975	18	14mm f/2.7	$29.95 $34.50
KODAK Instamatic M24 Movie camera Improved model: End-of-film indicator in the viewfinder	June 1969 July 1971	May 1972 Jan. 1975	18	14mm f/2.7	$49.50
KODAK Instamatic M26 Movie camera Improved model: 1. End-of-film indicator in the viewfinder 2. Rubber eyecup	June 1969 July 1971	May 1972 Jan. 1975	18	13mm f/1.8	$64.50
KODAK Instamatic M28 Movie camera Improved model: 1. End-of-film indicator in the viewfinder 2. Rubber eyecup	June 1969 July 1971	May 1972 Jan. 1975	18	13mm to 28mm f/2.7	$84.50
KODAK Instamatic M30 Movie camera Improved model: 1. End-of-film indicator in the viewfinder 2. Rubber eyecup	June 1969 July 1971	May 1972 Jan. 1975	18	13mm to 28mm f/1.9	$104.50
Kodak Ektagraphic 8 Super 8 Movie Camera	July 1967	Nov. 1969	12, 18, 24, 32, SF	9.5mm to 45mm f/1.8	$239.50
Kodak Supermatic 24 Super 8 Movie Camera	Feb. 1973	Dec. 1977	18, 24	9mm to 21mm f/1.2	$189.50
Kodak Analyst Super 8 Camera (Surveillance Camera)	June 1971	April 1982	Variable from 1 per 1.75 sec. to 1 every 90 sec.	13mm to 28mm f/1.9	$239.50
Kodak Monitor Super 8 Camera (Surveillance Camera)	June 1971	May 1981	18	13mm to 28mm f/1.9	$199.50

KODAK SUPER 8 XL MOVIE CAMERAS, 1971-1981

CAMERA NAME	FROM	TO	FRAMES PER SEC.	LENS	LIST PRICE
KODAK XL33 Movie Camera	Aug. 1971	July 1975	9, 18	9mm f/1.2	$119.50
KODAK XL55 Movie Camera	Aug. 1971	May 1977	9, 18	9mm to 21mm f/1.2	$199.50
KODAK XL10 Movie Camera (Also in Kodak Fun Saver Movie Outfit with M10 projector, case, etc.)	Mar. 1973	Dec. 1975	18	9mm f/1.2	$114.50
KODAK XL320 Movie Camera For use with KODAK Type G EXTACHROME 160 Movie Film only. With "Our Gang" decal from March 27, 1978.	July 1974	June 1981	18	9mm f/1.2	$99.50
KODAK XL330 Movie Camera	July 1974	June 1981	18	9mm f/1.2	$117.50
KODAK XL340 Movie Camera	July 1974	Apr. 1978	18	9mm to 21mm f/1.2	$182.50
KODAK XL350 Movie Camera	July 1974	Aug. 1977	18	9mm to 21mm f/1.2	$209.50
KODAK XL360 Movie Camera	July 1974	Aug. 1978	18	9mm to 21mm f/1.2	$232.50
KODAK XL342 Movie Camera	Apr. 1977	June 1981	18	9mm to 21mm f/1.2	$216.50
KODAK XK352 Movie Camera	Apr. 1977	June 1981	18	9mm to 21mm	$246.50
KODAK XL362 Movie Camera	Apr. 1977	June 1981	18	9mm to 21mm f/1.2	$281.50

KODAK SUPER 8 SOUND MOVIE CAMERAS, 1973-1979
(Accept both sound and silent cartridges)

CAMERA NAME	FROM	TO	FRAMES PER SEC.	LENS	LIST PRICE
KODAK Ektasound 130 Movie Camera	Aug. 1973	July 1977	18	9mm f/1.2	$189.50
KODAK Ektasound 140 Movie Camera	Aug. 1973	July 1977	18	9mm to 21mm f/1.2	$274.50
KODAK Ektasound 150 Movie Camera	April 1975	July 1977	18	9mm to 21mm f/1.2	$363.50
KODAK Ektasound 160 Movie Camera	Aug. 1974	July 1977	18	9mm to 21mm f/1.2	$398.50
KODAK Ektasound 230 Movie Camera	June 1976	Jan. 1979	18	9mm f/1.2	$274.50
KODAK Ektasound 240 Movie Camera	June 1976	Jan. 1979	18	9mm to 21mm f/1.2	$399.50
KODAK Ektasound 250 Movie Camera	April 1977	Jan. 1979	18	9mm to 21mm f/1.2	$444.50
KODAK Ektasound 260 Movie Camera	April 1977	Jan. 1979	18	9mm to 21mm f/1.2	$486.50
KODAK Supermatic 200 Sound Camera for 50 ft. and 200 ft. cartridges	June 1975	Jan. 1979	18, 24	9mm to 21mm f/1.2	$425.50

KODAK 8MM SILENT PROJECTORS

PROJECTOR NAME	FROM	TO	LAMP AND SPECIAL FEATURES	REEL SIZE	PRICE AT INTRODUCTION
Kodascope 8 Model 20 Projector	1932?		32 CP Candelbra base	200 ft.	$24 f/2.5 lens
Kodascope 8 Model 50 Projector	1932	1948	Same	200 ft.	$39 f/2.0 lens
Kodascope 8 Model 80 Projector	1938	1948	300W coil or T-10 biplane	200 ft.	$97.50 f/1.6
Kodascope 8 Model 70 Projector	1940	1950	300W, 400W, or 500W	200 ft.	$68.50 f/1.6 lens w/case
Kodascope Eight-33 Projector	1948	1958	300W, 400W, or 500W	200 ft.	$78.00 w/500W lamp $77.12 w/30W lamp $11.00 for case
Kodascope Eight-90A Projector	1948?		750W maximum	400 ft.	$185 1 inch f/1.6 lens w/case
Kodascope Eight-71 Projector	1950	1951	750W or 1000W T-12	400 ft.	Price on request
Kodascope Eight-71A Projector	1952	1954		400 ft.	$111.80 including tax
Ciné-Kodak Showtime 8 Projector	1955	1958	500W	400 ft.	$115
Ciné-Kodak Showtime Variable Speed Projector	1958		500W	400 ft.	$139
	Rheostat speed control. Self-threading, turns off room light, projects film, rewinds film in 15 seconds, turns on room light, shuts off projector				
Ciné-Kodak Automatic 8 Model 1 Projector (variable speed control)	1964	1966		400 ft.	$109.95
Kodak Chevron 8 Model 1 Projector	1964	1966	Dichroic DKR	400 ft.	$149.95
Kodak Chevron 8 Model 1 Zoom Projector	1962	1966	As above	400 ft.	$174.95
	As above but with 15 to 25mm Ektanar f/1.2 zoom lens				
Kodak Hi-Mat 8 A5 Projector	1962		150W DLG	400 ft.	$164.95 with f/1.0 lens $169.95 with f/1.5 zoom lens
	400 ft. geared reel arms, self-threading, variable speed				
Kodak Caralux 8 Projector	1964	1966	150W	400 ft.	$159.50 with f/1.5 lens $179.95 with f/1.2 15-25mm zoom lens
	Flickerless 6 fps slow motion, 18 and 54 fps speeds				
Kodak Chevron 8 Model 10 Projector	1963	1966	Dichroic DKR	400 ft.	$189.95 with f/1.2 lens $214.95 with 15-25mm zoom lens or with Ektar f/1.0 lens
	Automatic threading 400 ft. reel, air-jet cooling for single frame projection.				

KODAK 8MM SOUND PROJECTOR

PROJECTOR NAME	FROM	TO	LAMP AND SPECIAL FEATURES	REEL SIZE	PRICE AT INTRODUCTION
Kodascope Sound 8 Projector Model 1	1960		150W		$345
Built-in speaker or outlet for external f/1.6 Ektanar lens, record and playback on 8mm sound-stripe film.					

KODAK 8MM BROWNIE MOVIE PROJECTORS

PROJECTOR NAME	FROM	TO	LAMP USED	REEL SIZE	SPECIAL FEATURES	PRICE AT INTRODUCTION
Brownie Projector	1952		300W	200 ft.	1 inch f/2 lens	$62.50
Brownie Projector f/1.6	1954		300W	200 ft.	Improved pull-down and shutter	$69.50
Brownie Projector 500	1956		500W			
Brownie Projector 500 Model B	1957					
Brownie 8 Projector Model 10	1959	1963	150W	200 ft.		$49.95
Brownie 300 Projector	1957	1961	300W	300 ft.		$69.50
Brownie 8 Projector Model A-15	1960	1966	150W		Automatic threading	$55.00
Brownie 310 Projector	1960	1966	150W	200 ft.	Self-threading	$74.50
Brownie 500 Projector Model A-5	1960	1966	500W T-10	400 ft.	Self-threading, power rewind	$94.50

KODAK SUPER 8 SILENT PROJECTORS

PROJECTOR NAME	YEAR	LENSES	SPECIAL FEATURES	PRICE AT INTRODUCTION
Instamatic M50 Projector	1965	28mm f/1.5	200 ft. reel, 150W DFC lamp	$62.50
Instamatic M60 Projector	1965	28mm f/1.5	200 ft. reel, 150 W DFC lamp, auto speed rewind	$84.50
Instamatic M70 Projector	1965	28mm f/1.5 20-30mm zoom f/1.5	400 ft. reels, forward and reverse, 150W DNE lamp Same	$149.95 $169.95
Instamatic M80 Projector	1965	20-30mm zoom f/1.5	Similar to M70 but accepts 8mm	$209.95
Instamatic M90 Projector	1965	20-30mm zoom f/1.5	Similar to M40 but accepts 8mm 150W DNF lamp	$194.50
Instmatic M68 Projector	1967	20-30mm zoom f/1.5	400 ft. reels, auto thread, 3 speeds	$99.50
Instamatic M95 Projector	1968	20-30mm zoom f/1.5	400 ft. reels, sprocketless transport, 7 speeds, 6-54 fps	$199.50
Instamatic M105 Projector	1970	f/1.5 fixed or zoom	Loads with 50 ft. cartridge or 400 ft. reel	From $139.95
Instamatic M109 Projector	1970	f/1.5 fixed or zoom	Similar to M105 except accepts both Super 8 and regular 8mm	From $159.95
Instamatic M110 Projector	1970	f/1.5 fixed or zoom	Accepts Super 8 and 8mm in both reels and cartridge, including new 400 ft. cartridge	From $194.50
Instamatic M67 Projector	1972	f/1.5 fixed or zoom	Accepts reels up to 400 ft. of 8mm or Super 8	From $114.50
Instamatic M77 Projector	1972	f/1.5 fixed or zoom	As above, but with 6 fps forward and reverse as well as 18 fps	From $129.95
Moviedeck 425 Projector	1974	20-30mm f/1.5 zoom	As above, but with 6 fps forward and reverse, Super 8 or single 8 400 ft. reel, sprocketless film transport, 18 fps, rapid rewind, ENZ Halogen lamp	$137.50
Instamatic M435 Projector	1974	22mm f/1.8 lens	Similar to 425 but has reverse projection, single frame, auto rewind	$179.50
		20-30mm f/1.8 lens		$209.50
Instamatic M447 Projector	1977	22mm f/1.8 lens	Similar to 425 but has 18 fps forward and reverse, single frame, built-in viewing screen	$217.50
		20-32mm f/1.5 zoom		$242.50
Instamatic M457 Projector	1977	22mm f/1.8	Similar to 425 but has 6, 18 fps forward and reverse, still frame, auto rewind, viewing screen	$254.50
		20-32mm f/1.5 zoom		$279.50
Instamatic M467 Projector	1977	22mm f/1.8	Similar to 425 but has 6, 18, and 54 fps forward and reverse. Rest as in 457	$274.50
		20-32mm f/1.5 zoom		$299.50
Moviedeck 477 Projector	1977	22mm f/1.8	Similar to 425 but has 3, 6, 18, and 54 fps, forward and reverse, still frame, off/low/high lamp switch and viewing screen	$299.50
		20-32mm f/1.5 zoom		$324.50

Author's Note: The descriptions of Moviedeck Models 447, 457, 467, and 477 were only available from a 1979 Directory and may not accurately describe these models when they first came on the market in 1974.

KODAK SUPER 8 SOUND PROJECTORS

PROJECTOR NAME	YEAR	LENSES	SPECIAL FEATURES	PRICE AT INTRODUCTION
Ektasound 235 Projector	1973	Unknown	50 ft. to 400 ft. reels, fast forward, 18 or 24 fps projection, wood cabinet	$234.50
Ektasound 245 Projector	1973	Isco-Gottingen Vario-Kiptagon 15-30mm f/1.3 zoom	As above, but also records sound	$299.50
Supermatic 60 Projector	1974	13mm f/2	400 ft. reels or Kodak Supermatic cassettes, magnetic plyback only, 5W amplifier, built-in 6 inch 6 x 9 inch screen	$460
		15-30mm f/1.3 zoom		$490
Supermatic 70 Projector	1974	13mm f/2	Similar to 60 but has recording capability	$550
		15-30mm f/1.3 zoom		$580
Ektasound 235B Projector	1975		Improved projection system	Less than $245
Ektasound 245B Projector	1975		Same	Less than $330
Ektasound Moviedeck 265 Projector	1976	22mm f/1.4	400 ft. Super 8, 8mm, sound or silent, playback only, 17-24 fps speeds	$299.50
Ektasound Moviedeck 265Z Projector	1976	20-32mm f/1.5 zoom	Same as 265 except zoom lens	$324
Ektasound Moviedeck 275 Projector	1976	22mm f/1.4	Similar to 265 but with recording capability	$374.50
Ektasound Moviedeck 275Z Projector	1976	20-32mm f/1.5 zoom	Same as above except with zoom lens	$399.50
Ektasound Moviedeck 285 Projector	1976	22mm f/1.4	Same but has full record sound-on-sound auto gain control	$435.50
Ektasound Moviedeck 285Z Projector	1976	22-32mm f/1.5 zoom	Same as above except with zoom lens	$459.50
Eastman Super 8mm Videofilm Projector Model TV-M100A	1972-1982	f/1.6 2 inch Kodak Projection lens or f.2.0 3 inch or f/2.5 4 inch Kodak Projection Ektanon lens		
		Modified Kodak Instamatic M100-A Sound Projector with 5-bladed shutter		

APPENDIX 7: CHRONOLOGY OF REVERE AND WOLLENSAK CAMERAS, 1939-1966

Model No.	Description	Price	Year
Revere 16mm Cameras			
C-26 Camera	Magazine loading, 3-lens turret, 12-16-32-48 fps	$152 with f2.5 fixed focus lens	1947?-1956
C-29 Camera	Identical to above, except with f1.9 scale focus lens	$187.50	1947?-1953
C-16 Camera	Magazine loading, single lens, 12-16-24-32-48 fps	$127.50 with f2.5 fixed focus lens	1947-1956
C-19 Camera	Identical to above, except with f1.9 scale focus lens	$155	1947-1950?
36 Camera	Magazine load, thru-body finder, Wollensak 2.5 lens	$139.50	1955
38 Camera	Same as above, except with 3-lens turret, matching finder lenses	$169.50	1955
101 Camera	Upright body, roll-loading, 5 camera speeds, single or double perforated film	$139.50 with f2.5 fixed focus lens	1955
103 Camera	Same as above except with 3-lens turret	$169.50 with f2.5 lens	1955
Revere 8mm Cameras			
Revere C-8 Super 8 Camera	Took special pre-split 8mm film	$21.95	1939-1941?
88 Camera	For double 8mm	$29.50	1940
99 Camera	Same as 88 except with 3-lens turret	$65	1941
70 Camera	8mm, magazine load, single lens	$127.50 with f1.9 lens	1947
60 Camera	Similar to above except with 3-lens turret	$152.50 with f2.8 lens $187.50 with f1.9 lens	1948
C-77 Camera	Same as C 70 but with eye level finder	$87.50	1950
C-67 Camera	Same as C 60 but with 2-lens turret	$104.50	1950
55 Camera	Built in fade and dissolve, recessed lens, roll load, f2.8 lens	$73.50 with case $69.50 with out case	1951
B-61 Camera	Magazine load, interchangeable lens, 4-speeds	$116.50 to $141.50 Depending on case and lens	1951, 1957
B-63 Camera	Similar to B-61 except with 3-lens turret	$142.50 with f1.9 lens	1951
40 Camera	Magazine load, 5-speed, single lens	$99.50 with f2.8 lens $124.50 with f1.9	1952
B44 Camera	Magazine load, 3-lens turret	$129.50 to $154.50	1952
44 Camera	MaMagazine load, 3-lens turret	$129.50 to $154.50	1952
50 Camera	Roll load, single lens	$49.50 with f2.8 lens	1952
80 Camera	Roll load, single lens	$97.5$74.50 with f2.5 lens	1956
81 Ranger Camera	Roll load, similar to 88 except single lens	$74.50 with f2.5 lens	1956
82 Ranger Camera	Similar to 81 but with scale focusing	$99.50 with f1.9 lens	1956
03 Camera	Same as 80 except scale focusing	$122.50 with f1.9 lens	1957
84 Camera	Similar to 80 except 3-lens turret	$122.50	1957
87 Camera	Lite-Dial exposure control, 5 speeds, footage indicator	$72.50 with f2.5 fixed focus lens	1957
89 Camera	Same as 84 (Description given does not support or explain this reference)	$147.50	1957

APPENDIX 7: CHRONOLOGY OF REVERE AND WOLLENSAK CAMERAS, 1939-1966

MODEL NO.	DESCRIPTION	PRICE	YEAR
Revere 8mm Cameras (Continued)			
CA-1 Electric Eye-matic Camera	Roll loading, with fully automatic exposure control	$139.50	1959
CA-2 Camera	Same as above but with turret with wideangle & telephoto conversion lenses	$169.50	1959
CA-3 Camera	Same as CA-1 but magazine load	$169.50	1959
CA-4 Camera	Same as CA-2, except magazine loadi	$199.50	1959
CA-7 Cine Zoom Camera	Roll load, automatic exposure control, 9mm-30mm zoom lens, automatic back-light compensation	$179.50	1960
CA-8 Cine Zoom Camera	Similar to CA-7, but magazine load	$209.50	1960
C-141 Cine Zoom Camera	Roll load, 9-30mm f1.8 zoom lens, automatic exposure control	$145	1962
C-142 Cine Zoom Camera	Similar to C-141, but loads with 8mm magazine	$165	1962
C-143 Power Zoom Camera	Similar to C-141, but with spring powered zoom	$200	1962
C-144 Power Zoom Camera	Similar to C-143, but loads with 8mm magazine	$220	1962
C-153 Reflex Camera	Roll load, 10-28mm zoom f1.8 lens, electric eye exposure control, power zoom	$210	1963
C-154 Reflex Camera	Similar to C-153, but with magazine load	$230	1963
C-98 Reflex Electric Camera	Roll load, automatic and manual exposure, reflex viewing, battery film drive	$116	1964
Revere Super 8 Camera – By 3M Company			
Automatic S1 Camera	Electric film drive, 16mm f2.5 fixed focus lens, 16fps camera speed, pistol grip	$29.95	1966
Wollensak 8mm Cameras – Manufactured by Revere beginning in 1954			
23 Camera	Roll load, 3-lens turret, 2 in focus mts.	$239.50 – Case $17.50	1954
28 Camera	Magazine load, single lens	$139.50 with f1.9 lens	1954
53 Camera	Roll load, 3-lens turret: 13 mm f 1.9, 6.5mm f 1.9 WA, 38mm f2.5 teleplots	$199.50	1954
58 Camera	Roll load, single lens, 5 operating speeds	$124.50 with f .9 lens	1954
42 Camera	Roll load, f1.9 lens fixed focus, 12-16-24-32-48 fps, exposure computer	$69.50	1957
43 Camera	Like 4, turret, f 1.9 plus converter lenses	$99.50	1957
46 Tru-Automatic Camera	Roll loading, 3-lens turret, electric eye for automatic exposure control	$144.50	1959
47 Tru-Automatic Camera	Same as above, but with single f1.8 lens	$94.50	1959
72 Camera	Roll loading, 12-16-24-32-48 fps	$99.50 with f1.8 lens	1959
73 Camera	Same as 72 except with turret and telephoto & wide-angle conversion lenses	$149.50	1959
C-76 Cine Zoom Camera	Roll load, 9-30mm f1.8 zoom lens, auto exposure control	$145	1962
C-77 Cine Zoom Camera	Similar to C-76, but loads with 8mm magazine	$165	1962
C-78 Power Zoom Camera	Similar to C-76, but with power zoom	$200	1962
C-79 Power Zoom Camera	Similar to C-77, but power zoom	$220	1962

APPENDIX 8: CHRONOLOGY OF VICTOR ANIMATOGRAPH EQUIPMENT, 1910-1941

Model	Serial Nos.	Years of Manufacture
Stereotrope		1910
Motion Picture Stereotrope		1911
Professional Stereotrope (with 5-amp Arc)		1911
Model 1 Portable Stereopticon (Arc) 3-1/4 x 4 Slides)		1912
Model 1 Viopticon (2-1/2 x 2-3/4 Slides)		1912
Model 2 Viopticon (2-1/2 x 2-3/4 Slides)		1913
Victor Postcard Projector (Arc)		1913
Model 2 Stereopticon (Mazda & Acetylene) (3-1/4 x 4 Slides)		1914
Model 1 Animatograph (35mm Arc)		1914
Model 2 Animatograph (35mm Mazda)	5001 to 5782	1915 to 1919
Model 3 Stereopticon (Square) (3-1/4 x 4 Slides)		1917
Safety Cinema (28mm – 165 w. 30 v. Mazda)	555 to 2657	1918 to 1924
Model 3 Animatophone (35mm Revised Cinema)		1918
High Power Stereopticon (30-20 lamp & tripod) (3-1/4 x 4 Slides)		1919
Dissolving Stereopticon (3-1/4 x 4 Slides)		1919
Home Cinema (28mm Hand Drive)		1922
Model 4-10 Spot Lights		1922
Model 1 victor Cine Camera (16mm Hand Drive)		1923
Model 1 Victor Cine Projector (16mm Hand Drive)	1 to 432	1923 to 1927
Model 2 Victor Cine Projector (16mm Motor Drive)	5000 to 5397	1925 to 1928
Model 3 Victor Cine Camera (Spring Drive)		1927
Model 3-T Victor Cine Camera (Turret)		1928
Model 3-B and 3-C Victor Cine Projectors	5700 to 7077	1930 to 1933
Model 3-O and 3-R Victor Cine Projectors	30000 to 31000	1930 to 1933
Model 4 Victor Cine Projector	40000 to 40041	1930
Model 5 Sound-On-Disc Animatophone	50000 to 50322	1930 to 1931
Model 5-O Sound-On-Disc Animatophone	51000 to 51080	1930 to 1931
Model 6 Sound-On-Disc Animatophone	60000 to 60294	1931 to 1932
Model 7 Victor Cine Projector	70000 to 70190	1931 to 1932
"ERPI" Sound-On-Disc (16mm Head Only)	M-101 to M-421	1931 to 1934
Model 8 H.S. Victor Cine Projector (16mm Silent)	80000 to 80180	1932
Model 8-H Victor Cine Projector (16mm Silent)	81000 to 81019	1932
Model 10-FH Victor Cine Projector (16mm Silent)	82000 to 83947	1932 to 1936
Model 11 Victor Cine Projector (16mm Silent)	84201 to 85765	1936 to 1939
Model 12-A and 12-B Sound-On-Film Animatophone	12000 to 12474	1933 to 1934
Model 20 Victor Cine Projector (16mm Silent)	85000 to 86102	1934 to 1936

APPENDIX 8: CHRONOLOGY OF VICTOR ANIMATOGRAPH EQUIPMENT, 1910-1941

Model	Serial Nos.	Years of Manufacture
Model 21 Victor Cine Projector (16mm Silent)	85200 to 90300	1935 to 1936
Model 22 Victor Cine Projector (16mm Silent) (Cabinet)	90501 to 91629	1936 to 1939
Model 24-A and 24-B Sound-On-Film Animatophone	24000 to 25624	1934 to 1939
Model 24-A and 24-B Sound-On-Film Animatophone	26650 to 26727	1934 to 1939
Model 24-C (32 volt) Sound-On-Film Animatophone	25625 to 26649	1934 to 1939
Model 4 Victor Cine Camera	32200 to 33531	1935
Model 25 AC-DC Sound-On-Film Animatophone	38201 to 39984	1935 to 1937
Model 25 AC Sound-On-Film Animatophone	33532 to 33773	1936 to 1939
Model 26 Sound-On-Film Animatophone	42201 to 42603	1937 to 1938
Model 38 Sound-On-Film Animatophone	60501 to 61308	1937 to 1939
Model 31, 33, 36 Sound-On-Film Animatophone	10201	1938 to 1939
Model 50 Continuous (16mm Silent)	10210	1938
Model 50-S Continuous (16mm Sound-On-Film)	62502 to 121302	1939
Model 40-A, 40-B, 400-C Sound-On-Film Animatopone		1939 to 1947
Model 16 Victor Cine Projector (16mm Silent)		1939
Model 41-B and 41-C Sound-On-Film Animatophone		1939
Model 41-B Sound-On-Film Animatophone		1940
Model 40-E Sound-On-Filmm Animatophone		1941

A Comparison of Running Times and Formats of 8mm, Super 8, and 16mm Motion Picture Films

RUNNING TIMES AND FILM LENGTHS FOR COMMON PROJECTION SPEEDS

Film Format	8mm (80 Frames per Foot)				Super 8 (72 Frames per Foot)				16mm (40 Frames per Foot)			
Projection Speed in Frames per Second	18*		24*		18†		24†		18‡		24§	
Running Time and Film Length	Feet	+ Frames	Feet	+ Frames	Feet	+ Frames	Feet	+ Frames	Feet	+ Frames	Feet	+ Frames
Seconds 1	0	18	0	24	0	18	0	24	0	18	0	24
2	0	36	0	48	0	36	0	48	0	36	1	8
3	0	54	0	72	0	54	1	0	1	14	1	32
4	0	72	1	16	1	0	1	24	1	32	2	16
5	1	10	1	40	1	18	1	48	2	10	3	0
6	1	28	1	64	1	36	2	0	2	28	3	24
7	1	46	2	8	1	54	2	24	3	6	4	8
8	1	64	2	32	2	0	2	48	3	24	4	32
9	2	2	2	56	2	18	3	0	4	2	5	16
10	2	20	3	0	2	36	3	24	4	20	6	0
20	4	40	6	0	5	0	6	48	9	0	12	0
30	6	60	9	0	7	36	10	0	13	20	18	0
40	9	0	12	0	10	0	13	24	18	0	24	0
50	11	20	15	0	12	36	16	48	22	20	30	0
Minutes 1	13	40	18	0	15	0	20	0	27	0	36	0
2	27	0	36	0	30	0	40	0	54	0	72	0
3	40	40	54	0	45	0	60	0	81	0	108	0
4	54	0	72	0	60	0	80	0	108	0	144	0
5	67	40	90	0	75	0	100	0	135	0	180	0
6	81	0	108	0	90	0	120	0	162	0	216	0
7	94	40	126	0	105	0	140	0	189	0	252	0
8	108	0	144	0	120	0	160	0	216	0	288	0
9	121	40	162	0	135	0	180	0	243	0	324	0
10	135	0	180	0	150	0	200	0	270	0	360	0

*AN Standard PH22.22-1964   †AN Standard PH22.155-1967   ‡AN Standard PH22.10-1964   §AN Standard PH22.16-1965

NOTE: Diagrams of the three film formats, including dimensions to indicate size and location of both image area and sound stripe, are given in the following American National (AN) Standards:

8mm—PH22.88-1963, PH22.19-1964, PH22.20-1969
Super 8—PH22.157-1967, PH22.161-1968, PH22.154 (Draft Standard)
16mm—PH22.7-1964, PH22.87-1966, PH22.8-1969

APPENDIX 9: COMPARISON OF RUNNING TIMES AND FORMATS

TYPICAL RUNNING TIMES OF FILMS

Film Format	8mm				Super 8				16mm			
Projection Speed in Frames per Second	18		24		18		24		18		24	
Inches per Second	2.7		3.6		3.0		4.0		5.4		7.2	
Film Length and Screen Time	Minutes	Seconds	Minutes	Seconds	Minutes	Seconds	Minutes	Seconds	Minutes	Seconds	Minutes	Seconds
Feet 50	3	42	2	47	3	20	2	30	1	51	1	23
100	7	24	5	33	6	40	5	0	3	42	2	47
150	11	7	8	20	10	0	7	30	5	33	4	10
200	14	49	11	7	13	20	10	0	7	24	5	33
300	22	13	16	40	20	0	15	0	11	7	8	20
400	29	38	22	13	26	40	20	0	14	49	11	7
500	37	2	27	47	33	20	25	0	18	31	13	53
600	44	27	33	20	40	0	30	0	22	13	16	40
700	51	51	38	53	46	40	35	0	25	56	19	27
800	59	16	44	27	53	20	40	0	29	38	22	13
900	66	40	50	0	60	0	45	0	33	20	25	0
1000	74	4	55	33	66	40	50	0	37	2	27	47
1100	81	29	61	7	73	20	55	0	40	44	30	33
1200	88	53	66	40	80	0	60	0	44	27	33	20

NUMBER OF FRAMES SEPARATION BETWEEN SOUND AND PICTURE*

	8mm	Super 8†	16mm
Magnetic Track	56	18	28
Optical Track	—	22	26

*Figures given are for reel-to-reel projection in which the sound precedes the picture. A proposed standard places the sound 28 frames behind the picture for cartridge-loaded films.

†Proposed AN Standard Dimensions.

Motion Picture and Education Markets Division

EASTMAN KODAK COMPANY · ROCHESTER, N.Y. 14650

31-3-70-AE-Major Revision
KODAK Pamphlet No. S-42

Printed in the United States of America

Authors's Note: The reader should be aware that prior to the introduction of Super8 in 1965, 16 frames per second was the standard silent speed for both 8mm and 16mm cameras and projectors.

APPENDIX 10 – COMPILATION OF MOTION PICTURE FILM FORMATS

Henry "Dutch" Van Lieshout, of Great Falls, Montana, assembled this compilation of motion picture film formats over a number of years of patient research beginning before he left Holland, his native land. "Dutch" started working at Station KFBB Channel 5 in Great Falls in 1969 as Director of Photography, where he did most of the filming and processing for the News Department and all of the still photography and films for the Production Department. He retired in January 1983 or as he often said, "thrown out with the film processor." "Dutch and his wife Betty were founding members of the Movie Machine Society and his compilation first appeared in the Society's journal, SIXTEEN FRAMES, Spring 1990 issue. As this was a "work in progress" when Dutch lost his long battle with cancer, there are some incomplete and questionable entries.

Compilation of Motion Picture Film Widths, Perforations, Formats and Configurations
By Henry "Dutch" Van Lieshout

"This compilation of formats was copied from available sources, see list supplied, plus some museum visits and calls. It is by no means complete and there are many unknowns, re dates and perforations. I found 43 actual film widths, not counting Cinerama or differences in perforation or image sizes in the 16, 17.5, 28, 35mm etc. nor the disc, plate, and cylinder projectors. The total would be 95 plus the 11 disc/plate units. People in the know, such as Brian Coe, told me some sizes may have been measured from shrunken film; others may have only existed on paper drafts and were never actually manufactured. If anyone can fill in some of the missing data or knows of a format I missed let it be known."

SOURCE LISTING

A   Ariel, Pete. *Ariel's Cinematic Register*. Deutsches Filmmuseum, Frankfurt AM, Germany.

B   Matthews, Glenn E. and Raife G. Tarkinton. "Early History of Amateur Motion Picture Film." *Journal of SMPTE*. March '55 Vol. 64 pages 129-140.

C   Coe, Brian. *History of Movie Photography*. Taplinger Publishing, New York 1977.

D   Auer, Michel, and Michele Ory. *Histoire de la Camera cine amateur*. Les Editions de l'Amateur, Paris, 1979.

E   Eastman Kodak Co.

F   Kattelle, Alan D. "The Vitalux Story," *Photographica Journal,* Vol. 2, No. 4, August 1985.

G   _____. "The Vitak Story," *Photographic Canadiana* 25, 1 May/June 1999.

H   MacGowan, Kenneth. *Behind the Screen*, Delacorte Press, New York 1986.

K   Niver, Kemp. "Motion Picture Film Widths." *Journal SMPTE,* Vol. 77, August 1968. (See Note 1, page 366.)

L   Limbacher, James L. *Four Aspects of the Film,* New York, Arno Press, 1978.

M   The Museum of the Moving Image (MOMI), London.

P   British Kinematograph Sound and Television Society (BKSTS), London.

X   Caulfield, William. *International Photographer,* October, 1985.

Y   *News Letter.* Projected Picture Trust, No. 47, Summer 1989, London.

Z   Viewmaster Ideal Group Inc., Box 490, Portland, Oregon 09207-0490.

R   Gregory, C. L. "Early History of Wide Film, *Journal SMPTE,* January 1930.

BASE OR CARRIER Abbreviations

G   Glass.

O   Ozophane non-flammable cellophane (very thin).

N   Nitrate base film.

S   Safety base film: acetate, diacetate, triacetate, mylar.

APPENDIX 10 – COMPILATION OF MOTION PICTURE FILM FORMATS

Format in mm	Base	Name If Known	Perforation Location	Inventor or Manufacturer	Source	Year	Remarks, Page Numbers of Source
3	S		Center of frameline	Eric Berndt	K	1960	Used by NASA? See Note 1
4.75	S	Monoplex	Center frame-horizontal	Pathe Freres	C	1955	Page 172
6	S	Experimental	On side frameline	Not known	M	?	Small piece at MOMI
8	S	Regular 8	On side frameline	Eastman Kodak	E	1932	16mm split after proc.
8	S	Super 8	On side frameline	Eastman Kodak	E	1965	Single 8 Cartridge
8.75	S	Early TV film			P	1968	2 b&w or single color
9	S	Early TV film	Center frameline	?	M	?	9.5 possibly shrunken?
9.5	S	Pathé Baby	Center frameline	Pathé Cinema Paris	K	1922	
11	S	Vitak	1 center frameline	E.J. Rector	G	1902	Mail order only
11	N	Duplex	1 center frameline	Project-A-Graph	K	1910	
11	N	Duplex	2 round each edge	Gerald J. Badgley	B	1915	See Note 2
12 or 12.5	N	Jr. Prestwich	No other info	English	H/R	1899	470-28
13			1 center frameline	British	K	1920	
13			Quadruple on frameline	French	K	1925	
15	S	Pocket Chrono	1 center frameline	Gaumont-Paris	D	1900	58-64
16	S	Stubstandard	1 each edge on frameline	AGFA Germany	K	1920	
16	S	Cine Kodak	1 each edge on frameline	Eastman American	E	1923	
16	O	Ozophane	1 each l & r outside frame	AGFA-Germany	K	1928	Cellophane thin
16	S	Harper sound	1 & 2 on alternate frameline	British	Y	1938	No rewind necessary
16	S	Viewmaster	4 inside 12 x 12mm	Viewmaster Ideal	Z	1975	Bx 470 Portland, OR
16	S	Kemco HoMovie	1 each side frameline	Kodel Elec. & Mfg. Co	A	1929	ACR 155. See Note 3
17	S?		2 outside frameline	Pathé French	K	1920	For South Am export
17	S?		Single, sound	French	K	1930	
17.5	N	Birtac	Dual one side	Birt Acres-London	B	1898	
17.5	N	La Petite	1 square center frameline	Hughes-London	B	1900	
17.5	N	Biokam	1 square center frameline	Wrench & Son - London	B	1900	
17.5	N	Duoscope	2 square center frameline	Duoscope, Ltd.	P	1912	
17.5	N	Movette	2 each side frame	Movette Co-Roch.	P	1917	Neg nitrate, pos safety
17.5	N	Kino Einlock	1 center frameline	Erneman-Germany	B	1903	
17.5	N	Ikonograph	1 center frameline	E.J. Rector	B	1905	
17.5	S	Proposal	Dual sound outside	Germany	P	1968	
17.5	N	Sinemat	?	Sinemat Motion Picture Co.	B	1915	New York, NY
17.5	N	Autograph	?	Eric W. Nelson	B	1916	
17.5	N	Actograph	?	Willart Instrument Co.	B	1918	New Rochelle
17.5	N	Clou	2 each side of frame	Austria	B	1920	Austria
17.5	N	Coco	?	Linhof	B	1921	Germany
17.5	?	?	4 each side	? German sound	K	1930	Export to So. America
17.5	S	Pathé Rural	Single	Pathé French	K	1930	
17.5	S		Double sound	German	K	1930	

APPENDIX 10 – COMPILATION OF MOTION PICTURE FILM FORMATS

Format in mm	Base	Name If Known	Perforation Location	Inventor or Manufacturer	Source	Year	Remarks, Page Numbers of Source
18	?		2 square on frameline	Russian	K	1925	Used by NASA?
19	?	Proposed French			L		No evidence of Mfd
20	?	Proposed American			L		No evidence of Mfd
21	N	Mirographe	Edge notched	Reulos, Goudeau & Co.	K, L	1900	French
22	S	Home Kinetoscope	2 rows bet 3 row film	Thomas A. Edison	K	1912	
22	S	Gaumont	2, one each side frameline	French	K	1920	
22	O	Ozophane	2 sq each side frame	Soc. Cinema Res.		1924	
24	S		Dual each side frame	Soc. Cinema Res.	K	1925	
24	S		Quadrple perforated	French	K	1925	Page 817, Fig. 27
26	O	Ozophane	None, prism projection	Soc .Cinelux French	K	1920	Page 817, Fig. 23
26	O	Ozophane	One edge at frame	Soc .Cinelux French	K	1920	
26	S	Pathé Freres	?	French	L	1912	
28	S	Pathé KOK	3 left, 1 right side	Pathé French	B	1912	
28	S	Pathescope	3 left, 3 right side	Pathescope NYC	B	1913	
28	S	Home Cinema	3 perfs each side	A.F. Victor	K	1920	
28	S	Safety Standard	3 perfs each side	A.F. Victor	K	1918	
30	?		3 thru frameline	European	K	1910	
32	S	Twin 16	Perf both sides	Vincennes-French	K	1920	
32	S	Twin 16	Single perf sound	American	K	1925	
35	N	Lumiére	One round each side	Lumiére Bros	K	1895	
35	N	Toy film	45 frame horizontal	Ernst Planck	K	1900	For Toy Magic Lantern
35	N	Picturescope	?	Chas E Dressler	B	1910	Double row images
35	S	Duplivision	4 each side of frame	Walter Beyer	Y	1960	Dual inverted image
35	N	CUB		American Cin-Corp	B	1917	Chicago
35	-	Campro	4 each side		C	1927	Used paper film
38	N	Color		Lee & Turner	C	1901	For Lee Turner pg 47
40?	N	3 image rows	Four each side	French	K	1910	3-10mm episodes
40	N	LePrince	None, notch on side	English	C	1888	55
42		Tri Ergon	2 rows, 4 per frame	Experimental sound film	C	1922	108 German
48	N	Viventoscope	1 round each side of frame	A.S. Newman	C	1897	Manufactured for Blair
50	N	Grapho-Phonoscope		Skladowski-French	K	1899	Sound-on-film
51	N	Latham Corp		Woodville Latham	R	1900	29
55.625	S	Cinemascope-55		20th Century Fox	L	?	Early Cinemascope
56	N	Magnafilm		Paramount Pictures	C	1929	
60	N	Kinesigraph		Donisthorpe/Crofts	C	1890	
60	N	Chrono-photographe	5 each side	Georges Demeny	K	1895	
62	N	Mutoscope	6 each side	American Motoscope & Biograph Co.	K	1895	Modified biograph

APPENDIX 10 – COMPILATION OF MOTION PICTURE FILM FORMATS

Format in mm	Base	Name If Known	Perforation Location	Inventor or Manufacturer	Source	Year	Remarks, Page Numbers of Source
62	N	Burton Holmes	4 each side	Prestwick	K	1897	(or 2/38 in)
63	N	Veriscope	6 each side	E.J. Rector	K	1897	
63.5	N	Natural Vision		Spoor-Berggren	C	1929	p. 144-5
65	N	?		Skladowski	R	1899	28
68	N	Biograph		Casetler/Dickson	C	1894	142
70	N	Fox		Grandeur American	C	1920	
70	S	Pick a movie	1 perf per frame row	Leo W Wells	P	1972	12 row picture-sound
70	S	Imax	15 perfs each side	Wm A Shaw-Canada	X	1969	5 x 7 cm Horiz image
70	S	Panavision	5 perfs each side		L	1957	Todd ad 59-66
70	S	Single Cinerama		Fred Waller	C	1963	p. 147-150
75	S	Todd-AO	5 perfs each side	Michael Todd-Brian O'Brien	C	1954	Neg 65mm Prt 70mm
3 ea. 35	S	Cinerama triple	6 each side-3 vert. 35mm	Waller-American	C	1952	148
250mm 10"	N	Disc Kinemaphotograph	2 perfs in between rows	Baker	K	1904	Canadian
263mm 10.5"	N	Spiral Disc	None	A.F. Victor Animatograph	K	1911	U.S. See Note 4
250mm-10"	N	Spirograph	Center round-1 drive hole	Chas Urban	K	1913	(Til 1923)
6.5 x 90m	G	Olikos	None-glass plates	Societe Cinema	D-C	1912	12 rows of 7 frames
120mm	N	Oko	Both sides	Kasimir Proszynski	C	1914	15 picture rows
305mm-12"	G	Kammatograph	None	L.U. Kamm	G	1900	600 exposures circular
9 x 12 cm	G	LeSeul	None	Courvoiser-Paris	D	1920	Glass plates
12.5 x 44.5	S	Vitalux	2 rows each side	H.C. Schlicker	F	1914	1922 (1664 images/film)
Cylinder	N	Kinetograph	? Experimental	Edison	H	1898	Scrapped project
150mm	N	Cinephote	Disc.	M Clermont Huey	D	1907	58
131 x 216mm	G	Cinematographe		Gianni Bettini	D	1910	Glass Plate
?	?	L' Aelethorama	1 perf each side frame In	Paul Mortier	D		59

Notes:

1. The reader is cautioned to examine Kemp Niver's examples carefully, as there are some errors; for example Fig. 10 is described as 30mm, but is obviously much wider.

2. Matthews and Tarkington have the inventor's name misspelled as "Bradley."

3. The Kemco HoMovie 16mm frame held four images. See Chapter 5.

4. See Rose, Samuel G., "Alexander Victor - Motion Picture Pioneer," *Journal of SMPTE*, Vol. 72, August 1963.

Other excellent sources are "A Potpourri of Film Widths and Sprocket Holes." *American Cinematographer*, January 1969, pp. 99-103, and "One Hundred Years of Film Sizes," by Michael Rogge, which can be found at this website: **www.xs4all.nl/~wichm/filmsize.html**

APPENDIX 11: IDENTIFICATION MARKS USED IN SUBSTANDARD MOTION PICTURE CAMERAS

Cine Kodak Processing Dept., Kodak Park, Rochester, New York, Revised August 4, 1949

From the Estate of Harris B. Tuttle, Gift of Martin L. Scott, August 1993

Explanatory Notes

All drawing are approximately five times actual size.

In routine correspondence and record keeping it has been found convenient to refer to the Ciné Kodaks by number. The numbers are assigned as the cameras come out by the Service Department of the Main Office of the Eastman Kodak Company, Rochester, New York, U.S.A.

The number and code letter will be found just to the right of drawings. For example, C-1, C-2 etc. on the Ciné Kodak marks.

The term "Ciné-Kodak" being a trade name is used as applying specifically to the 16 and 8 mm motion picture camera of Eastman Kodak manufacture.

Author's Note

The term "Identification Marks" as used in this appendix refers to the practice of altering the margins of the camera aperture plate or cutting holes of various shapes in the margins of the aperture plate, in a unique manner for each make and model of camera. The result is a distinctive frame image left on film exposed in such cameras. While it would appear that this practice was industry-wide, it is not known when it was instituted, nor by what agreement among the various manufacturers.

This appendix is a verbatim copy of a booklet issued by the Cine-Kodak Processing Department of Eastman Kodak and is from the estate of Harris B. Tuttle. There are certain unexplained illustrations, such as on Plates 6A, 7A, etc. If any reader can identify those illustrations or point out other errors, such information will be much appreciated. The author gratefully acknowledges the gift of this booklet by Martin L. Scott of Rochester, New York.

Identification of Plates

Code No	Cine Kodaks	Plate No.
C-1	Model A f/1.9 and 3.5	1
C-2	B f/6.5	1
C-3	B f/3.5	2
C-4	B f/1.9	2
C-5	BB f/1.9 and 4.5 first mark	3
C-5	BB f/1.9 and 4.5 second mark	3
C-6	BB f/3.5 first mark	4
C-6	BB f/3.5 second mark	4
	Harrow Model BB f-3.5	4a
	Harrow Model BB f-1.9	4a
C-7	Model K f/1.9 and 3.5	5
C-8	Model M f/3.5	5
C-9	Special f/1.9	6
C-10	Magazine Cine Kodak f/1.9	6
C-9	Cine Special New Type Chamber	6a
C-11	Model E f/3.5	7
C-12	Model E f/1.9	7
C-13	Royal f/1.9 and f/2.8	7a
C8-1	Cine Kodak Eight Model 20 f/3.5	8
C8-2	Cine Kodak Eight Model 60 f/1.9	8
C8-3	Cine Kodak Eight Model 25 f/2.7	9
C8-4	Bedaux Measurement Camera f/1.9	9
C8-5	Magazine Cine Kodak Eight Model 90	9.1
H8-1	Cine Kodak Eight Model 55	9-2
C8-6	Cine-Kodak Eight Reliant f/2.7	9-2
C8-7	Brownie f/2.7	9-3

APPENDIX 11: IDENTIFICATION MARKS USED IN SUBSTANDARD MOTION PICTURE CAMERAS

Competitors' Cameras – 8mm Cameras	**Plate No.**
Stewart Warner Eight f/3.5	9a
Keystone Eight Model B-8 f/3.5	9a
Emel Cine Eight	9b
Cine Nizo Eight Model 8 - E	9b
Eumig Eight f/1.3	9c
Ditmar Eight	9c
Bell and Howell Double Eight	9d
Zeiss Movikon Eight f/3.5	9d
Siemens-Halske Double Eight Magazine Camera	9e
Revere Double Eight - Model 88	9e
Cine- Eight Magazine Cameras	9f
Univex Cinemaster Eight	9g
Competitors' CAMERAS – 16 mm. Cameras	
Bell and Howell Filmo 70D	10
Bell and Howell Filmo 75	10
Bell and Howell Filmo 121	10a
Movikon f/1.4	10a
Bell & Howell Filmo 141	10b
Zeiss Ikon Kinamo S - 10	11
Stewart - Warner	11
Bangsberg	12
Ansco Risdon Model A	12
Cine Ansco	13
Agfa Ansco	13
Agfa Movex Model 30	13a
Agfa Movex Model 16-12	13a
Ruby (formerly Oxford)	14
Ensign	14
Filmograph	15
Keystone	15
Victor	16
Victor Model 3	16
Vitascope	17
De Vry	17
Q. R. S.	18
Kodel	18
Kinatone	19
Peko	19
Simplex Pockette	20
Cine Nizo Model 3	20
Siemens-Halske	21
Bolex	21
Essex News Reel f/3.5	22
Paragon f/1.5	22
R.C.A. Sound Camera f/3.5	23
Berndt Sound Camera	23
Maurer Professional	24
Berndt-Bach Auricon - BB	25
Berndt-Maurer Sound - BM	25

APPENDIX 11: IDENTIFICATION MARKS USED IN SUBSTANDARD MOTION PICTURE CAMERAS

① Cine Kodaks

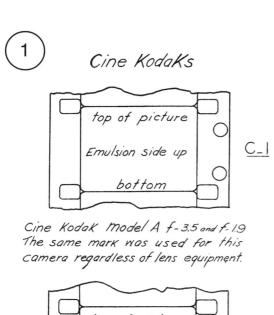

C-1

Cine Kodak Model A f-3.5 and f-1.9
The same mark was used for this
camera regardless of lens equipment.

C-2

Cine Kodak model B f-6.5

② Cine Kodaks

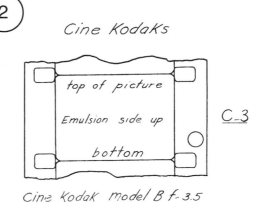

C-3

Cine Kodak model B f-3.5

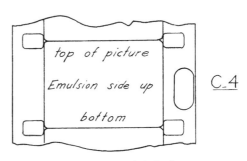

C-4

Cine Kodak model B f-1.9

③ Cine Kodaks

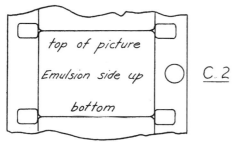

C-5

Cine Kodak Model BB f-1.9 and f-4.5
1500 cameras made using this mark.

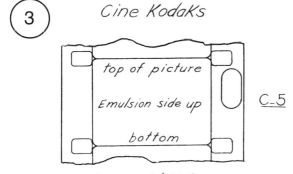

C-5

Cine Kodak model BB f-1.9 and f-4.5
This camera mark was adopted subsequently to
prevent confusion with the mark of the model B f-1.9.

④ Cine Kodaks

C-6

Cine Kodak model BB f-3.5
1500 cameras were made using this mark

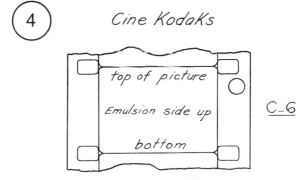

C-6

Cine Kodak model BB f-3.5
This camera mark was adopted subsequently
to prevent confusion with the mark of the model B f-35

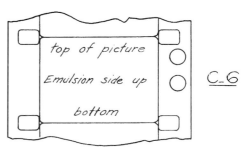
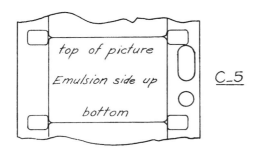

APPENDIX 11: IDENTIFICATION MARKS USED IN SUBSTANDARD MOTION PICTURE CAMERAS

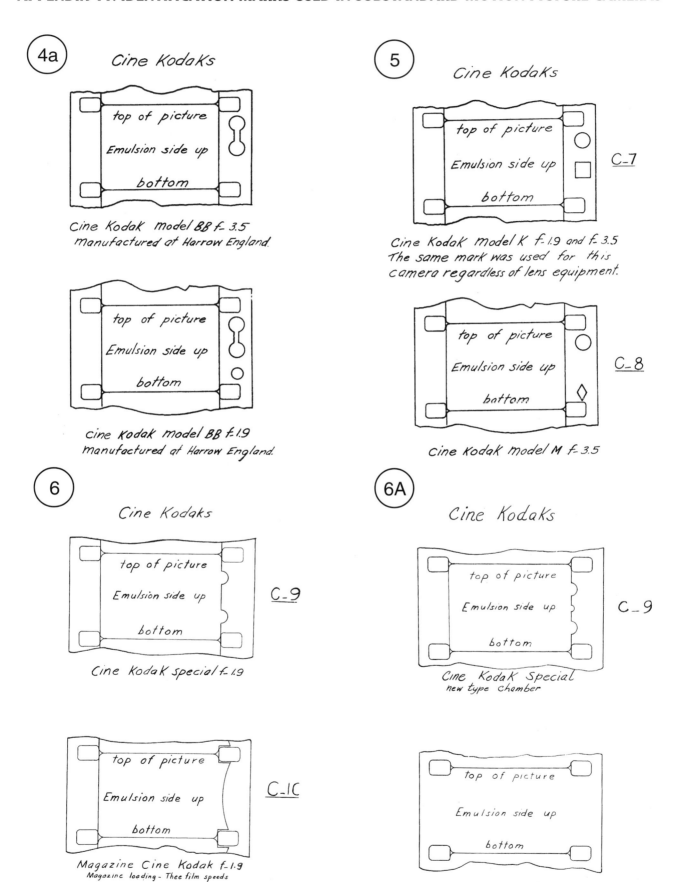

4a Cine Kodaks

top of picture

Emulsion side up

bottom

Cine Kodak model BB f. 3.5 manufactured at Harrow England.

top of picture

Emulsion side up

bottom

Cine Kodak model BB f.1.9 manufactured at Harrow England.

5 Cine Kodaks

top of picture

Emulsion side up

bottom

C-7

Cine Kodak model K f.1.9 and f.3.5 The same mark was used for this camera regardless of lens equipment.

top of picture

Emulsion side up

bottom

C-8

Cine Kodak model M f-3.5

6 Cine Kodaks

top of picture

Emulsion side up

bottom

C-9

Cine Kodak special f.1.9

top of picture

Emulsion side up

bottom

C-IC

Magazine Cine Kodak f.1.9
Magazine loading - Thee film speeds

6A Cine Kodaks

top of picture

Emulsion side up

bottom

C-9

Cine Kodak Special
new type chamber

top of picture

Emulsion side up

bottom

APPENDIX 11: IDENTIFICATION MARKS USED IN SUBSTANDARD MOTION PICTURE CAMERAS

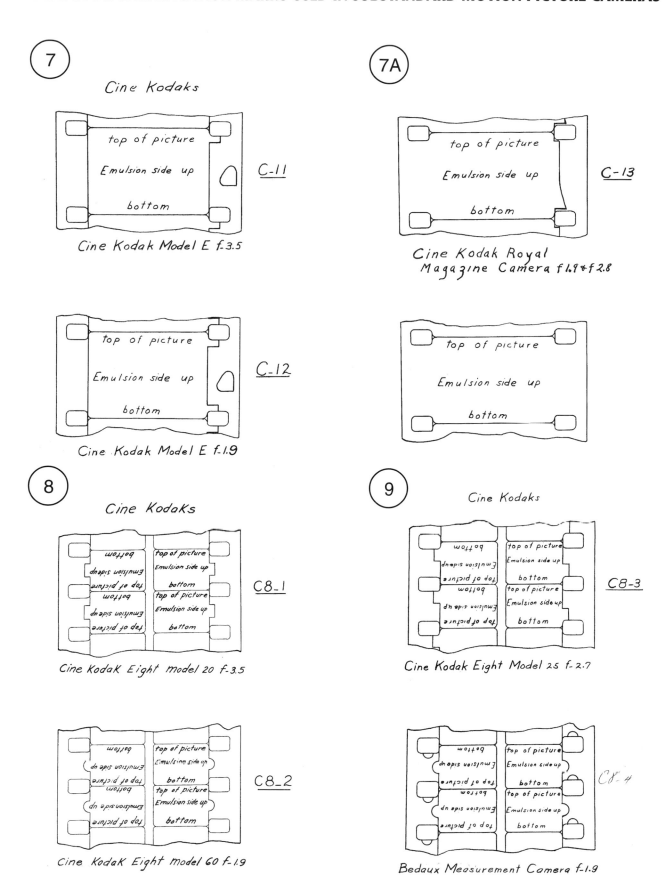

(7) Cine Kodaks

C-11 — Cine Kodak Model E f.3.5

C-12 — Cine Kodak Model E f.1.9

(7A)

C-13 — Cine Kodak Royal Magazine Camera f.1.9 & f.2.8

(8) Cine Kodaks

C8-1 — Cine Kodak Eight model 20 f.3.5

C8-2 — Cine Kodak Eight model 60 f.1.9

(9) Cine Kodaks

C8-3 — Cine Kodak Eight Model 25 f.2.7

C8-4 — Bedaux Measurement Camera f.1.9

APPENDIX 11: IDENTIFICATION MARKS USED IN SUBSTANDARD MOTION PICTURE CAMERAS

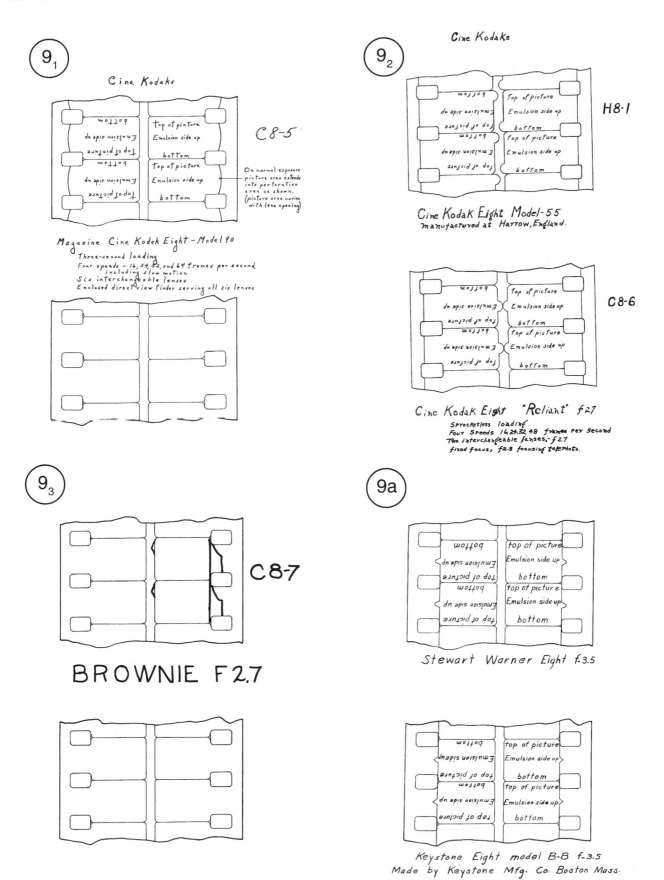

9₁

Cine Kodaks

C8-5

On normal exposure picture area extends into perforation area as shown. (picture area varies with lens opening)

Magazine Cine Kodak Eight – Model 90
Three-second loading
Four speeds – 16, 24, 32, and 64 frames per second, including slow motion
Six interchangeable lenses
Enclosed direct view finder serving all six lenses

9₂

Cine Kodaks

H8-1

Cine Kodak Eight Model-55
manufactured at Harrow, England.

C8-6

Cine Kodak Eight "Reliant" f2.7
Sprocketless loading
Four Speeds 16, 24, 32, 48 frames per second
Two interchangeable lenses,- f2.7 fixed focus, f2.8 focusing telephoto.

9₃

C8-7

BROWNIE F2.7

9a

Stewart Warner Eight f.3.5

Keystone Eight model B-8 f-3.5
Made by Keystone Mfg. Co. Boston Mass.

APPENDIX 11: IDENTIFICATION MARKS USED IN SUBSTANDARD MOTION PICTURE CAMERAS

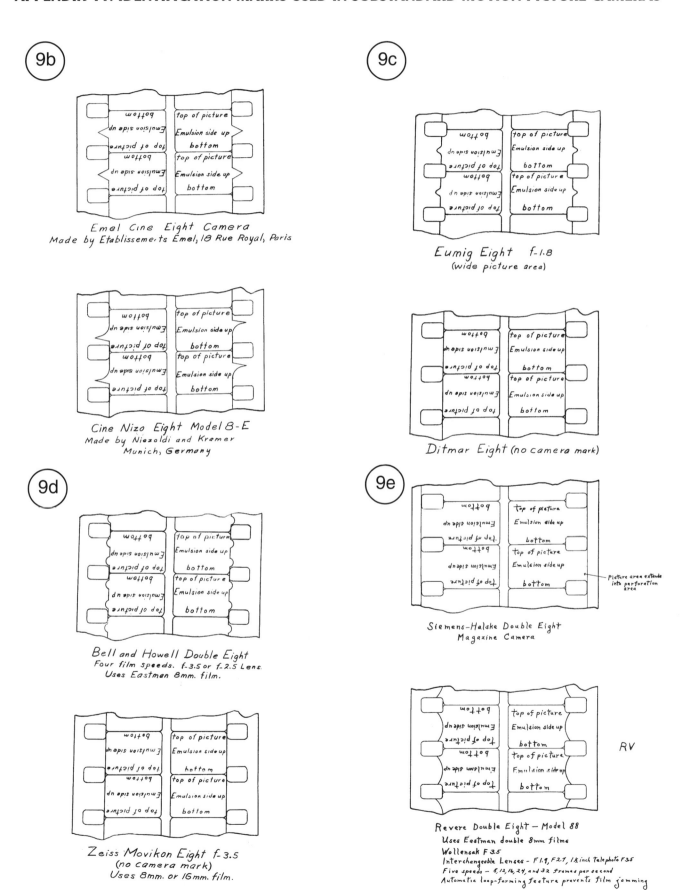

9b

Emel Cine Eight Camera
Made by Etablissements Emel, 18 Rue Royal, Paris

Cine Nizo Eight Model 8-E
Made by Niezoldi and Kramer
Munich, Germany

9c

Eumig Eight   f-1.8
(wide picture area)

Ditmar Eight (no camera mark)

9d

Bell and Howell Double Eight
Four film speeds. f-3.5 or f-2.5 Lens.
Uses Eastman 8mm. film.

Zeiss Movikon Eight f-3.5
(no camera mark)
Uses 8mm. or 16mm. film.

9e

Siemens-Halske Double Eight
Magazine Camera

Picture area extends
into perforation
area

RV

Revere Double Eight — Model 88
Uses Eastman double 8mm. films
Wollensak F 3.5
Interchangeable Lenses - F 1.9, F 2.7, 1½ inch Telephoto F 3.5
Five speeds - 8, 12, 16, 24, and 32 frames per second
Automatic loop-forming feature prevents film jamming

APPENDIX 11: IDENTIFICATION MARKS USED IN SUBSTANDARD MOTION PICTURE CAMERAS

Cine-Eight Magazine Cameras

Cine-Eight Magazine Cameras for the most part do not make a definite identification mark.

The perforation areas of the following listed cameras appear similar to that of the Siemens-Halske Double Eight Camera listed on page (9e):

Manufacturer	Camera
Bell & Howell	Filmo Auto-8
Briskin Camera Co.	Briskin
Camera Corporation of America	Cine Perfex Double Eight
DeJur Ansco	DeJur 8, Model B-100
Franklin Photo Ind.	Franklin Eight M.115
	Franklin Model 115T
	Franklin Model 115-E
Revere Camera Company	Revere "60" Turret
	Revere "70"

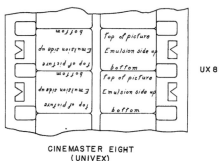

UX 8

CINEMASTER EIGHT
(UNIVEX)
MODELS II, D8, E8, F8
Made by UNIVERSAL CAMERA CORP.

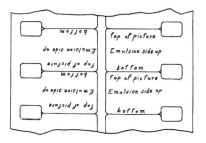

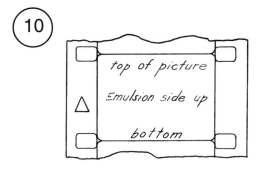

Bell and Howell Filmo 70 D
Three lens turret head-Seven film speeds-
Variable area view finder.

Bell and Howell Filmo 75 f-3.5
Universal focus or focusing mount - One speed
This is the thin vertical model.
Made by Bell and Howell Co. 1843 Larchmont Ave. Chicago, Ill.

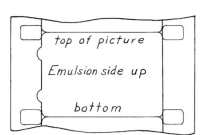

Bell and Howell Filmo 121 f-1.8 and f-3.5
The same mark is used regardless of lens equipment
Magazine loading - two film speeds.

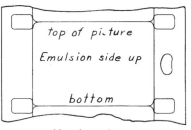

Movikon f-1.4
Made by Zeiss Ikon
Dresden, Germany

APPENDIX 11: IDENTIFICATION MARKS USED IN SUBSTANDARD MOTION PICTURE CAMERAS

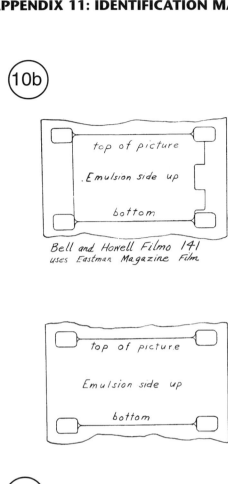

(10b)

Bell and Howell Filmo 141
uses Eastman Magazine Film

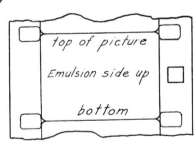

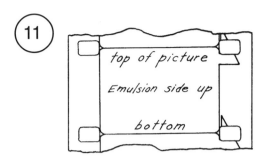

(11)

Zeiss-IKon Kinamo S-10
Made by Zeiss IKon   Dresden, Germany

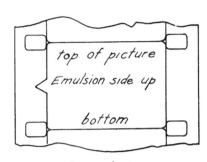

Stewart-Warner
Made by Stewart-Warner Corporation
1826-1852 Diversey Parkway Chicago Ill.

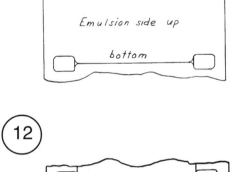

(12)

Bangsberg
Made by Bangsberg Cine Production Corp.

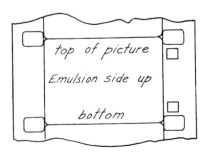

Ansco Risdon model A
Made by Agfa-Ansco Binghamton N.Y

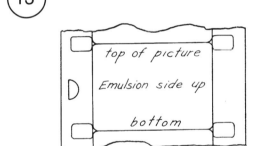

(13)

Cine Ansco
Made by Agfa-Ansco, Binghamton N.Y.

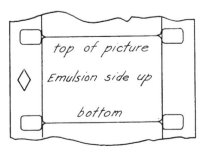

Agfa Ansco
made by Agfa-Ansco, Berlin Germany

APPENDIX 11: IDENTIFICATION MARKS USED IN SUBSTANDARD MOTION PICTURE CAMERAS

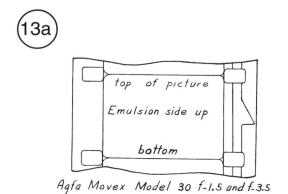

(13a)

Agfa Movex Model 30 f-1.5 and f-3.5

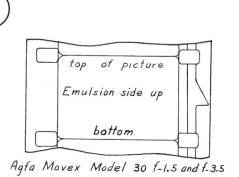

(14)

Agfa Movex Model 30 f-1.5 and f-3.5

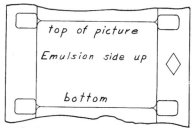

Agfa Movex Model 16-12
Magazine loading, Two film speeds, f-3.5
Made by Agfa-Ansco, Berlin Germany

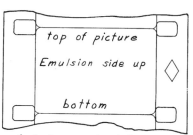

Agfa Movex Model 16-12
Magazine loading, Two film speeds, f-3.5
Made by Agfa-Ansco, Berlin Germany

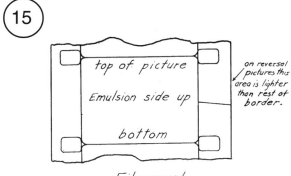

(15)

on reversal pictures this area is lighter than rest of border.

Filmagraph
Note: different densities on edge of film

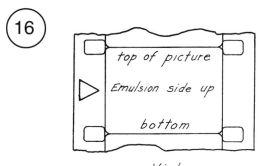

(16)

Victor
made by Victor Animatograph Corp. Davenport, Iowa

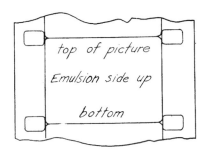

Keystone (no Camera mark)
made by Keystone Manufacturing Co., Boston Mass.

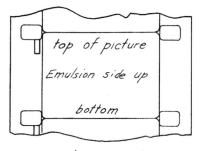

Victor model 3
Variable speeds - double springmotor - hand crank
built-in exposure meter - compensating View finder.
self - setting film measure.

APPENDIX 11: IDENTIFICATION MARKS USED IN SUBSTANDARD MOTION PICTURE CAMERAS

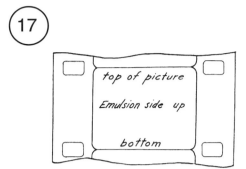

Vitascope - Hand cranked (narrow picture area)
made by the Vitascope Corporation Providence R.I.

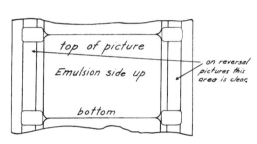

DeVry
Made by Q.R.S.-DeVry Corporation
333 N. Michigan Ave. Chicago Ill.

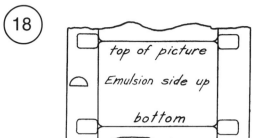

Q.R.S.
made by Q.R.S.-DeVry Corporation
333 N. Michigan Ave. Chicago Ill.

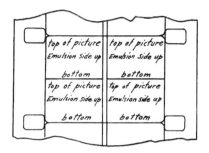

Kodel - four pictures per frame
(No Camera mark)
made by Kodel Electric and Manufacturing Co.
507 Pearl St. Cincinnati, Ohio

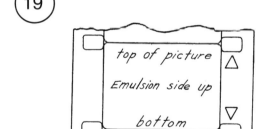

Kinatone (Warren D. Foster)
4 Wilsey Square Ridgewood N.J.

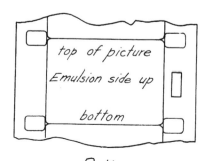

Peko
Made by Peko Inc. 2400 W. Madison Ave. Chicago, Ill.

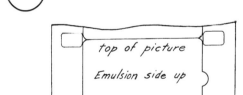

Simplex Pockette f.1.9 and f.3.5
The same mark is used regardless of lens equipment.
Made by International Projector Corporation
90-96 Gold St. New York, N.Y.

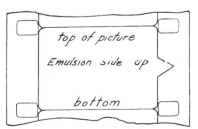

Cine Nizo model 3
made by Niezoldi and Kramer
Munich, Germany

APPENDIX 11: IDENTIFICATION MARKS USED IN SUBSTANDARD MOTION PICTURE CAMERAS

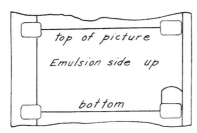

Siemens-Halske Kino Kamera
made by Siemens-Halske Berlin, Germany

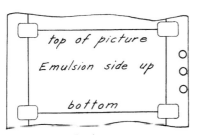

Bolex
made by Bolex Co. Geneva, Switzerland

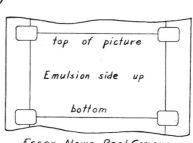

Essex News Reel Camera
Wollensack f-3.5

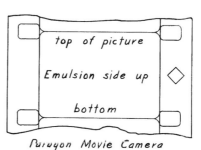

Paragon Movie Camera
Three speeds, 20' one winding, f 1.5
Mfg. by Paragon Camera Co. Fond du Lac, Wis.

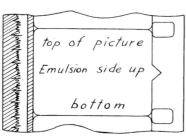

RCA Sound Camera f-3.5
Variable area - Turret lens front
Made by RCA Victor Co. Inc.
Camden, N.J.

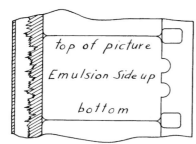

Berndt Sound Camera
Variable area - 400 foot magazines
Made by Eric Berndt
112 East 73rd. St. N.Y. City

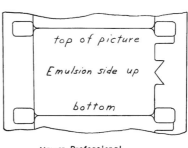

Maurer Professional
Made by J.A. Maurer, Inc.

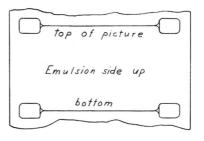

APPENDIX 11: IDENTIFICATION MARKS USED IN SUBSTANDARD MOTION PICTURE CAMERAS

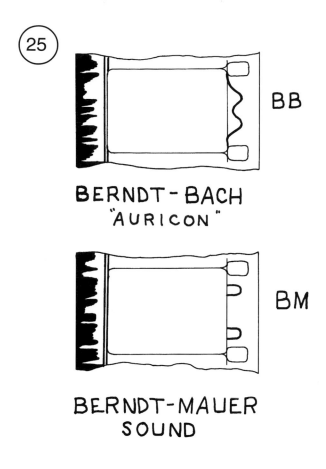

BB

BERNDT - BACH
"AURICON"

BM

BERNDT-MAUER
SOUND

APPENDIX 12: 1952 LIST OF MANUFACTURERS OF 16MM AND 8MM CAMERAS AND PROJECTORS

April 3, 1952

Dr. A. C. Robertson
Kodak Park

In connection with revision of the standards that specify the width of 16mm film, you already have been supplied with a list of U. S. manufacturers and importers of 16mm motion picture equipment. When we discussed this the other day, it seemed like a simple matter to obtain such a list from our files. But so many names came up that it was deemed advisable to do a rather complete job, even though some of the companies are no longer in business.

As the attached list shows, the data were taken from several sources. Although the list is long, it is far from complete. We tried to cover the important manufacturers in this country. In addition, the list includes the names of some European concerns, but that phase of it is very incomplete. It seems best to add 8mm cameras and projectors. However, no attempt was made to cover manufacturers of accessories only, or of auxiliary equipment such as printers.

You will note that some of the larger manufacturers are merely listed, with their addresses, while in the case of some of the lesser known concerns, descriptions of their equipment are included. That was done because most of us are familiar with the general lines of the big manufacturers, but are not acquainted with the products sold by the smaller companies.

D.F. Lyman
Development Department

SOURCES:

Card File in Patent Museum, Motion Picture Cameras, Motion Picture Projectors, Sound Cameras, and Sound Projectors, Sound Equipment.

POPULAR PHOTOGRAPHY, Giant Directory Issue, May, 1951.

PHOTO DEALER, Section 1, February 1952.

PHOTO DEALER, Section 2, Directory Section, February, 1952.

Files of the Development Department, Camera Works.

Ace Manufacturing Company, Milwaukee, Wisconsin

The Ace 16mm projector is a very cheap ($6.50) hand-cranked toy. See Development Department report No. 2647.

Acme Process Camera

See Producers Services Company.

Agfa AG, I. G., Farbindustrie, Germany

Made both cameras and projectors.

Gustav Amigo, Feinmechanik

Amigo Electra Electric Cine Camera, 16mm. Berlin S42

Shown in Messrs Dallmeyer Ltd. Showrooms. See THE AMATEUR PHOTOGRAPHER, 11/4/31, page 439. See PHOTO WOCHE, 2/26/36, page 230. Received from Germany 6/2/36 fitted with Tacharett 1:1.5 – 25mm lens No. 15045. Price we paid RM 409.15. See Catalog received 3/23/37. Price fitted with 1:3.5 – 25mm lens—PM 450.

Ampro Corporation, 2835 N. Western Avenue, Chicago 18, Illinois

Ansco, Binghamton, New York

Arnold & Richter, K. G., Munich, Germany

Arriflex 16mm camera. Imported by Camera Mart Inc., U. S. From FILM WORLD, March 1950, page 148. See AMERICAN CINEMATOGRAPHERS, July, 1951, page 258. Will soon be available in this country according to Kling Photo Supply Corp. which has been appointed U. S. agent for the camera by the makers, Arnold & Richter KG, Munich, Germany, (U. S. Zone).

Associated Photo, Products Co., 136 W. 32nd St., New York, N. Y.

Simplex and Lektro cameras. Lektros are not now available.

Automotion Pictures Inc., 14 West Fortieth St., New York, N. Y.

Automotion 16mm Double Purpose Projector. See MOVIE MAKERS, Oct. 1935, page 416. Straight projector equipped with 2" f/1.65, 40mm lens and 500 watt bulb. Price $127.50

Bangsberg Cine Production Corp.

Bass Camera Co., Chicago, Ill., Sound Sales Division
Bass DeFranne Sound Projector. Fr. PHOTOGRAPHIC DEALER, September, 1939, page 460.

Eugene Bauer, G. m. b. H., Stuttgart, Germany

Bauer 8mm Pantalux Projector. There is another for 16, 9 1/2, and 8mm. Also, Bauer Selecton Projector (sound). See pamphlet received in Model Room 4/19/34. See report on "Leipzig Spring Fair", 1934—page 3. See PHOTO WHOCHE, March 15, 1938, page 265 (750 watt lamp)

Bell & Howell Company, 7100 McCormick Road, Chicago 45, Ill.

Berndt-Bach, Incorporated, 7393 Beverly Blvd. ,Los Angeles 36, Calif.
16mm Sound Cameras, also Recorders, Blimps, Motor Drives, etc.

Bing Werke, Dresden, Germany
American Agent, Bing Corp., 31 East 17th St., New York, N. Y.
Projectors selling for $4.50 to $25 in 1927, also, toy projector was received in 1930.

Bosch AG, Stuttgart, Germany
Projectors. New Competitive Goods report, Germany, 2/18/34. Price RM 380, RM 800. Also Bosch 16mm projector with a sound attachment. See New Comptitive Goods Report 2/23/34. Price RM 2,000 2/18/34

Briskin Camera Corp., 2103 Colorado Avenue, Santa Monica, Calif.
Briskin Magazine 8 Camera, Model No. 301-352/1 and B52/2. Photostate announcement is in Patent Dept. 1/10/1947. Fitted with " Fl.9 Focusing Mount Coated Lens $122.50. Received 3/10/1947. Mr. Moyes purchased this camera from Willoughby's fitted with f/2.5 lens. 301-B52/2 Received 5/9/1947. See NATIONAL PHOTO DEALER Feb. 1949, page 44. Price with 1/2 in. f/2.5 universal focus coated lens - $59.50

British Acoustic Films, Ltd.
British Acoustic 16mm Home Sound-Film Equipment. See Kodak Limited's reports on New Competitive Goods report, 7/9/33. Complete equipment, suitable for A. C. or D. C., costs £125.

British Thomson-Houston Co. Ltd., London, England
From THE BRITISH JOURNAL OF PHOTOGRAPHY 11/30/34, p. 719. Price complete £160. From THE BRITISH JOURNAL ALMANAC, 1939, page 58. See THE AMATEUR PHOTOGRAPHER Oct 9, 1946, advertising 2 New B T-H 16mm. Sound Projectors (Type 301)

Burke & James, Inc., 321 S. Wabash Ave., Chicago 4, Ill.
See Paragon Camera Co. and Peko, Inc., Ditmar.

Camera Corporation of America, 844 Adams Street, Chicago, Ill.
Perfex Cinc Eight Camera. Magazine camera. Not now available. See International Camera Corporation.

Cameraflex Corp., 1947 Broadway, New York 23, N. Y.
Cameraflex 35mm and 16mm silent camera. 200 and 400 ft. rolls. 12, 24, or 115-volt motors. Detachable spring motor available. Built-in tachometer; critical focus; governor controlled speeds from 8 to 135 fr/sec. 3-lens turret. Motor mounted underneath for hand operation, or on side for operation on tripod. See POPULAR PHOTOGRAPHY, May, 1951.

Camera Specialty Co. Inc., 50 W. 29th St., New York 1, N. Y.
Euming C-3, C-4, 8mm camera.

Capital Projector Corp., 814 10th Avenue, New York, N. Y.
Porto-Sound 16mm; sound only; line voltage 120 a-c; 60 cycles; 500-watt lamp; direct lighting; _-inch coated Wollensak f/1.9 lens; sliding focusing; combination belt and chain drive; 16 frames per second speed; rotary disc shutter; blower cooling; film snubbers; special threading and framing; max. undistorted output, 2 _ watts; self-contained 15 x 20" screen for visibility in fully lighted areas. Price including case, $495.

Carpenter and Richardson Ltd., Beresford Ave., Wembley, Middlesex, England
Carpenter DeLuxe 16mm Sound Film Projector. From THE BRITISH JOURNAL OF PHOTOGRAPHY, Jan. 3, 1947—p. 8. The price of the projector is £186:0:0 (plus tax £41:6:8). Speaker £15:0:0, transformer £13:0:0, making a total of £255:6:8.

J. Chotard, 22, Rue Bobillot, Paris – XIII
Jubilar 16B Projector. From LE PHOTOGRAHE, July 20, 1948 – ad. In front of magazine.

Cinematic Developments, 2125 Thirty-second Ave., San Francisco 16, Calif.
Custom built cameras. President Arthur H. Hart. Make a four-lens turret for Cine-Kodak Special.

Cineric, 111 Rue Villiers, Paris, France
Cineric Ericsson Projector Model SD from LE PHOTOGRAPHE, Jan. 5, 1950 – ad. In front. 16mm, silent or sound. See folder received 8/21/1950, 32-78.

Cinetechnic Ltd., 169 Oldfield Lane, Greenford, Middlesex, England
Sound Projector. Cinetechnic "D16" Sound Film Projector (750 watt lamp). From THE BRITISH JOURNAL PHOTOGRAPHIC ALMANAC", 1946—page 167.

Cinklox Camera Co.

Cincinnati Clock & Instrument Co., 1113 York Street, Cincinnati 14, Ohio

Continental Products Corp., 1103 East Fifteenth St., Kansas City 6, Missouri
Movie Sound 8 Synchronous sound Projector. From PHOTOGRAPHIC TRADE NEWS, Apirl 1946 – p. 48 & 53. 8mm, sound in accomplished by the use of a turntable playing a twelve-inch record (the sound track) synchronized to the projector's motor. See MINICAM MAGAZINE, July-August 1949 – page 86. Price with case $295.00 plus Federal tax. This was our Kodascope Eight 33, equipped with a synchronous motor that they supplied to us.

Establissements André Debrie, 111 – 113 rue Saint Maur, Paris, XI, France
DeBrie 16, a 16mm. Proejctor (Arc). From LA TECHNIQUE CINEMATOGRAPHIQUE No. 72– July 1948 (on front cover)

De Jur Amsco Corporation, 45-01 Northern Blvd., Long Island City 1, N. Y.

Dekko Camera Ltd., Telford Way-East Action, London – W – 3
Dekko 8mm Cine Camera (available in the summer of 1947) Dekko 8mm, Projector, 300-ft. capacity. From THE PHOTOGRAPHIC DEALER, Jan. 1939 (ad. on front cover.) See PHOTOGRAPHIC TRADE BULLETIN, Nov. 1949, p. 12, Model 118A-Has a film capacity of 400 ft. Finally the price has been kept down to £39 10s.

De Mornay. Budd, 475 Grand concourse, New York 51, N. Y.
8mm battery-driven camera. Camera not now available.

Delta (Nottingham) Mfg. Co., 46 High Pavement, Nottingham, England
Delta Home Projector. From THE PHOTOGRAPHIC DEALER, Aug. 1939, p. 241, (British Magazine). Hand turned Model 25/-. Motor (Universal) Driven Model £3-17-6.

De Vry Corporation, 1111 Armitage Ave., Chicago 14, Ill.

Dimaphot, Paris, France
Dimaphot Type A, 16mm Camera

Director Products Corp., 570 Fifth Ave., New York 19, N. Y.
Pathe Super "16" Camera (Pathe Webo)

Ditmar, Germany
Ditmar camera was sold by Burke and James.

Dual Projector Corp., Industrial Trust Bldg., Providence 3, R. I.
Dual Projector. From NATIONAL PHOTOGRAPHIC DEALER, Feb. 1946 p. 100. Something radically new in Motion picture projectors is the Dual projector which "does the work of two projectors." The projector holds two sets of reels and permits the shifting from one reel to another without interruption, a task normally requiring the use of two projectors.

Dunning Color Corporation, 932 N. LaBrea Ave., Hollywood 38, Calif.
Dunning "Animatic" Sound Porjector. Catalog loaned to us by Mr. G. N. Graham, Cine Kodak Processing Department 3/12/1947. Of particular interest are the automatic film advance system and the "cold light" principle. 500 watt pre-focus projection lamp (300 or 750-watt can be used) Price $285.00 complete fitted with 2-inch f/1.6 coated lens.

Duograph, Inc., New York, N. Y.
Cameras and projectors. For a preliminary, pre-market report, see Development Department Report No. 2008. See Jan. 1929 MOVIE MAKERS, p. 840. A projector was received Jan. 1929. $35.00, hand wound (cranked).

Eastman Kodak Company, 343 State Street, Rochester 4, New York

Edco Electronic Devices, Inc., 112 W. 21st Street, New York, N. Y.
Edco 16mm Sound-on-Film Projector 21-826. From MOVIE MAKERS, May 1934, page 209, price $295. See article in MOVIE MAKERS, Feb. 1935, p. 91 (an improved and newly designed model).

Elmo Projector Corp.
See General Photographic Supply Co.

Empire Projector Corp., 60 McLean Ave., Yonkers, N. Y.
King 16mm Sound Projector. From PHOTOGRAPHIC TRADE NEWS, May 1947, page 15. Retail Price $289.50. See ditto June 1947, page 84, Error on price – should be $297.50.

Ensign Ltd., High Holborn, London, W. C. 1, England

Epimo, 15 Rue Simon-Dereure, Paris 18, France
Handy Type B Projector – 9.5mm or 8mm.,

Establissements Emel, 77 Rue Fondary, Paris, France
Emel 8mm Motion Picture Camera.

Eumig, Wien (Vienna), Austira
Photoelectric-cell cameras. See Camera Specialty Co., Inc.

Excedl Movie Products, Inc., 853 Dundee, Elgin, Ill.
Apollo projectors.

Fearless Camera Co., 8572 Santa Monica Blvd., Hollywood, Calif.
Fearless 16mm Sound Camera. From AMERICAN CINEMATOGRAPHER, May 1935, p. 220, article on page 214. Price of camera without equipment, $1500.00. Complete equipped with 3 magazines, Matte box, tripod, sound recording attachment & universal motor, $2500.00.

Filmagraph Corp., S. Easton, Mass.
Very cheap equipment; see Development Department Report No. 2282.

Film Crafts Engineering Co., New York, New York
Cine Pro 16mm camera. 10/1/46

Forway Industries, Inc., 245 W. 55ᵗʰ St., New York 19, N. Y.
Forway "Opera Voice" 16mm Sound Projector. 16mm; sound and silent; 2000 ft. capacity with extension arm supplied; 105-125 line voltages; 25-60 cycles; 750 or 1000-watt Westinghouse lamp recommended; reflected lighting; Separate light switch; coated 2-inch Simpson f/1.6 lens; sliding focusing belt drive; governor speed control; rotary disc shutter; blower cooling; motor rewind; tilting device; 10 watts maximum undistorted output; steel pressure shoe and gate. Price $366 including tax and case.

Warren D. Foster
See Kinatome Patents Corporation

Franklin Photo Industry
See Photographic Industries Corporation

Gaumont British Equipments, Ltd., Kingsway, London, England,
G. B. E. Standard 16mm. Sound Film Projector. From THE BRITISH JOURNAL OF PHOTOGRAPHY 11/30/ 34 - P. 719. Price of complete outfit £135. Also, GoBescope Projectors (Sound) From THE PHOTOGRAPHIC DEALER Nov. 1935 – P. 300 (There are four models in the range of equipment's, A, B, C, and D, the new Superlux Projector). See page 398 for article and price on Model D, 250.

General Photographic Supply Co., Distributor, 136 Charles St., Boston 14, Mass.
Distributor for the Elmo. 16mm; sound and silent; 750-watt; 10-watt amplifier; speed control; microphone and phonograph jack; coated 2-inch f/1.6 projection lens; focusing control; 2000 feet capacity; single unit containing projector and amplifier. Prince $495.

Glore Industries, 29 S. Desplaines St.
Allen 8 movie camera using double 8 roll film. Camera not now available.

Edwin Gorse, 86 Accrington Rd., Blackburn, England
8mm Egofix Super Camera. Egofix Projectors for 8mm. & 16mm. From THE PHOTOGRAPHIC DEALER, Feb. 1936—page 52. Price for 16mm £25, 8mm £12 12s.

Gumbiner Suncro-Sound Co., 3337 Wilshire Blvd., Los Angeles, Calif.
Syncro-Sound 16mm. Professional Sound-on-film camera. Ampro Corp., Chicago are exclusive United States sales Agents. Price $2975, including list below. From AMERICAN CIMEMATOGRAPHY, Dec. 1938 – page 503. (The equipment packs into three black fabrikoid cases with chromium trim. The complete sound picture equipment consisting of camera, amplifier, tripod, two magazines, microphone, one picture lens, carrying case with all cables.)

Walter Gutlohn Inc.
Globe Projector, 750-watt model and 1000-watt model.

Heuztier & Cie, Saint-Etienne, France
Heuztier Monofilm Projector – Model 8mm, 9.5mm & 16mm.

Holmes Projector Company, 1813 N. Orchard St., Chicago, Ill.
From EDUCATIONAL SCREEN, Feb. 1936 – Page 57 21-360.

Home Cine Cameras Ltd., 18 Gary's Inn Rd., London, England
H. C. C. Super Projector for 16mm & 9.5mm. From THE PHOTOGRAPHIC DEALER, March 1936 – P. 101. Price £10 – 10 – 0.

R. F. Hunter Ltd., Agent, Celfix House, 51 Gray's Inn Road, London
Celfix 16mm Cine Camera. Swiss apparatus assembled in England. Bingoscope Projector. From THE PHOTOGRAPHIC DEALER, Nov. 1936 – 455. Price – Battery model – £14/6. Mains model – suitable for A. C. or D. C. complete with lamp and resistance £22/6.

Ihagee Ihagee, Kamerwerke, Germany
16mm Projector. Received 12/9/31.

Walter Illge, Berlin SO 36, Germany
Illge Camera. Received in Model Room 4/20/28.

International Camera Corp., 844 West Adams, Chicago, Ill.
(Formerly Camera Corperation of America)
Perfex 88, 8mm, Magazine Loading Camera. From NATIONAL PHOTO DEALER, Feb. 1949 – page 46. 5 operating speeds; three-lens turret front. Price with f/2.5 Lens $69.50 including tax, with f/1.9 lens $105.50 including tax. See NATIONAL PHOTO DEALER, Dcc. 1950 – page 18. International Camera Corp. sucessor to Camera Corp. of America, 844 West Adams St. Chicago 7, Ill. Camera not now available.

International Film Library (General Office), 220 West 42ⁿᵈ St., New York, N. Y.
Peerless 16mm. Sount-on-Film Projector. See catalog received 2/3/1948 (1933) from Mr. J. Scott's office. 21- 830. Price $295.00. See correspondence file 51,929.

Irwin Corporation, 27 W. 20ᵗʰ St.,New York, N. Y.
Later Superior Products Mfg. Corp. See the entry under that heading.

A. Kershaw & Son, Leeds, England (Sold by Soho Ltd.)
Kalee NP3 Cine Projector – 16mm. From the BRITISH JOURNAL OF PHOTOGRAPHY, 10/5/34 – page 597. Price, including carrying case, reels, and tools is £60. See THE PHOTOGRAPHIC DEALER, Jan. 1935 – Page 14 (Victor Projector construction) per Mr. Naramore.

Keystone Manufacturing Company, Boston 24, Mass. (151 Hallet St., Dorchester P. O.)
They have made their own products for years, but apparently they also have taken over the products originally marketed by Stewart-Warner.

Kinatome Patents Corporation (Warren D. Foster)
The book of identification marks for motion picture cameras put out by the Processing Department shows a 16mm marking for a camera made by this company, which never really placed a camera on the market. We made a camera for him in our shop, much like the B & H, according to Mr. Stewart. Foster was the inventor who had large numbers of claims in his patents, and who seemed to be making a business of covering the ficid with blanket patents that would make others pay tribute. The camera had a novel gate and pulldown, and moved away when a button was pressed. They also made advertising projectors.

Klangfilm, G. m.b. H., Frankfurt, Germany
Projectors.

Kling Photo Supply Corporation, 235 Fourth Ave., New York 3, N. Y.
Distributors of Arriflex 16mm and 35mm cameras. See Arnold & Richter.

Kodel Electirc & Mfg. Co.
Kemco Home Movie Outfit, now obsolescent. Four pictures were taken on a 16mm frame, but the film was not slit. It was taken and projected in a zig-zag pattern.

Kolograph
See National Sound Projector Corporation

A. Lehmann, Furth, Bayern (Bavaria), Germany
Alef Alcinn projector. In the toy class. See Development Department Report No. 2266. Has cheap Geneva pull-down mechanism.

Lehmann & Knetsch, Breslau, Germany
Juwel and Alef Alcino projectors.

Lytax-Werke G. m.b. H., Freiberg, Germany

N. Marshall, Moorgate St., Nottingham, England
N. M. 16mm. Sound Film Projector. From THE BRITISH JOURNAL OF PHOTOGRAPHY, 12/7/34 – p. 734. Price £125.

J. A. Maurer, Inc., 37-01 31ˢᵗ Street, Long Island City 1, N. Y.

Mavco Inc., 14 E. 38ᵗʰ Street, New York, N. Y.
Disney-Land Toy Projector (electrically operated). From THE CAMERA, Nov. 1949 – page 157. See HOME MOVIES, Dec. 1949 – page 638, Price $4.95.

Micro Tecnica , Turin, Italy, Via Madama, Christina, 149
Projectors.

Miles Reproducer Co. Inc., 812 Broadway, New York, N. Y.
Filmgraph 16mm Projector. See pamphlets received 2/16/39   21-571.

Mitchell Camera Corporation, 666 West Harvard Street, Glendale 4, California

The Morton Co., 86 S. 6ᵗʰ St., Minneapolis 2, Minn.
Morton Soundmaster Camera. 16mm sound-on-film, single system, 200 ft. magazine interchangeable with 400 ft. magazine. 3-lens turret, amplifier, microphone, headset, operated by portable power pack. Price $645.00. Morton Soundmaster 16mm Sound-on-film Camera. From NATIONAL PHOTO DEALER, April 1950, page 52. The complete outfit weighs 24 lbs. Price $495.00. See BUSINESS SCREEN MAGAZINE, Number 3, Vol. 12, 1951 – page 45. Price $670.00 complete with Amplifier, Head-Phones, Batteries, Microphone, and 200-foot magazine.

The Mostow Co., 540 N. La Salle St., Chicago 10, Ill.
Da-Brite "first" 16mm, movie projector. From POPULAR PHOTOGRAPHY, Feb. 1947 – page 145. Capacity for 400 ft. of 16mm, film. 2" Focusing Projection Lens, 120 watt lamp. Price $17.95.

Movie-Mite Corporation, 1105 E. Truman Rd., Kansas City 6, Missouri
16mm. Sound Projector.

Natco, Inc., 4401 W. North Ave., Chicago 39, Ill.
Sound Projectors.

National Sound Projector, 8044 N. Ridgeway Corp., Skokie, Ill.
Kolograph Sound Projector. 16mm; sound and silent; 2000 feet capacity; extension arm for 4000-foot reels; line voltage 110 a-c, d-c; 50-60 cycles; 1000-watt T-20 Or T-12 lamp; direct lighting; separate light switch; 2-inch f/1.6 coated lens; helical focusing; combination belt drive; governor speed control; 16 and 24 frames

per second; 2-blade shutter; blower cooling; sealed lubrication; film snubbers; motor rewind; tilting devices; maximum undistorted output, 20 watts; sprocket intermittent film movement; speaker and all necessary cords; weighs 65 pounds; price including case, $585.

Neoton – J. Salardon, 125 Boulevard Du General, Koeing, Neuilly – Sur-Seine, Seine
Ducati 16mm. Projector. From LE PHOTOGRAPHE, March 20, 1949, ad, in front of magazine.

Niezoldi & Kramer, Munich, Germany
Cine Nizo and Model J projector. Nizo Model 2-ST 8mm silent, roll loading. Distributed by Ercona Camera Corp., 527 5th Ave., New York 17, N. Y.

The Nord Co., 254 1st Ave. N., Minneapolis, Minn.
Nord Professional camera. 16mm roll, 200 ft., 24 fr/sec. 240° shutter, electric motor, etc., rackover, microscope Focusing, $2500.00.

Oxford
See Thornton & Pickard

Paillard Products, Inc., 265 Madison Avenue, New York 16, N. Y.
Bolex products, cameras and projectors, 8mm and 16mm.

Pacent Reproducer Corp., 91 Seventh Ave., New York, N. Y.
Pacent Home Talkie Portable Projector. See catalogs received 2/3/1948 (1931) from Mr. J. Scott's office 21-829. Price $275.00.

Par Products Corp., 926 N. Citrus Ave.
Custom-built cameras and fittings, for example, a four-lens turret for the Cine-Kodak Special.

Paragon Camera Co., Fond du Lac, Wisconsin
Paragon cameras, Models 3515 and 3535, not now available. Some of these Paragon cameras were sold by Burke & James.

Par-a-Gon of Hollywood, 5549 Sunset Blvd., Hollywood, Calif.
Par-a-Gon 16mm. Sound Movie Projector. From FILM WORLD, Feb. 1947 – page 102 & 103. Listing at $199.50, the 15 pound sound projector utilizes a radio as amplifier And speaker. Two models are available; one model plugs directly into radio and the other comes equipped with speaker and amplifier. Projector is said to be more than ample for school and home use.

Pathe, France
Pathe Joinville 9.5mm or 16mm Projector. From LE PHOTOGRAPHE, Jan. 5, 1950 – ad. on back cover.

Peko, Inc., 2400 W. Madison Ave., Chicago, Ill.
Projectors, at least, were sold by Burke & James.

Phillips Lamps, Ltd., 145 Charing Cross Rd., London, England
Cinesonor Sound Projector. From THE BRITISH JOURNAL OF PHOTOGRAPHY, 7/26/35 – Page 476. See "New Competitive Goods report," 12/4/35 (sold in Holland).

Photographic Electrical Co. Ltd., 71 Dean St., London, England
Sonitola sound projector. From THE BRITISH JOURNAL OF PHOTOGRAPHY, Jan. 17, 1947 – p. 32.

Photographic Industires Corp., 223 W. Erie St., Chicago 10, Ill.
See 1951 may POPULAR PHOTOGRAPHY. 4 Corona 8mm magazine. Franklin camera. Franklin cameras not now available.

Producers Service Company, 2704 W. Olive Ave., Burbank, Calif.
Acme Process Camera. This camera is made in 16mm and 35mm sizes. See AMERICAN CINEMATOGRA-PHER, October, 1951, pages 401 and 420. A paper on these cameras was given by John P. Kiel at the Chicago convention of the Society of Motion Picture & Television Engineers, on April 28, 1950. It is printed in the May, 1951, issue of the Journal of the Society of Motion Picture & Television Engineers. Vol. 56.

Radio Corporation of America, RCA Victor Divison, Camden 2, New Jersey
Sound projectors. They also made a single-system sound camera.

RCSAM, 221 Rue Lafayette, Paris, France
RCSAM Major Projector. 8mm. – 9.5mm.

Reger Manufacturing Co., Mt. Clemens, Michigan
U. S. CAMERA, Jan. 1950 – page 85. Reger "Advanced Design" Toy Projector. Priced at $15.95 – Photo-Tak Corp., 21 No. Loomis St., Chicago 7, Ill. Is exclusive sales representative.

Revere Camera Company, 320 E. 21ˢᵗ Street, Chicago 16, Ill.

Ruby
See Thornton & Pickard.

Sales Producers, Ltd., 13/14 Golden Sq., London, England
S. P. Cine Projector for 16mm. Sound Film. From THE BRITISH JOURNAL OF PHOTOGRAPHY, 11/2/34—page 655. See "New Photographic Goods report" 7/15/35. Price £80 complete.

Schalie & Collee, Rotterdam, Holland
S-C 16mm. Camera made in Switzerland. See Development Department Report No. 2782.

Sears Roebuck & Co., 925 S. Honan Ave., Chicago, Illinois
Tower Sound Projector – 16mm., 2000' capacity. From MINICAM MAGAZINE, July-August 1949 – page 91. Sound or silent; 110V. AC or DC: 750 watt or 1000 watt Lamp. F:1.6 coated lens. Price with Case - $288.00.

Siemens & Halske, Berlin, Germany
Cameras and projectors.

S. C. S. Cinema Supply Corp., 602 W. 52ⁿᵈ St., New York 19, N.Y.
S. O. S. Cinemaphone 16mm. Sound Projector. From MOTION PICTURE HERALD, July 27, 1935 – p. 63.

Sound Products Co., 150 Nassau St., New York, N. Y.
Nulite 16mm Film-Sound Projector. From MOVIE MAKERS, Sept. 1935 – page 400. Price $198.50.

Specialized Sound Products Inc., Northport, New York
Cine-Compacto projector. Portable automatic motion picture projectors with sound 7/26/49. Official Guide 998.

Standard Projectors, Inc., 72 Spring Street, New York, N. Y.

Steatit-Magnesia, A. G., Germany
Dralowid 8mm. Projector. See Development Department Report No. 3308.

Stewart Warner, Inc.
See Keystone Manufacturing, Company.

Superior Products Mfg. Corp., 589 Essex Street, Lynn, Mass.
Formerly Irwin Corporation. The Irwin camera was very cheap, selling for $112.50. See Development Department Report No. 3183, Parts I and II. This camera used Gevaert film in magazines. For their projector, see Development Department Report No. 3229.

Technical Devices Corp., Roseland, N. J.
Fodeco Model 8. Fodeco 16mm Projector.

Technical Service Inc., 693 Monroe St., Detroit, Mich.
Technical Automatic 16mm. Sound-on-film Projector. From BUSINESS WEEK, Jan. 12, 1946 – page 74. Weighs 40 lb. And contained in a carrying case complete with amplifier, speaker, and screen.

Thornton & Pickard, England
Ruby camera, formerly Oxford – 1927.

E. Richard Turnham & Son Ltd., 14 Cornfield Rd., Eastbourne, England
Burville 16mm Sound and Silent Projector. From PHOTOGRAPHIC TRADE BULLETIN, Jan. 1948 – page 126.

Universal Camera Corporation, 28 West 23rd St., New York 10, N. Y.
Univex line of camera and projectors.

University Cameras, 1 S. Mary's Passage, Cambridge, England
Sofil Minor Sound Projector. From AMATEUR PHOTOGRAPHER, Feb. 28, 1951 – p. 21 Compact in one case; Price complete 99.

Valette, Inc., 215-T W. Ohio St., Chicago 10, Ill.
Projectors.

Van Der Schalie Corp., 347 Madison Ave., New York, N. Y.
Contimovie Continuous 16mm. M. P. projector. From PHOTOGRAPHIC TRADE NEWS, Nov. 1949 – page 84. This company is listed in the PHOTO DEALER directory section as putting out 8mm, projectors, too.

Victor Animatograph Corporation, Hickory Grove Road, Davenoprt, Iowa
Camera and Projectors.

Vitascope Corporation, Providence, Rhode Island
Cameras and Projectors.

Weber Machine Corp., 59 Rutter St., Rochester, N. Y.
Synchrofilm Sound Projector. 750-watt, 2-inch lens, $450.00. Synchrofilm Sixteen Sound-on-Film Projector, 750-watt lamp. From THE EDUCATIONAL SCREEN, Sept. 1934—P. 198 & P. 192. See MOVIE MAKERS, Oct. 1934—Page 435. 21-828. Price $450.00 from market Research 11/29/35.

Willoughby's, 110 West 32nd Street, New York, N. Y.
Willoscope Senior.

Wollensak Optical Co., 872 Hudson Ave., Rochester, N. Y.
High-speed Fastax Camera.

Zeiss-Ikon, Dresden, Germany

APPENDIX 13: SOME UNITED STATES PATENTS OF INTEREST IN THE DEVELOPMENT OF MOTION PICTURES

Amet, Edward H. #1,162,433. November 30, 1915, *Combined Phonographic and Motion Picture Apparatus for Producing Indexed Synchronous Records* (His sound camera); #1,065,576 (His projector)

Armat, Thomas #578,185. March 2, 1897, *Vitascope* (His first projector)

Armat, Thomas #673,992. May 14, 1901, *Vitascope* (Edison bought the rights and marketed it under his name.)

Bell, Donald J. #879,355. February 18, 1908, *Moving Picture Machine* (Appears to be the Kinodrome Projector.)

Brown, O. B. #93,594. August 10, 1869, *Magic Lantern* (A lantern equipped with a rotating two-bladed shutter for showing moveable lantern slides.)

Casler, Herman #549,309. November 5, 1895, *Mutoscope*

Chandler, Jasper S. and McNair, Hugh R #3,949,952. April 13, 1976, *Film Cartridge and Associated Drive Means* (200 foot cartridge for the Kodak Supermatic 200 Sound Camera)

DeVry, Herman A. #1,758,221. May 13, 1930, *Motion Picture Camera* (Assigned to QRS-DeVry Corp.)

DeVry, Herman A. #2,067,893. January 19, 1937, *Portable Projector*

Easterly, Donald O. #4,281,807. August 4, 1981, *Web Transport Apparatus* (The Last Super 8 Project. (See Chapter 5.)

Eastman, George #306,594. October 14, 1884 (Stripping Film)

Eastman, George #471,469. March 22, 1892 (Machine for forming flexible film)

Edison, Thomas A. #589,168. August 31, 1897, *Kinetographic Camera*

Edison, Thomas A. #493,426. March 14, 1893, *Apparatus for Exhibiting Photographs of Moving Objects.*

Farnum, W. C. #547,775. October 15, 1895. *Viviscope* (See Chapter 1)

Fuerst, C.C. #1,736,436. November 19, 1929, Assigned to Eastman Kodak Co. Removable Lens Mount (The two-pin mount used on many Ciné-Kodaks)

Gall, A. F. #1,204,424. November 14, 1916 *Kinetoscope* (The Edison Home Kinetoscope)

Harris, Varian M. #1,291,865. 1919 - Combined Motion Picture Camera and Projector (Assigned to Klix Mfg. Co.)

Hayden, A. C. #1.722.088. July 23, 1929, *Motion Picture Camera* (Patent is for audible signal for length of film exposed, drawing appears to be the Filmo.)

Howell, Albert #862,559. August 6, 1907, *Picture Exhibiting Machine* (This patent covers a novel framing device.)

Howell, Albert S. #1,038,586. Sepember 17, 1912 *Motion Picture Machine* (The company's first, wooden-body camera.)

Howell, Albert S. #1,507,357. Sepcmber 9, 1924, *Reel and Spindle Mount Therefor.*

Howell, Albert S. #1,571,670. February 2, 1926, *Photographic Camera* (Drawing is of first Filmo)

Howell, Albert S. #1,767,849. June 24, 1930, Plural Lens Adjusting Means (Patent drawing shows Filmo with three lens "spider turret")

Jenkins, C. Francis #1,017,672. 1912, *Phantoscope* (A wooden body camera) Jenkins, C. Francis #536,539 Mar 26 1895 *Phantoscope* (In a 1935 memoir for the SMPE, Armat described this machine as "a modification of the Edison Kinetoscope.")

Jenkins, C. Francis. and Armat, Thomas #586,953. July 20, 1897, *Phantoscope* (Armat claims this was the first machine giving intermittent motion with long period of rest, but a mechanical failure!)

Land, Edwin H. #3,709,588. January 9, 1973, *Motion Picture System with Unique Projector and Method* (The Polavision System)

Latham, Woodville #707,934. August 26, 1902, *Projecting Kinetoscope*

LePrince, Auguste #376,247. January 10, 1888, *Method of and Apparatus for Producing Animated Pictures of Natural Scenery and Life* (The multi-lens camera.)

Lincoln, William E. #64,117. April 23, 1867. *Toy,* Assigned to Milton Bradley Co. (The Zoetrope)

Marks, Isidore #1,345,793. July 6, 1920, *Motion Picture Machine* (Assigned to Keystone Corp.)

Moomaw, Lewis H. #2,082,505. June 1, 1937, *Motion Picture Camera* (Assigned to Keystone Camera Co. and drawing shows Keystone 8mm camera.)

Muybridge, Eadweard. #212,865. March 4, 1879, *Method and Apparatus for Photographing Objects in Motion*

Nelson, Nicolay #594,094. November 23, 1897, *Kinetographic Camera*

Oxberry, John W. #2,912,898. November 17, 1959, *Film Gate for Combined Camera and Projector* (The Wittnauer Ciné Twin)

Phillmore, Charles E. #2,019,767. *Motion Picture Camera* (Assigned to Tobin Tool & Die Works. Appears on Cinklox cameras)

Rector, Ernest J. #849,499. April 9, 1907, *Moving Picture Machine* (The Vitak).

Reichenbach, Henry A. #417,202. December 10, 1889 (Flexible celluloid film)

Schlicker, Herman C. #1,256,931. February 19, 1918, *Kinetograph* (The Vitalux Camera)

Schlicker, Herman C. #1,504,722. August 12, 1924, *Moving Picture Projector*

Sellers, Coleman #31,357. February 5, 1861, *Exhibiting Stereo Pictures of Moving Objects.*

Smith, Albert E. #673,329. April 30, 1901, *Framing Device* (Cited by Thomas Armat as "one of the 8 most important inventions of the motion picture art."

Tessier, Julien #1,572,252. February 9, 1926, *Motion Picture Apparatus* (The Original Ciné-Kodak)

Townsley, Malcolm G. #3,200,411. *Motion Picture Camera* (One of the claims reads: "to provide a motion picture camera having a zoom lens which may be driven from the drive of the camera selectively while feeding and exposing film *and while not feeding nor exposing film.* This is the Zapruder Camera.)

Victor, Alexander F. #976,954. November 29, 1910, *Moving Picture Machine* (Pictures are arranged in a spiral on a disc.)

Wilkins, L. A. et al. #2,910,911. November 3, 1959, *Portable Sound and Motion Picture Camera* (The Fairchild Cinephonic 8.)

Appendix 14: Amateur Motion Picture Film Prices As Advertised in *Movie Makers, Popular Photography*, etc., 1935-1975

(All prices include processing)

YEAR	ADVERTISER	MAKE OF FILM	DOUBLE 8MM B&W ROLL	DOUBLE 8MM B&W MAGAZINE	DOUBLE 8MM COLOR ROLL	DOUBLE 8MM COLOR MAGAZINE	16MM B&W ROLL	16MM B&W MAGAZINE	16MM COLOR ROLL	16MM COLOR MAGAZINE
1935	Eastman Kodak	Ciné Kodak Pan	25' $2.25				50' $3.25 / 100' $3.25			
		Ciné Kokak Safety					100' $4.50			
		Super Sensitive Pan					50' $4.00 / 100' $7.50			
		Kodachrome							50' $4.75 / 100' $9.00	
1948	Wholesale Photo Supply Co., Chicago, IL	Geveart Micro Pan	25' $2.21				100' $4.12			
		Ultra or Super Pan	25' $2.21				100 $4.94			
1952	Sears, Roebuck	EKC Day ASA 10	25' $3.95			25' $4.59			100' $10.85	50' $6.98
		Tung. ASA 16	25' $3.95			25' $4.59			100' $10.85	50' $6.98
		Agfa Day ASA 12		25' $4.60					100' $10.00	50' $6.91
1955	Delta Photo Supply New York City	100 ASA (Make Not Shown)	25' $1.11	25' $2.95	25' $2.25		100' $2.75	Plus x - $2.28	100' $5.95	50' $3.75
		200 ASA	100' $3.15				50' $1.57 / 100' $5.75	Sup x - $1.98 / 50' - $3.95		
1960	Kolor-Brite New York City	Kodachrome Daylight or Type A Prices for 3 rolls			25' $10.75 / 100' Bolex $35.25 - Box of 4 rolls	25' $12.95			100' $28.75 / 100' $28.75 (Super Ansco)	50' $19.75
	Eversnap	Kodachrome Film Re-Spooled 3-Roll Price			25' $8.95	25' $11.95			100' $25.00	
1965	Ever-Snap Color Labs	Kodachrome II		100' Double 8 Bolex - $13.25	25' $3.25 / Super 8 - $3.60	25' $4.20			100' $10.95	50' $6.95
1970	Kolor Brite Mail Order New York, Chicago, and Los Angeles	All prices are for 3 rolls of Kodachrome II unless otherwise noted	Prepaid Processing Mailers Included		25' $12.10 / 100' Bolex $44.85 / Fujichrome Single 8 - $12.10	Super 8 - $13.25 / 8mm. - $15.50			100' $36.40 / 100' $47.95 Ektachrome	50' $23.85 / Ektachrome
1975	Glo-Color Labs	Kodachrome 40				Super 8 - $3.90				
		Kodachrome 25			$3.75					
		Ektachrome 40				Super 8 - $4.15				
		Ektachrome 160				Super 8 - $4.60				

APPENDIX 15 – EDGE PRINTED CODES FOR EASTMAN KODAK FILM STOCK

Beginning in 1922 all Eastman Kodak Company motion picture film carried a date code printed on the edge of the film, indicating the year of manufacture. The code was repeated every twenty years, as shown in the table below. Prior to 1951, the plant of manufacture was also shown by the position of the asterisk in the word "SAFETY" as shown in the small table.

1922	1942	1962	● ■	1982	● ■ X
1923	1943	1963	● ▲	1983	X ▲ X
1924	1944	1964	▲ ■	1984	▲ ■ ▲
1925	1945	1965	■ ●	1985	■ ● ▲
1926	1946	1966	▲ ●	1986	▲ ● ▲
1927	1947	1967	■ ▲	1987	■ ▲ ▲
1928	1948	1968	+ +	1988	+ + ▲
1929	1949	1969	+	1989	X + ▲
1930	1950	1970	▲ +	1990	▲ + ▲
1931	1951	1971	● +	1991	X + X
1932	1952	1972	■ +	1992	■ + ▲
1933	1953	1973	+ ▲	1993	+ ▲ ▲
1934	1954	1974	+ ●	1994	+ ● ▲
1935	1955	1975	+ ■	1995	+ ■ ▲
1936	1956	1976	●	1996	X ● ▲
1937	1957	1977	■	1997	X ■ ▲
1938	1958	1978	▲	1998	X ▲ ▲
1939	1959	1979	● ●	1999	● X ▲
1940	1960	1980	■ ■	2000	■ ■ ▲
1941	1961	1981	▲ ▲	2001	▲ ▲ ●

Where Kodak stock was manufactured:

S * A F E T Y	Rochester
S A * F E T Y	Canada
S A F * E T Y	England
S A F E * T Y	France

Author's Note: The above information was retrieved from the following website:

www.geocities.com/hollywood/hills/2438/filmstockdates.gif

Index

A

Index

N

T

Index